LEGAL PAPERS OF
Andrew Jackson

LEGAL PAPERS OF
Andrew Jackson

JAMES W. ELY, JR.
THEODORE BROWN, JR.

EDITORS

WILLIAM J. HARBISON
Consulting Editor

THE UNIVERSITY OF TENNESSEE PRESS
KNOXVILLE

*Publication of this volume was assisted by grants from
the National Historical Publications and Records Commission, the
Tennessee Bar Foundation, the Ladies' Hermitage Association, and
the University of Tennessee.*

Frontispiece: Andrew Jackson, an engraving by H. B. Hall &
Sons, after Longacre, courtesy of the Ladies' Hermitage
Association.

The paper used in this book meets the minimum requirements of the American National Standard for Permanence of
Paper for Printed Library Materials. ♾ Binding materials
have been chosen for durability.

Library of Congress Cataloging in Publication Data

Jackson, Andrew, 1767–1845.
  Legal papers of Andrew Jackson.

  Includes index.
    1. Law—Tennessee—Miscellanea. 2. Jackson, Andrew,
1767–1845. 3. Lawyers—Tennessee—Biography. I. Ely,
James W., Jr., 1938–   . II. Brown, Theodore, Jr., 1949–
III. Title.
KF213.J29E59   347.73′32   82–2635
ISBN 0-87049-355-8   347.3072   AACR2

Contents

PART IV
A Biographical Register
Jackson's Legal Colleagues in Western North Carolina,
the Territory South of the River Ohio,
and Tennessee, 1787–1804

353

Acknowledgments

THE EDITORS WISH TO EXPRESS their gratitude to the following individuals for their review of and comments upon portions of the manuscript for the present edition: L. Kinvin Wroth, Hiller B. Zobel, Herbert A. Johnson, Charles T. Cullen, Maxwell Bloomfield, Mary K. Bonsteel Tachau, David J. Bodenhamer, Kermit L. Hall, Harriet C. Owsley, and Harold D. Moser.

The editors are very much indebted to Sam B. Smith and Harriet C. Owsley, the editors of the initial volume of *The Papers of Andrew Jackson,* for their assistance and encouragement during the early stages in the production of the present edition.

Invaluable assistance was rendered by each of the following persons toward the publication of this volume: George Rooker, Clerk of the Davidson County Circuit Court; Ramsey Leathers, Clerk of the Supreme Court of Tennessee; John McDonough, Manuscript Division of the Library of Congress; James R. Bentley, The Filson Club; Robert L. Byrd, William R. Perkins Library, Duke University; Francis James Dallett, University of Pennsylvania Archives; Sara Dunlap Jackson and Mary A. Giunta, National Historical Publications and Records Commission; Drew N. Greunburg, the Maryland Historical Society; Howard Hood, Vanderbilt University School of Law Library; Carese Parker, Luke Banker, Ann Bailey, Ted R. Bright, Linda Keeton, and Donna Zocolla, Andrew Jackson Papers Project staff; Jonathan Schmerling, Kay Eileen Stephenson, and Susan Bostick, student research assistants; and Alexa Selph, who prepared the index. A special expression of gratitude is due Elizabeth W. Pitha for her invaluable editorial assistance.

The editors also are deeply indebted to Frank G. Burke, Executive Director of the National Historical Publications and Records Commission, and his staff, without whose assistance and good offices the publication of this volume would not have been possible.

Editorial Method

PARTS I AND II OF THIS VOLUME consist of two sections each. The first section includes various licenses, commissions, and documents that bear upon Jackson's legal career but that do not relate to litigation. The second section includes numbered cases arranged according to the date of the final judicial action of each case. Part III, the Chronology, containing the numbered cases, other cases, and Jackson biographical data, places the numbered cases into the larger context of Jackson's developing legal career and personal life.

The documents published in the litigation sections of Parts I and II are arranged and presented with the cases to which they apply. Each of the numbered cases consists of one or more separate documents. When more than one document is printed, each is designated by roman numerals. Preceding each document, the editors have provided a brief descriptive heading and, when appropriate, a designation of the court and, in cases from the judicial period, of the presiding judges. The date, both when it occurs elsewhere in the text and when supplied by the editors in brackets from other sources, occurs at the head of each document. The cases presented in this volume are referenced by the numbers assigned to them.

PREPARATION OF TEXTS

To the extent possible, the editors have followed the general editorial principles relating to spelling, capitalization, and punctuation that are set forth in the initial volume of *The Papers of Andrew Jackson* (I, xxxi–xxxii). The specialized nature of the present edition has, however, required the formulation of certain additional editorial principles.

Official seals, if originally attached to the document, are rendered [SEAL]. Wafer seals and signatures followed by "L.S." or variations thereof have been rendered as follows:

Andrew Jackson	L.S.	:	Andrew Jackson L.S.
Andrew Jackson	[LS]	:	Andrew Jackson [LS]
Andrew Jackson	(LS)	:	Andrew Jackson (LS)

Andrew Jackson ⟨Seal⟩   :   Andrew Jackson (Seal)

Andrew Jackson ⟨SEAL⟩   :   Andrew Jackson (SEAL)

Andrew Jackson ⟨L.S.⟩   :   Andrew Jackson (L.S.)

Words and phrases deleted by authors other than Jackson have been provided in notes to the pertinent portions of the text only when the deletions vary significantly with the text. Transcribed texts of documents extracted from court record books have been conventionalized only to the extent that all date lines and signatures that appear in linear text in the record book have been brought to the center of the page. When the first word appearing on a page of a court minute or record book also appears below the last word on the preceding page, the insertion has been deleted by the editors. Inadvertent repetition of words and phrases within the text, however, has been retained. As a rule, clerical marginal notations in the court minute and record books have not been retained when they merely repeat information provided in the portion of the text reproduced. In those instances when the marginal notations do contain information not found in the text or when they clarify and amplify the text, the editors have included them in notes to the pertinent portions of the text.

Because many of the printed sources cited in the annotations are legal in nature, the editors have elected to follow a hybrid citation system. Citations to constitutions, statutes, cases, legal treatises, and to all periodicals follow the Harvard Law Review's *A Uniform System of Citation* (12th ed., 1976). Citations to nonlegal reference works appear in the standard bibliographical format.

ANNOTATION

To avoid an inordinate amount of editorial intrusion into the texts of the documents, the editors have kept textual annotations to a minimum. Footnotes thus have been limited to identification of all cases, statutes, and legal treatises cited in the texts. Biographical data for the most significant lawyers and judges mentioned in the volume are provided in Part IV, the Biographical Register. For the most part, the editors' rule has been that the documents must speak for themselves. When explanatory notations to individual documents are necessary, they have been supplied in additional paragraphs in the endnotes to the pertinent documents.

The editors have viewed their task not as providing exhaustive identification of every petit juror and geographical feature mentioned in the texts, but rather as one of placing the documents into a proper legal and historical context. To accomplish this purpose, the editors for the most part have relied upon editorial notes that precede the presentation of the case documents and supply the pertinent factual, procedural, and legal background for the documents that follow. Biographical data about the parties to the cases, when available, are provided in the editorial notes. Related cases are dealt with in single editorial notes.

When the only case documentation that has been located consists of entries from the Bland Casebook (see page lxv below), generally no editorial notes have been provided unless the legal issues are of unusual significance. Bland's statement of the case, with few exceptions, is sufficient to stand alone. Pertinent biographical data, when available, have been provided in the endnotes to the Bland document(s).

SELECTION OF CASES AND DOCUMENTS

Of necessity, this edition of Jackson's legal papers is a selective one. Because the great majority of the documents that have been collected relate either to litigation in which Jackson participated as counsel or to matters that he heard as a member of the Superior Court, the editors concluded that arrangement of the documents by cases provided the most efficient method of presentation.

The selection process included two steps. First, the editors made an initial selection of the cases that were to be published. The editors chose to follow criteria similar to those set forth by L. Kinvin Wroth and Hiller B. Zobel in the *Legal Papers of John Adams* in making this initial determination:

(1) whether the case in question illuminates a particular legal issue;
(2) whether the case contained an unusual document;
(3) whether the case, when considered with others, accurately illustrated the development of Jackson's legal career;
(4) whether the case was of interest for historical, social, or cultural reasons if not from a purely legal point of view; and
(5) whether there was any justifiable reason for not including the case.

Second, once each case had been selected for inclusion, two additional principles were applied:

(1) any Jackson document relating to the case—*i.e.*, any manuscript in Jackson's hand or addressed to Jackson and any document about Jackson— would be printed, except for the most perfunctory of items, and
(2) any other document would be printed if it explained or illuminated the case or was of interest for any other reason and was not merely cumulative of other documents.

The editors have chosen not to treat in the text of this edition the anecdotes and legends that, despite the editors' best efforts, have not been documented. For these, the reader is referred to the bountiful treatment that has been accorded them by Jackson's many biographers. When verified only in part or when the available documentation refutes tradition, however, the pertinent evidence and the account or accounts to which it relates have been included as a rule in the notes. (For the editors' treatment of the familiar Russell Bean anecdote, see the Appendix to this volume.)

TEXTUAL DEVICES

The following devices are employed throughout the present edition to clarify the presentation of the text.

[. . .], [. . . .]	One or two words missing or illegible and not conjecturable.
[. . .],¹ [. . . .]¹	More than two words missing or illegible and not conjecturable; subjoined note estimates number of missing or illegible words.
[ ]	Number or part of a number missing or illegible.
[roman]	Conjectural reading for missing or illegible matter. A question mark follows when the reading is doubtful.

The omission of irrelevant or duplicative material from court minute book and record book entries is indicated by ellipses without brackets.

DESCRIPTIVE SYMBOLS

The following symbols are employed throughout this edition to describe the various kinds of manuscript originals.

Dft   Draft
MS   Manuscript (arbitrarily applied to most documents other than letters)
RC   Recipient's Copy

All manuscripts of the above types are assumed to be in the hand of the author of the document to which the descriptive symbol pertains. Minute book entries, for example, are assumed to be in the hand of the clerk for the particular court. Documents not in the hand of the author are so identified. The following types of manuscripts are assumed not to be in the hand of the author, and exceptions will be noted.

FC   File Copy (applied to all forms of retained copies, such as letter-book copies, etc.)

Tr   Transcript (applied to both contemporary and later copies; if other than contemporary, period of transcription will be provided if known)

REPOSITORY SYMBOLS

DLC	Library of Congress
DNA	National Archives
ICHi	Chicago Historical Society
L-M	Louisiana State Museum
MHi	Massachusetts Historical Society
MdHi	Maryland Historical Society
MiU-C	William L. Clements Library, University of Michigan
Nc	North Carolina Department of Cultural Resources
NcD	William R. Perkins Library, Duke University
OHi	Ohio Historical Society
PHi	Historical Society of Pennsylvania
PVT	Private Collector
T	Tennessee State Library and Archives
TAnCo	Anderson County Courthouse
TDaCo	Metropolitan Davidson County Courthouse
THer	Ladies' Hermitage Association
THi	Tennessee Historical Society
TKL	Knoxville-Knox County Public Library (formerly Lawson-McGhee Library)
TMM	Memphis State University Library
TNJ	Jean and Alexander Heard Library, Vanderbilt University (formerly Joint University Libraries)
TSumCo	Sumner County Courthouse
TWashCo	Washington County Courthouse
WHi	State Historical Society of Wisconsin

COUNTY AND COURT ABBREVIATIONS

CPQS	Court of Pleas and Quarter Sessions
DaCo	Davidson County, Tennessee
HDSC	Hamilton District Superior Court
K.B.	English Court of King's Bench
MDSC	Mero District Superior Court

N.P.	Nisi Prius
Q.B.	English Court of Queen's Bench
SumCo	Sumner County, Tennessee
WashCo	Washington County, Tennessee
WDSC	Washington District Superior Court

Short Titles

The following list includes only those short titles of published works cited with great frequency throughout this edition. For works cited less frequently, short titles also are used subsequent to the initial full citation.

AHM / *American Historical Magazine*.

ASP / *American State Papers*.

Bacon, *Abridgment* / Matthew Bacon, *New Abridgment of the Law*, 5 vols. (London, 1736–1766).

Barnhart, "The Tennessee Constitution of 1796" / John D. Barnhart, "The Tennessee Constitution of 1796," 9 *J. Southern Hist.* 534 (1943).

Bassett, *Correspondence* / John Spencer Bassett, *Correspondence of Andrew Jackson*, 6 vols. (Washington, D.C., 1926–1934).

BDAC / *Biographical Directory of the American Congress, 1774–1961* (Washington, D.C., 1961).

BD–Tenn. Assembly / Robert M. McBride and Dan M. Robison, *Biographical Directory of the Tennessee General Assembly, 1796–1861*, Vol. I, Robert M. McBride, ed. (Nashville, 1975).

Black. W. / William Blackstone, *Reports, Courts of Westminster Hall, 1746–1779*, 2 vols. (London, 1781).

Blackstone, *Commentaries* / William Blackstone, *Commentaries on the Laws of England*, 4 vols. (Oxford, 1765–1769).

Blount, *Journal* / William Blount, *The Blount Journal, 1790–1796* (Nashville, 1955).

Brown, "Tennessee County Courts" / Theodore Brown, Jr., "The Tennessee County Courts Under the North Carolina and Territorial Governments: The Davidson County Court of Pleas and Quarter Sessions, 1783–1796, as a Case Study," 32 *Vand. L. Rev.* 349 (1979).

Burr. / James Burrow, *Reports, King's Bench, 1756–1772*, 5 vols. (London, 1766–1780).

Caldwell, *Bench and Bar* / Joshua W. Caldwell, *Sketches of the Bench and Bar of Tennessee* (Knoxville, 1898).

Carter, *Territorial Papers* / Clarence E. Carter, ed., *The Territorial Papers of the United States*, 26 vols. (Washington, D.C., 1934).

Caruthers, *History of a Law Suit* / Abraham Caruthers, *History of a*

Law Suit, in the Circuit Court of Tennessee, Addressed to a Law Student (Lebanon, Tenn., 1852).

Cheney, *North Carolina Government* / John L. Cheney, ed., *North Carolina Government, 1585–1974: A Narrative and Statistical History* (Raleigh, 1975).

Clayton, *Davidson County* / W. Woodford Clayton, *History of Davidson County, Tennessee, with Illustrations and Biographical Sketches of its Prominent Men and Pioneers* (Philadelphia, 1880).

Comyns, *Digest* / J. Comyns, *Digest of the Laws of England,* 5 vols. (London, 1762–1767).

DAB / Allen Johnson and Dumas Malone, eds., *Dictionary of American Biography,* 20 vols., supplements, indexes (New York, 1928–   ).

Doug. / Sylvester Douglas, *Reports of Cases Argued and Determined in the Court of King's Bench in the Nineteenth, Twentieth, and Twenty-first Years of the Reign of George III,* 2d ed., pt. 1 (Dublin, 1789).

Eng. Rep. / *The English Reports,* 176 vols. (Edinburgh and London, 1900–1930).

Eq. Cas. Abr. / *General Abridgment of Cases in Equity, argued and adjudged in the High Court of Chancery, etc., with several cases never before published, alphabetically digested under proper titles,* 2 vols. (London, 1732–1756).

Espinasse, *Actions at Nisi Prius* / Isaac Espinasse, *A Digest of the Law of Actions at Nisi Prius* (London, 1789).

ETHS *Publ.* / East Tennessee Historical Society *Publications.*

Green, *Lives of the Judges* / John W. Green, *Lives of the Judges of the Supreme Court of Tennessee, 1796–1947* (Knoxville, 1947).

Hale, *Pleas of the Crown* / Matthew Hale, *Historia Placitorum Coronæ: The History of the Pleas of the Crown,* 2 vols. (London, 1736).

Hening, *Laws of Virginia* / William W. Hening, *The Statutes at Large; Being a Collection of All the Laws of Virginia,* 13 vols. (Richmond, 1809–1823).

Iredell, *Laws of North Carolina* / James Iredell, *Laws of the State of North-Carolina* (Edenton, 1791).

Jackson Papers, I / Sam B. Smith and Harriet Chappell Owsley, eds., *The Papers of Andrew Jackson,* vol. I (Knoxville, 1980).

Jackson Papers, II / Harold D. Moser, Sharon Macpherson, and Charles F. Bryan, Jr., eds., *The Papers of Andrew Jackson,* vol. II (Knoxville, 1984).

JES / *Journal of the Executive Proceedings of the Senate of the United States,* vol. I (Washington, D.C., 1828).

Lilly, *Entries* / John Lilly, *Collection of Modern Entries; or, Select Pleadings in the Court of King's Bench, Common Pleas, and Exchequer* (1771).

McLemore, *Mississippi* / Richard A. McLemore, ed., *A History of Mississippi*, 2 vols. (Hattiesburg, Miss., 1973).

Mallory, *Modern Entries* / J. Mallory, *Modern Entries in English; being a select collection of Pleadings in the Courts of King's Bench, Common Pleas and Exchequer, and also all kinds of Writs, with readings and observations on the cases in the Reports*, 2 vols. (London, 1734–1735).

Mod. / *Modern Reports; or, Select Cases adjudged in the Courts of K.B., Chancery, C.P. and Exchequer* (London, 1682–1738).

Morgan, *Vade Mecum* / J. Morgan, *Attorney's Vade Mecum and Client's Instructor; treating of Actions, of prosecuting and defending them, of the Pleadings and Law, also of Hue and Cry [with] precedents*, 3 vols. (London, 1787).

N.C. *State Records* / Walter Clark, ed., *The State Records of North Carolina, 1776–1790*, 16 vols. numbered XI–XXVI (Winston-Salem and Goldsboro, N.C., 1895–1914).

Quarles and White, *Three Pioneer Documents* / Robert T. Quarles and Robert H. White, eds., *Three Pioneer Documents: "Donelson's Journal," "Cumberland Compact," "Minutes of the Cumberland Court"* (Nashville, 1964).

Ramsey, *Annals* / James G. M. Ramsey, *Annals of Tennessee to the End of the Eighteenth Century: Comprising Its Settlement, as The Watauga Association, from 1769 to 1777: a Part of North-Carolina from 1777 to 1784; the State of Franklin, from 1784 to 1788; a Part of North-Carolina, from 1788 to 1790; the Territory of the U. States, South of the Ohio, from 1790 to 1796; the State of Tennessee, from 1796 to 1800* (Charleston, S.C., 1853).

Rothrock, *French Broad-Holston Country* / Mary U. Rothrock, ed., *The French Broad-Holston Country: A History of Knox County, Tennessee* (Knoxville, 1946).

Rowland, *Courts of Mississippi* / Dunbar Rowland, *Courts, Judges, and Lawyers of Mississippi 1798–1935*, 2 vols. (Jackson, 1935).

Salk. / William Salkeld, *Reports of Cases in the Court of King's Bench, with Some Special Cases in the Courts of Chancery, Common Pleas and Exchequer, Alphabetically Digested under Proper Heads, from the 1st of William and Mary to the 10th of Anne*, 3 vols. (London, 1795).

Scott, *Laws of Tennessee* / Edward Scott, comp., *Laws of the State of Tennessee*, 2 vols. (Knoxville, 1821).

Sevier, *Commission Book* / John Sevier, *Commission Book of Governor John Sevier, 1796–1801* (Nashville, 1957).

Str. / John Strange, *Reports of Cases in the courts of Chancery, King's Bench, Common Pleas and Exchequer*, 2 vols. (London, 1755).

THQ / *Tennessee Historical Quarterly*.

T.R. / C. Durnford and E. H. East, *King's Bench Reports*, 8 vols. (London, 1787–1800); known as *Term Reports*.

Tidd, *Practical Forms* / W. Tidd, *Practical Forms; chiefly designed as an appendix to the Practice of the Court of King's Bench in Personal Actions* (London, 1799).

Tucker, *Blackstone's Commentaries* / St. George Tucker, ed., *Blackstone's Commentaries: With Notes of Reference, to the Constitution and Laws, of the Federal Government of the United States; and of the Commonwealth of Virginia* (Philadelphia, 1803).

White, *Messages* / Robert H. White, *Messages of the Governors of Tennessee*, 7 vols. (Nashville, 1952–   ).

WMQ / *William and Mary Quarterly*.

Williams, *Lost State of Franklin* / Samuel C. Williams, *History of the Lost State of Franklin* (New York, 1933).

Wils. / G. Wilson, *Reports, King's Courts at Westminster*, 2 vols. (London, 1770–1775).

Introduction

ALTHOUGH ANDREW JACKSON engaged actively in the practice of law for nearly ten years and served as a member of the Superior Court of Law and Equity in the new state of Tennessee for more than five years, his career as an attorney has not been treated in detail by any of his numerous biographers. The *Legal Papers of Andrew Jackson* seeks to provide documents for the understanding of Jackson's formative experiences as lawyer and judge and to shed light on the practice of law on the trans-Appalachian frontier. The cases and documents have been selected to illustrate the nature, quality, and variety of both Jackson's practice and the disputes that he and his colleagues on the bench were called upon to resolve. The editors hope that this introductory essay and the legal papers in this volume will result in a better understanding and appreciation of the function of law on one of the earliest of American frontiers.[1]

THE TENNESSEE COURT SYSTEM

County Courts of Pleas and Quarter Sessions
These courts, a direct inheritance from North Carolina, constituted the basic unit of the judicial system in early Tennessee. Precinct courts were established in Albemarle County in North Carolina as early as the 1670s and evolved into the county courts. A series of colonial measures enlarged their jurisdiction and importance. Inevitably, the North Carolina legislators modeled the colonial county courts on those of the mother country. Indeed, one historian has concluded: "The power which the North Carolina county court had gained by 1750 permitted that body to exercise a

---

1. For the impact of the frontier upon the legal system, see Elizabeth G. Brown, "The Bar on a Frontier: Wayne County, 1796–1836," 14 *Am. J. Legal Hist.* 136 (1970); William W. Blume, "Civil Procedure on the American Frontier," 56 *Mich. L. Rev.* 161 (1957); William B. Hamilton, *Anglo-American Law on the Frontier: Thomas Rodney and His Territorial Cases* (Durham, N.C., 1953); Malcolm J. Rohrbough, *The Trans-Appalachian Frontier: People, Societies, and Institutions, 1775–1850* (New York, 1978), 49–57.

jurisdiction comparable to that which the quarter sessions court in England had enjoyed for several centuries."[2]

The members of the county courts were the justices of the peace. Appointed as individual magistrates, these justices were authorized to conduct county courts by virtue of a commission of the peace. The governor named a varying number of prominent citizens as justices of the peace for each county, but at least three justices were necessary to hold a term of county court. The tribunals met once every quarter, typically in January, April, July, and October. The opening dates of court frequently were staggered to accommodate litigants who had business in more than one county.

After the Revolution, North Carolina lawmakers did not significantly alter the system of county courts. The Carolina Constitution of 1776 in section 33 provided that the governor should appoint justices of the peace upon the recommendation of the legislature; once commissioned, they held office "during good behavior" and could not be removed "unless for Misbehavior, Absence, or Inability." The Judiciary Act of 1777, although giving little attention to the county courts, nevertheless vested the tribunals with sweeping jurisdiction

> to hear, try, and determine, all Causes whatsoever at the common law, within their respective Counties, where the Debt, Damages, or Cause of Action is above five pounds, (actions or Trespass in Ejectment, Formedon in Defeender, Remainer and Reverter, Dower, Partition, Perjury, and such Felony and criminal Causes where the Judgment, upon Conviction, shall be for the loss of life, Limb, or Member, excepted) and all petit Larcenies, Assaults, Batteries, and Trespasses, . . . Breaches of the Peace, and other Misdemeanors of what kind soever, of any inferior Nature.[3]

Sessions of the county courts could not exceed six days a quarter. A 1785 measure extended the jurisdiction of the county courts to actions of ejectment, dower, partition, and trespass quare clausum fregit.[4] Apart from their purely judicial duties, the county courts exercised significant executive, legislative, and administrative functions. For example, they regulated weights and measures, issued licenses for ferries and taverns, and set tavern prices. After 1777, all judgments by the county courts, in both civil and criminal actions, were subject to appeal to the Superior Court for the district in which the pertinent county was located.

As North Carolina's population moved westward, local courts were regularly instituted in newly organized counties. Indeed, the administra-

---

2. Paul M. McCain, *The County Court in North Carolina before 1750* (Durham, N.C., 1954), 145.

3. Ch. 2, 1777 Laws of N.C. (Nov. Sess.), reprinted in Iredell, *Laws of North Carolina* 296, 1 Scott, *Laws of Tennessee* 165.

4. Ch. 2, 1785 Laws of N.C., reprinted in Iredell, *Laws of North Carolina* 547, 1 Scott, *Laws of Tennessee* 330.

tion of justice at the county level was a prime concern for the legislature. For instance, when Davidson County, in what is now middle Tennessee, was established in 1783, the lawmakers declared that "a considerable Number of Inhabitants have settled on the Lands of the Cumberland River in this State, at a very great Distance from any Place where County Courts are held, and it is represented that erecting a County to include the said Inhabitants, and appointing Courts to be held among them, would be very beneficial and advantageous."[5]

In 1789, responding to congressional efforts to settle conflicting state claims over the western lands, North Carolina ceded the area that encompasses Tennessee to the United States.[6] Congress in May 1790 organized "the Territory of the United States South of the River Ohio" and provided that the government of the territory should be similar to that already established under the Northwest Ordinance (1787).[7] The shift from a North Carolina to a territorial government did not, however, significantly change the functions of the county courts. The Judiciary Act of 1794 simply provided that "courts of pleas and quarter sessions shall continue to be held as heretofore, in each and every county in this territory," and the jurisdiction of the courts was restated in language similar to that of the 1777 North Carolina act.[8]

When Tennessee became a state in 1796, neither the constitution nor the legislators of the new state gave much attention to the county court system—continuity with earlier institutions was the dominant theme. Still, throughout the late eighteenth and early nineteenth centuries, few institutions had a more pervasive impact upon the daily lives of Tennessee citizens than did the county courts.[9]

The Superior Court of Law and Equity
The North Carolina Constitution of 1776 in section 13 provided for "the Supreme Courts of Law and Equity," but neither mandated the tribunal nor specified the composition and operation of the judiciary. The constitution did, however, state that Supreme Court judges should be selected by joint ballot of the legislature; thus, implementation of a supreme or superior court was deemed a legislative responsibility.

In 1777 the North Carolina lawmakers fulfilled that responsibility by organizing a full court system and establishing the Superior Court of Law.

5. Ch. 52, 1783 Laws of N.C., reprinted in Iredell, *Laws of North Carolina* 473, 1 Scott, *Laws of Tennessee* 282.
6. Ch. 3, 1789 Laws of N.C., reprinted in Iredell, *Laws of North Carolina* 663, 1 Scott, *Laws of Tennessee* 405.
7. 1 Stat. 123 (1790).
8. Ch. 1, 1794 Terr. S. of River Ohio Acts, reprinted in 1 Scott, *Laws of Tennessee* 457.
9. For a detailed analysis of the operations of the county courts, see Brown, "Tennessee County Courts."

This tribunal, consisting of "three Judges, being Men of Abilities, Integrity, and learned in the Law," was directed to hear cases in each of six judicial districts. The jurisdiction of the Superior Court was extensive:

> all Pleas, real, personal, and mixt; and also all Suits and Demands relative to Legacies, Filial Portions, and Estates of Intestates; all Pleas of the State, and criminal Matters, of what Nature, Degree, or Denomination soever, whether brought before them by original or mesne Process, or by Certiorari; Writ of Error, Appeal from any Inferior court, or by any other Ways or Means whatsoever.

Furthermore, the statute authorized members of the court to "use, exercise, and enjoy, the same powers and Authorities, Rights, Privileges, and Preheminences, as were had, used, exercised, and enjoyed, by any former judges in this Territory." In the event of the death or absence of one or more judges, the remaining jurists were empowered to hold court sessions. The power of a sole judge, however, was restricted by a requirement that demurrers, exceptions to evidence, and motions in arrest of judgment be argued before at least two judges.[10]

Proceedings in the Superior Court were limited in two important respects. The lawmakers established strict venue requirements, and failure to bring an action in the proper district was a ground for a plea in abatement. For example, actions involving real property, ejectment, or trespass had to commence in the district where the cause of action arose. The legislature also set a monetary prerequisite for original actions in the Superior Court: the tribunal had no jurisdiction over lawsuits for less than one hundred pounds when the parties lived in the same district or fifty pounds when the parties resided in different districts.

Equity law in North Carolina throughout the colonial period had been dispensed by the Court of Chancery. Modeled on the English High Court of Chancery, the tribunal had consisted of the royal governor and his council.[11] This court was no longer suitable following the Revolution, but the lack of a tribunal to handle equity matters was perceived as a serious problem. Declaring that the existing courts were "not equal to the Redress of all kinds of Injuries, but many innocent Men are with-held of their just Rights," the Carolina legislature in 1782 provided that

> each Superior Court of Law in this State shall also be and act as a Court of Equity for the same District, and possess all the Powers and Authorities within the same, that the Court of Chancery which was formerly held in this State under the late Government used and exercised.

10. Ch. 2, 1777 Laws of N.C. (Nov. Sess.), reprinted in Iredell, *Laws of North Carolina* 296, 1 Scott, *Laws of Tennessee* 165. See generally John Haywood, *Reports of Cases Adjudged in the Superior Courts of Law and Equity of the State of North Carolina, 1789–1798* (Halifax, N.C., 1799).

11. William S. Price, Jr., ed., *North Carolina Higher-Court Minutes, 1709–1723* (Raleigh, 1974), xl, xli.

The statute further required that two judges must sign a final equity decree, but allowed a single jurist to grant temporary injunctions.[12]

Even as this post-Revolutionary court structure was being fashioned, the westward migration of settlers into the trans-Appalachian region created a severe strain on the administration of justice. Parties and witnesses found it extremely inconvenient to attend the scheduled terms of the Superior Court in the eastern portion of the state. Accordingly, the lawmakers enacted a series of measures extending the court's geographic reach. In 1782 they organized the six western counties into the new judicial district of Morgan and mandated two sessions of the Superior Court annually in Morgan. The statute also made special arrangements for Washington and Sullivan counties, a part of the Morgan District. The legislators recognized that "the extensive Mountains that lie desolate" between Washington County and the place of trial for the Morgan District rendered "the Transportation of Criminals from the former to the latter difficult." They provided that one Superior Court judge, or "some other Gentleman commissioned for that Purpose," should hear criminal cases in Washington County twice a year. By 1784 this arrangement no longer sufficed, and the North Carolina legislature created a "distinct and separate" Washington District. Abandoning the circuit-court scheme employed elsewhere, the lawmakers selected a single Superior Court judge for the Washington District and granted him the same powers as those exercised by other members of the Superior Court.[13]

With the 1783 organization of Davidson County, the Carolina legislators were again confronted with extending the court system to a remote outpost. At first Davidson County was part of the Washington District, but in 1785 the lawmakers instituted a separate Superior Court for Davidson County to be held at Nashville. As in the Washington District, a single judge enjoyed the same power and authority as did other Superior Court jurists. The court met twice a year. The statute also erected a jurisdictional barrier by directing that no resident of Davidson County should be subject to any lawsuit "in any of the Courts on the East Side of the Appalachian Mountains." Three years later the Davidson Superior Court was broadened to include adjacent Sumner and Tennessee counties and was renamed Mero in honor of the Spanish governor of Louisiana.[14]

12. Ch. 11, 1782 Laws of N.C., reprinted in Iredell, *Laws of North Carolina* 432, 1 Scott, *Laws of Tennessee* 261.

13. Ch. 22, 1782 Laws of N.C., reprinted in Iredell, *Laws of North Carolina* 439; ch. 28, 1784 Laws of N.C., reprinted in Iredell, *Laws of North Carolina* 544, 1 Scott, *Laws of Tennessee* 328.

14. Ch. 47, 1785 Laws of N.C., reprinted in Iredell, *Laws of North Carolina* 567, 1 Scott, *Laws of Tennessee* 349; ch. 31, 1788 Laws of N.C., reprinted in Iredell, *Laws of North Carolina* 643, 1 Scott, *Laws of Tennessee* 402. See John Allison, "The Mero District," 1 *AHM* 115 (1896).

Since final equity decrees required the signatures of two judges, there was uncertainty as to the scope of power exercised by the Mero Superior Court judge. In 1789 the North Carolina legislature, turning its attention to the Mero District for the last time before the cession of the western lands, resolved the problem by a statute giving the Mero jurist the same power as two judges had elsewhere in the state. Moreover, the lawmakers felt that the existing salary of the Mero Superior Court judge was "very inadequate to the Fatigue and Trouble of attending to his Duty" and raised his compensation to £100 for each term of court attended.[15]

The congressional measure of 1790 organizing the territory established "a court to consist of three judges, any two of whom to form a court, who shall have a common law jurisdiction." The principal territorial officers were nominated by the President, subject to Senate confirmation.[16] Thereafter, two judges usually presided at Superior Court trials and traveled between the districts to hear cases. In spite of the requirements of the Northwest Ordinance, a single judge occasionally held court as before.

The territorial government made relatively few changes in the structure of the Superior Court. In 1793 the territorial legislature organized the new judicial district of Hamilton, with court terms to be held at Knoxville. A year later the lawmakers enacted a comprehensive measure establishing courts and regulating judicial proceedings. The statute, however, simply confirmed the existing Superior Court:

> this territory shall remain divided into three districts as heretofore, viz. the district of Washington, Hamilton, and Mero, in each of which a court for the trial of causes civil and criminal shall continue to be held at the times and places already by law appointed, and shall be known as heretofore by the name of the superior court of law in the district where the same shall be held.

Although the tribunal was composed of three judges, appointed pursuant to Act of Congress, a single jurist was authorized to hold court, award judgments, and issue executions if other judges were absent. The territorial Superior Court was given the identical broad original and appellate jurisdiction as had been previously conferred under the 1777 North Carolina statute. Venue and monetary requirements were also reenacted.[17]

The Tennessee Constitution of 1796 was sketchy in its treatment of the court system and lodged a good deal of discretion over it in the legislature. Article V simply declared that

15. Ch. 66, 1789 Laws of N.C., reprinted in Iredell, *Laws of North Carolina* 692, 1 Scott, *Laws of Tennessee* 421.

16. 1 Stat. 50 (1789).

17. 1793 Terr. S. of River Ohio Acts, reprinted in 1 Scott, *Laws of Tennessee* 454; ch. 1, 1794 Terr. S. of River Ohio Acts, reprinted in 1 Scott, *Laws of Tennessee* 457.

[t]he judicial power of the state shall be vested in such superior and inferior courts of law and equity, as the legislature shall, from time to time, establish.

The constitution did include several specific provisions governing the judiciary. Judges were to be elected by joint ballot of both houses of the legislature and were commissioned during good behavior. The constitution mandated that Superior Court judges receive a compensation set by law not to exceed $600 annually, but denied them "any fees or perquisites of office." Judges were also barred from charging juries "with respect to matters of fact" but were permitted to "state the testimony and declare the law." Furthermore, the constitution (Article I, section 20) authorized Superior Court judges "in all civil cases, to issue writs of certiorari" to remove cases from lower tribunals.[18]

Over the next few years the Tennessee legislature turned its attention to the organization and operation of the Superior Court. In essence, the new state fashioned its highest tribunal after the North Carolina and territorial models. In 1796 the lawmakers mandated a Superior Court of three judges, yet permitted any one jurist to conduct court sessions. Two terms a year for each district were scheduled. In the Washington District the tribunal met on the first Monday in March and September. Sessions in the Hamilton District opened on the fourth Monday of the same months. Court terms in the Mero District commenced in May and November. The terms of the court could not exceed fifteen business days. The statutes did not address the jurisdiction of the Superior Court or the location of the existing judicial districts.[19]

Judicial nonattendance was particularly bothersome to the legislators, and the 1796 enactment included several provisions designed to discourage this practice. The statute required the judges to attend every court session and further provided that "in case of failure so to attend without sufficient cause for such failure be shown, it shall be deemed a misdemeanor in office." This was a serious matter because, under Article IV of the constitution, all civil officers were subject to impeachment for any misdemeanor in office. Indeed, in December 1798 the state House of Representatives adopted articles of impeachment against Judge David Campbell, charging, among other things, his failure to attend a regular court session.[20] On a more routine level, the salary paid to Superior Court

18. See generally Barnhart, "The Tennessee Constitution of 1796," p. 534; Sanford Wilson Higginbotham, "Frontier Democracy in the Early Constitutions of Tennessee and Kentucky, 1772–1799" (M.A. thesis, Louisiana State Univ., 1941).

19. Ch. 7, 1794 Terr. S. of River Ohio Acts; ch. 1, 1796 Tenn. Pub. Acts; ch. 7, 1797 Tenn. Pub. Acts, reprinted in 1 Scott, *Laws of Tennessee* 497, 545, 595.

20. Campbell was narrowly acquitted by the Senate. White, *Messages*, I, 73–86; *Journals of the Senate and House, 1797–1798* (Kingsport, Tenn., 1933), 329–330. In 1803 Judge Campbell was again impeached and acquitted for allegedly accepting a bribe. White, *Messages*, I, 154–160.

judges was conditioned upon attendance at court. Each jurist was to receive $83.33 for each session attended, provided he was present during the entire term. The statute even specified a reduced compensation for appearance for only part of a term and required the clerk of the court to file a certificate of attendance for each judge. Thus, if a jurist faithfully attended both of the biannual court sessions in each district, he could earn $500 a year.

This compensation scheme became an early subject of controversy. In a 1798 petition Judge Archibald Roane protested that the attendance requirement violated the Tennessee Constitution, which referred to "annual salaries" for governmental officials. Moreover, Roane observed, "[T]here are a number of official duties required of the Judges in Vacation for which no compensation [is] provided" by the statute. He urged the legislature to set a salary level that would "best tend to secure the Independence of the Judges which Independence the Laws contemplate to be one of the best securities for the rights and privileges of the People."[21]

Perhaps in response to Roane's plea, the legislature modified the scheme of judicial compensation in 1801. The salary of a Superior Court judge was raised to $100 "for each and every court he may attend." Accordingly, judges regularly present could earn the constitutional maximum of $600 a year. The lawmakers also relaxed the attendance requirement. While still insisting that it was the duty of the jurists to be present at all sessions, the 1801 measure declared that when a judge was "prevented by sickness or some unforeseen accident," he might nonetheless receive his salary for one absent term.[22]

It is clear that by the first decade of the nineteenth century the jurisdiction of the Superior Court, determined by an overlapping series of North Carolina, territorial, and Tennessee statutes, was extensive. The court heard all types of criminal cases; although the county courts exercised concurrent jurisdiction over a limited number of minor offenses, all major crimes were tried before the higher court. Subject to venue and monetary requirements, the Superior Court also heard all types of civil actions. Before 1801 the court exercised original and exclusive jurisdiction over equity proceedings; in that year the legislature removed the equity power over suits with a value of less than $50. Finally, the Superior Court provided appellate review of both civil and criminal matters by means of appeal, certiorari, or writ of error.

Even while Jackson sat on the Superior Court, the tribunal was coming under increased criticism from all quarters. Decrying "the great and insurmountable Delay occasioned to Suitors," in 1799 Judge Campbell

21. Petition of Judge Archibald Roane, Dec. 26, 1798, Legislative Papers: Petitions and Memorials, 1799–1809, T.
22. Ch. 28, 1801 Tenn. Pub. Acts, reprinted in 1 Scott, *Laws of Tennessee* 715.

urged the legislature to lengthen court sessions and to set aside certain days for the equity docket. Two years later the Hamilton District grand jury requested the creation of a new district between Washington and Hamilton to "contribute to the convenience of your fellow Citizens." In 1803 the Tennessee House of Representatives adopted a resolution to ascertain the number of lawsuits heard at the sessions of the Hamilton District. The following year an unsuccessful bill before the legislature proposed to revamp the Superior Court on the ground that it was "inconvenient in form." Limited in scope, this measure would have merely renamed the tribunal the Circuit Court and mandated that one judge must be a resident in each district.[23]

The initial court structure of Tennessee did not long survive Jackson's retirement from the bench. In November 1809, the lawmakers abolished the Superior Court.[24] Briefly, they divided the state into five circuits and authorized a single judge to hold court twice a year in each county within the circuit. The new tribunals were vested with "original jurisdiction over all matters and causes at common law and in equity, whereof the present superior courts of law and equity have jurisdiction; also, exclusive jurisdiction over all criminal causes." Circuit judges heard appeals from the county courts. In addition, Tennessee lawmakers instituted a Supreme Court of Errors and Appeals composed of "two judges in error, and one circuit judge." Unlike the Superior Court, the Court of Errors had no original jurisdiction but exercised appellate review through writs of error. This new appeals court met once annually in each circuit.[25] Fur-

---

23. Petition of Judge David Campbell, ca. October 1799, and Petition of Hamilton District Grand Jury, Oct. 3, 1801, Legislative Papers: Petitions and Memorials, 1799–1809, T; *Journal of the House of Representatives, Fifth General Assembly* (1803), 65; "A Bill to Abolish the Superior Courts of Law and Equity and for Erecting Others in their Stead," July–August 1804, 5th General Assembly, 2d Sess., Secretary of State Papers: Rejected Bills, T.
 Historians have echoed this displeasure with the operations of the Superior Court. One student of Tennessee judicial history remarked: "For lack of a reviewing court and of authoritative precedents to make the law uniform throughout the Commonwealth, our jurisprudence reached a low ebb in the first decade of the nineteenth century. Everything was in confusion; different decisions were made on the same points by different judges." Samuel Cole Williams, "History of the Courts of Chancery of Tennessee," 2 *Tenn. L. Rev.* 6, 16 (1923).
 24. Thomas Hart Benton, then at the beginning of his long political career, penned a devastating attack upon Tennessee's court system during 1808. Writing under the pseudonym of Sir John Oldcastle, Benton published a series of newspaper articles that championed sweeping judicial reform. Although he recognized that "[o]n the score of impartiality and ability our bench will rank with those of other states," he contended that the system itself was defective. Benton was primarily concerned about the county courts, but the Superior Court did not escape his barbs. Specifically, Benton maintained that the Superior Court was incapable of rendering prompt administration of justice and that litigants were compelled to travel away from their homes at great expense and inconvenience. For selected extracts from Benton's Oldcastle articles, see White, *Messages,* I, 295–313.
 25. Ch. 49, 1809 Tenn. Pub. Acts, reprinted in 1 Scott, *Laws of Tennessee* 1148.

thermore, the legislature required that the judges of both the Circuit
Court and the Supreme Court submit written opinions, thus laying the
basis for the publication of case reports. The first volume of decisions was
collected and published by John Overton in 1813.

THE PRACTICE OF LAW
IN JACKSON'S TENNESSEE

Sources of Law

The substantive law of early Tennessee, as the discussion of the court system has indicated, was drawn from several sources. The 1789 North
Carolina statute ceding the western lands provided in part:

> That the laws in force and use in the state of North Carolina at the time of
> passing this act, shall be and continue in full force within the territory hereby
> ceded, until the same shall be repealed, or otherwise altered by the legislative
> authority of the said territory.[26]

Similarly, the 1796 Tennessee Constitution (Article X, section 2) declared:

> All laws and ordinances now in force and use in this territory, not inconsistent
> with this constitution, shall continue to be in force and use in this state, until
> they shall expire, be altered or replaced by the legislature.

Since the territorial and early Tennessee legislatures enacted few measures
changing the substantive law, judges and attorneys naturally looked to
North Carolina's practice for guidance. Unfortunately, the legal history
of North Carolina has not received much attention from scholars, and the
governing rules cannot be established with certainty.

In 1715 the North Carolina lawmakers passed a reception statute
which provided that, with few exceptions, "the Common Law is, and
shall be, in Force in this Government" and that various categories of parliamentary acts should be adopted. The legislators passed an even more
comprehensive reception statute in 1749. This measure, however, was
disallowed by the Crown in 1754, a move that seemingly revived the earlier law.[27] Whatever the legislative authority, North Carolina settlers believed that both the English common law and certain acts of Parliament
were effective in the colony. In his 1774 justice's handbook, James Davis
observed:

---

26. Ch. 3, 1789 Laws of N.C., reprinted in Iredell, *Laws of North Carolina* 663, 1
Scott, *Laws of Tennessee* 405.

27. Ch. 31, 1715 Laws of N.C., reprinted in Iredell, *Laws of North Carolina* 17, 1
Scott, *Laws of Tennessee* 20; ch. 1, 1749 Laws of N.C., reprinted in *N.C. State Records,*
XXIII, 317.

All the Laws and Statutes of Great Britain made before the Fourth Year of the Reign of James I, or before the Settlement of this Province, are binding here, as the first Settlers of a Colony always carry with them the Laws and Constitutions of the Mother Country.[28]

The American Revolution did not alter Carolina's attachment to the English legal tradition. In 1777 Waightstill Avery, as the attorney general of North Carolina, instructed the grand jury for Salisbury District:

Those who have maintained and propagated this erroneous opinion, that there was no Law immediately after Independence was declared; Might be corrected and convinced by looking into the History of Nations and examining what has been the State of their Laws in like cases. They may convince themselves that a Revolution or Change of Govt. does not induce or infer the Abolition or Destruction of the Laws—This might be illustrated & proved by numerous examples from almost every Country and Nation upon Earth who have had Laws & suffered Revolution.

Avery advised the jurors that the Revolution was directed "against such laws, and such only as America had no share in making."[29] A year later the Carolina legislature declared that "all such Statutes and such Parts of the Common Law, as were heretofore in Force and Use within this Territory," not repealed or repugnant to independence, were in full force.[30] Hence, the substantive laws of North Carolina, which prevailed in Jackson's Tennessee, were grounded on an English base.[31]

The purchase of English law books and the frequent citation of British authorities by Tennessee attorneys and judges in the post-Revolutionary era underscore this legal conservatism. For example, Judge Archibald Roane, Jackson's colleague on the Superior Court, concluded in a 1799 opinion that "we must in this case take the Laws of England for our guide."[32] Accordingly, the astute Tennessee lawyer was required to fashion arguments from a confusing mixture of sources: English common law; acts of Parliament effective in colonial North Carolina; statutes enacted by the Carolina, territorial, or Tennessee legislatures; and English or local judicial opinions. The outcome of a case could well turn on which provision was deemed controlling.

Criminal law in particular posed difficulties for attorneys. During the colonial era North Carolina enacted few criminal statutes, and the settlers evidently continued to rely upon English common law as a basis for

28. James Davis, *The Office and Authority of a Justice of Peace* (New Bern, N.C., 1774), 351.
29. Speech to the Salisbury District Grand Jury, 1777, Draper Coll., WHi.
30. Ch. 5, 1778 Laws of N.C., reprinted in Iredell, *Laws of North Carolina* 353, 1 Scott, *Laws of Tennessee* 226.
31. Elizabeth G. Brown, *British Statutes in American Law, 1776–1836* (Ann Arbor, 1964), 138–146, 176–180.
32. Massengill v. Humphreys, Bland Casebook, 20–21, MdHi (WDSC 1799).

criminal prosecutions. Indeed, James Davis's justice of the peace handbook for North Carolina listed murder, manslaughter, larceny, robbery, piracy, and burglary as felonies at common law. Such an attitude may have been founded on the 1715 reception statute, although it contained no express reference to criminal offenses. In any event, English criminal law played a crucial role in Carolina and remained strong in Jackson's Tennessee.[33]

Civil Procedure

Common-law pleading had been established in America during the colonial era. While it is questionable whether the full technicalities of the English system ever prevailed in the American colonies, the classic common-law pleadings were prolix, cumbersome, and laden with pitfalls for the unwary. The plaintiff was required to name the form of action under which he was bringing suit. Once the lawsuit was instituted, the parties exchanged a series of successive pleadings, each framed in precise fashion, designed to define the issues of law and fact in dispute. Any error in pleading, however, could result in dismissal of the proceeding. For instance, if the plaintiff selected the wrong form of action for a particular situation, the suit would abate.[34]

The system of common-law pleadings was subject to increasing criticism in the post-Revolutionary era. Reformers maintained that the plead-

33. Joseph H. Smith, "The English Criminal Law in Early America," in Smith and Thomas G. Barnes, *The English Legal System: Carryover to the Colonies* (Los Angeles, 1975), 20, 39; Davis, *The Office and Authority of a Justice of Peace*, 174–175. For a discussion of crime in colonial North Carolina, see Donna J. Spindel, "The Administration of Criminal Justice in North Carolina, 1720–1740," 25 *Am. J. Legal Hist.* 141 (1981).

There is little evidence of hostility to English law on the Tennessee frontier and no sustained effort to undercut the authority of English precedents. In October 1803, Governor John Sevier voiced the only significant criticism of this reliance on English law in Tennessee. Declaring that "the common law of England, or any other European nation, are not suitable for republican states to adopt," Sevier called upon the legislature to enact statutes supplanting English laws. A Senate committee, however, was unpersuaded. Noting that British statutes had "been in a great measure ingrafted into the American code of laws," the committee did not recommend any specific action on the governor's message. White, *Messages*, I, 137–138, 150–151.

In contrast, both New Jersey and Kentucky attempted to ban the citation of post-1776 British authorities. See Brown, *British Statutes in American Law*, 130–135; Lawrence M. Friedman, *A History of American Law* (New York, 1973), 97–98; Mary K. Bonsteel Tachau, *Federal Courts in the Early Republic: Kentucky, 1789–1816* (Princeton, 1978), 78. For a discussion of English law in post-Revolutionary America, see James W. Ely, Jr., "Law in a Republican Society: Continuity and Change in the Legal System of Post-Revolutionary America," in Richard A. Preston, ed., *Perspectives on Revolution and Evolution* (Durham, N.C., 1979), 46–65.

34. Theodore F. T. Plucknett, *A Concise History of the Common Law*, 5th ed. (Boston, 1956), 399–418; John Adams's Pleadings Book, 1771–1773, L. Kinvin Wroth and Hiller B. Zobel, eds., *Legal Papers of John Adams* (Cambridge, Mass., 1965), I, 26–86; Friedman, *A History of American Law*, 49–51; F. W. Maitland, *The Forms of Action at Common Law* (Cambridge, 1948); David Thomas Konig, ed., *Plymouth Court Records, 1686–1859* (Wilmington, 1978–), I, 149–172. And see No. 33.

ings were repetitious and delayed a final determination of lawsuits. Even worse, they charged, the system was expensive to litigants and frequently prevented a decision on the merits.[35]

On the surface, the traditional system of pleading governed Tennessee practice. Indeed, there was no comprehensive procedure statute, and attorneys instinctively followed English models. All Tennessee lawsuits were brought in the style of one of the customary forms of action, and a plaintiff's case could be dismissed for failure to state the form of the proceeding (No. 33).

Moreover, the highly fictitious pleadings of the common law were regularly utilized. For example, the action of ejectment, widely used to determine the title or recover possession of land, had evolved from a proceeding to recover a leasehold. Since in theory the action was only for a leasehold interest, the plaintiff was obliged to allege that the actual parties had leased the land to imaginary persons and that one such lessee had evicted the other.[36] These nominal parties were most often named John Den and Richard Fen, but imaginative Tennessee counsel occasionally designated John Doe and Richard Roe or Miles Goodtitle and Mark Notitle. Not until 1852 did Tennessee abolish the fictitious ejectment pleadings and permit the action in the name of the real claimants. Similarly, actions in trover contained a fictitious allegation that the defendant had found the lost property of the plaintiff. In actuality, trover was a remedy for the wrongful conversion of real property.[37]

Notwithstanding its traditional English origin, legal practice in Tennessee was undergoing piecemeal modification during the late eighteenth century. There were numerous departures, some perhaps unconscious, from the classic system of common-law pleadings. Extended pleadings were unusual, and most cases were tried upon only the plaintiff's declaration and the defendant's plea. Pleadings almost never continued beyond the replication stage; hence, the rejoinder, surrejoinder, and rebutter were virtually extinct by Jackson's day.[38] Likewise, demurrers were infrequent. The use of the sham demurrer, utilized in other American jurisdictions to move a case to a higher court without the expense of a trial below,[39] was

---

35. Friedman, *A History of American Law*, 128–129; William E. Nelson, *Americanization of the Common Law: The Impact of Legal Change on Massachusetts Society, 1760–1830* (Cambridge, Mass., 1975), 71–72.

36. 4 Tucker, *Blackstone's Commentaries* 200, and see No. 15.

37. Ch. 152, 1851–1852 Tenn. Pub. Acts, reprinted in *Acts of Tennessee Passed at the First Session of the Twenty-Ninth General Assembly* (1852); Timothy Walker, *Introduction to American Law* (Philadelphia, 1837), 508–509. For an example of pleadings in trover, see No. 25.

38. For a rare instance of a rejoinder during Jackson's tenure as a judge, see White v. Smith, MDSC Law Min. Bk., 1788–1803, p. 236 (1799).

39. Nelson, *Americanization of the Common Law*, 16, 73.

unknown in Tennessee practice. Tennessee courts were casual about the forms of action. Rejecting a defendant's argument that a proceeding could not be maintained in trespass, the Superior Court declared in 1801: "The line of distinction between trespass and case, in many instances, is so nice, that it seems difficult to discover it" (No. 37). Indeed, it was not common for lawsuits to be resolved on the pleadings.

This relaxed concept of the role of common-law pleadings reflected a statutory policy against dilatory pleas. As early as 1777 the North Carolina legislature directed that "in all actions where the declaration shall plainly set forth sufficient matter of substance for the court to proceed upon the merits of the cause, the suit shall not abate for want of form in the proceedings." Similarly, the lawmakers provided that if an appeal or writ of error raised substantive questions "the same shall not be dismissed for want of form." Even writs of attachment were protected against abatement for technical defects once essential requirements were met. These provisions, reenacted in virtually identical language by the territorial legislature in 1794, regulated the practice while Jackson was at bar and bench. In 1809, as part of the measure creating the circuit-court system, the legislators again emphasized their displeasure with technical pleadings. Declaring that "no summons, writ, declaration, return, process or other proceedings, in any civil suit or action" should be dismissed for any defect, the lawmakers mandated "that all civil causes shall be tried on their merits, without being entangled in the nice formalities of law." It is hardly surprising that classic common-law pleadings withered in the face of this persistent legislative command.[40]

Outline of a Civil Lawsuit

A review of the proceedings commonly employed in civil litigation on the law side will illustrate the basic practice in early Tennessee:[41]

1. The first process to issue from the clerk of court was the writ of capias ad respondendum, which directed the sheriff to hold the body of the defendant to answer the plaintiff's suit at the next term of court. Ostensibly to prevent frivolous lawsuits, the plaintiff was required to file a prosecution bond covering the court costs should the plaintiff be found

40. Ch. 2, 1777 Laws of N.C. (Nov. Sess.), reprinted in Iredell, Laws of North Carolina 296, 1 Scott, Laws of Tennessee 165; ch. 1, 1794 Terr. S. of River Ohio Acts, reprinted in 1 Scott, Laws of Tennessee 457 (but see Huser v. Phillips, MDSC Law Min. Bk., 1788–1803, p. 388 [1800], in which the court sustained a plea in abatement on the ground that the defendant had been misnamed in the writ); ch. 49, 1809 Tenn. Pub. Acts, reprinted in 1 Scott, Laws of Tennessee 1148.

41. In addition to an examination of the case law and the relevant statutes, this discussion of civil litigation is based upon Davis, Office and Authority of a Justice of Peace, and Caruthers, History of a Law Suit.

to have initiated a frivolous action. The defendant could then obtain his release by posting a bond with two securities to the sheriff, ensuring his appearance in court.

2. If the defendant could not be located within the county or was about the leave the jurisdiction, the plaintiff could obtain a writ of attachment. This writ ordered the sheriff to seize sufficient property of the defendant to satisfy the claim. The property was held until the defendant either posted a bond for his appearance in court or was discharged by judgment. Attachments used to institute actions were known as original attachments.

3. At the ensuing term of court the plaintiff filed his declaration, a written statement of the facts constituting his cause of action. If the plaintiff neglected to file his declaration in the time required by law, he could be nonsuited upon motion of the defendant.

4. The defendant then entered a general or special plea, which set forth his answer to the declaration. The defendant could enter several inconsistent defenses:

(a) A plea of traverse denying the plaintiff's allegations.

(b) A plea in bar that set up a defense, such as the statute of limitations, to the declaration.

(c) A plea in abatement alleging some defect in the writ or declaration.

(d) A demurrer in which the defendant admitted that the facts alleged in the declaration were true, yet contended that they failed to state a cause of action. If the court overruled the demurrer, the defendant was permitted to file another plea setting up his defense.

5. If the defendant's plea alleged some additional facts that would constitute a defense, the plaintiff could answer the defendant with a replication.

6. Instead of entering a plea of demurrer, the defendant might admit the facts set forth in the plaintiff's declaration. In that event, judgment by confession would be entered against him.

7. Similarly, the defendant might fail to appear at the time of trial, and the court would enter a judgment by default. Despite the defendant's absence, the plaintiff was still obligated to prove the extent of his damages. Accordingly, the court issued a writ of inquiry directing a jury at the next term of court to determine the plaintiff's damages. Upon good cause shown, a default judgment could be set aside and the defendant allowed to enter a plea.

8. Each party had the right to demand subpoenas to ensure the appearance of witnesses or the production of documents at the trial.

9. Following the trial and judgment, if the plaintiff prevailed he could obtain a writ of capias ad satisfaciendum commanding the sheriff to hold

the defendant until the judgment was satisfied. In the alternative, the plaintiff might seek a writ of fieri facias ordering the sheriff to seize and sell the goods and lands of the defendant to satisfy the plaintiff's award. If the plaintiff delayed his execution for a year and a day, he was obligated to revive his judgment by a scire facias, a writ ordering the defendant to show cause why an execution should not be issued. Scire facias was also used as a means of proceeding against sureties on a bond.

10. The losing party could move for a new trial at any point during the term in which the judgment was rendered. Such a motion would be based upon the contention that the verdict was contrary to the law or the evidence or upon the discovery of new evidence. Less frequent was the motion in arrest of judgment, grounded on a material defect on the face of the record or the pleadings.

11. If the judgment were rendered at the county court level, the losing party could file an appeal to the Superior Court of Law and Equity, posting a bond, with sufficient securities, to prosecute the appeal and perform the judgment of the Superior Court. Alternatively, the losing party could seek a writ of certiorari from the Superior Court. By this writ the Superior Court ordered the county court to deliver a record of its proceedings so that the case could be heard by the higher tribunal.

The Role of Juries

Although Tennessee deemphasized the significance of common-law pleadings, trial by jury played a central role in determining lawsuits. Lay influence on the administration of justice was one of the most distinctive features of the English legal system, and the colonists were quick to claim trial by jury as their birthright. The 1776 North Carolina Declaration of Rights contained two provisions concerning jury trials:

  1. That no freeman shall be convicted of any crime, but by the unanimous verdict of a jury of good and lawful men, in open court, as heretofore used. [section 9]
  2. That in all controversies at law respecting property, the ancient mode of trial by jury is one of the best securities of the people, and ought to remain sacred and inviolate. [section 14]

Twenty years later the Tennessee Constitution's Declaration of Rights broadly declared that "the right of trial by jury shall remain inviolate." The constitution further maintained: "The judges of the superior court and inferior courts shall not charge the jury with respect to matters of fact, but may state the testimony and declare the law."[42] Jurors were the only arbiters of factual questions presented in a lawsuit. Neither the state

---

42. Tenn. Const. Art. V, §5, Art. XI, §7 (1796). On the function of the jury, see Mark DeWolfe Howe, "Juries as Judges of Criminal Law," 52 *Harv. L. Rev.* 582 (1939); Com-

constitution nor any statute required judges to instruct the jury on the law, and the extent to which this was done is uncertain.

Since juries were drawn from the locality, they inevitably brought community sentiments to bear on the resolution of disputes. Throughout the Jackson period juries in Tennessee usually returned general verdicts, deciding all of the issues and finding in favor of the plaintiff or defendant. Juries were not expected to explain or justify their verdicts. This practice underscored the power, but not the right, of jurors to pass upon both the law and the facts. In contrast, a special verdict restricted the jury to deciding specific questions of fact and left to the court the application of the law to the facts. Use of the special verdict, however, was infrequent except in equity proceedings.[43]

Judges had relatively limited techniques to control the jury's ability to decide cases and return general verdicts. Once jurors rendered a verdict, the only method by which the court could exercise jury control was to set aside a jury's verdict. The principal post-verdict relief was the motion for a new trial. Either party could request a new trial on the ground that the verdict was contrary to the evidence or the law or on the basis of newly discovered evidence. Jackson, for example, appearing before the Davidson County court in October 1793, "alleged to the court that the Damages Given by the Jury Was Inadequate to those Sustained and Moved for, and Obtained a new Trial."[44]

The courts were reluctant to grant new trials, and most such motions were denied. Occasionally, however, the parties were able to secure retrials, and one proceeding was tried five times before a jury.[45] Doubtless concerned about judicial economy, in 1801 the legislature mandated that "Not more than two new trials may be granted to the same party in the same cause at law, or upon trial of an issue of fact in equity."[46] Even when granted, the motion for a new trial was often unsatisfactory as a mode of jury control. The new trial frequently produced a verdict in favor of the party that had prevailed in the initial trial.

---

ment, "Changing Role of the Jury in the Nineteenth Century," 74 *Yale L. J.* 170 (1964); Robert M. Ireland, "The Nineteenth Century Criminal Jury: Kentucky in the Context of the American Experience," 4 *Ky. Rev.* 52 (1983).

43. For special verdicts, see Nos. 13, 14, and 42. In equity the special verdict was frequently employed when the court submitted contested issues of fact to a jury. 4 Tucker, *Blackstone's Commentaries* 452.

44. 4 Tucker, *Blackstone's Commentaries* 388; Caruthers, *History of a Law Suit*, 57; Nelson, *Americanization of the Common Law*, 27; Ross v. Cannon, DaCo CPQS Min. Bk. B, 139 (1793–1794).

45. McConald v. Danforth, HDSC Law Rec. Bk. C, 359 (1798–1803), was tried three times by the county court and twice by the Hamilton District Superior Court. Likewise, an ejectment matter was tried on three occasions before the Hamilton District Superior Court. English v. Bean, HDSC Law Rec. Bk. C, 161 (1801).

46. Ch. 6, 1801 Tenn. Pub. Acts, reprinted in 1 Scott, *Laws of Tennessee* 685.

JACKSON THE LAWYER, 1787–1798

In late 1784 or early 1785, several months before his eighteenth birthday, Andrew Jackson began to read law in the Salisbury office of Spruce Macay, a prominent lawyer and later a judge. Aspiring young lawyers in eighteenth-century America customarily learned their profession through apprenticeship with members of the bar. Presumably Jackson copied documents and read law books, but the extent of his legal education remains uncertain, and his biographers have devoted most of their attention to his propensity for horseplay during his stay in Salisbury.[47]

By early 1787 Jackson had shifted to the office of John Stokes, where he completed his legal studies. In September of that year he was examined before two judges of the North Carolina Superior Court and was admitted to practice in the county courts.[48] For several months he drifted from county to county, presenting his license to the local magistrates and seeking business. During the early part of 1788 he practiced in Rockingham and Randolph counties, serving for a brief period as county solicitor for Randolph County. He prosecuted one defendant for "profane swearing" and sued the coroner for failure to return a writ of fieri facias,[49] but apparently found it difficult to attract clients.

Then chance intervened to propel Jackson's career in a different direction. In December 1787 the legislature had elected John McNairy judge of the recently created Davidson County Superior Court. Probably through oversight the statute had made no provision for a prosecuting official, although there is some evidence that judges were authorized to appoint a prosecutor. McNairy and Jackson had become friends while clerking for Macay, and McNairy, acting on his own initiative, offered the post to his friend. It is an indication of Jackson's initial discouragement at the bar that he accepted such a doubtful and unsalaried appointment at the fringe of the western settlement.[50]

47. See John S. Bassett, *The Life of Andrew Jackson* (New York, 1911), 11–12; Burke Davis, *Old Hickory: A Life of Andrew Jackson* (New York, 1977), 8–9; James Parton, *Life of Andrew Jackson* (New York, 1860), I, 101–109; Robert V. Remini, *Andrew Jackson and the Course of American Empire, 1767–1821* (New York, 1977), 29–33. See Part IV of this volume for sketches of Jackson's contemporaries on bench and bar.

48. License to Practice in the North Carolina County Courts, Sept. 26, 1787, p. 3 below.

49. State v. Pearce, Randolph Co. Criminal Action Papers, 1788–1792, Nc (1788); Tatum v. Tate, Randolph Co. CPQS Min. Bk., 1787–1794, p. 31, Nc (1788).

50. For McNairy's appointment, see *N.C. State Records,* XX, 262, 270. When the legislature created the Washington District Superior Court in 1784, it provided for a salary for "the attorney general, or in his absence such gentleman as the court shall appoint to transact the business in his department." Ch. 28, 1784 Laws of N.C., reprinted in Iredell, *Laws of North Carolina* 544, 1 Scott, *Laws of Tennessee* 328. McNairy and Jackson may have

In the spring of 1788 Jackson moved across the mountains, passing some months in Jonesboro, where he defended at least one lawsuit. Arriving in Nashville that fall, Jackson was admitted to practice in the Superior Court by order of McNairy.[51] He acted as state's attorney at the November and May terms of the court.

In November 1789 Jackson petitioned the legislature for "some allowance" for his service. Not only was he voted a salary of £40, but also he was duly elected attorney general for the Mero District by joint ballot of the legislature.[52] Nor did North Carolina's cession of the western lands to the federal government terminate his official position. On December 15, 1790, William Blount, the territorial governor, licensed Jackson to practice law in the territory and in February of the following year named Jackson attorney general for the Mero District.[53] It is interesting to note that years later Jackson found it necessary to petition both Congress and the Tennessee legislature to secure compensation for his work as attorney general on behalf of the territory. In 1799 the Tennessee lawmakers paid Jackson $400 "as a full compensation for his services as Attorney General, for the district of Mero, under the Territorial government."[54]

In the Mero District Superior Court Jackson prosecuted eighty-nine criminal cases on behalf of the North Carolina and territorial governments. The largest category was assault and battery, followed by petty larceny, perjury, and horse stealing (see No. 2). Jackson prosecuted one defendant for a robbery on the Mississippi River (No. 1) and another for the theft of five gallons of brandy.[55] Only infrequently did he handle the most serious felonies, prosecuting just two accusations of murder and a single rape. As always, the criminal docket gives a glimpse of the underside of society; the pattern of Jackson's cases, however, may call into question the

---

assumed that the same provision applied to the Davidson County Superior Court. Still, the wording of the statute lends no support to such a conclusion, and Jackson may have reasoned that he could present the lawmakers with a *fait accompli* by performing the duties of prosecutor. He was officially appointed prosecutor on Nov. 3, 1788, the opening day of the Davidson County Superior Court. MDSC Law Min. Bk., 1788–1803, p. 1.

51. Jackson presented his license to the Washington County court on May 12, 1788, and to the Greene County court on Aug. 5, 1788. *Jackson Papers*, I, 13. For Jackson as defense counsel, see Writ, Aug. 19, 1788, Carney v. Mitchell, Paul Fink, PVT. See License to Practice in the Superior Court of Law and Equity, Nov. 3, 1788, p. 4 below.

52. In his petition Jackson noted that the governing statutes "made no provision for the attorney General." Petition to the North Carolina General Assembly, November 1789, *Jackson Papers*, I, 18. For his election, see *N.C. State Records*, XXI, 412, 637, 717.

53. Blount, *Journal*, 43, 46.

54. Petition to the U.S. House of Representatives, [Mar. 6, 1792], *Jackson Papers*, I, 35–36; Petition to the Tennessee General Assembly, Apr. 11, 1796, *id.* at 87–88; ch. 58, 1799 Tenn. Pub. Acts, *Acts Passed at the First Session, Third General Assembly of the State of Tennessee* (Knoxville, 1799).

55. Territory v. Rider, MDSC Law Min. Bk., 1788–1803, p. 182 (1794–1796).

stereotype of the lawless frontier.[56] While doubtless there were unreported offenses, the level of prosecution for major crimes is strikingly low.

In those cases for which a final judgment can be determined, Jackson secured thirty guilty verdicts against nineteen not-guilty, for a conviction rate of approximately 62 percent. While not outstanding by modern measures, Jackson's record as a prosecutor was similar to the experience in other jurisdictions.[57] He handled all aspects of the prosecution, preparing the indictments and personally appearing in court. Nearly every criminal case was submitted to a jury. Defense counsel can be identified in just two of Jackson's prosecutions. Post-conviction remedies were infrequent: only three defendants were awarded new trials. One defendant convicted of manslaughter in 1790 was granted benefit of clergy.[58] In addition to his prosecutory role, Jackson instituted more than thirty scire facias proceedings on behalf of the territorial government, presumably to collect fines for statutory offenses against the court.[59]

Although he had moved west to act as public prosecutor, Jackson seems to have tired of his official responsibilities, even though the post was a part-time one. In May 1795 and in May 1796 he was absent from sessions of the Mero District Superior Court; on both occasions he was in Philadelphia negotiating the sale of land to the speculator David Allison.[60] The court named Jackson's brother-in-law Samuel Donelson as at-

56. For a similar finding, see David J. Bodenhamer, "Law and Disorder on the Early Frontier: Marion County, Indiana, 1823–1850," 10 *Western Hist. Q.* 323 (1979).

57. Between 1969 and 1975 the conviction rate in federal district courts averaged approximately 75 percent. Michael J. Hindelang et al., *Sourcebook of Criminal Justice Statistics—1976* (Washington, D.C., 1977), 600. Of adults charged in 1976 with offenses on the FBI Crime Index, 66 percent were found guilty as charged, and 7 percent were found guilty of lesser offenses. Federal Bureau of Investigation, *Uniform Crime Reports for the United States—1976* (Washington, D.C., 1977), 215. One study found that 71.5 percent of those tried in antebellum South Carolina were convicted. Michael S. Hindus, *Prison and Plantation: Crime, Justice and Authority in Massachusetts and South Carolina, 1767–1878* (Chapel Hill, 1980), 91. Other scholars have found a large gap between indictments and convictions. See Douglas Greenberg, *Crime and Law Enforcement in the Colony of New York, 1691–1776* (Ithaca, 1976), 70–98; Jack K. Williams, *Vogues in Villainy: Crime and Retribution in Ante-Bellum South Carolina* (Columbia, S.C., 1959), 38; David J. Bodenhamer, "Crime and Criminal Justice in Antebellum Indiana: Marion County as a Case Study" (Ph.D. dissertation, Indiana Univ., 1977), 188–198.

58. State v. White, MDSC Law Min. Bk., 1788–1803, pp. 23, 26 (1790). For a treatment of benefit of clergy, see No. 38.

59. Apart from brief procedural minute book entries, the only extant records of these scire facias proceedings are entries in the court's execution docket. E.q., Territory v. Bushnell, MDSC Law Min. Bk., 1788–1803, p. 47 (1791), MDSC Execution Docket, 1792–1803, pp. 6, 10 (1792–1793). Various offenses, such as forfeiture of recognizance and failure to respond to a subpoena to give testimony, were prosecuted by scire facias. Ch. 2, 1777 Laws of N.C., reprinted in Iredell, *Laws of North Carolina* 296, 1 Scott, *Laws of Tennessee* 165.

60. See Promissory Note, David Allison to AJ, May 13, 1795, Box 25, Middle Tennessee Supreme Court Records, T; AJ to Rachel Jackson, May 9, 1796, *Jackson Papers*, I, 91–92; various transactions, June 11, 1796, *id.*, App. III, 443–444.

torney general pro hac vice for each term.[61] Jackson's resignation cannot be precisely determined, but apparently he stepped down sometime in the spring of 1796.[62]

Most of Jackson's energies during his period as attorney general were devoted to his expanding private practice. Between 1788 and 1798 he represented clients in more than 400 lawsuits, largely confined to the Mero District.[63] He appeared regularly before the Davidson and Sumner county courts and the Mero District Superior Court (see Part III). This geographic limitation was not surprising since the nearest important tribunals, the Washington District Superior Court in Jonesboro and the Hamilton District Superior Court in Knoxville, were some two hundred miles from Jackson's home near Nashville.[64] Because the federal district court for Tennessee was not established until 1797, Jackson never developed a federal practice. By far the majority of his cases were tried in the Davidson County court, with his appearances in the Mero Superior Court about equally divided between appeals and original actions. In one instance Jackson submitted a hypothetical question to the Superior Court concerning the assignment of a bond and obtained an advisory opinion (No. 13). Jackson occasionally tried matters before a single justice of the peace and then handled appeals to the county court.[65]

Jackson's caseload before the Davidson County court was unpredictable. Although he regularly represented clients in eight to fifteen separate matters each quarter session, a heavy term would produce between twenty and thirty items of business. On the other hand, Jackson sometimes experienced a light call for his services. There were a few terms in which he made no court appearances, and in January 1793 he secured only three

---

61. MDSC Law Min. Bk., 1788–1803, pp. 130, 164.

62. Howell Tatum was elected attorney general for the Mero District by the legislature in April 1796. *Senate Journal*, 64 (1796). He was commissioned in July but evidently never served in an official capacity. Sevier, *Commission Book*, 2.

63. As mentioned above, the Mero District Superior Court also exercised jurisdiction over the Tennessee County court, but the records for this county have been lost.

64. The surviving contemporary records do not support Remini's conclusion, apparently based upon the account of an interview with Jackson two years before his death and nearly forty-five years after the termination of his practice (James A. McLaughlin to Amos Kendall, Mar. 13, 1843, AJ Papers, DLC), that "in trying these cases [Jackson] traveled regularly, principally between Nashville and Jonesborough." Remini, *Andrew Jackson and the Course of American Empire*, 45.

Although an intercounty practice developed on a limited basis, a circuit bar never flourished in the Cumberland region. For a treatment of lawyers in antebellum Tennessee, see Daniel H. Calhoun, *Professional Lives in America: Structure and Aspiration, 1750–1850* (Cambridge, Mass., 1965), 59–87.

65. See Skelly v. Betts, DaCo CPQS Min. Bk. B, 211 (1793–1794); Archer v. Skinner, DaCo CPQS Min. Bk. A, 311 (1789). All judgments rendered in civil actions by individual members of the county court were subject to appeal to the full court. Ch. 2, §70, 1777 Laws of N.C. (Nov. Sess.), reprinted in Iredell, *Laws of North Carolina* 311, 1 Scott, *Laws of Tennessee* 187.

default judgments. Likewise, Jackson's schedule varied widely during sessions of the county court. On some days he represented numerous clients, while on others he did not handle any matters. Certain dates must have been especially hectic for him. Several times he tried more than three jury cases in a day. On April 10, 1793, he conducted eight jury trials and won five judgments by default.[66]

Jackson also appeared often at the Sumner County court, but he never handled a large volume of cases there. Since the Sumner County court met during the same time period as the Davidson court, Jackson was compelled to stagger his schedule in order to practice before both bodies, and this partially explains the uneven distribution of cases tried in Davidson County.

Jackson was retained by plaintiffs more often than by defendants, but he regularly represented both. Although the surviving records are not complete, it appears that Jackson's clients prevailed in approximately two-thirds of these suits. It is revealing, however, to compare Jackson's record in representing plaintiffs and defendants. In those cases for which a final outcome is known, Jackson emerged victorious on behalf of plaintiffs in 215 trials, against only 26 defeats. Conversely, he lost nearly two-thirds of his appearances for defendants.[67]

The overwhelming majority of those cases actually tried were submitted to a jury. Even default judgments were presented to jurors in order to fix the amount of damages. Pursuant to statute, appeals to the Mero Superior Court were tried de novo with a jury. Since, traditionally, juries have been viewed as favorable to plaintiffs, this mode of trial may be a significant factor in the outcome of Jackson's trials. Further, more than one hundred of Jackson's cases on behalf of plaintiffs ended in confessions of judgment or in defaults.

While the jury trial was the dominant form of conflict resolution, arbitration was also employed on occasion. The parties would agree to submit their differences to a panel of arbitrators, often attorneys, and to abide by the results. The court then entered an order referring the case to arbitration. If the arbitrators could not resolve the conflict, they were authorized to elect an umpire whose decision was final. Upon motion the court would confirm the arbitration award. Eight cases in which Jackson appeared were referred to arbitration, and he acted as an arbitrator him-

66. For the distribution of his workload, see DaCo CPQS Min. Bk. A, 259–448 *passim;* DaCo CPQS Min. Bk. B, 3–325 *passim;* and for specific dates, see, for example, Oct. 6, 1789, July 15, 1791, Apr. 10–11, 1793, and Apr. 15, 1795. DaCo CPQS Min. Bk. A, 320–323, 442–448; DaCo CPQS Min. Bk. B, 78–93, 253–260.

67. Jackson's record on behalf of defendants is more impressive than may be immediately apparent. One scholar found that in Kentucky during this period, "jurors almost invariably found for the plaintiffs." Tachau, *Federal Courts in the Early Republic,* 78.

self several times. For instance, in 1793 Jackson represented the plaintiff in a lawsuit seeking damages for the defendant's alleged breach of a promise to convey a lot in Nashville. The case was submitted to arbitration, and the Superior Court confirmed an award against Jackson's client (No. 9).[68]

The most commonly used forms of action in Jackson's practice were trespass on the case, debt, covenant, and attachment. Although many of these cases involved routine collection of debts and suits to collect promissory notes and to enforce contracts, they reflected a vigorous economy of land speculation and burgeoning commerce. One case involved a "writing obligatory" under seal to deliver 1,453 pounds of beaver fur (No. 14). Jackson handled relatively few tort cases. He tried two actions for deceit. In one case he argued for a plaintiff who alleged that a lame horse had been misrepresented as sound.[69] This was a period in which reputation was zealously guarded, and Jackson had several cases for slander. Thus, in 1794 he represented a client who secured a judgment of $18.75 because the defendant had accused the plaintiff of horse stealing (No. 11). Another significant group of cases involved real property. Jackson participated in actions of *caveat* to claims of public land and ejectment (Nos. 7, 15). Several actions sued in covenant concerned agreements to deliver title to parcels of real property. Jackson's role as attorney general for the Mero District precluded a large criminal defense practice. Nevertheless, on three occasions he represented defendants accused of petty larceny or assault and battery before the Davidson County court, winning each time.[70]

Jackson, as might be expected, was inevitably concerned with the law of slavery. In 1791 Jackson defended two men against a complaint of trespass vi et armis, alleging that the defendants had committed an assault on the plaintiff's slave that resulted in his death (No. 5). He successfully appeared on behalf of one John Williams, who was charged with being a slave (No. 6). Most of his cases involving slavery, however, were routine, indicating the extent to which slaves were treated like other forms of chattel property. Thus, Jackson levied attachments on slave property and, in the last trial of his career, defended a suit asserting ownership of four slaves held by his client.[71]

68. Resort to arbitration was common in colonial North Carolina. McCain, *The County Court in North Carolina before 1750*, 59–60. For Jackson as arbitrator, see No. 15 and *Jackson Papers*, I, 27.

69. Wells v. Anderson (1794), SumCo Records, T.

70. Territory v. Clark (1793), Territory v. Hutchison (1793), Territory v. Shearman (1791), DaCo CPQS Min. Bk. B, 9, 123, 132.

71. Sevier v. Cox, DaCo CPQS Min. Bk. B, 201 (1794); Lenier v. Hadley, MDSC Law Min. Bk., 1788–1803, p. 204 (1798).

Jackson's services to his clients involved more than preparation of pleadings and arguments in court. He functioned partly as a collection official and land agent. One client, on the losing side of a lawsuit, requested Jackson to convey a portion of a tract "to the use of Setling the Judgment . . . obtained against me." He further instructed Jackson: "Sell the Balance for any kind of Trade and we can Settle when I return in the Spring." In 1796 a nonresident called upon Jackson to post bail in order to lift an attachment on real property. At least twice Jackson signed as security on his clients' prosecution bonds.[72]

Occasionally Jackson appeared before the county court in his capacity as a private citizen. For instance, in October 1793 Jackson and John Overton, "professing themselves to appear only for the good of Society," opposed William Terrell Lewis's application for a tavern license. After hearing the arguments, the court revoked a license previously granted to Lewis. One may speculate that there was some personal animosity between Jackson and Lewis, who had recently moved from North Carolina. During 1793 and 1794 Jackson appeared as defense counsel in several lawsuits in which Lewis was the plaintiff.[73]

During the years of his practice Jackson had a group of regular clients. While little is known about many of them, several can be identified as prominent in the community. He represented James Bosley, owner of a large plantation, in twenty-four separate lawsuits and another landowner, George Sugg, in twelve proceedings. He also represented William Tait, a merchant and later mayor of Nashville, and John Boyd, a tavern owner and subsequently sheriff of Davidson County, in eight matters each. David Hay, a justice of the peace, militia major, and landowner, called upon Jackson in four cases. Jackson frequently appeared in court as counsel for Tait & Company and Quarles & Company, two merchant partnerships. For example, in 1797 Jackson unsuccessfully sued to collect a debt "for diverse goods, wares and merchandise" for Quarles & Company.[74]

Moreover, Jackson regularly appeared on behalf of nonresident clients.

---

72. Squire Grant to AJ, Nov. 7, 1793, *Jackson Papers*, I, 42. Jackson had unsuccessfully represented Grant in Loggins v. Grant, DaCo CPQS Min. Bk. B, 69 (1793). The nonresident client promised to "execute any instrument to you giving you a Lien on the Lands to secure you." John Hinds to AJ, July 23, 1796, *Jackson Papers*, I, 96. For Jackson's signing as security, see No. 10, Doc. II; Sharp v. McNairy, DaCo CPQS Min. Bk. B, 116 (1793).

73. DaCo CPQS Min. Bk. B, 131. For Lewis as plaintiff, see, *e.g.*, Lewis v. Hay, DaCo CPQS Min. Bk. B, 253 (1794–1795); Lewis v. Bosley, DaCo CPQS Min. Bk. B, 228, MDSC Law Min. Bk., 1788–1803, p. 137 (1794–1795); Lewis v. Worldly, SumCo CPQS Min. Bk., 1787–1805, p. 62 (1793).

74. For Bosley, see Clayton, *Davidson County,* 58. For Sugg, see SumCo Tax Lists, 1787–1794, p. 60, T. For Tait, see Clayton, *Davidson County,* 58, 203, and Nos. 8, 15. For Boyd, see A. W. Putnam, *History of Middle Tennessee* (Nashville, 1859), 284, 384; Provine Papers, Box 1, T. For Hay, see Brown, "Tennessee County Courts," 384. And see Quarles & Co. v. Sharp, MDSC Law Min. Bk., 1788–1803, p. 197 (1797).

He represented two firms, Edgar & Company and Edgar & Tait, which handled the extensive commercial interests of John Edgar. A resident of Kaskaskia, then a political and economic center on the Mississippi River, Edgar was the leading merchant and landowner in the Northwest Territory. Jackson instituted a lawsuit for Marguerite Bentley, another Kaskaskia resident, growing out of her long battle with John Dodge over his administration of her husband's estate. In 1794 John Rice Jones, also from Kaskaskia, asked Jackson to file a claim against the estate of Josiah Love. Jackson tried a suit on behalf of George Meldrum, a Detroit businessman (No. 4), and represented the interests of Squire Grant of Kentucky.[75]

In common with most attorneys of the late eighteenth century, Jackson was a sole practitioner and argued alone for his clients in the majority of cases. Yet it was not unusual for two lawyers to represent one side. Jackson appeared as co-counsel in more than twenty-five proceedings. He was most often paired with Josiah Love and his close friend John Overton, although he opposed them far more than he joined them. Jackson's participation in these arrangements flew squarely in the face of a statutory prohibition. Declaring that "the frequent abuses of attorneys have occasioned distresses to many of the good People of this state," the North Carolina legislature in 1786 provided that

> it shall not be lawful for each Plaintiff or Defendant to employ in any matter of Suit whatever more than one Attorney to speak in any Suit in Court; and the Courts in this State are hereby directed not to suffer more than one Attorney as aforesaid in any Matter whatever to plead for either Plaintiff or Defendant to any Suit. . . .

This restriction was not repealed by the territorial legislature until late 1794 and was in effect during most of Jackson's years at the bar. Still, such post-Revolutionary restrictions on lawyers were often futile, and this statute seems to have been totally ignored by both judges and counsel.[76]

Jackson apparently maintained a working relationship with other at-

---

75. James H. Roberts, "The Life and Times of General John Edgar," *Transactions of the Ill. State Hist. Soc'y* (1908), XII, 70. William Tait apparently handled Edgar's business operations in Nashville. See No. 15, note 18, and accompanying text. The Bentley suit is Bentley v. Dodge, DaCo CPQS Min. Bk. A, 342 (1789). For a discussion of the dispute between Bentley and Dodge, see Clarence W. Alvord, ed., *Kaskaskia Records 1778–1790*, Collections of the Illinois State Historical Library, V (Springfield, 1909), 397 n.2. For Jones, see John Rice Jones to AJ, Nov. 30, 1794, *Jackson Papers*, I, 51. For Grant, see note 72 above and No. 14.

76. Ch. 14, 1786 Laws of N.C., reprinted in Iredell, *Laws of North Carolina* 584; 1 Scott, *Laws of Tennessee* 368; ch. 1, 1794 Terr. S. of River Ohio Acts, reprinted in 1 Scott, *Laws of Tennessee* 457. In the 1780s, for example, Massachusetts enacted statutes that limited the number of attorneys a litigant could employ. Yet this prohibition was widely evaded. Gerald W. Gawalt, *The Promise of Power: The Emergence of the Legal Profession in Massachusetts, 1760–1840* (Westport, Conn., 1979), 64, 69; Nelson, *Americanization of the Common Law*, 69.

torneys whereby they would handle court matters for one another. For example, declaring that he had left Nashville before instituting a lawsuit, Overton requested that Jackson "file a Bill against Egnew respecting his claims to Neelys Lick." At the May Term of the Mero District in 1795, while Jackson was in Philadelphia, several lawsuits and appeals in which he was attorney of record or counsel below were tried. Jackson likely retained overall management of the proceedings and engaged another attorney to appear for him during his absence. Possibly Samuel Donelson, who substituted for Jackson as attorney general, also handled any necessary civil business.[77]

Trial work claimed most of Jackson's legal time. Surviving records show that his practice was exclusively in the common-law courts, but this is misleading since the Mero District equity records were destroyed by fire early in 1796.[78] Office work, such as drafting deeds and wills, was seemingly not a major activity.

As a lawyer, Jackson experienced considerable success and enjoyed a favorable reputation. One litigant wrote to a friend: "I wish you to put my Papers into the hands of an Attorney Lawyer Jackson if you can or into Mr. Overton or some good attorney."[79] During Jackson's years at the bar sixteen attorneys practiced before the Davidson County court, but the bulk of the litigation was handled by only five—Josiah Love, Jackson, Howell Tatum, John Overton, and Bennett Searcy. Love, who had been the first attorney in the area, presenting his license to the county court shortly before Jackson arrived, had the largest case load in 1793 (the year of his death), while Jackson handled the second heaviest volume. Nonetheless, Jackson represented more clients than any other attorney for the period 1788–1796. Another measure of his standing in the profession is that both Searcy and Love asked Jackson to represent them in private litigation.[80]

The years 1794 and 1795 were the apex of Jackson's career as a lawyer.

---

77. In 1795 Samuel Donelson asked Jackson either to handle Donelson's pending business in the Tennessee County court or to ask Bennett Searcy to do so. Samuel Donelson to AJ, June 29, 1795, *Jackson Papers*, I, 62–63. See also John Overton to Robert C. Foster, May 8, 1827, Box 60, Dickinson Papers, T, and Overton to AJ, Mar. 10, 1796, *Jackson Papers*, I, 84–85.

78. Noting that the Mero District equity office "was lately destroyed by fire, and the books, records and papers thereof were lost," the Tennessee legislature in April 1796 provided that the parties could establish equity decrees by oral proof under oath. Ch. 21, 1796 Tenn. Pub. Acts, reprinted in 1 Scott, *Laws of Tennessee* 566.

79. William Cook to Lewis Elliott, June 2, 1797, Box 1, Correspondence by Author, T.

80. See Brown, "Tennessee County Courts," 394. Calhoun found that such a concentration of practice among a few leading Tennessee attorneys continued well into the nineteenth century. Calhoun, *Professional Lives in America*, 67–69. For Searcy and Love, see, *e.g.*, Searcy v. Armstrong, DaCo CPQS Min. Bk. B, 214 (1794); Nelson v. Love, *id.* at 81 (1792–1793).

Starting in 1796, the demands of public office began to dominate his life. His service in the convention to draft Tennessee's first constitution and subsequent election to Congress markedly reduced his legal business. Yet Jackson probably did not expect that official duties would terminate his law practice. Between brief stints in the House of Representatives and the Senate, he continued to handle a small number of matters. While in Philadelphia he purchased a sizable collection of law books.[81] Concerned about a land dispute, a client asked Jackson in August 1797 to "make every necessary arrangement to bring the matter to a decision at next Court." Nonetheless, the lure of public office proved too strong. Jackson tried his last case in May 1798, only months before he was named judge of the Superior Court of Law and Equity.[82]

Jackson's financial remuneration is difficult to determine. Following a series of colonial statutes, in 1786 the North Carolina legislature mandated the fees that attorneys could receive for lawsuits and appeals in both the county courts and the Superior Court. Violation of the fee schedule constituted a misdemeanor, and upon conviction a lawyer was "thenceforth dismissed from his Practice as an Attorney, for one Year, in every Court of Law and Equity within this State." The statutory attorney's fee was regularly taxed as part of the court costs to be paid by the losing party. This legal ceiling curtailed the income that attorneys could derive from the practice of law and possibly encouraged them to seek financial rewards through other ventures.[83]

Of course, the statutory scheme provided no guarantee that attorneys would in fact be paid. Judging from the large number of unsatisfied writs of execution, lawyers must have often looked to their clients for compensation. In 1793 several Knoxville attorneys publicly declared that "for the future no application need be made to them for advice on any matter of law, or to appear in any cause, either in the superior or inferior courts, without first paying the fees established by law, or giving their notes for the same."[84]

81. See Invoice for Law Books Purchased from Robert Campbell & Company, Jan. 7, 1797, pp. 5–6 below.
82. David Shelby to AJ, Aug. 4, 1797, *Jackson Papers,* I, 149. See also John Sevier to AJ, May 13, 1797, *id.* at 145. Jackson's last case was Lenier v. Hadley, note 71 above.
83. For the colonial statutes, see Ernest H. Alderman, "The North Carolina Colonial Bar," 13 *James Sprunt Hist. Publ.* 5 (1913). See ch. 14, 1786 Laws of N.C., reprinted in Iredell, *Laws of North Carolina* 584, 1 Scott, *Laws of Tennessee* 368. In 1796 Tennessee lawmakers reenacted the limitation on attorneys' fees but omitted the penal sanction for violators. Ch. 7, 1796 Tenn. Pub. Acts, reprinted in 1 Scott, *Laws of Tennessee* 552. The assessment of attorneys' fees as costs followed the practice in colonial North Carolina. McCain, *The County Court in North Carolina before 1750,* p. 62. And see Clement Eaton, "A Mirror of the Southern Colonial Lawyer: The Fee Books of Patrick Henry, Thomas Jefferson, and Waightstill Avery," 8 *WMQ* (3d ser.) 520 (1951).
84. *Knoxville Gazette,* Mar. 23, 1793.

On the other hand, it is likely that the legislative limit on fees was partially evaded. A 1770 Carolina statute regulating fees included an escape clause:

> That it may be lawful for any Person, after the determination of his Suit, to make his Lawyer a Larger Compensation for his Trouble, if he thinks he has merited the same . . . .[85]

While this provision was not repeated in the 1786 measure, it may well have reflected the prevailing custom. Moreover, anxious clients might not have argued about fees. For example, in October 1793 one client wrote Jackson: "Now Sir as Mr. Wilcox is about running his property out of this district I wish you to Transact This business for me in the Same manner as if it was your own and your charge shall be paid."[86] In 1796 an individual signed a promissory note to pay Jackson $50 from a judgment of $500 upon satisfaction of the award.[87] Jackson estimated that he was entitled to £28 from the judgment in one case, an amount well in excess of the statutory scheme.[88] Probate work was not covered by the fee limitation. Jackson received a note in the amount of $10 "for his undertaking to transact the business of the Estate of Christopher Lightholder" and two payments totaling $16 for handling another estate.[89] On occasion Jackson was paid in kind (see No. 11). One conclusion seems fully warranted: Jackson's financial return was dependent upon his ability to secure relatively small fees from a great number of cases, not large payments from a few clients.[90]

The intellectual dimension of Jackson's practice is also obscure. Extant court records and pleadings contain few references to statutes, judicial authority, or legal treatises. Only fragments remain of the arguments presented by counsel. Without these sources, the best evidence as to the

---

85. Ch. 5, 1770 Laws of N.C., reprinted in *N.C. State Records,* XXIII, 788.

86. Robert King to AJ, Oct. 23, 1793 (No. 10), pp. 51–52 below.

87. John Caffery purchased the $500 judgment that William Cotter had obtained against Elijah Robertson. Promissory Note, Caffery to AJ, May 18, 1796, *Jackson Papers,* I, App. III, 443. Jackson had represented the plaintiff, Cotter. See Cotter v. Robertson, MDSC Law Min. Bk., 1788–1803, p. 167, MDSC Execution Docket, 1792–1803, p. 38 (1796).

88. AJ to John Overton, June 23, 1799, *Jackson Papers,* I, 221. The case was *Protzman v. Robertson,* No. 14.

89. Promissory Note, Haydon Wells to AJ, July 12, 1794, AJ Papers, DLC (Reel 1); Receipts, AJ to Moses Shelby, Jan. 22 and Oct. 29, 1794, *Jackson Papers,* I, App. III, 436–437.

90. In 1827 the Tennessee Supreme Court rejected the legislative fee limitation and permitted attorneys to seek a reasonable compensation. "It cannot be seriously thought," the court ruled, "that the General Assembly intended the fee tax, which is directed to be included in the bill of costs in each suit, as the sole reward of professional exertion." Newnan v. Washington, 8 Tenn. (1 Mart. & Yer.) 79 (1827). This nineteenth-century view of the lawyer as entrepreneur did not prevail during Jackson's years at the bar.

source of law may be the variety of legal books available in the Mero District. Jackson brought with him in 1788 an appendix to William Blackstone's *Commentaries,* and doubtless he was conversant with Blackstone.[91] In 1795 he bought the *Miscellaneous Essays and Occasional Writings of Francis Hopkinson* (Philadelphia, 1792), a three-volume set that contained several legal essays. Two years later Jackson purchased from Robert Campbell & Company in Philadelphia some twenty-four sets of law books, ranging from legal dictionaries to case reports. The case reports were devoted to Chancery Court decisions, suggesting that Jackson maintained an equity practice. Treatises included Geoffrey Gilbert's *The Law of Evidence,* William Hawkins's *Pleas of the Crown,* Emmerich de Vattel's *The Law of Nations,* and Edward Coke's *Institutes.*[92] Significantly, with the exception of two volumes of laws of the United States, all of the works purchased by Jackson concerned English or international law.

In assessing Jackson's career at the bar it is important to remember that legal duties never claimed his undivided attention. Like many others, Jackson had moved west to seek his fortune, and the practice of law was only one route to this end. Almost from the moment of his arrival in Nashville he engaged in extensive land speculations. He also was a participant in several commercial ventures, trading regularly with businessmen in Spanish Natchez. Even a successful frontier lawyer could find a more lucrative return in other pursuits.

Then, too, Jackson's years at the bar were also marked by his emergence as a prodigious litigant. In connection with his commercial activity, Jackson was a party in numerous proceedings during the 1790s. Usually the plaintiff, he instituted lawsuits to collect unpaid obligations and pursued elusive debtors with attachments.[93] In one instance, however, he was successfully sued in detinue before the Sumner County court. The jury set his damages at £300 and costs, "or a delivery of the negro specified in the declaration to the plaintiff."[94] Jackson never represented himself. Rather, he called upon other counsel to handle his legal affairs, most frequently Bennett Searcy, but Howell Tatum and John Overton also appeared for him.

91. *An Interesting Appendix to Sir William Blackstone's Commentaries on the Laws of England* (Philadelphia, 1773), inscribed on the flyleaf, "Andrew Jackson August 25th 1788," T.

92. Invoice for Law Books Purchased from Robert Campbell & Company, Jan. 7, 1797, pp. 5–6 below.

93. *E.g.,* Jackson v. Waller, DaCo CPQS Min. Bk. B, 259 (1795); Jackson v. Marney, *id.* at 235, 246 (1795).

94. Head v. Jackson, SumCo CPQS Min. Bk. 1, p. 40 (1791).

JACKSON AS JUDGE OF THE SUPERIOR COURT, 1798–1804

Only months after Jackson had resigned from the Senate in the spring of 1798, he was afforded another opportunity to enter public life. By early summer, Governor John Sevier was under pressure from the Blount faction to consider Jackson as judge of the Superior Court of Law and Equity. William Blount undertook to sound out Jackson on the subject, and Blount's half-brother Willie advised Sevier that it was "the wish of the people in this district" that "Andrew Jackson should be appointed." [95] Because of the distance between judicial districts, there was a compelling need to fill the vacancy with a candidate from the Mero District. As William Blount noted:

> I have also receved another Letter a friend of mine in the Mero District stating that there are several Decisions in the Courts of law now which the Parties upon one side or the other will pray for Relief in equity and that if a Judge is not shortly appointed in the place of Mr. Tatom who shall reside in that District that the Parties injured will be compelled to pass the Wilderness to Judge Roane or Judge Campbell to obtain Injunctions. [96]

With his years of law practice and experience in public office, Jackson was an obvious choice. "I now do myself the honour of informing you," Sevier wrote Jackson in August 1798, "that in case the office of a judge of the Superior Courts of Law and equity meets your Approbation, you will please Consider yourself as Already appointed." [97] Under the Tennessee Constitution of 1796 the legislature elected Superior Court judges. The governor, however, was authorized by Article II, section 14, to make recess appointments in order temporarily to fill vacancies. Accordingly, Jackson sat on the bench at the September Term in the Hamilton District and the November Term in the Mero District. His appointment was apparently popular: "While his fellow citizens have to lament the loss of his abilities in the Senate," the *Knoxville Register* of October 9, 1798, declared, "they have a consolation of hoping for his long continuance in his present honorable, and important office." When the lawmakers convened in December, Jackson was elected judge, defeating Bennett Searcy by a vote of 18–13, and was duly commissioned "during good behavior." [98]

Jackson's motives for accepting this assignment are a topic for speculation. After a disappointing stint in Congress, he might well have decided to forgo public office at this time. On the other hand, the Superior Court

---

95. Willie Blount to John Sevier, Aug. 13, 1798, John Sevier Papers, THi.
96. William Blount to John Sevier, July 6, 1798, *Jackson Papers*, I, 199 n.3.
97. John Sevier to AJ, Aug. 29, 1798, *id.* at 209.
98. See *Journals of the Senate and House, 1797–1798*, pp. 323, 435. Jackson's temporary and full commissions are given at pp. 101 and 103–104 below.

post carried a secure salary, and the duties kept Jackson closer to home. Moreover, a Superior Court judge enjoyed stature in the community and an opportunity to make contacts across the state.

The disposition of litigation was the most important function performed by Tennessee judges. Twice a year, at legislatively mandated intervals, Jackson joined his fellow jurists on circuit to conduct trials, hear appeals, and pass upon motions. It may facilitate an understanding of Jackson's judicial responsibilities to reconstruct a typical term of the Superior Court. One must remember that the extant records are incomplete, particularly with respect to equity practice and the motion docket, and hence some degree of conjecture is unavoidable.

The length of court terms fluctuated between twelve and fifteen days. When in session, the tribunal met six days a week, working on Saturdays. Administrative duties occupied the entire opening day of each term. The justices of the peace and sheriffs of the counties in the district made return of recognizances, scire facias, and other writs. Constables were summoned and a grand jury impaneled. Occasionally the judges decided motions pending from the previous term of court.

On the following day, and throughout the remainder of the session, the judges, sitting en banc, heard original actions and appeals from county courts in an undifferentiated manner. Appeals were tried de novo and were interspersed among the rest of the docket. Invariably there were far more original actions than appeals. Similarly, criminal prosecutions were scattered among the civil proceedings. The judges and jurors would hear and resolve several cases each day, indicating that jury trials were more expeditious than their modern counterparts. Jackson often presided over three or four jury deliberations daily, and during one hectic day he sat on seven trials.[99]

Between trials, perhaps while jurors were deliberating, the judges decided a wide variety of motions and applications. Jackson and his colleagues passed upon demurrers, requests for a jury of view and survey, motions in arrest of judgment and for new trials, motions for a writ of error, applications for a writ of mandamus, motions for a commission to take depositions, and requests for subpoenas. In addition, they entered orders directing the sale of land under attachment and referring cases to arbitration. A 1798 statute provided that applicants for admission to practice law "shall undergo an examination before two or more judges of the superior courts of law and equity"; if such applicant were found "to possess a competent share of law knowledge" and to be "a person of upright character," the judges were required to "grant him a license under

99. This practice of multiple trials in a day was consistent with the litigation experience during the colonial era. Wroth and Zobel, eds., *Legal Papers of John Adams*, I, xlix.

their hands." The court thus regularly admitted attorneys to practice, and Jackson participated in the qualifying examinations.[100]

In cases instituted on the law side of the Superior Court the most frequently employed forms of action were trespass on the case, covenant, debt, and ejectment. The court also heard many other matters, including trespass quare clausum fregit, detinue, divorce (No. 45), qui tam proceedings (No. 42), and presentments of local officials for neglecting their duties.[101] Trespass on the case was a general action seeking redress for wrongs inflicted without force. Suits filed in case covered a range of tort matters, such as attorney malpractice (No. 33), slander, and loss of services for a daughter seduced by the defendant.[102] More commonly, however, suits in case sought payments for services rendered, such as surveying or carpentry, or for goods sold and delivered to the defendant.[103] In addition, case was employed to collect rent and money due on promissory notes. Lastly, actions "on the case sur trover" were used to recover the value of personal property, typically slaves or cattle, wrongfully converted by another to his own benefit.[104]

Covenant actions customarily involved the recovery of damages for the breach of a contract under seal. During Jackson's years at the bar and bench, suits in covenant lay for the failure to perform agreements to convey real property and to deliver such chattels as slaves, cattle, and salt.[105] Suits in debt concerned a broad range of unpaid obligations for specific sums. The action of ejectment lay for the recovery of the possession of land. Given the unsettled state of land titles in early Tennessee, disputes over possession and ownership of real property were common.[106]

Criminal cases did not occupy much of the court's time. The Superior

100. Ch. 2, 1798 Tenn. Pub. Acts, reprinted in 1 Scott, *Laws of Tennessee* 615; see License of Samuel Powel, Sept. 15, 1803, Jones Memorial Library, Lynchburg, Va.

101. State v. Johnston, MDSC Law Min. Bk., 1788–1803, p. 401 (1800) (presentment of overseer of roads for failing to keep road in repair).

102. *E.g.,* Cowan v. Frankland, HDSC Law Rec. Bk., 1798–1803, p. 401 (1803) (alleged perjury); Hutchison v. Meek, *id.* at 133 (1801) (alleged sodomy); Thompson v. Carr, *id.* at 6 (1798) (alleged fornication). See also McBee v. Gordon, HDSC Law Rec. Bk., 1798–1803, p. 58 (1799) (loss of services).

103. Evans v. Huffaker, HDSC Law Rec. Bk., 1798–1803, p. 318 (1802); Kimble v. Bosley, MDSC Law Min. Bk., 1788–1803, p. 438 (1801); Nelson v. Taite, MDSC Law Min. Bk., 1788–1803, p. 222 (1798); Metcalf v. Douglass, MDSC Law Min. Bk., 1788–1803, pp. 358, 450 (1800–1801); Caffery v. Siglear, *id.* at 240 (1799).

104. Gordon v. Cummins, MDSC Law Min. Bk., 1788–1803, p. 109 (1803); Welch v. Morris, HDSC Law Rec. Bk., 1798–1803, p. 144 (1801).

105. Morris v. Able, MDSC Law Min. Bk., 1803–1805, p. 95 (1803); Barton v. Moore, MDSC Law Min. Bk., 1788–1803, p. 682 (1802); Young v. Shackler, MDSC Law Min. Bk., 1788–1803, p. 460 (1801); Hodge v. Burns, HDSC Law Rec. Bk., 1798–1803, p. 54 (1799).

106. *E.g.,* English v. Bean, note 45 above. Although land suits were common in Tennessee, such litigation never dominated judicial business in the state, as was the case in neighboring Kentucky. Tachau, *Federal Courts in the Early Republic,* 167–190.

Court never heard more than ten criminal matters at a term and averaged only six. Criminal cases were usually tried during the same term at which the indictment had been returned. Assault, horse stealing, and riot were the most commonly prosecuted offenses while Jackson served as a judge. Reflecting the pattern that had prevailed while Jackson was a prosecutor, the Superior Court rarely tried such felonies as murder (No. 38), rape, and burglary. Appeals of criminal cases from the county courts were infrequent, although in March 1803 Jackson heard a larceny appeal involving the theft of a note valued at ten cents.[107]

Contrary to modern practice, relatively few defendants entered guilty pleas. Nearly all criminal cases tried on the merits were submitted to juries. While jurors often acquitted, conviction resulted in the imposition of a sentence by the court. Sentences were monetary, corporal, or capital. Jackson joined in many of the harsh sentences characteristic of the era (No. 26). Thus, he concurred in a sentence of five lashes for the theft of a half pint of whiskey worth five cents and in an order of thirty lashes for the larceny of a pair of stockings. Moreover, he participated in rendering the death penalty on at least ten occasions. For instance, in May 1802 at a single term of court, Jackson handed down three capital sentences for horse stealing.[108]

Slave crimes were handled separately in special justices' and slaveholders' courts.[109] Since Tennessee law permitted no appeal from these tribunals, Jackson never heard prosecutions of slave offenses. Nonetheless, slavery was indirectly involved in several cases tried before Jackson. In 1800 a white man was indicted for an assault upon a slave (No. 29). The prosecution ended when the jury could not agree upon a verdict and the state's attorney dismissed the case. Two years later a white defendant was tried and acquitted for inciting a slave to commit murder (No. 44).

Although the free Negro population of Tennessee was not large, at least

107. State v. Landrum, HDSC Law Rec. Bk., 1798–1803, p. 419 (1803).

108. State v. Roarke, MDSC Law Min. Bk., 1788–1803, p. 690 (1802); State v. McClure, HDSC Law Rec. Bk., 1798–1803, p. 31 (1799); State v. Powel, State v. West, State v. Black, MDSC Law Min. Bk., 1788–1803, p. 640 (1802). Jackson also imposed capital punishment for burglary and murder. State v. Ryley, WDSC Law Min. Bk., 1803–1809, p. 55 (1804); State v. Carman, MDSC Law Min. Bk., 1788–1803, p. 566 (1801). See also note 119 below and Nos. 26, 40.

109. Until 1815 slaves accused of major offenses were tried "without the solemnity of a jury" before a special slave court composed of three justices of the peace and four slaveowners. Tennessee law made no provision for an appeal from the judgment of such a tribunal. This system was gradually altered over the next two decades, and in 1835 the legislature gave the circuit courts exclusive jurisdiction over trials of slaves for capital crimes. Ch. 24, 1741 Laws of N.C., reprinted in Iredell, Laws of North Carolina 85, 1 Scott, Laws of Tennessee 62; Chase C. Mooney, Slavery in Tennessee (Bloomington, Ind., 1957); H. M. Henry, "The Slave Laws of Tennessee," 2 Tenn. Hist. Mag. 175 (1916); Arthur F. Howington, What Sayeth the Law: The Treatment of Slaves and Free Blacks in the State and Local Courts of Tennessee (New York, 1986).

one black, Jeffery, successfully brought suit before the Superior Court. Represented by two attorneys, Jeffery sued two white defendants for assault and battery and false imprisonment. He alleged that the defendants had beaten him with clubs and swords and had held him for forty days. The defendants answered that Jeffery was a slave, suggesting that the incident grew out of an attempt to recapture a runaway slave. On appeal, a Superior Court jury in 1801 found one defendant liable for damages in the amount of $12 and costs.[110]

The growth of equity as a separate branch of English law was reflected in early Tennessee. Litigants turned to equity in order to secure relief when the common law was unduly harsh or afforded no remedy. Jackson and his colleagues maintained the traditional distinction between law and equity. Denying a motion for a new trial in a 1799 suit at law, Jackson ruled, "If there has been fraud in the sale the party must be relieved in Equity" (No. 22). The Superior Court followed no set procedure in handling the equity docket. Although law and equity cases were carefully segregated, they were, of course, argued before the same judges. Typically the tribunal would start hearing equity matters during the second week of every term, often splitting each day thereafter between law and chancery business. Frequently, one entire day or more was devoted to equity cases. Unquestionably the judges gave most of their attention to civil and criminal proceedings on the law side, perhaps reflecting the infrequent use of juries in equity deliberations and the large number of continuances or dismissals by the parties.[111]

Bills to enjoin the enforcement of judgments obtained in a court of law were by far the most common type of equity litigation during Jackson's years on the bench. Usually the law judgment that was the subject of such a proceeding had been secured by a jury verdict in the same Superior Court. This equitable relief had originated in England and had been recognized in North Carolina's Court of Chancery through the colonial years.[112] An injunction against a judgment at law was granted only under limited circumstances: when the defendant at law had a valid defense on the merits and was prevented from making that defense by fraud or accident; when the defendant at law had a valid defense on the merits that was unavailable in law; or when the defendant at law was subject to a void decree, such as one vitiated by fraud, mistake, or lack of jurisdiction.

---

110. Jeffery, a free Negro man v. Lewis and Harness, MDSC Law Min. Bk., 1788–1803, p. 454 (1801).

111. See generally William W. Blume, "Chancery Practice on the American Frontier," 59 *Mich. L. Rev.* 49 (1960). The parties in equity could submit specific questions of fact for determination by a jury. George Jeremy, *A Treatise on the Equity Jurisprudence of the High Court of Chancery* (Philadelphia, 1830), 295–299; 4 Tucker, *Blackstone's Commentaries* 452. E.g., King v. Wilson, HDSC Eq. Rec. Bk. B, 260 (1802). See also note 43 above.

112. Price, ed., *North Carolina Higher-Court Minutes, 1709–1723*, pp. 469, 481.

Parties seeking to enjoin the enforcement of a judgment would usually apply ex parte to a judge of the Superior Court for a temporary injunction pending a disposition of the bill by the full court (No. 51).

The equity side of the Superior Court did not exercise any general appellate review over cases decided on the law side. Rather, the power to enjoin judgments at law was merely a supplemental aspect of the legal system. It is significant that the Superior Court rarely granted permanent injunctions against legal judgments.[113] Usually the tribunal dissolved the temporary injunction and allowed the defendant to have the benefit of his judgment at law.

Since courts of equity exercised a wide-ranging jurisdiction over all matters concerning fraud, the Superior Court also heard suits to set aside deeds, bonds, or sales of personal property when the transaction was allegedly tainted by fraud, duress, or forgery.[114] The rights of creditors were a traditional concern of equity. On at least one occasion during Jackson's tenure the Superior Court granted relief to a creditor seeking to reach a debtor's equitable interest under a contract to convey land.[115] In addition, several applications to foreclose mortgages came before the tribunal while Jackson was a judge.[116] Petitions for the partition of land between co-owners were presented to the Superior Court sitting in equity (No. 50). As with the law docket, much of the tribunal's equity calendar consisted of routine matters. Thus, the court issued writs of scire facias, passed upon motions seeking leave to amend pleadings, appointed guardians ad litem, and entered decrees pro confesso.

It is difficult to probe the intellectual dimension of Jackson's years on the bench. Notes that he made during the argument of one case indicate that counsel relied heavily upon statutes and English treatises (No. 41). Since Superior Court judges were not expected to submit written opinions, Jackson apparently wrote few. Indeed, given the authority of Tennessee juries to resolve questions of law as well as fact, judges had little opportunity to render decisions. The handful of judicial rulings that survive are primarily concerned with procedural questions. Decisions were delivered seriatim by the individual judges. Although Jackson was pre-

---

113. *E.g.*, Donelson v. McMillin, HDSC Eq. Rec. Bk. B, 36 (1800); Grant v. Gordon, *id.* at 10 (1800). For the authority of equity to enjoin the enforcement of judgments at law, see Joseph Story, *Commentaries on Equity Jurisprudence,* 2d ed. (Boston, 1839), II, 166–167, 874–877; William S. Holdsworth, *A History of English Law* (London, 1903–1966), I, 457–465.

114. *E.g.*, McMillin v. White and Delancy, HDSC Eq. Min. Bk. 1, p. 320 (1804).

115. Irwin v. Hickman and Colquhoun, Order dated May 28, 1800, Stanley Horn Coll., TNJ.

116. *E.g.*, Humes v. Shelly, HDSC Eq. Rec. Bk. B, 377 (1803–1804); Adair and McClellan v. Wilson and Whiteside, *id.* at 63 (1800); Buckingham's Ex'rs v. Richardson and King, HDSC Eq. Rec. Bk., 1793–1801, p. 221 (1799–1800).

pared to exercise an independent judgment and to disagree with his colleagues, his opinions were brief and lacked extensive citation to legal authorities (see, for example, No. 34). Unfortunately, the extent to which judges instructed jurors as to the law cannot be ascertained from the available documents.

Although the extant records reveal that Jackson regularly attended the scheduled terms of court, he missed a brief portion of several sessions. For example, he missed the opening day of the 1804 March Term in the Washington District and was absent for three calendar days (two court days) of the November 1801 session in the Mero District. These absences can be explained by travel difficulties, health problems, or the press of business activities. The longest lapse in Jackson's attendance to judicial duties came in 1803. He missed the last seven calendar days (six court days) of the March Term in the Hamilton District, the entire May Term at Mero, and nine calendar days (eight court days) of the September session at the Washington District. His business activities and a subsequent illness were responsible for this long absence. He left for Philadelphia in mid-April and spent May in that city purchasing merchandise for Jackson, Watson & Company. The clerk of the Washington District certified that Jackson had "Discharged the Duties of his office" during the September 1803 Term "except when prevented by indisposition." Jackson was also absent from the May 1804 session in the Mero District, the last scheduled court term before he resigned. Once again, he journeyed to Philadelphia to buy goods for his store.[117]

Jackson's judicial duties were by no means confined to hearing trials and motions during terms of court. When court was not in session, litigants called upon Jackson for various types of ex parte relief. Pursuant to statute, bills in equity and divorce petitions were regularly verified before him (Nos. 45, 51). He issued numerous temporary injunctions restraining the enforcement of judgments at law pending a hearing and subpoenas ordering defendants to appear in court. In addition, Jackson released insolvent debtors from custody upon the required oath and granted property attachments.[118]

117. Some twenty certificates of attendance for Jackson are located in the Treasurer's Records, RG 29, T. For absences, see WDSC Law Min. Bk., 1803–1809, pp. 1, 40; MDSC Law Min. Bk., 1788–1803, pp. 518–540 passim; HDSC Eq. Min. Bk., 1793–1808, pp. 139–153 passim; HDSC Law Min. Bk. 3, pp. 314–319 passim; MDSC Law Min. Bk., 1788–1803, pp. 719–747 passim; WDSC Law Min. Bk., 1803–1809, pp. 23, 25–37 passim; see Promissory Note, Jackson & Hutchings to John Morrell & Son, May 7, 1803, Jackson Papers, I, App. III, 453; AJ to Rachel Jackson, May 26, 1803, Jackson Papers, I, 331. See Certificate of Attendance, Sept. 17, 1803, Treasurer's Records, RG 29, T; AJ to John Coffee, May 3, 1804, AJ to Coffee, May 13, 1804, Jackson Papers, II, 21–23.

118. See Papers Relating to the Discharge of William Journey, pp. 104–105 below; Sanders v. Watson, MDSC Law Min. Bk., 1803–1805, p. 174 (1803).

Under particular circumstances the governor was empowered to commission the judges of the Superior Court to hold a court of oyer and terminer. Courts of oyer and terminer were extraordinary tribunals established for a limited time specifically to hear criminal cases in need of immediate prosecution. In July 1803 the sheriff of Knox County certified that the jail was "very insufficient for the safe keeping" of three accused murderers, whereupon Governor Archibald Roane authorized Jackson and the other Superior Court judges to hold a court of oyer and terminer. This special tribunal, however, was never convened, and the accused were tried for murder before the regular fall term of the Hamilton District Superior Court.[119]

Jackson seems never to have been comfortable with his position as judge. As early as 1801, only three years after his appointment, Jackson considered resigning from the bench, and the subject appeared regularly in his correspondence.[120] In the last analysis, Jackson's restless nature was not suited for the inevitable constraints upon a judge.

A series of specific problems eventually induced Jackson to quit the bench. Judicial service interfered with his personal life and business activities. Circuit travel to the Washington and Hamilton districts was arduous and necessitated long absences from home. In a 1799 letter written upon his arrival in Knoxville from Jonesboro between court sessions, Jackson complained about "a touch of the Reumatick—and a head ach today which I Suppose proceded from a Cold I caught riding in the night, last night." He promised his wife, Rachel, that he would "Stay not a moment longer, than the business of the Court requires." Four years later, while in Jonesboro, Jackson had to save his horse from a stable fire. He explained to his wife:

> During this distressing Scene I was agreat deal Exposed, having nothing on but my Shirt. I have caught a verry bad cold which has Settled on my lungs, occasioned a bad cough and pain in my breast.

Shortly thereafter Jackson considered resignation to "retire to domestic exile, there to regain my health, and repair a broken constitution." He declared: "Retirement to private life has been, for some time, to me a very desirable event."[121]

---

119. Ch. 26, 1801 Tenn. Pub. Acts, reprinted in 1 Scott, *Laws of Tennessee* 713; 5 Tucker, *Blackstone's Commentaries* 269–271. See Archibald Roane to David Campbell, AJ, and Hugh Lawson White, July 15, 1803, *Jackson Papers,* I, 336–337. The accused were convicted of murder in October 1803 and were sentenced to hang. State v. Duncan, State v. Duncan, State v. Childress, HDSC Law Min. Bk. 3, pp. 337–341 (1803).

120. See, *e.g.,* AJ to Robert Hays, Aug. 24, 1801, *Jackson Papers,* I, 252–253; AJ to Hays, Sept. 9, 1801, *id.* at 254–255.

121. AJ to Rachel Jackson, Sept. 17, 1799, *id.* at 223–224; AJ to Rachel Jackson, Mar. 22, 1803, *id.* at 326; AJ to George Rutledge and John Tipton, Oct. 7, 1803, *id.* at 373.

Jackson's commercial dealings and land speculations continued unabated during his years on the bench. As has been seen, business travel caused him to miss two entire terms of court. Litigation in which Jackson had an interest came before the Superior Court on several occasions, posing an awkward problem for him. The Tennessee Constitution of 1796 (Article V, section 8) provided that:

> No judge shall sit on the trial of any cause where the parties shall be connected with him, by affinity or consanguinity, except by consent of parties.

Although primarily directed against blood or marriage ties between a judge and litigants, this prohibition would seemingly apply when the judge himself was a party. Such a construction is bolstered by other language in the constitution (Article V, section 8) which authorized a special tribunal if all the judges "shall be interested in the event of any cause or related to all or either of the parties." Still, as G. Edward White has observed, "The specter of judicial conflicts of interest did not loom large to nineteenth-century Americans." Reflecting the more relaxed judicial standards of the day, Jackson sat on two trials in which he had a personal stake (Nos. 27, 36). He also considered filing a bill in equity against a former partner. Nonetheless, he may well have experienced some judicial embarrassment because of his extensive business dealings and felt compelled to forgo some legal claims.[122]

Perhaps the most pressing reason for Jackson to resign, however, was his controversial election in February 1802 as major general of the Tennessee militia.[123] Once again he arguably ran afoul of the Tennessee Constitution (Article V, section 3), which declared that judges of the Superior Court could not "hold any other office of trust or profit under this state, or the United States." Jackson had long desired military office, but had been previously defeated in a contest for this particular post. When his name was again advanced as a candidate for major general, Jackson, concerned that his selection would violate this clause of the constitution, sought the counsel of friends. David Campbell advised, "I must confess at first I had my doubts wheather your holding such an appointment would be consistent with the constitution or not but on examining the constitu-

---

122. G. Edward White, *The American Judicial Tradition* (New York, 1976), 40. In May 1803, during a term when Jackson was absent, the Mero District Superior Court confirmed an arbitration award growing out of litigation in which Jackson was a party (No. 46). Jackson heard at least one case in which he had originally appeared as counsel for one of the parties (No. 16). On the other hand, Jackson recused himself in another matter because he was related by marriage to the maker of the deed in dispute. Yet Jackson joined in signing the court's final decree. Anderson v. Justice and Gayley, HDSC Eq. Min. Bk. 1, pp. 91, 119–122 (1801–1802). And see AJ to Thomas Watson, Jan. 25, 1804, Bassett, *Correspondence*, I, 81–82.

123. Remini, *Andrew Jackson and the Course of American Empire*, 118–119.

tion, and consulting Governor Roane Judge Campbell and Col. McClung my doubts are nearly removed." While Campbell promised his support, he warned Jackson: "I expect some will object to the propriety of your holding the appointment."[124]

Also troublesome was Jackson's irrevocable break with John Sevier, his rival in the militia canvass. Jackson and Sevier had quarreled before. In 1796 Sevier had ridiculed Jackson as a "poor pitifull petty fogging Lawyer," but the two had patched up their differences and maintained cordial relations for several years. Now the feud was resumed in full fury. Sevier doubtless believed that Jackson owed him a debt of gratitude, and he was deeply chagrined over the election. Moreover, Jackson rejected Sevier's proposal that they submit to a new ballot. Sevier, who was reelected governor in 1803 over Jackson's opposition, induced his supporters in the legislature to enact a measure dividing Tennessee into eastern and western military districts. Jackson's command was reduced to the less populated western district. An embittered Sevier also sought to have Jackson impeached. The enmity between Jackson and Sevier reached a climax during the fall of 1803, when the judge and the governor publicly exchanged blows and insults in Knoxville. Thereupon Jackson challenged Sevier to a duel, a practice illegal in Tennessee. The Sevier incident did not reflect well on Jackson's judicial temperament and widened the gulf between his official post and his military ambitions. This affair must also have been a compelling factor in Jackson's decision to resign less than a year later.[125]

Militia duties themselves created other complications in Jackson's judicial career. Command claimed a share of Jackson's attention and energy. He was placed in a prosecutory role at odds with his responsibilities as a judge, directing, for example, the arrest and court-martial of an officer who was suspected of illegally attacking an Indian camp.[126]

Additional factors also influenced Jackson's thinking about the bench, foremost among them financial remuneration and the ability of his colleagues. In 1801 he candidly wrote:

> I am in Possession of a verry independant office, but I Sink money—the Salary is too low—another thing I dread the Successor of Mr. Roane. it is well known

124. David Campbell to AJ, Jan. 25, 1802, *Jackson Papers,* I, 273–274.

125. See AJ to John Sevier, May 8, 1797, *Jackson Papers,* I, 136; Carl S. Driver, *John Sevier: Pioneer of the Old Southwest* (Chapel Hill, 1932), 171–172; Thomas J. Vandyke to AJ, Nov. 5, 1803, *Jackson Papers,* I, 392–393. A killing in the course of a duel had long been treated as murder. 5 Tucker, *Blackstone's Commentaries* 198. In 1801 a Tennessee statute established penalties for both principals and seconds for sending challenges or otherwise attempting to fight a duel. Ch. 32, 1801 Tenn. Pub. Acts, reprinted in 1 Scott, *Laws of Tennessee* 718. For Jackson's quarrel with Sevier, see Driver, *John Sevier,* 176–189; *Jackson Papers,* I, 367–385 passim, App. VI; Remini, *Andrew Jackson and the Course of American Empire,* 121–124.

126. AJ to Henry McKinney, May 10, 1802, *Jackson Papers,* I, 294–295.

I cannot Expect much beneficial aid from the Talents of Judge Campbell, altho an agreable companion—and Should one be appointed whose Legal abilities were not Superior to ours the responsibility on me would be too great and perhaps frequent divisions make the office disagreable. My real wish would be, would my circumstances permit, to retire from the busy scenes of the world, and entirely domesticate myself, but I am got a little involved and untill I extricate myself must give out that Idea, and I fear that a seat in congress would not with my family [be] a profitable employment, and I am determined if I should offer and be elected to take them with me. the Judiciary scar[c]ely bears my Expence and the assembly cannot add more to it than $100 per annum, but perhaps it would be better to have that Secure, than to beat upon the fluctuating waves of popularity.[127]

Given these concerns, Jackson must have been tempted by various offers of political nomination or legal business should he quit the bench. On the other hand, a judicial salary, while not large, was at least secure. Further, Jackson expressed a strong sense of public duty as a reason for continuing to hold office. Responding to a request that he remain on the bench, Jackson in 1803 noted that he would "abandon for the present my resolution and obey the call of so respectable apart of my fellow citizens, as the dictates of duty to a grateful country."[128]

Jackson's resignation from the Superior Court was presented to the legislature on July 24, 1804.[129] While the immediate motive for this move cannot be determined, historians have traditionally attributed the step to health and financial concerns.[130] Considering his frequently expressed desire to leave public life, his decision cannot have been a surprise. He was replaced on the bench by his close friend John Overton.

Before he became a judge, Jackson had declared: "[A] good Judiciary lends much to the dignity of a state and the happiness of the people When on the Contrary a bad Judiciary involved in party business is the greatest Curse that can befall a Country."[131] Perhaps it is not unfair to inquire how well Jackson lived up to his own standards. Certainly he was a conscientious, hardworking jurist who was unafraid to express his individual opinion. Yet Jackson's tenure was marred by conflicts of interest, nonattendance at court sessions, and the unseemly quarrel with Sevier.

Although he was never accused of partisan bias in the discharge of his official duties, at least one case that Jackson heard on the bench threatened to plague him during his later political career. On March 28, 1802, Jackson, sitting alone, presided at the murder trial of Andrew White in

127. AJ to Robert Hays, Aug. 24, 1801, *id.* at 252–253.
128. See Martin Armstrong to AJ, Aug. 29, 1803, *id.* at 356; AJ to George Rutledge and John Tipton, Oct. 7, 1803, *id.* at 373.
129. *House Journal*, 5th General Assembly, 2d Sess., 11.
130. *E.g.*, Amos Kendall, *Life of Jackson*, No. 3 (New York, 1843), 103; Remini, *Andrew Jackson and the Course of American Empire*, 129.
131. AJ to William Blount, Feb. 29, 1796, *Jackson Papers*, I, 83.

Knoxville. Because the defendant was his brother, Judge Hugh Lawson White evidently recused himself. Following a jury trial, the defendant was acquitted.[132] Presumably in preparation for the acrimonious presidential campaign of 1828, Charles Hammond, a Cincinnati newspaper editor, noted the following about the case:

> Hugh Lawson White's brother Andrew murdered a man in Knoxville (an inoffensive country man) for which he was tried before Jackson as Judge and acquitted. Benj Parker was with White when he committed the Murder; trial took place without Parker's testimony, P having left the country.[133]

The implication, of course, is that Jackson either was negligent in the performance of his duties or was showing favoritism to his colleague's brother. The surviving records shed no light on this matter, but it is noteworthy that there was apparently no contemporary controversy about Jackson's handling of the case.

Jackson's strong concern in 1801 that "Some legal Charector in whose Legal talents I can place as much confidence" be named to fill the vacancy created by Judge Roane's departure from the bench that year may reveal a lingering realization that his own legal training was skimpy. Clearly Jackson did not relish deciding cases without the assistance of a competent colleague. Yet, whatever his limitations, contemporaries highly valued Jackson's judicial performance. Numerous citizens signed petitions in 1803 urging him to stay at his post. "In your talents and uprightness we have the highest confidence," proclaimed one such document. As late as 1810 Jenkin Whiteside declared that Jackson had "served as a Judge . . . with much credit . . . & satisfaction to the Lawyers & Suitors."[134]

One must be careful to keep Jackson's departure from the Superior Court in proper perspective. Short tenures on the bench were the practice throughout Tennessee's early years as a state. Describing judicial salaries as "inadequate," Samuel C. Williams noted: "Resignations in order to return to practice at the bar or to accept more lucrative positions in public life led to frequent changes in personnel."[135] In fact, Jackson served as a judge for a longer period than several of his contemporaries.

Nonetheless, Jackson's resignation marked an important event in his career. Thereafter, he renounced law as an avenue of advancement and concentrated his energy on planting, business, and the military. The sole

---

132. State v. White, HDSC Law Min. Bk., 1793–1809, pp. 275–276.

133. Hammond Notebook, Charles Hammond Papers, OHi.

134. AJ to Robert Hays, Sept. 9, 1801, *Jackson Papers*, I, 254; Patrick Campbell et al. to AJ, Oct. 7, 1803, *Jackson Papers*, I, 373–374; John Tipton et al. to AJ, Oct. 5, 1803, *id.* at 372–373; James Robertson to AJ, Sept. 7, 1803, *id.* at 358; [Jenkin Whiteside] to AJ, Mar. 11, 1810, AJ Papers, DLC (Reel 75).

135. Williams, "A Remarkable Bench: Campbell, Jackson and White," 16 *Tenn. L. Rev.* 907, 908 (1941).

attempt to renew a judicial calling came in 1810, when he unsuccessfully expressed an interest in being selected a judge of the Mississippi Territory. Characteristically, he was much concerned about the compensation for such a post. Jackson remained a frequent litigant throughout his life, but his thinking about the legal system took on a pessimistic tone. Thus, shortly before he left the bench he warned one adversary that "Law is disagreeable an[d] investigation in a court of chancery expensive." In 1823, while involved in protracted land litigation, Jackson wrote to John McNairy, "[Y]ou know my detestation for law suits." He forgetfully maintained that the pending matter was "the only suit but one I have ever had in my own name and I hope it will be the last."[136]

SOURCES

Disappointingly little in the way of legal correspondence, memoranda, research notes, and accounts that Jackson might have kept during the course of his legal career has been located. Responding to an inquiry by an early biographer into the availability of the papers from his tenure on the bench, Jackson wrote in 1843: "[A]ll of my papers and commissions as judge . . . was consumed with my House" when the Hermitage burned in 1834. The extent of this loss is difficult to determine. Jackson's recollection, for example, was not entirely accurate, for his commission as judge of the Superior Court and a few of his other judicial papers have survived. Moreover, Jackson evidently failed to preserve his personal papers systematically until well after his legal career had terminated. In any event, the editors have not had the carefully drafted correspondence and courtroom arguments or the notebooks, research notes, and courtroom minutes that some of Jackson's eastern colleagues, such as Adams and Jefferson, left behind.[137]

In addition to the general search for Jackson documents conducted by the Jackson Papers Project since 1971, the editors of this volume made

---

136. AJ to Jenkin Whiteside, Feb. 10, 1810, *Jackson Papers*, II, 223–224. For his litigation see, *e.g.*, Pryor v. Jackson & Hutchings [Mero District Superior Court] Order Bk. A, 206–220, Box 3, Middle Tennessee Supreme Court Records, T (1808–1812); Jackson v. Jackson, DaCo CPQS Min. Bk. F, 315, DaCo Circuit Ct. Trial Docket, 1810–1816, p. 11 (ca. 1807–1810); Jackson et al. v. Ward, Record Bk., 1842–1843, pp. 130–139, Box 69, Middle Tennessee Supreme Court Records, T (1840–1842); Jackson v. Erwin et al., Record Bk., 1824–1829, pp. 1–96, Box 25, Middle Tennessee Supreme Court Records, T (1814–1824). AJ to Thomas Masten, July 17, 1804, Bassett, *Correspondence*, I, 98–99; AJ to John McNairy, Sept. 6, 1823, Bassett, *Correspondence*, III, 207–208.

137. AJ to Amos Kendall, Nov. 2, 1843, Bassett, *Correspondence*, VI, 239–240. See, *e.g.*, Commission as Superior Court Judge, Dec. 22, 1798, pp. 103–104 below. Jackson appears not to have begun preserving his papers until during the Creek War. See Bassett, *Correspondence*, I, xix; *Jackson Papers*, I, xxv.

inquiries of institutions and individuals in the United States, Scotland, and England for documentation relating to cases that Jackson handled as a lawyer and heard as a judge and to his colleagues and clients. Such efforts, however, were not always fruitful. Few of Jackson's professional colleagues and fewer still of his clients left papers that have been located. The searches of those collections that have survived likewise brought about meager results.[138] Newspaper accounts of even the most notorious cases were scarce in the Knoxville papers published before 1805. Nashville was without a newspaper before 1800, and, except for occasional legal notices from the Tennessee courts, the *Kentucky Gazette* carried virtually no accounts of Tennessee litigation for the period of Jackson's legal career.

The Jackson Legal Papers
The few personal papers that have been located relating to cases from both the practice and the judicial periods were retrieved from private and institutional collections of Jackson's papers in the United States. The most significant of these were the Andrew Jackson Papers at the Library of Congress and the collections in the Tennessee Historical Society, the Tennessee State Library and Archives, the Jean and Alexander Heard Library at Vanderbilt University in Nashville, and the Ladies' Hermitage Association.

Court Records
The editors of the present edition concur with the editors of John Adams's legal papers that the largest source of information about a lawyer's career exists not always in the subject's own legal papers, but in "that legal and historical treasure which, largely unexplored by lawyers and historians alike," remains in the offices of the various courts, or their successors, at whose bar the subject practiced and whose bench he may eventually have come to occupy.[139] The primary sources of information about Jackson's career both as a practicing lawyer and as a judge thus have been the court records that have survived for the Tennessee and North Carolina superior and inferior courts.

Beginning in 1971, the staff of the Jackson Papers Project at the Hermitage conducted a search for county court records for more than thirty Tennessee, North Carolina, Kentucky, and Georgia counties. This under-

138. A further significant hindrance has been the absence of census records for Tennessee prior to 1810. Hence, although an attempt has been made to identify every party to the litigation from both the practice and the judicial periods, these efforts have frequently proved unsuccessful.

139. Wroth and Zobel, eds., *Legal Papers of John Adams*, I, xxxiii.

taking consisted of on-site searches of courthouse records for most of the counties; an examination of the Tennessee and North Carolina county court records on film at the Tennessee State Library and Archives and at the Division of Archives and History, North Carolina Department of Cultural Resources; an examination of the Works Project Administration transcripts of court records for which the originals were not found; a search of the Tennessee Historical Society's collection of Davidson County court records and of the unprocessed collection of Sumner County records at the Tennessee State Library and Archives; and an examination of the county court records that have been printed in the various state historical publications. Superior Court records were retrieved from the archives of the Tennessee Supreme Court in Nashville, from the collection of Supreme Court Records at the Tennessee State Library and Archives, and from the Circuit Court Archives at the Davidson County courthouse in Nashville, the Knoxville-Knox County Public Library (formerly the Lawson-McGhee Library) in Knoxville, and the William R. Perkins Library at Duke University. The staff also conducted a search of the United States district and circuit court records at the Federal Records Center, East Point, Georgia.

The court records that provide most of the documentation for Jackson's legal career consist of three major categories—record books, minute books, and case files—each of which survives in varying degrees of fullness.

Record Books. Of the three types of court records, the record books are the most complete and without question the richest source of documentation for the cases that Jackson handled as a lawyer and heard as a judge. Legal historians and historical editors only recently have come to appreciate fully the value of court record books as sources for the transcribed texts of documents that have not survived in original manuscript form.[140] Following a practice more characteristic of the civil-law courts than of the common-law courts, the clerks for the Tennessee Superior Court of Law and Equity and for the Davidson County Court of Pleas and Quarter Sessions transcribed the texts of the most important documents filed in each case—pleadings, orders, and decrees—into the courts' record books.

Superior Court record books survive for most of the years spanned by

140. For a discussion of record books as a neglected source for the texts of documents that have not survived in manuscript form, see Herbert A. Johnson, "Opportunities and Challenges in Editing Legal and Judicial Papers," unpublished paper presented at the Center for Textual and Editorial Studies in Humanistic Sources, University of Virginia, 1971, pp. 5–6.

Jackson's legal career. The clerks for the Mero District Superior Court of Law maintained such a volume between 1788 and 1803 (labeled Mero District Superior Court Law Minute Book; so cited here). Into most trial entries David Allison, Andrew McNairy, and Randal McGavock transcribed the texts of indictments, the parties' pleadings, and the court's orders and decrees. This manuscript volume now is in the custody of the Clerk of the Circuit Court for Davidson County in Nashville. The law record book for the Hamilton District for the period 1789–1803 is preserved in the Old Records Room at the Knoxville-Knox County Public Library. Equity record books for the Superior Court survive for the Mero District for the period 1803–1806 and for the Hamilton District for the period 1797–1804 in the same repositories. Equity record books for the Washington District for the periods 1791–1804 (labeled Washington District Superior Court Equity Minute Book; so cited here) and 1804–1810 are among the microfilmed holdings of the Tennessee State Library and Archives.

Although record books have not been located for Sumner and Tennessee counties, an unbound portion of the Davidson County Court of Pleas and Quarter Sessions Record Book that was maintained by the court's clerk, Andrew Ewing, between 1783 and 1790 survives in the Tennessee Historical Society's collection of Davidson County records.

Minute Books. Less significant as sources for the texts of missing documents, the minute books maintained by the clerks of the superior and county courts nonetheless provide succinct summaries of the procedural history of most cases that went to trial and of the final disposition of each case by the particular court. Although the minute books vary in degrees of completeness with each court, the typical minute book entry provides the parties' full names and the form of action, followed by a statement of the disposition of the case at the particular term of court. Trial entries in addition normally provide a brief account of each case's procedural history by term, an identification of each party's counsel and pleadings, a listing of jurors, and a recitation of the final disposition of the case. Significantly, trial entries often include the texts of factual questions submitted to juries and of the resulting special verdicts (for example, *Protzman v. Robertson*, No. 14, Document IV).

For the Superior Court, law minute books survive for the Mero District, 1788–1805, and for the Hamilton District, 1793–1809. Equity minute books survive for the Hamilton District, 1793–1808, and for the Washington District, 1791–1804.

Minute books survive for two of the three county courts in which Jackson practiced. Those for the Davidson County court are available from the date the court first met in 1783. Minute books survive for the Sumner County court, 1787–1808.

Supplementing the Superior Court minute books are a criminal docket for the Mero District, 1792–1809; an execution docket for the Mero District, 1792–1803; and an execution docket for the Hamilton District, 1793–1803. Trial and appearance dockets survive for the Sumner County court, 1787–1801, as does that court's execution docket, 1801–1812.

Case Files. Case files as a general rule are maintained by the court in which litigation is initiated and typically contain all of the documents submitted to the court by the parties and the originals of all orders and decrees entered by the court during the pendency of each case. Although for the early Tennessee courts the texts of most of these documents have survived by way of the courts' record books, very few of the case files themselves have been found. For the Superior Court cases, the scattered and incomplete case files that survive are to be found in the office of the Clerk of the Tennessee Supreme Court in Nashville; in the Supreme Court Records, Tennessee State Library and Archives; in the court papers, Old Records Room, Knoxville-Knox County Public Library; and in the Washington County court and the Washington District Superior Court papers, 1774–1893, at Duke University. For the county court cases, none of the case files for the Davidson County court has been located for the years that Jackson practiced at its bar. A rich assortment of Sumner County court case files is among the small, still unprocessed collection of records for the county at the Tennessee State Library and Archives. Although most of the files retrieved from this collection related to cases in which Jackson was a party litigant after he left the bench in 1804, some virtually complete files were found for cases tried by Jackson before the Sumner court (for example, *Cummins v. Peairs*, No. 12).

All of these case files initially were searched comprehensively for Jackson holographs, for documents bearing Jackson's signature, and for documents addressed to Jackson individually, as opposed to those addressed to the full Superior Court when he was one of its members. The files also were later searched for collateral documents relating to cases that Jackson handled as a lawyer. The editors subsequently examined the Superior Court files for the years 1798–1804 only for those cases that, after a review of the court's record and minute books and other available documentation, tentatively had been selected for publication (see Editorial Method: Selection of Cases and Documents, above). Since this volume was designed as a selective edition of Jackson's legal papers and not a collection of judicial documents, the editors made no attempt to collect and to reconstruct complete case files for each case initiated in the three districts of the Superior Court between 1798 and 1804. The volume of such litigation and the distant relationship between Jackson the judge and the parties before the court also militated for such a course.

Other Manuscript Sources
The editors have drawn documents from the sources that follow in addition to those to whom recognition is given on an individual basis in the appropriate notes.

The Bland Casebook. This 140–page notebook containing reports of Superior Court cases tried in the Washington and Hamilton districts between 1799 and 1801 is in the hand of Theodorick Bland, a young Virginia lawyer and later chancellor of the High Court of Chancery of Baltimore, who evidently began his career in the courts of eastern Tennessee. The editors discovered this manuscript among the Bland Family Papers at the Maryland Historical Society in Baltimore in 1978. The manuscript bears no author's name, but the editors were able to establish Bland as the author by the similarity between the hand in which it is written and Bland's handwriting as it occurs in letters written to his sister Sophia from Jonesboro and Bluff City, Tennessee, during the same period as that spanned by the casebook entries. The editors determined the document's credibility by matching, with very few exceptions, the reported cases with minute and record book entries or other records for the same cases that had been maintained contemporaneously by the court's clerks in Tennessee. Perhaps not surprisingly, Bland served as counsel in several of the reported cases, a fact that the editors had documented long before their discovery of the casebook in Baltimore. Among Bland's reports of the decisions by the court as announced, presumably orally, from the bench are eleven attributed to Jackson. All are published in this edition for the first time.

The Claybrooke and Overton Papers. Maintained by the Tennessee Historical Society, this collection contains many of John Overton's private and legal papers, including a notebook of Overton's own research and courtroom notes and accounts.

The Stanley Horn Collection. Among the holdings of the Jean and Alexander Heard Library at Vanderbilt University in Nashville, this collection contains several important documents from Jackson's legal career, most of which are included in the present edition.

The Archives Section, Tennessee State Library and Archives. The Archives holds several collections of state papers that have provided important collateral documents and data for the present edition, including the

Governors' Papers, Treasury Records, Executive Petitions and Pardons, and the Legislative Papers.

Private Collections.   Jackson documents from collections held by William Waller, Sr., Paul Fink, Horace J. Stepp, Jr., Mrs. G. James Packard, and Paul C. Richards have been of great significance in the preparation of the present edition.

PART I

Jackson the Frontier Lawyer, 1787–1798

Nonlitigation Documents

License to Practice in the
North Carolina County Courts

September 26, 1787

State of North Carolina Ss.

To the Justices of the several courts of pleas & quarter sessions within the said State.

Whereas Andrew Jackson in Rowan County in the state aforesaid, gentleman, hath applied to us the Judges of the Superior Court of Law & Equity in the said State, to be admitted to plead & to practise as an attorney in the several County Courts in the same state; And whereas the said Andrew Jackson hath resided in the said State for the space of two years last past, and is sufficiently recommended to us as a person of unblemished moral character, and upon examination had before us, appears to possess a competent degree of knowledge in the Law for the purpose aforesaid.

We therefore in pursuance of the power and authority committed to us by the act of the General Assembly in that case made and provided, do he[re]by admit the said Andrew Jackson to plead and practise as an Attorney in the said several courts of pleas and quarters Sessions within the said state; with all and singular the priviledges and emoluments which of right appertain to attorneys and practisers of the law in the same; he the said Andrew Jackson taking the several oaths appointed by law for his qualification.

Given under our hands and seals the twenty sixth day of September in the year of our Lord one thousand, seven hundred & eighty seven, & in the twelfth year of our independence.

Saml. Ashe   [SEAL]

Jno. Williams [SEAL]

MS, THer. Endorsed: "State of North Carolina Anson County. Ss. October Sessions 1787 These may Certify that Andrew Jackson Esquire produced the within Commission Authorising him to practise as an Attorney within the severale County Courts within this State; before the Justices of the County Court of Anson &c. and was Qualified in due form. Certified ℔ Mich Auld C C."

License to Practice in the
Superior Court of Law and Equity

November 3, 1788

State of North Carolina Ss

To the Judge or Judges of the Superior Court of law and Equity for the County of Davidson

Whereas Andrew Jackson Esquire hath applied to me the Subscriber, Judge of the Superior Court of law and Equity for the County aforesaid to be admitted to plead and practice as an attorney in the Said Court of law and Equity and whereas the Said Andrew Jackson from proper credentials to me produced appears to be of an unblemished Moral character, and from a previous examination before me had likewise appears to possess a competent degree of law Knowledge for the purpose aforesaid

I therefore in pursuance of the Authority vested in me by the Act of the General Assembly to that purpose do hereby admit and impower the said Andrew Jackson to plead and practice in the said Courts of law and Equity within the Said county as an Attorney thereof with all and Singular the Rights priviledges and emoluments belonging or in any wise appertaining to Attorneys and practisers of the law in the Said courts he the said Andrew Jackson taking the Several Oaths appointed by law for his quallification

Given under my hand and Seal this third day of November A. D. 1788—and in the XIIIth year of our independance

John McNairy. J. S. C. L &E

MS, DLC-AJ Papers (Reel 1); Bassett, *Correspondence,* I, 5–6.

License to Practice
in the Tennessee Courts

July 5, 1796

SEAL   State of Tennessee, John Sevier
Governor in and over the same.

To all who shall see these presents: Greeting, Know ye, that I do license Andrew Jackson esquire to practice as an Attorney at law, in the several

Courts of law and equity in the State aforesaid, with all the privileges and emoluments thereto or right appertaining

Given under my hand and Seal at Knoxville this 5th day of July, 1796.

By the Governor:

JOHN SEVIER.

Wm. MACLIN, Secretary.

(With the following endorsement on the back in the hand writing of Andrew Jackson.) Governor of the State of Tennessee License to A. Jackson to Practice law within said state in all the courts therein.

Printed copy, *Nashville Tennessean*, Apr. 18, 1909.

Invoice for Law Books Purchased
by Jackson from
Robert Campbell & Company

Philada. Jany. 7 1797

Genl. James Winchester

Bot. of Robt. Campbell & Co.

1 Vatell's Law of Nations	1 ..	2 .. 0
1 Powell on Contracts	16 ..	10½
1 Espinasse Nisi Prius	1 .. 10	
1 Gilberts Law of Evidence	1 .. 10	
1 Bullers Nisi prius	16 ..	10½
1 Comyns's Digest 6 Vols	6 .. 15	
2 Vesseys Reports	5 .. 5	
1 Browns Do.	6	
1 Vernons Chancery	2 .. 12 ..	0
1 Peere Williams's reports 3 Vols	3 .. 7 ..	0
1 Impeys practice 2 Vols	1 .. 10	
1 Laws of the United States 2 Vols	1 .. 10	
1 Equity Cases abridged	3 .. 7 ..	6
1 Hawkins pleas of the Crown	2 .. 10	
1 Hindes Practice	16 ..	10½
1 Gilbert on Equity	11 ..	3
2 Atkyns's Reports	9	
1 Coke upon Lyttleton 3 Vols	5 .. 5	
1 Bacons abridgmt. 5 Vols	9	
1 Wilsons Reports 3 Vols	3 .. 7 ..	6

1 Raymonds Do.   . . . .   3 . . 7 . . 6
1 Barns Law Dictiony.   . . . .   1 . . 10
1 Sheridans Dictionary   1
1 Barnes Notes London Edition   . . . .   1 . . 8

Chd. to A Jackson   £73 . . 19 . . 10½

MS, DLC-AJ Papers (Reel 1).

Jackson's purchases included: Emmerich de Vattel, *The Law of Nations; or, Principles of the Law of Nature, Applied to the Conduct and Affairs of Nations and Sovereigns* (1787); John Joseph Powell, *Essay Upon the Law of Contracts and Agreements* (1790); Isaac Espinasse, *A Digest of the Law of Actions at Nisi Prius* (1789); Sir Geoffrey Gilbert, *The Law of Evidence* (1760); Sir Francis Buller, *An Introduction to the Law Relative to Trials at Nisi Prius* (1781); Sir John Comyns, *A Digest of the Laws of England, by the Right Honourable Sir John Comyns . . . Continued Down to the Present Time, by a Gentleman of the Inner Temple* (1785); Francis Vessey, *Cases Argued and Determined in the High Court of Chancery, in the Time of Lord Chancellor Hardwicke, from the Year 1746–7, to 1755* (1771); William Brown, *Reports of Cases Argued and Determined in the High Court of Chancery, During the Time of Lord Chancellor Thurlow, and of the Several Lords Commissioner of the Great Seal, and Lord Chancellor Loughborough, from 1778 to 1794* (n.d.); Thomas Vernon, *Cases Argued and Adjudged in the High Court of Chancery [1680–1719], Originally Published by Order of the Court, from the Manuscripts of Thomas Vernon* (1726–1728); William Peere Williams, *Reports of Cases Argued and Determined in the High Court of Chancery 1680–1719* (1740–1749); John Impey, *The New Instructor Clericalis, Stating the Authority, Jurisdiction and Modern Practice of the Court of Common Pleas . . . to which Are Added the Rules of the Court, Modern Precedents* (1785); *A General Abridgement of Cases in Equity, Argued and Adjudged in the High Court of Chancery, etc., [1667–1744] with a Large Collection of Cases Never Before Published* (1792–1793); William Hawkins, *A Treatise of the Pleas of the Crown; or, A System of the Principal Matters Relating to that Subject, Digested Under Proper Heads* (1788); Robert Hinde, *The Modern Practice of the High Court of Chancery . . . with . . . Forms of Practical Precedents . . . from the Original Bill to the Decree* (1786); either Geoffrey Gilbert, *Reports of Cases in Equity, Argued and Decreed in the Courts of Chancery and Exchequer, Chiefly in the Reign of King George I* (1742), or Geoffrey Gilbert, *Cases in Law and Equity, Argued, Determined and Adjudged in the King's Bench and Chancery [1714–1715]* (2nd ed. 1792); John Tracy Atkyns, *Reports of Cases Argued and Determined in the High Court of Chancery, in the Time of Lord Chancellor Hardwicke [1736–1754]* (1765–1786); Sir Edward Coke, *The First Part of the Institutes of the Laws of England; or, A Commentary upon Littleton; Not the Name of the Author Only, but of the Law Itself* (1628); Matthew Bacon, *A New Abridgment of the Law, Alphabetically Digested under Proper Titles* (1736–1759); George Wilson, *Reports of Cases Argued and Adjudged in the King's Courts at Westminster [1742–1774]* (n.d.); Robert Raymond, *Reports of Cases Argued and Adjudged in the Courts of the King's Bench and Common Pleas, in the Reigns of the Late King William, Queen Anne, King George the First, and King George the Second [1694–1732] Taken and Collected by the Right Honorable Robert Lord Raymond* (1792); Richard Burns, *A New Law Dictionary* (1792); Thomas Sheridan, *A Complete Dictionary of the English Language Both with Regard to Sound and Meaning* (1789); and Henry Barnes, *Notes of Cases in Points of Practice, Taken in the Court of Common Pleas at Westminster . . . 1732 to . . . 1756 . . . to Which Is Added a Continuation of Cases to the End of the Reign of King George the Second* (1790).

Jackson's acquisition contained numerous volumes found in the collections of prominent American lawyers of the eighteenth century. Herbert A. Johnson, *Imported Eighteenth-Century Law Treatises in American Libraries, 1700–1799* (Knoxville, 1978). Similarly, many of the books purchased by Jackson appeared in the collections of other frontier lawyers during this period. William W. Blume, "Civil Procedure on the American Frontier," 56 *Mich. L. Rev.* 161, 167 (1957); Blume, "Criminal Procedure on the American Frontier," 57 *Mich. L. Rev.* 195, 246 (1958).

Litigation

1. State v. Dollison

1788
(Criminal Law)

EDITORIAL NOTE

The prosecution of James Dollison for robbery was one of the first criminal cases that Jackson undertook after his appointment in November
1788 as state's attorney for Mero District. Jackson's indictment charged
that Dollison on December 29, 1784, had assaulted "Peter Tardivo &
Israel Todd" on the Mississippi River and had robbed them of certain
goods and chattels and two swivel guns. When the case went to trial on
November 8, a jury returned a verdict of not guilty.[1]

The indictment that is presented here and a corresponding trial entry
in the Mero District Superior Court's minute book constitute the only
documentation that has been located for the case.

1. MDSC Law Min. Bk., 1788–1803, pp. 5–6.
The North Carolina General Assembly in 1783 extended the state's western boundary
from the Virginia line "west to the *Missisippi,* thence down the *Missisippi* to the thirty fifth
degree of north lattitude." Ch. 2, § 3, 1783 Laws of N.C. 4. The western boundary of Davidson County, and later of the Mero District, was defined by the legislature as the western
portion of the Tennessee River from the Virginia line southward to the mouth of the Duck
River, a line that lay a substantial distance east of the Mississippi River. Ch. 52, 1783 Laws
of N.C., reprinted in Iredell, *Laws of North Carolina* 473, 1 Scott, *Laws of Tennessee* 282;
see ch. 3, 1788 Laws of N.C., reprinted in Iredell, *Laws of North Carolina* 643, 1 Scott,
Laws of Tennessee 402; ch. 47, 1785 Laws of N.C., reprinted in Iredell, *Laws of North
Carolina* 567, 1 Scott, *Laws of Tennessee* 349. The Mero District court's criminal jurisdic-
tion was limited to the punishment of offenses committed within the district. See ch. 47, §§
1, 4, 1785 Laws of N.C., reprinted in Iredell, *Laws of North Carolina* 567, 1 Scott, *Laws of
Tennessee* 349. Referring to the Mississippi in the indictment that he filed against Dollison
as "one of the navigable Waters" of North Carolina and apparently considering the Mero
District court as the most convenient forum for the trial of one of the district's residents,
Jackson proceeded with the prosecution of Dollison despite the ambiguities in the statutory
limitations upon the court's criminal jurisdiction.

Dollison has not been further identified.

The "Peter Tardivo" whom Jackson describes in the indictment as having been one of the victims of the 1784 robbery probably was Pierre Tardiveau of Louisville, whose given name frequently occurs in the records as Peter. Tardiveau and his brother Barthélemi had been the subjects of an incident similar to the present one in May 1783, when they were attacked by pirates on the Mississippi near the present site of Memphis.[2] Both of the Tardiveau brothers owned property in Mero District.[3]

The "Israel Todd" to whom Jackson refers in the indictment probably was Israel Dodge, a close friend of Barthélemi Tardiveau's from Kaskaskia.[4]

2. Inventory, May 2, 1783, Laura L. Porteous, ed., "Index to the Spanish Judicial Records of Louisiana," pt. 56, 21 *Louisiana Hist. Q.* 326–327 (1938); see Barthélemi Tardiveau to Jean Holker, Aug. 4, 1783, quoted in Howard C. Rice, Jr., "News from the Ohio Valley as Reported by Barthélemi Tardiveau in 1783," 16 *Bulletin of Hist. and Philosophical Soc'y of Ohio* 274 (1958). See also the MS case file in Judicial Records of the Spanish Cabildo, 826 (June 2, 1783), L–M. For further biographical information about the Tardiveau brothers, see Account, Jean Holker with Michael Lacassagne, Barthélemi Tardiveau, and Pierre Tardiveau, January 1782–August 1783, Holker Papers, DLC (Container 23, Reel 11); Expense Account of Pierre Tardiveau, July–August 1784, Holker Papers, MiU-C; Howard C. Rice, Jr., *Barthélemi Tardiveau: A French Trader in the West* (Baltimore, 1938), 2–3, 40–48; Robert A. Burnett, "Louisville's French Past," 50 *Filson Club Hist. Q.* 7 (1976); Ludie J. Kinkead and Katharine G. Healy, comps., "Calendar of Bond and Power of Attorney Book No. 1, Jefferson County, Kentucky, 1787–1798," 7 *Filson Club Hist. Q.* 37 (1933); Thomas C. Cherry, "Robert Craddock and Peter Tardiveau: Two Revolutionary Soldiers of Warren County, Kentucky," 4 *Filson Club Hist. Q.* 84–88 (1930).

Subsequent to the present case, Pierre Tardiveau served as an interpreter for Citizen Genêt's agents in the west and in 1795 was tried at Bayou Pierre for having participated in a plot to incite an uprising among Louisiana's French inhabitants to regain control of their former colony. By the end of the century, Tardiveau had exhausted the private fortune that he had made in the mercantile business and in 1800 joined his friend Robert Craddock at the latter's home, the Hermitage, in Kentucky and remained with him and his family until his death in 1835. Cherry, "Robert Craddock and Peter Tardiveau," 84–88.

3. See DaCo Deed Bk. A, 309; Montgomery County Deed Bk., 7.

4. Rice, *Tardiveau*, 10; Rice, "News from the Ohio Valley," 278–279. Described as "an active young man, faithful, enterprising, familiar with the woods, and accustomed to the Indians' tricks," Dodge in 1783 had been hired by Barthélemi Tardiveau to transport, trade, and sell in Kentucky a substantial shipment of merchandise owned by himself and the Philadelphia commercial speculator Jean Holker. Barthélemi Tardiveau to Jean Holker, Aug. 4, 1783, in Rice, "News from the Ohio Valley," 278–279.

INDICTMENT OF
JAMES DOLLISON

Mero District Superior Court, Nashville

State of North Carolina ⎱ Ss   November Term 88
Davidson County   ⎰   The Jurors for the state upon their
Oath present that James Dollison late of the County of Davidson and
State of North Carolina, Yeoman, On the twenty ninth day of December
in the Year One Thousand seven hundred & Eighty four with force &
arms at the County aforesaid on the Mississippi One of the said State's
navigable River, then & there in and upon One Peter Tardivo & Israel
Todd in the peace of God & our said State then & there being, feloniously
did make an assault, and they the said Peter Tardivo & Israel Todd in
bodily fear & danger of their Life on the said River Mississippi one of the
navigable Waters of the said State then & there feloniously put, and Two
Swiwell Guns of the Value of Eighteen pounds, of the Goods & Chattels
of the said Peter Tardivo & Israel Todd from their persons and against the
Will of the said Peter Tardivo & Israel Todd on the River Mississippi
aforesaid then & there feloniously and violently did steal, take & carry
away against the peace & dignity of our Said State.

Andw. Jackson atty.
for the State

MS, THi-Hurja Coll. Endorsed: "A true Bill Lardner Clark Foreman   The State vs. James
Dollison Indict Robert   November Term 88 (pro se)   Thomas Green prosecutor   Samson
Williams   Sworn and Sent   Test J Macay   A Jackson atto." A Tr of the indictment occurs
at MDSC Law Min. Bk., 1788–1803, pp. 5–6. Green possibly was the Thomas Green who
had resided in Natchez and who had been an acquaintance of John Donelson's. See *Jackson
Papers,* I, 17 n.1. Green's association with the Tardiveau brothers may have dated from
1786, by which time he had moved from Natchez to Louisville. William E. Cox, "The
Greens of Jefferson County, Mississippi," 36 *J. Mississippi Hist.* 77, 88 (1974).

2. State v. Hendrix

1789
(Criminal Law)

EDITORIAL NOTE

Although horse stealing was one of the most commonly prosecuted offenses during Jackson's tenure as a Superior Court judge, only seven recorded instances in which Jackson sought horse-stealing convictions during his service as state's attorney for the Mero District between 1788 and 1796 survive (see Part III). Juries returned not-guilty verdicts in three of Jackson's cases, including the present prosecution of Thomas Hendrix of Sumner County.

The survival of two different indictments in the present case (Documents I, II) suggests that Jackson might have attempted to obtain convictions of Hendrix for two distinct offenses. Jackson's description of the offense in Document I is of a theft that occurred on October 29, 1785, of a "mare of a brownish coulour" valued at six pounds. His description of the offense in Document II is of a theft that occurred nine months later, on July 29, 1786, of a "mare of a blackish coulour" valued at six pounds. Moreover, Jackson in Document I charges only Hendrix with the offense, while in Document II he charges not only Hendrix, but also two confederates, John Hendrix and James Hays.

Jackson, however, actually pursued only the prosecution of Hendrix for the latter offense, which resulted in an acquittal at the court's May Term 1789 (see Document III). The absence of endorsements on Document I similar to those on Document II by the court's clerk and by the grand jury foreman indicating whether the indictment was returned a true bill suggests that Jackson probably chose not to file the first indictment with the grand jury at all.

The court's records are silent about the final disposition of the charges against Hendrix's two co-defendants. The most likely explanation is that the court was unable to secure custody of them and that Jackson, once his evidence had proved insufficient to convict Hendrix, decided that it was not worthwhile to seek their arrest and conviction.[1]

1. None of the defendants has been further identified.

I. INDICTMENT OF THOMAS HENDRIX

Mero District Superior Court, Nashville

State of North Carolina ⎱ Ss   November Term at 1788
Davidson County   ⎰

The Jurors for the State upon there Oaths present that Thomas Hendrix—late of the county of Sumner and state of North Carolina on the twenty ninth day of October—in the year of our lord one thousand Seven hundred and Eighty five with force and arms at the County aforesaid one mare of a brownish coulour of the price of Six pound of the goods and chattles of philip Shickler then and there being found feloneously did Steal take and lead away to the great damage of him the Said philip Shickler—contrary to the Statute[1] in that case made and provided and against the peace and Dignity of the Said State

Andrew Jackson atto.
for the State

MS, THi-Misc. Files. Endorsed: "State vs. Thos. Hendrix Indictm. H. S. November Term 88 philip Shickler prosecutor Joshua Campbel Elisabeth Hacker Sworn and Sent Test A Jackson atto."

1. Ch. 7, 1786 Laws of N.C., reprinted in Iredell, *Laws of North Carolina* 579, 1 Scott, *Laws of Tennessee* 366.

II. INDICTMENT OF THOMAS HENDRIX, JOHN HENDRIX, AND JAMES HAYS

Mero District Superior Court, Nashville

State of North Carolina Ss   Superior Court
Mero District   May Term 1789

The Jurors for the State upon their oath present that Thomas Hendricks John Hendrix and James Hays late of the county of Sumner and District of Mero yeomen on the twenty ninth day of July in the year of our lord one thousand Seven hundred and Eighty six with force and arms at the county aforesaid in the District aforesaid one mare of a blackish coulour of the price of Six pounds of the goods and chattels of Philip Shackler then and there being found feloneously did Steal take and lead away to the

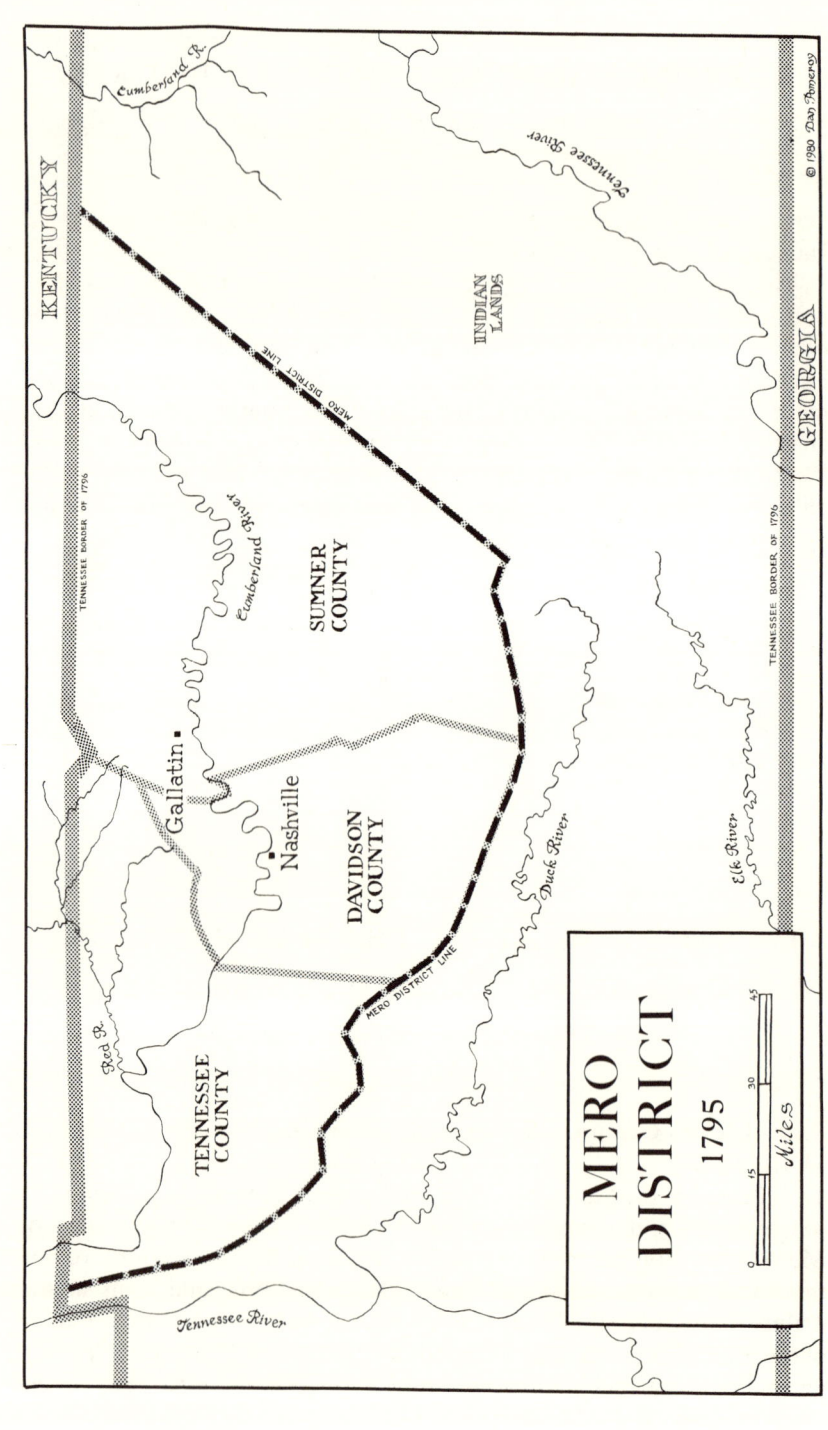

MERO DISTRICT

1795

Miles

0   15   30   45

KENTUCKY

GEORGIA

Cumberland R.

Tennessee River

INDIAN LANDS

MERO DISTRICT LINE

TENNESSEE BORDER OF 1796

TENNESSEE BORDER OF 1796

Cumberland River

SUMNER COUNTY

Gallatin

Nashville

DAVIDSON COUNTY

Duck River

Elk River

Red R.

TENNESSEE COUNTY

Tennessee River

MERO DISTRICT LINE

© 1980 Dan Pomeroy

great damage of him the Said philip contrary to the Statute in that State mad and provided and against the peace and dignity of the State

Andrew Jackson
Atto. for the State

MS, MHi-Colburn Coll. Endorsed: "A True Bill   Thos. James formn. State vs Thos. Hendricks and others   Horse Stealing   May Term 89   Philip Shackler prosecutor   Joshua Campble Elisabeth Hacker David Hacker Senr. John Chisolm John McCombs   Sworn & Sent Test Dd. Allison CSC   A Jackson atto for the State   John Hendricks Thomas Hendricks   Plead not Guilty."

III. MINUTE BOOK ENTRY

Mero District Superior Court, Nashville

the State

vs

Thomas Hendrix

[May 7, 1789]

Indictment   Horse Stealing

Plea   Not Guilty

the Prisonir Thomas Hendrix being Called to the Bar was Charged on the Bill of Indictment[1] . . . to which Indictment the Prisoner Thomas Hendrix Plead not Guilty, and for his Trial put himself upon God and his Country whereupon Came a good & Lawfull Jury (viz) Robert Looney, John Wilson, John Hamilton, Thomas Hamilton, John Norris, John drake, david Wilson, Chrisley Couts, Robert deshea Elmore Douglass, Alexander Neely, John Bell, who being impanelled & Sworn truly to Try the issue of Traverse betwen the State and Said Hendrix Defendant, Say they find Thomas Hendrix the Prisoner at the Bar not Guilty of the Felony & Horse Stealing in manner & form as Charged in the Bill of Indictment

MS, TDaCo-MDSC Law Min. Bk., 1788–1803, pp. 14–15. Date is taken from *id*.

1. At this point in the MS the text of Document II is repeated.

3. Barton and Shaw v. Robertson

1789
(Contracts)

EDITORIAL NOTE

In October 1791 Jackson received an appointment to the Board of Trustees of Davidson Academy, the Cumberland region's first educational institution.[1] He had become acquainted with the academy's president, the Reverend Thomas B. Craighead, and with the institution's future site as early as July 1789, when he defended Elijah Robertson in the present litigation, initiated by Samuel Barton and James Shaw.

Early in 1785 the Reverend Mr. Craighead, a Presbyterian minister who had been educated at the College of New Jersey and who had settled in Kentucky shortly after his ordination in 1780, offered to move to Davidson County and establish a Presbyterian church there.[2] The condition that Craighead attached to his proposal was that a 640-acre tract of land north of Nashville be purchased for him as a suitable church site. Twenty of the town's residents responded on July 4, 1785, by agreeing, under penalty of £1,000, to contribute proportionately to the still undetermined purchase price for the tract (Document I). Although not specified in the text of this subscription agreement, all of the parties thereto subsequently stipulated that they also had agreed (a) that their annual subscription payments were to be made for a total of three years; (b) that all of the proceeds from the subscription payments were to be used to pay for the land except for the sum of £50 that was to be paid Mr. Craighead annually for three years for his subsistence; and (c) that the anticipated surplus in proceeds was to go to the two agents appointed by the subscribers to purchase the land, Samuel Barton and James Shaw, as compensation for their services.[3]

1. *Jackson Papers*, I, 29. Jackson resigned from the Board of Trustees in 1805. *Id.* at 321–322.
2. A. W. Putnam, Memoir of Rev. Thomas B. Craighead, n.d., Misc. File, THi; Walter B. Posey, *The Presbyterian Church in the Old Southwest 1778–1838* (Richmond, 1952), 19; Ernest T. Thompson, *Presbyterians in the South* (Richmond, 1963), I, 355.
3. Complaint of Samuel Barton (typescript), Sept. 4, 1797, Provine Papers, THi.

Three days later, on July 7, 1785, Barton and Shaw purchased a 640-acre tract from John Buchanan for £640 and executed a personal agreement under the terms of which Barton and Shaw were to pay Buchanan, under £1,000 penalty, £320 on or before July 7, 1786, and the balance on or before July 7, 1787 (Document II).[4] The parties to the original subscription agreement, possibly fearing that a default by Barton and Shaw would result in individual liability to Buchanan for far more than their proportionate share of the purchase price, refused to sign the agreement of July 7, 1785, with Buchanan.[5]

The amount collected by Barton and Shaw from the subscribers before the initial installment was due Buchanan is not entirely clear. Nor is it certain whether the full amounts claimed by the subscribers to have been paid to Barton and Shaw actually were remitted by the two agents to Buchanan. Buchanan's records, which were submitted to the Davidson County court in 1794 to support his recovery of the full purchase price plus interest from Barton and Shaw, indicate that he received only one payment for the tract from Barton and Shaw, a sum of £63, 11 shillings, and 7 pence, which was paid to him on April 14, 1787, more than nine months after the initial installment was due.[6] Neither the amount due Buchanan in 1786 nor the balance due on July 7, 1787, appears to have been paid.

That Barton and Shaw did make some attempt to collect from the subscribers, however, is apparent from the present action that they brought against Elijah Robertson in the spring of 1787 (see Document III).[7] Under the subscription agreement of July 4, 1785, Robertson had agreed to make an annual payment of £10 toward the land's purchase price (see Document I). In their declaration (Document IV), Barton and Shaw alleged that Robertson had "hitherto failed to pay to the Said Shaw and Barton his proportionate Sum as Afforesaid Or in Anywise to Content them in Lieu thereof."

Jackson's first recorded appearance for Robertson occurred on July 6, 1789, the date on which the cause went to trial. No records of Jackson's pretrial pleadings have been located. Although Barton and Shaw sought damages in the amount of £80, the jury returned a verdict for the plaintiffs "'According to the Bond'" (Document V). Jackson used the apparent discrepancy as a ground for obtaining an appeal of the judgment to the

4. Provine Papers, THi.

5. Answer of Ephraim McLean, 1787, Misc. File, THi; Answer of Samuel Shannon, May 14, 1798, Coffee Papers, Dyas Coll., THi.

6. Enclosure, Answer of John Buchanan, Nov. 11, 1797, Provine Papers, THi.

7. On the same date Barton and Shaw initiated a parallel action to collect from Robertson's brother James, whom Jackson represented at the Davidson County court's July Term 1789. DaCo CPQS Min. Bk. A, 369.

Mero District Superior Court (Document VI).[8] No records for the final disposition of Jackson's appeal have been located.

Shaw subsequently became insolvent, and when the Davidson County court in January 1794 awarded Buchanan a judgment against Barton and Shaw for the balance of the purchase price plus interest, a total of £728, 3 shillings, 9 pence,[9] it was Barton who bore full responsibility for satisfying the judgment.[10] His attempt to do so apparently rendered him nearly insolvent as well,[11] and he finally sought equitable relief in the form of a petition for contribution from the other subscribers in the Superior Court in 1797. In the meantime, the Reverend Mr. Craighead had moved to Davidson County and had erected a structure on the Buchanan tract that served as both a church and the Davidson Academy.[12] One month after recovering his judgment in February 1794, Buchanan, for the consideration of £40, formally executed a deed transferring title to the tract upon which Mr. Craighead's meetinghouse had been constructed.[13]

Shaw, one of the many subscribers to the Cumberland Compact of 1780, had been a member of the Cumberland Association Committee in 1783 and had received a legislative appointment in 1784 as one of three trustees of Nashville.[14] After the present action had been tried, Jackson represented Shaw frequently in litigation before the Davidson and Sumner county courts.[15]

For additional identification of Barton and Robertson, see Part IV.

8. The other two grounds were (a) that plaintiffs had brought their action as trespass on the case, whereas, presumably, it should have been brought as a debt or covenant action, and (b) that apparently new evidence had been introduced and submitted by the court to the jury after the jury had returned from their deliberations. See Document VI.

9. DaCo CPQS Min. Bk. B, 753.

10. Complaint of Samuel Barton, Sept. 4, 1797, note 3 above.

11. Ephraim McLean described Barton as having been jailed, where he "almost perished with cold for want of Bed clo[th]es." Answer of McLean, 1798, Misc. File, THi.

12. In 1786 Mr. Craighead was named president of the Board of Trustees for Davidson Academy, a position that he held until 1809. Putnam, Craighead Memoir; Thompson, *Presbyterians in the South*, I, 355.

13. John M. Bass, "Rev. Thomas Craighead," 7 AHM 91 (1902).

14. Ch. 47, §2, 1784 Laws of N.C. (Apr. Sess.), reprinted in *N.C. State Records*, XXIV, 616, 617; Quarles and White, *Three Pioneer Documents*, 18, 23–39 *passim*.

15. See, *e.g.*, Shaw v. Martin, DaCo CPQS Min. Bk. B, 78 (1792), Hadley v. Shaw, DaCo CPQS Min. Bk. A, 442 (1791); Cartwright v. Shaw, SumCo CPQS Min. Bk., 1787–1805, p. 40 (1791).

I. SUBSCRIPTION AGREEMENT
FOR THE
SUPPORT OF THE REVEREND
THOMAS B. CRAIGHEAD

July 4, 1785

Know all men by these presents that We the Under Subscribers Inhabitants of Davidson County in the State of No. Carolina Are held and firmly Bound unto James Shaw & Samuel Barton of the County & State Affsd. in the penal Sum of One thousand Pound's Current Money of the sd. State, To Which payment Well & Truly to be made We bind ourselves our heirs Extrs. & Admrs. Jointly and Severally firmly by these presents. Sealed Wt. our Seals & Dated this 4th day of July 1785. The Condition of the Above Obligation is Such, that Whereas We the Subscribers have this day Appointed the Above named James Shaw & Saml. Barton to purchase a Certain Tract of Land known by the name of Bucchanon's Spring including a pond lying and Situate on the Road from the french lick to Manskers Station, to and for the use of the Revd. Thomas Craighead his heirs And Assigns. Provided that the sd. Thomas Craighead doth Remove himself Into Said County & Shall Take charge of the Congregation's hereafter to be formed. Now if the sd. James Shaw & Samuel Barton, Shall procure and purchase the beforementioned Tract of 640 Acres of land for the purposes & Use's Afsd. We hereby Obligate Ourselves to pay unto the sd. James Shaw & Saml. Barton our proportionable part to and With Them, the sd. James Shaw and Saml. Barton of the sd. purchase, Agreeable to the Condition of the Contract by them made and According to our Subscriptions at Such times as the Said Payments Shall become due: On failure of Which the Above Obligation to be and Remain In full force, And Virtue:

James Robertson [1]
Samuel Barton
James Shaw
Lardner Clark
Ephm. McLane
James Bosley
Frederick Stump
Anthony Crutcher
Wm. Gubbins
Thomas James

David Hay
Elijah Robertson
John Rice
William Stuart
Saml. Shannon
William Stuart
Eusibus Bushnell
John Bucchanan
William Overall
Thomas Thompson

Tr, THi-DaCo CPQS Rec. Bk., 1783–1790, p. 147.

The record book entry also includes the annual amounts pledged by each of the subscribers: "James Robertson £8—Samuel Barton £5, James Shaw £5, Lardner Clark £12; Ephm. McLane £5—James Bosley £4, Frederick Stump £2, Anthony Crutcher £5, Wm. Gubbins £6[,] Thomas James £6, David Hay £2, Elijah Robertson £10, John Rice—William Stuart £1 . . 10s, Samuel Shannon £2, William Stuart £3, Eusebius Bushnell £4[,] John Buchanan, £2, Wm. Overall £1, Thomas Thompson £3."

1. The names of the subscribers are preceded in the Tr by "To Which Was marked the name's of."

II. AGREEMENT OF SAMUEL BARTON AND JAMES SHAW WITH JOHN BUCHANAN

July 7, 1785

Know all men by these presents tha[t] We Samuel Barton & James Shaw of the county of Davidson And State of North Carolina Are held and Firmly bound unto John Bucchanan of the county and State Aforesaid his Assigns &c. the Sum of Twelve hundred pounds current Money of said State Which payment Well and Truly to be made We hereby bind our selves our heirs Executors and Administrators Jointly and Severally Firmly by these presents Sealed With our Seals and Dated this Seventh day of July 1785 The condition of the Above Obligation is Such that If the Above bounden Samuel Barton & James Shaw Shall Well and truly pay or cause to be paid to the Said John Bucchanan Three hundred and Twenty pounds In Gold or Silver at the Rate of Eight Shillings for each Spanish Dollar at on or before the Seventh day of July in the year of our Lord One thousand Seven hundred and Eighty Six and Three hundred and Twenty pounds like Money on the Seventh day of July in the year of our Lord One thousand Seven hundred and Eighty Seven Without fraud or Delay Then the Above Obligation to be Void Otherwise to And Remain in full force and Virtue

Samuel Barton (LS)

&

James Shaw (LS)

Signed Sealed and Delivered
in the presence of
    John Brown and
    Martin Armstrong

Tr, T-DaCo Wills & Inventories, I, 222. The Tr indicates that the original agreement contained the following endorsements: "Cr. To the Within Bond by fifty Two pounds thirteen Shillings and three pence on Account of Ephraim McLane Senr. April 14th 1787 And by

Samuel Barton £10. .18. .4 And by my own Proportion of Mr. Craighead's Subscription
£14. .15s 11¼d Amounting in the Whole to £78. .7. .6¼."
    The agreement was acknowledged in open court by Shaw in July 1791 and was recorded
on Aug. 6, 1794.

III. WRIT

*Davidson County Court of Pleas and Quarter
Sessions, Nashville*

[ca. April 1787]

The State of No. Carolina
To the Sheriff of Davidson County Greeting.
    You Are hereby Commanded to take the Body of Elijah Robertson if to
be found in your County and him Safely keep so as you have him before
the Justices of our County Court of Pleas & quarter Sessions to be held
for the said county at our Courthouse in the Town of Nashll. on the first
Monday in April next: Then and there to Ansr. James Shaw & Samuel
Barton in a Plea of Trespass on the case To the Damage of the Plaintiffs
Eighty Pounds. herein fail not: And have you Then this Writ. Witness
Andrew Ewing Clerk of our sd. Court at Office this 13th day of April in
the year of our Lord 1787.
                        "Signed" Andrew Ewing C D C

Tr, THi-DaCo CPQS Rec. Bk., 1783–1790, p. 146. On its face, a writ normally was dated
as of the first day of the preceding term, and the clerk was required to endorse the document
by providing his signature and the date on which the writ actually was issued. Caruthers,
History of a Law Suit, 13. Because only a Tr of the writ in the *Robertson* case has been
located, the actual date of issuance remains unknown.

IV. DECLARATION OF SAMUEL
BARTON AND JAMES SHAW

*Davidson County Court of Pleas and Quarter
Sessions, Nashville*

[ca. April 1788]
Davidson County Ss.
    James Shaw and Samuel Barton Complain of Elijah Robertson &c. For
that Whereas the sd. Shaw and Barton heretofore became bound unto
John Bucchano[n] for the payment of £640 Principal money in Consideration of Which the said Elijah Robertson Wt. Sundry others each one
for himself promised to pay to the sd. Shaw and Barton When thereto

Required a proportionable part of the Afforesaid Sum According to the Amount of his Subscriptio[n] Made for the Support of the Revd. Mr. Craighead: Nevertheless the said Robertson Tho' often thereto Requested has hitherto failed to pay to the Said Shaw and Barton his proportionate Sum as Afforesaid Or in Anywise to Content them in Lieu thereof to their damage Eighty pound as they Say. &c.

Tr, THi-DaCo CPQS Rec. Bk., 1783–1790, p. 146. Approximate date is derived from initial appearance at April Term 1788. DaCo CPQS Min. Bk. A, 295.

V. MINUTE BOOK ENTRY

*Davidson County Court of Pleas and Quarter
Sessions, Nashville*

[July 6, 1789]

James Shaw & Saml. Barton Plaints. Against Elijah Roberton Defendant, "Case" To Which the Defendant April Term 1788 Appeared prayed & Obtained An Imparlance: And Afterwards October Term 1788 pleaded the "General Issue" And now at this day comes here into Court the plaints. by Josiah Love Esqr. their Attorney Likewise the Defdt. by Andrew Jackson Esqr. his Attorney And thereon comes a Jury To Wit, Elisha Rice Randal Johnston Thos. Smith Geo. A Suggs Patrick kelly, Saml. McCutchen David Crow Robert Kennedy Danl. Frazer, John Quales, Thos. Murry & Geo. Blackamore Who being Elected Tried & Sworn Well and Truly to try the Issue Joined &c. Say they find for the Plaintiffs "According to the Bond" Therefore it is considered of by the court that the plaints. Recover Against the Defdt. According To the Afforesd. Verdict Wt. his costs of Suit Expended &c. From Which Verdict & Judgment the Defdt. by his Attny. Affsd. prayed and Obtained an Appeal to the Honbl. the Superior Court of Law and Equity of Mero District And gave Bond of Two hundred pounds Wt. Andw. Jackson And James Cole Montflorence his Securities And filed his Reasons of Appeal: &c.

Court Adjourns untill Tomorrow at Eight OClock

MS, TDaCo-DaCo CPQS Min. Bk. A, 295. Date is taken from *id*.

VI. JACKSON'S STATEMENT
OF THE
GROUNDS FOR AN APPEAL

*Davidson County Court of Pleas and Quarter
Sessions, Nashville*

[July 6, 1789]

That the Writ in the sd. Cause is on A Trespass on the Case. That the
Declaration Corresponds With the Writ by Which the plaintiffs Lay their
Damages at Eighty pounds, Notwithstanding of Which the Jury Gave a
Verdict on A Bond the penalty of Which is One thousand pounds & no
Particular Sum in the condition the sd. Bond Being in the Nature of a
Covenant That After the Jury had Wt. drawn from the Barr, to make Up
their Verdict having returned into Court New Testimony & Other then
that Which Was produced on the Trial: Was Ruled by The Court to be
given them;

"Signed" Andw. Jackson Attny. for the Defdt.

Tr, THi-DaCo CPQS Rec. Bk., 1783–1790, p. 147. Date is taken from DaCo CPQS Min.
Bk. A, 295.

4. Meldrum v. Clark

1789
(Commercial Law)

EDITORIAL NOTE

Jackson numbered among his clients several nonresident litigants, including George Meldrum, a partner in the Detroit mercantile firm of Meldrum & Park. This action, in which Meldrum sought to recover from Lardner Clark an unpaid judgment that the latter had obtained for him in the Davidson County court in 1785, had been pending for more than a year when Jackson was retained to try the case. Jackson tried the suit in the Davidson court in July 1789, lost, and filed an appeal of the adverse judgment to the Superior Court. Whether he continued to represent the Detroit merchant on appeal has not been determined.

The trial and appeal constituted the final phases of an effort by Meldrum between 1785 and 1790 to collect a debt of more than 5,400 livres from one Antoine Harmand. Harmand operated a trading business in the Cahokia District of the Northwest Territory, and, although none of his records have been found, surviving court records indicate that he customarily purchased goods from suppliers like Meldrum & Park for resale to customers in the Cumberland settlements.[1]

It thus was probably for goods purchased from the Detroit firm for resale either in the Cumberland settlements or in the Northwest Territory that Harmand, on July 14, 1783, executed a note payable to Meldrum for the sum of 5,478 livres, 15 sous. Harmand subsequently defaulted on the note. When Meldrum thereafter sought to collect the debt, Harmand was no longer to be found in the Cahokia District.

Harmand in fact had defaulted on several other obligations in Cahokia

---

1. See, *e.g.*, Harmand v. Donaldson, DaCo CPQS Rec. Bk., 1783–1790, p. 79 (1788); Harmand v. Gower, *id.* at 42 (1787). Harmand had prospered sufficiently in Cahokia by June 1780 to warrant an appointment by the governor as a justice of one of the district's county courts. Clarence W. Alvord, ed., *Cahokia Records 1778–1790*, Collections of the Illinois State Historical Library, Virginia Ser., II (Springfield, 1907), 51.

between 1780 and 1784.[2] When the Cahokia court in June 1786 finally granted the petition of several of Harmand's creditors for a judicial sale of all of the debtor's real and personal property,[3] he had left the district and had moved to Davidson County.[4]

Unable to locate Harmand in Cahokia, Meldrum early in 1785 executed a power of attorney authorizing one of the firm's Nashville customers, Lardner Clark,[5] to collect the debt. Meldrum's power of attorney was delivered to Clark in April 1785[6] by Timothy Demonbreun, deputy county lieutenant at Kaskaskia.[7] Clark was authorized to recover the debt from Harmand and to deliver the amount recovered either to Meldrum himself or to Meldrum's agent, John Dodge.[8] On July 30 Clark secured a judicial attachment of certain property of Harmand's that was in the possession of John Boyd and Samuel Martin, who were summoned to appear as Harmand's garnishees before the Davidson court in October. When Clark's action for Meldrum went to trial on October 3, Harmand made a personal appearance and entered a confession of judgment. Boyd and Martin were dismissed, and a judgment was entered against Harmand for £438, 2 shillings.[9]

Meldrum apparently never received any payment on the judgment against Harmand. In December 1787 Meldrum instituted the present action against Clark in the Davidson County court (Document I). He asserted that, although the court's execution docket indicated that the judgment had been satisfied, Clark had not turned over the amount recovered from Harmand.

At the court's April 1788 Term, Clark secured an imparlance in the instant action and instituted a separate proceeding, purportedly on Meldrum's behalf, against Harmand. In the latter, Clark sought to recover the expenses necessary to transport from Nashville to the Northwest Territory an unspecified quantity of furs and skins that he claimed to have demanded from Harmand in satisfaction of the 1785 judgment.[10] Al-

2. See, e.g., Prevost v. Harmand, in Alvord, *Cahokia Records,* 185, 187 (1784); Beaulieu v. Harmand, *id.* at 171 (1784); Beaulieu v. Harmand, *id.* at 142 (1782); Cerré v. Harmand, *id.* at 135, 137 (1782).

3. *Id.* at 243, 245. The court provided, however, that Harmand's house and its appurtenances were to be sold only if his other property was insufficient to satisfy the demands of his creditors.

4. See DaCo CPQS Rec. Bk., 1783–1790, p. 153.

5. W. A. Provine, "Lardner Clark, Nashville's First Merchant and Foremost Citizen," pt. 1, 3 *Tenn. Hist. Mag.* 29, 48 (1917).

6. DaCo CPQS Rec. Bk., 1783–1790, p. 153.

7. Alvord, *Cahokia Records,* cxxiv–v, cxxxii.

8. DaCo CPQS Rec. Bk., 1783–1790, p. 153.

9. *Id.* at 19.

10. *Id.* at 70. Clark claimed that he had demanded that Harmand satisfy the judgment in furs and skins because Harmand's original obligation to Meldrum was to have been dis-

though the records for this later action against Harmand are not entirely clear, Clark seemingly argued that he had collected from Harmand but that the recovery had not yet been forwarded to Meldrum. When his claim against Harmand met with no success, Clark secured the court's permission in October to admit into evidence in the present case an account by which he hoped to prove that a parcel or parcels of land had been conveyed to Meldrum in lieu of whatever had been collected from Harmand.

Jackson tried Meldrum's action against Clark on July 7, 1789. Although the details of the trial remain unknown, the jury found, evidently on the basis of the account produced by Clark, that a conveyance of land to Jackson's client had satisfied his judgment against Harmand except for £46, for which sum a verdict was returned (see Document III). Jackson appealed the resulting adverse judgment to the Mero District Superior Court on the ground that the court's admission of Clark's account "as a Sett off. . . . Deprived the Plaint. of Any Remedy of Compelling the Defdt. to make a Title to the sd. Land or to Recover the Whole Debt" (Document IV).

Although Meldrum prevailed in the Superior Court, it cannot be determined whether Jackson remained as counsel of record for the Detroit merchant during the appellate proceedings.[11]

Meldrum (ca. 1737–1817) had begun a trading operation at Detroit as early as 1768 and supplied rations and matériel to the American troops there during the Revolutionary War. By the end of the conflict, he had accumulated substantial amounts of real estate in the growing trading post.[12] The firm of Meldrum & Park was one of six mercantile shareholders in the Miami Company, an association of Detroit businesses that was organized in 1786 to outfit traders throughout the Northwest Territory.[13] Meldrum & Park was one of the principal suppliers for Clark's Nashville store,[14] but the full extent of the firm's business in Nashville and in the Northwest Territory has not been determined.

For further identification of Clark, see Part IV.

---

charged in the Illinois settlements and because the currency then in circulation in Davidson County was "of No consequence at the Illinois." *Id.* A jury subsequently returned a verdict for Harmand.

11. Clark was less successful in convincing the jury on appeal that Meldrum's judgment against Harmand had been paid. The Mero District jury on May 4, 1790, returned a verdict for Meldrum in the amount of £487, 12 shillings—very nearly the amount of the 1785 judgment recovered from Harmand. The court denied a subsequent motion in arrest of judgment by Clark and entered judgment on the verdict for Meldrum. MDSC Law Min. Bk., 1783–1803, pp. 20–21.

12. Milo M. Quaife, ed., *John Askin Papers* (Detroit, 1928), I, 71 n.11, 293 n.14.

13. Wayne E. Stevens, "The Northwest Fur Trade 1763–1800," 14 *U. Ill. Studies in the Social Sciences* 137 (1926).

14. Provine, "Lardner Clark, Nashville's First Merchant," 48.

I. WRIT

Davidson County Court of Pleas and Quarter Sessions, Nashville

[ca. December 1787]

The State of No. Carolina—

To the Sheriff of Davidson County: Greeting

You are hereby commanded to take the Body of Lardner Clark if to be found in your County and him Safely Keep So as you have him before the Justices of our County Court of pleas and Quarter Sessions to be held for sd. County at our Courthouse in the Town of Nashle. on the first Monday in January next thereto Answer George Meldrum in a plea of Trespass on the Case to the damage of the plaint[iff] two thousand Pounds—Herein fail not And have there this Writ. Witness Andrew Ewing Clerk of our sd. Court office this 29th day of Decr. in the year of our Lord 1787

Signed   Andrew Ewing C D C

Tr, THi-DaCo CPQS Rec. Bk., 1783–1790, pp. 152–153. On its face, a writ normally was dated as of the first day of the preceding term, and the clerk was required to endorse the document by providing his signature and the date on which the writ actually was issued. Caruthers, *History of a Law Suit*, 13. This procedure apparently was not followed in the present case, since the Davidson County court did not meet for a December term. Because only a Tr of the writ has been located, the actual date of issuance remains unknown. The record book indicates that the writ was executed and returned to the court at its January Term 1788 endorsed: "Danl. Rowan D Shff."

II. DECLARATION OF

GEORGE MELDRUM

Davidson County Court of Pleas and Quarter Sessions, Nashville

[ca. January 1788]

Davidson County Ss—

George Meldrum Complains of Lardner Clark &c. For that Whereas he the sd. Clark on the [. . .] day of Apl. 1785 did receive of Timothy Demumbre a Power of Attorney to Collect & Recei[ve from] Anthony Harmand 5478 Livres 15 Sous, in behalf of John Dodge as Agent or Agency for him the sd. Meldrum and for the payment of which the sd. Harmand had given His Obligation dated July 14th 1783 As Appears by

Sundry Reciepts given by sd. Clark. In Consequences of Which Power of Attorney the sd. Clark did Appear in our Court in behalf of [Plaint.] Meldrum and Obtain Judgment in his name Against the said Harmand for the Sum of £438..2 s As Appears by Record thereof made October 4th 1785 And for Which execution did Issue Against the Estate of the sd. Harmand: Whereon Thomas Masten then Shff [. . .] Return that the Plaint. Debt was Satisfied to the sd. Clark his Attorney in fact:[1] as Appears by the Execution Dockett.—Nevertheless Although he did Engage to Acct. for the sd. Bond or Monies When Recd. Yet has he never made Any Remittances to the sd. Meldrum or Dodge but hitherto has and Still does Refuse to Account for the Same: To the damage of the said [Meldrum] One thousand Pounds as he Saith &c.

Tr, THi-DaCo CPQS Rec. Bk., 1783–1790, p. 153. Plaintiffs were required to file their declarations during the term to which process was returned. See Caruthers, *History of a Law Suit,* 17. The approximate date of Document II is established from the indication in the record book that the writ (Document I) was returned to the court at its January Term 1788.

    1. An attorney in fact was an agent authorized to act for another for some particular purpose or for the transaction of business. For example, when payment of a debt or judgment was made to an attorney in fact for the creditor, it was treated as having been paid to the creditor himself. This authority was commonly conferred by a written instrument known as a power of attorney. John Bouvier, *Institutes of American Law* (Philadelphia, 1851), I, 314–315, II, 6.

III. MINUTE BOOK ENTRY

Davidson County Court of Pleas and Quarter
Sessions, Nashville

[July 7, 1789]

George Meldrum Plaint. Agt. Lardner Clark Defendant. Case To Which April Term 1788 the Defendant by Edward Douglass his Attorney in fact Appeared prayed & Obtained an Imparlance, And Afterwards Oct. Term 1788 by James Cole Mountflorence his Attny. in fact pleaded the General Issue And Sett of:[1] And now at this day comes hereinto court the plaint. by Andrew Jackson Esqr. his Attorney Likewise the Defendant by Josiah Love Esqr. his Attorney And thereon comes a Jury Viz Wm. Ellis Wm. Stuart Thos. McCrory Eusibius Bushnel David Ralston James Shaw Thos. Johnston Frederick Stump Robert Mitchel Danl. Frazer Samuel Wilson and Griswell Latimore Who being Elected tried & Sworn Will and truly &c. try the Issue Joined &c. And John Bucchanan and Samuel Martin the Witnesses in behalf of the Defendant being Sworn Examined and heard the Jury Whereas Returned Say they find for the plaint. and Do Assess his damage on the Occasion to Forty Six pounds: Therefore it is Considered of by the Court that the plaint. Recover Against the defendant The Affsd. Sum of Forty Six pounds So Assessed to him by the Jury As Afforesd. Together Wh his cost of Suit on that behalf Expended sd. And from Which Judgment the plaint. by his Attny. Affsd. prayed and Obtained An Appeal to the Honble. Superior court of Law and Equity Mero District And gave Bond of Ninety Two pounds Wt. James Cole Mountflorence & Timothy Demembre his Securities And filed his Reason of Appeal &c.

MS, TDaCo-DaCo CPQS Min. Bk. A, 297. Date is taken from *id.*

1. A setoff allowed the defendant in an action to set up against the plaintiff's claim any debt that the plaintiff owed him. A 1756 North Carolina statute declared that "in all Cases where there are, or shall be, mutual Debts subsisting between the Plaintiff and Defendant . . . one Debt may be set against the other . . . notwithstanding such Debts shall or may be deemed in Law to be of a different Nature." Ch. 4, 1756 Laws of N.C., reprinted in Iredell, *Laws of North Carolina* 171, 1 Scott, *Laws of Tennessee* 89. See generally Timothy Walker, *Introduction to American Law* (Philadelphia, 1837), 535–536; 4 Tucker, *Blackstone's Commentaries* 304. Despite the description in the pleadings, it seems unlikely that Clark employed a setoff against Meldrum. There is nothing in the record to indicate that Meldrum was indebted to Clark. Rather, it appears that Clark attempted an accord and satisfaction by tendering real property as a substitute payment.

IV. JACKSON'S STATEMENT OF THE GROUND FOR AN APPEAL

Davidson County Court of Pleas and Quarter Sessions, Nashville

[July 7, 1789]

[T]he Defendant Introduced An Open Account as a Sett. off. in Which he Charges the Plaint. for Recieving Land in Payment of the Debt by Virtue of a Power of Attorney and letter Which he there Produced, And it was decreed by the Court that the Account Should be Admitted as a Sett off. for £442 And Deprived the Plaint. of Any Remedy of Compelling the Defdt. to make a Title to the sd. Land or to Recover the Whole Debt &c.

                          Signed   Andrew Jackson Att. for
                          the plaint.

Tr, THi-DaCo CPQS Rec. Bk., 1783–1790, p. 153. Date is taken from *id.*

5. Hampton v. Boyd and Foster

1790
(Slavery)

EDITORIAL NOTE

As has been indicated, Jackson was inevitably concerned with the law of slavery. Most of his cases involving slavery were routine levies upon slave property or actions relating to the disputed ownership of slaves. This case, in which Jackson represented two defendants who allegedly had committed an assault upon the plaintiff's slave that resulted in his death, and the case that follows, in which Jackson successfully appeared on behalf of a defendant who was charged with being a slave, were thus out of the ordinary.

In the winter or early spring of 1788, Thomas Hampton of Sumner County[1] brought this action of trespass vi et armis in the Davidson County court to recover damages for the death of his slave Caesar (see Document I). Hampton alleged that John Boyd, the proprietor of the Red Heifer distillery in Nashville, and James Foster had assaulted Caesar and broken his leg and that the assault had caused the slave's ensuing death.[2] Hampton sought compensation in the amount of £1,000, the alleged value of the slave (Document II).

Jackson made his first recorded appearance in the action at the Davidson court's October Term 1789 as counsel for the defendants with Howell Tatum. When the case finally went to trial on April 13, 1790, the jury returned a judgment for the plaintiff in the amount of £200 plus costs (Document III). Jackson and Tatum obtained an appeal of the decision to the Mero District Superior Court and filed the appropriate documentation with the court on April 19.

---

1. See State v. Hampton, MDSC Law Min. Bk., 1788–1803, p. 40 (1791). Hampton has not been further identified.

2. Boyd Sketch, Provine Papers, T. Albigence W. Putnam, *History of Middle Tennessee* (Nashville, 1859), 284, 384. Neither Boyd nor Foster has been further identified.

Although the record is unclear, Jackson evidently did not represent the defendants during the appellate proceedings.[3]

3. The county court's judgment was reversed on May 2, 1791. MDSC Law Min. Bk., 1788–1803, pp. 30–31. Plaintiff's counsel, John Overton and James Cole Mountflorence, moved for a new trial on the grounds that the Superior Court jury's verdict was contrary to the evidence, that the defendants since the trial had admitted that the slave at the time of the supposed assault had been on the premises where the injury occurred, and that the admission was a material fact that had not been available to the jury before the verdict was returned. *Id.* at 45. The court granted Hampton's motion and scheduled a new trial for the ensuing November Term.

The case went to trial for the second time at the appellate level on Nov. 7. The jury returned a special verdict apparently on the factual issue of whether the defendants' conduct in evicting the slave from the premises had been a cause in fact of the slave's broken leg. The jury found that, although the defendants had been accessories to injuring the slave by evicting him from the premises, the defendants had not intended to cause the resulting injury. The jury's verdict was an alternative one, depending upon whether the facts they had found were sufficient at law to constitute an action of trespass vi et armis. If so, the jury concluded, Hampton should be awarded only £100; if not, then Boyd and Foster should be awarded judgment. *Id.* at 50–51. On Nov. 11, the court announced that the facts found by the jury were insufficient to support the plaintiff's action and awarded judgment to the defendants. *Id.* at 61.

I. WRIT AND RETURN

Davidson County Court of Pleas and Quarter Sessions, Nashville

[ca. January–March 1788]

The State of No. carolina To the Sheriff of Davidson county Greeting: You Are hereby commanded to take the Bodies of John Boyd and James Foster If to be found in yr. county and them Safely keep So as you have them before the Justices of our county court of pleas & Quarter Sessions to be held for sd. County at our courthouse in the Town of Nashville on the first Monday in April next: Then and there to Answer Thomas Hampton in a plea of Trespass, to [the] damage of the sd. Hampton One thousand pounds &c. Herein fail not and have then & there [this] Writ. Witness Andrew Ewing Clark of our sd. Court at office this Ninth day of Jany. 1788   and   in the 12th year of our Independence: "Signed" Andrew Ewing &c. Which Writ So Issued was Executed and Returned to April Term 1788 by Daniel James [DS]

Tr, THi-DaCo CPQS Rec. Bk., 1783–1790, p. 203. Exact date of preparation and issuance is unknown. On its face, a writ was dated not as of the time of its actual preparation and issuance, but as of the first day of the preceding term (here, Jan. 9, 1788). The clerk was required to endorse the reverse of the writ by providing his signature and the date on which the writ actually was issued. Caruthers, *History of a Law Suit,* 13. Because only a Tr of the writ has been located, the exact date of preparation and issuance cannot be determined, although these must have occurred before the writ's return to the court, according to the text of the Tr, in April 1788.

II. DECLARATION OF
THOMAS HAMPTON

*Davidson County Court of Pleas and Quarter
Sessions, Nashville*

[ca. April 1788]

Davidson county To Wit Thomas Hampton complains of John Boyd and James Foster in Custody &c. of a plea of Trespass, for that Whereas the sd. plaint. on the   ¹day of   ¹in the year One thousand [seven] hundred and Eighty   ¹at county Afforesd. was possessed of a Certain Negro man slave named Cesar. as of his own proper Slave. And being so thereof possessed, the said defendants on the day and year Afforesaid at the County Afforesd. Contriving & Maliciously intending to injure the plaint. did Assault and threaten Violently to beat and Abuse the sd. slave, and did then and there break or Cause to be broken the leg of the sd. Slave, of Which wound the sd. Slave Languished and died; by Reason Whereof the plaint. hath lost not only the service, but the life of the sd. Slave Wherefore he saith he hath Sustained Damages to the Amount of One Thousand pounds, And therefore he Brings Suit &c.

Tr, THi-DaCo CPQS Rec. Bk., 1783–1790, p. 203. Plaintiffs were required to file their declarations during the term to which process was returned. See Caruthers, *History of a Law Suit,* 17. The approximate date of Document II is established from the indication in Document I that the writ was returned to the court at its April Term 1788.

1. Thus in Tr.

III. RECORD BOOK ENTRY

Davidson County Court of Pleas and Quarter Sessions, Nashville

[April 13, 1790]

Thomas Hampton Plaint.

vs

John Boyd & James Foster Defdts.

. . . .[1] And to Which the defendants Appeared April Term 1788 and prayed and Obtained a General Imparlance: And afterwards October Term 1788 pleaded the "Genl. Issue" Which proceedings so Remained untill Octr. Term 1789 at Which Time comes here into court the Plaint. by Josiah Love Esqr. his Attorney, Likewise the Defendants by Andrew Jackson & Howel Tatum Esqrs. their Attorneys, And by Consent of parties it was Agreed on that the plaint. plea laid in the Writ Should be Taken and Considered as a plea of Trespass Viet-Armis"[2] Which Afterwards continued Without Any Determination had, untill April Term 1790 At Which time comes Again into court [sd.] plaint. by Josiah Love, John Overton & James Cole Montflorence Esqrs. his Attorneys, Likewise [sd.] defendants by Andrew Jackson, & Howel Tatum Esqr. their Attorneys and thereon named a Jury; Alexander Cambell, Thomas Smith, Frederick Stump, John Edmondson, Wm. Bosley Headon Wells, Dan Hill, Ezekiell Smith, Jas. Byrns, David Hood Thomas Peal and Wm. Marrs Who being Elected Tried and Sworn well and Truly to try the Issue joined &c. And the Witnesses for the plaint. Sarah Lucas, Cynthia Gower, Elizabeth Hinslar William Loggins and Adam Hampton Likewise for the Defendant Sarah Lucas Senr. being all sworn Examined & heard the Jury With drew Return and Say They find for the plaintiff & do assess his Damages on the Occassion to Two hundred pounds: Therefore it is considered of by the court that the plaintiff Recover against the Defendants the Affsd. Sum of Two hundred pounds So assessed to him by the Jury as Afforesd. together Wt. his costs of Suit in that behalf Expended: &c. from Which Judgment the Defendants prayed and Obtained an Appeal to the Honble. Superior court of Law for Mero District having given bond of four hundred pounds Wt. Gade Gibson, Richard Shaffer & Pleasant Lockett their Securities, and filed their Reasons of Appeal:[3]

MS, THi-DaCo CPQS Rec. Bk., 1783–1790, p. 203.

1. Documents I and II originally occurred at this point in the MS.
2. The parties agreed to treat this case as an action of trespass vi et armis. Trespass vi et armis was a civil action for immediate injury to the plaintiff's person or property, such as a battery or wounding committed with force.
3. The grounds for the appeal are missing both from the MS and from the corresponding entry in DaCo CPQS Min. Bk. A, 352.

6. Gilmore v. Williams

1791
(Slavery)

EDITORIAL NOTE

By statute, the county courts under both the North Carolina and territorial governments heard complaints by persons held as slaves who claimed to have been free in another jurisdiction.[1] Yet the only suit during Jackson's practice to raise the question of slave status arose procedurally in a manner different from that prescribed by the statute. The action was brought not by a person claiming to be free, but by a plaintiff, William Gilmore, who alleged that the defendant, John Williams, was one of his slaves.

The suit went to trial at the Davidson County Court of Pleas and Quarter Sessions on July 15, 1791. Gilmore was represented by Howell Tatum. Jackson represented Williams. The only document for the case that has survived, the trial entry in the court's minute book, indicates that Jackson called three witnesses for Williams, including John Montgomery, the former commander of the Virginia troops at Kaskaskia and sheriff of the Cumberland District in 1783,[2] and Lardner Clark, a future justice of the Davidson court. The jury returned a verdict for Williams, finding him to be "a free man."[3]

1. Ch. 24, § 24, 1741 Laws of N.C., reprinted in Iredell, *Laws of North Carolina* 89, 1 Scott, *Laws of Tennessee* 68.

2. Ursula S. Beach, *Along the Warioto; or, A History of Montgomery County, Tennessee* (Nashville, 1964), 82; Quarles and White, *Three Pioneer Documents*, 23, 29.

3. Neither of the parties has been further identified.

MINUTE BOOK ENTRY

Davidson County Court of Pleas and Quarter Sessions, Nashville

[July 15, 1791]

William Gillmore Plaintiff With Protestation Against John Williams Alias James Charged by Plaintiff With being a Slave Whereupon now comes hereinto As Well the Plaintiff by Howel Tatum Esqr. his Attorney as the Defendant by Andrew Jackson Esqr. his Attorney and Pleads the "General Issue" And thereupon Comes a Jury To Wit, William Marshall Andrew Boyd Alexander Campbell John Marshall William McMoon, Jonathan Philips, James Byrns Isaac Evans, John Caffery James Todd, Judinian Cartwright & Frederick Stump Who being Elected tried and Sworn well & truly to try the Issue Joined Between the Parties Aforesaid And Anthony Hart & his Wife, the Witnesses in behalf of the Plaintiff and Adam Pinkley John Montgomery & Lardner Clark the Witnesses for the Defendant being all Sworn Examined and heard the Jury Withdrew Return and Say they find the Issue for the Defendant And that he is a free man Therefore it is considered of by the court that the Defendant be Discharged from the custody of the Sheriff And that he Recover Against the Plaintiff his costs of Defence.

MS, TDaCo-DaCo CPQS Min. Bk. A, 448. Date is taken from *id.*

7. Murfree v. Leeper

1791
(Procedure)

EDITORIAL NOTE

This *caveat* action in which Jackson and John Overton were counsel of record for the defendant is of significance primarily because of the Mero District Superior Court's procedural decision in the case in November 1791. The court's opinion (Document IV) is the only published decision known to have arisen from a case in which Jackson was counsel of record.

Caveat litigation was rare in the course of Jackson's practice. A formal notice to an official informing him to suspend proceedings until the merits of another claim could be decided, *caveat* was widely employed in American law to stay the granting of land patents.

Ostensibly the disposition of public land was closely governed by statute. Any citizen could file a written claim for previously ungranted land, typically a tract of 640 acres, with the county entry taker. Payment of the required sum was made to this officer. If no other person claimed the same land within three months, the entry taker delivered a copy of the entry to the claimant and directed the county surveyor to survey the tract. The surveyor would prepare two plats, often a difficult task given the primitive state of surveying, and forward them to the office of the secretary of state. The secretary then issued a grant based upon the survey. Finally, the claimant was required to register this grant in the register's office where the land was located.

In the event that a *caveat* was filed with the entry taker, he would transmit the disputed claim to the county court. This tribunal was charged with summoning a jury and going with the jurors to the contested premises. The jury was expressly authorized to return either a general or a special verdict, and the prevailing party could then obtain an order of survey and proceed to perfect a grant.[1] A 1779 measure altered the *caveat* proce-

---

1. Ch. 1, 1777 Laws of N.C. (Nov. Sess.), reprinted in Iredell, *Laws of North Carolina* 292, 1 Scott, *Laws of Tennessee* 159. Land claims in Kentucky were handled in a similar

dure in two important respects. Upon complaint, the governor could suspend the execution of land grants already made and refer the matter to the appropriate county court for a jury trial "in the same manner as they might do if a *caveat* had been made in the office of the entry taker." Further, the judgment of the county court was "final and conclusive, without any appeal to the Superior Court."[2]

Acting upon a complaint by Hardy Murfree, Governor Richard Caswell in 1786 suspended the execution of a grant to Hugh Leeper of 640 acres in Davidson County. Pursuant to the governor's order, Secretary of State James Glasgow issued a *caveat* certificate on December 22, 1786, to the Davidson County court, directing the court to initiate the proceedings provided by statute for settling the dispute between Murfree and Leeper (Document I).

Although the Davidson County court on April 6, 1787, and again at several succeeding terms, directed the county sheriff to summons a jury to try the case, the initial trial of the action did not occur until July 1789. When at the trial a juror was withdrawn and a mistrial declared, the court directed that the cause be continued until its April Term 1790.[3]

Jackson's first recorded appearance with John Overton as counsel for Leeper occurred at the second trial of the suit at the Davidson County court on April 17, 1790. After hearing testimony from five witnesses for Murfree and four for Leeper, the jury retired and returned a general verdict for the caveator. The court entered judgment on the verdict for Murfree (Document II).

Although Jackson remained as co-counsel with Overton for Leeper until the subsequent certiorari phase of the litigation terminated in 1794,[4] he apparently was not present when Overton, in the late spring or early summer of 1790, filed a petition with the Mero District Superior Court for the issuance of a writ of certiorari.[5] Jackson likewise was absent at the county court's July Term 1790, when Overton successfully moved that a transcript of the case be forwarded to the Superior Court.[6]

Between the entry of the Davidson County court's judgment on April 17 and the filing of Overton's motion with the court in July, the Superior Court granted Leeper a writ of certiorari. The court's action came despite

fashion. Herbert A. Johnson, ed., *The Papers of John Marshall* (Chapel Hill, 1974), I, 103–104. See also 3 Tucker, *Blackstone's Commentaries* 66–67, App. D.

2. Ch. 4, 1779 Laws of N.C., reprinted in Iredell, *Laws of North Carolina* 384, 1 Scott, *Laws of Tennessee* 238.

3. DaCo CPQS Min. Bk. A, 169, 218, 243, 314.

4. See MDSC Execution Docket, 1792–1803, p. 24.

5. MDSC Law Min. Bk., 1788–1803, p. 62.

6. DaCo CPQS Min. Bk. A, 381.

the terms of the 1779 statute, which provided that such judgments in *caveat* actions were final and not subject to appeal.[7]

A transcript was filed with the Superior Court on September 27. Because the court met only for two days in November 1790, the initial proceedings at the Superior Court level did not occur until May 1791. On May 4, the court on the motion of Murfree's counsel ordered Leeper to show cause why he should not post bond for costs upon filing a petition for certiorari with the court. Jackson and Overton moved for a continuance, which the court granted on May 9.[8]

At the court's November Term 1791, Murfree's counsel moved to quash the writ of certiorari on the ground that, under the 1779 statute, the court was without authority to issue such a writ in a *caveat* action. Although no record of Jackson and Overton's response has been located, the court, with Judges McNairy and Anderson presiding, denied the motion on November 11, ruling that the authority to issue the writ was derived from the court's common-law supervisory power over all inferior courts. The court further held that a writ of certiorari, even in a *caveat* action, was an appropriate means of exercising that power and that the court's authority to issue such writs could not be abrogated by the legislature "without express negative words." The court concluded that, although the legislature clearly had intended that no appeals to the court should be granted in *caveat* actions, it did not follow that the legislature also had meant to prevent removing a *caveat* proceeding to the Superior Court upon a writ of certiorari (Document IV). The court did grant Murfree's motion of May 4 that Leeper, whom Murfree claimed was a nonresident with no property within the jurisdiction, post a bond for costs in the certiorari proceeding (Document IV, endnote).

On November 12, Murfree's counsel objected to Overton's having filed the petition for certiorari, arguing that Leeper himself should have filed the petition. The court overruled the objection (Document V).

A final verdict for Jackson and Overton's client was not rendered for another two and a half years. On May 6, 1794, a jury returned a verdict finding that Leeper held title to the disputed 640 acres in Davidson County (Document VI).

Murfree (1752–1809) resided in Hertford County, North Carolina, until well after the Revolution. Appointed by President Washington as a revenue inspector for the District of North Carolina in December 1793, Murfree subsequently moved to middle Tennessee to occupy land granted

---

7. Ch. 4, 1779 Laws of N.C., reprinted in Iredell, *Laws of North Carolina* 384, 1 Scott, *Laws of Tennessee* 238.
8. MDSC Law Min. Bk., 1788–1803, pp. 27–28, 38, 47, 112.

him for services rendered as a lieutenant colonel during the war. The city of Murfreesboro, Tennessee, was named in his honor in 1811.[9]

It has not been determined whether Leeper was the Hugh Leeper whose signature appears on the Cumberland Compact or the Hugh Leaper whose name occurs on a Hawkins County, Tennessee, tax list for 1809.[10] The court's ruling in November 1791 (Document IV, endnote) indicates that, at least as of that date, Leeper was not a resident of the Mero District.

9. Weston A. Goodspeed, *A History of Tennessee from the Earliest Time to the Present* (Nashville, 1886), 826; Philip M. Hamer, ed., *Tennessee: A History, 1673–1932* (New York, 1953), IV, 463; *JES*, I, 143–144; Worth S. Ray, *Tennessee Cousins: A History of Tennessee People* (Baltimore, 1966), 613; John H. Wheeler, *Historical Sketches of North Carolina from 1584 to 1851*, rpnt. ed. (New York, 1925), 208; "The North Carolina Society of Cincinnati," 4 *AHM* 316–318 (1899).

10. Quarles and White, *Three Pioneer Documents*, 20; Pollyanna Creekmore, "Early East Tennessee Taxpayers," pt. 8, ETHS *Publ.* No. 32 (1960), 124.

I. CAVEAT CERTIFICATE

December 22, 1786

State of No. Carolina

The Honorable Jas. Glasgow Esqr. Secretary.

To the Worshipfull the Justices of Davidson County, Greeting

Whereas his Excellency the Governor hath Certified that on Complaints of Hardy Murfree on Oath he hath Suspended the Execution of a grant to Hugh Leeper for a Tract of Land in sd. County Containing Six hundred & forty Acres in the main West fork of Big-harpeth: And Required me to Certify the Suspension of the sd. grant to you the sd. Justices to the End the Dispute be Determined According to Law. I Do hereby persuant thereto hereby Certify the Suspension of the sd. Grant to you the sd. Justices, Accordingly; Given under my hand at Fayette this 22d of Decr. 1786;

Signed   J: Glasgow

Tr, THi-DaCo CPQS Rec. Bk., 1783–1790, p. 209.

II. MINUTE BOOK ENTRY

*Davidson County Court of Pleas and Quarter
Sessions, Nashville*

[April 17, 1790]

Colo. Hardy Murfree Caveator Against Hugh Leeper Caveattee: To Which
the Caveator Appeared by Josiah Love Jas. Cole Montflorence & Howel
Tatum Esqrs. his Attorneys Likewise the Caveattee by John Overton, &
Andrew Jackson Esqrs. his Attorneys And thereon Came a Jury To Wit
Thomas Smith Ezekiel Smith, Alexander Campbel John Edmondson
Saml. Bucchanan, William Marshall James Hamilton Thomas James,
Wm. Donelson, Hugh Thompson John Caffrey and Wm. Shaw Who
being Elected tried and Sworn to do equal Right between the Caveator,
and Caveattee &c. And the Witnessess for the Caveator James Robertson,
Wm. Stuart, James McSherin Russell Gower and Jonathan Drake. And
for the Caveattee Robert Thompson, Elijah Robertson, Julius Sanders &
B Wm. Pollock being all Sworn Examined and heard: The Jury Wt. drew
Return and Say they find for the Caveator: And the Court gave Judgment
According to their Verdict And Order that the Clerk Certify the Same to
the Governor.

MS, TDaCo-DaCo CPQS Min. Bk. A, 361. Date is taken from *id.*

III. MINUTE BOOK ENTRY

Mero District Superior Court, Nashville

[November 11, 1791]

Moved the following question for the opinion of the Court (viz) whether
Certiorarii Can issue in particular Cases of hardship and injustice to Correct the proceedings of all inferiour Courts and arguments had by Council
Learned in the Law It is Considered by the Court that the writ of Certiorari will Lie and ought to issue to the inferiour Courts to Correct Errors
in the proceedings below even after Judgment had in the Said Courts.

The Honble. Court adjourned till tomorrow morning 9 oClocke

MS, TDaCo-MDSC Law Min. Bk., 1788–1803, p. 61. Date is taken from *id.* at 60.

IV. THE DECISION OF
THE COURT

Mero District Superior Court, Nashville

MURFREE *v.* LEEPER, Nov., 1791.

CAVEAT in the County Court. Verdict for the Caveator; a petition was presented to a judge of this court, praying that the cause might be removed by *certiorari*. The judge granted the writ, and now at this term, it was moved to quash it, on the ground that the court have no authority in cases of caveats to grant writs of certiorari. The first section of an act passed in the year 1779, c. 4, was referred to. By that section, the legislature have said that the judgment of the (County) Court, in all cases of vacant and unappropriated land, shall be final and conclusive without any appeal to the Superior Court. Ird. 384.

The cause was elaborately argued on both sides, when the court decided, that this court by the common law, had a control over all inferior jurisdictions; that this writ was the proper means of exercising this control in a case situated like the present; and that the power of this court to issue writs of *certiorari* could not be taken away without express negative words.[1]

The will of the legislature when known is the law; but to exclude the general superintending power of this court, it should be clearly and unequivocally expressed, and not left to be collected from doubtful inferences. The legislature have clearly said, that no appeal shall be allowed to this court, but it does not thence follow that the cause cannot be brought here by *certiorari*.

Take nothing by the motion.

The counsel for the caveator then observed, that the caveatee was a nonresident, that he had no property within the jurisdiction of this court, except the land now in dispute; and therefore moved that the caveatee should be ordered to give security for costs, within a limited time, or the certiorari be dismissed, which after argument was ordered accordingly.

Printed decision, 1 Tenn. (1 Overton) 1–2 (1791). Editorial headnotes inserted by reporter between style of the case and text have been omitted.

The minute book contains the court's decision on the question of whether a party seeking a writ of certiorari must post a bond similar to that required in the case of an appeal. The court held that "Security Should be given on Granting Said Certiorari either before the Judge at the time of Granting Said writ or in open Court and it is further the opinion of the Court, that, where a matter has been determined in any Inferior Court, where the Plaintiff hath good and Sufficient Security and the defendant praying a Certiorari and Suggesting

Some irregularities in the proceedings, that the Security had in the inferior Court Shall Still be Considered as Such till Security be Given on the Certiorari." MDSC Law Min. Bk., 1788–1803, p. 62.

1. Sources cited in the margin at this point: "2 Term. Rep. 735; 5 Term Rep. 251, 626; 6 Term. Rep. 194."

V. MINUTE BOOK ENTRY

Mero District Superior Court, Nashville

[November 12, 1791]

[Murfree v. Leeper], upon Certiorari motion that the affidavit filed for the obtaining a writ of Certiorari was filed by John Overton Esqr. Atto. for Leeper and being Suggested by the Councils of Murfee that it was not Legal & ought to have been filed by Leeper himself, and after arguments being heard on both Sides it is the opinion of the Court that the affidavit is good, and that the Cert well Lies Hugh Leeper Enters into a recognizance of the Sum of two hundred and fifty pounds With Samson Williams his Security for the prosecuting his writ of Certiorari against Hardee Murfee.

MS, TDaCo-MDSC Law Min. Bk., 1788–1803, p. 62. Date is taken from *id.* at 61.

VI. MINUTE BOOK ENTRY

Mero District Superior Court, Nashville

[May 6, 1794]

Hardee Murfee
   vs   Certiorari
Hugh Leeper   Be it remembered that this Certiorari with the Proceedings thereon was brought up and filed in the office of the Honble. Superior Court the 27th of September 1790 and Continued from Term to Term untill this Term, the Cause Came on for Trial and thereon Came a good and Lawfull Jury (viz) John Childers, David Beaty, Badly Gambrel Josiah Fort, Nemrod Williams, James Dean, Thomas Harney, Robert Shaw, Gasper Mansker, Archibald Marlin, Robert Bell,

John Gilbert Who being impannelled and Sworn, the Council being heard on both Sides Witnesses (to wit) James Robertson, Robert Thomson, Julius Sanders &c. Examined & heard, Say they find the right and Title of the whole Land now in dispute Wherein Hardee Murffee is Caveator and Hugh Leeper is Caveatee to be in Said Hugh Leeper Caveatee

MS, TDaCo-MDSC Law Min. Bk., 1788–1803, p. 112. Date is taken from *id.* at 111.

8. Tait v. Deaderick

1792
(Commercial Law)

EDITORIAL NOTE

Although in his civil practice Jackson was retained by plaintiffs more often than by defendants, he regularly represented both, as his defense of Elijah Robertson in No. 3 and of John Deaderick in this debt action indicate.

In February 1790 Deaderick executed a bond payable upon demand to David Hay in £100 paper money, £50 specie, or an equivalent in merchandise. In April, Hay assigned the bond to William Tait, a Nashville merchant. In May of the following year, Tait initiated the present litigation in the Mero District Superior Court to recover damages from Deaderick for the latter's alleged failure of performance (Document I).

By May 1792 Deaderick had retained Jackson as counsel in the case. In his client's answer to Tait's declaration, Jackson pleaded alternatively (1) that Deaderick had attempted performance under the bond by tendering to the plaintiff merchandise valued at £100, which Tait had refused to accept, and (2) that Deaderick had paid Hay in merchandise of the same value before the 1790 assignment of the instrument (Document II).

Jackson prevailed when the case went to trial on May 9, 1792. A jury found that the defendant had in fact tendered payment to Tait in the manner described by Jackson (Document III). Although Tait moved for a new trial on the ground that a juror had left after retiring to deliberate upon the case, the court on May 12 denied the motion and entered a judgment for Deaderick (Document IV).

Jackson's plea of tender was that the debtor, Deaderick, had attempted to perform his contractual obligation and that his offer had been refused by the creditor. A successful defense of tender did not discharge the underlying obligation, but did relieve the debtor of subsequent liability for interest and costs.[1] Perhaps Tait refused the tender of merchandise in the

---

1. William S. Holdsworth, *A History of English Law* (Boston, 1926), IX, 79–80; 4 Tucker, *Blackstone's Commentaries* 302.

hope of receiving payment in money. Under the terms of the bond, however, Deaderick had three alternative means of performance, and Tait could not insist upon a cash settlement.

John Deaderick (d. 1797) entered into a mercantile partnership with his brother George Michael Deaderick soon after their arrival in Davidson County from Virginia in 1790. He was a substantial landowner and, after July 1795, a justice of the Davidson County court.[2]

For Tait, see *McNairy v. Edgar & Tait*, No. 15.

2. Harriette S. Arnow, "Education and the Professions in the Cumberland Region," 20 *THQ* 153 (1963); Blount, *Journal,* 111. For Deaderick's property holdings, see, *e.g.,* DaCo Deed Bk. C, 133, 200; DaCo Wills & Inventories, I, 105, 132. Shortly after his death more than five years after the successful termination of this case, Deaderick was characterized by Jackson as his "worthy friend" and as one of Nashville's "invaluable citizens" whose "Loss . . . time cannot repair." AJ to John Overton, Jan. 22, 1798, *Jackson Papers,* I, 170.

I. DECLARATION OF
WILLIAM TAIT

Mero District Superior Court, Nashville

[ca. May 1791]

William Taitt Complains of John Deaderick in Custody &c. of a Plea of debt, &c. for that Whereas the Said John Deaderick did on the 13th day of February 1790 Signed & Sealed a Bond, with his own proper hand and Seal, to pay unto a Certain David Hay, on his return to Nashville one hundred pounds, paper money or fifty pounds in specie or the value thereof in M[erchandise] which the Said John then and there undertook and promised to [pa]y the aforesaid David when he Should be thereto required and Whereas, the Said David Hay did on the twelth day of April 1790, assigned the Said writing obligatory to a Certain William Taitt, of Davidson County which Said Bond or writing obligatory the Said Williams brings into Court and afterwards (to wit) on the 12th day of april 1790 the Said John Deaderick then and there undertook and promised to pay to the Said William Taitt the Sum aforesaid (to wit) the Sum of one hundred pounds, paper money or fifty pounds in Specie or the value thereof in Marchandize when he Should be thereto required, Yet Nevertheless, the Said John Deaderick not regarding his Several promises made to the Said William nor fearing the Laws of the Country hath not paid or Contented, the Said Sums aforesaid to the Said William but Craftily and

Subtely intending to defraud, and deceive the Said William hath altogether refused and Still doth refuse, to pay the aforesaid Sums Whereupon the Said William Saith he is damaged fifty pounds & therefore he brings Suit

Tr, TDaCo-MDSC Law Min. Bk., 1788–1803, p. 72. Date is derived from Jackson's reference to the commencement date in Document II.

II. ANSWER OF JOHN

DEADERICK

Mero District Superior Court, Nashville

[ca. May 1792]

And the said John Deaderick by Andrew Jackson his attorney come and Defends the force and Injury When &c. and saith that the said William Ought not to have or maintain his said Action against him because he saith that he the said John after his return to the town of Nashville as in the writing set forth in the Declaration of the plaintiff is specified and previous to the commencement of this suit to wit on the Twentieth day of May 1791 gave notice to him the said William then being present that he was ready to pay the said sum of one hundred pounds in Merchandize according to the form of the said Writing and then and there immediately on his the said Johns return to NashVille he the said John at the town of NashVille did afterwards to wit on his the said Johns return to NashVille and before the issuing of the writ he offered to deliver to the said William at the house of David Hay Merchandize to the value of one hundred pounds according to the form and effect of the said writing and the said William then and there refused to receive the said Merchandize of him the said John and the said John further saith that he always from his return to the town of Nashville to this time hath been ready and now is ready to deliver the said sum of one hundred pounds value in merchandize to him the said William according to the form and effect of the said Writing if he the said William will receive the same and this he is ready to verify &c. and for further plea in this behalf the said John by leave of the Court here for that purpose first had and obtained according to the form of the Statute in such case made and provided says that before the indorsement of the said writing he the said John paid to David Hay the indorsor the said sum of one hundred pounds in Merchandize at the Town of NashVille agreeable to the intent form and effect of the said writing and this he is ready to verify &c. wherefore he prays Judgment of the said William ought to have and maintain his said suit against the said John

Andrew Jackson

atto. pro Defendant

MS, PVT-William Waller, Sr. Endorsed: "Plea Taitte vs Deaderick." Date is derived from trial date (see Document III).

A North Carolina statute provided that the defendant "may plead as many several matters as may be necessary for his defence." Ch. 2, 1777 Laws of N.C. (Nov. Sess.), re-printed in Iredell, *Laws of North Carolina* 296, 1 Scott, *Laws of Tennessee* 178. An identical measure was enacted by the territorial government. Ch. 1, 1794 Terr. S. of River Ohio Acts, reprinted in 1 Scott, *Laws of Tennessee* 468.

III. MINUTE BOOK ENTRY

Mero District Superior Court, Nashville

[May 9, 1792]

William Taitt
vs   Debt, Plea Tender & refusal and
John Deaderick   always ready, & payt. Joinder.

Be It remembered that John Deaderick was Attached to answer William Taitt of a Plea of Debt, and at this Term the parties appearing in Court by their Attornies, and praying that a Trial might be had, thereon, therefore They were ordered to proceed upon[1]. . . to which Charge the defendant Plead Tender & refusul and always ready, payment, & Joinder and for the Truth of his Plea he put himself upon the Country &c. thereupon there came a good and Lawfull Jury (viz) Joseph Motheral, Joseph Hart, James Byrns, John Caffry, Thomas French, William Overall, James Hall, Allexander Ewing James Rutherford, Joseph Hooper, William Stuart, John Shanon who being impannelled and Sworn Truly to Try the issue Joined between the aforesaid parties, Counsil being heard on both Sides Say the find that the defendant did Tender in manner and form as Pleaded therefore find for defendant, motion by the Plff Council for a new Trial

MS, TDaCo-MDSC Law Min. Bk., 1788–1803, p. 72. Date is taken from *id.* at 71.

1. The text of Document I occurs in the MS at this point.

IV. MINUTE BOOK ENTRY

Mero District Superior Court, Nashville

[May 12, 1792]

William Taitt
vs
John Deaderick

} Motion for a new Trial was made by the Plff. Council and the reasons being duly Considered by the Court, which was Whether a new Trial Should be granted upon the Misbehaviour of one of the Jurors, (to wit) that he Left his fellow Jurors after retiring from the Bar, and it is the opinion of the Court that no new Trial be Granted

MS, TDaCo-MDSC Law Min. Bk., 1788–1803, p. 82. Date is taken from *id.* at 81.

9. Hay v. Hickman

1793
(Contracts)

EDITORIAL NOTE

One of the most prominent of Jackson's local clients was David Hay, a justice of the Davidson County court and a former sheriff of the county. Jackson represented Hay in at least four cases, including this action against Thomas Hickman.

In the present litigation, Hay claimed that in 1791, for the consideration of $100, Hickman had permitted him to go into possession of one half of Lot 6 in the town of Nashville and further had agreed to convey the half lot to him upon demand. Hay also claimed that Hickman had agreed to pay him the market value of the lot should he breach the agreement and refuse to convey the lot upon Hay's demand.

Jackson filed a declaration for Hay in the Mero District Superior Court in May 1793 (Document I). Judge McNairy referred the case to a panel of three arbitrators, two of the parties' choosing and a third appointed by the court. When the arbitrators reduced their award to writing and submitted it to the court on November 6, 1793, they concluded that Hay had "not Supported his Contract" and awarded judgment to Hickman (Document II).

No written agreement between Hay and Hickman and no memoranda thereof have been located in either manuscript or transcript form. It seems unlikely, however, that Jackson would have relied upon a verbal contract to convey the lot at issue. The English Statute of Frauds, enacted in 1677, required that contracts to convey real property be in writing or deemed unenforceable. The North Carolina reception measure of 1715 specifically declared that statutes "for preventing Immorality and Fraud" were effective in the colony.[1]

---

1. Ch. 31, 1715 Laws of N.C., reprinted in Iredell, *Laws of North Carolina* 17, 1 Scott, *Laws of Tennessee* 20.

Although few of Jackson's cases were resolved by arbitrators, the reference of legal disputes to arbitration was a common practice during the period. Jackson himself served as an arbitrator on occasion.[2]

For additional data about Hay, see Part IV.

In July 1788 Hickman, a surveyor, succeeded Hay in the office of sheriff. The brother of one of Hay's former colleagues on the bench, Hickman himself received a commission as a justice of the Davidson County court in January 1799.[3]

2. For Jackson as arbitrator, see *Jackson Papers*, I, 27, 81–82, and *McNairy v. Edgar & Tait*, No. 15, Doc. III.

3. DaCo Wills & Inventories, I, 212; see MDSC Law Min. Bk., 1788–1803, pp. 188, 264; William C. Moore, "Notes on the Childress, Hickman, Smith, and Cabler Families" (unpublished typescript, 1967), 45, T. Thomas Hickman's brother was Justice Edwin Hickman (d. 1791). Moore, "Notes," 34.

I. DECLARATION OF DAVID HAY

Mero District Superior Court, Nashville

Mero District Ss   Superior Court of Law
                                     May Term 1793

David Hay Complains of Thomas Hickman in Custody &c. &c. For that whereas, to wit, on the ¹day of ¹in the year our lord one thousand Seven hundred & Ninety one at the Town of Nashvill in the District aforesaid in and for the Consideration of one hundred Dollars to him the said Thomas Hickman in hand paid by the said plfft he the said Thomas did Bargain and Sell and promise to Convay to the said plff one half of a Certain Lott No. 6 situate Lying and being on water Street in the Town of Nashvill being the Lower half & he the said Thomas being so bound by his promises and assumpsits as aforesaid afterwards to wit, on the same Day and year aforesaid and in and for the consideration by him the sd. Deft. Recd. from the sd. plfft. then and there undertook and faithfully promised to Convay to the sd. plfft said half Lott when he should be there unto required by the said plaintiff and gave the sd. plfft Possession of the same and in and for the Consideration above said by the said Deftd. Recd. he on the same day & year aforesaid undertook and faithfully promised in case he the sd. Deft Should fail to Convay the sd. Lott above Described agreable to his assumpsit and undertaking that he would well & Truly pay and Content and pay the said plfft what the said Lott Should be Reasonably worth when he should be thereunto required by the sd.

plfft and this Defendant Does aver that it is now worth the Sum of one hundred pounds   Nevertheless the said Defendant will Knowing the premises, but not reguarding his said several promises and assumpsit & undertakings made and Entered into with the plaintiff but contriving and intending to Deceive and Defraud the plfft in this particular tho often Required by the sd. plfft hath not Convayed the said half Lot agreable to his promise and undertaking nor has this Deft tho often Requested by the said plfft paid the sd. Plaintiff was reasonable worth or in any wise Contented the said plfft for the same but to Do this has hitherto Refused and still Doth Refuse to perform the same wherefore he saith he is Injured to his Damage   [1]pounds & thereupon brings his suit

Andrew Jackson pro Quer

MS, PVT-William Waller, Sr.

   1. Thus in MS.

II. ARBITRATION AWARD

Mero District Superior Court, Nashville

Mero District Novr. Term 1793

We John Gordon, and Jonathon Phillips being Mutually Chozen by David Hay & Thos. Hickman, and Moses Shelby by the Court to arbitrate decide and determine a matter of Controversy now pending in the Superior Court of Law for the district of Mero, wherein said Hay is Plaintiff and said Hickman defendant We the arbitrators aforesaid do hereby award that the Plaintiff david Hay has not Supported his Contract, that he hath declared against Said defendant Hickman respecting a half lot in the town of Nashville therefore we award in favor of the defendant Given under our hands and Seals this 6th day of November 1793

John Gordon (Se[al])
Jona Phillips (Se[al])
Moses Shelby (Se[al])

Tr, TDaCo-MDSC Law Min. Bk., 1788–1803, pp. 104–105.

10. King v. Cox

1794
(Commercial Law)

EDITORIAL NOTE

As has been noted, much of Jackson's civil practice consisted of suits to collect debts. The present case, which Jackson filed for Robert King in the Mero District Superior Court in December 1793, is representative of this class of litigation.

On October 23, 1793, King wrote to Jackson from Southwest Point in east Tennessee to solicit his assistance in collecting two promissory notes that had been executed by one William Cox. The notes evidenced Cox's indebtedness to King for a slave and for £6 Virginia currency (see Document I). Upon the receipt of King's request, Jackson on December 16 instructed Andrew McNairy, clerk of the Mero District Superior Court, to issue a writ against Cox and to execute a prosecution bond bearing a representation of Jackson's signature as surety for King (Document II). McNairy issued the writ, which has not been located, and executed a prosecution bond for King (Document III) as Jackson had instructed. While the court's minutes do not contain any entries for the case at the ensuing May Term 1794, King was awarded a conditional default judgment by the court, because at the court's next term a jury, following the routine procedure with respect to default judgments, assessed King's damages at $208.50 (Document IV). Ten days later, on November 14, 1794, the sureties to Cox's appearance bond delivered the defendant into the court's custody.[1] For unknown reasons, King's judgment nonetheless remained unsatisfied as late as May of the following year,[2] and indeed it is unclear whether King ever received payment.

At some time in the spring or early summer of 1795, Cox did give King two bills, one for $100 and another for $50, evidently in partial payment of the outstanding judgment. These were of little use to King, however, for

1. MDSC Law Min. Bk., 1788–1803, p. 154.
2. MDSC Execution Docket, 1792–1803, p. 26.

on July 8 of that year he wrote in exasperation to Jackson that he longed to hear "what you have done for me respecting the debt that Will. Cox owed me, the Bills that he [ga]ve me ha[ve] appeared to have been Counterfeit" (Document V). No response from Jackson has been found.

King has not been further identified.

Cox's identity likewise remains uncertain. It is possible, although the evidence is only circumstantial, that the defendant in the *King* suit was the William Cox who had fled trial at the Washington District Superior Court in September 1793 on an indictment for counterfeiting. King's initial letter to Jackson (Document I) was written a month later. The fugitive Cox headed north to Kentucky, where, only by virtue of a pardon by Governor Isaac Shelby, he escaped being hanged in June 1794 on still another counterfeiting charge.[3] By May 1795—certainly in time for the passing of the two counterfeit bills about which King informed Jackson the following July—Cox had returned to east Tennessee to stand trial in Jonesboro on another indictment by the Washington District grand jury for "passing ten or more counterfeit dollars."[4]

3. *Knoxville Gazette,* July 17, 1794; see "The Journal of Needham Parry—1794," 34 *Register Kentucky State Hist. Soc'y* 382 (1938). While Cox awaited execution in Kentucky, Tennessee's future governor John Sevier on May 18, 1794, wrote to Governor Shelby to urge him to pardon Cox. Sevier to Shelby, May 18, 1794, reprinted in Cora B. Sevier and Nancy S. Madden, *Sevier Family History* (Washington, D.C., 1961), 116.

4. *Knoxville Gazette,* May 22, 1795. Cox was acquitted. *Id.*

I. FROM ROBERT KING

South west point   October 23rd 1793

Sir,

Inclosed is two notes on William Cox   one is for a negro   the other for Six pounds Virginia money assigned from me to Martin Armstrong   Now Sir as Mr. Wilcox [William Cox?] is about running his property out of this district I wish you to Transact This business for me in the Same manner as if it was your own and your charge shall be paid   I understand Mr. Wilcox has a negro woman and five children living in Nashville and I Expect his Negro man Holloway will go there with the Guard as he made his escape from me at this place today which, property will be fully Sufficient to Satisfy my Demand, pray Sir be as Expeditious as possible in bringing Suit as I am Suspicious The Negroes will be run out of your country as Soon as Holloway gets the[re]   consult Capt. Gordon on the buisness who is able to give you any information you may want   nothing more   but remains with Esteem & affection your friend & Humble servt.

Robert King

MS, DLC-AJ Papers (Reel 1); *Jackson Papers*, I, 41. Addressed: "Andrew Jackson Esqr. Davidson County." Enclosures not found.

II. TO ANDREW MCNAIRY

December 16th 1793

Dr. Sir

Issue a writ Robert King against William Cox Tresspass on the Case Damage Two hundred pounds, and be so obliging as to Convay the writ to the Sheriff Should he not be in Town; If you Cannot Convay it to the Shff apply to Mr. Gorden who I am Certain will Contrive it to the Sherriff   I am &c

Andrew Jackson

I do by these presents authorise and empower Andrew McNairy to sign My name as security to the prosecution Bond in the Suit Robt. King vs Wm. Cox in witness whereof I have hereunto set my and seal this 16th day of Decbr. 1793

Andrew Jackson

Test
Jno. Overton
N. B. I wish the writ to be served on Cox this Day &c

A. J.

MS, TNJ-Stanley Horn Coll.

III. PROSECUTION BOND

Mero District Superior Court, Nashville

December 16, 1793

KNOW *all men by these presents that* we Robert King & Andrew Jackson *are held and firmly bound unto* Wm. Cox *in the just and full sum of one hundred pounds, to be paid unto the said* Wm. Cox *his certain At-*

torney, Heirs, Executors, Administrators, or Assigns; to which payment, well and truly to be made, we *bind* ourselves our *Heirs, Executors, and Administrators, jointly and severally, firmly by these presents. Sealed with our Seals and dated this* 16th *day of* December *Anno Dom. one thousand seven hundred and ninety-3*

THE condition of the above obligation is such that *Robert King* who hath this day obtained a writ against *Said Cox* returnable to the Superior Court of Law, to be held for the district of Mero, at the Courthouse in Nashville, on the first Monday in *May* next, do well and truly prosecute the same, or otherwise pay into the Clerk's office, all such costs and charges as shall be awarded against him, for wrongfully issuing the same, then this obligation to be void otherwise to remain in full force and virtue.

Witness.   *[LS]*
    Andrew McNairy   *Andrew Jackson [LS]*

Printed form, filled in and signed, TNJ-Stanley Horn Coll. Initial paragraph, except for the first word, is set in italics in original; those portions of the paragraph rendered in regular roman here are in the hand of Andrew McNairy. Second paragraph and "Witness" are set in regular roman in original; those portions of the paragraph rendered in italics here and the signatures are in McNairy's hand.

IV. MINUTE BOOK ENTRY

Mero District Superior Court, Nashville

[November 4, 1794]

Robert King ⎱
    vs   ⎰   Case Judgment by default taken the
William Cox ⎰   following Jury viz Joseph Hanah
Adam Lynn, Phillip Shute, George Ridley, Nimrod Williams Thomas Talbott John Walker John Motheral, Joseph Motheral Thomas Johnston, Martin Duncan John Williamson who being impannelled and Sworn Say they find for the Plaintiff and assess the Damages to two hundred & eigh Dollars fifty Cents & Costs

MS, TDaCo-MDSC Law Min. Bk., 1788–1803, p. 118. Date is taken from *id.* at 115.

V. FROM ROBERT KING

[Southwest] point July 8[th 1]795

Dear Sir.

I think long to hear from you to hear what you have done for me respecting the debt that Will. Cox owed me, the Bills that he [g]ave me ha[ve] appeared to have been Counterfeit. I have two inpossessoon one of 100 Dollars & the other 50 Dollars. both have been proved back on me. please to Get Mr. Simpson to make me Such a Gun, as I was Speaking to you about and let me know when. I spoke to Mr. Hays about the Same Gun. I wish you to talk to Genl. Robertson to assist you about the pay coming to me for marking the road through the Cumbeland mountain & let me Know, Something respecting the Same in a Letter directed to me at Knoxville or to the Care of Colo. Donelson, & it will ever be esteem'd by Sir Your Obt.

Robert King

NB. remember me to all my acquaintences. R.K.

MS, DLC-AJ Papers (Reel 1); *Jackson Papers,* I, 63–64. Addressed: "Andrew Jackson esq. Cumberland hond by."

11. Hannah v. Cummins

1794
(Slander)

EDITORIAL NOTE

During the summer of 1794, Jackson initiated this slander action in the Mero District Superior Court on behalf of James Hannah (see Document I). Jackson's client alleged that the defendant, John Cummins, on at least three occasions had publicly accused him of stealing an unspecified number of his horses, either alone or in concert with others, and that the defendant on at least one of those occasions also had accused him of profiting from the sale of the stolen horses. Hannah sought to recover £1,000 in damages.

At the court's November Term 1794, Cummins entered pleadings denying Hannah's allegations, asserting the truth of any public statements that he might have made about the plaintiff, and setting forth the statute of limitations as a defense (see Document III). The case went to trial on November 5. A jury returned a verdict for Hannah, but assessed his damages at only $18.75 (Document III).

An action for words, or slander, was brought for false and malicious defamation of character, in either written or verbal form. In Jackson's time, slander was generally sued as trespass on the case. Although historically the plaintiff was required to prove actual damages in order to prevail, by the eighteenth century certain allegations, such as charges of criminality, raised a presumption of injury to the plaintiff.

Actions for slander were highly technical. The plaintiff was obligated to plead and prove: (a) that the defendant's words were defamatory; (b) that they were spoken about the plaintiff; (c) that the defendant's remarks were communicated to a third person; and (d) that the defendant spoke maliciously and without justification. The plaintiff's declaration had to contain a colloquium, which set forth the conversation in which the slander was made. For his part, the defendant could plead the general issue, denying the plaintiff's allegations, or enter special pleas such as truth or the statute of limitations.[1] The defendant in *Hannah* unsuccessfully relied upon both general and special pleas.[2]

Little is known about Cummins, other than that he resided in Sumner County and that, as the case that follows, No. 12, demonstrates, he had on at least one occasion freighted goods between Nashville and Redstone, Pennsylvania.[3] No documentation has been located for the theft of Cummins's horses or for the circumstances surrounding the incidents out of which Hannah's action arose.

Hannah, who also was a Sumner County resident,[4] was the defendant in *Barton v. Hannah,* No. 13, which was pending before the Sumner County court when his slander action against Cummins was initiated during the summer of 1794.

1. 4 Bacon, *Abridgment* 480–522; Caruthers, *History of a Law Suit,* 12. See also Hamilton v. Dent, 2 N.C (1 Hayw.) 135 (1794).
2. Jackson argued at least one other slander action. See Cummins v. Wyer, SumCo CPQS Min. Bk. 2, p. 72 (1794). Jackson represented the plaintiff.
3. See DaCo Wills & Inventories, I, 281.
4. See SumCo CPQS Min. Bk. 1, p. 24.

I. DECLARATION OF
JAMES HANNAH

Mero District Superior Court, Nashville

[ca. June 1794]

James Hanah Complains of John Commons in Custody &c. for that whereas the sd. James Hanah, is a good true faithfull Subject of our Territory of good name fame credit and reputation and So was held Esteamed & [. . . .] As well amonghts his Neighbours as amonghts other faithfull Subjects of the Said Territory and free from all manner of felony, Stealing or violation of truth or honesty in any manner whatever from the time of his Nativity hath Lived and Continued to live free, Clear, unsuspected of any Such Crimes, and always hath hitherto Carried & demeaned himself in a pious and honest way of living, and Yet the Said John Commons not Ignorant in the Premises, but Contriving and fraudulently intending him the Said James, Greatly to predudice in his good name fame Credit & reputation and his fame to hurt detract and Blaken on the   [1]day of   [1]in the year of   [1]in the County of Sumner in the district of Mero, upon a discourse then and there had, of the Said James in the presence and hearing of many of the good Citizens of our Said Territory, openly and Publickly Said pronounced, and pubblished the Words following (to wit) that James Hanah Meaning the Said James Hanah now Plff was one of three that Stole his Horses Meaning the Horses of him the Said John deft and the Said John as aforesaid Contriving and Maliciously intending the Sd. James in form aforesaid to preduce & damnify afterwards (to witt) they day and year aforesaid at the County and district aforesaid upon a discourse then & there had and held of the Said James Hanah Certain other false and Scandalous words of the Said James in the presence and hearing of Several of the good Citizens of Said Territory and Publickly Said pronounced and published, in these words to wit, James Hanah meaning the Said James Now Plff, hath Stole his Horses meaning the Horses of the Said John Commons, deft, and the Said John aforesaid Contriving and Maliciously intending the Said James in form aforesaid to prejudice & damnify, afterward to wit on the Same day and year aforesaid at the County and district aforesaid upon a discourse then and there had of the Said James Certain other false & Scandalous words of the Said James in the presence and hearing of Several good Citizens of our Said Territory openly and Publickly Said, pronounced and Published in these words (to wit) that he blames James Hanah, (meaning the Said James now Plff) for Stealing his Horses meaning the Horses of him the Said John, and that he the Said James Hanah, meaning the Said Plaintiff had Red. the Benefits arising from the Sales of his Horses that was Stole meaning the Horses that was Stole from this deft. by reason of the Speaking pronouncing and Publishing of which Said Several false and Scandalous words of the Said James is not only Greatly prejudiced in his good name fame Credit and reputation but is also brought into Great infamy & Lost the good Esteem of his Neighbours & Citizens, Greatly hindred from going about his lawfull business wherfore the Said James Saith he hath damage of the value of one thousand pounds and therefore he brings Suit

[Andrew Jackson for the plaintiff]

Tr, TDaCo-MDSC Law Min. Bk., 1788–1803, pp. 118–119; preceded by: "and the Plff by his atto. declared as follows viz)." The identity of Jackson as counsel for Hannah is established at MDSC Execution Docket, 1792–1803, p. 28. Jackson probably drafted Hannah's declaration at some time in June, after the court had completed its May Term but before Hannah's pretrial payment for Jackson's services on July 1 (see Document II).

1. Thus in Tr.

II. BILL OF SALE FROM
JAMES HANNAH

July 1, 1794

Know all men by these present that I James Hannah have this day Bargained and sold unto Andrew Jackson five Cows & Calves Viz; one large Red cow & heifer calf it being the same the sd. James Purchased at Widow Hays Vendue one Black Cow & calf Marked a crop of the Right Ear one Red Cow & Calf with white Back and face Marked a Crop of the Right Ear & a hole in the left which hole is tore out, one Brended heifer & white yearling for a Cow & calf marked a Crop in the Right a hole in the left and an upper Bit in the left, a Black Cow with white Back Springing to Calf marked a Crop and a Slit in the Right Ear and an upper bit and under bit in the left and Branded on the Cushion with A D Two Large white Sows and one Blew listed Sow marked a Crop off the Right and a hole in the left one of the white Sows with no Bristles on her Back and the Hole tore out also fourteen Shoats four months old Marked with a Crop and a slit in the Right Ear and a hole and upper Bit in the left, and in and for the Consideration of Twenty one pounds ten Shillings to me in hand paid as also for Services done and performed by the Said andrew as attorney at law for the Said James to the amount of Eight Cows & calfs I the Said James do bind myself my heirs &c to warrent and for Ever Defend the Said Bargained Cows Calfs & hogs to the Said Andrew Jackson his heirs and assigns for Ever from the Claim or Claims of all and Every Person Legally Claiming in witness whereof I have hereunto Set my hand and Seal this first day of July 1794

Test   John White   his
        Seth Lewis   James I H Hannah
                                           mark   (Seal)

MS, DLC-AJ Papers (Reel 1). Text is in AJ's hand. Endorsed in AJ's hand: "Hannah to Jackson Bill of Sale."

III. MINUTE BOOK ENTRY

Mero District Superior Court, Nashville

[November 5, 1794]

James Hanah
vs
John Commons

} Slander Plea Not Guilty Justification & Sta Lim[1] Be it Known that the defendant was attached to answer the Plaintiff of a Plea of Trespass on the Case for words, and at this Term the Cause Came on for Trial[2] . . . to which Charge the defendant Plead not Guilty Justification and Sta Lim and of this he put himself upon the Country therefore there Came a good and Lawfull Jury (to wit) Thomas McCrory, George Perry, James Franklin James Frazier Peter Looney, Ephraim McLain, Robert Nelson Joseph Hanah, Mathew Talbott, William Starks, William DeLoach, William Mitcheal who being impannelled and Sworn the Council Being heard on both Sides Witnessess Examined Say they find for the Plaintiff and assess his damage to eighteen Dollars Seventy five Cents.

his

James   ×   Hanah

mark

this Judgt. assigned to Wm. T. Lewis
Signed in open Court

MS, TDaCo-MDSC Law Min. Bk., 1788–1803, pp. 118–119. Date is taken from *id.* at 118.

    1. A 1715 measure provided that "the said Action upon the Case for words" should be instituted "within Six Months after the Ratification of this Act or within Six months next after the words spoken & not after." Ch. 27, 1715 Laws of N.C., reprinted in Iredell, *Laws of North Carolina* 12, 1 Scott, *Laws of Tennessee* 13.

    2. Document I follows at this point in the MS, preceded by: "and the Plff by his atto. declared as follows viz)."

12. Cummins v. Peairs

1795
(Commercial Law)

EDITORIAL NOTE

Commerce between Philadelphia and the southwestern frontier was a recurring source of litigation in the Tennessee courts throughout Jackson's legal career.[1] Beginning well before the end of the eighteenth century, the Pennsylvania city supplied many Tennessee merchants, including Jackson between 1795 and 1804, with a substantial portion of their retail inventories.[2] Although normally arising between Tennessee retailers and their eastern suppliers in connection with the purchase of inventory on credit (*e.g.*, No. 41), legal disputes occasionally resulted from the practice followed by some frontier merchants of sharing in the expense of transporting their goods from Philadelphia to Nashville or Knoxville.[3]

Goods that were purchased in Philadelphia for resale in Tennessee ordinarily were carried by wagon westward to Pittsburgh, shipped down the Ohio River to the falls at Louisville, and, once past the falls, either freighted further down the Ohio and up the Cumberland River to Nashville or conveyed overland from Louisville southward to Nashville or Knoxville.[4] To shorten the overland route between Philadelphia and Pittsburgh, cargoes at times were hauled by wagon to Redstone, Pennsylvania,

---

1. See, *e.g.*, No. 41; Magoffin & Son v. King, HDSC Law Rec. Bk. C, 1798–1803, p. 295 (1802); Magoffin & Son v. Johnston, *id.*
2. See Stanley J. Folmsbee, Robert E. Corlew, and Enoch L. Mitchell, *Tennessee, A Short History* (Knoxville, 1969), 118–119; *Jackson Papers*, I, 54, 58–59, 329–330. See also Stanley J. Folmsbee, *Sectionalism and Internal Improvements in Tennessee, 1796–1845* (Knoxville, 1939), 10, 14.
3. For examples of Jackson's participation in joint shipments of goods from Philadelphia to Tennessee, see Bassett, *Correspondence*, I, 92–93; *Jackson Papers*, I, 62.
4. Folmsbee at al., *Tennessee, A Short History*, 119; Folmsbee, *Sectionalism and Internal Improvements*, 10 n.9, 14; see Bassett, *Correspondence*, I, 94–95; Thomas P. Abernethy, "The Early Development of Commerce and Banking in Tennessee," 14 *Miss. Valley Hist. Rev.* 311–312 (1927). Most retail goods for east Tennessee, however, appear to have been imported by wagon through Virginia. Folmsbee, *Sectionalism and Internal Improvements*, 10.

where they were transferred to boats on the nearby Monongahela for the trip downstream to Pittsburgh and beyond.[5]

This case, which Jackson tried in the Sumner County court in October 1795, resulted from the freightage of a shipment of goods along this latter route between Redstone and Nashville by John Cummins and Isaac Peairs in November or December 1791. Most, if not all, of the goods in the shipment appear to have belonged to third parties (see Document IV). Cummins and Peairs evidently supplied a boat and crewmen. Jackson's client, Cummins, sought to recover damages from Peairs in part at least as reimbursement for the latter's share of the expenses that had been incurred during the trip.

Perhaps impressed by Jackson's handling of James Hannah's slander action against him in the latter part of 1794 (No. 11), Cummins retained Jackson to represent him in the present case in the autumn of that year. By early December, Jackson had secured the issuance of a writ against Peairs. On December 5, Peairs filed an appearance bond with the Sumner court (Document I). Jackson prepared and submitted a declaration for Cummins the following month (Document II). At the Sumner court's January Term, Peairs's counsel entered pleadings and obtained a continuance until the April Term. In March, Peairs subpoenaed two witnesses to testify on his behalf at the trial that was scheduled to occur in April (Document III). The trial was further continued in April and July, however, as both parties deposed additional witnesses.[6]

Jackson tried Cummins's suit on October 5, 1795. A virtually indecipherable account in Jackson's hand of the expenses incurred by Cummins and Peairs survives as part of the case file (Document IV). Notes in Jackson's hand on the verso of the account suggest that Jackson argued that Peairs had deceived his client by failing to protest his payment for provisions for both of the parties' crewmen and for other supplies.[7] The

5. See, e.g., AJ to John Coffee, May 3, 1804, and AJ to Coffee, May 13, 1804, *Jackson Papers*, II, 21–23.
6. SumCo CPQS Min. Bk., 1787–1805, pp. 89, 91.
7. One of the persons Cummins had paid for provisions was Amos Bird. Bird later recalled that when the vessel bearing Cummins and Peairs had docked near Clarksville to take on supplies, he had thought them to be partners: "Somtime in the Month of Deceb. 1791 John Cummins applyd to me at Clarksvill (Tennessee County) for a quantity of provisions to Suply his Boat Crew and Som familys Which were then on the River at or near Clarksvill—that I furnishd. the Sd. Cummins to a Considderable amot. perha[ps] twelve Dollars or upwards Including Some provisions Which Mr. Isaac Pearce Got of me on acct of the Sd. Cummins at the time the Boat of Cummins or Cummins & Pearce Left Clarksville as from aperences I Judged. them to hav bin In partnership In the Expence of the voyage." Deposition of Amos Bird, Nov. 16, 1796, Stanley Horn Coll., TNJ. Bird's recollection of the incident is recorded in a deposition that he gave in 1796 in an equity case then pending in the Mero District Superior Court; there Cummins apparently sought to enjoin collection of the double costs with which the court had assessed him in his unsuccessful attempt to recover from Peairs his share of the trip's expenses. See note 10 below and accompanying text.

jury, however, returned a verdict in Peairs's favor (Document V). The court denied a motion by Jackson for a new trial and entered a judgment for the defendant. Jackson then obtained an appeal of the judgment to the Mero District Superior Court.

It is doubtful that Jackson remained as counsel of record for Cummins on the appeal. Although the Superior Court's minutes rarely identify counsel in any trial entries, the entry for the trial of Cummins's appeal at the court's November Term does name Bennett Searcy as counsel for Peairs.[8] The court's minutes do not indicate who represented Cummins. Moreover, the court's execution docket entry for the case bears Searcy's initials as Peairs's attorney, but contains no initials for Cummins's counsel.[9] When the appeal did go to trial in November 1795, the jury returned a verdict for Peairs, and the court awarded the defendant double costs.[10]

8. See MDSC Law Min. Bk., 1788–1803, pp. 154–155.
9. See MDSC Execution Docket, 1792–1803, p. 34.
10. Cummins v. Peairs, MDSC Law Min. Bk., 1788–1803, pp. 154–155; see MDSC Execution Docket, 1792–1803, p. 34. Cummins subsequently filed a petition in the Mero District Superior Court of Equity against Peairs (see Deposition of Amos Bird, note 7 above), apparently to enjoin the collection of the court's award of double costs. The ultimate success of Cummins's effort on the equity side is suggested by the final annotation entered in the court's execution docket entry for Cummins's appeal in the present case: "Stopped by Bill of Injunction R Cage." MDSC Execution Docket, 1792–1803, p. 34.
Neither Cummins nor Peairs has been further identified.

I. APPEARANCE BOND

Sumner County Court of Pleas and Quarter Sessions

December 5, 1794

Teritory of the United States South [of] The River ohio Sumner County we Isaac Pearce & Jonithan Pearce do acknow[ledge] our Selves justly indebted unto Willia[m] Cage Sherriff of Sd County in the Su[m of] two hundred dollars the above to be nul & void on Conditions t[hat] Isaac Pearce does make his personal appearance at our next County Court to be held at the house of Ezekiel Douglass on the first monday in January Next to answer John Cummins of a pl[ea] of trespass on the Case damage one hundred Dollars and not depart with out leave of the Court. Given under our hands this 5th day of December 1794

Isaac Peairs (Seal)
Jonathan Peairs (Seal)

MS, T-SumCo Records (unprocessed).

II. DECLARATION OF
JOHN CUMMINS

Sumner County Court of Pleas and Quarter Sessions

Sumner County Sst.   January[1] Term 1795

John Cummins complains of Isaac Purs in Custody &c. of a plea of
trespass on the Case for that whereas the aforesaid Defendt. on the   [2]
day of   [2] in the year of our lord Seventeen hundred &c. in the County
aforesaid was indebted to the aforesaid Plaintiff the Sum of Ninety one
Dollars & Seventy one Cents for work & labour before that time at the
Special instance & request of the said Defendt. done by the Said Plaintiff
and being so indebted he the said Defendt. afterward towit on the same
day & year in the County aforesaid undertook & then & there faithfully
promised that he sd. Defdt. would well & truly pay & Satisfy the aforesd.
Plaintiff the said Sum of Ninety one Dollars & 71 Cents when he should
be thereunto required. And also whereas the aforesaid Defendt. the same
day & year in consideration that the aforesaid Plaintiff had done other
work & labour at the Special Instance & request of the sd. Defdt. the sd.
Defdt. did thereupon undertake & to the sd. Pllf did then & there faithfully promise that he the said Defendt. would well & truly pay the said
Plaintiff such Sum of money as the said work & labour was reasonably
worth and the said Plaintiff in fact saith that the said last mentioned
work & labour was reasonably worth the sum of Ninety one Dollars &
71 Cents. And also whereas the aforesaid Defendant afterwards to wit
the same day & year & in the County aforesaid in consideration that the
aforesaid plaintf [h]ad at the like instance & request of him the sd. Defendt. sold & Delivered to him the sd. Defdt. divers Goods wares and
Merchandize the same Defendt. did thereupon undertake and to the
same Plaintiff did then & there faithfully promise that he the said Defendt. would likewise well & truly pay & Satisfy to the said Plaintiff when
he should be thereunto required such sum of money as the said Goods &
Merchandize were reasonably worth and the aforesaid Plaintiff in fact
saith that the Goods sd. wares & Merchandize were reasonably worth
the sum of Ninety one Dollars and 71—Cents of which the aforesaid Defendt. the same day & year in the County aforesaid had notice: yet the
aforesaid Defdt. in no wise regarding his several promises & undertakings aforesaid but craftily intending to deceive & defraud the said plaintiff the aforesd. several Sums of money or any part thereof, hath not paid
tho' often thereto requested but hitherto hath refused & Still doth refuse

to pay the Same to the damage of the said Plaintiff one hundred Dollars & therefore he brings his suit &c

Jackson pro ptff

MS, T-SumCo Records (unprocessed).

    1. Originally "October."
    2. Thus in MS.

III. SUMMONS FOR THE APPEARANCE OF JOHN HAWKINS AND ANDREW HOOVER

Sumner County Court of Pleas and Quarter Sessions

March 30, 1795

Territory of the united States South of the River Ohio Sumner County

To the Sheriff of Davidson County Greeting. You are hereby commanded to summons John Hawkins & Andrew Hoover personaly to appear before our ensuring Court of pleas & Quarter Sessions to be held for said County at the house of Ezekiel Douglass on the first Monday in April next then & there to give testimony in behalf of the Defdt. in amatter of controversy depending in our said Court wherein John Cummins is Plt & Isaac Pearce defendant & this they shall in no wise omit under the penalty prescribed by law,[1] fail not, Witness D Shelby Clk at office this first Monday in January 1795 & nineteenth year of our Independence

Issd. 30th March 1795   David Shelby

MS, T-SumCo Records (unprocessed).

    1. A 1794 territorial measure provided that "every witness being summoned to appear in any of the said courts . . . shall appear accordingly . . . and in default thereof shall forfeit and pay to the party at whose instance the subpoena issued, the sum of one hundred and twenty-five dollars, and shall be further liable to the action of such party for the full damages which may be sustained for want of such witness's testimony." Ch. 1, 1794 Terr. S. of River Ohio Acts, reprinted in 1 Scott, *Laws of Tennessee* 457, 469.

IV. JACKSON'S NOTES ON THE
ACCOUNT OF JOHN CUMMINS

Sumner County Court of Pleas and Quarter Sessions

[ca. October 5, 1795]

Isaac Peirce to John Cummins Dr.

November 1791	Dollars Cents
[. . . .][1]	[ ]
To 27 lb. Iron one fourt Dollar pr. lb.	6.[75]
To one note on John Bosley by Joshua	4.17
Deal freightage for 600 lb. or	
700 lb. from red river[2] to Nashville @	
2 S pr. Centum.	—————
	26.92
	2.00

Credit for /6 Pens Money[3] Recd. on acct	
of Mr. Bets.	
[Con]tra Credit	Dollars Cents
To Sixteen Dollars pd. for Boat	16.
To the Freitage of Zacariah Betts	
goods from Red Stone to Nashvill	
£2.13.4 Pens money[3] Recd.[4] by	
Isaac Peirce one half Due me.	3.53
Cash Recd. from Aspee & McQuillam	
by Isaac Pierce fifty Eight[5] Dollars	
one half: for freitage from Red Stone	
to Gaspers Creek half Due me.	29.25.[6]
Cash paid by me to John Beason for him	1.00
To wiskey on the passage furnished by	
me Sixteen gallons @ one Dollar pr.	
Gallon one half Due me from Peirce.	8.00
one quarter of Pork bought of Sutton at	
one Dollar pd. by me for the use of	
the Boatmen.	0.50
To 20 lb. Beacon Bought of Epraim	
McClain @ ⅙ pr. lb. paid for by me.	0.81
To Two Days work of Ross at Red River	
at ½ Dollar pr. Day.	1
To one large Kettle Wright 67 lb.	
@ one fourt of a Dollar pr. lb.	16.75
To fraitage of a Still from Red Stone	

to Jones Bent for Mr. Moor for which
he Recd. 8 Dollars one half Due me.   4.00
furnished 3 hands 30[7] days more than
    Pearce at 50 Cents pr. day one half
    Due me fro[m Peirce]   [   ]
to 2 Do. more than him for 9 day @ Do.[8]   [   ]
                                          19.½   [   ]

So Cummins taken advantage. Clearly proven.

════════

Deceipt of Deft.

════════

Dispute of the han[ds] all. no.

════════

Deft sd. had Six hands

════════

Test Mrs. P.

════════

Cummins Demands What. [. . .] 3 contra

════════

no Count Recd.

════════

D. not say ½ Doz words [. . .]

════════

Big Kettle.

════════

Settlement proven Huver Taken in to Ballance P.
[. . .] to have been in all the way to go against
    one of the pierces
Deal &c &c Joth. Pierce &c &c.

MS, T-SumCo Records (unprocessed). Entirely in Jackson's hand. Endorsements in Jackson's
hand: "acct pr." and
                      16.75
                      4. .81
                  Espy. 15 25 or 29.25
Endorsement in court clerk's hand:
     Cummins
        vs
     Peairce
     Plea non assumsit with leave set off & Stat
     limetation
          Z Betts   D5 50
          I Dale.   1.50.5
          A Hoover.   2.91.
          Tho Waller   1 8
          Cath Moore   1. 8
          H Bradford   1 50

W Frazer 2.50
S Kanstro 2 50

Approximate date is derived from the date the action went to trial at the Sumner County court. See SumCo CPQS Min. Bk., 1787–1805, p. 93.

1. The following entry appears to have been subsequently stricken from this point in the MS: "To s[. . .] half of [a?] b[oa?]t."
2. The Red River flows into the Cumberland River at Clarksville. *Tennessee Gazetteer 1834* rpnt. (Nashville, 1971), 242.
3. Pennsylvania currency.
4. Originally preceded by "one half."
5. Originally preceded by "of" and inserted above "fifteen," which subsequently was stricken.
6. Originally "15.00."
7. Originally "39."
8. The preceding entry was subsequently stricken: "To 4350 lb. loading frieghted from Red Stone to Cumberland at   pr. hundred weight half freightage as pr. agreement Due me."

V. MINUTE BOOK ENTRY

Sumner County Court of Pleas and Quarter Sessions

[October 5, 1795]
Territory of the united States South of the River Ohio &c.}
John Cummins vs. Isaac Pearce} Case

To which at January term 1795 the Plt. appeared by Andw. Jackson esq his Attorney, likewise the Defdt. by his Attorney Bennet Searcy esq.; and the said defendant by his attorney aforesaid Pleaded Non Assumpsit with leave set off & Statute of limitation,[1] & thereon the Plt & defendt. Joined issue, after which the cause was continued to each Succeeding Term until October term 1795 at which time comes hereinto Court as well the Plt as the Defendant by their attornies aforesaid & then comes a Jury Vizt. John Dunihoo William Snoddy Edward Gwin James Hays John Sereker Francis Bird Sion Perry John Dawson James Wilson Isaac Lowel George Hamilton Thomas Patton who being elected tried & Sworn well & truly to try the issue Join'd between the Parties as aforesaid, the Jury withdrew return & on their oaths do Say that they find the issue in favour of the Defendant, wherupon the Plt by his attorney aforesaid moved for a new trial which motion on Argument is overuled, and the verdict confirmed by the Court from which the Plt pray & obtains an appeal and enters into bond in the sum of two hundred Dollars with William Hankins Security

MS, TSumCo-SumCo CPQS Min. Bk., 1787–1805, p. 93. Date is taken from *id*.

1. The statute of limitations required that all actions "upon the case" be commenced within three years after the cause of action accrued. Ch. 27, 1715 Laws of N.C., reprinted in Iredell, *Laws of North Carolina* 12, 1 Scott, *Laws of Tennessee* 13.

13. Barton v. Hannah

1795
(Contracts)

EDITORIAL NOTE

Shortly after having initiated Robert King's suit against William Cox in Davidson County in December 1793 (see *King v. Cox*, No. 10), Jackson appears to have secured for Samuel Barton the issuance of a writ in Sumner County in this debt action against James Hannah.

The case had its origins in a series of transactions that began in 1786, when one Thomas Ring executed a bond to convey land in favor of Anthony Rogers (Document I). Under the terms of the bond, Ring agreed to pay Rogers the sum of £1,000 in the event that Ring had failed to convey 500 acres of land to Rogers by October 1, 1787. Rogers subsequently assigned his rights under the bond to two different individuals. First, in January 1791 he made an assignment to one Robert Dean (Endorsement I, Document I). Dean in turn assigned his rights under the bond to Barton, the plaintiff in this action (see Document II). Second, in July 1792 Rogers assigned his rights to Hannah, the defendant in the case, "without recours to me or my heirs for ever" in exchange for a note executed by Hannah payable to Rogers in the amount of £35 (Endorsement II, Document I; see Document VIII).

It was Jackson who appears to have secured the issuance of Barton's writ against Hannah in January 1794 (Document II). Hannah's counsel, Bennett Searcy, entered a plea of "non est factum & Paymt. fraud & Covin no consideration & duress" when the court reconvened in April. Both Jackson and John Overton represented Barton at this stage in the proceedings.[1] In July the parties secured commissions from the court to take the depositions of several witnesses who resided in Kentucky.[2]

1. The pertinent portions of the form writ appear to be in Jackson's hand. See Document II. When Barton made his initial appearance at the Sumner court's April Term 1794, he was represented by both Jackson and John Overton. SumCo CPQS Appearance Docket, 1787–1800, p. 31. "Covin" refers to a secret conspiracy or agreement between two or more persons to injure or defraud another. E. Coke, *First Institute of the Laws of England,* ed. J. H. Thomas (Philadelphia, 1826), III, 188.

2. Jackson and Overton obtained a commission directing Archibald Woods, a Madison County, Kentucky, justice of the peace, to depose Benjamin Estill and Peter Carlin on Au-

The case went to trial more than a year later. On October 6, 1795, a jury returned the following special verdict: "that in case the Defdt. can have recourse on Anthony Rogers they find a verdict for the Plt otherwise for the Defendant."[3] The court took the case and the jury's special verdict under advisement, and "a case [was] agreed to be made for the determination of the Supr. Court which is to determine the case."[4]

Jackson and James Dohertie, whose status in the proceedings remains unclear, thereafter submitted the Request for an Advisory Opinion to the Mero District Superior Court that is published here as Document IX. Jackson sought a determination by the court of whether the effect of the language used in Rogers's assignment was to leave Hannah without a remedy against Rogers. The court on November 17 concluded that such language released Rogers of any liability to Hannah (Document X). On January 6, 1796, the Sumner County court read the Superior Court's opinion into its minutes and entered a judgment upon the jury's verdict for Hannah.[5]

The case, although richer than most in Jackson documents, nonetheless poses a number of questions upon which the surviving records shed little light. First, Jackson's role at different stages in the litigation is not easily ascertainable. The documents seem to indicate that Jackson withdrew as counsel of record for the plaintiff during the course of the litigation. The records clearly indicate that Jackson and Overton represented Barton until October 1794, a year before the case went to trial. The docket entry for the case in January 1795, however, identifies only Overton as Barton's counsel and Searcy as Hannah's. None of the subsequent docket entries identifies Jackson as counsel for either of the parties.[6] The implication is that Jackson at some time prior to January 1795 withdrew as co-counsel of record for Barton, perhaps in part because of his representation of Hannah beginning in the summer of 1794 in the latter's slander action against John Cummins (*Hannah v. Cummins*, No. 11). Jackson nonetheless continued to perform an active, although uncertain, role in the litigation. For instance, when the case was taken under advisement by the Sumner court in October, it was Jackson who, with James

gust 22, 1794. Commission of Archibald Woods, July 18, 1794, SumCo Records (unprocessed), T. Estill on August 22 testified "that he Saw James Hannah make his mark and Acknowledged it to be his Act and deed to a Certain Obligation of Thirty five pounds Virginia Money to Anthony Rogers." Affidavit of Archibald Woods, Aug. 22, 1794, SumCo Records (unprocessed), T. Hannah secured commissions to take the depositions of Thomas Smith and Jonathan Skinner. Blank Commissions, July 18, 1794, SumCo Records (unprocessed), T; SumCo CPQS Min. Bk., 1787–1805, p. 76.

3. SumCo CPQS Min. Bk., 1787–1805, p. 94.

4. SumCo CPQS Trial Docket, 1787–1800, p. 43. A similar entry occurs at SumCo CPQS Min. Bk., 1787–1805, p. 94.

5. SumCo CPQS Min. Bk., 1787–1805, pp. 99–100; SumCo CPQS Trial Docket, 1787–1800, p. 43.

6. SumCo CPQS Trial Docket, 1787–1800, pp. 33, 35. See *id.* at 37, 39, 41, 43.

Dohertie, submitted the Request for an Advisory Opinion to the Mero District Superior Court (Document IX). The documents thus clearly establish that Jackson continued to participate in the litigation after withdrawing as counsel of record for Barton but do not reveal the capacity in which he performed his services.

Second, the nature of the dispute between Barton and Hannah is not at all clear. That both of the parties were assignees of Rogers's does not explain why Barton in the present suit sought to recover from Hannah in a debt action. It is possible, of course, that Rogers assigned Hannah's £35 note to Barton. Such an assignment of a note, if not under seal, would have given the assignee a cause of action against the maker, but the proper form of action would have been a suit in assumpsit, not debt. By statute, such an assignment of a note under seal would have given the assignee a cause of action in debt against the maker,[7] but because Hannah's note has not be located, this explanation remains merely a matter of speculation. It does seem to be clear that Barton in the present case was not suing Hannah on the assigned bond. No performance was required of Hannah under the bond.

Finally, although the suit represents the only instance that has been found during the years spanned by Jackson's legal career in which the ultimate resolution of an action pending in a county court depended upon the issuance of an advisory opinion by the district Superior Court, the relationship between the question submitted to the judges and Barton's right to recover from Hannah is unclear. Hannah's position evidently was that he had been fraudulently induced into executing the £35 note in exchange for Rogers's nonrecourse assignment. The grounds for Hannah's position appear to have been intoxication at the time that the note was executed and a false representation to Hannah at that time that the original obligor on the bond owned land in the Cumberland area with which to satisfy the condition of the bond (see Document VII). Fraud in the inducement commonly consisted of a false representation of an existing or pre-existing fact. A contract also would be set aside, however, as having been fraudulently induced when one of the contracting parties was found to have been taken advantage of by reason of intoxication at the time of its execution and when the intoxication was found to have been at the design of the other party.[8] Unless the jury considered Rogers's nonrecourse language to be further evidence that Hannah had been taken advantage of while intoxicated,[9] which again seems to presuppose that Barton in

7. Olive v. Napier, 3 Tenn. (Cooke) 11 (1811).
8. White v. Cox, 4 Tenn. (1 Hayw.) 79, 82–83 (1816).
9. The prevailing view at the time was that, in the absence of special provisions or circumstances, the assignment of a bond rendered the assignor liable to the assignee upon nonpayment of the bond by the original maker. M'Gee v. Lynch, 4 Tenn. (1 Hayw.) 105 (1816);

the present case was suing upon Hannah's note, the reasoning underlying the conditioning of a recovery by Barton upon a resolution of the question sought from the Superior Court remains inexplicable.[10]

<hr>

Mackie's Ex'rs v. Davis, 2 Va. 219 (1796); Joseph Story, *Commentaries on the Law of Promissory Notes* (Boston, 1845), 133–135. Jackson's Request for an Advisory Opinion, however, stipulated that the assignor specifically had intended to prevent recourse against himself.

The Tennessee courts subsequently held that "without recourse" language was not a defense in an action to rescind a contract procured by false representations once such representations had been made and relied upon. See Smith v. Cozart, 39 Tenn. (2 Head) 526, 531 (1859); Hamilton v. Galbraith, 15 Tenn. App. 158, 168 (1932). No cases have been found holding that the use of nonrecourse language constituted an indicium of overreaching or fraud.

10. For biographical data about Barton, see Part IV; for Hannah, see *Hannah v. Cummins*, No. 11.

I. BOND, THOMAS RING TO ANTHONY ROGERS

August 23, 1786

Know all Men by these presents that Thomas Ring of hallifax County in the State of North Carrolina am held and firmly bound to Anthony Rogers of Lincoln County & State of Virginia in the Sum of one thousand pounds Current money of Virginia to be paid to the sd. Anthony Rogers his heirs Exrs. Admrs. or assigns to which payment well and truely to be made I bind myself my heirs Exrs. and Admrs. firmly by these presents Sealed with my seal and Deated this twenty third day of August one thousand Seven hundred and Eighty Six

The Condition of the above obligation is such that if the above bound Thomas Ring his heirs and &c shall well and truely make or Cause to be made unto Anthony Rogers his heir[s] or assigns a good and a Lawful Deed of fi[ve] hundred acres of Land between the first and Second [. . .] on the south side of Cumberland River Down below Nashveal well watered not to Exceed thirty miles from Nashveal the Deed to be obtained on or before the first day of October in the year one thousand Seven hundred and Eighty seven then the above obligation to be void Elce to Remain force and [. . .].

Thos. Ring (Seal)

Sighnd. seald. & Delivered }
In Presenc of us   }
        Jerh. Parker
        Michael Woods

the words Not to Exceed thirty Miles from Nashveal in the Condition
Enterlined before Sighned. ˙

MS, T-SumCo Records (unprocessed). Endorsement I:
> I assign the within Bond to Robert Dean it Being for value Receved of him as witn[ess]
> my hand this [   ] day of January 1791
>   a[nthony rogers]
>
> test
> [. . . .]
> [. . . .]

Endorsement II:
> I do assign over my right and title of the within bond unto James hannah without re-
> cours to me or my heirs for ever anthony rogers.
> Test
> Jno. Ford

II. WRIT

January 6, 1794

Territory of the united States South of the River Ohio Sumner Co[unty]

To the Sheriff of said County greeting. You are hereby commanded to
take the body of *James Hanah* if to be found in your bailiwick & him the
said *Hannah* Safely keep so as you have him before the Justices of our
ensuing Court of pleas & quarter Sessions to be held for said County at
the House of Ezekiel Douglass on the first Monday in *April* next then
& there to answer *Samuel Barton assinee of Robert Dean assinee of
Anthony Rogers* of a plea of *Debt that he Render to him the sum of thirty
five pounds Virginia Currency of the Vallue of Forty six pounds 13 S 4
No. Carolina Currency which he owes and unjustly detains* damage
Twenty pounds herein fail not & have you then & there this writ witness
D Shelby Clerk of our said Court at office this first Monday in *January*
Anno Domini 1794 & XVIIIth. year of American independence
                          David Shelby

Issd. 6th January 1794

MS, T-SumCo Records (unprocessed). Italicized portions of the text appear to be in Jackson's hand. The appearance and trial docket entries for the case indicate an actual commencement date of Dec. 28, 1793, eight days before the issuance of the writ.

III. HANNAH'S APPEARANCE BOND

February 4, 1794

Teritory of the United States South the River Ohio Sumner County we James Hannah & Henry Bradford do acknowledg our selves indebted unto William Cage Sheriff of said in the afsd. two Hundred pounds to be void on Condition that James Hannah make his personal appearence at out next Court to be held for the County of Sumner at Ezekel Douglass on the first monday in April Next to answer Samuel Barton and others In a plea of Debt Forty Two pound thirteen Shillings & fore pence and not depart the same without Leave. giving under our hands & seal this 4 day of February 1794

his
James I H Hannah (Seal)
mark
H. Bradford (Seal)

MS, T-SumCo Records (unprocessed).

IV. JAMES HANNAH TO
SAMUEL BARTON

February 16, 1795

Sir

Take notice that on the Tenth and Eleventh days of March next I intend to procede to take the Depossitions of Thomas Smith Joseph & James Carlin   [1] Parks Thomas Ring James Donelly Robert McClellen & Jonathan Skinner at the House of Robert McClellin at Mans Lick Kentuckey to be read in Evidence in the Suit now pending in Sumner Court wherein you are Plaintiff and I am Deftd. I am sir &c

James Hannah

February 16th. 1795

RC, T-SumCo Records (unprocessed). Inside address: "Colo. Samuel Barton."

1. Thus in RC.

V. SAMUEL BARTON TO
JAMES HANNAH

July 7, 1795

Mr. J. Hannah will take notice that on the 10 Day of August I shall take the Deposition of Benja. Estil and Peter Carlin at the House of Archibald Woods in Madeson County State of Kentucky in the Suit now pending in Sumner County So. W. Teritory Wherein I am Plft. and you are Deft. at which time and Place you may attend and cross examine

Samuel Barton

7th Day July 1795

RC, T-SumCo Records (unprocessed).

VI. COMMISSION OF ARCHIBALD
WOODS TO TAKE DEPOSITIONS

July 7, 1795

Territory of the united States South of the River Ohio

To Aarcbald Woods Esquire greeting

Know you that pursuant to an order of the worshipful [court] of Sumner County We have appointed you & do hereby Commissionate & give unto you full power & authority to cause to come before you at such time & place as shall be appointed such witnesses as may be required in behalf of Samuel Barton and them examine on oath as well in behalf of the said Samuel Barton Plt as James Hannah Deft. in a Suit not depending in our said Court between the said parties and such depositions so taken send plainly & distinctly inclosed under your hand & Seal to gether with this writ to our said Court to be held for said County at the house of Ezekeil Douglass on the first Monday in October next Witness D Shelby Clk of our Said Court at office this first Monday in July Anno Domini 1795 & XX year of our independence

David Shelby Clk

Issd. 7th July 1795

MS, T-SumCo Records (unprocessed). Endorsed: "De Po Saml Barton vs. James Hannah to examine Witnesses for Plt To Octer. term 95." A similar but blank commission for the taking of depositions on Hannah's behalf is in the case file and is dated July 8, 1795.

VII. JACKSON'S
INTERROGATORIES

[Before August 10, 1795]
Questions to be put to the Subscribing witnesses, for the Deftd. (Viz) was the Deftd. intoxicated or had he been Drinking when he Signed the instrument of writing to Rogers, did he wright his name or not, what did he receive in Consideration for sd. bond, did he know or was he informed that Ring had any land in Cumberland, what circumstances was Ring in at the time, was he Solvent or not, and how long had he owed the land to Rogers, Set forth all you know of the Circumstance to the best of your Knowledge & belief, and whether the said Rogers did not impose upon the said Deftd. in obtaining the said note from him

MS, T-SumCo Records (unprocessed). Entirely in Jackson's hand. Endorsed in Jackson's hand: "Interrogatories." Date is derived from Benjamin Estill's Answers to Interrogatories, Aug. 10, 1795 (Document VIII).

VIII. BENJAMIN ESTILL'S
ANSWERS TO INTERROGATORIES

August 10, 1795
Agreeble to a Dedamoce to me directed by the Worshipful Court of Sumner County & District of Mero South o the River Ohio. I have caused Benjamin Estill to appear before me at my House this Tinth day of Augus 1795 being first Swor on the Holy Ebangalist of almighty God Saith That he Saw James Hanah acknewledg and Deliver to Anthoney Rodgers an obligation for Thirty five five pounds on Demand given on the tenth day of July 1792 To Said obligation the abovementioned Benjn. Estill is a witness Questn. Was James Hanna Intoxacated when he signed the Instrument of Wrighting to Rogers or had been drinking, Ansr. They were Drinking at the time but appeared to be Sensible of the Buisiness they were a doing Quest. did Said James Hanna write his name or not, Ansr. He made his mark and desired me to wright his name which I did, Quest. What did he receive in Compensation for said Bond. Ansr. He recd. a Bond of a Certain Mr. Ring for a Quantity of Land the Number of Acres I donot remember, Quest., do you know or was you informed if Ring had any land on Cumberland Ans. I donot know to my own knowledge but

Sd. Ring Informed me he had, Quest. what circumstance was Ring in at that time was he Solvant or not Ansr. I do not know, Quest. how long had he Owed the Land to Rogers, Ansr. I know not Questn. do you know if Said Rogers Imposed on Said Hanna in obtaining Sd. obligation Ansr. I do not know, And further Saith Not,

Benjamin Estill

Sowern to before me the day & date are within Mentioned.

Archd. Woods

MS, T-SumCo Records (unprocessed).

IX. REQUEST FOR AN ADVISORY OPINION FROM THE MERO DISTRICT SUPERIOR COURT

[Before November 17, 1795]

A gives a Bond to B. conditioned to convey 100 acres of land. B. transfers sd. Bond to C. by these words viz. "I do assign over my right & title [to] the within Bond to C. without recourse to me or [my] heirs for ever. Will this assignment Give C recourse against B. for the value of the Bond in [case] A becomes insolvent

James DoHe[rtie]

Andrew Jack[son]

MS, T-SumCo Records (unprocessed). Text in unidentified hand; autograph signatures. Endorsed: "These papers to be carried to the Superior Court." Approximate date is taken from MDSC Law Min. Bk., 1788–1803, p. 158, and from Document X.

X. THE SUPERIOR COURT'S ADVISORY OPINION

[November 17, 1795]

Mero District } November Term 1795

Case Agreed

A gives a Bond to B Conditional to Convey 100 acres of Land B Transfer Said Bond to C by these words (viz) I do assign over my right & title to the within Bond to C without recourse to me or my heirs forever; Will this assignment give C a recours against B for the Value of the Bond in Case A becomes insolvant. It is the opinion of the Court he cannot, for that it oporates as a release to assignor.

Teste

Andrew McNairy C. S. C.

MS, T-SumCo Records (unprocessed). Date is taken from MDSC Law Min. Bk., 1788– 1803, p. 158, where both the text of the question and the text of the court's opinion are repeated.

14. Protzman v. Robertson

1795
(Commercial Law)

EDITORIAL NOTE

This covenant case, which Jackson tried before the Mero District Superior Court in November 1795, further illustrates the regularity with which he represented the interests of nonresident clients. Here Jackson represented first Laurence Protzman, a Maryland merchant and land speculator, and then Protzman's assignee, Squire Grant of Kentucky.

At issue was the validity of a sealed agreement between Protzman and Elijah Robertson that had been executed on July 8, 1788, for the delivery to the plaintiff of 1,453 pounds of beaver fur before July 1790. The 1788 agreement canceled and superseded a similar but substantially unperformed contract between the parties dated October 7, 1786, in which Robertson, John Montgomery, and James Allen had agreed to deliver 1,136½ pounds of fur to the falls of the Ohio River at Louisville by May 1, 1787. By 1788, Robertson and the other obligors had delivered 123⅓ pounds of fur to Protzman, leaving a balance, including interest from the date of the 1786 agreement, of 1,115½ pounds.[1] In exchange for the cancellation of the 1786 contract, Robertson agreed to deliver to Protzman during the next two years a total of 1,453 pounds of fur, a figure that included (a) the balance of the fur that was due under the old agreement plus (b) an additional 337½ pounds of fur "as a recompence and in Leu of all Interest for the forbearance" of Protzman from demanding the 1,115½ pounds under the delivery terms of the 1786 agreement. Robertson subsequently failed to transfer the fur under the terms of the 1788 agreement, and Protzman brought this action to recover £3,000 in damages as a result of the breach (Document I).

Robertson defended by claiming that the 1788 agreement was rendered void by a 1741 North Carolina usury statute, which limited the in-

---

1. Protzman's interest, which consisted of approximately 102⅓ pounds of fur, accrued on the original principal amount of 1,136½ pounds at a simple interest rate of slightly more than 5 percent per annum.

terest chargeable on all contracts to 6 percent per annum.[2] Robertson argued in effect that the maximum statutory interest allowable on the 1,115½ pounds of fur, computed from the date of the original 1786 agreement to the 1790 delivery date, was approximately 268 pounds. The 337½ pounds that had been added under the 1788 agreement in lieu of interest, he contended, thus exceeded the 6 percent statutory limit (Document II).[3]

In his replication, Protzman urged that he should not be barred from his recovery on the 1788 agreement, because the 337½ pounds of fur had been added to the undelivered balance still due him in valid consideration for his having extended the date for delivery of the fur from 1787 to 1790 (Document III).

Protzman, or more likely an agent, had filed his declaration in the Mero District Superior Court by May 1793. When the action first went to trial on November 3, 1794, a jury returned a verdict awarding him damages in the amount of $1,830.78. On November 10, the court granted a motion by Robertson's attorney for a new trial.[4]

Jackson made his first recorded appearance for Protzman when the case went to trial again before the Mero District Superior Court in November 1795. In a special verdict returned on November 10, a jury found that Protzman had canceled the 1786 contract and had returned it to Robertson "in Consideration of another Bond" from Robertson dated July 8, 1788, and made payable to Protzman in 1,453 pounds of fur on July 8, 1790, "without Interest" (Document IV). The jury concluded that if the facts as found did not render the 1788 agreement void under the terms of the usury statute, then the plaintiff was entitled to recover damages in the amount of £767, 3 shillings, 6 pence. Eight days later, on November 18, Judges McNairy and Anderson ruled that the 1788 contract did not violate the usury statute and entered judgment on the special verdict for Protzman (Document V).

English statutes had long proscribed charging interest in excess of a legal rate as usury. The 1741 North Carolina statute limiting interest on any contract to 6 percent a year declared that "the settling of Interest at a reasonable Rate, will greatly tend to the Advancement of Trade, and Improvement of Lands." All agreements assessing a higher charge were declared "utterly void," and persons who received an illegal rate of interest

2. Ch. 14, 1741 Laws of N.C., reprinted in Iredell, *Laws of North Carolina* 77.
3. Robertson's computations are very nearly accurate. Simple interest on the principal amount of 1,115½ pounds calculated at the legal rate of 6 percent per annum for the period of time in question is approximately 250½ pounds. The 337½ pounds specified in the 1788 agreement are the equivalent of interest accrued on the principal amount of 1,115½ pounds at a simple interest rate of approximately 8 percent per annum.
4. See MDSC Law Min. Bk., 1788–1803, pp. 88, 115, 124.

were subject to forfeiture of the "double Value" of the goods or money loaned.[5] The defense of usury, raised unsuccessfully in this case against Jackson's client, required a special plea by the defendant.[6]

Protzman's judgment remained substantially unsatisfied at the time of Robertson's death in April 1797.[7] Within the next year, Protzman assigned to Squire Grant his rights under the 1788 agreement with Robertson.[8] In November 1798 Jackson was appointed to the Superior Court bench. Two months later, Jackson, as attorney in fact for Grant, and John Overton filed for Grant a petition in the Mero District Superior Court of Equity seeking the issuance of an execution against Robertson's executors for the unsatisfied portion of the judgment.[9] The court, with Jackson not sitting as one of its members, awarded the execution. Robertson's executors satisfied the unpaid balance of the judgment, a sum amounting to $1,778.11, on May 2, 1799 (Document VI).

It was in his capacity as Grant's attorney in fact that Jackson on May 2, 1799, issued the receipt to Robertson's executors for payment of the $1,778.11 judgment (Document VI). On the same day Jackson turned the sum over to John Overton, who had represented Grant as his attorney at law since Jackson's elevation to the bench (Document VII). Jackson nonetheless wrote to Overton more than a month later, on June 23, that

> the amount yet coming to me out of the Judgmt. of Sproutzman vs. Robertson you said was Twenty Eight pounds. can that amount be retained out of the money in your hands. If it can apply it to your use and I will receipt to you for it on sight, the ballance I will pay you as soon as I am furnished with the amount and go to Nashville. take notice I only make the enquiry with respect to the 28 lb. that if it can with prop[riety] I wish it to remain in your hands.[10]

In the interim, on June 7, Grant had addressed a letter alternatively to Overton or, in his absence, to Jackson, requesting that they turn over to his agent, John Fowler, the money that had been recovered from Robertson's executors (Document VIII). Although on July 12 Fowler collected Grant's money from Overton, less nearly $700 that Overton retained for fees and in reimbursement for funds that he had expended on Grant's be-

---

5. See note 2 above. See also Glisson v. Newton's Ex'rs, 2 N.C. (1 Hayw.) 385 (1796); Carter v. Brand, 1 N.C. 167 (1800).

6. Joseph Story, *A Selection of Pleadings in Civil Actions* (Salem, 1805), 113–118.

7. A portion of the judgment had been paid by May 1796. See MDSC Execution Docket, 1792–1803, p. 34.

8. See Hannah v. Grant, DaCo CPQS Min. Bk. C, 303 (1800). Although it is possible that Grant had been associated with the Robertson litigation before the assignment, the only evidence of any earlier connection occurs in Grant's letter to Jackson of May 19, 1796, in which Grant wrote that he hoped "the business of Robertson is setled on amicable Terms" and that he was anxious to hear about "my Little business in you[r] Country." Grant to AJ, May 19, 1796, *Jackson Papers*, I, 92.

9. See Overton Notebook, 25–26, Claybrooke and Overton Papers, THi.

10. AJ to Overton, June 23, 1799, *Jackson Papers*, I, 221.

half (Document IX), Grant did not acknowledge receipt of the amount of the judgment until more than two years later, in December 1801 (Document X). The reason for the delay has not been determined. No documentation has been located, however, for any further involvement in the case by Jackson beyond the transfer of funds to Grant's agent in July 1799.

Laurence Protzman, a dry-goods dealer in Hagerstown, Maryland, whose surname appears in the records also as Sproutzman and Sprotzman,[11] had begun speculating in Kentucky land with two Maryland partners as early as 1784.[12] In July 1788, the same month in which he executed the agreement with Elijah Robertson that was the basis for the present case, Protzman entered into a partnership with James Lanier of Davidson County to keep a tavern in the settlement of Bourbon in Kentucky.[13] During the next year, however, Protzman left Kentucky and returned to Hagerstown. It is possible that Lanier, who remained in Kentucky after Protzman's departure, or perhaps Thomas Jones, whom Protzman had designated as his attorney in fact in Bourbon County,[14] initiated the present litigation against Robertson and retained Jackson to try the case the second time in November 1795.

Squire Grant (1764–1833), a nephew of Daniel Boone's, probably was the "S. Grante" who had witnessed the July 1788 partnership agreement between Protzman and Lanier. As deputy land surveyor for the state in the military district, Grant surveyed and located entries in North Carolina, Kentucky, and Tennessee before settling in Campbell County, Kentucky, in 1794. In December 1795, Grant received appointments as a justice of the county court and as lieutenant colonel commandant of the county militia. He represented Campbell County in the Kentucky Senate between 1801 and 1806.[15]

For additional identification of Robertson, see Part IV.

11. Protzman's given name appears as Laurence in newspaper advertisements in the *Kentucky Gazette* in 1792 and in court records for Davidson County and for Jefferson County, Kentucky. See, *e.g.*, *Kentucky Gazette*, May 5, 1792, Aug. 25, 1792; Ludie J. Kinkead, comp., "Minute Book No. 1, Jefferson County Kentucky April 6, 1784–December 7, 1785," 6 *Filson Club Hist. Q.* 129 (1932).

12. See T. Thomas Scharf, *History of Western Maryland* (Philadelphia, 1882), II, 1170; Ludie J. Kinkead and Katharine G. Healy, comps., "Calendar of Bond and Power of Attorney Book No. 1, Jefferson County, Kentucky, 1783–1798," 7 *Filson Club Hist. Q.* 39 (1933).

13. Julia S. Ardery, ed., "Bourbon Circuit Court Records," 37 *Register Kentucky State Hist. Soc'y* 380 (1939). One of the witnesses to the partnership agreement was "S. Grante." For additional identification of Lanier, see *McNairy v. Edgar & Tait*, No. 15.

14. Ardery, "Bourbon Circuit Court Records," 378–379.

15. Alice R. Rouse, "The Pioneer Grants," 33 *Register Kentucky State Hist. Soc'y* 5, 6 (1935); "Department of State Archives: Campbell County," 26 *Register Kentucky State Hist. Soc'y* 24, 25 (1928). It was with Grant's brother John that Protzman entered into a number of business transactions on the eve of his departure for Maryland in 1789. Ardery, "Bourbon Circuit Court Records," 379.

I. DECLARATION OF
LAURENCE PROTZMAN

Mero District Superior Court, Nashville

[n.d.]

Laurence Sproutzman complains of Elijah Robertson in Custody &c. of a Plea of Covenants Broken, For that whereas the aforesaid Elijah by his Certain writing obligatory Signed with the proper hand and Sealed with the Seal of the Said Elijah made the eight day of July in the Year of our Lord Seventeen hundred and Eighty eight it was Covenanted and agreed by and between, the aforesaid Laurence, by the name of Laurence Sproutzman, & the aforesaid Elijah by the name of Elijah Robertson (which writing obligatory Signed and Sealed as aforesaid Baring date the Same day & year the Said Laurence brings here into Court) that the aforesaid Elijah should pay and diliver, unto the Said Laurence on or before the Experation of two years from the date of the Said writing obligatory aforesaid one thousand four hundred and fifty three pounds of Beaver fur, under the Penalty of two thousand and Seven Dollars and one half in Silver or the value thereof in paper Currency, as by the aforesaid writing obligatory doth more fully appear. and the Said Laurence the Plaintiff, in fact Saith that the aforesaid writing obligatory was Signed Sealed and delivered on the day and Year aforesaid, and the aforesaid Laurence doth further in fact Say that the aforesaid Elijah, on the day of the Sealing and delivering of the Said writing obligatory or any time afterwards altho' often required by the Said Laurince hath not delivered, unto the Said Laurence, the Said one thousand four hundred and fifty three pounds of good Merchantable Beaver fur, the Said Laurence further in fact Saith, that the aforesaid Elijah altho' often thereunto required by the Said Laurence hath not performed all or any part of the Covenant, in the aforesaid writing obligatory Contained, [as upon?] the part and Behalf of the aforesaid Elijah ou[gh]t to have been [don]e, and performed according to the form and Effect of the Said writing obligatory or Covenant aforesaid but to do or perform the Same hath hitherto refused & denied and Still doth refuse from whence the Said Laurence Saith he is injured and hath been Damaged to the value of three thousand pounds North Carolina Currency and thereupon he brings Suit

Tr, TDaCo-MDSC Law Min. Bk., 1788–1803, p. 144. Enclosure missing. The date of the declaration and whether Jackson drafted the document cannot be determined with certainty. Although the Tr occurs in the trial entry for the case at November Term 1795, the action had been pending in the court at least as early as May 1793 and had been tried once before, in November 1794 (MDSC Law Min. Bk., 1788–1803, pp. 88, 115). It thus is likely that the declaration had been filed with the court more than two years before the Tr was entered into the court's minute book. Moreover, the appearance of AJ's initials on the execution docket as sole counsel of record for the plaintiff at the November 1795 trial might well indicate that he entered the case only at the second trial stage and inherited a declaration that had been drafted and filed with the court more than two years earlier by someone other than himself.

II. ANSWER OF ELIJAH
ROBERTSON
Mero District Superior Court, Nashville

[n.d.]

[T]he said Elijah Saith that he ought not to be Charged with the Damages Set for[th] and declared upon for a breach of the Covenants Contained in the writing obligatory aforesaid, because he Saith, that at the time of, & before the Sealing and delivering the Covenant & writing obligatory aforesaid, to wit, the Same eight day of July Seventeen hundred and eighty eight at the County of Davidson, it was Corruptly agreed between the Said Laurence and Elijah that the Said Laurence Should deliver unto the Said Elijah one other writing obligatory which he the Said Laurence had then & there in his possession, Sealed with the proper Seals of John Montgomry, James Allen and the Said Elijah, wherein: it was Covenanted that the Said John, James, and Elijah Should pay or Cause to be paid unto the Said Laurence one thousand one hundred and thirty Six pounds & one half of good Merchantable Beaver furr at the fals of Ohio on or before the first day of May then next insuing with Lawfull Interest from the date thereof, which date was as appears from the Said writing obligatory, the Seventh day of October in the year of our Lord, Seventeen hundred and eighty Six, on which writing obligatory there was an agreement Signed with the proper hands & Seals of the Said Montgomry and Sproutzman, that one hard Dollar Should be Deemed a payment for each pound of Beaver Furr, so Contracted to be paid provided the Said Dollars, were paid by or before the aforesaid first day of May Seventeen hundred and eighty Seven, in Consequence of which agreement there appears on the Said writing obligatory a Credit for thirty seven pounds Virginia Currency which Sum reduced to Dollars amounts to one hundred and twenty three and one third Dollars, which by virtue of the Said agreement ought to be Considered as a payment for one hundred and twenty three & one third pounds of Beaver furr, and would leave a Balance Due by virtue of the Said writing obligatory from the Said John, James, & Elijah to the Said Laurence after ading full interest from the date of the Said writing obligatory to time of Sealing & delivering the writing obligatory no[w] declared on of Eleven hundred & fifteen & one half pounds or thereabouts of the aforesaid Furr to be delivered as aforesaid and that the Said Elijah Should give unto the Said Laurence his own Bond, for the quantity of furr, mentioned in the obligation declared on amounting to one thousand four hundred and fifty three pounds as therein Specified, and that the quantity of three hundred and thirty seven & one half pounds or thereabouts over and above the quantity that remained Due & owing on the Bond or writing obligatory Sealed with the proper Seals of the Said John James & Elijah as aforesaid Should be added as a recompence and in Leu of all Interest for the forbearance of the aforesaid Eleven hundred and fifteen and one half pounds of Beaver Furr, or thereabouts Due and owing on the writing obligatory of the Said John, James & Elijah for two years then next insuing which Said quantity of three hundred and thirty seven & one half pounds of Beaver Furr, doth Exceed the rate of six pounds for the Interest and forbearance of one hundred pounds of the aforesaid furr, and So in proportion for a greater or Less quantity for one whole year; Contrary to the true interest and meaning of the act of the Genl. assembly in th[at] Case made & provided and afterwards (to wit) the Same eight day of July, [se]venteen hundred and eighty eight in the County aforesaid the Said Laurence in pursuance of the Said Corrupt agreement, did assign and deliver unto the said Elijah the writing obligatory aforesaid Sealed with the Seals of the said John Montgomry James Allen & Elijah Robertson, and the Said writing mentioned in the said declaration, was Sealed and delivered to the said Laurence by the Said Elijah as his act and deed; By means whereof the Said writing obligatory Set forth in the declaration of the Said Laurence, by virtue of the act of the Genl. assembly in that Case made and provided, is void in Law, and this he is ready to verify; Whereupon he prays Judgment wether he ought to be Charged with the Damages Set forth to have been Sustained by the Said Laurence for the non performance of Covenants Contained in the writing obligatory aforesaid by virtue of the Said writing obligatory and the Covenants therein Contained &c.

Tr, TDaCo-MDSC Law Min. Bk., 1788–1803, pp. 144–145.

III. REPLICATION OF
LAURENCE PROTZMAN

[n.d.]

[A]nd the Said Laurence Says that he, by any thing by the said Elijah above in Pleading Alledged, ought not to be Barred from having his Said action thereupon against the Said Elijah, because he Says that the Said Elijah made, Sealed and as his act and deed delivered to the Said Laurence the Said writing obligatory in the Said Declaration mentioned, for a true and Just Debt Due from the said Elijah, to the Said Laurence, without this, that it was Corruptly agreed between the Said Laurence and the Said Elijah—manner and form as the said Elijah above in pleading has alledged and this he is ready to verefy wherefore he prays Judgment and his said Debt, Together with his Damages by occasion of the not performing of the Said Covenant to be adjudged to him

Tr, TDaCo-MDSC Law Min. Bk., 1788–1803, pp. 145–146.

IV. SPECIAL VERDICT
Mero District Superior Court, Nashville

[November 10, 1795]

We the jurors taking to Consideration the Law and fact Introduced on trial of the present Suit wherein Laurence Sproutzman is Plaintiff and Elijah Robertson defendant do find that on the 7th day of October 1786 John Montgomry Elijah Robertson & James Allin, give their obligation to Laurence Sproutzman for the Sum of one thousand, one hundred thirty Six pounds & one half of Beaver furr to be paid on or before the first day of May 1787: and by an agreement on the Back of Said the Beaver Furr was to be rated at one Silver Dollar per pound, provided the Same was paid by Said or first day of May 1787: but no Longer which bond was payable at at the falls of Ohio with Interest from the date: We find further that on that Bond there was Thirty seven pounds VCurrency paid, we further find that on the eight day of July 1788 the Said Bond Signed by said Montgomry, Robertson, & Allin was Transferred to Elijah Robertson by said Sproutzman in Consideration of another Bond Given by said Robertson to the Said Sproutzman on the Said 8th day of July 1788 for the Sum of fourteen hundred and fifty three pounds Merchantable Beaver furr, to be paid two years after date without Interest; now if the Law Considers these facts to bring the Cause within the Statute of usury we find for defendant; if not we assess the Plaintiff's Damages to the Sum of Seven hundred and Sixty Seven pounds three Shillings and Six pence and find that sum for the Plaintiff

Tr, TDaCo-MDSC Law Min. Bk., 1788–1803, p. 146. Date is taken from *id.* at 143.

V. MINUTE BOOK ENTRY

Mero District Superior Court, Nashville

[November 18, 1795]

The Honble. Court met agreable to adjournment. Present the Honble.

John McNairy &
Joseph Anderson } Esquire Judges &c.

Laurence Sproutzman
vs
Elijah Robertson } Special Verdict. The matter being Solemly argued by the Council on both Sides The Court are of opinion that It is not within the Statute of Usury It is therefore decreed by the Court that the Plft. have J[udg]ment for the sum agreable to the verdict of the Jury (viz) Seven hundred Sixty seve[n po]unds three Shillings & Six pence

MS, TDaCo-MDSC Law Min. Bk., 1788–1803, p. 159. The court convened on Nov. 9, 1795. *Protzman* went to trial on the second Wednesday of the term (Nov. 18). See *id.* at 143.

VI. RECEIPT ISSUED TO JAMES
ROBERTSON

May 2, 1799

Laurence Sproutzman	
vs	} In Equity
Exr of Elijah Robertson, Decd.	
James Robertson & Isaac Robert	

Dol. Ct.

Judgment for   1013.17
Interest untill
the 1s[t] day of
May 1799 from   764.94
7 Octo. 1786
              ————
          1778.11

Recd. from James Robertson the Sum of one thousand Seven hundred and Seventy Eight Dollars Eleven Cents, it being the principal and Interest up the first day of May 1799, of the Judgment obtained by Laurence Sproutzman against the executors of Elijah Robertson and James Robertson and Isaac Roberts in the Court of Equity for Mero District, Recd. by me Andrew Jackson attorney for Squire Grant this 2d day of May 1799.

Teste   Squire Grant
B Searcy C   by
                      Andrew Jackson his
                      attorney in fact,

MS, TNJ-Stanley Horn Coll. Text in the hand of Bennett Searcy; autograph signature.

VII. RECEIPT FROM JOHN
OVERTON

May 2d. 1799 This day Andrew Jackson Esq. deposited in my possession for the use of Squire Grant of Kentucky the sum of Seventeen hundred & Seventy eight Dollars 11/100, to award the orders of said Grant.

$1778.11   Jno. Overton

MS, DLC-AJ Papers (Reel 2). Endorsed: "Overton to Jackson Receipt for Grants money."

VIII. SQUIRE GRANT TO JOHN OVERTON

June 7th 1799

Dr. Sir

There is a probibility of Capt. John Fowler calling on You on his rout through Tennessee   If he should call You will please to let Him have what Money You have collected on the Judgment I have obtained against Elijah Robertson and his Receipt will be good against me   I wish If Capt. Fowler should be good anough to call You will Try not to disappoint him as I am in Great want of Money

I am with Esteem Yr. obt. Huml. Svt.

Sqr. Grant

RC, THi-Claybrooke and Overton Papers. Addressed: "John Overton Esqr. or in his abstance The Honourable Andw. Jackson State Tennessee Davidson County John Fowler esq." Inside address: "John Overton esqr." Endorsement in Overton's hand: "Jno. Fowler for Sq: Grant Rect. $1079:20 July 12th 1799."

IX. RECEIPT, JOHN FOWLER TO JOHN OVERTON

Nashville July 12th 1799

Then Received of John Overton one thousand and seventy nine Dollars 20/100 upon the within order

Test   John Fowler

J. Overton

MS, THi-Claybrooke and Overton Papers. Text in the hand of John Overton; autograph signature. Filed with Squire Grant to Overton, June 7, 1799 (Document VIII).

The sum that Overton turned over to Fowler was, of course, $698.91 less than the sum that Overton had received from Jackson on May 2 (Document VI). The difference consisted of $598.91, which Overton retained as reimbursement for sums that he had paid to William T. Lewis and others for Grant in November 1798, and an additional $100, which he retained as his fee for services rendered in the equity proceeding that terminated the following May. Overton Notebook, 25–26, Claybrooke and Overton Papers, THi.

X. SQUIRE GRANT TO JOHN OVERTON

Frankfort Decr. 19th 1801

This day I acknowledge to have received from John Overton full satisfaction of a Judgment obtained in the name of Laurance Sproutzman agt. Elijah Robertson and endorced against his Heirs and Executors after his death which Judgment was for my benefit, and was obtained in the Superiour Court for the District of Mero State of Tennessee, in Equity: Except about the sum of $139: for which a subsequent Decree passed in said Court of Equity and which I have not yet received

Test   Sqr. Grant
Geo Walker

MS, THi-Claybrooke and Overton Papers. Endorsed: "S Grant To Overton Rect. in full Decr. 19th 1801." No records have been located for the award of the $139 to which reference is made in the text.

15. McNairy v. Edgar & Tait

1796
(Property)

EDITORIAL NOTE

As Nos. 4, 12, and 14 suggest, the increasing commercial development of the southwestern territory during the final two decades of the eighteenth century generated a substantial portion of Jackson's civil practice. The simultaneous growth of land speculation and land ownership in the territory likewise accounted for much of the litigation that Jackson handled as a practicing lawyer. As *McNairy* illustrates, however, Jackson's real-property cases as a general rule were not in the nature of proverbial boundary-line disputes.

The North Carolina General Assembly in April 1784 set aside two hundred acres on the south side of the Cumberland River as the site for the town of Nashville. The legislators directed the trustees of the new town to divide the site into one-acre lots and to offer the first fifty lots to subscribers by lottery. Each lot was to be sold for £4 on the condition that the purchaser within three years would construct a sixteen-foot-square house upon the premises.[1]

The lot that the trustees subsequently designated as Lot 9 was drawn later in the same year by James Robertson, and, in August 1784, the trustees deeded the one-acre tract to him for the prescribed consideration of £4. Whether Robertson had completed the improvements on Lot 9 within the time specified by statute is not known, but on September 3, 1787, he deeded out a half interest in the lot to James Lanier. Lanier in turn conveyed his interest in Lot 9 to Eusebius Bushnell and his partner William Dobbins in October of the same year.[2]

The series of conveyances that eventually resulted in the ejectment action that Judge John McNairy and his wife, Mary, brought against the mercantile firm of Edgar & Tait began on June 23, 1788, when Lanier's

---

1. Ch. 47, 1784 Laws of N.C. (Apr. Sess.), reprinted in N.C. *State Records*, XXIV, 616.
2. DaCo Deed Bk. A, 13, 69–70, 285.

grantees, Bushnell and Dobbins, executed a deed for their half of Lot 9, "a house and half acre lot in the town of Nashville," and for nine tracts of land along the Cumberland River to David Hay and Adam Hampton. In return, Hay and Hampton became sureties for Bushnell and Dobbins on a note for the sum of £598, 16 shillings, that the latter executed payable in December 1789 to the estate of Mark Robertson, brother of James Robertson. Bushnell and Dobbins subsequently defaulted on the note, and Robertson's executors promptly brought an action in the Davidson County court to recover from their sureties, Hay and Hampton. Hay and Hampton satisfied their obligation on the note on January 11, 1790, merely by conveying to Robertson's widow, Mary, to whom the executors had indorsed the note, their half of Lot 9 and the other nine tracts of land that Bushnell and Dobbins had conveyed to them a year and a half earlier.[3]

In February 1791 Bushnell and Dobbins executed a deed of release to Mary Robertson. In this instrument they sought to confirm that, by virtue of the 1790 conveyance, their interests in Lot 9 and the other nine tracts had passed to her. Because Robertson's widow by February 1791 had married John McNairy, the grantees recited in the deed of release were both Mary Robertson McNairy and her husband, Judge John McNairy.[4]

Unfortunately for Mary Robertson and her new husband, Hay and Hampton had never recorded the 1788 deed from Bushnell and Dobbins. To make matters worse, the latter's interests in the lot had been sold at a sheriff's sale to Edgar & Tait in satisfaction of two outstanding judgments against Bushnell and Dobbins. Moreover, Edgar & Tait had had their deeds to Lot 9 proved and recorded by Jackson on April 23–24, 1789,[5] eight months prior to Hay and Hampton's transfer to Mary Robertson and more than a year before she recorded the conveyance in July 1790.[6]

In the autumn of 1793, more than two years after Bushnell and Dobbins had sought to confirm the conveyance of title to their half of Lot 9 to Robertson's widow, McNairy initiated in the Davidson County court an ejectment action and an action to recover mesne profits against William

3. See Deed, Hay and Hampton to Robertson, Jan. 11, 1790, DaCo Deed Bk. B, 107–108.

4. Deed of Release, Bushnell and Dobbins to McNairy, February 1791, DaCo Deed Bk. B, 212.

5. DaCo Deed Bk. A, 322–323. Bushnell's interest in half of Lot 9 was sold to Edgar & Tait for £26, 1 shilling, to satisfy a judgment awarded Guifford Dudley by the Cumberland County, Kentucky, court in January 1789. Dobbins's interest in Lot 9 was sold to Edgar & Tait for £57, 10 shillings, to satisfy a judgment awarded Henry Lenier by the Davidson County court in October 1788.

6. DaCo Deed Bk. B, 107. McNairy recorded the February 1791 deed of release from Bushnell and Dobbins on July 27, 1791. Id. at 212.

Tait, one of the partners in the firm of Edgar & Tait. At the court's October Term 1793, Jackson made his initial appearance for Tait and secured a continuance with leave to file an answer at next term. After having obtained still another continuance at the court's January Term 1794, Jackson by April of that year apparently had filed Tait's answer, which has not been located. The court at its April Term 1794 consented to a request by Jackson and McNairy's counsel, John Overton, that Mary McNairy be admitted as a party plaintiff and that John Edgar of Kaskaskia be admitted as a party defendant with his business partner Tait.

The two actions went to trial on April 15, 1794. Inexplicably, the jury in the ejectment action returned the following verdict:

> [T]hey find the Defendants Guilty in manner and form as charged in the Plaintiffs Declaration, With Regard to the one half of the half of Lott Number Nine, And Do Assess the Plaintiffs Damages . . . to Twelve pence, and not Guilty as to the Other half of the half of the sd. Lott No. Nine.

The court thereupon awarded the McNairys possession of only one half of the half of the lot that had been deeded to Bushnell and Dobbins in 1787, plus damages in the amount of 12 pence (Document II). A separate jury returned a verdict on the plaintiffs' mesne profits claim for the sum of £37, 16 shillings, which was computed from the date of Edgar & Tait's deed to the contested half of Lot 9 in 1789 (Document II). Both judgments were appealed to the Mero District Superior Court.

Presumably, the appeals were filed in time for the cases to be heard when the Superior Court reconvened in Nashville on May 5, 1794. There are no entries for the cases in the court's minutes before November 1795, however. Because McNairy was the only one of the three territorial judges in attendance at the court's May Term 1794, it is probable that the appeals were in fact filed with the Superior Court shortly after the April judgments in the Davidson County court and that McNairy, to avoid the conflict of interest that would have arisen had he heard the matter, merely issued unrecorded continuances in the cases until a later term when either Judge Anderson or Judge Campbell was in attendance. This explanation appears all the more likely in view of the court's attendance records for the two succeeding terms. McNairy presided alone at both the court's November Term 1794 and its May Term 1795. Judge Anderson again joined McNairy on the bench in Nashville only at the court's November Term 1795, when the first recorded entries for the cases occur in the court's minutes. On November 12, 1795, Judges McNairy and Anderson referred both cases to Jackson and Overton and to a third arbitrator of their choosing.[7]

7. MDSC Law Min. Bk., 1788–1803, pp. 148, 149.

Jackson and Overton selected Howell Tatum to join them in arbitrating the two cases. The three arbitrators reduced the terms of their award to writing on February 23, 1796 (Document III). They awarded McNairy and his wife title to the disputed half of Lot 9 plus their litigation costs, but denied them any recovery for damages or for mesne profits. The arbitrators awarded Edgar & Tait only their costs in defending the mesne profits action. Because the litigation costs for both parties were nearly identical,[8] the net result of the award, which the court confirmed on May 12, 1796, was to vest title to the contested half of Lot 9 in McNairy and his wife.

Since the purpose of an ejectment suit was to regain possession of real property, the jury usually awarded only nominal damages. If the plaintiff wished to recover the profits derived from the land while it was unlawfully possessed by the defendant, it was necessary to institute a separate but parallel action of trespass quare clausum fregit for mesne profits. The judgment in the ejectment action was sufficient proof of title for an award of mesne profits.[9]

It is difficult to reconcile the arbitration award in *McNairy* with the prevailing law. Edgar & Tait had recorded their deed obtained from the sheriff's sale well before the plaintiffs registered the 1790 instrument. Since Hay and Hampton never had recorded their 1788 deed, the plaintiffs did not receive their later deed in reliance upon a complete record title. A North Carolina statute had long provided that no conveyance of real property "shall be good and available in Law" unless recorded within twelve months "after the Date of the said Deed."[10] The wording of this measure indicates that recording was a condition precedent to the passing of title by deed.[11] Although the period for recording had temporarily been enlarged in November 1788,[12] the plaintiffs could not have benefited from this action by the legislature because Hay and Hampton failed to register the 1788 deed at any time. Hence, the plaintiffs seemingly received a void deed and thus could not have ejected Edgar & Tait from possession of the lot. Of course, some irregularity in the sheriff's sale may have clouded the title conveyed to the defendants, but the record contains no hint of such a defect. The arbitrators' divided award upholding the plaintiffs' claim to

8. The ejectment costs included a clerk's fee of £7, 75 shillings; attorney's fees amounting to £12, 50 shillings; and court costs of £16, 14½ shillings. The mesne profits costs were the same, except that the court costs amounted to £16, 27 shillings. MDSC Execution Docket, 1792–1803, p. 38.

9. 5 Tucker, *Blackstone's Commentaries* 205–206.

10. Ch. 38, 1715 Laws of N.C., reprinted in Iredell, *Laws of North Carolina* 22, 1 Scott, *Laws of Tennessee* 25.

11. See Stinson's Lessee v. Russell, 2 Tenn. (2 Overton) 40, 49 (1809).

12. Ch. 24, 1788 Laws of N.C., reprinted in Iredell, *Laws of North Carolina* 640, 1 Scott, *Laws of Tennessee* 400.

the lot but denying them any mesne profits thus may well indicate a compromise decision.

When Jackson made his first appearance in the *McNairy* litigation in October 1793, he had represented Edgar & Tait in at least five earlier actions[13] and had represented Edgar's Kaskaskian firm of John Edgar & Company in at least one case.[14] By 1793, John Edgar had become one of the most prominent and financially successful merchants in the Northwest Territory. A native of Belfast, Edgar had amassed a fortune in trade while living in Detroit during the Revolutionary War. Placed under arrest by the British in 1779 for sympathizing and corresponding with the Americans, Edgar eventually moved to the Mississippi River trading center of Kaskaskia.[15] In Kaskaskia, Edgar formed the mercantile firm of John Edgar & Company[16] and soon began trading in flour, salt, and other commodities as far south as Nashville and New Orleans.[17] Subsequently, Edgar entered into a separate partnership in Nashville with one of the town's established merchants, William Tait. As the ejectment suit by McNairy demonstrates, Tait apparently managed the firm's business operations in Nashville.[18] Although Sheriff Thomas Hickman had executed deeds to Bushnell and Dobbins's interests in Lot 9 in April 1789 to the firm of Edgar & Tait, McNairy initially brought his action only against Tait individually (see Document II). Moreover, the Superior Court's Execution Docket clearly indicates that it was Tait who in November 1796 paid the plaintiffs' litigation costs in the ejectment action pursuant to the arbitration award.[19] The firm owned at least one additional half-acre lot in Nashville[20] and was still conducting its business in the town as late as 1802 (see *Edgar & Tait v. Neville*, No. 43). It is not known whether the firm had survived when Tait was elected mayor of Nashville in 1811.[21]

13. Edgar & Tait v. Forde, DaCo CPQS Min. Bk. A, 323 (1789), Min. Bk. B, 6 (1791); Edgar & Tait v. Brock and Forde, DaCo CPQS Min. Bk. A, 388 (1790); Edgar & Tait v. Forde, DaCo CPQS Min. Bk. A, 323 (1789); Edgar & Tait v. Hay, DaCo CPQS Rec. Bk., 1783–1790, p. 162 (with Josiah Love, 1789); Edgar & Tait v. Grant, DaCo CPQS Rec. Bk., 1783–1790, p. 150 (1789).

14. John Edgar & Company v. McPherson, DaCo CPQS Min. Bk. B, 22 (1792).

15. James H. Roberts, "The Life and Times of General John Edgar," *Transactions of the Illinois State Historical Society*, XII, 66–67, 70 (1908).

16. See Clarence W. Alvord, ed., *Kaskaskia Records 1778–1790*, Collections of the Illinois Historical Library, V (Springfield, 1909), 523, 526.

17. Roberts, "John Edgar," 70; see John Edgar & Company v. Cunstock, MDSC Law Min. Bk., 1788–1803, pp. 89–90.

18. The *McNairy* litigation is not the only evidence, of course. See, *e.g.,* Edgar & Tait v. Donelson, MDSC Law Min. Bk., 1788–1803, p. 117 (1794); Riston and Shelby v. Tait, *id.* at 57 (1791).

19. MDSC Execution Docket, 1792–1803, p. 38.

20. DaCo Deed Bk. A, 73.

21. Clayton, *Davidson County*, 198.

I. DECLARATION AND NOTICE
IN EJECTMENT

Davidson County Court of Pleas and Quarter
Sessions, Nashville

[ca. April 1794]

Davidson county To Wit, John Den complains of Richard Fen being in custody &c. For that Whereas on the fourth day of June in the year 1788, John McNairy & Wife in the county of Davidson Demised and [for wood?] & to farm let, to the sd. John Den a certain Lott in the Town of Nashville, known in the Plat of the sd. Town by Number Nine With the Appurtenances Situate Lying and being, in the sd. county the Place Where the Premises lie in the county Afsd. To have and to hold, the sd. Tennements With the Appurtenances Afsd. to the sd. John Den and his Assigns from the fourth day of June 1788 untill the Expiration And End of Seven years from the sd. fourth day of June 1788 by Virtue of Which sd. Demise the sd. John Den Entered into the sd. Tennements With the Appurtenances and Was Possessed thereof untill the sd. Richd. Fen Afterward To Wit on the fourth day of June 1788 With force and Arms &c. Entered on the Tennements Aforesd. With the Appurtenances, in and Upon the Possession of the said John Den, And Ejected, Drove, out and Removed the sd. John Den from his said Lott Number nine With its Appurtenances and Still keeps out the said John Den, So Ejected Drove out And Removed from his said possessions and then did Other Injuries to him, And Against the peace & dignity of the State and to the Damage of the said John Den And therefore he brings Suit.

John Overton Pro. Plaints.

And John Doe and Richd. Roe are Pledges to Prosecute.

Mr: William Taitt & John Edgar.

I Am informed that you are in Possession and claim title to the sd. Premises in this Declaration Mentioned or to Some part thereof. I being Sued in this Action as causual Ejector, and having no claim or Title the sd. premises Do Advise you to Appear on the first day of the Ensuing court for Davidson county by Some Attorney of that court, And there And then to cause your Selves to be made Defendants in my Stead, Otherwise I Shall Suffer Judgment to be Entered Against me, and you Will be Turned out of Possession.

John Den

To William Taitt Merchant in Nashville.

Tr, TDaCo-DaCo CPQS Min. Bk. B, 174. The plaintiffs' declaration apparently was not filed with the court until April Term 1794 (see Document II, note 1), from which fact the present document has been assigned its date.
    For a discussion of the use of pseudonyms in ejectment actions, see Introduction, p. xxxi.

II. MINUTE BOOK ENTRIES

Davidson County Court of Pleas and Quarter Sessions, Nashville

[April 15, 1794]

[The Ejectment Proceedings]

John McNairy Esq:
    & Wife Plaints.
        vs   }   "Ejectment"
William Taitt & John
    Edgar Defendants

Service of the Writ Acknowledged. And by consent of Parties all kind of Error and Informality is Waved, Merely to try on the Merits, Whose Title is best.

To Which at October Sessions 1793 the Plaintiff Appeared John Overton Esquire his Attorney Likewise the Defdt. by Andrew Jackson Esquire his Attorney and in the mean time Pleads "Not guilty With Leave &c." After Which the cause Was continued to January Sessions 1794 at Which time, by a Previous Agreement of the Parties that Cause Was to have been tried; But was then continued Without further Proceedings had thereon untill April Sessions 1794 at Which time by consent of John McNairy Esquire & William Taitt and their Attorneys and Assent of the court, Mrs. Mary McNairy, and John Edgar became Plaintiff and Defendant, With the Aforesaids[1]. . . .

At Which Sessions of April 1794 comes hereinto court as Well the plaints. by their Attorney Aforesd. As the sd. Taitt & Edgar by Andrew Jackson Esquire their Attorney and is considered as the Defendants in the cause, and Confesses Lease Entry, and Ouster and Stands on the Merit of the Title only, And Saith that they are in nowise Guilty of the Trespass in Ejectment as Set forth in the Plaintiffs Declaration, and of this they put themselves on the Country and the Plaintiffs Do likewise. Therefore a Jury comes thereon To Wit, Jessee Reed, Benjamin cassellman, Frederick Stump Joseph Hannah, William Murry William Marshall John Anderson Gadi Gibson Lach. Stull John Sharp, George Payne and Alexander Moore Who being Elected tried and Sworn Well and truly to try the Issue Joined between the Plaintiffs and the Defendants as Aforesd. &c. Upon their Oaths Do Say that they find the Defendants Guilty in manner and form as charged in the Plaintiffs Declaration, With Regard to the one half of the half of Lott Number Nine, And Do Assess the Plaintiffs Damages on the Occasion to Twelve pence, and not Guilty as to the Other half of the half of the sd. Lott No. Nine. Therefore it is considered of by the court that the Plaints. Do Recover Against the Defendants the Possession of the one half of the half of Lott Number Nine, Also the Damages So Assessed to them by the Jury as Aforesd., And With Regard to the Other half of the sd. half Lott, be the Defendants Acquitted.[2]

[The Mesne Profits Proceedings]

John McNairy Esquire
   & Wife Plaints.
      vs
William Taitt & John
   Edgar Defendants

For the mesne Profits of half the Lott No. 9 in the Town of Nashville.

Service of the Writ Acknowledged. And by consent of parties, all kind of Error & Informality is Waved; Merely to try on the Merits of the cause.

To Which at October Sessions 1793 the Plaintiff Appeared by John Overton Esquire his Attorney Likewise the Defendant by Andrew Jackson Esquire his Attorney And Pleads "Not Guilty With leave &c." And thereon the Plaint. & Defendant Were at Issue, After Which the cause Was continued to January Sessions 1794 at Which time by a Previous Agreement of the Parties the cause Was to have been tried, But Was then continued Without further proceedings had thereon untill April Sessions 1794 at Which time by consent of John McNairy Esquire, and William Taitt & their Attorneys, and Assent of the court, Mrs. Mary McNairy, and John Edgar became Plaintiff & Defendant With the Aforesds., the Defendants Still Relying on the Issue Joined as Aforesd: And thereon comes a Jury To Wit; Daniel Young, Thos. Talbott, William Marshall, Mathew Payne, James Hamilton, Daniel James, Joseph Hannah, James Marshall, Alexander Moore, Frederick Stump, George Payne, and Flowers McGriggor Who being Elected tried and Sworn, Well and truly to try the Issue Joined Between the Plaintiffs and Defendants as Aforesd. &c. And David Hay, Andrew McNairy, & Seth Lewis the Witnesses in the cause being called, Sworn, Examined and heard, the Jury Withdrew Return, And on their Oaths Do Say, that they find for the Plaintiffs Damages thirty Seven pounds Sixteen Shillings, Currency hard money computed from the Date of the Defendants Deed to part of sd. Lott. Therefore it is considered of by the court that the Plaintiffs Do Recover Against the Defendants the Sum of Thirty Seven pounds Sixteen Shillings currency hard Money So Assessed to them by the Jury as Aforesd. as Also their costs of Suit in that behalf Expended. From Which Judgment the Plaintiffs Prayed and Obtained an Appeal to the Honorable Superior Court of Law and Equity for Mero District, having given bond and Security as by Law is Required

MS, TDaCo-DaCo CPQS Min. Bk. B, 174–175. Date is taken from *id.*

1. The text of Document I follows at this point in the MS, preceded by: "And then the Plaints. by their Attorney Afds. Declared as follows."
2. Marginal notation at this point: "Appealled & Security given."

III. ARBITRATION AWARD

Mero District Superior Court, Nashville

February 23, 1796

Andrew Jackson & John Overton having been mutually chosen by John McNairy & William Taitt to abritrate and determine, two Suits now depending in the Superior Court of the district of Mero, wherein the Said John McNairy & wife are Plaintiffs and the Said Taitte & Edjar are defts. do Chose Howel Tatum Esquire umpire or third person; one of Said Suits being an Ejectment instituted for the recovery of the half Lott No. 9 in the town of Nashville, the other for mesne profits of Said Lott, We do arbitrate and determine and award, the right of property and possession in & to the Said half Lot No. 9 in John McNairy & wife and that the recover the Same of the Said Taitt & Edjar; and that the Said McNairy & wife recover their Legal Costs in the Said Ejectment against the Said defendants. We are also of opinion that the Said McNairy & wife are not entitled to any thing for mesne profits of Said half Lot and they take nothing by their for, and that the Said Edjar, & Taitt recover their Legal Costs in the Suit respecting mesne profits against the Said McNairy & wife In Testimoney whereof we have hereunto Set our hands & seals this 23rd day of February 1796

Signed

Andrew Jackson	(Seal)
John Overton	(Seal)
Howel Tatum	(Seal)

Tr, TDaCo-MDSC Law Min. Bk., 1788–1803, pp. 168–169. The award was confirmed by the court on May 12, 1796.

PART II

Jackson as a Judge of the Superior Court of Law and Equity, 1798–1804

Nonlitigation Documents

Temporary Commission
as Superior Court Judge

September 20, 1798
State of Tennessee:
[SEAL] John Sevier Governor in and over the said state.

To all who shall see these presents: Greeting. Know ye, that by the powers in me vested I do appoint, and hereby commission Andrew Jackson esquire of the district of Mero, one of the Judges of the Superior courts of law and equity, in and for the State aforesaid, until the end of the next Session of the General Assembly, in the place and Stead of Howell Tatum esquire, who has resigned: And do authorize and empower the said Andrew Jackson to execute and fulfil the duties of that office according to the constitution, and laws of the said state: And to have and to hold the said office, of one of the Judges of the Superior courts of law and equity until the end of the next session of the General Assembly, with all the powers, privileges and emoluments thereto of right appertaining. Given under my hand and seal at Knoxville this twentieth day of September, in the year of our Lord, one thousand seven hundred and ninety eight.

John Sevier

By the Governor.
Wm. Maclin, Secretary.

MS, T-AJ Papers. Text in the hand of William Maclin; autograph signature. Endorsed: "State of Tennessee Hamilton District Septr. Term 1798. The Honble Andrew Jackson on the first day of said term produced the within Commission and was quallifyed by taking the necessary oaths of office Test F A Ramsey Clk."

Petition of Jackson and Others to the Tennessee General Assembly

[ca. December 12, 1798]

To the honorable the general assembly of the State of Tennessee,

The petition of the subscribers humbly sheweth that whereas a law was passed at   [1] Session of   [1] whereby it was enacted that no attorney should be admitted to practice in any of the courts of this commonwealth unless he shall have previously resided twelve months within the limits of this State.[2] Your peti[t]ioner humbly concieve, the above law to be impolitic as its tendency is to prevent the emigration, of attornies from other States of the union to this State, and the only reasonable and generous reason for the above law can be answered by obliging the emigrants to bring with them sufficient Testimonials of their moral character, we concieve the above law to be inconsistent with the spirit of the federal constitution which declares that citizens of the United States shall be entitled to all the priviledges of citizenship in the several states, so that it appears to accord with the laudable intention of the federal constitution, that no citizen of the United States, should be subjected to greater difficulties, in the prosecution of a lawful occupation, in any of the United States than the natural born citizens of that State; It casts a reflection on the gentlemen of the bar, of this State which we humbly concieve they by no means merit, as tho' they ungenerously wished to monopolize the whole of the business, without allowing strangers to come in for a share, or that they felt a consciousness of their inability to maintain their ground if attornies from other States should be admitted on an equal footing with them, neither of which we are confident is the case. We believe that no other State of the Union, has at present any such law in force, and wish that the State of Tennessee would not be singular in retaining such a one. The State of Kentucky at their last Session taking into consideration the above mentioned act and finding that the citizens of Tennessee were admitted to practice as attornies in the State of Kentucky but that the citizens of Kentucky were not admitted to practice in the State of Tennessee, without a previous residence of twelve months, passed a law prohibiting attornies of this State from practicing as attornies in the State of Kentucky, unless they shall have previously resided one year in the state of Kentucky, which law shall be in force until the State of Tennessee shall repeal the above law, and no longer.[3]

For these and other reasons your petitioners pray that the said law may

be repealed, or such alterations made in it as may be consistent with reci-
procity and a generous spirited policy and your petitioners as in duty
bound will ever pray &c.

J. Whiteside	Saml. Donelson
Andrew McNairy	Jos. Herndon
Wm. P. Anderson	Jno. C Hamilton
Geo. Smith	Isaac McNutt
Thos. Stuart	J. Wharton
Andrew Jackson	R. McGavock
	I. A. Parker
	John McNairy
	Robt. Searcy
	Jno. Overton

MS, T-Legislative Petitions, 1799; *Jackson Papers,* I, 214–215. Text in the hand of Samuel
Donelson; autograph signatures. Approximate date is derived from endorsement: "In Senate, Decr. 12, 1798. Read & referred to the House of Representatives, with the bill to repeal
so much of the 4th Section of an act, as respects the residence of Attornies. G Roulstone CS."

Shortly after the receipt of this petition, the legislature repealed the residency requirement for attorneys. Ch. 2, 1798 Tenn. Public Acts, reprinted in 1 Scott, *Laws of Tennessee* 615.

1. Blank in MS.
2. Ch. 1, 1794 Terr. S. of River Ohio Acts, reprinted in 1 Scott, *Laws of Tennessee* 457.
3. Ch. 19, 1798 Kentucky Acts.

Commission as Superior Court Judge

December 22, 1798
State of Tennessee
[SEAL] John Sevier Governor in and over the same.

To all who shall see these presents: Greeting. Know ye, that Andrew
Jackson esquire of Davidson County Mero District, was on the twentieth
Instant December, by joint ballot of both Houses of the Legislature, duly
elected one of the Judges of the Superior courts of law and equity in and
for the said State agreeably to the Constitution thereof; and that in pursuance of the said constitution I the said John Sevier Governor &c., do
hereby commission the said Andrew Jackson one of the Judges of the Superior courts of law and equity aforesaid, to have and to hold the said
office of one of the Judges of the Superior courts of law and equity, dur-

ing good behaviour, with all the power and privilegs of right thereto appertaining.

    Given under my hand and seal at Knoxville this
22nd day of December 1798.

John Sevier

By the Governor.
Wm. Maclin, Secretary.

MS, THer; *Jackson Papers,* I, 215. Endorsed: "State of Tennessee Washington District March Term 1799 I James Aiken Clerk of the Superior Court of Law for Washington District in the State aforesaid do Certify that the Honble. Andrew Jackson appeared in open Court and produced the within Commission, and took an Oath to Support the Constitution of the United States, State of Tennessee, and also the Oath of Office required by Law. Given under my hand this fourth Day of March A D 1799, and in the 23 Year of our Independence. Jas. Aiken."

Papers Relating to the Discharge
of William Journey

I. WILLIAM JOURNEY
TO SETH LEWIS

May 28th 1800

Sir
    you will take notice that on the fourth Monday in june next I mean to take the benefit of the insolvent Debtors Act, in the suit Wm. & Andrew Neely against me in the County Court of Davidson to be done at the house of Mr. Parkers in Nashville between the Hours of Eight in the Morning & sunset when and where you May attend and shew Cause if any you have why I should not do so I am yours &c.

Wm. Journey
to
Seth Lewis esqr.

this day personaly apeared before Me Andrew Jackson one of the Judges of the Superior Court of Law for the State of Tennessee Isaac McNutt & made oath that he Delivered a true Copy of the within Notice to Seth Lewis Esqr. attorney for William and Andrew Neely on the 28th day of May 1800.

Isaac McNutt

Sworn to before me this
23d day of June 1800.
  Andrew Jackson
I Delivered a copy of the within Notice to Seth Lewis the 28th of
May 1800
                    Isaac McNutt
State of Tennessee Ss.
  on this 23rd day of June Eighteen hundred William Journey was brought
before me Andrew Jackson one of the Judges of the Superior Courts of
law & Equity on a petition for the benefit of the insolvant Debtors act, at
the Suit of Wm. & Andrew Neely, under which he is confined and being
duly Sworn deposeth & Saith that the said plaintiffs are not Inhabitants
of this State.
                    Andrew Jackson

MS, T-AJ Papers. Only the text of the second attestation of June 23, 1800, is in Jackson's
hand; autograph signatures.
  For further discussion of the Insolvent Debtors Act, see Editorial Note to No. 41.

II. JACKSON'S DISCHARGE OF
WILLIAM JOURNEY

                    June 23, 1800
[. . . .   Da] ¹vidson County or
[. . . .   ]
[. . . .   Willi]am Journey did on this
[date . . . .   ] take the oath of
[. . . .   debt]ors in the Suits for
[. . . .   im]prisoned to wit. one
[. . . .   ]ntgomery in Jonesborough
[. . . .   i]n Washington District
[. . . .   ] County Court of Davidson
[. . . .   ] Andrew Neeley's, and
[. . . .   ] commanded that
[. . . .   ] said Journey from
his imprisonment on them two Suits & this Shall be your Warrant for the
Same Given under my hand and Seal this 23rd day of June 1800.
                    Andrew Jackson (Seal)

MS, THi-Coffee Papers, Dyas Coll.; large fragment of text torn away from upper left corner.
Text in unidentified hand; autograph signature.

  1. Approximately five to ten words are missing from the bracketed portion of this line
and from the similarly marked portions of the lines that follow.

Statement of Issues
to be Submitted to a Jury
in *Parker v. Payton et al.*

Benjamin Parker	July 15, 1802
vs	Issue of Fact to be Submitted
	to a Jury, made up by
Ephraim Payton	Andrew Jackson one of the
John Gardner &	Judges of the Superior
John Delotch	courts of law and Equity at
	his office this 15th day of
	July 1802

Whether William Parker Deceased purchased the improvement mentioned in the complainants Bill from the Said Thomas Sharp Spencer. If he did at what time and for What consideration and whether it is the same improvement claimed to have been purchased by Ephraim Payton and now in the possession of the two Defendants, John Gardener and John Delotch.

Andrew Jackson

MS, T-AJ Papers. Endorsement in Jackson's hand: "Parker vs Payton and others Issue Made up by A. Jackson one of the Judges &c." Endorsement in an unidentified hand: "We cant agree."

No further records for the case have been located. Jackson's dating of the document remains especially puzzling, since the court's May 1802 Term in the Mero District had concluded more than a month and a half earlier and since the court was not scheduled to convene again until September in the Washington District. Notes in the hand of Robert Whyte, one of the lawyers in the litigation, and a typescript of a letter addressed to Whyte by John C. Hamilton in May 1804 suggest that the case remained before the court until after Jackson had resigned from the bench. See Whyte Notes and Hamilton to Whyte, May 20, 1804, Robert Whyte Papers, THi.

Litigation: Law Cases

16. Reading v. Douglass

1798
(Bailment)

EDITORIAL NOTE

This action posed for Jackson the first instance of a conflict of interest between his earlier representation of a client and his newly assumed position as one of the judges of the Superior Court. Jackson had hardly practiced law at all while serving in the House of Representatives in 1796 and 1797. Two months after his election to the Senate in September 1797, however, he filed a declaration on behalf of William Reading in the Mero District Superior Court (Document I). Less than a year later, Jackson was appointed to the bench.

There is no evidence that Jackson was still counsel of record when a jury returned a judgment for Reading on May 18, 1798.[1] The court granted a new trial, however, and when the cause went to trial for the second time, on November 15, 1798, Thomas Stuart had replaced Jackson as counsel of record for Reading. There is no indication that Jackson recused himself from hearing the case because of his earlier representation of the plaintiff. A jury on November 15 returned a verdict for the plaintiff (Document II).

During Jackson's tenure on the bench, there were primarily three circumstances under which a judge might be required or expected to recuse himself from hearing litigation tried before the court. First, Article V, section 8, of the Tennessee Constitution of 1796 forbade judges from sitting at the trial of "any cause where the parties shall be connected with him, by affinity or consanguinity except by consent of the parties." Second, Article V seemingly required judges to recuse themselves from presiding

1. MDSC Law Min. Bk., 1788–1803, p. 208.

at the trial of suits to which they were either litigants themselves or interested parties.[2] Third, although arguably not within the purview of Article V, judges nonetheless frequently recused themselves from presiding at the trial of actions in which they previously had represented one of the parties. Judge Hugh Lawson White, for example, recused himself on numerous occasions for this reason.[3]

As the *Reading* case illustrates, Jackson was not as sensitive as some of his colleagues to the conflict of interest arising from the prior representation of litigants who subsequently appeared before him as a judge. In all fairness, of course, *Reading* appears to have been the only case tried during Jackson's tenure on the court that raised this particular variety of conflict of interest. Jackson, however, appears to have been no more sensitive to other conflicts of interest, as Nos. 27, 36, and 46 illustrate. Indeed, based upon the records that have been located, Jackson appears to have recused himself on only one occasion from presiding at the trial of an action in which he had even a potential conflict of interest, and his action on that occasion apparently was based upon the clear constitutional proscription of Article V. At the Hamilton District Superior Court's final hearing in October 1801 on petitioner's bill for an injunction in *Anderson v. Justice*, Jackson recused himself because he was related to Stockley Donelson, the maker of the deed at issue in the litigation.[4]

In the present case, Reading alleged, probably in the alternative, (a) that Douglass, the keeper of an inn at the courthouse in Sumner County, had caused the loss of one of the plaintiff's horses by allowing it to escape from where it had been put up at the inn and (b) that he had lost one of his horses and that the defendant, knowing that the horse belonged to the plaintiff, had converted it to his own use rather than return it to its owner (see Document I).

The common law had long subjected innkeepers to extraordinary responsibility for the money and goods of their guests. "Travellers, who must be numerous in a rich and commercial country," James Kent observed in 1827, "are obliged to rely almost implicitly on the good faith of innkeepers, and it would be almost impossible for them, in any given case, to make out proof of fraud or negligence in the landlord."[5]

2. This apparently had been the case, for example, in *McNairy v. Edgar & Tait*, No. 15.

3. For example, *Magoffin & Son v. Acklin* and *Magoffin & Son v. Acklin, Perrin, and Combs*, No. 41; *Williams et al. v. Henderson & Company*, No. 50.

4. HDSC Eq. Min. Bk. 1, 1793–1808, p. 91. Because Judge White also recused himself due to his service as counsel of record originally in the cause, the court's disposition of the petition was left entirely to Judge Campbell. Both Jackson and White, however, signed the court's final decree in the action in March 1802, apparently on the ground that the affixing of their signatures to the decree incorporating a decision for the court made only by Judge Campbell was merely a ministerial function not within the purview of the constitutional article. *Id.* at 122.

5. William S. Holdsworth, *A History of English Law* (London, 1903–1966), VIII, 452; James Kent, *Commentaries on American Law* (New York, 1827–1828), II, 460.

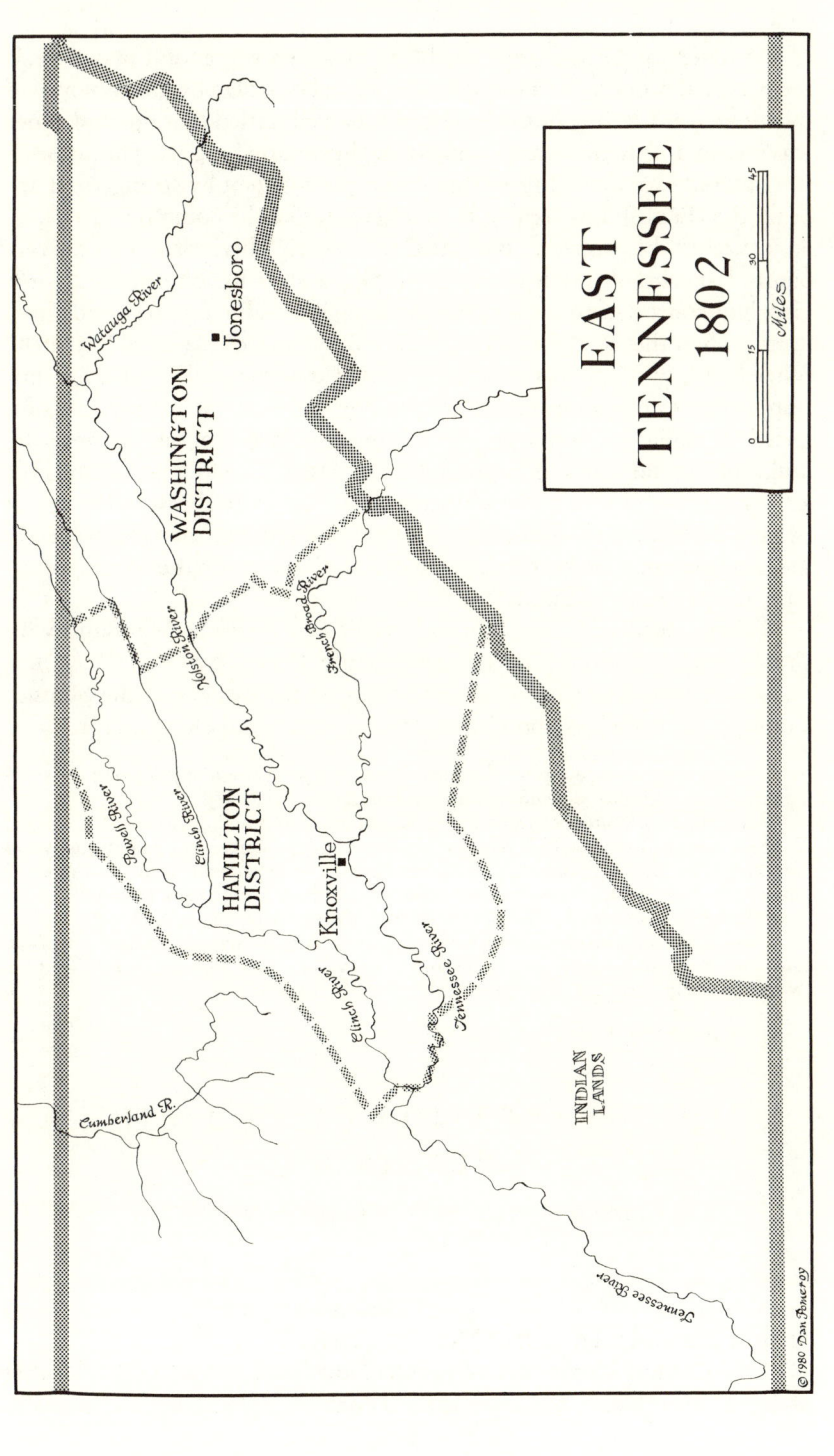

EAST
TENNESSEE
1802

Miles

0   15   30   45

Watauga River

Jonesboro

WASHINGTON
DISTRICT

Nolston River

French Broad River

Powell River

Clinch River

HAMILTON
DISTRICT

Knoxville

Clinch River

Tennessee River

INDIAN
LANDS

Cumberland R.

Tennessee River

© 1980 Dan Pomeroy

The extent of the innkeeper's liability, however, was a topic of debate. If the personal property of a guest was damaged or stolen by an employee of the innkeeper's or by another guest, it was well settled that the innkeeper was answerable without a showing of negligence on his part. The authorities differed over the liability of an innkeeper for theft by strangers. It appears that English law treated the innkeeper, like the common carrier, as an insurer of the property committed to his care. This strict view was recognized in early America. For example, a post-Revolutionary North Carolina court declared that "the inn-keeper is liable for the goods lost, unless when the guest is robbed by a companion of his own."[6] On the other hand, in 1832 Joseph Story stressed that the innkeeper was "not responsible to the same extent as common carriers." While the loss of a guest's personal property was "presumptive evidence of negligence," the innkeeper could rebut this presumption. Story concluded that an innkeeper was not "liable (it should seem) for a loss by robbery and burglary by persons from without the inn."[7] Despite subsequent changes, however, the law governing innkeepers during Jackson's tenure on the bench apparently imposed strict liability for theft.

William Reading is reported to have been a native of Maryland who subsequently practiced law in Logan County, Kentucky.[8]

Ezekiel Douglass was a brother of one of the justices of the Sumner County Court of Pleas and Quarter Sessions, Edward Douglass, Jr.[9]

6. Quinton v. Courtney, 2 N.C. (1 Hayw.) 51 (1794). Kent initially adopted the strict liability theory. Kent, *Commentaries on American Law,* II, 458–462.

7. Joseph Story, *Commentaries on the Law of Bailments* (Cambridge, 1832), 308, 309. By 1840, Kent had modified his position, declaring that an innkeeper's responsibility did not extend "to loss occasioned by inevitable casualty, or by superior force, as robbery." James Kent, *Commentaries on American Law,* 5th ed. (New York, 1840), II, 592.

8. James F. Hopkins, ed., *The Papers of Henry Clay* (Lexington, 1959), I, 53n.

9. Jay G. Cisco, *Historic Sumner County, Tennessee, with Genealogies of the Bledsoe, Cage and Douglas Families, and Genealogical Notes of Other Sumner County Families* (Nashville, 1909), 203, 204. For Edward Douglass, Jr., see Part IV.

I. DECLARATION OF WILLIAM
READING

Mero District Superior Court, Nashville

November 1797

State of Tennessee, District of Mero November Term 1797
William Reading Complains of Ezekiel Douglass in Custody &c for that whereas according to the Law and Custom of England, which Law is in

forse in the State and district aforesaid Inn keepers who keep Common Inns to entertain persons travelling by the Places where Such Common Inns are kept by day and night are to keep and preserve Such Guests and their Goods and Chattles and also the goods and Chattles of any other, being in the Lawfull Custody of Such in keepers, within the Said Inns without Subtraction or Loss, so that by the default of the said Inn keeper or their Servants any Damage or loss should in no wise happen to the Said Guests or any other, having goods and Chattles in the Lawfull Custody of Such Innkeepers in Such inns and whereas the Said Ezekiel, the fourth day of October one Thousand seven hundred and ninety four was an Inn keeper and held a Common Inn, at Sumner County in the district aforesaid at the Court House in Said County to entertain persons travelling by Said Court House & Sojourned in the Said inn and the Said William reading travelling by Said Court House Sojourned in the Said inn of the Said Ezekiel the Same day and year aforesaid and then and there delivered into the Lawfull Custody of the Said Ezekiel a Certain Bay Horse of the Value of two hundred Dollars money of the united States belonging to the Said William and which Horse the Said Ezekiel then and there had in his Lawfull Custody in the Said Inn, Yet the Said Ezekiel by the default and Negligence of himself and his Servants did then and there permit the Said Horse to Escape and run away out of his Said Lawfull Custody as aforesaid whereby the Said Horse was wholly lost by Said William to wit at the Court House aforesaid and other wrongs to the Said William did against the Law and Custom aforesaid and to the Damage of the Said William of two hundred Dollars, and also whereas the Said William the said fourth day of October one thousand Seven hundred and Ninety four at Sumner County aforesaid was possessed of a Certain other bay Horse of the value of two hundred Dollars as of his own proper Goods and Chattles and being So possessed thereof the Said William Casually lost the Said Horse out of his hands and possession which Said Horse afterwards to wit the Same day and year at Sumner County aforesaid Came to the hands and possession of the Said Ezekiel by finding: yet the Said Ezekiel knowing the Said last mentioned Horse to be the property of the Said William and of right to belong to him, but Contriving and fraudulently intending craftily and Subtelly to deceive and defraud the Said William in this Behalf, hath not delivered the Said Horse to the Said William (Tho' often requested) but afterwards to wit, the Same day and year aforesaid at Sumner County aforesaid Converted and disposed of the Said Horse to the Said Ezekiel's own proper use to the Damage of the Said William of two hundred Dollars and thereupon he brings Suit

Andrew Jackson pro Quer.

Tr, TDaCo-MDSC Law Min. Bk., 1788–1803, pp. 223–224.

II. MINUTE BOOK ENTRY

Mero District Superior Court, Nashville
Judges Jackson, Roane, and Campbell Presiding

[November 15, 1798]

Thursday the Honble. Court met agreable to adjournment.
Present the Honble. Archibald Roane ⎫
               Andrew Jackson & ⎬ Esquires, Judges &c.
               David Campbell ⎭

. . . .

William Reading ⎫
     vs   ⎬   Case, Be it remembered that
Ezekiel Douglass ⎭   Ezekiel Douglass was attached
to answer William Reading in a Plea of Trespass on the Case and at this
Term the Parties appearing in Court by their attornies and being ready for
trial[1] . . . and the defendant in this Suit by James DoHertie his attorney
Comes into Court and defends the forse and injury &c when and where
he ought &c and Says that he is not Guilty of the premises in manner or
form as the Plaintiff in either of his Counts in his declaration against him
has Alledged and of this he puts himself upon the Country, James DoHertie atto. for deft and the Said Plaintiff in like manner T Stuart atto. for
Plff, and thereon Came a Good and Lawfull Jury to wit, David Hamilton
James Dean, Isaac Phillips, John Buckhanon, Michael Gleaves, Nimrod
Williams, William Murray, James Wilson, Peter Luna (H), Griswold Latimer, John Wilson, James Rankin, who being Elected tried and Sworn
truely to try the issue Joined between the Parties, the Witnessess being
Examined and Counsel heard on both Sides, retire, return and Say they
find the issue in favor of the defendant.

MS, TDaCo-MDSC Law Min. Bk., 1788–1803, pp. 223–224. Date is taken from *id.* at
223.

    1. The text of Document I occurs at this point in the MS.

17. Embree v. McFerran

1799
(Contracts)

BLAND'S STATEMENT OF THE CASE
AND MINUTES OF THE OPINIONS
OF THE COURT

Washington District Superior Court, Jonesboro
Judges Jackson, Roane, and Campbell Presiding

[September 1799]
Thomas Embree vrs Andrew McFerran

This was an action of assumpsit commenced in the County Court of Washington, and was brought here by Certiorari. the action was founded on an open account which the Plaintiff was allowed to prove by virtue of the Act of Assembly;[1] several items of the Account were for *Timber* & the like *Lent,* with out specifying the price or quantity.

On the trial it was urged by Mr. Rhea in the defence that such itims ought to be struck out.

[The Opinion of Judge Jackson]

Jackson J: If such accounts were admitted it would be opening a door to infinite fraud, which never could have been the intention of the makers of the Book debt Law. Every item of an account proven by the party's own oath ought to be specifically described so that the opponent may have it in his power to rebut the charge.

[The Opinion of Judge Roane]

Roane J: It appears to me that whenever Debits of that general nature are allowed; Credits of as general a nature may also be proven.

MS, MdHi-Bland Casebook, 15–16, Bland Papers (MS 134). Date is taken from *id.* at 11. Bland's statement of final disposition: "upon which the pa[r]ties agreed to strike out all vague items both debit & credit. Verdict & Judgment for the Plaintiff." *Id.* at 16. No further records have been found.

Embree, father of the Rogersville abolitionist newspaper editor Elihu Embree, had moved to Washington County from Pennsylvania about 1780. Originally a Quaker minister, Embree in January 1797 had called for the formation of a society in Washington and Greene counties whose members were to work for "the relief of such of their fellow creatures as are illegally held in bondage." Embree operated an ironworks in east Tennessee near Bumpass Cove until about 1800. *Knoxville Gazette*, Jan. 28, 1797; Raymond F. Hunt, Jr., "The Pactolus Ironworks," 25 *THQ* 181 (1966). McFerran has not been identified.

1. Ch. 4, 1759 Laws of N.C., reprinted in 1 Scott, *Laws of Tennessee* 89.

18. State v. Thompson et al.

1799
(Criminal Law)

BLAND'S STATEMENT OF THE CASE
AND MINUTES OF THE ARGUMENT
OF COUNSEL AND OF THE OPINIONS
OF THE COURT

Washington District Superior Court, Jonesboro
Judges Jackson, Roane, and Campbell Presiding

[September 1799]
State vrs John Thompson et al:

This was an Indictment against one Jones & two others for an Assault and Battery committed on the body of one Amis in Hawkins County, Jones and his companion in guilt had been apprehended by virtue of warrant from a Justice of peace, and on their being bro't before the Magistrate he demanded of them security for their appearanc at the next county Court, John Thompson became their security, The Recognizance into which they entered made no difference between Thomson the Bail and the persons charged with the offence so that it appeared from the face of it that the person therein named were equally culpable. This Recognizance had been in some way lodged among the records in the County Court of Hawkins but was not regularly certified up. In   ¹ term of Hawkins Court there were Indictments found against Jones & others for committing the said Battery and Capias issued accordingly; af[t]er two nihils Judgment was entered up against John Thompson as Bail for their appearance. thus stood the case when it was bro't here by Certiorari

It was now proposed by the Court as a question previous to the consideration of any thing else whether the Errors on the Record could be taken advantage of in the shape in which the case now presents itself to the court to wit after final Judgment has been entered up?

[John Rhea and Joseph Hamilton for the State]

Rhea & Hamilton on the part of the state contended that the party's only relief was a writ of Error

[Theodorick Bland and Townshend Stuart Dade for Defendant Thompson]

Bland & Dade on behalf of Thompson urged that the record stands here in the same situation that it did in the Court below; a Certiorari removes a cause from an inferior to a superior Court liable to and incumbered with all its errors & imperfections and gives the Court to which it is removed as full power over it as if it had originated in that court. that being the case this Court may at any stage of the case as in other Cases see 4 Bacon 44[2] ex officio, inorder to save time trouble & expens lay their hands on an Erroneous record arrest its vicious proceeding and say that it shall be a mere nullity. The Errors in this Record are so glaring manifest and egregious that they cannot escape the observation of the Court. It seems from 2 H.H.P.C. 210[3] that this was the old practice in England instead of a writ of Error Why were the makers of our Cons[ti]tution so attentive to secure to the citizens of this state the right of obtaining a Certiorari were it not that they conceived that writ to be of such a general nature as to comprehend almost every possible case.

[The Opinion of Judge Jackson]

Jackson J: There is no doubt but the record stands here in the same situation it did in the inferior Court: but the question is whether the Court below could take notice of errors apparent on the record after final Judgment entered up. I think not, without a writ of Error; for all the cases prove to my mind that the Court can only ex officio take notice of the errors so long as the proceedings remain *in fieri* which is not the case after final Judgment; Therefore I am clearly of opinion that the party's only relief is by writ of Error

[The Opinion of Judge Campbell]

Campbell J: From the Constitution I am clearly of opinion the Errors may be taken advantage of by writ of Certiorari & I have been long of this opinion.

[The Opinion of Judge Roane]

Roane J: It has been the practice heretofore in this country to take advantage of Errors in this manner by Certiorari; and the Law read by the Bar from Hale seems to insinuate that such was the practice in England I am therefore of opinion the Deft Thompson may proceed to take advantage of the errors on this record in this way.

R[h]ea & Hamilton were then heard in behalf of the state in support of
the Recognizance.

Dade was about to proceed in behalf of Thompson but was stoped by
the Court who said the Errors were too apparent and egregious to need
any argument

The proceedings were quashed as to John Thompson. The others not
appearing in person or by Counsel the Court would take no notice of the
record as to them.

MS, MdHi-Bland Casebook, 25–29, Bland Papers (MS 134). Date is taken from *id.* at 11.
No further records have been found. Thompson has not been identified.

1. Blank in MS.
2. 4 Bacon, *Abridgment* 44.
3. 2 Hale, *Pleas of the Crown* 210.

19. Mitchell v. Berry

1799
(Procedure)

EDITORIAL NOTE

At the same court term in Jonesboro at which he delivered the opinions in the two preceding cases, Jackson rendered brief rulings for the court in the present case and in the case that follows, No. 20, upon the nature of the writ of certiorari as a procedural feature of the Tennessee court structure.

The pertinent facts in this case arose before Jackson's elevation to the bench. On December 21, 1795, James Berry and Gideon Smith executed a promissory note for £150 payable to Jesse Dodd on March 1, 1796 (Document I). On March 15, 1796, Dodd assigned the note to Richard Mitchell in exchange for Mitchell's becoming surety on bail bonds in several suits then pending against the assignor in the Hawkins County court (Document II).[1] On December 1, 1796, Dodd executed a release of Berry and Smith on the note in exchange for $500 (Document III), with which sum Dodd evidently was to have repurchased the note from Mitchell. Mitchell refused to relinquish the note, however, and instead on January 18, 1797, brought the present debt action in the Hawkins County court against Berry to recover on the note.[2]

Berry entered a confession of judgment in the action. He later claimed that he had done so on the assurance of both Dodd and Mitchell that a credit would be entered upon the record of the judgment for the sum of £50, which Berry claimed he had paid Dodd in partial liquidation of the note before he had had notice of the assignment of the instrument to Mitchell. When Mitchell refused to enter any credit upon the record after judgment had been entered, Berry secured from one of the Superior Court judges a writ of certiorari removing the action to the Washington District Superior Court of Law.[3]

1. Answer of Richard Mitchell, Berry v. Mitchell, WDSC Eq. Rec. Bk., 1791–1803, p. 129.
2. Declaration of James Berry, *id.* at 118.
3. *Id.* at 120–121.

The case came before the court in September 1799. After Berry's counsel had failed to secure from the court a continuance to the next term, Mitchell's counsel entered a motion to set aside the writ of certiorari on the ground that Berry's petition had failed to set forth sufficient grounds for the removal of the action to the court (Document IV).

Jackson, speaking for the court, granted Mitchell's motion, set aside the writ of certiorari, and granted Mitchell a writ of procedendo returning the action to the Hawkins court for further proceedings. In his ruling for the court, Jackson held that a writ of certiorari properly would be issued by the court or any of its judges only (a) when the facts in a complainant's petition, assuming them to be true, revealed that an injustice had been sustained by the complainant or (b) when the nature of the complainant's case was such that relief could not properly be sought in a court of equity. When an individual member of the court during recess granted a writ of certiorari in the absence of either of these requirements, Jackson continued, then the full court would set the writ aside as having been improvidently granted (Document IV).

Berry subsequently sought relief on the equity side of the court in the form of a petition submitted to Jackson for the issuance of an injunction against execution of the judgment Mitchell had obtained against him in the Hawkins County court. Jackson issued the injunction and subpoenaed Mitchell, Dodd, and a third party to appear and answer Berry's complaint at the court's March Term 1800. When a final hearing was held on Berry's bill on March 15, the court dissolved the injunction.[4]

Mitchell had been commissioned by Governor Blount as clerk of the Hawkins County court in November 1790 and had served as county treasurer in 1792. He had represented the county at the convention that met in Knoxville in February 1796 to frame the state's first constitution, where both he and Jackson were aligned with the faction led by Governor Blount.[5]

Berry likewise had represented Hawkins County at the 1796 constitutional convention, where he was aligned with the moderate block of delegates. He had been commissioned by Governor Blount as a justice of the Hawkins County court in November 1790.[6]

Dodd has not been identified. Smith, who also has not been identified, does not appear to have participated in the litigation in any way.

---

4. *Id.* at 123–124, 131.
5. Blount, *Journal,* 36; Barnhart, "The Tennessee Constitution of 1796," p. 543 n.41. See *Knoxville Gazette,* Jan. 12, 1793.
6. Blount, *Journal,* 36; Barnhart, "The Tennessee Constitution of 1796," p. 543 n.41.

I. PROMISSORY NOTE,
JAMES BERRY AND
GIDEON SMITH TO JESSE DODD

December 21, 1795
Hawkins County

we or either of us do promise to pay to Jessee Dodd or his order the Just and full sum of one hundred and fifty pounds on or before the first day of March Ensuing the date hereof for Value received of him as Witness our hands this twenty first day of December one thousand seven hundred and Ninety five.

Test Dav Larkin   James Berry
        his   Gidion Smith
James X Johnson
      mark

Tr, TWashCo-WDSC Eq. Rec. Bk., 1791–1803, p. 124; Exhibit No. 1, Declaration of James Berry, *Berry v. Mitchell* (1800).

II. ASSIGNMENT, JESSE DODD
TO RICHARD MITCHELL

March 15, 1796

I do assign over unto Richard Mitchel a Note of hand on James Berry and Gidion Smith for one hundred and fifty pounds bearing date the 21st day of December 1795 and due the first day of March 1796 for Value Received of him the said Richard Mitchel this 15th March 1796.

Jes. Dodd

Tr, TWashCo-WDSC Eq. Rec. Bk., 1791–1803, p. 125; Exhibit No. 3, Declaration of James Berry, *Berry v. Mitchell* (1800).

III. RELEASE OF JAMES BERRY
AND GIDEON SMITH

December 1, 1796

Know all men by these presents that I Jessee Dodd of Hawkins County have Remised Released & for ever quit Claim & by these presents for me my heirs excrs. adm[rs.] do remise release James Berry and Gideon Smith of a bond bearing date the twenty first day of december Ninety five for the Sum of five hundred Dollars Given unto said Dodd—all of Hawkins County also James Berry & Gideon Smith Heirs Excrs. adm[rs.] in all manner of Suits actions or Causes whatever the said Dodd has forwarned Richard Mitchel who detained the bond under no pretens whatsoever to bring suit or make use of his Name in bringing Suit against the above Named persons—as I the said Dodd have Receivd. full Satisfaction for the amount of the bond in Witness my hand and Seal this 1st day of December 1796

Test David Larkin   Jessee Dodd (Seal)

Tr, TWashCo-WDSC Eq. Rec. Bk., 1791–1803, p. 124; Exhibit No. 2, Declaration of James Berry, *Berry v. Mitchell* (1800).

IV. BLAND'S MINUTES OF THE
ARGUMENT OF COUNSEL AND
OF JACKSON'S RULING FOR THE
COURT

Washington District Superior Court, Jonesboro
Judges Jackson, Roane, and Campbell Presiding

[September 1799]
Richard Mitchell Assee. vrs James Berry

This was an Action of Debt brought here from the County Court of Hawkins by Certiorari.

[The Argument of Counsel and the Court's Response]

Rhea in the Defence urged that this case ought to be continued of course like a case just put at issue, and also the Jury cannot try any case not at issue when the venire facias is awarded.

By the Court[:] as to that Jurors are summoned to try all cases regularly triable this is such a one, and the court will not continue this sooner than any other cause without reasons shewn.

No cause being shewn for a continuance. Miller for the Plaintiff then moved to set aside the Certiorari merely on the insufficency of the Petition on which it was granted.

[The Ruling of Judge Jackson]

Jackson J: Where it appears by the facts stated in the Petition (admitting them to be true), the party has not had injustice done him, or that the nature of his case is such that he ought to go into a Court [of] Equity this Court will not grant a Certiorari and if granted during vacation they will set it aside. Now it is manifest from the Petition that there has been no injustice done consequently the Certiorari must be set aside

By the Whole Court Certiorari and Supersedeas set aside & Procedendo awarded.

MS, MdHi-Bland Casebook, 17–19, Bland Papers (MS 134). Date is taken from *id.* at 11.

20. Craft v. Flora

1799
(Procedure)

BLAND'S STATEMENT OF THE CASE
AND MINUTES OF JACKSON'S OPINION
FOR THE COURT

Washington District Superior Court, Jonesboro
Judges Jackson, Roane, and Campbell Presiding

[September 1799]
Jacob Craft vrs Daniel Flora

This was an action of assumpsit brought here from Hawkins County court by Certiorari together with several other cases of a like nature between the same Parties.

Miller on the part of Craft agreed to submit this with the rest entirely to the Court on the Petition for the certiorari alone—and all but this one were remanded to the court below on the principles of the case of Mitchell vrs Berry ante 17.[1]

[The Opinion of Judge Jackson]

As to this case Judge Jackson said It appears to me to be the object of our Constitution in allowing a certiorari, that the parties might have complete justice done them; consequently whenever that is on oath stated not to have been done the Superior Courts will grant a Certiorari in order that a full rehearing may be had in the case; but otherwise where tis plain from the party's own shewing that, that is not the case, or that he cannot have relief in this Court. In this case the Defendant has sworn that injustice has been done him and also states the reasons why; therefore the Court will not quash this Certiorari. of this opinion were the whole Court Cause Continued.

MS, MdHi-Bland Casebook, 22–23, Bland Papers (MS 134). Date is taken from *id.* at 11.
   Neither of the parties has been identified. No further records have been found; final disposition of case is unknown.

   1. *Mitchell v. Berry,* No. 19.

21. Love v. Duncan

1799
(Procedure)

EDITORIAL NOTE

Afflicted with an occasional flare-up of rheumatism and a cold contracted while traveling, Jackson arrived in Knoxville on September 17, 1799, from the session in Jonesboro during which the preceding four cases had been decided.[1] Docketed for a hearing when the court convened on the following Monday was a motion in arrest of judgment in the present case, which was before the court on a writ of certiorari from the Knox County court.

The case had arisen nearly three years earlier. Late in 1796, John Love obtained from Justice Joseph Greer, a member of the Knox County court, a judgment against Stephen Duncan for the sum of $8.45 plus costs. The judgment represented the balance Duncan owed for brick that he had purchased from Love earlier that year. Greer erroneously omitted the word "dollars" from the execution that he issued upon the judgment. When a constable attempted to collect the judgment, Duncan evidently convinced him that the judgment was for only forty-five cents. Paying the constable fifty cents and assuring him that he would himself return the execution to Justice Greer to correct the mistake, Duncan retained the execution and procured a receipt from the constable either for the fifty cents or for an unspecified sum. Love refused to accept the amount tendered by Duncan and returned the money. Duncan, however, refused to relinquish any of the documents that the constable had turned over to him. When he also refused to settle the matter amicably, Love obtained a writ of certiorari to remove the proceedings to the full county court.[2]

The case eventually was tried in the Knox County court in January 1798. At the trial, Duncan introduced into evidence a document purported to be a receipt signed by the constable for the full amount of the

1. AJ to Rachel Jackson, Sept. 17, 1799, *Jackson Papers*, I, 223–224.
2. Duncan v. Love and Robertson, HDSC Eq. Rec. Bk. B, 1797–1804, pp. 50–57 (1800).

judgment. Love disputed the authenticity of the document but was unable to produce the original receipt, because that document and all others relating to the proceedings before Justice Greer were still in Duncan's possession. A jury returned a verdict for Love for the same amount as the judgment that Greer had awarded (Document II). After the court denied a motion by the defendant for a new trial, Duncan obtained a writ of certiorari to remove the cause to the Hamilton District Superior Court.

When the case went to trial there on March 28, 1799, a jury returned a verdict for Love.[3] Duncan entered a motion in arrest of judgment during the court's ensuing summer recess. In his motion, Duncan asserted that the county court had erred in denying his similar post-verdict motion on two grounds (see Document III). First, although the records are not entirely clear on the point, Duncan evidently asserted either that Love had failed to produce any of the original documents from the proceedings before the justice of the peace or that Justice Greer had entered Love's judgment without first having summoned Duncan to appear before him to enter a defense in the action.[4] Second, Duncan asserted that there had been no issue properly joined before the county court.

The court denied the motion after a hearing in late September. Jackson delivered an opinion in which he declared that, on the first ground asserted by Duncan, the jury's verdict in the county court had cured any prior defects in the proceedings and that, on the second ground, any defect in the proper joining of an issue below likewise had been cured by the jury's verdict (Document III). Judge Roane delivered an opinion concurring with Jackson's views on the latter issue.

Jackson's views on the curative effect of a jury verdict in an appeal from a determination by a single justice upon a failure to join issue properly were reflected in at least two subsequent Tennessee decisions. In *M'Cutchen v. Owen*, 1 Tenn. (1 Overton) 365 (1808), an action had been initiated before a justice of the peace, appealed to the county court, and removed to the Superior Court upon a writ of certiorari. The court in a per curiam opinion held that, because suits before individual justices were determined without pleadings, the county court jury on an appeal from a single magistrate's determination was required to try "the matter in dispute" rather than the issue as in other cases. The court reaffirmed

3. HDSC Law Min. Bk. 3, 1793–1809, p. 173.
4. The uncertainty arises from Bland's version of this ground as "for the want of an original prceipt" (Document III). It cannot be determined whether Bland's "prceipt" was intended as "receipt" or "precept," a warrant or order by an individual justice to bring a party before him. Henry C. Black, *Law Dictionary*, 4th ed. (St. Paul, 1968), 1340. The latter seems as plausible as the former in the light of the attention that Justice Greer devoted in Document I to his issuance of a warrant and in the light of Greer's acknowledgment that Love's judgment had been entered without Duncan's having made an appearance.

this view in *Baker v. Allen,* 2 Tenn. (2 Overton) 175 (1812), in which the defendant in an action initiated before a single justice but later tried before a jury at the county court level sought to reverse the decisions below on the ground, *inter alia,* that no issue had been joined for the jury to try. Judge White delivered an opinion for the court affirming the lower proceedings:

> [I]n proceedings before justices there is no law which requires any pleadings to be made up, nor is there any law requiring a written statement of the nature of the demand. If the defendant is a second time sued for the same claim, he must protect himself by averring and proving that there was a previous recovery thereof. The defendant is not, in this case, in a worse situation than many defendants in actions of assumpsit, where the declaration does not show precisely how the demand accrued, and the defendants have no other protection against a second suit than that which this defendant has.
>
> . . . [T]he law does not require that any issue should have been made up. The jury are sworn to try the matter in controversy, and if this objection were to prevail, it would be a total departure from the universal practice for at least the last fifteen years.
>
> Proceedings in actions of this kind, which are directed by law to be conducted in a summary way, ought to be favored as much as the rules prescribed by the legislature will permit; and it is not perceived that any of those rules have been departed from in this case.

2 Tenn. (2 Overton) at 175–176 (citations omitted).

Love has not been further identified.

Duncan, a Knoxville merchant, subsequently was a defendant in a murder trial that attracted as much, if not more, public attention as any during Jackson's years on the bench. In May 1803 the Knox County sheriff and a party attempted to serve an arrest warrant upon Joseph Duncan and John Childress, both of whom evidently had taken refuge in a vacant house along with Stephen Duncan, the present defendant, who was not named in the warrant. The three refused to surrender, an altercation ensued, and, when the sheriff and his party attempted to storm the house, Stephen Duncan "poured the contents of his piece into the bowels of Joseph Ravenhill, who expired in ten hours after."[5] The three eventually were captured, confined in the district jail, and charged with Ravenhill's murder. In mid-July, after learning from the sheriff that the jail was "verry insufficient" for the prisoners' safekeeping, Governor Roane authorized Jackson and the other two judges to convene a court of oyer and terminer and to try the three defendants prior to the court's September Term.[6] No such proceedings ensued, however, and the prisoners were not tried until

5. *Tennessee Gazette,* June 8, 1803. See Hunt v. Duncan, HDSC Law Rec. Bk. C, 1798–1803, p. 13 (1799).

6. Archibald Roane to AJ, David Campbell, and Hugh Lawson White, July 15, 1803, *Jackson Papers,* I, 336–337.

October. Jackson presided at the trials, along with Judges White and Campbell. A jury found Stephen Duncan guilty on October 5. On October 6, Joseph Duncan was convicted only of the felonious slaying of the deceased, and Childress was convicted of murder two days later. Stephen Duncan and Childress were sentenced by the court to be hanged.[7] In response to a letter from Judge White and petitions signed by Judge Campbell, the jurors who convicted Joseph Duncan, virtually every member of the Tennessee legislature, and several prominent Knoxville citizens, Governor Sevier pardoned all three of the defendants. Jackson, possibly because the trial and the requests for executive clemency occurred at the height of his controversy with Sevier and at a time when rumors were circulating about his retirement from the bench, was the only one of the three judges who declined to join in petitioning the governor.[8]

7. HDSC Law Min. Bk. 3, 1793–1809, pp. 337–340. For an additional account of the trials, see Marquis James, *Andrew Jackson, the Border Captain* (New York, 1933), 98–99, which erroneously states that Stephen Duncan was acquitted. The results of the trials were reported in the *Tennessee Gazette*, Oct. 19, 1803.

8. The petitions, White's letter, and Sevier's pardons are in Governors' Papers, 1803–1809, T. For Jackson's controversy with Sevier, see the Introduction and *Jackson Papers*, I, 367–384 *passim*; for Jackson's response to rumors about an impending retirement, see *id.* at 372–374.

I. JUSTICE JOSEPH GREER'S RETURN
TO THE KNOX COUNTY COURT'S
WRIT OF CERTIORARI

Knox County Court of Pleas and
Quarter Sessions, Knoxville

July 28, 1797

John Love ⎫
vs.   ⎬
Stephen Duncan ⎭

In Obedience to a writ of Certiorari to me directed I do hereby Certify the following return viz "That on the   [1] day of   [1] 1797 John Love applied to and obtained from me a warrant against Stephen Duncan for Debt directed to the proper Officer to execute and return that on the   [1] day of   [1] the warrant was returned to me executed At the day appointed for trial before me John Love the Plaintiff appeared but the Defendant did not appear, That after the Plaintiff having established his Debt by proof, I gave Judgment against the said Defendant Stephen Duncan for the sum of eight Dollars and forty five Cents that with a Copy of the Plaintiff['s] account and the paper on which Judgment was rendered I issued execution against the said Defendant Stephen Duncan for (as I at the time Conceived) the sum of eight Dollars and forty five cents together with the Costs of suit; But I am now Convinced that by mistake in issuing the Execution the word Dollars is omitted to be inserted which makes the Execution as to the sum therein expressed read thus eight forty five Cents, instead of eight Dollars and forty five Cents that the Execution issued as aforesaid was put into the hands of James Robertson a Constable for Knox County, that the said Constable has never returned the said Execution or any of the papers which Accompanied it to me that I have applied to the said Constable to return the papers to me, together with the execution, That the said Constable informed me he coould if he could get them of the Defendant Duncan and understood by the Constable at the same time that the Defendant Duncan paid to him fifty Cents, and that a receipt was given to the said Duncan for the said sum of fifty on the said Execution, and left it Together with the other papers before mentioned in the possession of the said Defendant Stephen Duncan—All which I do Certify to the worshipful the Court to be held for Knox County as I was Commanded to do by the said writ of Certiorari Witness my hand & Seal at Knoxville in the County of Knox this 28th day of July Anno Domini 1797.

Joseph Greer (LS)

Tr, TKL-HDSC Law Rec. Bk. C, 44–45.

1. Blank in Tr.

II. TRANSCRIPT OF THE COUNTY
COURT PROCEEDINGS

Knox County Court of Pleas and Quarter
Sessions, Knoxville

January 1798

Be it remembered that at a Court of Pleas and Quarter Sessions began and held for the County of Knox at the Court house in Knoxville on the last Monday of July One thousand seven hundred and Ninety seven Joseph Greer esquire made the following return to a writ of Certiorari to him directed, to wit[1] . . . .

Which cause was entered upon the trial Docket and Continued from

Term to Term until January Sessions 1798 at which time came the Plaintiff
by Hugh L White and Drury W Breazeale his Attornies and also the Defendant by Joseph Anderson and John Rhea his Attornies and thereupon
came a Jury, to wit Richard Richardson, Robert Patterson, John Preston
James Black, Peter McNamee, James Bartley, John Bryan, James Thompson
John Bounds, Hiram Geran, Martin Pruit and Henry Roberts who being
elected tried and sworn well and truly to try the matter in dispute between
the Parties upon their Oath do say they find for the Plaintiff his Debt of
eight Dollars and forty five Cents and Costs of suit, Whereupon the Plaintiff was put under a rule to shew cause why a new trial should not be
granted which rule was discharged. It is Therefore considered by the
Court that the Plaintiff do recover against the said Defendant the aforesaid
sum of eight Dollars forty five Cents and Costs in the Verdict of the Jury
aforesaid assessed and the said Defendant be in mercy &c.

Tr, TKL-HDSC Law Rec. Bk. C, 44–45.

1. The text of Document I follows at this point in the Tr.

III. BLAND'S MINUTES OF THE
OPINIONS OF THE COURT

Hamilton District Superior Court, Knoxville
Judges Jackson, Roane, and Campbell Presiding

[September 1799]
John Love vrs Stephen Duncan

This case had been brought by Certiorari from before a Magistrate
into the County Court of Knox and from thence here by Certiorari.
While the case remained in the County Court reasons in arrest of Judgment were filed which were overruled and they were now taken up and
argued the four first in substance were for the want of an original prceipt[1]
the last was for the want of an issue in the County Court.

[The Opinion of Judge Jackson]

Jackson J: As to the four first reason which go to the want of an original 'tis now too late for the party to avail himself of them; they should
have been taken advantage of before Verdict as they are cured by it. so
also is the want of an Issue cured by Verdict. However as this case originated before a Justice of the Peace it is entirely different from those em-

braced by the Statutes of Jeofail,[2] for our Act of Assembly seems to intend they should be tried speedily just in the situation they come up in[3]

[The Opinion of Judge Roane]

Roane J: I shall not give any opinion as to the four first points But as to the last I think the reason is of no weight. In all cases except such a one as is now before the Court the Court have some legal mode of compelling the parties to make up an issue; but in the case of an appeal from a Justice of the Peace there is no way of doing it. Besides the Law says appeals must be tried the first Term, from hence we may resonably infer that it is the intention of the Act that in such cases the usual formularies of the proceedings in Courts should be dispensed with and the cause heard sans cerimonei upon the merits merely.

MS, MdHi-Bland Casebook, 32–34, Bland Papers (MS 134). Date is taken from *id.* at 30 and corresponds with HDSC Law Rec. Bk. C, 45. Bland's statement of the final disposition of the case: "Reasons overruled Judgment for the Plaintiff."

1. See Editorial Note, note 4 above.
2. One of the purposes of the English statutes of amendment and jeofails, which enabled a pleader to acknowledge and amend any error in the form of his pleadings, was to avoid frivolous appeals by writs of error brought upon slight and trivial grounds. See 3 Blackstone, *Commentaries* 406.
3. Ch. 1, § 54, 1794 Terr. S. of River Ohio Acts, reprinted in 1 Scott, *Laws of Tennessee* 457. The corresponding provision of the 1777 North Carolina statute had provided that such appeals were to be tried "in a summary Way." Ch. 2, § 70, 1777 Laws of N.C. (Nov. Sess.), reprinted in Iredell, *Laws of North Carolina* 296, 1 Scott, *Laws of Tennessee* 165.

22. Finley v. McClung

1799
(Property)

EDITORIAL NOTE

This ejectment action arose between a judgment debtor whose land had been sold at a sheriff's sale and a defendant who had purchased from the original buyer of the debtor's land (see Document IV). John Finley, the debtor, filed his declaration against the ultimate purchaser, Charles McClung, in the Hamilton District Superior Court in April 1798 (Document I). The matter came on for trial late in the court's September Term 1799, on October 1, at which time a jury returned a verdict for McClung (Document II). Finley's counsel, Jenkin Whiteside, filed a motion for a new trial on the grounds (a) that the judgment giving rise to the sale of his land had already been satisfied and (b) that the sheriff's sale had been illegal because it had not been advertised as required by law and that, as a result, Finley had had no notice that the property was to be sold (Document III). Whiteside argued that there was English precedent for the authority of the court to examine the legality of sheriff's sales. McClung's counsel, Townshend S. Dade, argued that the uncertainty that would result from the court's scrutinizing the legality of sheriff's sales would have the undesirable effect of discouraging purchasers at such sales.

The court denied Finley's motion for a new trial. Speaking for the court, Jackson asserted that, as a rule, the legality of sheriff's sales was not subject to court scrutiny. A party alleging fraud in the conduct of a sheriff's sale, Jackson declared, must seek relief on the equity side (Document IV). Judge Roane concurred in Jackson's decision.[1]

1. Finley has not been further identified; for biographical data about McClung, see Part IV.

I. DECLARATION AND NOTICE
IN EJECTMENT

Hamilton District Superior Court, Knoxville

[April 1798]

State of Tennessee Hamilton District Superior Court of Law John Den Complains of Richard Fen now in Custody of the Sheriff &c. for that Whereas John Finley on the first day of March in the year of our Lord One thousand seven hundred and Ninety eight at 　　¹to wit at Knoxville in the County of Knox within the District aforesaid, had demised, granted and to farm let unto the said John Den a certain parcel and tract of Land in the County of Knox, in the said District and State situate lying and being as follows, Containing four hundred Acres on the North side of Holston river On the West fork of third Creek, Beginning at a white Oak then North two hundred & forty three poles to a stake, then West two hundred and fifty four poles to a stake then South One hundred and sixty poles to a stake then West sixty five poles to a pine then South eighty four poles crossing the Creek at forty four poles to a stake then East three hundred poles to the Beginning with the Appurtenances to have and to hold the said Lands tenements, and Appurtenances to the said John Den his Assigns from the said First day of March in the year aforesaid to the full end and Term of Ten Years, thence next ensuing and fully to be Complete and ended By Virtue of which said Demise he the said John Den entered into the said Lands and Tenements with the Appurtenances and was thereof possessed until the aforesaid Richard Fen afterwards that is to say On the third day of March in the year aforesaid entered with force and Arms, into the said Tenements with the Appurtenances in And upon the possession of the said John Den, & ejected drove out expelled and removed the said John Den from his said farm during his Term aforesaid, then not yet expired, and the said John Den being so ejected drove out expelled and removed, the said Richard Fen hitherto hath withheld from him & Still doth withold the possession of the said farm, and then and there other injuries did against the peace and dignity of the State to the Damage of him the said John Den One hundred pounds &c. therefore he brings his suit &c. and there are pledges to prosecute &c.

Go. W. Campbell Atto.

Mr. Ignatius Chisolm

I am informed you are in Possession of or claim title to the premises mentioned in the above Decleration of Ejectment, or to some part thereof & I being sued as casual ejector in this Action and having no title to the said Premises do advise you to appear on the fourth Monday in September next at Knoxville, then and there in the Superior Court of Law to be held at said place & time for the District of Hamilton, by some Attorney of said Court, or (by yourself) & by a rule of said Court to cause yourself to be made Defendant in my stead otherwise I shall suffer Judgment to be entered up against me and you will be turned out of possession[.] I am your Friend

Richard Fen

Tr, TKL-HDSC Law Rec. Bk. C, 53–54. The record book indicates that the declaration and notice were filed with the court in September 1798 and that the document contained the following endorsements from which its date has been derived: "Issued April 14th 1798 Delivered the tenant in possession a true Copy of the within Decleration of Ejectment, R Houston, Shff."

1. Blank in Tr.

II. RECORD BOOK ENTRY

*Hamilton District Superior Court, Knoxville
Judges Jackson, Roane, and Campbell Presiding*

[October 1, 1799]

Whereupon[1] came into Court Charles McClung and upon his agreeing to confess lease entry & ouster is Admitted Defendant and by Hugh L White esquire his Attorney defends the force and injury when and where &c and for plea saith that the Plaintiff ought not to have and maintain his Action against him because he saith he is not Guilty as the Plaintiff in his Decleration hath alledged and of this he puts himself On the Country. And the Plaintiff by his Attorney aforesaid doth the same. Whereupon let a Jury Come &c. at March Term 1799 at which Term On Affidavit of the Defendant this cause was Continued until September Term 1799 at which Term came the parties aforesaid by their Attornies aforesaid and thereupon came a Jury, to wit, Isom Gwin Jeremiah Jack, Daniel McPherson, David Adair, Samuel McMullin, William Haislet, John Adair, Andrew Evans, Henry Regan, Thomas Gillespie, Oliver Alexander, Josiah Gamble, who being elected tried and sworn the truth to speak upon the issue joined upon their Oaths do say that the Defendant is not Guilty of the

Trespass in Ejectment in manner and form as the Plaintiff against him hath Complained. Therefore it is Considered by the Court that the Plaintiff take nothing by his bill but for his false Clamor be in mercy &c. and that the Defendant go hereof without day & recover against the Plaintiff his Costs by him about his Defence in this Behalf expended.

MS, TKL-HDSC Law Rec. Bk. C, 53–54. Date is derived from the corresponding trial entry in HDSC Law Min. Bk. 3, p. 191. The minute book indicates that the plaintiff entered a motion for a new trial and that the motion was denied. Argument by counsel and the court's decision on the motion are set forth as Documents III and IV

    1. The text of Document I precedes the entry.

III. BLAND'S STATEMENT OF THE CASE AND MINUTES OF THE ARGUMENT OF COUNSEL ON THE MOTION FOR A NEW TRIAL

Hamilton District Superior Court, Knoxville
Judges Jackson, Roane, and Campbell Presiding

[October 1, 1799]
Den on Dem John Finley vrs Char: McClung

There had been a Verdict in this Case for the Defendant, The Plaintiffs counsel obtained a Rule to shew cause why a new trial should not be granted and the verdict set aside upon the affidavit of Finley to this effect That the Land in dispute had been sold to satisfy an execution against him (Finley) which was at that time satisfied, and also that the sale made by the Sheriff was illegal because he had not advertised the Land for sale as he was directed by Law, by reason of which he (Finley) knew nothing of the sale

[Townshend Stuart Dade for Defendant]

Mr. Dade now shewed cause why a new trial should not be granted

The ground principally relied on is surprize but if Shiriffs sales were allowed thus to be ript up who would purchase at them; the inconveniences of such doctrine are so numerrous & monsterous that the Law will in no case allow it to be done; 2 Bacon 370[1] See 1 Salk: 320 Smallcomb vrs Buckingham[2] a case precisely similar to the one before the Court.

[Jenkin Whiteside for Plaintiff]

Whiteside in support of the Rule[:] The Court have at any time a right and ought to examine into the legality of an execution against real property to prove which he cited & read 2 Bacon 369[3] where an Elegit improperly executed is said to be void much more so ought an execution to be so in this State when the Fee Simple is disposed of. If an Elegit improperly executed is void, there certainly must be a power in the Court to examine into the validity of it indeed the Book last cited expressly says so.

MS, MdHi-Bland Casebook, 35–37, Bland Papers (MS 134). Date is from HDSC Law Min. Bk. 3, p. 191. The term "Den" that Bland includes in the style refers to the fictitious declarant in ejectment, for which see Introduction, p. xxxi; the term "Dem" is an abbreviated form of "demise."

    1. 2 Bacon, *Abridgment* 370.
    2. Smallcomb v. Buckingham, 1 Salk. 320, 91 Eng. Rep. 283; Smallcomb v. Cross and Buckingham, 1 Ld. Raym. 251, 91 Eng. Rep. 1064 (K.B. 1697). This was a trover action against the sheriff of London and the purchaser at a sheriff's sale. Two judgment creditors of one Fox secured writs of fieri facias upon their judgments. Creditor A delivered his writ to the sheriff at nine o'clock in the morning. Creditor B delivered his writ to the sheriff an hour later. The sheriff nevertheless ran an execution upon B's writ, levied upon Fox's goods, and sold them to Smallcomb. Subsequently, the sheriff ran an execution upon A's writ, levied upon the same goods, and sold them to Cross. A unanimous court ruled: "[I]f two writs of execution are delivered to the sheriff the same day, he has not an election to execute which he pleases, but he must execute that which was first delivered. But if the sheriff levies goods in execution by virtue of the writ last delivered, and makes sale of them (whether the last writ was delivered upon the same day or a subsequent day) the property of the goods is bound by the sale, and the party cannot seize them by virtue of his execution first delivered; but he may have his remedy against the sheriff. For sales made by the sheriff ought not to be defeated, for if they are, no man will buy goods levied upon a writ of execution." 1 Ld. Raym. at 252, 91 Eng. Rep. at 1064.
    3. 2 Bacon, *Abridgment* 369.

IV. BLAND'S MINUTES OF JACKSON'S DECISION FOR THE COURT ON THE MOTION FOR A NEW TRIAL

Hamilton District Superior Court, Knoxville
Judges Jackson, Roane, and Campbell Presiding

[October 1, 1799]

Jackson J: Were I of opinion that under the circumstances of this case the Plaintiff could on a new trial go into a scrutiny of the Sheriffs sale agreeable to the rules of Law I would cheerfully grant one but I am of opinion that cannot be done; this case is not at all similar to that in Bacon, the contention here is not between the original parties but between the person against whom the execution issued and one who has bona fide purchased from the person who bought the Land at the Sheriffs sale[.] If there has been fraud in the sale the party must be relieved in Equity. Roane concurred

Rule Discharged

MS, MdHi-Bland Casebook, 37, Bland Papers (MS 134). Date is taken from HDSC Law Min. Bk. 3, p. 191.

23. Crinder v. Willson

1800
(Property)

BLAND'S STATEMENT OF THE CASE
AND MINUTES OF JACKSON'S DECISION
FOR THE COURT

Washington District Superior Court, Jonesboro
Judges Jackson, Roane, and Campbell Presiding

[March 1800]
Joseph Crinder vrs Sam: Willson

This was an Action of Trespass Quaeri Clausum Fregit, to which the Defendant Pleaded first not Guilty—secondly Justification. After both Plff and Deft had produced their Titles The counsel for the Plff moved to introduce testimony to shew that the Defts title was surreptitiously obtained and that a third Person has a better title.

[The Opinion of Judge Jackson]

Jackson J: The issue is first that he (Deft) is not Guilty; secondly Deft says that he is justifiable in doing that with which he is charged because he has good title to the Lands in question, which last issue can only be determined by the title of the *Parties* and the title of a *third Person* cannot be taken into view in this Action; if it were otherwise as has been justly observed (Whiteside)[1] the Deft might be called on to rebut that which he had no conception of. It would be opening a door to strengthen the title of a third Person when he was not a Party and draw him in to take a benefit or sustain an injury without his consent Of this opinion was the whole Court. Testimony not admitted.

MS, MdHi-Bland Casebook, 38–39, Bland Papers (MS 134). Date is taken from *id.* at 38. No further records have been found; neither Crinder nor Willson has been identified.

1. Jenkin Whiteside, for whom see Part IV.

24. McKinley and Holmes v. Rogers & Hagan

1800
(Contracts)

BLAND'S STATEMENT OF THE CASE
AND MINUTES OF THE ARGUMENT
OF COUNSEL AND OF THE OPINIONS
OF THE COURT

Washington District Superior Court, Jonesboro
Judges Jackson, Roane, and Campbell Presiding

[March 1800]
McKinley & Holmes vrs Rogers & Hagan

This was an Action of Assumpsit; the Declaration contained four Counts the first for Goods Wares & Merchandizes, second Quantum Valebant, third Money had & received and the fourth for money Paid laid out & expended—To which, as it had only been filed this term the Defendant had not pled.

[Edward Scott for Defendant]

Scott for the Defendant moved to have the two first Counts in the Declaration struck out because of there being no Account filed with the De[c]laration. He then Read the Act of Assembly (Ire 171 [1] and contended that it embraced all cases it being evidently the object of the Legislature to compel the Plaintiff to shew the Defendant with what he was charged in order that he might be the better enabled to make his defence otherwise it can't be known till trial what testimony the Plaintiff means to rely on; therfore could this Act be eluded the Defendant might be unguardedly drawn in to plead that which he would not have done had he known fully the nature of the demand; which is surely what this Court will never Permit.

[George Duffield for Plaintiff]

Duffield contra. The only question here is whether the Plaintiff is obliged to File his account with his Declaration or not? I do humbly contend he is not, since the Act does not apply in all cases, but only to those individual species of Actions where the Party means to rely on a Book Account substantiated by his own oath & in those cases only to the Evidence. In order to prove this let us take a survey of the manner in which this doctrine relative to Book Debts has been introduced, and the mutations it has undergone. In 3 Black 368[2] we are told it is derived from the civil Law and was admitted merely from necessity, Proof of an open Account by the Party's own oath being often the best which the nature of the case would admit of; but lest this dangerous species of Evidence should be carried to too great lengths the Statute of 7 Jac: 1 cap: 12[3] was passed (which see 2 Bacon 307)[4] to limit define and ascertain in what cases it should be resorted to, leaving the party at his option by bringing himself within the restrictions of the Statute to use the n[e]w statutory evidence, or the common Law mode of Proof for the Support of his Action

this it is clear is the intention & construction of the British Statute from a view of every decision on the subject. That the regulation of a new species of Evidence is manifestly all that Statute contemplates may be seen from a slight glance of the act itself for it leaves the proceedings in all Actions, so far as respects any thing else wholly untouched. Thus stood the Law in England and of course in this Country until the year 1739 (Iredell 83),[5] when there appears to have been an Act Passed in North Carolina on the subject, which Act was repealed by the passage of the one now under consideration (Ire 171)[6] From a general view of the subject from the striking similarity of the English and North Carolina Statutes the intention and construction of the two acts must be the same—and that intention can be nothing else than to regulate a new mode of Proof. and if the Plaintiffs in the present instance have not bro't thems[e]lf within those limits chalked out by the Act, the only consequence is that they cannot avail themselves of that mode of supporting their Action, but must pursue it agreeable to the rules of the Common Law. Our Act of Assembly is in affirmance of and also cumulative to the common Law and such Statutes says 4 Bacon 648[7] leave the Com: Law unimpaired. But if as it has been contended the Account ought indispensably to accompany the Declaration, Why (permit me to ask) Why was it not pled in Abatement or Demurred to. Upon the whole I hope the Court will not, in this summary manner compel us to File an Account or Strike out those Counts when we wave the advantage of this new statutory evidence.

[Jenkin Whiteside for Defendant]

Whiteside in support of the Motion[:] I admit that the object of both the Statutes is to regulate a new species of Evidence The British Statute ascertains and defines that which was vague, our Statute extends and enlarges that which was so defined. The evident intention of the makers of our Act was to do two things, first to regulate a particular sort of Testimony and secondly to regulate & new modle certain Action and the proceedings therein, A view of the whole act will shew this, the first words of the Statute and the 4th Sect manifest it. It is an axiom well settled, that where a statute or positive Law requires a certain thing to be done that thing cannot be dispensed with. This Act does expressly require that the Account should be filed with the Declaration, which has not been done therefore the Declaration must be bad. To recur back to the Law as it stood at the time when this act was passed I think the reason and necessity of filing an account with the Declaration will appear yet more plain. At that time a Defendant could not plead as many several matters as he thot proper, he was obliged to rest his Whole defence on a single plea, and consequently might by the Plaintiff's producing on trial an Account to support his Action of which he had no conception be entraped, wheras had he known of it he might have pled so as to bar a recovery therefore was this Law made, and it is as beneficial to the Defendn[t] as to Plaintiff. I contend further that this fault could not be taken advantage in any other way than this, it could not be pled in abatemen[t] because the Judgment on such Plea must be that the Action be wholly quashed or a Respondeat ouster; neither could it be Demurred to because that must be to something that is apparent on the face of the Record. Superfluous or vicious Counts says Tidd's Practi 140 & 198[8] may be struck on motion   on that authority I think this motion supportable.

[The Opinion of Judge Roane]

Roane J: I am of opinion on the whole Law taken together that an Account must be filed with the Declaration when any of the remedies is pursued that are mentioned in the Act of Assembly. No doubt there may be certain Species of Actions which will not come within this Act, as where there had been goods sold & delivered and a special promis[e] made to pay for them   there an Account would not be necessary   But in other cases within this Act, in order to use that mode of Proof and to prepare the Defendant for his defence the Act must be complied with.

[The Opinion of Judge Jackson]

Jackson J: I concur with the opinion that has been delivered but if it were confined to the first Section of the Law the strong argument that have been adduced would go a great way in opposition   yet considering this Statute with the latter part, as being beneficial for the Defendant as well as for the Plaintiff; I agree with his Honor Judge Roane.

By the whole Court the Motion sustained, the two first Counts struck out of Declaration.

MS, MdHi-Bland Casebook, 40–51, Bland Papers (MS 134). Date is taken from *id.* at 38. No further records have been found; final disposition is unknown.

The Hawkins County mercantile firm of Rogers & Hagan, organized ca. 1787 by Joseph Rogers and James Hagan, had opened the first store at Hawkins Courthouse before 1789. Rogers and Hagan also were brothers-in-law. Weston A. Goodspeed, *A History of Tennessee from the Earliest Time to the Present* (Nashville, 1886), 874. Neither McKinley nor Holmes has been identified.

1. Iredell, *Laws of North Carolina* 171.
2. 3 Blackstone, *Commentaries* 368–369: "[T]he one general rule that runs through all the doctrine of trials is this, that the best evidence the nature of the case will admit of shall always be required, if possible to be had; but, if not possible, then the best evidence that can be had shall be allowed. For if it be found that there is any better evidence existing than is produced, the very not producing it is a presumption that it would have detected some falsehood that at present is concealed. . . . yet in some cases . . . the courts admit of *hearsay* evidence, or an account of what persons deceased have declared in their life-time: but such evidence will not be received of any particular facts. So too, books of account, or shipbooks, are not allowed of themselves to be given in evidence for the owner; but a servant who made the entry may have recourse to them to refresh his memory: and, if such servant (who was accustomed to make those entries) be dead, and his hand be proved, the book may be read in evidence: for, as tradesmen are often under a necessity of giving credit without any note or writing, this is therefore, when accompanied with such other collateral proofs of fairness and regularity, the best evidence that can then be produced. However this dangerous species of evidence is not carried so far in England as abroad; where a man's own books of accounts, by a distortion of the civil law (which seems to have meant the same thing as is practised with us) with the suppletory oath of the merchant, amount at all times to full proof. But as this kind of evidence, even thus regulated, would be much too hard upon the buyer at any long distance of time, the statute 7 Jac. I. c. 12. (the penners of which seem to have imagined that the books of themselves were evidence at common law) confines this species of proof to such transactions as have happened within one year before the action brought; unless between merchant and merchant in the usual intercourse of trade. For accounts of so recent a date, if erroneous, may more easily be unravelled and adjusted."
3. An Act to Avoid the Double Payment of Debts, 7 Jac. 1, ch. 12 (1609).
4. 2 Bacon, *Abridgment* 307.
5. Iredell, *Laws of North Carolina* 83.
6. *Id.* at 171.
7. Probably 4 Bacon, *Abridgment* 647:
    32. The best Construction of a Statute is to construe it as near to the Rule and Reason of the Common Law as may be, and by the Course which that observes in other Cases.
    . . . .
    34. When the Provision of a Statute is general, it is subject to the Controul and Order of the Common Law.
    35. If a new Remedy be given by a Statute in a Particular Case, this shall not be extended to alter the Common Law in any other than that Case.
    . . . .
    37. An obscure Statute ought to be construed according to the Rules of the Common Law.
8. Tidd, *Practical Forms* 140, 198.

25. Smith v. Fitzgerald

1800

(Slavery)

EDITORIAL NOTE

Several months before Jackson's elevation to the bench, Samuel Smith, Sr., brought this trover action in the Hamilton District Superior Court to recover possession of one of his slaves, Neptune. In actions of trover to recover personal property, the plaintiff typically asserted that the defendant had found lost property belonging to the plaintiff. This was, of course, a legal fiction. Because of the fictional nature of the pleadings in trover actions, the allegations in the declaration that Smith filed with the court (Document I) almost certainly do not represent the actual facts that gave rise to the litigation; the facts themselves remain undetermined.

Both of the parties filed pleadings in September 1798. The court, with Jackson sitting for his first session, scheduled a trial of the cause for March Term 1799. Because Smith died before the trial, the court on April 3, 1799, granted Smith's executors, Samuel Smith, Jr., and James Lea, leave to prosecute the suit further at September Term.[1] The action finally went to trial on March 26, 1800, with Jackson and his colleagues Judges Roane and Campbell presiding. A jury returned a verdict for Fitzgerald (Document II).

At common law the death of either the plaintiff or the defendant at any time before final judgment caused a lawsuit to abate automatically.[2] This rule was modified, however, by a 1786 North Carolina statute which declared that "in future it shall and may be lawful for the heirs, executors, administrators or guardians, to carry on every suit or action in courts after the death of either plaintiff or defendant."[3] For instance, if a plain-

---

1. HDSC Law Min. Bk. 3, 1793–1809, p. 179.
2. 4 Tucker, *Blackstone's Commentaries* 301–303.
3. Ch. 14, 1786 Laws of N.C., reprinted in Iredell, *Laws of North Carolina* 584, 1 Scott, *Laws of Tennessee* 368. The statute further provided that a lawsuit should not abate because a term of court intervened between the death of a party and the appointment of a personal representative. Ch. 57, 1789 Laws of N.C., reprinted in Iredell, *Laws of North Carolina* 687, 1 Scott, *Laws of Tennessee* 420. In 1794, the territorial legislature directed

tiff died during a lawsuit, his attorney or the defendant could inform the court of the death. Upon motion, the heir, administrator, executor, or guardian of the deceased would be substituted as plaintiff. If no representative of the plaintiff appeared to continue the suit, the court would then abate the proceeding.[4]

The plaintiff probably was Samuel Smith, Sr., of Sullivan County, a justice of the Court of Pleas and Quarter Sessions in the county since 1780.[5] Garret Fitzgerald, a partner in an unsuccessful lead-mining venture in Greene County that had dissolved in 1791–1792, had been appointed a justice of the Jefferson County court by Governor Sevier in April 1796. He had moved to Smith County by October 1799 and was a justice of the county court when the present action went to trial.[6]

---

that "no appeal in any cause or court whatsoever shall be abated by the death of either plaintiff or defendant." Ch. 1, 1794 Terr. S. of River Ohio Acts, reprinted in 1 Scott, *Laws of Tennessee* 457.

4. Caruthers, *History of a Law Suit*, 24, 29–30.

5. Pollyanna Creekmore, comp., "Early East Tennessee Taxpayers," pt. 7 (Sullivan Co.), ETHS *Publ.* No. 31, pp. 113, 120 (1959).

6. *Knoxville Gazette*, Mar. 10, 1792, Sept. 8, 1792; Sevier, *Commission Book*, 26. See Sevier, *Commission Book*, 50.

I. DECLARATION OF SAMUEL
SMITH, SR.

Hamilton District Superior Court, Knoxville

[ca. September 1798]

Samuel Smith Senr. by John Rhea esquire his Attorney Complains of Garret Fitzgerald of the County of Knox in the District of Hamilton in Custody of the Sheriff &c. of a plea of Trespass on the Case Sur trover and Conversion of One Negro Male Slave, named Neptune &c. for that Whereas the said Samuel Smith Sr. on the ___[1] day of ___[1] in the year of our Lord one thousand seven hundred and Ninety eight at viz at Hamilton in the District of Hamilton aforesaid was possessed of One Negro Male Slave named Neptune about the age of Nineteen years old and of the Value of Seven hundred Dollars current money as of his Own proper goods and Chattles, and being so thereof possessed he the said Negro Male Slave named Neptune On the day and year and at the place aforesaid did come by casualty out of his possession did loose which Negro Male Slave afterward, by finding or otherwise on the day and year and at the place aforesaid did come into the hands and possession of him the said Garret Fitzgerald Nevertheless the said Garret Fitzgerald altho he well knew that the said Negro male Slave named Neptune was of the proper goods and Chattles of him the said Samuel Smith Sr. and to him of right to belong and appertain hath not delivered the said Negro Male slave named Neptune unto him the said Samuel Smith Senr. but hitherto hath refused and still doth refuse to deliver the said Negro Male Slave named Neptune altho Demanded to deliver him but on the day & year and place aforesaid hath Converted and disposed of the said Negro Male Slave to his Own use whereby the said Samuel Smith Senr. saith he is injured and hath sustained One thousand Dollars Damages and thereof brings suit and there are pledges to prosecute &c

Tr, TKL-HDSC Law Rec. Bk. C, 1798–1803, pp. 73–74. Plaintiffs were required to file their declarations during the term to which process was returned. See Caruthers, *History of a Law Suit*, 17. The approximate date that has been assigned to Document I is derived from the sheriff's return of process to the court at September Term 1798 (see Document II).

    1. Thus in Tr.

II. RECORD BOOK ENTRY

Hamilton District Superior Court, Knoxville
Judges Jackson, Roane, and Campbell Presiding

[March 26, 1800]

Be it remembered that on the 4th day of April Anno Domini 1798 a Capias ad Respondendum was issued Commanding the Sheriff of Knox County to take the body of Garret Fitzgerald to answer Samuel Smith Sr. of a plea of Trespass on the Case Sur trover &c. of One Negro Male slave named Neptune to the Damage of the said Plaintiff One thousand Dollars. Upon which writ at September Term 1798 Robert Houston esquire Sheriff returned "Executed"[1] . . . .

And the Defendant by Joseph Hamilton esquire his Attorney comes into Court and Defends &c and pleads not Guilty And the Statute of Limitation[2] and of this he puts himself on the Country

And the Plaintiff by his Attorney aforesaid doth the same. Whereupon let a Jury hereon Come &c at March Term 1799 at which Term the Death of the Plaintiff was suggested in Abatement of this suit and a rule entered to notify his Executors upon which rule this cause was Continued until September Term 1799 at which Term it appearing to the satisfaction of the Court that James Lea and Samuel Smith Junr. Have taken upon them the Execution of the last will and Testament of Saml. Smith decd. they were admitted as Executors to prosecute this suit and by Consent of the parties & assent of the Court it was Continued until March Term 1800 at which Term came the parties aforesaid by their Attornies aforesaid and Thereupon came a Jury, to wit, John Blackburn, Thomas Snoddy, Robert Armstrong, Peter Fine, James Ore, John Daniel, Ambrose Yancy, Thomas Henderson, Mitchell Childress Ebenezar Byram, William Hays and John Trimble who being elected tried and sworn the truth to speak upon the issue joined upon their Oath do say the Defendant is not Guilty as pleading he hath pleaded. Therefore it is Considered by the Court that the Plaintiffs take nothing by their bill but for their false Clamor, as Executors be in mercy &c and that the Defendant go hereof without day and recover against the Plaintiff his Costs by him about his Defence in this behalf expended

MS, TKL-HDSC Law Rec. Bk. C, 1798–1803, pp. 73–74. Trial date is taken from HDSC Law Min. Bk. 3, 1793–1809, pp. 199–200.

   1. The text of Document I occurs at this point in the MS.
   2. Ch. 27, 1715 Laws of N.C., reprinted in 1 Scott, *Laws of Tennessee* 15.

26. State v. McKee

1800
(Criminal Law)

EDITORIAL NOTE

McKee was one of several horse-stealing cases that Jackson heard during his tenure on the bench. In this case, the Hamilton District grand jury's indictment charged that Thomas McKee had stolen a horse from Patience Carter in Jefferson County on Christmas Day 1799 (Document I). When the case went to trial before Judges Jackson, Roane, and Campbell on April 1, 1800, a jury returned a guilty verdict (Document II). Counsel for McKee filed a motion in arrest of judgment, alleging in part that the indictment had varied improperly from the form prescribed by statute and that the statute under which McKee had been convicted was unconstitutional because of its prescription of capital punishment for the offense of horse stealing (Document III).

After hearing argument on McKee's motion on April 7, Jackson, Roane, and Campbell denied the motion and sentenced the defendant to death by hanging (Document IV). In response to a petition signed by a considerable number of the jurors who had convicted the defendant and by several Knoxville citizens and members of the local bar, however, Governor Sevier pardoned McKee on April 9 (Document V).[1]

The contrast between the sentence that was imposed by Jackson and his colleagues in *McKee* and that which was imposed by the same court in *State v. Pierce* (No. 28) is rather striking, though explicable. McKee committed his offense only some six months after the theft in June 1799 by the defendant in *Pierce*. Unfortunately for McKee, the Tennessee legislature in October 1799 had adopted death as the penalty for horse stealing.[2] Hence, the defendant in *Pierce*, for having stolen a horse in June 1799, was sentenced to have his ears pinned to the public pillory and then cut off and to be whipped and branded, whereas McKee very nearly lost his life for having committed a similar offense in December of the same year.

1. The petition has not been located. McKee has not been further identified.
2. Ch. 20, 1799 Laws of Tenn., reprinted in 1 Scott, *Laws of Tennessee* 648.

I. INDICTMENT OF THOMAS
MCKEE

Hamilton District Superior Court, Knoxville

State of Tennessee   }   March Term 1800
Hamilton District   }

The Jurors for the State impannelled for the body of the district of Hamilton Upon their oath present that Thomas McKee late of the County of Jefferson Within the district of Hamilton and State of Tennessee labourer, on the twenty fifth day of december in the year of Our Lord one thousand Seven hundred and ninety nine With force and arms at Jefferson in the County of Jefferson Within the district of Hamilton one mare, of an Iron gray Colour, of the price of ten dollars, of the goods and chattels of one Patiance Carter, then and there being found feloniously, did Steal, take, and Lead away contrery to the form of the Statute in that case[1] made and provided and against the peace and dignity of the State of Tennessee

John Lowrey atto. fo Dst.

MS, THi-Sneed Papers. Endorsed: "186, Indictment horsestealing, State vs Thomas McKee, Patiance Carter prosecutor, George House John Hibbert Eres Witt Isaac Cofman witnesses, sworn and suit, F. A. Ramsey clk, a true Bill, William Snoddy, Foreman, copied."

1. Ch. 20, 1799 Laws of Tenn., reprinted in 1 Scott, *Laws of Tennessee* 648.

II. MINUTE BOOK ENTRY

Hamilton District Superior Court, Knoxville
Judges Jackson, Roane, and Campbell Presiding

Tuesday Morning 1st of April 1800
Court Met according to adjournment
Present all the Judges.

. . . .

State   }
  vs   }   Horse Stealing   Not guilty
Thomas McKee   }   A Jury sworn (to wit)

1 John Trimble	7 John Inman
2 Ebenezer Byram	8 Thomas Henderson
3 George McNutt	9 Mitchell Childress
4 William Hayes	10 Robert Armstrong

5 Robert Miller	11 Thomas Snoddy and
6 John Daniel	12 Hugh Montgomery

[Wh]o Say they find the Defendant Thomas McKee guilty of the Felony and Horse Stealing in [Ma]nner and form as charged in the bill of Indictment. Motion by Prisoners Counsel to file reasons arrest of Judgment. reasons filed

MS, TKL-HDSC Law Min. Bk. 3, 1793–1809, p. 205.

III. GROUNDS FOR
DEFENDANT'S MOTION
IN ARREST OF JUDGMENT

Hamilton District Superior Court, Knoxville
Judges Jackson, Roane, and Campbell Presiding

[April 1, 1800]

State
vs   }   Indictment for Horse Stealing
Thomas McKee

The said Thomas McKee comes in his proper person, and prays that Judgment may not be given on the verdict rendered against him in the aforesaid Case; but that Judgment may be arrested for the following reasons (viz)

1st Because in the body of the Indictment in the case aforesaid, The Said Thomas McKee is charged that he did Steal take and lead away a certain mare, contrary to the form of the Statute made and provided, altho the form of the Statute on which the said Thomas McKee was arraigned is in the following words, viz *Steal take or carry away.*

2d Because the said Indictment concludes in these words viz *of Tennessee* When the Constitution of the State directs that all Indictments shall conclude *against the peace and dignity of the State*

3d Because the Law on which the said Thomas McKee was arraigned is an Unconstitutional Law, and contrary to the rights of the people of the State of Tennessee, in having directed the infliction of Capitol punishment for Horse Stealing.

Love for the prisoner
A Copy Teste
F. A. Ramsey Clk

Tr, THi-Sneed Papers. Entirely in the hand of Francis Alexander Ramsey. Endorsed: "State vs McKee, reasons in arrest of Judgment, A Copy." Date is taken from Document II.

IV. MINUTE BOOK ENTRY

Hamilton District Superior Court, Knoxville
Judges Jackson, Roane, and Campbell Presiding

Monday Morning 7th of April 1800
Court Met According to adjournment
Present all the Judges
Thomas McKee who before this time was by the Jury found Guilty—was now led to the bar. It was then demanded of him What he had to Say Why the Sentence of Death Should not be passed against him. offers the following reasons in arrest of Judgment, (to wit) he files—And upon Solemn Argument had thereon it is considered by the Court, that the reasons are insufficient to arrest the Judgment. The said Thomas McKee being Again Asked if Any thing he had to say why the Sentence of the Law Should not be passed upon him, Saith nothing. The Sentence therefore passed that Thomas McKee be taken from hence to the place from Where he last came and there remain untill Friday the Second day of May next and that he be taken from thence to the place of execution and there be hanged by the neck untill dead and that the Sheriff of Knox County See this Sentence put in execution between the Hours of Twelve and Two O Clock of that day.

MS, TKL-HDSC Law Min. Bk. 3, 1793–1809, pp. 210–211.

V. PARDON BY GOVERNOR SEVIER

April 9, 1800
State of Tennessee
John Sevier Governor in and over the same.

To all who shall see these presents: Greeting. Whereas it is represented to me that Thomas McKee has lately in the Superior Court for the district of Hamilton been prosecuted, tried and convicted for the felonious crime of horse stealing, and sentenced to suffer death: And whereas I have been petitioned by a considerable part of the jurors who convicted him of the said crime, and sundry persons of the bar, and other respectable Citizens who were present at his trial, to pardon him of the felony and crime aforesaid.

Now know ye, that I the said John Sevier Governor &c. being desirous to extend mercy and clemency to those who are fit objects to obtain and receive the same, do by the power and Authority in me vested pardon the said Thomas McKee of the felony and crime by him committed, for which he has been prosecuted, tried, convicted and Sentenced as aforesaid.

Given under my hand and seal at Knoxville this 9th day of April 1800.

/signed/ John Sevier

By the Governor.

Wm. Maclin, Secretary.

FC, T-Sevier Letterbook, 105–106, Governors' Papers.
Under the Tennessee Constitution the governor was authorized "to grant reprieves and pardons, after conviction, except in cases of impeachment." Art. II, § 6, Tenn. Const. (1796).

27. Stothart v. Stuart

1800
(Commercial Law)

EDITORIAL NOTE

This case raises for the second time in Jackson's judicial career the possibility of a conflict of interest between his public responsibilities as a judge and his affairs as a private citizen before assuming those responsibilities.[1] In April 1796, William Blount, acting as Jackson's agent in Knoxville, sold approximately 30,000 acres of land to James Stuart for approximately $7,000.[2] Stuart agreed to make an initial payment in June 1796 of $2,800 to one of Jackson's Philadelphia creditors, John B. Evans & Company, and to pay the balance to Jackson two years later. Stuart subsequently indorsed a note for $4,539.94 that Blount executed to Jackson on June 11, 1796 (Document I).[3] Stuart paid Jackson $819.59⅔ on May 2, 1798. In turn, Jackson on July 12, 1798, assigned the note to Robert Stothart (see Document I). Stuart subsequently defaulted on the note. Jackson's assignee, Stothart, brought the present action in May 1799 to recover on the note from Stuart in the Mero District Superior Court (Document II).

Jackson had assumed his duties as a member of the court the previous September. Despite his having been a principal in the underlying transaction with Stuart in 1796 and despite his continuing capacity as assignor of the note to Stothart, Jackson did not recuse himself from presiding as a member of the court when Stothart's action at last came to trial in May 1800. A jury returned a verdict for Stothart in the amount of $4,636.19 plus costs. Stuart entered a motion for a new trial. Although the grounds for Stuart's motion are not known, the court denied the motion and entered judgment for Stothart upon the verdict (Document III).

1. The first was *Reading v. Douglass*, No. 16.
2. See *Jackson Papers*, I, 441.
3. Blount borrowed heavily from Jackson and others during the summer of 1796 to finance the purchase of more than 2 million acres of land. William H. Masterson, *William Blount* (Baton Rouge, 1954), 298–299.

The law governing the assignability of bills of exchange and promissory notes underwent considerable change in the eighteenth century.[4] Declaring that "promissory Notes are of great Utility, as well to Merchants as others," North Carolina legislators in 1762 provided that such notes "may be assignable over in the like Manner as Inland Bills of Exchange are by Custom of Merchants in England." The statute further declared that the assignee of a promissory note could maintain an action against either the maker or the indorser of the instrument.[5]

The conflict of interest question thus arose from Jackson's stake in the outcome of the lawsuit as assignor of the instrument sued upon by Stothart. When Stuart signed the note as a guarantor, he became liable in the event that Blount failed to discharge the obligation. Jackson's assignment of the note created additional rights in Stothart, since an indorser was liable to each successive holder of the instrument.[6] Upon nonpayment by the original maker, the plaintiff could proceed against either Stuart as guarantor or Jackson as indorser.[7] If Stuart was unable to pay, Jackson was a potential defendant on the assigned note.

The circumstances surrounding Jackson's assignment of the 1796 note to Stothart, a Nashville merchant with whom Jackson kept a regular account between 1798 and 1800, have not been determined. In 1802 Stothart was appointed postmaster at Nashville.[8]

Stuart, one of the first justices of the Washington County court, had represented Washington District in the North Carolina House of Commons, 1786–1788. He had represented Washington County in the state's first constitutional convention, where both he and Jackson were aligned with the faction led by Governor Blount. Just prior to concluding the

---

4. Julius Goebel, Jr., ed., *The Law Practice of Alexander Hamilton: Documents and Commentary* (New York, 1969), II, 211–222; J. Milnes Holden, *The History of Negotiable Instruments in English Law* (London, 1955), 127–132; Herbert A. Johnson, *The Law Merchant and Negotiable Instruments in Colonial New York 1664–1730* (Chicago, 1963), 28–43.

5. Ch. 9, 1762 Laws of N.C., reprinted in Iredell, *Laws of North Carolina* 576, 1 Scott, *Laws of Tennessee* 105. A later statute expanded the category of negotiable instruments. Ch. 4, 1786 Laws of N.C., reprinted in Iredell, *Laws of North Carolina* 576, 1 Scott, *Laws of Tennessee* 362.

6. James Kent, *Commentaries on American Law* (New York, 1827–1828), III, 43–80; Timothy Walker, *Introduction to American Law* (Philadelphia, 1837), 417–423.

7. In 1801, Tennessee lawmakers provided that the surety of a contract or note who was concerned that the principal debtor was about to become insolvent or migrate from the state could notify the creditor to commence an action on such instrument within thirty days. Creditors who failed to comply forfeited the right to recover from the surety. Ch. 18, 1801 Tenn. Pub. Acts, reprinted in 1 Scott, *Laws of Tennessee* 705.

8. Clayton, *Davidson County*, 199. See Account with Robert Stothart & Company, 1798–1800, AJ Papers, DLC (Reel 2).

transaction with Blount in April 1796, Stuart had been elected Speaker of the Tennessee House of Representatives, an office that he retained until 1799.[9]

9. *BD–Tenn. Assembly,* I, 704; Barnhart, "The Tennessee Constitution of 1796," p. 543 n.41; Pollyanna Creekmore, comp., "Early East Tennessee Taxpayers," pt. 10 (Washington County), ETHS *Publ.* No. 32 (1962), 118.

I. PROMISSORY NOTE,
WILLIAM BLOUNT TO JACKSON

Dollars 4539$\frac{94}{100}$ Phila. June 11th 1796.

Two years after date I promise to pay Andrew Jackson Esquire or order four thousand five Hundred thirty nine dollars ninety four Cents with Interest from the date for value received

A Copy   Wm. Blount

On the original are the following endorsements. I bind myself my Heirs &c. for the payment of the within sum.

                                        James Stuart

May the second 1798

Then received from James Stuart the sum of Eight Hundred & nineteen dollars 59 & $\frac{2}{3}$ cents for which a receipt was past to him for the same on that day.

                                        Andrew Jackson

I assign the within to Robert Stothart July 12th 1798.

                                        Andrew Jackson

Test   Andw. McNairy C. S. C.

Tr, DLC-AJ Papers (Reel 2); *Jackson Papers,* I, 89 n.1. Text and signatures in unidentified hand. Endorsed: "Copy Note Blount to Jackson 4539\frac{94}{100}$."

II. DECLARATION OF ROBERT
STOTHART

Mero District Superior Court, Nashville
Judges Jackson, Roane, and Campbell Presiding

May 1799

State of Tennessee, Mero District, May Term 1799, Robert Stothart assignee of Andrew Jackson complains of James Stuart in custody &c for
that whereas a certain William Blount, on the eleventh day of June in the
year One thousand Seven hundred and ninety six, in the District aforesaid,
& within the Jurisdiction of this Court made a certain writing, subscribed with his own hand, commonly called a promissory note, bearing
date the same day and year aforesaid, which is to the Court now here
shewn, "undertook & faithfully promised to pay Andrew Jackson esquire, or order, the just & full sum of four thousand five hundred &
thirty nine dollars ninety four Cents, with Interest from the date:" And
whereas the said Defendant James Stewart did on the   ¹ day of   ¹ one
thousand seven hundred &   ¹ bind himself his heirs &c on the back of
the aforesaid promissory note or writing signed and executed as aforesaid
by William Blount, for the payment of the within sum mentioned, to wit,
four thousand five hundred and thirty nine Dollars ninety four cents with
interest from the date of the aforesaid promissory note so signed and executed by the said William Blount as aforesaid. And for that whereas the
said Andrew Jackson afterwards to wit, on the twelfth day of July in the
year one thousand seven hundred and ninety eight in the District and Jurisdiction aforesaid, by his the sd. Andrews indorsement on the back of
the said Note or Writing with the proper name of him the said Andrew
Jackson, by his own hand there to subscribed, did then and there assign,
transfer and make over all his the said Andrews right and interest in and
to the said Writing or promissory note signed and executed as aforesaid
by William Blount, and so assumed by the said Defendant James Stewart,
with his proper name subscribed on the back of the said promissory note
a writing as aforesaid, which said indorsement, so made by the said
Andrew Jackson, the date whereof is the same day and year aforesaid last
mentioned, which is also to the Court now shewn, of which said indorsement and assignment so made as aforesaid, the said Defendant afterwards, to wit, on the   ¹ day of   ¹ in the year one thousand seven hundred and ninety   ¹ By reason whereof, and also by force of the Statute
in that case made and provided the said Defendant became liable to pay
to the said plaintiff the sum in the said note mentioned, according to the

tenor & effect of the said note, and being so liable, the said Deft. in consideration thereof afterwards, to wit on the same day and year aforesaid, and at the place aforesd. undertook and then and there faithfully promised the said plaintiff, that he the said Deft. would well and truly pay to the said Plt. the sd. sum of four thousand five hundred & thirty nine Dollars Ninety four cents in the said Note or Writing mentioned, according to the tenor & effect of the said note, whenever he Should be thereto afterwards requested. Nevertheless the said Defendant although often requested, the said sum of money to the said plaintiff hath not paid, but the same to pay, hitherto hath refused, and still doth refuse, to the damage of the plaintiff Six thousand Dollars, & therefore he sues &c. Pledges &c.

Wm. P. Anderson Atto pro plt.

Tr, TDaCo–MDSC Law Min. Bk., 1788–1803, pp. 293–294.

  1. Blank in Tr.

III. MINUTE BOOK ENTRY

Mero District Superior Court, Nashville
Judges Jackson, Roane, and Campbell Presiding

[May 22, 1800]

Robert Stothart assee. &c. Plt.
  vs.   In Case.
James Stewart   Deft.

James Stewart was attached to answer Robert Stothart, Assee. of Andrew Jackson, of a plea of Trespass on the case, Damage Six thousand Dollars—whereupon the said Robert Stothart, by William Preston Anderson Esq. his Attorney, at May Term 1799, filed his Declaration[1] ... And the said Defendant James Stuart, by George W. Campbell Esqr. his attorney, at the Term last mentioned, comes and defends the wrongs and injuries when &c. & for plea says that he did not promise, assume and undertake in manner & form as the said Robert hath above thereof complained against him, and of this he puts himself upon the Country. And the plaintiff likewise. And further the Deft. pleads payment, accord and satisfaction &c. Set off &c and of these he puts himself upon the Country and the plaintiff likewise. And the cause was continued from term to term until this term to wit May 1800, at which time came the parties, by their Attornies aforesaid, and a Jury, to wit, Benjamin Weakley, Charles Stuart, John Bradley, Wilson Cage, Andrew Grier, John Walker Senr. Michael Gleaves, Henry Rutherford, Richard Hightower, Charles Kavenaugh, Lewis Crane, & David M. Eewing being elected tried & sworn the truth to speak upon the issue joined on their oath do say that the Defendant did assume upon himself in manner & form as the plaintiff against him hath complained, and they do assess the plaintiffs damages by occasion of the Defts. non performance of that assumption to four thousand Six hundred and thirty Six Dollars and nineteen cents, besides his costs, whereupon the said Defendant obtained a Rule to shew cause why the verdict aforesaid should be set aside and a new trial granted, which, after argument, was discharged. Therefore It is considered by the Court that the plaintiff recover against the said Defendant his damages aforesaid in form aforesaid assessed, and his Costs by him, about his suit on this behalf expended, and the Defendant in Mercy &c.

MS, TDaCo-MDSC Law Min. Bk., 1788–1803, pp. 293–294. Date is taken from *id.* at 291.

    1. The text of Document I follows at this point in the MS.

28. State v. Pierce

1800
(Criminal Law)

EDITORIAL NOTE

As has been noted, and as the present case and Nos. 26 and 40 suggest, horse stealing was one of the most commonly prosecuted offenses while Jackson served as a judge. In this case, the indictment that was returned by the Mero District grand jury in November 1799 charged Andrew Pierce of Robertson County with having stolen two horses in June of that year (Document I).

The case went to trial before Judges Jackson, Roane, and Campbell at the Mero District Superior Court on May 25, 1800. The state produced three witnesses,[1] and, after hearing their testimony, the jury returned a guilty verdict (Document II). The defendant entered a motion in arrest of judgment on the ground that the property specified in the indictment as having been stolen was not described with such certainty as to bar another conviction of the defendant for the same offense (Document II). The court denied Pierce's motion and sentenced the defendant to stand in the pillory one hour, to receive thirty-nine lashes on his bare back, to have both his ears nailed to the pillory and then cut off, and to be branded on the cheeks with the letters *H* and *T* (Document II).[2]

1. See MDSC Law Min. Bk., 1788–1803, p. 336.
2. Pierce has not been further identified.

I. INDICTMENT OF ANDREW
PIERCE

Mero District Superior Court, Nashville

[November 1799]

Andrew Pierce, late of the County of Robertson, and District aforesaid, labourer, on the twentieth day of June in the year of our Lord One thousand Seven hundred and ninety nine, with force and arms in the County aforesaid, one Sorrel Mare branded on the rear buttock thus C. of the value of forty Dollars, and one year old mare colt, of the value of fifty Dollars of the Goods and Chattels of John Chowning, then and there found feloniously did steal, take and lead away, contrary to the Statute in such case[1] made & provided, and against the Peace & dignity of our said State.

John C. Hamilton Atto. for
the State.

Tr, TDaCo-MDSC Law Min. Bk., 1788–1803, p. 312. Date is taken from Document II.

1. Ch. 7, 1786 Laws of N.C., reprinted in Iredell, *Laws of North Carolina* 597, 1 Scott, *Laws of Tennessee* 366.

II. MINUTE BOOK ENTRY

Mero District Superior Court, Nashville
Judges Jackson, Roane, and Campbell Presiding

Monday Morning, May 25th 1800. Court met agreeably to adjournment. Present the Hon. Archibald Roane ⎫
⎪ David Campbell ⎬ Esquires Judges
⎪ Andrew Jackson ⎭

The State—— ⎫
vs ⎬ On an Indictment for Horse stealing.
Andrew Pierce ⎭

Be it remembered that heretofore, to wit, at Nashville, in the State of Tennessee, and District of Mero, November Term One thousand Seven hundred and Ninety nine, by the oath of twelve Jurors, honest and lawful men of the State & District aforesaid, then and there being sworn and charged to enquire for the body of the said District; It was presented that[1] . . . And the said Andrew Pierce was led to the bar, in custody of the Sheriff of Davidson County, and thereupon charged, and pleaded not guilty to the Indictment, and for his trial put himself upon his Country, therefore the trial is, on the affidavit of John Chowning the Prosecutor, continued till the next Court. At which Court, to wit, May Term 1800, came the said John C. Hamilton Atto. &c And the said Andrew Pierce was again led to the bar in Custody of the Sheriff &c And thereupon came a Jury to wit, John Bradley, John Walker Senr. John Payton, Henry Ruther-ford, Richard Hightower, Edmund Gamble, George McWhirter, Thomas Hudson Charles Miles, Robert Thompson, Benjamin Weakley and David McEwing who being elected tried & Sworn the truth of and upon the premises to speak, upon their oath do say that the said Andrew Pierce is guilty of the horse stealing aforesaid in manner & form as in the Indict-ment against him is alledged. And the said Andrew Pierce saith that Judg-ment on the Verdict aforesaid ought not to be given, for the following reason. "That the property, stated to have been stolen in the Bill of Indict-ment, is not described with that certainty, which by the laws of the Land it ought to be, so as to enable the Defendant to make his defence, or for the Court to pass Judgment on, so as to bar another conviction for the same offences." Whereupon he prays that Judgment upon the Verdict aforesaid may be arrested. And thereupon the plea of the said Andrew Pierce, in arrest of Judgment, being argued and overruled, by the Court; It is therefore considered, that the said Andrew Peirce shall stand in the Pillory one hour, and shall be publicly whipped on his bare back with thirty nine lashes well laid on, and at the same time shall have both of his ears nailed to the Pillory and cut off, and shall be branded on the right cheek with the letter H. of the length of three quarters of an Inch and of the breadth of half an Inch, and on the left cheek with the letter T. of the same dimensions as the letter H. in a plain and visible manner. And that execution of this Judgment be made and done upon him the said Andrew Peirce, by the Sheriff of Davidson County, immediately, and that the said Andrew Peirce pay the costs of the prosecution.

MS, TDaCo-MDSC Law Min. Bk., 1788–1803, pp. 311–313.

    The court correctly applied the punishment prescribed by law at the time of the commis-sion of the offense. In October 1799, between the time of the theft in *Pierce* and the indict-ment, the Tennessee General Assembly altered the punishment for horse stealing. Convicted offenders were to "suffer death without benefit of Clergy." Ch. 20, 1799 Laws of Tenn., re-printed in 1 Scott, *Laws of Tennessee* 648.

    1. The text of Document I follows at this point in the MS.

29. State v. Lavender

1800
(Criminal Law)

EDITORIAL NOTE

The *Lavender* case illustrates that, during Jackson's tenure on the bench, whites could be indicted for assaults upon blacks, here presumably upon a slave, and that even attorneys for the state occasionally initiated criminal prosecutions over which the Superior Court had no jurisdiction.

Lavender, a schoolmaster in Davidson County, was indicted in May 1800 for having assaulted "one black Negro man nam'd Bob" with a foot-adze, a cutting tool with a thin, arched blade used for rough-shaping wood (Document I). On May 26, Judges Jackson, Roane, and Campbell sat for Lavender's trial. According to the trial entry, the jury, which "could not agree in their Verdict," was discharged, and the case was dismissed for want of prosecution (Document II).

The disposition of the *Lavender* case is understandable in the light of the statutory division of jurisdiction between the Superior Court and the county courts to try prosecutions for such offenses. Document I seemingly charges Lavender with an assault with intent to kill. Under the Judiciary Act of 1794, the Superior Court was granted jurisdiction over all "criminal matters of what nature, degree or denomination soever . . . except where it is otherwise directed by this or some other act."[1] In 1797 the Tennessee General Assembly enacted a statute requiring that all actions for assault and battery be initiated in the county courts.[2] Although subject to being interpreted as having application only to civil actions, the language of the statute does refer to the county solicitor and thus might well have embraced all types of assault proceedings.[3] A 1799 stat-

1. Ch. 1, § 1, 1794 Terr. S. of River Ohio Acts, reprinted in 1 Scott, *Laws of Tennessee* 457.

2. Ch. 45, 1797 Tenn. Pub. Acts, reprinted in 1 Scott, *Laws of Tennessee* 613.

3. Only in November 1804 did the Superior Court limit the 1797 statute to assaults and battery and exclude from its purview assaults with intent to kill. In *State v. Anderson*, 2 Tenn. (2 Overton) 6 (1804), the defendant was indicted by the Mero District grand jury for an assault and battery with an intent to commit murder. Counsel for the accused argued

ute vested the Superior Court with original jurisdiction only over those assaults that were committed during the court's terms.[4] The alleged assault in *Lavender,* of course, occurred in April, at a time when the Mero District Superior Court was not in session. Uncertainty about whether the court had jurisdiction to try Lavender thus might well explain the jury's inability to agree upon a verdict and the court's subsequent dismissal of the case. This interpretation seems likely in the light of Lavender's subsequent indictment upon the same charge in the Davidson County court in July. In the county court proceeding, Lavender "confessed the charges" and was fined one penny.[5]

Lavender has not been further identified.

The "black Negro man nam'd Bob" possibly was the same "negro man called Bob" who by October 1801 had "by his indoustery and eoconomy: raised money & purchased himself" and who was the keeper of Black Bob's Tavern, a "prominent tavern" in Nashville during the first decade of the nineteenth century.[6]

---

that the 1797 measure had granted the county courts exclusive jurisdiction over all indictments for assault and battery and that the Superior Court thus was without jurisdiction to try the case. At least, they asserted, "it was their understanding that it had been so decided in this Court, when his Honor Judge Jackson presided." 2 Tenn. (2 Overton) at 7. The court disagreed. Judge Overton, Jackson's successor, held for the court that "the meaning of the act is that the county courts shall have exclusive jurisdiction of assaults and batteries barely, but not when united with an intent to murder."

4. Ch. 23, 1799 Tenn. Pub. Acts, reprinted in 1 Scott, *Laws of Tennessee* 649.

5. State v. Lavender, DaCo CPQS Min. Bk. C, 291 (1800).

6. Petition of Nashville Citizens to the Tennessee General Assembly, ca. Oct. 1801, Legislative Papers: Petitions and Memorials, 1799–1809, T; Clayton, *Davidson County,* 200.

1. INDICTMENT OF ANDERSON LAVENDER

Mero District Superior Court, Nashville

[May 1800]

Anderson Lavender late of the County of Davidson, Schoolmaster, on the twenty fifth day of April in the year of our Lord one thousand eight hundred, with force and arms at the County of Davidson aforesaid in the Town of Nashville, with a certain foot-adze which he the sd. Anderson then and there held in his right hand, in and upon one black Negro man nam'd Bob in the peace of God and our said State then and there being did make an assault and battery with an intent him the said Bob then and there feloneously, wilfully and of his malice aforethought to kill & murder, against the Statute in such case made and provided, and against the peace and dignity of our State.

John C. Hamilton Attor. for
the State

Tr, TDaCo-MDSC Law Min. Bk., 1788–1803, pp. 316–317. Date is taken from Document II.

II. MINUTE BOOK ENTRY

Mero District Superior Court, Nashville
Judges Jackson, Roane, and Campbell Presiding

Tuesday Morn. May 26th 1800 Court met agreeably to adjournment.
Present the Hon. Archibald Roane ⎤
     David Campbell ⎬ Esquires Judges.
     Andrew Jackson ⎦

. . . .

The State ⎯⎯⎯ ⎤
  vs   ⎬   On an Indt. for an Assault & battery &c
Anderson Lavender ⎦

Heretofore, to wit, at Nashville, in the State of Tennessee, & District of Mero, at May Term 1800, by the oath of twelve Jurors, honest & lawful men of the State and District aforesaid, then and there being sworn and charged to enquire for the body of the District aforesaid, it was presented that[1] . . . And the said Anderson Lavender appeared in Court and having heard the Indictment aforesaid pleaded not Guilty thereto, & for his trial put himself upon his Country. Whereupon came a Jury, to wit, William Edwards, William Stothart, William Lytle Junr. Thomas Hickman, Frederick Ward, Peter Edwards, James Dupree, Amon Davis, Isaac Roberts, Metcalf DeGraffinried, Henry Key, & Aquilla Carmack who being elected tried & sworn the truth of & upon the premises to speak, went out of Court to consult of their verdict, and after some time returned into Court and declared they could not agree in their Verdict; by consent of the Parties, and with the assent of the Court, William Edwards one of the Jurors is withdrawn, and the rest of the Jurors from rendering their Verdict are discharged. And John C. Hamilton Atto &c confesses that he intends no farther to prosecute the said Indictment. And the sd. Anderson Lavender assumes all costs. Therefore, by consent of parties, it is considered by the court that the said Anderson Lavender do pay the costs of the prosecution.

MS, TDaCo-MDSC Law Min. Bk., 1788–1803, pp. 316–317.

 1. The text of Document I follows at this point in the MS.

30. Craig v. Montgomery;
Craig v. Montgomery

1800
(Contracts)

I. BLAND'S STATEMENT OF THE CASE
AND MINUTES OF JACKSON'S RULING
FOR THE COURT

Washington District Superior Court, Jonesboro
Judges Jackson, Roane, and Campbell Presiding

[September 1799]
Craig vrs Montgomery

In an Action of Debt on a Bond the Plaintiff attempted to read a Deposition taken at Lancaster in Pennsylvania to prove the execution of the Bond, which was opposed by the Defendants counsel because there was no time fixed by the Court for the plaintiff's giving notice to the Defendant of the time and place of taking the Deposition.

[The Ruling of Judge Jackson]

Jackson J: It appears to me from the Law that the party at the time of his making application for a Dedimus Potestatem should also apply to the Court to fix the time for Notice; and as that has not been done in this case the Deposition cannot be read in evidence.

Roane & Campbell J: of the same opin[i]on.

Plaintiff suffered a non suit

MS, MdHi-Bland Casebook, 16–17, Bland Papers (MS 134). Date is taken from *id.* at 11.

The parties most probably are the same as those in the case that follows, Robert Craig and Michael Montgomery. Craig had opened a fulling mill in Washington County, Virginia, in 1792. See *Knoxville Gazette*, Mar. 10, 1792. Montgomery, who also was the defendant in *State v. Montgomery*, No. 32, and one of the defendants in *Vannerson v. Montgomery and McCormick*, No. 48, otherwise has not been identified.

II. BLAND'S STATEMENT OF THE
CASE AND MINUTES OF
THE ARGUMENT OF COUNSEL
AND OF JUDGE ROANE'S
DECISION FOR THE COURT

Washington District Superior Court, Jonesboro
Judges Jackson, Roane, and Campbell Presiding

[September 1800]
Robert Craig vrs Michael Montgomery

This was an Action of Debt on a Bond which had become payable in the year 1775. the Defendant plead Non est Factum, Payment at the Day—and Set off. The Bond was proven by the subscribing witness, no notice was taken of the plea of Set off. The whole cause turned upon the presumption in favor of the plea of Payment.

[Hugh Lawson White for Defendant]

White for Montgomery. There is a defence in this case which the Defendant may set up that ought in Law to aval him, and therefore I trust will have such weight with the Jury as to induc them to say the Plff shall not recover. The Bond on which this action is brought is payable in 1775. from that time to the commencement of this action more than 20 years has elapsed and during that long period of time there does not appear have been a payment even of interest a demand of the money or anything else to induce the Jury to believe that that Debt is still due. The strong presumption is, after such a lapse of time that the Bond has been discharged, The Law recognises such a presumption (1 Esp 254)[1] and on that legal presumption do we rest our cause

[Pleasant Moorman Miller for Plaintiff]

Miller for Craig The defendant relys on the presumption of payment of the lapse of 20 years on the Law read from Espinasse. I contend that on the bare plea of Solvit ad diem no such presumption can arise and this seems necessarily to be inferred from the next succeding case to that which was read. There should have been likewise a plea of payment after the day to have intitld the defendant to take complete advantage of the presumption in this case. But even were the Presumption applicable on this Plea as it now stands. Yet I think ther cannot remain a doubt on the act of 1777 and 1783 (Iredell 318, 453),[2] which completely precludes the operation of all limitation for eight years during the American Revolution and consequently this presumption cannot avail the Defendant.

[George Washington Campbell for Defendant]

Campbell for Mont. This case may be narrowed into a very small compass. This is a point which ought properly to be dec[i]ded by the Court and is such a one as I think would be highly improper for a Jury to determine. We rely on a presumptive payment after the lapse of 20 years which we are authorized in doing from the law that has been read. With respect to what has been said by the Gent last up respecting the plea of payment I cant conceive as a Lawyer he was serious in what he advanced, for payment at the day is the most general & comprehensive one that be of that nature it includes both the plea of payment before the day, and payment after and so say all the Books expressly The presumption in this case is founded on the strictest principles of Justice and is so strong that unless there be some circumstance can be adduced to rebut it the Jury have no election but are as much tied down to a Verdict for the Defendant as they would be by a positive Law.

In answer to what was said respecting the acts of Assembly, I shall address some few observations to your Honors. The act of 1777 can only have relation to the Statute of Limitations. The words "Shall not be allowed of in the County Courts hereby established in any Plea of Limitation, or in the computation of time allowed for proving Accounts &c" do in the plainest terms that can be inform us what was the meaning the Legislature in passing this Act.[3] The Act of 1783 does expressly say "That the statute of limitations, entitled, An Act concerning old Titles to Lands, and for Limitations of Actions, and for avoiding Suits in Law, be and is hereby suspended from its usual operation &c"[4] so that from both these acts themselves it may be clearly collected that they have no relation to the present qu[e]stion for in this case it is not a positive statute which prevents the plaintiff from recovering but an equitable presumption.

[Jenkin Whiteside for Plaintiff]

Whiteside Contra: We contend that under the circumstance of this case the Presumption ought not to run so as to bar the present Pltf. It ought to be recollected by the Jury that the cases read are decisions of the British Courts and principally founded on the nature of that country. Such is the narrow insular situation of Great Britain that it is almost impossible for a Debtor to remove out of the reach of his Creditor if the Debtor had gone to the most remote corner of the Island the Creditor could easily pursue or send after him have suit brot and enforce the payment but how different is the nature of the U. S. the citizens are spread over an immense tract of Country and so little social intercourse carried on amongst those citizens that an age almost might elapse before the Creditor could possibly discover the retreat of his absconding Debtor even if he were to use all the diligence in his power, in England this could never be the case. I think on an attentive consideration the Law read by the Gent it will be found that the Presumption was never meant to operate but in those cases where this Creditor and Debtor resided in the same neighbourhood for 20 years and during the whole of that time nothing prevented the Creditor from demanding and recovering his money. this I think is the true intent and meaning of that law. Now view the circumstances of the parties during that 20 years which the Gent says is to operate as a bar to the Plaintiff— Montgomery sometimes in Pennsylvania sometimes in Virginia and in this State has no settled place of residence for a number of years, and for several years in the army during that Revolutionary war which harrassed the Country and impeded the course of Justice every where

Whatever may be the expressions of the acts of 1777 and 1783 I think the Legislature of N Carolina never intended to make a distinction between the Positive Law of Limitations and the Presumtive Limitation as in this case. the Presumption arising on the lapse of 20 years operates as a Limitation and is in effect the same (4 Burr. 1963)[5] therefore must have been within the meaning of the Legislature in making those Acts

[The Opinion of Judge Roane]

Roane Judge. On the plea of Payment the Defendant has relied on the lapse of 20 years being full evidence of his having paid the Debt. There is a difference between the Statute of Limitation and the Presumption. the Statute is a positive Law which the Court are bound to notice and when the case comes within it is a complete bar. the Presumption is part of the common Law (1 Burr 434)[6] and grows out of the whole circumstances and matters of Fact attendant on the case (2 Morg. Ess. 331.[7] Oswold vrs Leigh)[8] and is therefore not within the saving of the two acts mentioned by the Bar It is a matter solely within the province of the Jury to say whether on taking into view the lapse of time the party's removing from place to place the revolutionary War in short all the curcumstances; the Plaintiff ought or ought not to recover. It seems to me this is a matter so peculiarly the part of a Jury [to be] judge of, that I do not know if the Court could take on them to decide were it brought before them in a special Verdict.

Jackson & Campbell Concurred in opinion with his Honor J. Roane.

The Plff's counsel entered a Rule to shew cause why a new trial should not be granted—and during the same term they shewed for cause that the

Verdict was contrary to evidence And argued as before that the intervention of the late war &c ought to prevent the Presumtion from running. The Court continued of the same opinion and Discharged the Rule

MS, MdHi-Bland Casebook, 62–71, Bland Papers (MS 134). Date is taken from *id.* at 62. Annotation at the foot of the casebook entry: "It had like to have escaped me to mention that so soon as mr. White had opened the Defence in this Case—The Plff introdu[c]ed testimony to shew that Montgomery lived in Pennsylvania about the time the Bond was given, that he moved away soon after and for a number of years during the Revolutionary war he had no fixed place of residence but was frequently backward and forward from that Country to this and settled here soon after the war. Mr. Craig moved out to this Country during the Revolution and settled where he now lives about thirty or 40 miles of where Montgomery did afterward settle." *Id.* at 72.

1. 1 Espinasse, *Actions at Nisi Prius* 254.
2. Ch. 4, § 9, 1783 Laws of N.C., reprinted in Iredell, *Laws of North Carolina* 453; ch. 2, § 98, 1777 Laws of N.C. (Nov. Sess.), reprinted in Iredell, *Laws of North Carolina* 318.
3. Ch. 2, § 98, 1777 Laws of N.C. (Nov. Sess.), reprinted in Iredell, *Laws of North Carolina* 318.
4. Ch. 4, § 9, 1783 Laws of N.C., reprinted in Iredell, *Laws of North Carolina* 453.
5. Winchelsea Causes, 4 Burr. 1962, 98 Eng. Rep. 22 (K.B. 1766). Rules were pending against a number of the borough's incorporators to show cause why informations in the nature of quo warranto should not be granted against them to show by what right they claimed to hold their offices. The incorporators had held their offices for varying periods of time, some for less than twenty years and some for more than twenty years. "The Court thought it would be right to fix a certain point of limitation, beyond which they would not go back, to disturb a possession so long acquiesced in. And having taken due time to consider how many years this quiet possession ought to have lasted, in order to protect it from future impeachment; they now publicly declared the resolution that they were unanimously come to; namely, that after twenty years unimpeached possession of a corporate franchise, no rule ought to be granted against the person in possession, to oblige him 'to shew by what right he holds it.'" 4 Burr. at 1962–1963, 98 Eng. Rep. at 22. The court declared that the rule thus enunciated was analogous to the rule that "Bonds which have lain dormant, shall be supposed to be satisfied, after twenty years." 4 Burr. at 1963, 98 Eng. Rep. at 22.
6. Rex v. Stephens, 1 Burr. 433, 97 Eng. Rep. 388 (K.B. 1757). This was an action on a motion for an information in the nature of a quo warranto against the defendant to show by what authority he held his office as one of the aldermen of the corporation of St. Ives in Cornwall. It was alleged that the defendant's election as alderman in 1741 and his election as mayor the next year were defective, because the election in 1728 of the first alderman to the seat now occupied by the defendant had been improper. The court unanimously refused to grant the information: "[I]t would be of very ill consequence to corporations, if the Court should, after so many years acquiescence, quieta movere, and call corporators to account for acting under such elections, depending upon the prior rights of others, whose rights had never been before objected to: which must occasion infinite confusion in corporations. . . . though there was indeed no statute nor even fixed rule of limitation, as to the length of time which should suffice to quiet the possession of these offices; yet the Court, in their discretion, ought to refuse granting these motions, after a great length of time." 1 Burr. at 433–434, 97 Eng. Rep. at 388.
7. Unidentified.
8. Oswald v. Legh, 1 T.R. 270, 99 Eng. Rep. 1089 (K.B. 1786). This was a debt action upon a bond that had been executed in January 1765. The obligee sued out a writ on the bond in June 1784, but died within the ensuing three months without ever having served it. The obligee's executors commenced the present action. When a jury found for the plaintiffs, the defendant moved for a new trial on the ground that, although both parties to the bond had lived in the same kingdom, no demand had been made for nineteen and a half years.

Justice Buller declared for the court, "I have always been of opinion that no less time than twenty years could of itself form a presumption that a bond had been paid; and as there was no evidence at the trial in aid of the presumption, I left the question to the jury with strong directions in favour of the plaintiff. For even with regard to the rule of twenty years, where no demand has been made during that time, that is only a circumstance for the jury to found a presumption upon, and is in itself no legal bar. In those cases where satisfaction of a bond has been presumed within a less period, some other evidence has been given in favour of such a presumption; such as having settled an account in the intermediate time, without any notice having been taken of such a demand." 1 T.R. at 271, 99 Eng. Rep. at 1089. The court followed the rule referred to in the Winchelsea cases that if a bond lay dormant for twenty years, it was to be presumed paid. 1 T.R. at 272, 99 Eng. Rep. at 1089.

31. Grundy's Executors v. Harmon

1800
(Conflict of Laws)

EDITORIAL NOTE

As the litigation between George Grundy's executors and John and Peter Harmon illustrates, the Superior Court during Jackson's tenure on the bench frequently provided a forum not only for nonresident litigants seeking to enforce their rights under Tennessee law, but also for nonresidents seeking enforcement of rights secured under the statutes and judicial decisions of other states. In the present case, the plaintiffs, residents of Virginia, sought to enforce against the defendants, residents of Tennessee, judgments that had been obtained in a Virginia county court against the defendants before the latter moved to Tennessee. To resolve the question of whether the plaintiffs could enforce the Virginia judgments in a manner that was permitted under Tennessee law but not under Virginia law required that the court on at least two occasions consider and apply conflict-of-laws principles.

Although the underlying facts and the procedural background of the present case in the Virginia court are not entirely known, it is possible to trace the litigation in the Tennessee courts. Before his death in late 1783 or early 1784, George Grundy brought a debt action against Peter Harmon in one of the Virginia county courts, probably that for Jefferson County in the Kentucky District where Grundy resided. Grundy obtained a judgment against Harmon, who at the time also was a resident of Virginia. After Grundy's death, the executors of his estate[1] attempted to enforce the judgment against Harmon. When the defendant was not to be found within the jurisdiction, the executors secured the issuance of a writ of scire facias against the surety on defendant's bail bond, John Harmon. After judgment had been entered by the Virginia court in the scire facias

---

1. Under the terms of Grundy's will, the decedent's widow, Elizabeth, and two of Grundy's sons, John and George, Jr., were designated as executors of the estate. Katharine G. Healy, "Calendar of Early Jefferson County, Kentucky, Wills," 6 *Filson Club Hist. Q.* 3 (1932).

proceeding against John Harmon, both the surety and his principal moved from Virginia to Greene County, Tennessee (see Document I).

In most American jurisdictions during the late eighteenth century, an action had to be brought upon a foreign judgment in the forum where enforcement of the judgment was sought and a new judgment rendered before execution issued against the defendant's property.[2] At some time prior to February 1797, Grundy's executors brought an action of debt in the Greene County Court of Pleas and Quarter Sessions against both Peter and John Harmon jointly, seeking to enforce the Virginia judgments. The defendants in February 1797 entered a plea of abatement in the Greene County court on the ground that, under Virginia law, the plaintiffs could not proceed against both the principal and his surety because the entry of a judgment against a surety upon a scire facias acted to discharge the principal. The court denied the defendants' plea and awarded the plaintiffs a respondeat ouster, an order directing the defendants to answer the plaintiffs' declaration. The defendants appealed the lower court's ruling to the Washington District Superior Court.[3]

The appeal did not go to trial until March 1799, at which time Jackson, speaking for the court, sustained the lower court's ruling and ordered the defendants to answer the plaintiffs' declaration (Document I).[4] Jackson held that the plaintiffs could proceed in the Tennessee courts against both the principal and his bail. Although the plaintiffs might not have been able to proceed against principal and surety jointly in a similar action under Virginia law, Jackson held that Tennessee law applied to the enforcement of the Virginia judgments against the defendants once they had become residents of Tennessee. Under Tennessee law, Jackson declared, judgment against the surety did not operate to discharge the principal but operated to bind the surety "conjointly with the Principal, [and] they are both liable at the option of the Plff" (Document I).[5] Plaintiffs,

---

2. Joseph Story, *Commentaries on the Conflict of Laws*, 2d ed. (Boston, 1841), 509.

3. Grundy's Executors v. Harmon, Greene Co. CPQS Min. Bk., 1796–1809, pp. 9–10. See Document I. The basis of the debt action in the present case against John Harmon was the statutory requirement that the sheriff assign all bail bonds to plaintiffs, so that the plaintiff subsequently could proceed directly against the defendant's surety in an action of debt upon the bond. See *Magoffin & Son v. Acklin* and *Magoffin & Son v. Acklin, Perrin, and Combs*, No. 41, Document IV, endnote.

4. Jackson also ruled that a principal and his surety could not join in a single writ of error (Document I).

5. Jackson correctly observed that, under Tennessee law, the awarding of judgment upon a writ of scire facias against the surety on a bail bond did not operate to discharge the principal. See ch. 1, §14, 1794 Terr. S. of River Ohio Acts, reprinted in 1 Scott, *Laws of Tennessee* 457; ch. 2, §19, 1777 Laws of N.C. (Nov. Sess.), reprinted in Iredell, *Laws of North Carolina* 296, 1 Scott, *Laws of Tennessee* 165. The only exception under Tennessee law appears to have been upon the discharge of the principal under the Insolvent Debtors Act. See *Magoffin & Son v. Acklin* and *Magoffin & Son v. Acklin, Perrin, and Combs*, No. 41.

Jackson concluded, were free under Tennessee law to secure writs of execution against either or both of the defendants. Both Judges Roane and Campbell concurred in Jackson's ruling on the defendants' plea.

At the court's September Term 1800, the defendants entered a demurrer to the declaration on the ground that an action in debt against the defendants jointly was an improper form of action in Tennessee to enforce the Virginia judgments (see Documents II and IV). The court, in a per curiam opinion delivered by Judge Roane, overruled the demurrer and entered judgment for the plaintiffs. The court held that an action of debt against defendants jointly was proper in Tennessee although such a method of recovery might not have been proper under Virginia law. The court recognized the conflict-of-laws principle that the law of the place where a contract was made governed, but ruled that it was limited to "the substantial object" of the contract and did not apply to the method in which performance of the contract was to be enforced. The substantive law of contracts in effect in Virginia, Roane declared, prevented the enforcement in Tennessee of a contract made in Virginia but invalid there. Such, however, was not the issue in the present case. Only the method of enforcing contracts that were admittedly valid in Virginia—Peter Harmon's debt obligation under the Virginia judgment and his surety's bail bond—was at issue, Roane concluded. A joint action of debt against both principal and surety, he asserted, was "perhaps the best and most simple mode that could be devised for enforcing the performance of the Judgments on which it is founded" (Document IV).

The court's decision was consistent with the prevailing American view. For instance, Joseph Story observed,

> It is universally admitted and established, that the forms of remedies, and the modes of proceeding, and the execution of judgments, are to be regulated solely and exclusively by the laws of the place, where the action is instituted.[6]

Tennessee long adhered to the position that the validity of a contract was determined by the substantive law of the place where the contract was made, while the enforcement of the contract was governed by the procedural law of the place where performance was sought to be enforced.[7]

George Grundy was the father of Felix Grundy (1777–1840), a future member of the United States Senate from Tennessee. There is no evidence that Felix Grundy, who had been practicing law in Kentucky for two years by 1799 but who did not move to Tennessee until 1807, participated in the present litigation in Tennessee in any way.[8]

---

6. See Story, *Commentaries on the Conflict of Laws*, 2d ed., 467–468.

7. See, *e.g.*, Deaton v. Wise, 186 Tenn. 364, 210 S.W.2d 665 (1948).

8. Joseph Parks, *Felix Grundy: Champion of Democracy* (Baton Rouge, 1940), 1, 3, 4 n.9.

John Harmon was probably the Greene County justice who had been commissioned in 1796 and who represented the county in the General Assembly, 1801–1807 and 1809–1811.[9] Peter Harmon has not been identified.

9. *BD–Tenn. Assembly*, I, 334.

I. BLAND'S STATEMENT OF THE CASE
AND MINUTES OF JACKSON'S RULING
ON DEFENDANTS' PLEA IN ABATEMENT

Washington District Superior Court, Jonesboro
Judges Jackson, Roane, and Campbell Presiding

[March 1799]
Geo. Grundy Ex. vs. P. Harman & J. Harman

This case was brought hither by appeal from the County Court of Green, where it had been commenced, founded on the transcript of a Record from one of the County Courts of Virginia, by which it appeared in an action of Debt between Geo. Grundy & P. Harmon the present parties after Judgment for the Plff, a Ca. Sa issued against the Defendant on which non est inventus was returned, then a Si. fa: issued against the Bail J Harman and Scire feci returned[.] Judgm was entered up against him; at that Stage of the Suit in Virginia both the Principal and Bail emigrated to this State; in consequence of which this action was brought here against the Principal & Bail jointly; To which they plead in abatement, that by the Plffs own shewing it appeared the Judgments against them were seperate and destinct, and that being actually the case they could not be joined in the same action: on which plea the Court below awarded Respondeat ouster.

And now after argument of Counsel on either side—

[The Ruling of Judge Jackson]

Mr. Jackson J: This is one of those Cases not governed by the Laws [of] a foreign Country   it matters not to us what would have been the proceedings on the case in Virginia, it appears here plain enough that the Defts are jointly bound, not severally. After Judgment is entered against the principal, and on the return of two nihils judgment is awarded against the Bail; the Principal is by no means discharged, for the judgment against the Bail binds him conjointly with the Principal, they are both liable at the option of the Plff; the Plff may have Executions against either or both of them at his pleasure; therefore an Action will lay against both jointly on those Judgments.

The reason why the Principal & Bail cannot join in a writ of Error, appears to me to be this Each is charged in a different manner The Judgments against them are entered up at different times, and it is necessary that each should shew how he is charged before he can take advantage of any inaccuracies in the Record.

Roane & Campbell J: concurred

Pr. Cur: Respondeat ouster Award.

MS, MdHi-Bland Casebook, 1–4, Bland Papers (MS 134). Date is taken from *id.* at 1.

II. DEFENDANTS' DEMURRER

Washington District Superior Court, Jonesboro
Judges Jackson, Roane, and Campbell Presiding

[September 1800]

Peter Harman and John Harman ⎫
       ads   ⎬   For Debt—Demurer
George Grundy Executor of   ⎪
George Grundy deceased.   ⎭

The defendants by their Attorney come into Court and defend the Wrong and injury when &c, and say that the said Plaintiff his said Action against them ought not to have and maintain, because, they say they are advised that the Declaration of the said Plaintiff and the Matters therein contained are not sufficient in Law, to enable the said Plaintiff to support his said Action against these Defendants, and that they are not bound by the Laws and Statutes of this State to answer to the said Declaration, and therefore they Demur thereto in Law, and thereupon they crave the Judgment of the Court, whether they ought to make answer to said Declaration &c

J. Whiteside

MS, NcD-Tennessee Court Records, Washington County Undated. Endorsed: "P. Harman & al, ads G. Grundy excer Demurrer." Date is derived from Document IV.

III. PLAINTIFFS' JOINDER IN DEMURRER

Washington District Superior Court, Jonesboro
Judges Jackson, Roane, and Campbell Presiding

[September 1800]

Grundys Executors
vs
Peter Harmon &
John Harmon

And the plaintiff saith that for anything alledged by the said Defendants in their plea saith he ought not be precluded from having his said Action against them for that the said Declaration and the matters and things therein contained are good & sufficient in law to enable the plaintiff to recover, wherefore he prays Judgment of the Court and that his Debt may be adjudged to him

Hamilton Atto.

MS, NcD-Tennessee Court Records, Washington County Undated. Endorsed: "Grundy vs Harmon Joinder plea Joinder in Demurer." Date is derived from Document IV.

IV. BLAND'S MINUTES OF JUDGE ROANE'S PER CURIAM RULING ON DEFENDANTS' DEMURRER

Washington District Superior Court, Jonesboro
Judges Jackson, Roane, and Campbell Presiding

[September 1800]

Per Curiam. The opinion entirely Roane's. By the Laws of Congress the Records and Judical procceeding of the Courts of a Sister state are of high authority as the Records of our own State Courts are[.][1] consequently an action of Debt is the proper Action on a Judgments given in a Sister State. The only question then in this Case is whether we must pursue the same mode of recovery here as would have been proper in Virginia? There can be little doubt that our own mode of recovery is the proper one to pursue. The Law of the place where the contract is made governs that contract only so far as respects the substantial object of it; but from the very nature of things can have nothing to do with the mode in which its performance is to be enforced—for in many instances it would be wholly impracticable to administer relief in the same mode that it should be in Virginia (our Neighbouring State) owing to the great difference in the Systems of Jurisprudence that have been adopted in the two States.

In the case of Robinson vrs Bland (2 Burr 1077)[2] no doubt had an action been brought in France on the Bill of Exchange against Bland, that it would have been different from the Action upon the case which was sustained in the K. B. in England—yet on that ground no objection was ever thought of. That case however shews that the Laws of Virginia ought govern the present case in some respects—as that none can be made liable who would not be so there, and what advantages the Bail could have in Virginia he may have here &c.

This joint action of Debt against both Principal and Bail is perhaps the best and most simple mode that could be devised for enforcing the performance of the Judgments on which it is founded

Therfore let the Demurrer be overruled

Judgment for Plaintiff.

MS, MdHi-Bland Casebook, 88–91, Bland Papers (MS 134). Date is taken from *id.* at 62.

1. Article IV, section 1 of the United States Constitution declares, "Full Faith and Credit shall be given in each State to the public Acts, Records, and judicial Proceedings of every other State." Congress is expressly authorized to prescribe the manner in which such public acts may be proved. Pursuant to this provision, Congress in 1790 mandated that the records and judicial proceedings of the several states "shall have such faith and credit given to them in every court within the United States, as they have by law or usage in the courts of the state from whence the said records are or shall be taken." Ch. XI, 1st Cong., 2d Sess., 1 Stat. 122 (1790).

2. Robinson v. Bland, 2 Burr. 1077, 97 Eng. Rep. 717 (K.B. 1760). This was an assumpsit action in three counts: (1) a bill of exchange drawn by the defendant's intestate, (2) money lent in France to the intestate by the plaintiff, and (3) money won by the plaintiff from the intestate in France. Robinson had lent £672 to Bland in Paris, which Bland in turn lost to Robinson at gambling. Bland then executed a bill of exchange for the full amount payable ten days later in England. Bland died before the bill's ten-day maturity date. Under the laws of England and France, a bill of exchange given for a gambling debt was void. Under the law of England, money won at gambling could not be recovered. Although such a recovery could be had in France as a debt of honor, jurisdiction over the person of the defaulting drawer was a prerequisite. Money lent for gambling purposes could be recovered under both the law of England and the law of France. The case was decided by a court consisting of Lord Mansfield and Justices Wilmot and Denison. The court unanimously held that the bill of exchange was void, that the money lost at gambling could not be recovered, but that the money lent could be recovered. Mansfield and Wilmot based their decisions upon a finding that, under the facts in the case before the court, the laws of England and the laws of France were identical on all of the issues and thus did not have to reach the question

of which law should be applied if the laws differed. The judges nonetheless each expressed views on the question in dicta. Assuming that the contract was valid where made, the judges suggested four possible views: the law of the forum, the law of the place of performance, the law intended by the parties, or the law of the place of performance as that presumably intended by the parties. Roane, Jackson, and Campbell appear in the present decision to have preferred to apply the law of the forum when the laws of the two jurisdictions differed. For additional discussion of *Robinson,* see Alexander N. Sack, *Conflicts of Law in the History of the English Law* (New York, 1937), 389.

32. State v. Montgomery

1800
(Criminal Law)

BLAND'S STATEMENT OF THE
CASE AND MINUTES OF
THE ARGUMENT OF COUNSEL
AND OF
THE OPINIONS OF THE COURT

Washington District Superior Court, Jonesboro
Judges Jackson, Roane, and Campbell Presiding

[September 1800]
State vrs Michael Montgomery

This was an Indictment for Perjury committed before the Court of
Pleas and Quarter Sessions for Sullivan County on the trial of John Young
and John Hoffmand who were there indicted for a Trespass Assault
and Battery committed by them and others on the Body of Michael
Montgomery on the 18th. of March 1799 at the Furnace of David Ross in
that County and on which trial Young & Hoffman were convicted and
fined 100$ each

The Indictment charged that Michael Montgomery being duly sworn
in Sullivan Court in behalf of the State in that trial deposed that the said
John Young was at the Place where the said Trespass Assault & Battery
took Place a "few minutes before and a few minutes after the fighting was
all over" whereas the truth was otherwise

After the Witnesses on behalf of the State were examined a certain
John Richardson was introduced by the Defendant to Prove what John
Young himself had said respecting his having been there [at the] Furnace
when the Fighting happened.

The Atty. Genl. objected[:] What Young has at any time said can only
be hearsay coming from this witness, besides if they want youngs Testi-

mony he is now in Court and let him be sworn. The Deft himself has objected to John Young and prevents him from being sworn   Let him wave that objection permit young to be sworn then perhaps such Testimony as this would be admissible

[George Washington Campbell and
Hugh Lawson White for Defendant]

Campbell in the Defence. Contended that this Testimony was Proper. Young's Sayings and confessions might certainly have been given in evidence in the court below to prove that he was at the Place where this Fight should have happened and thereby shew that he must have been guilty of the Battery &c there charged. a fortiori whatever would go to shew that young was Guilty on the trial in the Court below would corroborate and substantiate Montgomery's testimony in that Court and what ever supported his testimony there ought surely to be admitted here to shew his innocence of the crime of which he stands charged.

White on the same side. There is (I think) yet one other reason why this Testimony is Proper. No man shall be compelled to criminate himself. Now suppose for a moment that young did actually take a part in the engagement said to have happened at the Furnace   could he be compelled to say so on his oath, certainly not—or indeed would the court permit us to ask him whether he did or not? undoubtedly the Court would say the question was improper. Therefore I hope we shall be permitted to examine the witness.

[Jenkin Whiteside for the State]

Whiteside contra[:] I contend in this case Richardsons testimony was not admissible. Young is no way concerned with the present Indictment   he is in no shape a party. neither was Montgomery in the Indictment below   therefore there can be no kind of privity between the Parties. Whereever a man confesses himself Guilty of a crime, or acknowledges himself to be indebted to another in certain sum &c in a prosecution for the crime or suit for the money against the same man then such sayings and confessions as those may be given in evidence because of the privity between that of which the confession is made and which is then the subject of controversy and him who made the confession &c. In the present instance Young has no more to do with this case than any other man   therefore Richardson ought not to be examined as to his sayings

[The Opinion of Judge Jackson]

Jackson J: The only question in this case is whether the Defendant may give the sayings of a Person in evidence who is a competent witness as respects himself? There is no doubt in my mind but that he shall not. Far be it from me to exclude any Testimony that might be beneficial to the party. Yet the Principles of Law and Justice must be observed as well in behalf of the State as the Prisoner. I dont see how this Testimony can completely avail the Party even if admitted—for a man may commit Perjury in swearing to a fact which is litterally true, as if the fact sworn to be not within his own knowledg[e] at the time it is sworn to. he commits Perjury because tis plain he possesses that corruption of heart which is defined as Perjury and therefore he is punishable. In fine I would only state that if such testimony as this were permitted to be given (taking into consideration to corrupt morral of mankind in general) it would be impossible to convict any one of Perjury   every one might Shield himself under these kind of Confessions.

Campbell J: Concurred.

[The Opinion of Judge Roane]

Roane J: As the opinion of the Court is against me I would only briefly declare, that if Young had been introduc[ed] I should have rejected him, therefore I think this Testimony admissible.

Richardsons Testimony Rejected

This cause was opened about 9 o clock in the morning and the Testimony and Arguments continued until about 4 o clock next morning, when the Jury retired from the Bar and after some little hesitation returned with a Verdict of Not Guilty

Prisoner Acquitted.

MS, MdHi-Bland Casebook, 92–99, Bland Papers (MS 134). Date is taken from *id.* at 62. No further records found. A brief account of the trial survives in a letter addressed by Bland to his sister in Virginia: "Yesterday a certain Major Mongomery was tried for Perjury. his trial was the most lengthy and irksome I have known in this Country. The Jury were sworn about 10 o'clock and the testimony opened on the part of the Prosecution and was not closed on the part of the Prisoner until candles were lit. There were three advocates besides myself in behalf of the State and five in the defence. The arguments of counsel on both side were not got thro' until 4 o'clock in the morning when the Jury retired; and returned with a Verdict of Not Guilty a little before day. The perjury alleged was in swearing that a certain man was at a certain place 'a few minutes before' a certain affray took place and 'a few minutes after' who it was said was during that time at another place. The testimony was very strong against the Prisoner. his acquital was owing to nothing as I concieve but the mercy of the Jury." Theodorick Bland to Sophia Bland, Sept. 7–10, 1800, Bland Papers, MdHi.

Montgomery, who also was the defendant in No. 30 and one of the defendants in No. 48, otherwise has not been identified.

33. Cotton v. Lewis

1800
(Attorney Malpractice)

EDITORIAL NOTE

After returning early in the autumn of 1800 from a pleasure trip with Rachel and a niece to Warm Springs, Virginia,[1] Jackson presided at the hearing of the present case on appeal from the Sumner County court. The suit was one of at least three cases alleging improper behavior by lawyers that Jackson heard during his judicial career.[2]

Early in 1797 Seth Lewis, as counsel for Lazarus Cotton, initiated a trespass-on-the-case action against one George Norris in the Sumner County court. After initial appearances by both parties at the court's April Term 1797, a series of continuances delayed the scheduling of a trial until the following January. On January 4, 1798, the case came on for trial. It soon became apparent, however, that Lewis had failed to file a declaration for his client. The court thereupon declined to send out the jury that had been sworn to try the matter, granted a motion by the defendant for a nonsuit, and ordered Cotton to pay the defendant's costs.[3]

The following October, Cotton initiated the present action against his lawyer in the Sumner County court (Document I). At the court's January Term 1799, Cotton filed his declaration (Document II), and Lewis's counsel, Samuel Donelson and Isaac McNutt, entered a motion for summary judgment and a plea in abatement on the ground that the plaintiff's writ was defective in failing to include the language "trespass on" (Document III). Cotton's counsel, John C. Hamilton, responded by filing a demurrer to Lewis's plea in abatement, asserting that the plea was insufficient to

---

1. See *Jackson Papers*, I, 233–234.
2. The other cases were *Matter of Whiteside*, HDSC Law Rec. Bk., 1798–1803, p. 194 (1801), and *State v. Barry*, MDSC Law Min. Bk., 1788–1803, p. 690 (1802). The court heard a case similar to the present one several years before AJ's elevation to the bench, *Love's Ex'rs v. Payton*, MDSC Law Min. Bk., 1788–1803, p. 122 (1794).
3. Cotton v. Norris, SumCo CPQS Min. Bk. 3, p. 146 (1798).

abate the writ, and by likewise moving for summary judgment (Document IV). The court took the matter under advisement. On October 10, 1799, the court denied Lewis's motion for summary judgment, overruled the defendant's plea in abatement, and sustained Cotton's demurrer. Two days later, on October 12, the court granted Lewis leave to appeal its rulings to the next session of the Mero District Superior Court.[4]

Lewis filed his appeal in the Superior Court on November 13, 1799. The case on appeal came on for a hearing before Judges Jackson, Roane, and Campbell a year and a day later, on November 14, 1800. After argument by counsel upon Cotton's demurrer to the defendant's plea in abatement, Jackson and the other judges overruled the demurrer, sustained Lewis's plea in abatement, quashed the plaintiff's writ, and ordered Cotton to pay Lewis's costs (Document V).

At common law an attorney who betrayed or neglected a client's business was answerable to the injured client in an action of trespass on the case.[5] In 1743 North Carolina lawmakers provided that if a lawyer should "neglect to perform his duty in any action in which he shall be retained, or commit any fraudulent practice," he would be "liable to an action on the case, at common law." The plaintiff was authorized to recover double damages.[6] The legislators were particularly troubled about the neglect of lawyers to file pleadings in a timely manner. A 1794 territorial measure declared that if an attorney failed to file the plaintiff's declaration within the required time, he would be responsible for the court costs and "further liable to the action of such plaintiff for such damages as he or they may have sustained in consequence of such declaration not having been filed as aforesaid."[7]

As in other states during the post-Revolutionary era,[8] the role of the

---

4. Cotton v. Lewis, SumCo CPQS Min. Bk. 3, pp. 219, 229, 236 (1799). Lewis's bond was $500. His securities were Donelson and Thomas Stuart. McNutt evidently was no longer serving with Donelson as counsel of record for Lewis.

For a discussion of the procedure followed by counsel for Cotton in filing a demurrer to Lewis's plea in abatement and moving for summary judgment, see Caruthers, *History of a Law Suit*, 25.

5. 4 Tucker, *Blackstone's Commentaries* 165; see also Stephens v. White, 2 Va. (2 Wash.) 203 (1799).

6. Ch. 4, 1743 Laws of N.C., reprinted in Iredell, *Laws of North Carolina* 99, 1 Scott, *Laws of Tennessee* 77.

7. Ch. 1, 1794 Terr. S. of River Ohio Acts, reprinted in 1 Scott, *Laws of Tennessee* 457. This statute followed a similar measure enacted in North Carolina in 1786. Ch. 14, 1786 Laws of N.C., reprinted in Iredell, *Laws of North Carolina* 584, 1 Scott, *Laws of Tennessee* 368.

8. James W. Ely, Jr., "Law in a Republican Society: Continuity and Change in the Legal System of Post-Revolutionary America," in Richard A. Preston, *Perspectives on Revolution and Evolution* (Durham, N.C., 1979), 46–65; Maxwell Bloomfield, *American Lawyers in a Changing Society, 1776–1876* (Cambridge, Mass., 1976), 32–58.

attorney in early Tennessee might well have been a sensitive topic. It is noteworthy that *Cotton,* involving attorney malpractice, was one of a handful of cases during Jackson's career in which the Superior Court sustained a plea based on a technical defect in the writ.[9]

9. Cotton has not been further identified. Jackson as a practicing lawyer represented clients with interests adverse to Cotton's in at least three cases and as a private litigant was Cotton's adversary in at least one suit after he left the bench. Roberts v. Cotton, SumCo Records, T (1794); Cotton v. Turney, SumCo CPQS Trial Docket, 1787–1801, p. 27 (1791); Butler v. Cotton, SumCo CPQS Trial Docket, 1787–1801, p. 21 (1790); Jackson & Hutchings v. Cotton, SumCo CPQS Rec. Bk., 1808–1809, p. 74 (1808).

For Lewis, see Part IV.

I. WRIT AND RETURN

Sumner County Court of Pleas and Quarter Sessions

October 6, 1798

State of Tennessee, Sumner County Sst. To the Sheriff of said County Greeting. You are hereby commanded to take the body of Seth Lewis if to be found in your bailwick and him safely keep so that you have him before the Justices of our insuing County Court of pleas and quarter sessions to be held for said County at the House of William Gallaspie on the first monday in January next, then and there to answer Lazurus Cotton in a plea of Case to his damage fifty Dollars. Herein fail not, and have you then and there this writ, Witness David Shelby Clerk of our said Court at office this first monday in October Anno Domini 1798 and twenty third year of our Independance, issued October 6th

David Shelby Clk.

Tr, TDaCo-MDSC Law Min. Bk., 1788–1803, p. 390. The minute book indicates that the writ was returned by the sheriff to the Sumner County court's January Term 1799 endorsed: "Came to hand 6th October and executed the same day J. Cage."

II. DECLARATION OF
LAZARUS COTTON

Sumner County Court of Pleas and Quarter Sessions

State of Tennessee ⎱
Sumner County ⎰   January Term 1799

Lazurus Cotton by his attorney complains of Seth Lewis in custody &c.
for that, to wit, the said Plaintiff on the   ¹ day of   ¹ In the year of our
lord one thousand seven hundred and ninety eight at Sumner aforesaid
imployed the said Seth Lewis as his attorney (& The said Lewis having
a license to practise as an attorney in the different Courts in the State
aforesaid as well as the Court of Sumner aforesaid) in an action on the
case brought by the said Cotton against George Norris in the County
Court of Sumner aforesaid, the said Cotton having paid the said Lewis his
lawful fees in the suit aforesaid. Nevertheless the said Lewis intending
to defraud the said Cotton neglected to file a Declaration in said suit.
Wherefore the said Cotton for want of a Declaration was nonsuited at the
January term 1798, of the County Court of Sumner County in said action
as appears by the record of said County Court of Sumner County and
Judgment was given against him to pay the sum of thirty seven Dollars as
cost to the said Defendant Norris wherefore the said Plaintiff says he is
injured and hath sustained damage to the value of fifty dollars, and therefore he brings suit &

J. C. Hamilton

Tr, TDaCo-MDSC Law Min. Bk., 1788–1803, pp. 390–391.

   1. Thus in Tr.

III. DEFENDANT'S PLEA IN
ABATEMENT

Sumner County Court of Pleas and Quarter Sessions

[January 1799]

And the said Seth in his own proper person comes and prays oyer of
the said original writ of the said Lazarus Cotton and it is read to him in
these words, to wit, which being read and heard the said Seth prays Judt.

of the said writ for that he saith, that the said writ doth not agree with the form of the Register in that case made and provided true that the said writ wants the words "Trespass on" and this he is ready to verify wherefore he prays Judgment of the said writ and that it may be quashed.

Samuel Donelson pro Defendant.

Tr, TDaCo-MDSC Law Min. Bk., 1788–1803, p. 391. Date is taken from *id*. at 390.

IV. PLAINTIFF'S DEMURRER TO THE PLEA

Sumner County Court of Pleas and Quarter Sessions

[January 1799]

And the said Lazarus says that the plea of the said Defendant and the matter therein contained is insufficient in law to quash the said writ, wherefore for want of a sufficient plea in this behalf the said Plaintiff prays Judgment and his damages unless the Defendant answer over to the said Plaintiffs Declaration.

J. C. Hamilton pro querente

Tr, TDaCo-MDSC Law Min. Bk., 1788–1803, p. 391. Date is taken from *id*. at 390.

V. MINUTE BOOK ENTRY

*Mero District Superior Court, Nashville
Judges Jackson, Roane, and Campbell Presiding*

[November 14, 1800]

| Lazurus Cotton against Seth Lewis___ | } In Case Appeal |

Be it remembered that on the 13th day of November 1799, an appeal from the County Court of Sumner was filed in the office of the Clerk of the Superior Court of law for the District of Mero, in the words following, to wit[1] . . . . And the Cause was continued until this Term of the Superior Court to wit, November 1800, at which time came the parties by their Attornies, and there upon the Plaintiffs Demurrer to the Defendants plea in abatement was argued; and because it seems to the Court that the said Plea, and the matters therein contained are sufficient in law to abate the Plaintiffs writ; It is considered by the Court that the demurrer aforesaid be overruled and that the said Writ be quashed; and that the Plaintiff pay to the said Deft. his costs by him about his defence in That behalf expended &c.

MS, TDaCo-MDSC Law Min. Bk., 1788–1803, pp. 390–391. Date is taken from *id.*

    1. The texts of Documents I–IV follow at this point in the MS. The text of Document IV in the MS is followed by: "And after demurrer joined, the Cause was continued to each succeeding Term, until July sessions 1799, at which time the Court, after hearing the arguments of the counsel on both sides, took and advissare thereon until the succeeding term, to wit, October session 1799, when & at which time, the Court overrules the plea of the Defendant from which Judgment the Defendant by Samuel Donelson Esqr. one of his said Attornies prays an appeal, files reasons, & obtains the same, and enters into bond for the prosecution of said appeal with effect in the penal sum of five hundred dollars with Samuel Donelson and Thomas St[u]art securities, &c."

34. Hall v. Amis et al.

1801

(Commercial Law)·

EDITORIAL NOTE

When the North Carolina General Assembly created Hawkins County in January 1787, it also appointed seven commissioners to select a site for and oversee the construction of a courthouse for the new county. After having settled upon a site by June of that year, the commissioners apparently contracted with Hall for the actual construction of the building. The building was completed by 1792.[1]

Hall subsequently brought an action in debt in the Hawkins County court against Amis and the commissioners to recover his compensation for constructing the courthouse. He relied upon a bond executed by the commissioners and made payable to him upon the completed construction of the building. In the Hawkins County court, Hall obtained a judgment without producing the bond upon which his action was based. Before execution of the judgment, the defendants secured a writ of certiorari from one of the judges of the Washington District Superior Court returnable to the court's March Term 1801, presumably raising the question of whether production of the bond was a prerequisite for judgment in a debt action.

At trial in the Superior Court in March 1801, Hall again failed to enter the bond into evidence. The jury reversed the county court's judgment and returned a verdict for the commissioners. Hall's counsel, Pleasant M. Miller and Jenkin Whiteside, filed a motion for a new trial on the grounds that the Superior Court jury's verdict was contrary to the evidence and that the law did not require the production of the bond as the basis for an action in debt when both parties to the action stipulate the existence of

---

1. Ch. 34, § 5, 1786 Laws of N.C. 29; Prentice Price, "Early History of Hawkins County," *Rogersville Review,* Nov. 26, 1926, citing James W. Rogan's 1859 manuscript quotations from minutes of the Hawkins County court that no longer survive; see *Knoxville Gazette,* Nov. 3, 1792.

the obligation (Document I). Plaintiff argued that the burden of proving payment of the debt was upon the defendants. The commissioners' counsel, Joseph Hamilton, argued that the plaintiff's failure to produce the bond raised a strong presumption that the debt had been paid. Hamilton observed that, under the plaintiff's interpretation of the law, the rights of possible assignees of an obligee's bond would not be protected adequately and multiple actions upon the same debt instrument could arise for the purpose merely of harassing obligors like the defendants.

Jackson, finding the rule requiring the production of a bill of exchange as a prerequisite for recovery on the instrument analogous to the case at hand, rendered an opinion denying the plaintiff's motion for a new trial (Document II). Judge Roane disagreed, concluding that the jury had not been warranted in drawing a presumption of payment from the plaintiff's failure to produce the bond and that the jury's verdict thus was not merely contrary to but entirely without supporting evidence. Judge Campbell took the motion under advisement but several days later issued an opinion concurring with Jackson's. Plaintiff's motion for a new trial thus was denied.

The minutes of the Hawkins County court, which might have provided further information about the parties and the background of the litigation at the trial stage, apparently were destroyed by fire in 1863.[2] The status and identity of Amis as one of the named defendants thus remain uncertain. Bland's styling of the case as "Hall vrs Amis & al: Commissioners of Hawkins County" is subject to at least two interpretations. Amis was sued either in his private capacity, perhaps as surety for the commissioners, or in his public capacity as one of the commissioners himself. Since the bond itself has not survived, there is no evidence with which to confirm or refute the first possibility. Amis was not one of the commissioners originally appointed by the legislature in 1787. The legislative records through 1801 contain no references to his having been appointed to replace one of the original commissioners. Hence, the second possibility also remains undocumented. The identity of the named defendant is equally puzzling. There is no indication that the defendant was the John Amis whose name surfaces infrequently (see, *e.g.,* Hawkins County Deed Book 1, pp. 281, 374) in the few records that survive for the county. More likely, the defendant was either Thomas Amis, who had been the county's representative in the North Carolina senate and who was the father-in-law of the grantor of the land upon which the courthouse was constructed, or, more probably, the executrix of his estate, his widow,

---

2. Pollyanna Creekmore, comp., "Early East Tennessee Taxpayers: Hawkins County, 1809–1812," ETHS *Publ.* No. 32, p. 118 (1960).

Lucy Haynes Amis. Thomas Amis apparently had died by 1797. Had the case been initiated either before or after Amis's death, Hall is likely to have proceeded after 1797 against Lucy Haynes Amis, as the executrix of Amis's estate.[3]

3. See Amis Genealogical Records, Vertical File, T; Hawkins County Will Bk. 1, p. 1; *BD–Tenn. Assembly*, I, 10.
Hall has not been further identified.

BLAND'S STATEMENT OF THE
CASE AND MINUTES OF
THE ARGUMENT OF COUNSEL
AND OF
THE OPINIONS OF THE COURT

Washington District Superior Court, Jonesboro
Judges Jackson, Roane, and Campbell Presiding

[March 1801]
Hall vrs Amis & al: Commissioners
of Hawkins County.

This was an action of Debt which had been commenced in the County Court of Hawkins on a Bond given by the Commissioners to Hall for the Payment of certain sum due for the building of the Court House in that County. The Defendants relied on the Plea of Payment alone without oyer of the Bond.

In the County Court of Hawkins Hall obtained Verdict and Judgment in his favor but before Execution was returned satisfied the Defendants obtained a Certiorari and Supersedeas from one of the Judges of this court in vacation by which the cause was brought hither.

On the trial at this Term the Defendants insisted that the Plaintiff was bound to produc the Bond on which his action was founded before he could be entitled to a verdict, No Bond was shewn in evidence to the Jury and they found for the Defendants upon which the Plaintiff entered a Rule to shew cause why a new trial should not be granted.

[Pleasant M. Miller for Plaintiff]

Miller in support of the Rule: I contend in this case that a New Trial ought to be granted because the Verdict is clearly contrary to evidence—

we were not bound to produc the Bond on trial, he who pleads a Deed must always make Profert of it; and the Deed is regularly in Court only during that Term at which it is pr[o]ducd for after that the opposite Party can't have oyer of it because says the Books the Deed is then out of Court (4 Bac: Abr: 113)[1] On the Plea of payment in Debt, or Covenants Performed in Covenant no variance between the Deed and Declaration can be taken advantage of Hay: R: 149[2] from whence I deduce this argument that it is wholly unnecessary to pr[o]duce the Deed on trial for if it were so the Party ought not to be tied up by his tacit admission but be allowed to take all advantages that ever were in his power.

[Joseph Hamilton for Defendants]

Hamilton against the Rule. The Arguments of the Gent. last up have principally gone to shew that Oyer cannot be had of a Bond after the term at which it is declared on. that as I conceive has no relation to the present question. The Bond is the ground of the Plaintiffs action and without the cause ought not to be entertained any longer in this Court. What! will you ask 12 honest men on their oaths to give a Verdict in your favour, without shewing them any grounds or evidence of your demand? The Bond may have been assigned over to a third person, or it may be taken out of the files and another suit have been bro't on it and the Deft thus twice harrassed doubly charged for the sa[me] Debt[.] The Bond with its endorsements is the highest Evidence and ought in this case to have been the sole guide of the Jury. No doubt in this case the Defts relied on the Plea of payment with an express view to the endorsements on the Bond itself. and the Plaintiffs not Producing the Bond affords a strong presumption that full Receipts in full discharge of it are indorsed [on] it. Doubtless it was on this Presumption the Jury founded their Verdict. therefore I think it a good one & hope it will not be set aside.

[Jenkin Whiteside for Plaintiff]

Whiteside contra   I conceive it is not necessary to produc the Bond on which the action is founded on Trial in the present case. Let us examine the State of the pleadings. the Declaration states the date Sealing and delivery of a certain Bond and complains that the Defendants have not paid the sum in which they acknowledged themselves indebted to the Plaintiff. the Defendants make defence and say that the P[l]aintiff ought not to have his action against them because they have paid that Sum, on this Issue is joined. The Jury are sworn to try the issue joined. now how can the production of the Bond on such a trial as this affect the case[?] if produced can it prove a negative that the money has not been paid? No. It is certainly incumbent on the Defendants to prove that it has been paid, the sole question with the Jury was [whether it had been] paid or not and

the onus Probandi rested entirely on the Defendants and not having pro-
ducd any Testimony to support this issue which is an affirmative one on
their part I do contend the Verdict is without one tittle of Evidence to
support therefore ought to be set aside—Had the issue been non est Factum the case would have been otherwise because the validity of the Bond
would then have been at issue and the Production of it at the [trial] in that
case is essentially necessary, but in the present case the Bond is admitted
and there is no rule more fixed and well known than that whatever is admitted by the parties in pleading need not be proved on trial. As to what
was said respecting the Indorsements—I answer we are not bound to take
care of the Defendants vouchers and Receipts. if there are Receipts indorsed on the Bond why did they not pray oyer of the Bond and make it
part of the Record or give us notice to bring forward those receipts. The
Law that has been read from Haywood clearly supports my reasoning[.] a
variance can be taken no notice of by the Jury on Covenants Performed,
and why? because that is not the issue they are sworn to try. In answer to
the Genl. assertion that the Bond may be taken out of the files and another suit be brought on it—I say there is no Law of this State which requires him to leave his Bond in the office[.] there is no Law directing the
Clerk to take care of it for him. and if another suit should be brought on
the same bond the Defendants may Plead this action in Bar. Pleas must be
true at the time of Pleading and if the Defendants Plea is so no subsequent
assignment can affect him.

[The Opinion of Judge Jackson]

Jackson J. I have a doubt in my mind how far it will be necessary to
produce the Bond on trial to convince the Jury that the Plaintiff is entitled
to a Verdict even on the Plea of payment. It is a new case to me [I] confess.
I may be blended by custom and usage but in all the course of Practice I
have observed the instrument declared on has uniformly been produced
on the trial and I have from thence thought it necessary. In the case of a
Bill of Exchange it is necessary to shew it on the trial otherwise the Plaintiff would not be entitled to a recovery (3 Term Rep. 301).[3] The case in
Haywood is just. the party could not take advantage of the Variance but
on different ground from that contended for. For my part I conceive it
necessary in all cases to produc the Bond [on] trial in order to entitle the
Plaintiff to a Recovery 1 Esp. N.P. 233.[4]

[The Opinion of Judge Roane]

Roane J. In order to understand this case correctly it will be proper to
take a concise view of it in the natural order in which it presents itself. An
Action of Debt has been brought on a Bond the Declaration sets it out.
the Defendants come and say they have paid the Bond so set out, that is

the issue the Jury are sworn to try[.] their Verdict then in pursuance of that ought to be either that they have or have not paid off the Bond so set out. It seems to me to be going too far on the presumption of payment to say that the Plaintiff's not producing the Bond on the trial is evidence of the Defendants having paid it. Therefore I think that the verdict in this case is not contrary to but without evvidence.

The consiquence of what I have said is that the Plaintiff is by no means under the necessity of Producing the bond on the trial of an issue joined on the Plea of Payment. As to what was said about an assignment after Action bro't that (if at all) can only be taken advantage of by Plea puis darrein Continuance

[The Opinion of Judge Campbell]

Campbell J. I do not at present feel prepared to give an opinion[.] I had rather advise.

At a subsequent day in the Term his Honor J. Campbell concurred with his Honor J. Jackson. Doug 316, N.2.[5] 2 Str. 1149.[6] 2 Blac. R. 748.[7] 3 Wils 155.[8] Barnes 233.[9]

Rule discharged

MS, MdHi-Bland Casebook, 103–113, Bland Papers (MS 134). Date is taken from *id.* at 101.

1. 4 Bacon, *Abridgment* 113: "Oyer of the Deed cannot be demanded but during the Time it is in Court, and that is all the Term wherein it is produced, and then it may be entered in *hæc verba;* and there may be a Demurrer or Issue upon it; but it cannot be done of another Term, because the Deed is then out of the Court."

2. Anonymous, 2 N.C. (1 Hayw. 144, 149) 166, 171–172 (1795): "As to the other objection, that the name of the apprentice is put in a subsequent part of the instrument, instead of that of the Chairman [the presiding justice acting in his official capacity for the benefit of the apprentice, and orphan]; if upon the profert thereof made in the Plaintiff's declaration, the Defendant had craved *oyer,* and demurred for the variance between the covenant set forth and that which appeared to be in the indentures, the objection might then have been fatal; but where the covenant stated in the declaration, is once admitted to be as there stated, by a plea of covenants performed, he cannot afterwards be permitted to say there is no such covenant; and the production of the warrant afterwards upon the trial by the Plaintiff is irregular, although it is often done when a declaration is mislaid, or not readily to be come at, it being presumable that the declaration has been drawn in conformity to it; and the court ought to take no notice of an inconsistency in the writing itself, discovered upon such an irregular reading—they cannot do it without a departure from the record and the issue submitted to the jury, which is, whether the Defendant has performed that covenant that is set forth in the declaration. . . ."

3. Green v. Hearne, 3 T.R. 301, 100 Eng. Rep. 587 (K.B. 1789). In an action on a bill of exchange against the defendant as acceptor, the plaintiff won a default judgment. At the execution of the writ of inquiry, the bill was produced, but it did not appear to have been accepted. No other evidence was produced. The jury returned with a verdict on the amount of the bill of exchange produced. The defendant moved to set aside the default judgment and the writ of inquiry executed thereon on the ground, *inter alia,* that the defendant had not accepted. The court denied the motion. Justice Buller declared, "When a defendant suffers judgment to go by default, he admits the cause of action. And thus far an action on a bill of exchange, and an action for money had and received, are alike: but beyond that there

is no similarity. For, in the latter, the defendant only admits something to be due; and, as the demand is uncertain, the plaintiff must prove the debt before the jury. But, in the former, as the bill of exchange is set out on the record, the defendant, by suffering judgment to go by default, admits that he is liable to the amount of it: here then the defendant has admitted that he did accept the particular bill of exchange set out in the declaration; and the only reason for producing it to the jury on executing the writ of inquiry, is to see whether or not any part of it has been paid." 3 T.R. at 302–303, 100 Eng. Rep. at 587.

4. 1 Espinasse, *Actions at Nisi Prius* 233.

5. Thellusson v. Fletcher, 1 Doug. 315, 99 Eng. Rep. 203 (K.B. 1780): "In actions upon a bill of exchange, or a promissory note, nothing but the instrument is to be proved before the jury, the sum being thereby ascertained." 1 Doug. at 316, 99 Eng. Rep. at 204–205. In a note to this statement, the reporter adds, "In such cases, although the note or bill is stated, and the execution of it averred, in the declaration, it has been settled, in many instances, that it must be produced before the inquiring jury." 1 Doug. at 316 n.2, 99 Eng. Rep. at 204 n.2.

6. Bevis v. Lindsell, 2 Str. 1149, 93 Eng. Rep. 1093 (K.B. n.d.): "In assumpsit upon a promissory note, there was judgment by default, and on executing a writ of inquiry, the plaintiff did not produce the subscribing witness, but offered other evidence of its being the defendant's hand. And the Court held, this was sufficient, for the note being set out in the declaration is admitted, and the only use of producing it is to see whether any money is indorsed to be paid upon it."

7. Snowden v. Thomas, 2 Black. W. 748, 96 Eng. Rep. 438 (K.B. 1771). The plaintiff's declaration contained two counts, one on a promissory note and another for money expended. The defendant pleaded a setoff. The plaintiff denied the setoff and was awarded judgment for lack of a rejoinder. The note was produced upon a writ of inquiry, but the sum due thereon was not proved. The defendant's offer to confess damages on being allowed a month's stay of execution was not agreed to. The jury assessed the plaintiff's damages at six guineas, the value of the note. Chief Justice DeGrey held, "Damages must either be proved or admitted. The present case does neither, for the set-off confesses only general damages on both counts. The note therefore ought to have been proved. But the confession of the defendant's attorney makes this case particular in its circumstances, and on that ground only I am for discharging the rule." 2 Black. W. at 748–749, 93 Eng. Rep. at 438.

8. Anonymous, 3 Wils. 155, 95 Eng. Rep. 986 (K.B. 1771): "[U]pon a judgment by default in an action upon a promissory note, or a bill of exchange, the sum due thereon is admitted, and need not be proved upon the execution of a writ of inquiry."

9. Billers et al. v. Bowles, Barnes 233, 94 Eng. Rep. 892 (K.B. n.d.): "Rule to shew cause why inquisition taken on writ of inquiry of damages, made absolute; no evidence of plaintiff's demand having been given to the sheriff and jury. Plaintiff urged, that the demand was by promissory note indorsed set forth in the declaration, which was admitted by not pleading, and the damages found were only the amount of principal and interest due on such note. But the Court held, that the note indorsed ought to have been produced, and the note and indorsement proved."

35. Moore v. Gains

1801
(Procedure)

I. BLAND'S STATEMENT OF THE
CASE AND MINUTES
OF THE ARGUMENT OF COUNSEL
AND OF THE COURT'S DECISION

Washington District Superior Court, Jonesboro
Judges Jackson, Roane, and Campbell Presiding

[March 1801]
Matthew Moore vrs James Gaines senr.

This was an action on the Case. One Henry Maggot had given his Bond to Gaines (the Defendant in this action for the Sum of ———— conditioned to pay the sum of ———— one half in cash the other in trade that is good property. this Bond Gaines assigned to More in these words towit—

"I James Gaines do assign the within contents to Matthew Moore and enter myself security for the same

James Gaines"

Upon which Assignment Moore brought this action against Gaines in the County Court of Sullivan (1 Esp. N.P. 95)[1] The Defendant by John Rhea his Counsel, after oyer of the Bond Condition and Assignment Demurred and set down for causes of Demurrer first. That the Bond was not a negotiable instrument. Secondly. That the Plaintiff had not averred in his Declaration that he had used due diligence to obtain payment of the original obligor or even that he had made a demand of Payment. thirdly That the Plaintiff had not averred that the Defendant had Notice of the Default of the original obligor to make payment. On argument of this Demurrer in the County Court it was sustained and Judgment entered up for the Defendant from which decision the Plaintiff appealed to this Court, and at last September Term, the Record being filed, on the Motion of Theo Bland counsel for the Defendant this Court affirmed the Judgment of the Court below it appearing on the face of the Record that it had not been lodged in the Office fifteen days before that Term as the Law directs[2]

Afterwards the Plaintiff by his counsel P. M. Miller moved the County Court of Sullivan at its November Sessions to allow a writ of Error, which they did and accordingly security was given for the Prosecution and a complete Transcript of the Record there together with an assignment of Errors as filed in the County Court came here to this Term.

Bland for the Defendant on Wednesday moved the Court to quash this Writ of Error on the ground that a Writ of Error Coram vobis ought to have been brought on the Record which was already in this Court, and not as this is from the Court below. After some argument the Court postponed the case for further consideration until Saturday and suggested another point to the Bar which they desired might also be argued—to wit Whether under the Act of Assembly the County Court could allow a Writ of Error at any other Term than that at which the cause was tried.

[Hugh Lawson White for Plaintiff]

On Saturday, White in Support of the Writ of Error. I shall confine myself to the grounds already suggested by the Bench and Bar. In the first place I do contend that the County Court may grant a writ of Error after a Term has elapsed. this may clearly be deduced from the express words of the Statute itself—the words are, "That when any Person shall be desirous to prosecute a writ of Error, he shall move the County Court of Pleas and quarter Sessions, *where such suit is or hath been depending,* to allow a writ of Error, he first entering into bond &c[3] These words are general and seem to contemplate as well a cause that *is* depending during the Term at which the writ of Error is moved for as one that *hath been* pending at any time before. I say at any time previous, for words "*hath been*" are indefinite and limit us to no given portion of time past. This is a beneficial Statute intended to introduce a new and more expeditious and plain mode of prosecuting writs of Error for the case and benefit of the citizens, and as such the Court will never narrow down and cramp its meaning but will pursuant to the rule laid down in 4 Bac Ab: 647[4] give it the most liberal construction in order to effectuate the intention of the Legislature. This too is a remedial Statute. the obvious scope of which is to remove those numerous difficulties that obstructed the course of proceeding by writ of Error at the Common Law. The legislators meant by the passage of this Law to lay open to the citizens a plain and direct way to relief, and therefore has given them a right to make application for a writ of Error to that Court which has the immediate custody of the Record which they

wish to have examined and rectified. It may be objected that if my doctrine were admitted—a Record may be carried to a Superior and the
Judgment be reversed by one party without the other's having any notice
of it. To this I answer The Common Law has adapted a writ to this very
purpose. if the Defendant in Error were served with a Scire facias ad Audiendum errores, (as he ought in this case to be) all objections of this sort
must be wholly obviated.

Next—Is the Record of this here or in the Court below? Upon the so-
lution of this question depends the Gentlemans objection stated the other
day. There is a very striking distinction between the law of England concerning writs of Error and the law of this State respecting Appeals and in
order to elucidate this distinction more clearly, I shall for a moment call
the attention of the Court to that Law in 4 Bac. Ab. 648[5] which says that
in cases where a word known to the common law is used it shall be understood in the same sense it was at the Common Law. The Law of Tennessee
prescribing the mode of prosecuting appeals says that "A *transcript* of the
records and proceedings in the suit on which the appeal shall be made,
shall be delivered to the clerk of the superior Court at least fifteen days
before the sitting of the Term &c."[6] From hence it clearly appears that the
original record itself remains in the Court below,—In England the original Record itself was transmitted to the Superior Court—2. Bac. Ab.
202.[7] nothing was left in the inferior Court. therefore a writ of Error
Coram vobis there was the only mode that could be pursued after writ
that had legally brought up the record was quashed for insufficiency.
Some of the cases read by the Gent. the other day so far from supporting
his position rather go to prove the contrary. In 2 Bac. Ab. 203[8] Error
from the K.B. to Parlt. says the transcript only goes to Parliament and on
their reversing or affirming the Judgment, it is sent back to the K.B. there
to be carried into effect. this shews that where a transcript only is sent up
the Law recognizes the Record as continuing in the inferior Court. The
next case of Error from the K.B. in Ireland to the K.B. in England, I think
is still stronger to the same point. only a *Transcript* is sent up. and as
soon as the K.B. in England has decided on the Errors, it issues its mandate to the K.B. in Ireland to do execution. this mandate, surely can't be
the sole authority by which the Court below acts. No, their proceeding
are again from thence forward founded on the original Record which has
ever remained with them But had that gone up to the K.B. in England,
that would have been the only Court competent to do execution, and of
course it would have issued from thence. In 2 Mall. Ent. 371–2[9] the same
law is laid down, all which in my mind conclusively goes to shew, that the
law the Gent. so much relied on from 2 Bac. Ab. 216[10] only applies to
those cases where the original Record itself was removed, and not where
a *transcript* only has gone for in those cases the Law completely recog-

nizes the record in the C below. However, admitting the English practice in this particular to be as the Gent. has stated, yet I think the Court will say it can't apply in this Country, for if it does, such is the nature of our system of Jurisprudence, that the Plaintiff in this case will be wholly without relief from this erroneous adjudication, for taking this to be a record of this Court the decision can only be reversed by a Superior tribunal for errors in Law, and in Tennessee there is none such to which it may be carried for that purpose. Upon the whole I trust the Court will say that this writ of Error shall not be quashed.

[Theodorick Bland for Defendant]

Bland contra. The Gent. has transposed the order in which the objections to this writ of Error have been made. however as I conceive it can in no wise affect the subject, I will pursue his method. The first question then to be considered is wether a County court can allow a Wr. E. after a term has elapsed & it rests wholly upon the construction of our Act of Assembly. The rules laid down in the Books for the construction of Statutes are so entirely consonant with the principles of sound reason and common sense that I think it altogether needless troubling the Court with them. The object and intention of the legislature I agree ought to be effectuated if possible, but while we give a loose to liberallity for that purpose, let us be cautious not to o'erstep the bounds of the Law. let us take a well known Rule for our guide in this respect and look into various sections of this Statute and endeavour to draw forth those ideas with which the legislative mind was impress at the time of its passage, and see if we can find amongst them any that will warrant the Gentlemans deductions. The 87th section has a Proviso annexed in these words, "That if it shall so happen, that there shall not be thirty days between the last day of the Term or *hearing* in the County Court, and the next term of the Superior Court to which such appeal shall be made, or *writ of Error allowed,* then such appeal or writ of Error shall *be continued* and a transcript of the records shall be transmitted and filed in like manner in the office of the Superior Court the term suceding that which shall immediately follow such County Court term in which such *trial and hearing* shall be had as aforesaid." This of itself I think afords a complete refutation of the Gents doctrine, Appeals and writs of Error such as the Present are blended and put upon the same footing. Why say the writ of Error shall be continued to the succeeding term of the superior Court if there should not be thirty days between the *trial or hearing* in the County Court and the Court above, if the legislature meant or intended to impower the County Courts to allow writs of Error at any other term after that at which the cause was tried? would not a Proviso worded as this is (Permit me to ask) have been

altogether nugatory, indeed downright nonsense? it certainly would. That
the Power of the County Court to allow writs of Error is confined solely to
that term at which the cause was tried or heard, appears also from a com-
parative view of the 65th sec (the one now under discussion) and the 37th
which points out the mode by which this Court are empowrd to grant
such writs. In the former no notice is required. by the latter ten days notice must be given to the adverse party previous to the motion for the
writ, and an assignment of Errors must accompany the motion and
be filed at the time it is made. Why this difference? The answer is obvious   in the one case the Parties are in Court and are bound to take
notice of the suspension of the *Judgment, or its effects* by *new trial, Reason* in arrest of Judgment, Appeal or writ of Error and that therefore a
notice in this case is not required by the Law. In the other case the parties
are supposed to be entirely out of Court and the notice was intended to
supply the place of a Sci. fa. which in my mind is a strong presumption
that the legislature meant virtually to abrogate the English common Law
notification by Sci fa, even if ever were at all in use in this State—As to
the words "*is or hath been depending*" in the 65th section upon which
the Gentleman builds so much. The principles of the Law will (I think)
abundantly explain the propriety with which they used without impugn-
ing the doctrine I contend for in the least. So soon as judgment is
rendered in any cause the parties are in strictness out of and the cause no
longer pends—and again the whole Term is considered as one day and the
Records of that term are during the term in the breast of the Court liable
to be corrected amended or rescinded[.] Suppose then a Judgment be
rendered the first day of the term[.] the cause as respects the parties is no
longer depending even during that term. but as respects the Court if
pends until the end of the term and they may till then call the parties
again before them to a litigation de novo. When the legislature gave the
County Courts power to allow writs of Error on Judgments rendered during the term they were no doubt impressed with these principles which
led them very properly to use the expression "is or hath been depending."
I concur with the Gent. that this is a benefical Statute, but the only advantage that I can conceive was intended was to put it in the power of the
party who thot himself injured by an erroneous Judgment to stop the
effects and consequences of such a Judgt. instantly, and carry it immediately to a superior tribunal where it might be rectified. this is a benefit
the citizen had not at the Common Law, and no doubt is all the legislature meant he should have. So much for the first point.
    I proceed next to inquire, Whether a writ of Error ought to have been
brought on the Record which is in this Court, or on that which is in the
Court below[.] when I made this motion on this ground, I thought it suf-

ficient of itself and was aware that some handle might be made of the word *Transcript* in our Act of Assembly. I read therefore the case of a writ of Error from Ireland to shew that altho a transcript only had been legally lodged here yet so soon as that was done the record in the Court below ceased, this I think the case does evidently shew, and so far as respects that Point this and that case are in my humble conception precisely parallel. The danger of removing the record from Ireland to England is the only reason why it was not done, and it is (at least) highly *probable* our Legislature in directing a transcript to be carried to the superior Court were actuated by the same motives that they had only the safety of the Record in view, and were therefore cautious not to insert in the Law any words that might negative the Common Law in any other respect; but left it to its well known operation as in the case from Ireland. The case of the writ of Error from K.B. to Pal, and that from the K.B. in Ireland to the K.B. in England have been much relied on to prove that the [record] is in the Inferior Court because those two cases say that only a transcript is sent up, and Execution is done by the inferior Court. the reason of this in the Parl. case is because the Parl. may dissolve and there could then be any proceedings thereupon to have Execution. The reason why the KB in England can't issue execution in a case bro't from Ireland is not because the original Record remains in the inferior Court, but because (as the Law which The Gent. read from Mallory expressly States) there is no officer in Ireland who is bound to obey the Process of the K.B. in England. These cases are excceptions in this respect therefore out of the general Rule of the Common Law which in all cases directs that the Superior Court should not only examine the Errors, but proceed to complete that which the inferior Court ought to have done. 1 Morg. V.M. 308.[11] 5 Com D. 299.[12] 2 Mall. Ent. 372.[13] An additional argument to this deduced from the Com. Law may be drawn from the 68th section of this Act of Assembly which requires that the Clerk of the County Court shall "give an attested copy of such record with a taxation of all costs accrued; to the appellant, or Plaintiff in Error &c" this shew that it was intended not only a transcript of the Record but a Bill of Costs and every thing should go up that was necessary to enable the Superior Court to do complete justice without any further reference to the original record which was from thenceforth to be considered a[s] a mere nihility and ever more cease. In the consideration of the preceeding point I have had occasion to notice the strong affinity under our Act of Assembly between an appeal and a writ of Error. in many instances they are meer convertible modes of arriving at the same thing. this very case is an example, it was bro't here originally by appeal to reverse the decision of the County Court for errors in Law. but however they may differ in some respects yet as to the removal of the Record from the inferior to the Superior Court they have precisely the same effect. the Record in this case was legally and properly bro't here to last September term and of course from thence forward the record in the Court below ceased, the consequence of which is that a writ of Error Coram vobis is the proper indeed the only mode by which the supposed Error in the record of this case can be examined into. The case I before relied on from 2 Bac. Ab. 216,[14] so far as I am capable of understanding can in nothing be distinguished from the present. A writ of Error Coram vobis may be brought either to reverse the decision of the same Court for error in Fact or to rectify the errors both of Law and Fact of an inferior Court whose proceedings have been regularly and legally brought up. In Lillys Entries 231–2[15] there are examples of such writs. Entries are the most respectable evidence of the Law, and are with propriety of metaphor said to be its living voice. As to any thing the Gent said about this Courts not having the power to reverse its own proceeding for errors in Law it can't in any shape apply to this case because the writ of Error Coram Vobis would not examine this Courts proceedings but those of the County Court which have been legally lodged here. In fine trusting that your Honors are fully sensible of the weight of the objections that have been made to this writ of Error I humbly hope that you will without hesitation say it shall be quashed.

Miller on the same side with Mr. White and his argument was nearly to the same purport of Mr. Whites but as I took no Notes of it I could not undertake to report it

Dade in support of the Motion to quash his arguments I took no note of either.

Curia advisare until Monday

[The Court's Decision]

Monday Per Curiam[:] The County Court have no authority to allow a writ of Error at any term but at that at which the Cause was tried. On the other ground the Court will give no opinion. On the first ground therefore alone let this writ of Error be quashed.

MS, MdHi-Bland Casebook, 115–138, Bland Papers (MS 134). Date is taken from *id.* at 101.

Apart from Documents I and II, the only other records for the case are a MS fieri facias issued over the signature of James Aiken, clerk of the Washington District Superior Court of Law, on Apr. 23, 1801, and a MS alias fieri facias issued on May 10, 1802, both of which are in NcD-Tennessee Court Records, Washington County, 1801–1804.

Moore has not been identified. Gains, whose surname Bland spells "Gaines," was the owner of some 3,000 acres in Sullivan County in 1792 and, before 1800, had secured an appointment as one of three commissioners to lay off and sell lots in the town of Blountville. *Knoxville Gazette*, June 2, 1792; Oliver Taylor, *Historic Sullivan: A History of Sullivan County, Tennessee* (Bristol, Tenn., 1909), 139.

1. 1 Espinasse, *Actions at Nisi Prius* 95.
2. Ch. 1, § 66, 1794 Terr. S. of River Ohio Acts, reprinted in 1 Scott, *Laws of Tennessee* 481.
3. *Id.* at § 65.
4. 4 Bacon, *Abridgment* 647: "Such Construction ought to be put upon a Statute, as may best answer the Intention which the Makers had in View; for *qui hæret in Litera, hæret in Cortice.*"
5. 4 Bacon, *Abridgment* 647: "If a Statute make use of a Word the Meaning of which is well known at the Common Law, the Word shall be understood in the same Sense [as] it was understood at the Common Law."
6. Ch. 1, § 67, 1794 Terr. S. of River Ohio Acts, reprinted in 1 Scott, *Laws of Tennessee* 481.
7. 2 Bacon, *Abridgment* 202.
8. *Id.* at 203.
9. 2 Mallory, *Modern Entries* 371–372.
10. 2 Bacon, *Abridgment* 216.
11. 1 Morgan, *Vade Mecum* 308.
12. 5 Comyns, *Digest* 299.
13. 2 Mallory, *Modern Entries* 372.
14. 2 Bacon, *Abridgment* 216.
15. Lilly, *Entries* 231–232.

II. BLAND'S MINUTES OF THE SECOND HEARING OF THE CASE

Washington District Superior Court, Jonesboro
Judges Jackson, White, and Campbell Presiding

[September 1801]
Matthew Moore vrs James Gaines senr.

At September term 1801 this cause was again bro't up on a writ of Error granted by this Court directed to the County Court of Sullivan. On Motion of the Deft Counsel the writ of Error was quashed on the ground formerly taken that a writ of Error Coram Vobis was the only and proper mode of proceeding. Mr. Campbell on behalf of Mr. White now Judge for the Plff. Mr. Dade of Mr. Bland absent

ex relatione Mr. Dade

MS, MdHi-Bland Casebook, 140, Bland Papers (MS 134). Date is taken from *id.*
    Bland had left Tennessee by the time the present action came before the court for a second hearing. As is indicated in the MS, Townshend S. Dade was the source of Bland's information about the court's final disposition of the case.

36. Jackson v. Kearby

1801
(Property)

EDITORIAL NOTE

This was an ejectment action that Jackson brought against John Kearby in the Hamilton District Superior Court in September 1801. The case is of interest primarily because, like *Reading v. Douglass,* No. 16, and *Stothart v. Stuart,* No. 27, it illustrates the conflict of interest that occasionally arose between Jackson's position as a member of the court and his relationship either to a litigant or to the subject matter at issue before the court. *Kearby* was one of three actions that came before the court between 1798 and 1804 in which Jackson himself was one of the litigants.[1]

At issue in the ejectment action that Townshend S. Dade filed for Jackson on September 3, 1801, was title to Patent 5, a 640-acre tract of land in Knox County adjoining the southern boundary of the Henderson & Company grant (Document II).[2] Jackson had deeded into Patent 5 on October 2, 1800 (Document I). Nearly a year later, on September 1, 1801, Jackson leased Patent 5 to John Kearby (see Document II). The particular circumstances that prompted the present litigation have not been determined. When the action went to trial on October 7, 1801, a jury returned a verdict for Jackson and awarded him nominal damages plus costs (Document III).[3] The next day, on October 8, Jackson deeded to Kearby 453 of the 640 acres that had been at issue for a dollar an acre.[4]

1. The other two cases were *Witherspoon v. Jackson* and *Jackson v. Witherspoon,* No. 46.

2. Although Jackson's declaration does not refer specifically to Patent 5, its description of the tract follows virtually verbatim Jackson's description of Patent 5 in Document I. For further identification of the Henderson & Company grant, see No. 50.

3. An award of nominal damages was customary in an ejectment action. For actual damages, the plaintiff in ejectment brought a parallel action for mesne profits. See No. 15. There is no evidence that Jackson brought a parallel action for mesne profits in connection with the present case.

4. Anderson Co. Deed Bk. B, 209–211, TAnCo. The identity of the 453 acres conveyed to Kearby as part of Patent 5 occurs in the paragraph just above the signature line in the Tr of

Jackson's deed to Kearby of Oct. 8: "Before the Sealing and delivery of these presents, it is agreed to be the true intent and meaning of the parties, that all the land Contained in patent No. 5 that lies on the South Side of clinch River except What is Conveayd to Kerkpatrick is Expresley Conveayed to John Kearby." *Id.* at 210. Jackson on the same day deeded all but some 87 acres of what remained of Patent 5 to Alexander Kirkpatrick. Anderson Co. Deed Bk. A, 46–48, TAnCo.

Kearby has not been further identified.

I. DEED TO PATENT 5 FROM
RICHARD GILL

October 2, 1800

THIS INDENTURE Made this *Second* day of *October* in the year of our Lord, one thousand eight hundred, between *Richard Gill by George Gordon his attorney in fact* of the county of   [1] and state of *New York* of the one part, and *Andrew Jackson* of the county *of Davidson and State of Tennessee* of the other part, WITNESSETH, That the said *Richard Gill by the said George Gordon his attorney* for and in consideration of the sum of *Six hundred Dollars* to *him* in hand paid, the receipt whereof is hereby acknowledged, hath, and by these presents, doth grant, bargain, sell alien, enfeoff, and confirm unto the said *Andrew Jackson his* heirs and assigns forever, a certain tract or parcel of land, containing *Six hundred and forty* acres, lying and being in the county of *Knox, in the Eastern District, on both Sides of Clinch river adjoining the lower line of Hendersons and companys grant Beginning at a white oak on the Side of a hill on the South East side of the river, thence along Said line north forty five degrees west Sixty poles to a large forked poplar on the river bank, thence the same course continued one hundred and Sixty Six poles to a red oak, thence south forty five degrees west four hundred and forty Six poles to a stake, thence south forty five degrees East two hundred and and Twenty Six poles Cross the river to a stake & thence north forty five degrees East four hundred and forty Six poles Cross two Creeks to the Beginning, it being the same tract of land convey by George Gordon as attorney in fact for Stockley Donelson to the said Richard Gill on the Twelth day of April Ninety Six, and patented to Stockley Donelson by patent dated at fairfield the Eleventh day of July in the year Seventeen hundred and Eighty Eight and No. of the patent, five* With all and singular, the woods, waters, water courses, profits, commodities, hereditaments, and appurtenances whatsoever, to the said tract of land belonging or appertaining; and the reversion and reversions, remainder and remain-

ders, rents and issues thereof, and all the estate, right, title, interest, property, claim, and demand, of *him* the said *Richard Gill his* heirs and assigns forever, of, in, and to the same, and every part or parcel thereof,
either in law or equity; TO HAVE AND TO HOLD the said *Six hundred
and forty* acres of land, with the appurtenances unto the said *Andrew
Jackson his* heirs and assigns forever, against the lawful title, claim, and
demand of all and every person or persons whatsoever, *claiming from by
through or under him* will warrant and forever defend by these presents.
IN WITNESS whereof, the said   [1] hath hereunto set   [1] hand and seal
the day and year above written.

Signed, sealed, and
delivered in the   }
presence of
The words "claiming from by }
through or under him" inter-
lined before signed   }
Acknowledged as by him
Pleasant M Miller

Geo Gordon (Seal)
Attorney in Fact
for Richd. Gill

Printed form, filled in and signed, DLC-AJ Papers (Reel 2). Italicized portions of text are in
AJ's hand, except for signatures, which appear to be autograph, and "Acknowledged as by
him" and "Attorney in Fact for Richd. Gill," which appear to be in Gordon's hand. Endorsement in AJ's hand with autograph signature:
  State of Tennessee
    On the Second day of October Eighteen hundred personally came George Gordon
  before me Archibald Roane one of the Judges of the Superior Courts of law and Equity
  for the State aforesaid, and as attorney in fact for Richard Gill acknowledged the Signing Sealing and Delivery of the within Deed, for the purposes therein Expressed—in
  order that the Same might be registered—Let the Same be registered
                                        Archibald Roane
Endorsement in an unidentified hand with autograph signature:
  State of Tennessee
  Knox County Registers Office   1.64 Recd. C M
    The within Conveyance and the above probate thereof are Recorded in Said Office in
  Book F, page 284. Febry. 23rd. 1801
                          Tho Chapman Regr.
Endorsement in AJ's hand, except for "1.64," which is in an unidentified hand:
  Richard Gill by George Gordon his attorney
  in fact   }   640 acres both sides
  To Andrew Jackson }   clinch river on the
  lower line of Henderson & company Grant
  $1.64
Tr of the text and of Roane's affidavit is in Knox Co. Deed Bk. F2, v.1, p. 284.

  1. Thus in the original.

II. DECLARATION AND NOTICE
IN EJECTMENT

Hamilton District Superior Court, Knoxville
Judges Jackson, White, and Campbell Presiding

September 3, 1801

State of Tennessee Hamilton District,

John Den on the Demise of Andrew Jackson by his Attorney complains of Richard Fen in custody &c. of a Plea &c. for that whereas the said Andrew on the first day of September in the Year of our Lord eighteen hundred and one at Knoxville within the District of Hamilton afsd. had demised and to farm let to the Said John a certain tract or parcel of land containing Six hundred and forty acres lying and being within what is now called the County of Knox, within the afsd. District of Hamilton, and in what was formerly called the Eastern District on both sides of Clinch River adjoining the lower line of Henderson's & Companies Grant. Beginning at a white Oak on the side of a Hill on the South East side of the River. thence along said line North forty five degrees West sixty poles to a large forked poplar on the River bank. thence the Same course continued one hundred and Sixty Six poles to a red oak. thence South forty five degrees West four hundred and forty six poles to a Stake. thence South forty five degrees East two hundred and twenty six poles cross the river to a Stake And thence North forty five degrees East four hundred and forty six poles cross to Branches to the Beginning To have and to hold the said Tract or parcel of land with its appurtenances to the Said John and his assigns from the last day of August then last past to the end and term of Ten Years from then next following and fully to be complete and ended by Virtue of which Demise the Said John entered on the said tract or parcel of land with its appurtenances and was thereof possessed; And the Said John being so thereof possessed the said Richard afterwards—to wit—on the second day of September in the Year afsd. with force and Arms entered into the tract or parcel of land with its Appurtenances which the said Andrew demised to the said John in form aforesaid for the terme afsd. which is not Yet expired & ejected the said John out of the sd. tract or parcel of land and other wrongs to the sd. John there did, to the great damage of the Said John and against the peace of the State, Whereby the said John saith that he is injured and damaged to the value of one hundred Dollars, and thereupon he Sues &c. And there are pledges to prosecute &c.

John Doe
Richd. Roe   Dade Atty

Mr. John Kearby }   3rd day of September 1801
I am informed that you are in possession of, or claim title to the premises mentioned in this declaration of Ejectment or to some part thereof;
And I being sued in this action as a casual Ejector and having no claim or
title to the same, do advise You to appear at the Superior Court of law for
the District of Hamilton in the state of Tennessee to be held at the Court
House in Knoxville on the fourth monday of September next then and
there by a rule of said Court to cause yourself to be made Deft. in my
stead; otherwise I shall let Judgment be entered against me by default,
And You will be turned out of possession. Your loving friend &c.
                                        Richard Fen.

Tr, TKL-HDSC Law Rec. Bk. C, 1798–1803, pp. 188–189. The record book indicates that
the declaration and notice were endorsed: "John Kearby came personly into open Court at
September Term 1801 And Acknowledged the Service of the within Declaration of Ejectment in due time & waives all manner of exception on account of any informality in issuing
and returning the Same." *Id.* at 189.

III. RECORD BOOK ENTRY

Hamilton District Superior Court, Knoxville
Judges Jackson, White, and Campbell Presiding

[October 7, 1801]
Be it remembered that at September Term 1801 the following Declara-
tion in Ejectment & Notice were returned to Court—to wit.[1] . . .
Whereupon John Kearby comes into Court and is admitted Defendent
in the room & Stead of Richd. Fen. And confesses, lease, entry & Ouster,
And pleads not Guilty of the Trespass laid in the Plaintiffs declaration of
Ejectment And of this he puts himself on the Country. And the Plaintiff
also. And now by the mutual agreement of the parties, and by the assent
of the Court Here the trial of the issue aforesaid was directed to be had
Instanter.
Whereupon a Jury to try the Issue aforesaid at the Term aforesaid was
impannelled—to wit—Arthur Crozier, Andrew McCampbell, David Stu-
art, Oliver Alexander, James Grant, Phillip Love, Charles Hodge, Daniel
Hasteen, Samuel Givens, John Sterling, William Matlock & George Gordon who being elected tried and Sworn the truth to Speak upon the issue
Joined upon their oaths do say they find the Deft. Guilty of the trespass in
Ejectment in manner and form as set forth in the Declaration; And Assess
the Plaintiff's Damage by occation thereof to Six Cents, And Six Cents
Costs

Therefore it is considered by the Court that the Plaintiff recover against the Defendent his Damages and costs aforesaid in form aforesaid Assessed. And the said Defendant in mercy &c.

MS, TKL-HDSC Law Rec. Bk. C, 1798–1803, pp. 189–190. Date is taken from HDSC Law Min. Bk. 3, 1793–1809, p. 256.

1. The text of Document I follows at this point in the MS.

37. Greer v. Emerson

1801
(Slavery)

EDITORIAL NOTE

In November 1800 Andrew Greer, Jr., brought this trespass action against Pleasant Emerson, the overseer of Greer's Smith County plantation. Greer, through his counsel, John Overton, alleged that Emerson had caused the death of one of his slaves, Cato. Emerson, Greer claimed, had ordered Cato to ride an unbroken horse at full speed along a race track near the plantation. Cato, the plaintiff asserted, subsequently had died as a result of injuries sustained when he was thrown from the horse (Document I).

The suit went to trial a year later, on November 11, 1801. Emerson's counsel, George Washington Campbell, moved that Greer be nonsuited on the ground that, since Emerson's conduct was within his authority as his employer's overseer, the plaintiff's action should have been filed as a trespass-on-the-case action and not as a trespass action. Greer's counsel, Overton and Whiteside, argued that Emerson's authority as Greer's overseer extended only to actions in furtherance of his employer's business and that his ordering of Cato to race the unbroken horse had gone beyond the limit of his authority. The court, with Jackson and White presiding, denied Emerson's motion (Document II). A jury subsequently returned a verdict for Greer in the amount of $350. The court on November 25 denied a motion by the defendant for a new trial.[1]

1. MDSC Law Min. Bk., 1788–1803, pp. 514, 568. One of the jurors in this action was Thomas Hart Benton. *Id.* at 514. Chambers identifies the *Emerson* trial as the occasion for the retrospective description of Jackson in Benton's *Thirty Years' View*. William N. Chambers, "Thomas Hart Benton in Tennessee, 1801–1812," 8 *THQ* 296 (1949). Benton's service as a juror in *Emerson*, however, occurred at the November 1801 trial, which was two years after the occasion on which Benton recalled that he first had observed AJ in the courtroom: "The first time that I saw General Jackson was at Nashville, Tennessee, in 1799—he on the bench, a judge of the then Superior Court, and I a youth of seventeen, back in the crowd. He was then a remarkable man, and had his ascendant over all who approached him, not the effect of his high judicial station, . . . but the effect of personal qualities; cordial and graceful manners, hospitable temper, elevation of mind, undaunted spirit, generosity,

and perfect integrity. In charging the jury in the impending case, he committed a slight sole-cism in language which grated on my ear, and lodged on my memory, without derogating in the least from the respect which he inspired; and without awakening the slightest suspicion that I was ever to be engaged in smoothing his diction." Thomas H. Benton, *Thirty Years' View; or A History of the Working of the American Government for Thirty Years, from 1820 to 1850* (New York, 1856), I, 736.

Neither of the parties has been further identified.

I. DECLARATION OF
ANDREW GREER, JR.

Mero District Superior Court, Nashville

District of Mero Sct.   10th November 1800

Andrew Greer Jur. by his attorney John Overton Esq. complains of Pleasant Emmison in custody &c. for that the said defendant on the   [1] day of   [1] in the year of   [1] at the County and District aforesaid being then & there employed as the Overseer of the said Plaintiff in looking after his Plantation—slaves &c, with force and arms &c. menaces, threats &c. did unlawfully and without the direction of him the said Andrew, lead, order and compel a negro man Slave, (then the property and in the possession of the sd. Plaintiff) named Cato—of the price of five hundred Dollars, to get upon a wild and unruly Horse, in order to ride at full speed, and strain the said Horse along a raise path at one quarter of a Mile, to the manifest danger—of the life of the said Slave. And thereupon the said negro man Slave, being directed & ordered by the said Defendant, overseer as aforesaid did actually start the said Horse along the said rase Path, and the Horse running at full speed threw the said negro Slave, to wit at the Dist. aforesaid on the day aforesaid & from the fall or being thrown aforesaid he the said negro man Slave, soon afterwards died, to wit on the   [1] day of   [1] in the aforesaid year at the District aforesaid and other normities and injuries to the said Plaintiff then and there did with force and arms, against the peace of this State, and to the damage of the said Plaintiff of five hundred Dollars, and therefore he brings Suit &c.

Tr, TDaCo-MDSC Law Min. Bk., 1788–1803, p. 514.

1. Thus in Tr.

II. THE ARGUMENT OF COUNSEL

AND THE OPINION

OF THE COURT

Mero District Superior Court, Nashville
Judges Jackson and White Presiding

[November 11, 1801]
GREER *v.* EMERSON.

Trespass.—The defendant was employed by the plaintiff, and lived with him as an overseer.

The plaintiff being from home, the defendant ordered a negro, the property of the plaintiff, to catch a horse and go with him to the race paths, which were in the neighborhood, for the purpose of straining the horse and ascertaining his speed. The negro obeyed and started the horse, the defendant being present. The horse flew the way, threw the negro, and killed him.

[The Argument of Counsel]

CAMPBELL, for the defendant, moved that the plaintiff should be non-suited, on the ground that the evidence would not support an action of trespass. Case, and not trespass, was the proper form of action. He read several cases, showing the distinction between trespass and case, and concluded by saying, that it was lawful for the overseer to carry the negro and horse to the paths, and to direct him to strain the horse.

If the act itself was lawful, any consequences which might result could not make it a trespass.

OVERTON and WHITESIDE, *e contra,* contended that the overseer's being employed to look after the business of the plaintiff, did not authorize his ordering the slave to do an act which had no connection with that business.

The defendant, in ordering the negro to strain the horse, was completely beyond the limits of his authority, and stood in the same situation as if he had not been overseer. 6 D. & E. 125;[1] 2 Bl. 892,[2] 983,[3] 1028,[4] and 1055.[5]

[The Opinion of the Court]

Per Curiam. Let the evidence go to the jury. The line of distinction between trespass and case, in many instances, is so nice, that it seems difficult to discover it. This appears to be one of that description, but modern authorities seem rather to incline to trespass than case.

Verdict for the plaintiff, for $350. Rule for a new trial, which was discharged.

Printed decision, 1 Tenn. (1 Overton) 12–13 (1801). Editorial headnotes inserted by the reporter between style of the case and text have been omitted. Date and judges' attendance taken from MDSC Law Min. Bk., 1788–1803, p. 513.

The motion for a new trial actually was not denied by the court until Nov. 25. See MDSC Law Min. Bk., 1788–1803, p. 568.

1. Savignac v. Roome, 6 T.R. 125, 101 Eng. Rep. 470 (K.B. 1794). The plaintiff's declaration recited a plea of trespass on the case and alleged that the defendant's servant willfully had driven the defendant's coach into the plaintiff's coach to the latter's damage. The jury returned a verdict for the plaintiff. The defendant moved for an arrest of judgment on the grounds (a) that no action could be maintained against the defendant for the willful act of a servant accompanied by force unless done at the master's command and (b) that, if any action could be supported, it should have been an action of trespass and not an action on the case. The plaintiff responded (a) that, by statute, a judgment shall not be arrested by reason of the omission of "vi et armis" or "contra pacem" from declarations in trespass actions and (b) that the court's earlier decision in Day v. Edwards, 5 T.R. 648 (K.B. 1794), in which it had been held that trespass was the proper form of action when a defendant willfully drove his carriage into the plaintiff's, was distinguishable because the injury in Edwards had been inflicted by the owner himself and not by his servant. The court granted the motion, after finding that trespass was the proper form of action under the facts before it and after confining the statute to those cases which appear on the face of the declarations filed therein to have been intended as trespass actions. Chief Justice Kenyon declared, "It is of importance that the boundaries between the different actions should be preserved, and particularly in cases of this kind; for if in an action of trespass the plaintiff recover less than 40s., he is entitled to no more costs than damages; whereas a verdict with nominal damages only in an action on the case carries all the costs. Here the whole frame and structure of the declaration shew that this is an action on the case; the memorandum, which we were desirous of seeing, is of 'an action of trespass on the case.' But in reality it should have been trespass. And the stat. 16 and 17 Car. 2 was never meant to apply to a case of this kind. This is as much the cause of an action of trespass as if the servant had given the plaintiff a blow, because the injury was immediate. This falls directly within the principle of the case we so lately decided [Day v. Edwards, above]; and therefore the judgment must be arrested." 6 T.R. at 129–130, 101 Eng. Rep. at 472–473.

2. Scott, an Infant v. Shepherd, an Infant, 2 Black. W. 892, 96 Eng. Rep. 525 (K.B. n.d.). This was a trespass-and-assault action for the throwing of a lighted squib, or firecracker, that blinded the plaintiff in one eye. The defendant had thrown the firecracker into a crowded market, where it landed on a baker's stand. A customer or servant tossed the object off the stand, and it landed on a merchant's booth. The merchant threw it away from his stand, and it struck and injured the plaintiff. At trial, a jury returned with a verdict for the plaintiff. The court, holding that an action in trespass was maintainable, entered a judgment upon the verdict. Two of the justices took the view that an action of trespass would lie because the plaintiff's injury was the natural and probable consequence of the defendant's act, which had been made a nuisance by statute. Justice Blackstone disagreed, concluding that when an injury is immediate, an action of trespass will lie, but when an injury is only consequential, it must be sued upon in an action on the case. Chief Justice DeGrey agreed with the result reached by the majority: "This case is one of those wherein the line drawn by the law between actions on the case and actions of trespass is very nice and delicate. Trespass is an injury accompanied with force, for which an action of trespass vi et armis lies against the person from whom it is received. The question here is, whether the injury received by the plaintiff arises from the force of the original act of the defendant, or from a new force by a third person. I agree with my brother Blackstone as to the principles he has laid down, but not in his application of those principles to the present case. The real ques-

tion certainly does not turn upon the lawfulness or unlawfulness of the original act; for actions of trespass will lie for legal acts when they become trespasses by accident; as in the cases cited for cutting thorns, lopping of a tree, shooting at a mark, defending oneself by a stick which strikes another behind, &c.—They may also not lie for the consequences even of illegal acts, as that of casting a log in the highway, &c.—But the true question is, whether the injury is the direct and immediate act of the defendant; and I am of opinion, that in this case it is. The throwing the squib was an act unlawful and tending to affright the bystanders. So far, mischief was originally intended; not any particular mischief, but mischief indiscriminate and wanton. Whatever mischief therefore follows, he is the author of it . . . ." 2 Black. W. at 898–899, 96 Eng. Rep. at 528.

3. Rafael v. Verelst, 2 Black. W. 983, 96 Eng. Rep. 579 (K.B. n.d.). This was an action of trespass, assault, and false imprisonment against the president of Calcutta and chief civil officer of the East India Company and an East Indian prince of the province of Owd, which lay some distance from Calcutta. The prince had complained about liberties taken by a group of agents for English merchants who were under Verelst's protection. As a result, Verelst withdrew his protection and requested that the prince arrest the plaintiff, who was one of the agents against whom a complaint had been lodged. Otherwise, Verelst advised, he himself would issue orders to have the plaintiff arrested. The prince arrested the plaintiff and transported him to Calcutta. When a jury returned a verdict for the plaintiff, the defendant Verelst moved for a new trial. The issue was whether an action of trespass would lie against him for procuring the plaintiff's arrest. The court granted a new trial. Justice Blackstone declared, "My present opinion is . . . that no action of trespass lies for the imprisonment suffered at Owd. Even allowing that such imprisonment was owing to the request, the influence, instigation, or whatever else it may be called, (not amounting to absolute command or compulsion), of the defendant, . . . yet still, I think, no action of trespass lies against the defendant for any act committed by the [prince], by his persuasion or advice . . . . Possibly an action on the case might lie for persuading and procuring a foreign prince to imprison one unjustly, (though that, I believe, is without a precedent), as it certainly does lie for maliciously indicting one of felony, and causing him to be imprisoned thereby. But no action of trespass will lie in either case; because the principal act done is in itself no trespass . . . ." 2 Black. W. at 985, 96 Eng. Rep. at 579–580.

4. Presumably, Bolts v. Purvis, 2 Black. W. 1022, 96 Eng. Rep. 601 (K.B. n.d.). This was an action of trespass, assault, and imprisonment. The plaintiff, an alderman of Calcutta who had been evicted for engaging in illegal trade there, sought to recover from the captain of the vessel that transported him from Calcutta to England. The plaintiff asserted that the defendant's conduct had not been justified, because the East India Company had no authority to arrest and evict the plaintiff. The court found that the company was so authorized and that the company's authority thus justified the trespass: "When the King's charter for establishing this Court was obtained, the trading without consent of the Company was an offense by law. The King's charter could not repeal the law, nor annihilate the offense. Nor can the making a man an alderman give him an implied leave to exercise an illicit trade. It would be a harsh construction to suppose, that making one an officer of the Company, would give him a right to oppose and rival his masters. . . . It is sufficient to determine the present question, that there may be an unlawful trading and trafficking, as applied to the present plaintiff, which may authorise the Company to remove him . . . ." 2 Black. W. at 1027–1028, 96 Eng. Rep. at 603.

5. Rafael v. Verelst, 2 Black. W. 1055, 96 Eng. Rep. 621 (K.B. n.d.). At the second trial granted by the court in *Rafael v. Verelst*, 2 Black. W. 983, 96 Eng. Rep. 579 (K.B. n.d.), note 3 above, a jury returned a special verdict finding that the prince had acted out of fear of Verelst and against his will and that he thus had acted merely as Verelst's instrument. The court entered a judgment upon the verdict for the plaintiff: "If, in the doing of an act, there be several intervening agents, and one happens not to be amenable, will it be said that all the rest are excused? . . . [P]rocuring a felony to be committed makes an accessory to the felony; and I take it to be a settled rule, that whatever makes an accessory in felony will make a principal in trespass. Since, therefore, the jury have found the procurement of the defendant, it follows, that he is liable, as a principal, for this trespass." 2 Black. W. at 1058, 96 Eng. Rep. at 623.

38. State v. Childress

1801

(Criminal Law)

EDITORIAL NOTE

Although less commonly prosecuted during Jackson's tenure upon the bench than horse stealing, murder nonetheless recurred as the subject of criminal cases that were tried before Jackson and his colleagues with some regularity. The prosecution of Joel Childress for murder in the fall of 1801 is of particular interest because of the entry by the defendant of a plea of benefit of clergy.

On November 13, 1801, the Mero District grand jury returned a true bill upon the indictment of Childress, a "Hatter" who resided in Sumner County, for the murder the previous September of one John Regan (Document I). The defendant pleaded not guilty on November 16.[1] When the case went to trial two days later, a jury returned a verdict finding Childress not guilty of murder, but guilty of "the felonious slaying" of the deceased (Document II). On November 19, Childress appeared before Jackson and Judge White for sentencing and entered a plea of benefit of clergy. Jackson and White granted the plea and sentenced the defendant to be branded on the left hand with the letter *M* (Document III).

1. MDSC Law Min. Bk., 1788–1803, pp. 530, 541. There is no evidence that the defendant might have been the Joel Childress who was the father of Sarah Childress Polk, wife of James K. Polk. Before his death in 1819, Sarah Polk's father had been a merchant, tavern keeper, planter, and land speculator in Sumner County and, later, in Murfreesboro in Rutherford County. Charles Sellers, *James K. Polk, Jacksonian: 1795–1843* (Princeton, 1957), I, 74. A Joel Childress served as a juror at various terms of the Sumner County court between July 1803 and June 1805 and was still residing in the county as late as July 1805. SumCo CPQS Min. Bk. 4, 1802–1804, p. 385; SumCo CPQS Min. Bk. 5, 1804–1805, p. 544; *Tennessee Gazette*, July 3, 1805. Because such records as the census returns for Sumner County have not survived, however, it is not possible to eliminate the possibility that more than one Joel Childress was residing in the county in 1801. Sarah Polk, who recalled very little about her family in later years, shed little light on the possibility that her father was convicted for the killing of Regan. See, *e.g.,* Anson and Fanny Nelson, *Memorials of Sarah Childress Polk, Wife of the Eleventh President of the United States* (New York, 1892), 1–12; "Annals of a Scotch-Irish Family," 9 *AHM* 240–241 (1904).

The identity of Regan and the circumstances surrounding his death remain undetermined.

As the case illustrates, the ancient custom of benefit of clergy continued to function in early nineteenth-century Tennessee, although in a much truncated form. Originally confined to persons in holy orders, this privilege operated to excuse an accused of a crime from civil punishment and to turn him over to an ecclesiastical tribunal. During the fourteenth and fifteenth centuries, the privilege of benefit of clergy was extended to all persons who could read but was restricted in its scope to capital offenses. Persons not actually of the clergy who claimed the benefit were branded on the left thumb and were not permitted to assert this exemption again. Second offenses were not clergyable. Eventually women and persons unable to read became eligible to assert benefit of clergy.[2]

When a statute created a new felony, benefit of clergy was deemed incident thereto unless specifically removed. The exemption was claimed after conviction by a motion in arrest of judgment. While the privilege served to mitigate the harsh English criminal laws, it was subject to gross abuse. Accordingly, over the years Parliament abolished benefit of clergy for many serious crimes.

During the colonial era the offenses that remained clergyable were the relatively few capital crimes, such as larceny and manslaughter, for which the privilege had not been abolished. In 1790 Congress extinguished benefit of clergy for any capital crime against the United States. Eliminated in England in 1827, the privilege lingered in North Carolina until 1854. The limited vitality of clergy in early Tennessee was underscored by a 1799 measure which provided that the murderer of a slave "shall suffer death without benefit of clergy." This privilege was effectively ended in Tennessee with the 1829 enactment of a new criminal statute.[3] This measure restricted capital offenses to a handful of felonies, such as murder, from which the benefit had previously been excluded. Hence, there were no longer any crimes for which benefit of clergy could serve to mitigate the death penalty.

2. William S. Holdsworth, *History of English Law,* 3d ed. (Boston, 1923), III, 293–302; 5 Tucker, *Blackstone's Commentaries* 365–374.

3. Act of Apr. 30, 1790, ch. 9, § 31, 1 Stat. 119; ch. 9, 1799 Tenn. Pub. Acts, reprinted in 1 Scott, *Laws of Tennessee* 640; ch. 23, 1829 Tenn. Pub. Acts 27; George W. Dalzell, *Benefit of Clergy in America & Related Matters* (Winston-Salem, 1955), 11, 259–260, 281; John Haywood, *The Duty and Authority of Justices of the Peace in the State of Tennessee* (Nashville, 1810), 7; Arthur L. Cross, "Benefit of Clergy in the American Criminal Law," 61 *Proc. of the Mass. Hist. Soc'y* 154 (1928).

I. INDICTMENT OF JOEL
CHILDRESS

Mero District Superior Court, Nashville

November 1801

Be it remmembered that, at Nashville, in the State of Tennessee and District of Mero at November Term eighteen hundred and one, by the oath of twelve Jurors honest and lawful men of the State & District aforesaid, then and there being impannelled sworn & charged to inquire for the body of the sd. District, it was presented, that Joel Childress, late of the county of Sumner in the District aforesaid, Hatter, not having the fear of God before his eyes but being moved by the instigation of the Devil on the twenty fifth day of September in the year of our Lord one thousand eight hundred and one, with force and arms, at Madison Creek in said County of Sumner, within the District aforesaid, in and upon one John Regan, in the peace of God and the State, then & there being, feloniouslly, wilfully & of his malice of aforethought, did make an assault; And that he the said Joel Childress, with a certain piece of plank of Oak Wood, of the length of three feet six inches, of the Value of One Cent, which he said Joel Childress then & there in both his hands had and held, the said John Regan in and upon the left temple, above the left Eye of him the said John Regan, then & there feloniouslly, wilfully, and of his malice of forethought did strike and hit, giving to the said John Regan, then & there, by striking and hitting, with the said Piece of plank, in manner aforesaid, in and upon the above said left Temple, above the left eye of him said John Regan, one mortal bruise of the lenght of four Inches and of the breadth of two Inches, of which said Mortal bruise, the said John Regan, from the time of giving said mortal bruise to said John, by said Joel, with said piece of Plank, in manner aforesaid, during four houres on the said twenty fifth day of September in the year aforesaid, at Madison Creek aforesaid, in said County of Sumner, in the District aforesaid, did languish and languishing did live during said four houres and afterwards on the said twenty fifth day of September in the year aforesaid, the said John Regan, at Madison Creek aforesaid, in said County of Sumner in the District aforesaid, of the said Mortal bruise Died. And so the Jurors aforesaid, upon their oath aforesaid do say, that the said Joel Childress, the said John Regan in manner and form aforesaid, feloniouslly, wilfully and of his malice aforethought did kill and murder, against the peace and dignity of the State of Tennessee

Jenkin Whiteside Attorney General.

Tr, TDaCo-MDSC Law Min. Bk., 1788–1803, pp. 543–544.

II. MINUTE BOOK ENTRY

Mero District Superior Court, Nashville
Judges Jackson and White Presiding

[November 18, 1801]

The State of Tennessee
    against   Indictment for Murder.[1]. . . .
Joel Childress———

And the said Joel Childress, was again led to the Bar in custody &c and thereupon came a Jury of good and lawful men, to wit, William Bowen Asham A Parker, Benjamin Smith, George W Neville, Nicholas Scales, John Bosley, James Robertson, James Watson, George B Curtis, Joseph T Elliston, John McGaugh and James C Maclin who being [el]ected tried and sworn, the truth of and upon the premises to speak, upon their oath do say that the said Joel Childress is not guilty of the Murder aforesaid, above charged upon him; but that the said Joel Childress is guilty of the felonious slaying of the aforesaid John Regan. And it is ordered that the said Joel Childress be remanded to Jail.

MS, TDaCo-MDSC Law Min. Bk., 1788–1803, pp. 543–544. Date and judges' attendance are taken from *id.* at 543.

   1. The text of Document I follows at this point in the MS.

III. MINUTE BOOK ENTRY

Mero District Superior Court, Nashville
Judges Jackson and White Presiding

[November 19, 1801]

Joel Childress, who stands convicted of Manslaughter, was again led to the Bar in custody of the Sheriff of Davidson County and thereupon it is demanded of the said Joel Childress if he hath or knoweth any thing to say, whereupon the Court here ought not upon the premises and Verdict aforesaid to proceed to Judgment and Execution against him, and the said Joel Childress prayeth the benefit of Clergy, which is allowed him in this behalf. Whereupon all and singular the premises being seen. It is considered by the Court here, that the said Joel Childress be burned in his left hand with the letter M; and that the Sheriff of Davidson County put this Judgment in execution immediately, and he is immediately burned in the left hand with the letter M.

MS, TDaCo-MDSC Law Min. Bk., 1788–1803, pp. 546–547. Date and judges' attendance are taken from *id.* at 545.

39. State v. Whitford

1801

(Criminal Law)

EDITORIAL NOTE

Jackson and his colleagues on the bench occasionally were called upon to resolve disputes that reflected the changing social, economic, and religious climate on the trans-Appalachian frontier. The *Whitford* case illustrates this interaction, but at the same time is unique in that it was the only prosecution during Jackson's tenure on the court for disturbing a public worship.

In early October 1801, the Sumner County grand jury returned a true bill upon an indictment in which John Whitford was charged with having assaulted one Francis Catharine in September at the meetinghouse of the Reverend William McGee and with having "otherwise disturb[ed] the people attending said public worship" (see Document I). When the case went to trial in the county court, a jury acquitted the defendant of the assault upon Catharine, but found Whitford guilty of having disturbed a public worship. Whitford's counsel, Samuel Donelson, then moved for an arrest of judgment on the grounds, among others, that (a) the language of the indictment describing the site at which the alleged offense had occurred was insufficient for the court to determine whether the offense had occurred within its jurisdiction and (b) the indictment did not contain two distinct counts such that the jury could separate the alleged assault upon Catharine from the allegation that the defendant had disturbed a public worship (see Document II). The Sumner court overruled Donelson's motion in arrest of judgment and entered a judgment on the jury's verdict in the form of a fine of $25.[1]

---

1. SumCo CPQS Min. Bk. 3, 1796–1802, pp. 320, 332. Whitford has not been further identified.

The Reverend William McGee had begun his Presbyterian ministry in Sumner County shortly after 1787. He soon organized his congregation into Shiloh Church, became its first pastor, and led his congregation to erect a meetinghouse at the eastern edge of the present town of Gallatin. By 1800, Mr. McGee had left Shiloh Church to serve as pastor of Beech

On October 24, 1801, Donelson filed an appeal of the county court's determination with the Mero District Superior Court.[2] When the appeal came on to be heard on November 20, the State moved for a trial de novo. Jackson and Judge White denied the motion, held that the jury's verdict in the lower court finding the defendant not guilty of the assault had constituted a full acquittal, and reversed the Sumner court's judgment "as being illegal" (Document III).

The legal basis for the prosecution of Whitford for disturbing a public worship is not at all clear. It does not appear that disturbing a public worship was recognized as a separate offense at common law. Since 1785, actions of debt had been recognized under North Carolina and Tennessee law for the recovery of fines from persons obstructing access to places of public worship.[3] The statute, however, did not reach the disturbance of persons assembled for worship. Moreover, the statutory remedy was civil in nature and evidently had no criminal counterpart. Jackson and White in any event do not appear to have reached the issue, for the basis of their reversal of the county court seems to have been that the jury found the defendant guilty of an offense not adequately alleged in the indictment as a separate offense.

Church on Drake's Creek. Under his ministry, a campground adjoining the Beech congregation's log meetinghouse served as the site for several revival meetings that occurred in middle Tennessee in 1800 and 1801 at the height of the Great Revival that swept the western states during the first decade of the nineteenth century. Walter T. Durham, *The Great Leap Westward: A History of Sumner County, Tennessee, from Its Beginnings to 1805* (Gallatin, Tenn., 1969), 151, 159, 162–163.

2. It is not clear from the county court minutes whether Donelson's appeal was of the court's denial of his motion or of the court's judgment. Presumably in either case the appeal was based upon that section of the Territorial Judiciary Act of 1794 that provided for appeals to the Superior Court by either party dissatisfied with the sentence, judgment, or decree of any county court. Ch. 1, 1794 Terr. S. of River Ohio Acts, reprinted in 1 Scott, *Laws of Tennessee* 457.

3. Ch. 24, 1785 Laws of N.C., reprinted in Iredell, *Laws of North Carolina* 562, 1 Scott, *Laws of Tennessee* 345. See 4 Blackstone, *Commentaries* 41–65, 217–218.

I. INDICTMENT OF
JOHN WHITFORD

Sumner County Court of Pleas and Quarter Sessions

October 1801

State of Tennessee, Sumner County, to wit, Oct. Term 1801.

The Grand Jury for the State and County aforesaid upon their oath present that John Whitford, late of the County aforesaid, Labourer, with force and arms at the County aforesaid on the sixth day of September in the year of our Lord one thousand eight hundred and one an assault did make upon the body of a certain Francis Catharine in the peace of God and our said State then and there being, during public worship in the meeting House of the reverend William McGee, and did then and there beat, wound and otherwise ill treat the said Francis Catharine, during said public worship, and did otherwise disturb the people attending said public worship, to the great damage of the said Francis Catharine, and contrary to the peace and dignity of said State,

George Smith C. S.

Tr, TDaCo-MDSC Law Min. Bk., 1788–1803, p. 551. The minute book indicates that the indictment was endorsed: "State agaist John Whitford. Indictment assault and battery. Prosecutor Francis Catharine. Witnesses Robert Latimer John Kirkpatrick William McEleyros Dred Dugger, John Dugger, Luke Dugger, George Reper, Sworn & sent October 5th 1801 D Shelby C. S. C. A true Bill Jesse Johnston foreman."

II. THE GROUNDS FOR
DEFENDANT'S MOTION
IN ARREST OF JUDGMENT

Sumner County Court of Pleas and Quarter Sessions

State vs. John Whitford.   Indt. Oct. Term 1801
    Sumner County

The Deft. in this Indictment prays the Judgment of the worshipful Court, touching the above Bill of Indictment brought against him, by the said State, to the end that the said Court may arrest the Verdict of the Jury as rendered in open Court in said Indictment, for the following reasons, to wit,

1st   Because the offence of which this Defendant is charged with having committed, is expressed in the said Bill of Indictment in such general insufficient vague and uncertain language, that It does not appear to the Court whether he is charged with any disticnt offence or of which of the offences, if any, he is accused.

2d   Because the Bill of Indictment does not charge the Defendant with sufficient certainty of the act or thing wherein the offence was committed.

3d   Because the place alledged in the Bill of Indictment, to wit, the reverend William McGees meeting house where the offence was said to be committed is expressed in such repugnant language that altho, it is alledged to be in the County of Sumner, and within the Jurisdiction of this Court, it is alledged with repugnance and such as the Law does not admit of, by saying the rvd. Wm. McGees meeting house, without saying where it lies, when in fact there is two meeting houses of the same discription.

4th

5th   Because the Indictment charges the Deft. during public worship to have disturbed the people attending said worship without mentioning or alledging to the time when, the place where, the said act was done and which ought agreeably to law to have being repeated.

6th   Because the offence for which the Defendant is found guilty is not stated to be a several and distinct act, from the offence also stated in the Bill of Indictment of his having committed a Trespass assault and battery on the body of Francis Catharine.

7th   Because the Indictment does not charge the Deft with having disturbed the public worship with force and arms.

8th   Because the place called the revd. Wm. McGees meeting house is stated in the Bill of Indictment, by way of discribing the fact of which the Deft. is charged and not the place where the same was done.

9th   Because there is not two distinct Counts in the said Bill of Indictment contained, and in fact no count legally speaking, but if there is it is the one of T. B. and of which the Deft. is found not guilty, and therefore cannot agreeably to the Laws of his Country be fined and punished out of the Indictment

Saml. Donlson for Deft.

Tr, TDaCo-MDSC Law Min. Bk., 1788–1803, pp. 552–553.

III. MINUTE BOOK ENTRY

Mero District Superior Court, Nashville
Judges Jackson and White Presiding

[November 20, 1801]

State of Tennessee   }   Indictment AB Appeal.
    against
John Whitford

Be it remmembered that heretofore, to wit, on the 24th October 1801, an appeal from the County Court of Sumner, was filed in the Office of the Clerk, of the Superior Court of Law for the District of Mero, in the following words, to wit,[1] . . . .

And now at this Term of the Superior Court, to wit November 1801, the attorney for the State, moved for a trial of the issue *de novo* in this cause. And it appearing to the Court here from the Record filed, that the Defendant, in the court below, was, by the Jury, found not Guilty of the Assault and battery as charged in the Bill of Indictment, but guilty of disturbing public worship, only. It is therefore the opinion of the Court, that the Deft. by that Verdict, was acquitted—whereupon the motion was overruled. Therefore It is considered by the Court, that the Judgment of the County Court be reversed as being illegal.

MS, TDaCo-MDSC Law Min. Bk., 1788–1803, pp. 551–553. Date and judges' attendance are taken from *id.* at 548.

1. The texts of Documents I and II and of the transcript of the lower court proceedings follow at this point in the MS.

40. State v. Beeler

1801
(Criminal Law)

EDITORIAL NOTE

In November 1801 Jackson and Judge White also presided at the Mero District trial of a youth named Henry Beeler for horse stealing. The indictment charged that Beeler on August 14 of that year had stolen from Richard Hannan a brown gelding valued at $120 (Document I). The district grand jury returned a true bill upon the indictment on November 11. When the case went to trial on November 16, the jury returned a guilty verdict (Document II). More than a week later, on November 25, Judges Jackson and White sentenced Beeler to be hanged on December 29 (Document III).

Beeler was not executed as scheduled on the twenty-ninth, but rather, like the defendant in *State v. McKee*, No. 26, received a pardon from the governor. Beeler's pardon is of particular interest, because Jackson was among those who petitioned Governor Roane to issue the reprieve. At some time after the sentencing of Beeler on November 25, Jackson, Judge White, Attorney General Whiteside, the entire jury that had found Beeler guilty, and a substantial number of Nashville's lawyers took the unusual step of petitioning Governor Roane to exercise his power of executive clemency in the *Beeler* case (Document IV). The governor issued his pardon on December 5 (Document V).[1]

1. Beeler has not been further identified.

I. INDICTMENT OF
HENRY BEELER

Mero District Superior Court, Nashville

November 1801

Be it remmembered that at Nashville, in the State of Tennessee and District of Mero, at November Term one thousand eight hundred and one, by the oath of twelve Jurors honest and lawful men of the State and District aforesaid, then and there being sworn and charged, to inquire for the body of the said District, It was presented, that Henry Beeler late of the County of Davidson in the District aforesaid, Labourer, on the fourteenth day of August in the year of our Lord one thousand eight hundred and one, with force and arms, at Fontainbleu in the said county of Davidson and within the District aforesaid, one brown Gelding, about fifteen hands high, about six years old, branded on the left buttock with the letter S of the Value of one hundred and twenty Dollars of the goods & Chattels of one Richard Hannan, then & there being found, feloniously, did Steal, take and carry away against the form of the Act of the General Assembly in such case made provided,[1] and against the peace & dignity of the the state of Tennessee.

Jenkin Whiteside,
attorney General.

Tr, TDaCo-MDSC Law Min. Bk., 1788–1803, p. 540. The grand jury returned a true bill upon the indictment on Nov. 11. *Id.* at 515.

1. Ch. 20, Tenn. Pub. Acts, reprinted in 1 Scott, *Laws of Tennessee* 648.

II. MINUTE BOOK ENTRY

Mero District Superior Court, Nashville
Judges Jackson and White Presiding

Monday Morning November 16th
1801.

Court met agreeably to adjournment.
Present the Honr. Hugh L White ⎫
           Andrew Jackson ⎬ Esqrs Judges

The State of Tennessee ⎫
    against   ⎬ Indictment for Horse Stealing[1] . . . .
Henry Beeler ─────── ⎭

And the said Henry Beeler, was led to the bar in the custody of the Sheriff
of Davidson County, and thereupon arraigned and pleaded not Guilty to
the Indictment and for his trial put himself upon God and his Country.
Whereupon came a Jury of Good and Lawful men to wit, Chapman
White, Kasper Mansker, George Bell, James Maxwell, James Rankins,
Joseph B Neville, John Hope, Wyley Cerry, Archibald Lytle, Ewen Cameron, John Irwin, and James Stuart, who being elected, tried and sworn,
the truth to speak of & upon the premisses, and having tried the evidence, upon their oath do say that the said Henry Beeler is guilty of the
Horse Stealing aforesaid in manner and form as in the Indictment against
him is alledged; and thereupon he is ordered to be remanded to Jail.

MS, TDaCo-MDSC Law Min. Bk., 1788–1803, pp. 540–541.

1. The text of Document I follows at this point in the MS.

III. MINUTE BOOK ENTRY

Mero District Superior Court, Nashville
Judges Jackson and White Presiding

[November 25, 1801]

Henry Beeler, late of the County of Davidson, Labourer, who stands convicted of Horse Stealing, was again led to the Bar in custody of the Sheriff
of Davidson County and thereupon it being demanded of him if any thing
for himself he had or knew to say, why the Court here to Judgment and

execution of and upon the premises should not proceed, he said, he had nothing, but what he had before said. Therefore it is considered by that the Court that he be hanged by the neck until he be dead, and that execution of this Judgment be made and done upon him the said Henry Beeler by the Sheriff of Davidson County, on Tuesday the twenty ninth day of December next, between the hours of twelve in the forenoon and three in the afternoon of the same day at the Public Gallows of the County of Davidson—And that the said Henry Beeler be remanded to Jail.

MS, TDaCo-MDSC Law Min. Bk., 1788–1803, pp. 565–566. Date and judges' attendance are taken from *id.* at 564.

IV. PETITION OF JACKSON AND OTHERS TO GOVERNOR ROANE

[Before December 5, 1801]

To his Excellency Archibald Roane Governor of the State of Tennessee

Whereas Henry Beeler at November Term 1801 of the Superior court of Law for the District of Mero was found guilty of Horse stealing upon an indictment the copy whereof is here with transmitted to your Excellency. Now we the first twelve underwritten being the Jury Who found the said Henry Beeler guilty, together with others subscribers who were present at the trial of said Indictment do hereby earnestly recommend the said Henry Beeler to the mercy of your excellency concieving him to be a fit object thereof from his youth and the weakness of his understanding. We therefore pray your Excellency to grant a pardon to the said Henry Beeler, for the said crime of Horse stealing and your petitioners will ever pray &c.

John Hope ⎫
Kasper Mansker ⎪
Archibald Lytle ⎪
Willie Cherry ⎪
John Irwin ⎪
J B Nevill ⎬ Jurors.
James Stewart ⎪
Geo Bell ⎪
Ewen Cameron ⎪
C White ⎪
James Maxwell ⎪
James Rankins ⎭

Andrew Jackson one of the Judges of the Superior courts of law and Equity for State of T.

H L White one of the Judges of the superior courts of Law and Equity for the state of Tennessee.

J. Whiteside atty Genl. for the State of Tennessee.

Jno Overton

W. P. Anderson

Edley Ewing
Bennett Henderson
Jno. B. Johnson
Wm. Smith
Jno. Martin
Ninian Edwards
Robt. C Foster
B Seawell
William Lytle Jr.
Robt. Searcy
James Desha
James King
Tho Crutcher
Geo B. Curtis
Wm. Hickman
Jno. Anderson
Wm. T Lewis
Joseph Hooper
R. McGavock
Jno. Sommerville
G W Campbell
Thos. Stuart.

Saml. Donelson
Ho. Tatum
John Alcorn
P R Booker
Lemuel Henry
Joel Lewis
Josiah Fox
Elisha Rice
William Bowen
Ay. Crutcher
Isaac Walton
I A Parke[r]
Jas. Robertson
B Searcy.

MS, T-Governors' Papers. Text in unidentified hand; autograph signatures; enclosure missing.

The petition probably was executed on or shortly after November 25, the date on which the court adjourned its November Term (MDSC Law Min. Bk., 1788–1803, p. 581).

V. PARDON BY
GOVERNOR ROANE

December 5, 1801

Archibald Roane Governor of the State of Tennessee.

To all who shall see these presents: Greeting.

Whereas it has been represented to me, that at the November Term of the Superior Court of law for the District of Mero, in the year one thousand eight hundred and one, Henry Beeler was found guilty of horse Stealing upon an indictment.

And I have been petitioned by a number of respectable persons, Citizens of this State to grant a pardon to the said Henry Beeler for the said crime of horse Stealing.

Now know ye, that I the said Archibald Roane by virtue of the powers vested in me do hereby pardon the said Henry Beeler of the said crime of horse Stealing for which he has been found guilty upon an Indictment at the November Term of the Superior Court of law for the District Mero, in the year one thousand eight hundred and one as aforesaid.

Given under my hand and seal at Knoxville this 5th day of December 1801.

/signed/ Archibald Roane.

By the Governor,
    Wm. Maclin, Secretary.

FC, T-Roane Letterbook, 125–126, Governors' Papers.

41. Magoffin & Son v. Acklin; Magoffin & Son v. Acklin, Perrin, and Combs

1802
(Commercial Law)

EDITORIAL NOTE

The *Magoffin* litigation consisted of two separate proceedings that, taken together, occupied the attention of the Hamilton District Superior Court for more than four years. Initially, in January 1798, the Philadelphia mercantile firm of Joseph Magoffin & Son brought a debt action in the Hamilton court against Samuel Acklin, a resident of Grainger County, Tennessee. Magoffin & Son alleged that in November 1795 Acklin had executed a promissory note for £468, 8 shillings, or $1,249.33⅓, payable to the firm six months from the date of execution (Document I). After the court had granted both parties a continuance at its September Term 1798, the case went to trial in March 1799. On March 27, a jury returned a verdict for Magoffin & Son in the amount of $1,461.40 plus costs (Document II).[1]

The second stage in the *Magoffin* litigation began when Acklin sought relief under the Insolvent Debtors Act of 1773. Upon Acklin's discharge, Magoffin & Son sought the issuance by the Hamilton court of writs of execution against Acklin's sureties. When the litigation finally terminated in March 1802 with the withdrawal by the Philadelphia firm of its motion for writs of execution, the nonresident plaintiff had only produced what it must have regarded as disappointing results.

---

1. For Magoffin & Son, see Abraham Ritter, *Philadelphia and Her Merchants* (Philadelphia, 1860), 165; *Stephens's Philadelphia Directory of 1796* (Philadelphia, 1796), 122; see Magoffin & Son v. King, HDSC Law Rec. Bk. C, 1798–1803, p. 296 (1802). For Acklin, see Pollyanna Creekmore, comp., "Early East Tennessee Taxpayers," pt. 4 (Grainger County), ETHS *Publ.* No. 27, p. 118 (1955). One of Acklin's sureties, Perrin, is known also to have been a resident of Grainger County. Creekmore, "Early East Tennessee Taxpayers," 101. The other surety, Combs, has not been further identified.

The sheriff of the county in which the defendant in a civil action resided was required, upon receipt of the writ initiating the action, to attach the defendant's person or secure a bail bond signed by two sureties for the defendant. If the defendant was still in the sheriff's custody after judgment had been entered against him, the court, upon a motion by either the plantiff's or defendant's bail, could order that the defendant be detained until the plaintiff's judgment and costs were paid or until the defendant was "otherwise discharged by due Course of Law."[2]

The *Magoffin* litigation illustrates the tangled relations of debtor and creditor in early America. The English practice of imprisoning debtors gradually withered during the colonial period. Although debtors could still be arrested, the law was modified to improve the conditions of confinement and to reduce the period of custody. Under the prison bounds system, debtors were allowed access to the area surrounding the jail and could pursue a trade. Many colonies also moved to release, after some period of confinement, all debtors who could take an oath of poverty or who would assign their property for the benefit of creditors. Defrauding debtors, however, were still subject to imprisonment until their obligations were paid. Peter J. Coleman has observed that "by the Revolution creditors had lost, or were in the process of losing their absolute power of confinement."[3]

In the 1740s North Carolina had adopted both the prison bounds system and a scheme for the discharge of insolvent debtors. The county court was given power "to mark out such a parcel of land as they shall think fit, not exceeding six acres, adjoining to the prison, for the rules thereof." Debtors and nonfelony offenders were allowed "to walk therein out of prison" while remaining "in law, a true prisoner." In order to take advantage of the expanded bounds, however, each prisoner had to post "good security . . . to keep within the said rules." The statute required that the prison bounds be recorded in the county records.[4]

Concerned that the prison bounds system "hath been greatly abused," the legislators in 1759 provided that bonds for breach of prison rules should be assigned by the sheriff to the creditor. If any person should escape from prison without paying his debts, the appropriate court, upon motion by the levying party, was authorized "to award execution against such person and his securities, for the debt, or damages and costs." It was

2. Ch. 1, §§ 11, 16, 1794 Terr. S. of River Ohio Acts, reprinted in 1 Scott, *Laws of Tennessee* 457.

3. Peter J. Coleman, *Debtors and Creditors in America: Insolvency, Imprisonment for Debt, and Bankruptcy, 1607–1900* (Madison, Wis., 1974), 254.

4. Ch. 18, 1741 Laws of N.C., reprinted in Iredell, *Laws of North Carolina* 82, 1 Scott, *Laws of Tennessee* 60; Coleman, *Debtors and Creditors in America*, 215–221; Note, "Imprisonment for Debt in North Carolina," 1 *N.C. L. Rev.* 229 (1923).

a matter of dispute whether an invalid release constituted a voluntary escape and rendered the securities liable on their breach of bounds bond.[5]

The innovative Insolvent Debtors Act of 1773 prescribed the procedure by which a confined debtor could secure his release from custody and a complete discharge from the debt on which he was sued. Any debtor who had remained in jail for twenty days could secure his release in one of two ways. First, the debtor could secure an order from two justices of the county court or from one judge of the Superior Court by providing notice to the judgment creditor and taking an oath that his total assets amounted to less than forty shillings. Alternatively, the debtor could seek a discharge from the court issuing process in the suit by filing a petition and a schedule of the debtor's property with the court at least twenty days before its next session. Upon notice to the creditor, the court examined the petitioner in a summary manner. If the debtor took an oath that he had not concealed any assets, the court ordered the release of the debtor and the sale of his property for the benefit of creditors. A discharge of the debtor under either procedure constituted a full satisfaction of "all such debts so sued for." When the creditor was a nonresident of the state, the requisite notice under either procedure could be satisfied by serving notice upon the attorneys at law who prosecuted the suit for the nonresident creditor.[6]

The new state of Tennessee, choosing to rely upon the North Carolina provisions, did not enact a comprehensive debtor relief measure of its own. Still, the Tennessee Constitution of 1796 adopted a reform viewpoint by providing that

> the person of a debtor, where there is not a strong presumption of fraud, shall not be continued in prison, after delivering upon his estate for the benefit of his creditor or creditors, in such manner as shall be prescribed by law.[7]

Which of the two available procedures under the Insolvent Debtors Act Acklin employed cannot be determined from the records that survive. It is clear, however, that Acklin was discharged from the custody of the sheriff

---

5. Ch. 14, 1759 Laws of N.C., reprinted in Iredell, *Laws of North Carolina* 189, 1 Scott, *Laws of Tennessee* 93.

Most American jurisdictions adopted the position that an order discharging an insolvent debtor, regular on its face, constituted a defense to an action for escape. *E.g.,* Ammidon v. Smith, 14 U.S. (1 Wheat.) 447 (1816); Hayden v. Palmer, 2 Hill 205 (N.Y. 1842); Hathaway v. Holmes, 14 Vt. 405 (1828); Stevenson, Mackie & Co. v. Carothers, 3 Yeates 180 (Pa. 1801). But see Cable v. Cooper, 15 Johns. 152 (N.Y. 1818).

6. Ch. 4, 1773 Laws of N.C., reprinted in Iredell, *Laws of North Carolina* 262, 1 Scott, *Laws of Tennessee* 128. Disallowed by the Crown, the 1773 measure was revived and "declared to be in full Force" following the Revolution. Ch. 14, 1777 Laws of N.C., reprinted in *N.C. State Records* XXIV, 113; ch. 5, 1778 Laws of N.C. (Apr. Sess.), reprinted in Iredell, *Laws of North Carolina* 353, 1 Scott, *Laws of Tennessee* 266.

7. Art. 11, § 18, Tenn. Const. (1796).

of Grainger County and that Magoffin & Son subsequently proceeded in the Hamilton District Superior Court against Acklin's two sureties, Joseph Perrin and George Combs, to recover their judgment. After granting the parties an initial continuance on October 9, 1801, the court scheduled for March 23, 1802, argument on Magoffin & Son's motion for an execution against Perrin and Combs.[8]

According to the copious notes that Jackson kept of the argument of counsel on the plaintiff's motion, both Pleasant M. Miller and Jenkin Whiteside appeared for Magoffin & Son and argued that the discharge of Acklin under the provisions of the Insolvent Debtors Act had been ineffective because the requisite notice had not been given to either the plaintiff or its counsel (Document III). Edward Scott, Townshend Stuart Dade, and George Washington Campbell appeared for the defendants and argued that the release of Acklin under the Insolvent Debtors Act had fully discharged both Acklin and his sureties and that the bail bond signed by Perrin and Combs was void because no prison bounds had been laid off in the county at the time the bond was signed and because there existed a forty-cent variation between the language of the bond and the actual amount of the plaintiff's judgment (Document III).

Although Judge White was present on March 23, the court's minutes do not indicate that he delivered an opinion on the plaintiff's motion for the issuance of an execution against Acklin's sureties. White probably recused himself because of his representation of the Philadelphia firm in litigation against several of its east Tennessee debtors before his elevation to the bench in 1801.[9] Judge Campbell was of the opinion that the plaintiff's motion should be granted. Jackson disagreed. With the court thus divided, counsel for Magoffin & Son withdrew their motion (Document IV).

Acklin was only one of Magoffin & Son's recalcitrant east Tennessee debtors. At the conclusion of the present unsuccessful litigation against Acklin and his sureties in March 1802, for example, the firm still was attempting to collect a $623 judgment that it had obtained in the court three years earlier and was in the midst of two lengthy actions against John Johnston and Robert King. The $3,000 debt action against Johnston finally came to a successful conclusion in September 1802, while Jackson was on the bench. The debt action against King, however, went to trial, again with Jackson presiding, only in October of that year and with less success than in the Johnston litigation. The firm had sought to recover damages from King in the amount of $3,000 on a note executed by William Cocke for the defendant in Philadelphia in 1797 for some $1,250.

8. HDSC Law Min. Bk. 3, 1793–1809, p. 257.
9. See Magoffin & Son v. King, HDSC Law Rec. Bk. C, 1798–1803, p. 295 (1802); Magoffin & Son to Pleasant M. Miller, July 26, 1802, PVT (copy on file with Jackson Papers Project, Hermitage).

The jury that returned a verdict for the firm in October, however, awarded it just more than one-tenth of what it had sought in damages. Clearly disconcerted by the state of its western accounts, the firm in July had written in frustration to Miller in an attempt to sort out the King affair. Observing with the benefit of hindsight that they really never should have engaged in any business with the likes of King, Miller's clients concluded that "we have surely met with the worst men in Tennessee, perhaps in the world." [10]

10. Magoffin & Son v. Johnston, HDSC Law Rec. Bk. C, 1798–1803, p. 295 (1802); Magoffin & Son v. King, *id.* at 296; Magoffin & Son to Miller, July 26, 1802, note 9 above.

I. DECLARATION OF JOSEPH
MAGOFFIN & SON

Hamilton District Superior Court, Knoxville

[ca. March 1798]

Joseph Magoffin & son by Pleasant M. Millar their Attorney Complains of Samuel Acklin in Custody &c. of a plea that he render unto them four hundred and sixty eight pounds eight shillings equal to twelve hundred and forty nine Dollars and a third of a Dollar which to them he owes and from them unjustly detains for that whereas the said Samuel on the first day of November in the year of our Lord one thousand seven hundred and ninety five at Philadelphia to wit, at Knoxville in the County of Knox & District aforesaid entered into a certain writing Obligatory signed with his name and sealed with seal and to the Court now here shewn the date whereof is the same day and year aforesaid by which writing Obligatory he promised and Oblidged himself to pay to the said Joseph Magoffin & son six months after date the said sum of four hundred and sixty eight pounds eight shillings equal to 1249 Dollars and a third. Nevertheless the said Samuel Altho often required by the said Magoffin & son after the expiration of the said six Months to pay them the said last mentioned sum of money, the said sum of four hundred and sixty eight pounds eight shillings equal to 1249 Dollars & a third to them or either of them hath not paid but the same hath hitherto refused and still doth refuse to their Damage 1000 Dollars & Therefore they sue.

Tr, TKL-HDSC Law Rec. Bk. C, 1798–1803, pp. 17–18. Plaintiffs were required to file their declarations during the term to which process was returned. See Caruthers, *History of a Law Suit,* 17. The approximate date that has been assigned to Document I is derived from the sheriff's return of process to the court at March Term 1798 (see Document II).

II. RECORD BOOK ENTRY

Hamilton District Superior Court, Knoxville
Judges Jackson, Roane, and Campbell Presiding

[March 27, 1799]

Be it remembered that on the twenty ninth day of January A.D. 1798 a Capias ad Respondendum was issued Commanding the Sheriff of Knox County to take the body of Samuel Acklin to answer Joseph Magoffin and son of a plea that he render to them four hundred and sixty eight pounds eight shillings Pennsylvania currency which to them he owes as is said equal to One thousand two hundred forty nine and One third Dollars to their Damage One thousand Dollars Upon which writ at March Term 1798, Robert Houston esquire sheriff returned "Executed"[1] .... And the Defendant by Drury W. Breazeale esquire his Attorney comes into Court and Defends &c. and pleads the General issue payment and set of[f] accord & satisfaction a release and puts himself on the Country and the Plaintiffs by their Attorney aforesaid doth the same Whereupon let a Jury come &c. at September Term 1798 at which Term by Consent of the parties and assent of the Court this cause was Continued until March Term 1799 at which Term came the parties aforesaid by their Attorneys aforesaid and Thereupon came a Jury, to wit, William Coleman, John Dunnel, William Reed, James Lea, James Blair, George Hays John Childers John Bullard, Peter Looney, John Love, James Cochran and Benjamin Rector who being elected tried and sworn the truth to speak upon the issue joined upon their Oath do say the Writing Obligatory declared on is the Deed of the Defendant and that he hath not paid or made satisfaction for the whole or any part thereof to the Plaintiffs neither hath he received a release therefor and that they assess the Plaintiffs Damage to fourteen hundred and sixty one Dollars and forty cents besids their Costs Therefore it is Considered by the Court that the Plaintiffs recover against the Defendant their Damages in form aforesaid assessed and their Costs by them about their suit in this Behalf expended and the said Defendant in mercy &c.

MS, TKL-HDSC Law Rec. Bk. C, 1798–1803, pp. 17–18. Date is taken from HDSC Law Min. Bk. 3, 1793–1809, p. 170.

1. The text of Document I follows at this point in the MS, preceded by: "whereupon the said."

III. JACKSON'S NOTES ON THE
ARGUMENT OF
COUNSEL AND ON HIS OPINION
ON THE MOTION

Hamilton District Superior Court, Knoxville
Judges Jackson, White, and Campbell Presiding

[March 23, 1802]

McGuffin & son
vs   } motion for Execution
Acklin & others

2 points 1st. bond taken before bounds laid off. 2 discharged from bounds by order, of the Justices under the insolvant Debtors act. in Support it is urged, that the law with respect of notice was not complied with, therefore illegal and cannot exonerate Securities from their bond.

To the first point Mr. Miller did not say any thing.

Mr. Miller, in favour of the motion. urged that notice is a substantial part, to give Jurisdiction therefore without notice it must be considered, coram

4 Beacon 641[1] }   non Judice. Beacon says that
2 Salkuld 475[2]   the authority must be persued

Iredal P. 83.[3] The courts power to mark out P. bounds & record them. The amendatory act P. 189.[4] The bond to be assigned, & Judgt to be entered, in case the condition thereof Should be broke.

Bond Execd. a true prisoner. untill regularly discharged. the word regular—must mean discharged agreable to law—and not agreable to the oppinion of the court. quere.

Page 262 &3.[5] rules prescribed to be persued, before oath administred. Summons must issue before, the court can proceed. but suppose they do. can the Gaoller, inquire into the regularrity of the proceeding.

Will Shew this the only mode and this the only court, that relief can be had. cites, Haywood 414[6]

Plea. liberated under the act. presumed to be regular, if contra does not appear.

1 Salkd. 202.[7] escape. coram non Judice. T.[8] lies against the officer. 1 Salkud P 273.[9] Escape warrent. often a discharge by a [c]ourt not having Jurisdiction well lies. 4 Beacon 451.[10]

Mr. Scott. This bond not known at common law, but formed by particular Statute

1. no Such Judgt. as set forth in the bond. reads the bond capias & record. a differrence in bond & record of $\frac{40}{100}$.

2. at the time bond taken, no prison bound. consequently the Securities not bound untill bounds laid off, the Sh must keep him in the Public gaol. 3 Black. 415.[11] Escape. act of assembly P. 83.[12] an Escape Espinasse 203.[13]

3. point. as to the discharge &c 4 Beacon 641.[14] read by M. 2 Salk 475.[15] & 1-202.[16] 2-273.[17] Haywood 414.[18] act Iredal 189.[19] concluded by Saying this court has no such controling power over the acts of the Justices as to reverse their Judgt. and grant Judgt. on mere motion.

Mr. Dade. 1. the bond void, no bounds laid off &c. conditions impossible void 2 Beacon P. 772.[20] Espinass 191.[21]

Mr. Campbel. bond void ab onitia. the Variance fatal. and the discharge Judgt. of the Justices still in force & securities discharged by the Judgt. which is binding untill reversed.

Mr. Whitesides. contended that if there was not Legal notice it could not be a regular discharge.

1. contends that the bond is fair in the face of it and the[y] are Estopt to Say that there is a varience. and exonerate themselves, on that ground.

2. This court cannot say that the bounds were not laid off. Thi[s] court cannot say that the bond is void. agreed. but if the condition is broken the court cannot award execution.

reads Iredal P. 93 to Shew that the bond is the Judgt., and not necessary to set out the Precise Sum. P. 189.[22] the bond to be assigned filed in the office for safe Keeping. and in case the Prisoner Escapes, the court authorised to enter up Judgt. vs Principle & his Securities.

3 point. the case comes on between a Just and fair creditor and securities who placed confidence in Deftd.

The discharge must exonerate all or none.

the act gives an extraordinary Jurisdiction. not Known in ordinary cases. and it must be performed, in strict conformity with the provisions otherwise their acts cannot have the effect contended for.

reads Iredall 262.[23]

case in iredal, Judgt. as Excrs. Execution vs the real Property, without Sci. fa. vs the heirs, Ejectment brought insisted, on the Judgt. & Sale & the heirs bound. ruled that the were not Estoped. why Sci fa. was necessary to make the land liable.

McGuffin & son
vs

Acklin   motion for Exect. vs them

Perrin &   for breach of the Prison bounds

Combs

no Judgt. such as mentioned in the bond. &c.

against the motion. 1st point, that the bond was taken and executed before Prison bounds were laid off. therefore void, and a voluntary escape by the Sheriff. 2. that the Deftd. was admitted by a competant authority to the benefit of the insolvant Debtors act and legally discharged by his order, which exonerated the Bail. and if that authority did not Strictly persue the law. they were not under the controul of the Securities. and they cannot and ought not to be answerable for any illegallity in their procedings. and the Securities being once exonerated by a competant authority never can be made liable on their bond.

In support of the motion it was argued, as every requisite of the law was not complied with, Previous to the oath being ad[m]inistered and Deftd. & principle are Still bound.

MS, DLC-AJ Papers (Reel 60); Bassett, *Correspondence*, I, 78–80. Date is derived from HDSC Law Min. Bk. 3, 1793–1809, p. 262 (see Document IV). Bassett incorrectly assigns to the document the date of 1804.

1. 4 Bacon, *Abridgment* 641.

2. Inhabitants of Chittington v. Inhabitants of Penshurst, 2 Salk. 475, 91 Eng. Rep. 409; 5 Mod. 321, 87 Eng. Rep. 682 (K.B. n.d.). Two justices of the peace issued an order removing a poor man from one parish to another. "[I]t was objected, that the statute . . . enables two justices of peace to remove the party, one of whom is to be of *the quorum,* which word was omitted in that order. And the order was quashed for this exception, the Court being of opinion, that two justices cannot remove a poor man out of sessions, unless one of them be of *the quorum,* because they have a special jurisdiction given by the Act, which must be followed." 5 Mod. at 322, 87 Eng. Rep. at 682. Chief Justice Holt ruled, "[T]his being a special authority to justices out of sessions, it ought to appear that authority was exactly pursued." 2 Salk. at 475, 91 Eng. Rep. at 409.

3. Ch. 18, 1741 Laws of N.C., reprinted in Iredell, *Laws of North Carolina* 82, 1 Scott, *Laws of Tennessee* 60.

4. Ch. 14, 1759 Laws of N.C., reprinted in Iredell, *Laws of North Carolina* 189, 1 Scott, *Laws of Tennessee* 93.

5. Ch. 4, 1773 Laws of N.C., reprinted in Iredell, *Laws of North Carolina* 262, 1 Scott, *Laws of Tennessee* 128.

6. Pearle v. Folsom, 2 N.C. (1 Hayw. 414) 477 (1796), a covenant action in which a discharge under the Insolvent Debtors Act was asserted as a defense. The defendant produced a petition setting forth his imprisonment by the plaintiff and another creditor and his prayer for relief under the act. The defendant also produced the subsequent proceedings, which showed that he had taken the oath as prescribed by the statute and that he had been discharged. The plaintiff argued that the defendant must produce the notice served upon the plaintiff that relief was to have been sought under the act. The defendant responded that the giving of notice had been a circumstance incident to the granting of his discharge, that the giving of notice must have been proved to the justices of the peace before they proceeded, and that, since a discharge had been entered, the court should presume that all of

the prerequisites to the granting of a discharge had been properly satisfied. In a per curiam opinion, the North Carolina Superior Court held, in part: "Since there is a discharge ordered by the proper officers of justice, we will presume all circumstances required by law to precede the discharge, to have been regularly observed; otherwise, we must presume, that the Justices have acted illegally: which is a presumption never entertained against the proceedings of officers of justice. If in fact they have proceeded to discharge without notice, and the creditor will shew that, it will vitiate the proceedings. The presumption *omnia recte acta*, lasts only until proof of the contrary appear; but we will not require the Defendant to prove notice to have been given, the Plaintiff not being able to shew any irregularity in the proceedings. . . ." 2 N.C. at 477–478.

7. Lucking v. Denning, 1 Salk. 201, 91 Eng. Rep. 180 (K.B. n.d.). This was a trespass action against an officer for the escape of one in his custody by virtue of a process issued by the Court of the Sheriffs of London in an action of debt upon a bond sued upon there. When it appeared that the bond had been executed beyond the court's jurisdiction, it was claimed that the proceeding upon the bond was *coram non judice, i.e.,* brought in a court that had no jurisdiction in the matter, and thus void. It also was claimed that the officer was a trespasser. The court agreed: "Where an inferior jurisdiction is confined to persons, . . . if it appears on the face of the declaration, that the persons that sue are qualified to sue, though in fact they are not; yet if the defendant does not plead to the jurisdiction, but comes in and admits it, he shall never take advantage of this afterwards, but is estopped and concluded: but if it is not averred in the declaration that the person is qualified to sue, and within their jurisdiction, all the proceeding is void, and *coram non judice* and trespass lies against the officer." 1 Salk. at 201–202, 91 Eng. Rep. at 180.

8. An action in trespass.

9. Anonymous, 1 Salk. 273, 91 Eng. Rep. 239 (K.B. n.d.): "Debt for 200£ upon a bond, conditioned to pay 100£.: for want of bail the defendant was committed to the *marshall*, and he applied to the justices of peace of Surrey, and procured a discharge on the late Act, for the relief of insolvent debtors. The plaintiff obtained an escape-warrant, upon which he was taken up; and, upon a motion to be discharged, the Court held that this was an escape, for being a prisoner both indebted and also charged in above 100£. debt and damages, the justices had no authority for what they did, and therefore the discharge was illegal and void."

10. 4 Bacon, *Abridgment* 451.

11. Blackstone, *Commentaries* 415: "WHEN a defendant is once in custody upon this [execution] process, he is to be kept in *arcta et salva custodia:* and, if he afterwards [is] seen at large, it is an *escape;* and the plaintiff may have an action thereupon against the sheriff for his whole debt."

12. Ch. 18, 1741 Laws of N.C., reprinted in Iredell, *Laws of North Carolina* 82, 1 Scott, *Laws of Tennessee* 60.

13. Espinasse, *Actions at Nisi Prius* 203.

14. 4 Bacon, *Abridgment* 641.

15. See note 2 above.

16. See note 7 above.

17. See note 9 above.

18. See note 6 above.

19. Ch. 14, 1759 Laws of N.C., reprinted in Iredell, *Laws of North Carolina* 189, 1 Scott, *Laws of Tennessee* 93.

20. 2 Bacon, *Abridgment* 772.

21. Espinasse, *Actions at Nisi Prius* 191.

22. Ch. 18, 1741 Laws of N.C., reprinted in Iredell, *Laws of North Carolina* 82, 1 Scott, *Laws of Tennessee* 60; ch. 14, 1759 Laws of N.C., reprinted in Iredell, *Laws of North Carolina* 189, 1 Scott, *Laws of Tennessee* 93.

23. Ch. 4, 1773 Laws of N.C., reprinted in Iredell, *Laws of North Carolina* 262, 1 Scott, *Laws of Tennessee* 128.

IV. MINUTE BOOK ENTRY

Hamilton District Superior Court, Knoxville
Judges Jackson, White, and Campbell Presiding

[March 23, 1802]

McGoffin & Son
vs
Samuel Ackland
Joseph Perrin &
George Combs

On a motion Continued at last Term against the defendants for an Execu[tion] to issue against them upon a Bond Given by said defendants to Martin Ashbourne high Sheriff of Grainger County for keeping the prison bounds and assigned to the plaintiffs by said Ashbourne and now upon Argument had at the bar by Council on both sides it is Considered by the Court now here that before Judges Campbell & Jackson It was the opinion of his Honor Judge Campbell that the plaint. have their Execution agreeable to their Motion and his honor Judge Jackson was of opinion that the plaintiffs take nothing by their motion—whereupon the Council for the plaintiffs moved for leave to with draw his motion

MS, TKL-HDSC Law Min. Bk. 3, 1793–1809, p. 262. Date is taken from *id.* at 261.

The assignment of bail bonds by the sheriff to the plaintiff or plaintiffs in every civil action was required by statute. Ch. 2, § 17, 1777 Laws of N.C., reprinted in Iredell, *Laws of North Carolina* 296.

42. Vaughn v. Barnes

1802
(Slavery)

EDITORIAL NOTE

This was a qui tam action brought pursuant to a 1779 North Carolina statute prohibiting the enticement and harboring of slaves from their masters. In May 1798, David Vaughn and his wife, the owners of eight slaves in Davidson County, brought the action against Joseph Barnes in the Mero District Superior Court. Because the original case file has not been located, the circumstances that gave rise to the litigation remain unknown. The case first went to trial on May 23, 1800, and a jury returned a verdict for the Vaughns in the amount of $200. Jackson and his colleagues Judges Roane and Campbell, however, set aside the verdict and awarded Barnes a new trial (Document I).[1]

After a continuance at November Term 1800,[2] the action went to trial for the second time on May 12, 1801. The jury returned a special verdict finding Barnes "gui[l]ty in manner and form as the Plaintiff in declaring hath alledged" and assessing damages at £100 North Carolina currency in accordance with the 1779 statute. The jury stipulated, however, that if the law required that the plaintiffs' damages be "scaled agreeably to the depre[cia]tion," then the amount of the Vaughns' damages was to be assessed at only twenty-five dollars, whereas otherwise the amount of damages was to be assessed at $250 (Document II). After granting a continuance of the proceedings, the court on May 24, 1802, more than a year later, announced its decision to enter judgment for the Vaughns in the amount of twenty-five dollars (Document III).

The special verdict and the court's judgment remain a paradox. The purpose of the depreciation statute appears to have been to allow for the

---

1. Ch. 11, 1779 Laws of N.C. (Jan. Sess.), reprinted in 1 Scott, *Laws of Tennessee* 233, superseded by ch. 28, 1799 Laws of Tenn., reprinted in 1 Scott, *Laws of Tennessee* 650; DaCo Tax List, 1798, p. 20, T. The 1779 statute, upon which the prosecution was based, provided for a penalty of £100 current money.

2. MDSC Law Min. Bk., 1788–1803, p. 348.

adjustment of judgments to compensate for a rapidly depreciating currency.[3] Hence, under the facts in *Vaughn*, a larger sum than the £100 provided for by the 1779 statute would be necessary to compensate for the loss in the value of the North Carolina pound during the more than two decades that preceded the judgment in the case. The jury, however, specified that if the depreciation statute applied, the judgment was not to be increased, but rather was to be decreased to only one-tenth the penalty prescribed by the 1779 statute. In effect, the jury and the court in its judgment appear to have concluded that £100 (the equivalent, apparently, of $250) in 1779 was worth only one-tenth that sum two decades later.[4]

3. Noting that "much difficulty hath arisen in the adjusting and settling debts and demands . . . from the rapid depreciation of paper currency emitted in circulation," the North Carolina General Assembly in 1783 established a depreciation scale for paper money. The statute provided that the depreciation table "be read in evidence in all the courts of this state, to liquidate all debts and demands, and in entering up judgments thereon." Ch. 4, § 3, 1783 Laws of N.C., reprinted in Iredell, *Laws of North Carolina* 451, 1 Scott, *Laws of Tennessee* 275. It is to this statutorily imposed depreciation rate that the jurors apparently make reference in the special verdict. For a discussion of a similar measure that was adopted by the South Carolina legislature in 1783, see Michael S. Hindus, *Prison and Plantation: Crime, Justice and Authority in Massachusetts and South Carolina, 1767–1878* (Chapel Hill, 1980), 5.

4. The Vaughns and Barnes have not been further identified.

I. MINUTE BOOK ENTRY

Mero District Superior Court, Nashville
Judges Jackson, Roane, and Campbell Presiding

David Vaughn & wife Plts vs Joseph Barnes Deft.	[May 23, 1800] In Debt, on a Penal Statute.

Joseph Barnes was attached to answer David Vaughn & Wife of a Plea of Debt for One hundred pounds, upon the Statute of harbouring Negroes, Damage one hundred pounds. Whereupon the sd. David & wife, by Bennet Searcy their Attorney, at May Term 1798, filed their Declaration upon the same in the following words. "State of Tennessee, Mero District, May Term 1798, David Vaughn and his Wife Susanah complains of Joseph Barnes in Custody &c. in a plea of Debt for One hundred pounds upon the Statute of North Carolina, for seducing, inticing and persuading Negroes out of their owners possession and harbouring the same &c. And the said Joseph, by his attorney Seth Lewis comes and defends the force and injury when &c and saith that the said Plaintiffs ought not to have their action aforesaid against him, because he saith that he is not guilty in manner & form as the said plaintiffs above in their Declaration have alledged against him, and of this he puts himself upon the Country, and the said Plts. likewise. And the cause was continued from Term to Term until this Term, to wit May 1800. At which time came the said parties by their attorneys, and a good & lawful Jury to wit James Dupree, William Morgan, Thomas Hudson, James Wilson, Edmund Gamble, John Donelson, Michael Gleaves, Richard Hightower, John Payton, Andrew Grier, William Hartgrove & William Smith who being elected tried & Sworn to speak the truth upon the issue joined on their oath do say that the Defendant is guilty of harbouring &c the Negro in the Declaration mentioned as the plaintiffs in declaring have alledged, and they do find for the plts the Debt of two hundred Dollars, as in declaring they hath set forth. whereupon on the motion of the Defendant, by his attorney, & for reasons appearing to the Court, the said Verdict is set aside, and it is ordered that a new trial be had at the next Court. See Page 436–639.

MS, TDaCo-MDSC Law Min. Bk., 1788–1803, pp. 303–304. Date is taken from *id.* at 300.

II. SPECIAL VERDICT

Mero District Superior Court, Nashville
Judges Jackson, Roane, and Campbell Presiding

[May 12, 1801]

We find that the Defendant Joseph Barnes is gui[l]ty in manner and form as the Plaintiff in declaring hath alleged, and find his debt of one hundred pounds North Carolina Currency in the Declaration mentioned: If it be Law that the same be scaled agreeably to the depre[cia]tion, we find twenty five Dollars; if not, we find the value to be two hundred and fifty Dollars.

James Stuart[1]	Wiley Cerry
David McEwing	Andrew Greer
John Williamson	Daniel Miengle
David Weakley	John Bradley
John Harpole	John Johnston Junr.
Robert Ellis	William Maxey

Tr, TDaCo-MDSC Law Min. Bk., 1788–1803, pp. 436–437. Date is taken from *id.* at 430. For a discussion of the depreciation statute, see Editorial Note, note 3.

    1. The roster of jurors precedes the text in the Tr.

III. MINUTE BOOK ENTRY

Mero District Superior Court, Nashville
Judges Jackson, White, and Campbell Presiding

Monday Morning May 24th 1802

Court met agreeably to adjournment
Present the Hon. David Campbell
       Andrew Jackson &   Esquires Judges
       Hugh L. White

Pleas before &c. May Term 1802
David Vaughn & Wife Plts
    vs   Debt
Joseph Barnes————Deft

And this day came the parties by their attorneys, and thereupon the matters of law arrising upon the Special Verdict in this case, being argued, it seems to the Court that the law is for the Defendant. Therefore it is considered by the Court, that the plaintiffs recover agt. the said Defendant twenty five dollars only, and their Costs by them about their suit in this behalf expended. Vide 303..436.

MS, TDaCo-MDSC Law Min. Bk., 1788–1803, p. 639.

43. Edgar & Tait v. Neville

1802
(Judicial Officers)

EDITORIAL NOTE

In July 1791 the mercantile firm of Edgar & Tait[1] obtained a judgment in the Davidson County court against Anthony Crutcher for £103, 9 shillings, and 6 pence plus costs. Edgar & Tait revived the still unsatisfied judgment in July 1794 and secured from the Davidson court the issuance of a capias ad satisfaciendum directing Neville, the sheriff of Tennessee County, to take Crutcher into custody until he had satisfied the judgment. Neville took Crutcher into custody in July 1795. Crutcher, however, did not remain jailed and never satisfied the outstanding judgment against him.

In May 1801 Edgar & Tait brought a debt action against Neville to recover the amount of the unsatisfied judgment against Crutcher plus the court costs that they had expended in seeking an execution upon Crutcher. Edgar & Tait, through their counsel, Bennett Searcy, alleged that Neville had not made any attempt to apprehend Crutcher after his escape from the Tennessee County jail and that, as a result, their judgment against Crutcher remained unsatisfied. The plaintiffs sought to recover against Neville on the ground that because of "the neglect of the aforesaid Joseph [Neville] he became liable to pay the aforesaid Judgment and costs of the suit to the plaintiffs" (Document I).

Neville answered by claiming in part that there was no record of the plaintiffs' original judgment against Crutcher and, alternatively, that he had released Crutcher from custody at the direction of William Stothart, whom the sheriff claimed was an agent of William Tait's (Document II). The plaintiffs subsequently filed a replication denying each of the allegations in Neville's answer (Document III).

When the action went to trial at the Mero District Superior Court in May 1802, the court on May 14 granted a motion by Neville to nonsuit

1. For further identification of Edgar & Tait, see No. 15.

Edgar & Tait for having failed to prosecute the action and dismissed the jury that had been selected to try the suit. The court, however, subsequently granted a motion by Edgar & Tait to set aside the nonsuit and reinstated the action at the plaintiffs' cost (Document IV). The reinstated action went to trial on November 10, 1802, and a jury returned a verdict for the plaintiffs (Document V).

By April 1803, the judgment that Edgar & Tait had obtained against Neville in November 1802 remained unsatisfied. The firm then obtained from the court the issuance of a writ of fieri facias for the public sale of two slaves, three horses, and twenty head of cattle belonging to Neville to satisfy the judgment.[2]

The duties of a sheriff in Tennessee at the start of the nineteenth century embraced the execution of all writs and other judicial process. These executions included the collection of debts, the public sale of debtors' property, and the detention of the person of the debtor in the county jail. A sheriff was obligated to post a bond for the faithful performance of his office.

In the event that a sheriff either neglected to pay over money collected from a debtor or allowed a debtor to escape from custody, the creditor was authorized, upon motion in the court that issued the writ, to demand judgment against the sheriff. The court could "award execution against the Goods and Chattles, Land and Tenements, of such Sheriff."[3]

2. See *Tennessee Gazette,* Apr. 13, 1803.

3. Ch. 8, 1777 Laws of N.C. (Nov. Sess.), reprinted in Iredell, *Laws of North Carolina* 330, 1 Scott, *Laws of Tennessee* 209. An 1803 statute permitted such a judgment to be entered against the sheriff or his securities. Ch. 18, 1803 Tenn. Pub. Acts, reprinted in 1 Scott, *Laws of Tennessee* 780.

I. DECLARATION OF
EDGAR & TAIT

Mero District Superior Court, Nashville

May 1801

State of Tennessee, Mero District, May Term 1801.

John Edger and William Tait, by the firm of Edger & Tait complain of Joseph B. Neville in custody of the Sheriff &c. in a plea of Debt that he render to them the sum of two hundred & Seventy nine dollars thirty eight cents, which he owes & from them unjustly detains &c. for that whereas the aforesaid plaintiffs instituted their suit in the worshipful court of pleas & quarter sessions for the County of Davidson against a certain Anthony Crutcher, and at July Term of the said Court 1791 obtained a Judgment for the sum of one hundred and three pounds nine shillings and Six pence and cost of suit in that behalf expended, which said Judgment remained dormant for upwards of twelve months and a day, and by reason thereof the said Plaintiffs caused a Scire facias to issue against the said Crutcher to revive the said Judgment, which was accordingly done, and at July Term of the said Court of Davidson 1794 the said Judgment was revived according to the Scire facias amounting to the sum of £103.9.6, and cost of suit amounting in the whole to twenty dollars Sixty eight and three fourths of a Cent; in consequence of the aforesaid Judgment obtained by the plaintiffs aforesaid against the said Anthony Crutcher they caused a Capias ad satisfaciendum to issue out of the said Court of Davidson County, bearing teste of Andrew Ewing Clerk &c. from their April Term of said Court 1795. (and made returnable to their July Term of the same year,) to the County of Tennessee, now called Montgomery commanding the Sheriff to take the body of the said Crutcher, & him safely keep until he made satisfaction of the said Judgment to the plaintiffs, which said Writ aforesaid was put in the hands of the aforesaid Joseph B. Neville who was then Sheriff for the County of Tennessee, now Montgomery, who did then and there mark on the back of said Writ that it came into his hands on the 7th of July meaning 1795, who did then and there execute the said Writ of Capias ad Satisfaciendum on the said Anthony Curtcher and took him in custody &c. And that the aforesaid Joseph B. Neville did then & there put the aforesaid anthony into the Jail for the County of Tennessee, now Montgomery, and made a return of the aforesaid Writ of Capias ad satisfaciendum to the July Term of the County Court of Davidson 1795, and indorsed on the back of said Writ the following words, to wit, "Executed and refused to give Security, put to Goal, the Goal not sufficient to keep him." signed Jos. B. Neville. The plaintiffs further declare that after the said Anthony Crutcher broke the said Goal that the aforesaid Joseph did not file or take out an Escape Warrant nor did not pursue him but that the aforesaid Anthony went at large. The plaintiffs further declare that the aforesaid Anthony Crutcher was in company with the aforesaid Joseph on the same day he got out of the sd. Goal and frequently afterwards, and that the aforesaid Joseph did not apprehend the aforesaid Anthony but suffered him to go at large in the said County; and suffered the aforesaid Anthony to make a voluntary escape contrary to the duties of his office as Sheriff aforesaid in consequence whereof the aforesaid plaintiffs has not received the amount of the aforesaid Judgment so obtained by them aforesaid and the costs of suit which they have paid; and in consequence of the aforesaid escape, and the neglect of the aforesaid Joseph he became liable to pay the aforesaid Judgment and costs of the suit to the plaintiffs; which said Writ of Capias ad satisfaciendum the plaintiffs here produce to the Court. Yet nevertheless the Said Joseph not regarding the laws in that case made and provided, nor the duties of his office as Sheriff aforesaid for suffering Voluntary escapes hath not rendered the aforesaid Debt and costs to the plaintiffs, altho' oftimes required by the Plaintiffs to pay and satisfy the same, but that the said Joseph hath hitherto refused and still doth refuse to pay and satisfy the same, to the damage of the plaintiffs two hundred dollars, and therefore they bring their suit. Pledges to prosecute.

B Searcy Atto.

Tr, TDaCo-MDSC Law Min. Bk., 1788–1803, pp. 601–602.

II. ANSWER OF
JOSEPH B. NEVILLE

Mero District Superior Court, Nashville

[After May 1801]

Joseph B. Neville,[1] by Thomas Stuart his Attorney comes & defends the force and injury when and where &c. & for plea saith that the said Plaintiffs ought not to have or maintain their action thereof against him because he saith there is not any such record of the said Original recovery against the said Anthony Crutcher at the suit of the said Edger & Tait, as they the said Edger and Tait above in declaring have alleged, and this he is ready to verify; whereupon he prayeth Judgment if the said plaintiff ought to have or maintain their said action against him

And for further plea said Defendant saith said Plaintiffs ought not to have or maintain their action thereof against him because he saith there is not any such record of the said recovery on Scire facias against the said Anthony Crutcher at the suit of said Edger & Tait, nor is there any record of said Capias ad Satisfaciendum, and the return on the same as said plaintiffs above in declaring have alledged, and this he is ready to verify, whereupon he prayeth Judgment if the said plaintiffs ought to have or maintain their said action against him.

And for further plea said Defendant saith that he the said Joseph B. Neville doth not owe to the said plaintiffs the said two hundred and Seventy nine dollars and thirty eight Cents, nor any part thereof in manner & form as the said plaintiffs have above declared against him, and of this he putteth himself upon the Country—and the plaintiffs likewise do the same.

And for further plea said Defendant saith that the said Anthony Crutcher, at the County aforesaid, on the ² day of ² paid the whole amount of said Execution and Costs to the said plaintiffs, wherefore this Defendant prays Judgment if the said plaintiffs ought to have or maintain their said action thereof against him.

And for further pleas said Defendant saith that said Plaintiffs ought not to have or maintain their said action against him, because he saith that said Anthony Crutcher, on the ² day of ² at Montgomery County, was let out of Prison by this Defendant, by the direction of William Stothart agent for said William Tait, and this he is ready to verify wherefore he prays Judgment if the said plaintiffs, ought to have or maintain their said action against him. 6th. Plea. Accord & Satisfaction.

Tr, TDaCo-MDSC Law Min. Bk., 1788–1803, pp. 602–603. Date is derived from Document I.

    1. Preceded in the Tr by: "And the said."
    2. Blank in Tr.

III. REPLICATION OF
EDGAR & TAIT

Mero District Superior Court, Nashville

[ca. November 1801]

And the plaintiffs say that they, by any thing by the aforesaid Defendant above in his first plea alledged, ought not to be precluded from having their action against him because they say, there is such a record of the original recovery as mentioned in their declaration, of their obtaining a Judgment in the County Court of Davidson against the said Anthony Crutcher in manner they have there declared, and this they pray Judgment &c. and that the same may be inquired of by the record. And the said Defendant likewise.

And for Replication to the second plea the aforesaid Plaintiffs say that there is such a record of the said recovery on the Scire facias in manner & form as they have alledged in their declaration, against the said Anthony Crutcher, obtained by the plaintiffs in the County Court of Davidson. And further they say that there is such a record of a Writ of Capias ad Satisfaciendum issued out of the County Court aforesaid against the body of said Anthony Crutcher, and such a return made on the writ aforesaid by the said Defendant in manner & form as they have alledged in their declaration, wherefore they pray Judgment &c. and that the same may be inquired of by the Records and the said Defendant likewise.

And for replication to the fourth plea, the said plaintiffs say that the said Anthony Crutcher did not at the   [1] day of   [1] pay the whole or any part of the amount of the said Judgment and Cost contained in the said declaration to the plaintiffs, and this they pray may be inquired of by the Country; and the said Defendant likewise.

And the said plaintiffs for replication to the fifth plea, say that said William Stothart did not on the   [1] day of   [1] at the County of Montgomery let out or directed the said Defendant to let the sd. Anthony out of prison, nor neither was the said Stothart agent for the said William Tait in that particular in manner & form as the said Defendant hath alledged in his plea, and this they pray may inquired of by the Country and the said Defendant likewise.

And the plaintiffs, for replication to the sixth plea, say that they never agreed, nor neither did the said Anthony, nor neither did the said Defendant ever agree or satisfy them for the Said Sum aforesaid in manner & form as the said Defendant hath alledged in his plea, and this they pray may be inquired of by the Country.

Tr, TDaCo-MDSC Law Min. Bk., 1788–1803, pp. 603–604. Approximate date is derived from Document I.

    1. Blank in Tr.

IV. MINUTE BOOK ENTRY

Mero District Superior Court, Nashville
Judges Jackson, White, and Campbell Presiding

[May 14, 1802]

Pleas at Nashville before &c. May Term 1802.

John Edger & William Tait Plts. ⎫
             vs.   ⎬   In Debt.
Joseph B. Neville_____ ⎭

Joseph B Neville was summoned to Answer John Edger & William Tait, by the firm of Edger & Tait in a plea of debt that he render to them the sum of two hundred & seventy nine dollars & thirty eight cents which he owes and unjustly detains to their damage two hundred dollars. Whereupon the said Plaintiffs, by their Attorney Bennet Searcy, at May Term 1801, filed their declaration upon the same[1] . . . .

And the cause was continued until this Term, to wit, the first mentioned, at which day came the parties by their Attornies aforesaid, and a Jury, to wit, Robert Desha, Benjamin Meneis Junr. Thomas Edmiston, George Briscoe, Hugh Crafford, William T. Lewis, William Rutledge, Alexander Brown, Joel Lewis, John Buchanan, Edward Mitchel & William Wilson, who being elected & Sworn to try the issues joined to the Country. And the plaintiffs not further prosecuting their said Action, on the motion of the Defendant, it is considered by the Court that the Jury from rendering their verdict be discharged, and that the said plaintiffs be nonsuitted. And there upon a Rule by the Plaintiffs to shew cause why the nonsuit aforesaid should be set aside, and the cause reinstated. And on argument of the said Rule It is ordered that the nonsuit be set aside, and the Cause reinstated—and that the plaintiffs pay the Costs of this Term. Vide. 658.

MS, TDaCo-MDSC Law Min. Bk., 1788–1803, pp. 601–604. Date and judges' attendance are taken from *id.* at 593.

    1. The texts of Documents I–III follow at this point in the MS.

V. MINUTE BOOK ENTRY

*Mero District Superior Court, Nashville
Judges Jackson, White, and Campbell Presiding*

Wednesday morning November 10th
1802.

Court met agreeably to adjournment
Present the Hon. David Campbell
            Andrew Jackson &   } Esqrs. Judges.
            Hugh L. White.

John Edger & William Tait
            agt.   } Debt
Joseph B. Neville_____

And this day come the parties, by their attorneys, & a Jury to wit Charles M. Hall, Edward Settles, James Clendening, Isaac Phillips, John Brooks, George Gillespie Roger Qualls, William Anthony, Matthew Alexander, John K. Wynne, William Neely & George D. Blackamore who being elected tried & Sworn the truth to speak upon the issues joined upon their oath do say that the Defendant doth owe to the plaintiffs two hundred & fifty eight dollars & Sixty eight & three fourth cents as the plaintiffs declaring have alledged; and the Jurors aforesaid on their oath aforesaid further say that the said Anthony Crutcher did not pay the whole or any part of the Judgment aforesaid, as the plaintiffs in replying have alledged. And the Jurors further say that the said William Stothart did not let out, nor direct the said Defendant to let the said Anthony out of prison, as the plaintiffs in replying have also alledged. And the Records aforesaid being seen & inspected it seems to the Court here that there are such records as the plaintiffs, in their replications to the first and second pleas of the said Defendant, have alledged.

Therefore it is considered by the Court that the plaintiffs recover against the said Defendant their Debt of $258.68¾ aforesaid, together with their costs by them about their suit in their behalf expended. &c. See Page 601.

MS, TDaCo-MDSC Law Min. Bk., 1788–1803, p. 658.

44. State v. Watson

1802

(Criminal Law)

EDITORIAL NOTE

During the spring of 1802, Jackson devoted much of his attention to securing the post of major general in the state's militia and to procuring the court-martial of an officer accused of murdering an Indian.[1] Nonetheless, Jackson also attended to his judicial duties when the court met in Washington and Hamilton districts in March and in Mero District in May. Among the criminal cases that Jackson and the other judges were asked to hear in Nashville was the unusual prosecution of a slaveholder accused of having incited a slave to commit murder.

The victim, William Dennis, had traveled to middle Tennessee from Carteret County, North Carolina, in the spring of the same year, bringing with him at least one slave for sale to Jeremiah Watson in Sumner County.[2] The sale of Dennis's slave Powell to Watson duly took place.[3] Then, on April 24, Dennis was brutally bludgeoned to death.

On May 10, nearly three weeks after Dennis's death, Judges Jackson, White, and Campbell convened the Mero District Superior Court,[4] and the district's grand jury retired to inquire into the incident. Five days later, on May 15, the grand jury returned with a presentment in which a slave,

1. See *Jackson Papers*, I, 277, 291–292, 294–296; Robert V. Remini, *Andrew Jackson and the Course of American Empire, 1767–1821* (New York, 1977), 118–119.
2. See SumCo CPQS Min. Bk. 4, 1801–1804, p. 353. For Dennis's residence in Carteret County, see U.S. Bureau of the Census, Second Census, 1800, Population, North Carolina, Carteret County, III, 219 (original schedules on microfilm); *Tennessee Gazette*, Aug. 18, 1802; see also note 9 below.
3. Watson had his bill of sale proved and recorded in the Sumner court the following October. SumCo CPQS Min. Bk. 4, 1801–1804, p. 353. A statute mandated that all sales of slaves be in writing and attested by at least one witness. Further, slave bills of sale had to be recorded within nine months after they were prepared. Ch. 10, 1784 Laws of N.C. (Oct. Sess.), reprinted in Iredell, *Laws of North Carolina* 529, 1 Scott, *Laws of Tennessee* 311. The recording period was subsequently enlarged to one year. Ch. 59, 1789 Laws of N.C., reprinted in Iredell, *Laws of North Carolina* 689, 1 Scott, *Laws of Tennessee* 420.
4. MDSC Law Min. Bk., 1788–1803, p. 582.

Peter, was charged with having beaten Dennis to death with a gun and in which Watson was charged with having incited the slave to commit the offense (Document I).

Evidently on the theory that Watson could not be convicted of aiding and abetting Dennis's murder if the principal, the slave Peter, was not convicted of the underlying primary offense of murder, the court continued Watson's trial until a justices-and-freeholders court could try the slave. On May 26, Watson was permitted to post bond for his appearance at the court's November Term and was released from the district jail.[5]

The justices-and-freeholders courts that by statute exercised jurisdiction in the trying of slaves for capital offenses were not courts of record, and, although accounts of such trials occasionally were entered into the minutes of the county court where the trials occurred,[6] no such records have been located for the trial of the slave Peter. Peter's fate, however, and that of another slave are suggested by a single-sentence entry in the minutes of the Sumner County Court of Pleas and Quarter Sessions for its July Term 1802. On July 7, 1802, the Sumner court awarded to Patrick Gibson, a county constable, the sum of twenty-five dollars for the "trouble & expences attending the execution of two negro criminals the property of Jeremiah Watson." That one of the two slaves was Peter and that the offense for which both of the slaves were executed was the Dennis murder seem likely. On July 8, the day after paying the expenses for the execution of Watson's slaves, the Sumner court awarded five dollars to one Benjamin Morgan for his expenses in having arrested and confined Watson in the district jail subsequent to the county court's April Term.[7] The only criminal prosecution between April and July that would have warranted Watson's arrest and detention in the Mero District jail was the present proceeding against Watson for procuring Dennis's death.

Moreover, with the execution of Peter and his accomplice for committing the primary offense of murder, the state was free to proceed against Watson. When the Mero District Superior Court reconvened on November 8, the attorney general attempted to secure an indictment of Watson for the primary offense of murder.[8] This failing, Watson on November 19 was tried before Judges Jackson, White, and Campbell on the initial presentment as an accessory to Dennis's murder. The jury, evidently un-

5. MDSC Law Min. Bk., 1788–1803, p. 641. Watson posted a $3,000 appearance bond with sureties for an additional $4,000. *Id.*

6. See, *e.g.,* State v. Dick, DaCo CPQS Min. Bk. B, 119–120 (1793); State v. Cato, DaCo CPQS Min. Bk. A, 411 (1791).

7. SumCo CPQS Min. Bk. 4, 1801–1804, pp. 345, 349.

8. The grand jury returned a no true bill on Nov. 13. MDSC Law Min. Bk., 1788–1803, p. 690.

persuaded by the evidence presented to it, acquitted the accused (Document II).

Either Watson or his father, who bore the same name, resided in or owned property in Carteret County, North Carolina, before 1785. It was in Carteret County, of course, that Dennis had resided and filled several civil and military posts before his death in Tennessee. One or both of the Watsons had resided in Jones County, North Carolina, in 1790 before moving to Sumner County.[9]

9. Jean B. Kell and Thomas A. Williams, eds., *North Carolina's Coastal Carteret County During the American Revolution 1765–1785* (Greenville, N.C., 1975), 198; U.S. Bureau of the Census, First Census, 1790, Population, North Carolina, Jones County, 143 (original schedules on microfilm).
Dennis held the rank of first major in the county's militia in 1781. Kell and Williams, *Carteret County*, 140. He also served as sheriff of the county, 1784–1785, 1787–1789. *Id.* at 144; *N.C. State Records*, XXI, 1072. By 1784, Dennis had procured title to more than 22,000 acres in the county. Kell and Williams, *Carteret County*, 163.

I. PRESENTMENT OF
JEREMIAH WATSON

Mero District Superior Court, Nashville

[May 15, 1802]

Be it remembered that heretofore, to wit, at Nashville, in the State of Tennessee, and District of Mero, at May Term 1802 by the oath of William Tait foreman, William Alexander, Allen Grace, George Ridley, Thomas Bradley, John Brown, Henry Buren, Benjn. Hicks, Micajah Barrow, Matthew Alexander, John Nichols, Benjamin Drake, William Johnston, John Blackman and George Murphey honest and lawful men of the State & District aforesaid, then and there being Sworn and charged to enquire for the body of the said District it was presented that Peter, a Negro man Slave late of the County of Sumner and District aforesaid, not regarding the laws of this State, but being moved and instigated by the Devil, on the twenty fourth day of April eighteen hundred & two with force and arms at the county aforesaid, to wit, said Sumner County, in the District aforesaid, in and upon William Dennis in the peace of the State then and there being, feloniously, wilfully and of his malice afore thought did make an assault, and that he the said peter with a certain Gun of Iron Steell and wood of the value of five dollars which he the said Peter in both his hands then and there had and held, the said William Dennis in and upon the back part of thé head, the left Temple, and right under the Jaw-bone of

him the said William Dennis, then and there feloniously wilfully and
of his malice aforethought did strike beat and wound, giving to the said
William Dennis then and there with the Gun aforesaid, by the striking,
beating and wounding as aforesaid in and upon the above said back part
of the head, the left temple, and right under Jaw-bone of him the said
William Dennis in manner aforesaid several mortal wounds and bruises,
of which said several mortal wounds & bruises the said William Dennis
then and there instantly died: And so we the Grand Jury aforesaid upon
our oath aforesaid do say that the said Peter, the said William Dennis in
manner & form aforesaid feloniously wilfully and of his malice afore
thought did kill and murder against the peace & dignity of the State of
Tennessee. And we the Grand Jury aforesaid upon our oath aforesaid do
further present that Jeremiah Watson late of the said County of Sumner,
and in the District of Mero aforesaid, Yeoman, before the said felony and
Murder was committed in form aforesaid, to wit, on the said twenty
fourth day of April in the year aforesaid with force and arms at the County
aforesaid, to wit, Sumner County in the District of Mero aforesaid did
feloniously, wilfully and of his malice aforethought, incite counsel, move,
procure, hire, aid and abet the said Peter a Negro man Slave, as above, to
do and commit the said felony and murder in manner & form aforesaid,
against the peace and dignity of the State of Tennessee aforesaid &c.

Tr, TDaCo-MDSC Law Min. Bk., 1788–1803, p. 702. Date is taken from *id.* at 609.

II. MINUTE BOOK ENTRY

Mero District Superior Court, Nashville
Judges Jackson, White, and Campbell Presiding

Friday morning November 19th 1802, Court met agreeably to
adjournment.
Present the Hon. David Campbell ⎫
        Andrew Jackson & ⎬   Esquires Judges.
        Hugh L. White ⎭
Pleas at Nashville before &c. November 19th 1802.
The State——— ⎫
       v. ⎬   Presentment.[1] . . .
Jeremiah Watson ⎭
   And the said Jeremiah Watson was led to the bar in Custody of the
Sheriff &c. And forthwith it being demanded concerning the premises in
the said Presentment above Specified and charged upon him, how he will

acquit himself thereof, he saith that he is not guilty thereof, and thereof puts himself upon the Country. And the trial of the premises aforesaid is continued 'till the next Court. And now, to wit, the Term first mentioned, the said Jeremiah Watson was again led to the bar in Custody of the Sheriff, and thereupon came a Jury of good & lawful men, to wit, Joseph T. Elliston, James Caldwell, Edmund Jennings, Stephen Bean, James Garrett, William Lytle, Joseph McKean, John Witherspoon, Thomas Dillon, Thomas Tolbot, John Childress Junr. & William Searcy, who being elected tried & Sworn the truth of and upon the premises to speak, & having tried the evidince, do say, upon their oath, that the said Jeremiah Watson is not guilty of the premises aforesaid charged upon him, as in pleading he hath alledged. Therefore it is considered by the Court that the said Jeremiah Watson be acquitted & discharged.

MS, TDaCo-MDSC Law Min. Bk., 1788–1803, p. 702–703.

1. The text of Document I follows at this point in the MS.

45. Parker v. Parker

1802
(Domestic Relations)

On April 29, 1800, Mary Parker by her "next friend," her brother, Josiah Ramsey, delivered to Jackson a petition for divorce from bed and board against her husband, Nathaniel Parker. Mrs. Parker alleged that her husband's ill treatment had forced her to leave the farm on which they resided and that the couple had lived apart from each other for three years and six months. Mrs. Parker sought the issuance of a divorce decree and an award of separate maintenance (Document I).

Nathaniel Parker subsequently filed an answer with the court in which he alleged that his wife had left his house without cause about one year after their marriage. Parker denied ever having mistreated his wife or ever having threatened to do so. In addition to seeking a dismissal of his wife's petition, Parker requested that his wife's prayer for an award of separate maintenance also be denied on the ground that she had squandered some $300 of the defendant's money, which he asserted was more than the value of her share of his property (Document II).

At May Term 1802, the court entered an order that the depositions of Anne Ramsey and Susanah Penny be taken and that the cause be set for trial at the court's ensuing November Term.[1] At the trial of the matter on November 12, 1802, the court, with Judges Jackson, White, and Campbell presiding, sent the jury out to render a special verdict upon two questions of fact: (a) whether the defendant had mistreated the plaintiff as alleged and (b) whether the defendant's conduct had forced the plaintiff to leave his house as alleged. The jury found that, although the defendant had not treated his wife any worse than she had treated him, the defendant's conduct in fact had forced the plaintiff from his house (Document III).

1. MDSC Law Min. Bk., 1788–1803, p. 608.

Twelve days later, on November 24, the court entered its final decree, signed by Judges Jackson and White. The court granted the plaintiff a divorce from bed and board and awarded her separate maintenance in the amount of $200 per annum to be paid quarterly (Document IV).

In common with most American jurisdictions, Tennessee adopted the English common-law rule that a woman, upon marriage, became one with her husband, a feme covert. Accordingly, she could institute a lawsuit only under the protection of her husband. When a married woman asserted a right in opposition to her husband, she could not sue either in her own name, being under the disability of coverture, or in her husband's name, because he could not sue himself. To remedy this situation, the wife was permitted to maintain a lawsuit in the name of a next friend. In essence, the next friend acted as a guardian representing a party under a legal or natural disability. Originally the next friend was the nearest kinsman of the disabled person, but by the eighteenth century a married woman could select any individual willing to act in good faith and secure the court costs.[2]

Reflecting a break from English practice, Tennessee divorce law was relatively liberal during Jackson's years on the bench. English law did not recognize absolute divorce until the seventeenth century, and then such relief was available only by means of a private bill of divorce passed through Parliament. This effectively restricted absolute divorce to the wealthy or powerful. More limited remedies were available in the ecclesiastical courts, which had jurisdiction over matrimonial litigation. These church tribunals could grant an annulment or a divorce from bed and board (a mensa et thoro). The divorce from bed and board was essentially a legal separation that did not permit either spouse to remarry.[3]

The southern colonies generally followed the English view on the dissolution of marriage. Apparently the North Carolina legislature never granted a divorce during the colonial era. Moreover, because ecclesiastical courts were not established in North Carolina, there was no other divorce mechanism of any kind. The drive for a general divorce statute started during the 1790s, but such a measure was not enacted until 1814.

2. John Bouvier, *Institutes of American Law* (Philadelphia, 1841–1854), IV, 294–295. Tennessee's 1799 divorce statute authorized "the husband in his own proper name or the wife by her next friend" to institute proceedings. Ch. 19, 1799 Tenn. Pub. Acts (Sept. Sess.), reprinted in 1 Scott, *Laws of Tennessee* 645.

3. Nelson Manfred Blake, *The Road to Reno: A History of Divorce in the United States* (Westport, Conn., 1962), 22–33; Harvey Couch, "The Evolution of Parliamentary Divorce in England," 52 *Tulane L. Rev.* 513 (1978); Gerhard O. W. Mueller, "Inquiry into the State of a Divorceless Society: Domestic Relations Law and Morals in England from 1660 to 1857," 18 *U. Pitt. L. Rev.* 545 (1957).

Beginning in 1794, however, the legislature began to grant some absolute divorces by private act.[4]

Both legislative and judicial divorces were available early in Tennessee's history. In October 1797, the legislature granted a petition for absolute divorce,[5] and the practice continued until prohibited by the Constitution of 1834.[6] Prompted perhaps by the large number of divorce bills,[7] the lawmakers in 1799 enacted a general divorce statute authorizing the Superior Court to decree absolute divorce, divorce from bed and board, and annulment. Absolute divorce could be granted for impotence, bigamy, adultery, or desertion for two years. Divorce from bed and board was available when "any husband shall maliciously abandon or turn his wife out of doors, or by cruel or barbarous treatment endanger her life, or offer such indignities to her person as to render her condition intolerable, and thereby force her to withdraw." In cases of divorce from bed and board, the court could award the wife alimony not exceeding one-third of the husband's income.[8]

Mary Ramsey Parker (1734–1808) was the widow of Justice Anthony Bledsoe at the time of her marriage to Nathaniel Parker. A native of Augusta County, Virginia, she had married Bledsoe in 1760 and had moved with him to Davidson County in 1781. The couple settled on a 6,280-acre tract and erected upon it a fortification referred to as Greenfield. Five years after her husband's death, Mary Bledsoe, at the age of sixty, married Nathaniel Parker in 1794. By November of that year, however, she had left her second husband. Whether she returned before leaving him on the occasion specified in her divorce petition or whether the state-

---

4. Blake, *The Road to Reno,* 51–53; George E. Howard, *A History of Matrimonial Institutions* (Chicago, 1904), II, 366–376; Note, "Early Statutory and Common Law of Divorce in North Carolina," 41 *N.C. L. Rev.* 604 (1963). See generally Jane Turner Censer, "'Smiling Through Her Tears': Ante-Bellum Southern Women and Divorce," 25 *Am. J. Legal Hist.* 24 (1981); James W. Ely, Jr., and David J. Bodenhamer, "Regionalism and American Legal History: The Southern Experience," 39 *Vand. L. Rev.* 539, 562–566 (1986).

5. Ch. 32, 1797 Tenn. Priv. Acts, reprinted in *Acts Passed at the First Session of the Second General Assembly* (Knoxville, 1797), 92. See generally Lawrence B. Goodheart, Neil Hanks, and Elizabeth Johnson, "'An Act for the Relief of Females . . .': Divorce and the Changing Legal Status of Women in Tennessee, 1796–1860," pt. I, 44 *THQ* 318, pt. II, *id.* at 402 (1985).

6. "The legislature shall have no power to grant divorces, but may authorize the courts of justice to grant them for such causes as may be specified by law." Art. 11, §4, Tenn. Const. (1834).

7. See, *e.g.,* Jones v. Jones, 2 Tenn. (2 Overton) 2 (1804).

8. Ch. 19, 1799 Tenn. Pub. Acts (Sept. Sess.), reprinted in 1 Scott, *Laws of Tennessee* 645. While on the Superior Court, AJ heard several other divorce cases. *E.g.,* Thompson v. Thompson, MDSC Law Min. Bk., 1788–1803, pp. 677–678 (1802) (allegation that husband's first wife was still alive); Martin v. Martin, MDSC Law Min. Bk., 1803–1805, pp. 86–87 (1803) (allegation that wife had run off in a state of adultery).

ment in her petition merely was inaccurate has not been determined. Whether her departure might have been prompted by the litigation over the substantial Bledsoe estate in which she was engaged with Parker as executors of the estate likewise remains conjectural. Her divorce petition was filed by her brother, Josiah Ramsey.[9]

Nathaniel Parker (ca. 1730–1803), also a native of Virginia, apparently was a friend of the Bledsoes' who had lodged with them during his visits to the Cumberland area before becoming himself a permanent resident. A widower when he finally settled in Sumner County with his seven sons and constructed a house near the Bledsoes' Greenfield, Parker was named by Bledsoe as one of the executors of his estate. Parker married Bledsoe's widow when he was sixty-four years old. Unsuccessful in defending the present divorce suit, Parker in the final year of his life was forced to sell his residence and slaves to meet his support payments under the court's separate maintenance order.[10]

9. Bledsoe Sketch, McRaven Coll., THi; *Knoxville Gazette*, Nov. 29, 1794; Jay G. Cisco, *Historic Sumner County, Tennessee* (Nashville, 1909), 70–71; see Bledsoe's Ex'rs v. Hay, MDSC Law Min. Bk., 1788–1803, p. 116 (1794).
10. *Tennessee Gazette*, Mar. 23, 1803, and June 1, 1803; Cisco, *Historic Sumner County*, 287; see, *e.g.*, Bledsoe's Ex'rs v. Hay, note 9 above.

I. PETITION OF MARY PARKER

Mero District Superior Court, Nashville

April 29, 1800

To the Hon. the judges of the Superior Courts of law & Equity for the State of Tennessee: Your petitioner Mary Parker wife of Nathaniel Parker, by her next friend Josiah Ramsey, humbly complaineth and sheweth unto your honors, that the said Nathaniel Parker[,] husband of your petitioner, did for some time after their intermarriage, beat abuse, threaten and evilly treat your petitioner in such manner as to render her life and condition intolerable, and did thereby force her to withdraw from her home, & leave the house, farm and all the appurtenances thereunto belonging which by virtue of her said intermarriage with said Parker he became possessed: Your petitioner humbly and further sheweth that in consequence of the repeated ill treatment and unhusbandlike conduct of said Nathl. Parker she was compelled, in order to keep safe her life & person, to seperate and keep a part from all communion and intercourse with said Parker, and in that State have your said petitioner and the said Parker remained for the Term & space of three years and Six months; and whereas the said Parker has kept at an awful distance your petitioner ever since their seperation as aforesaid, and enjoyed all the priveledges & emoluments arrising from the property both real & personal of which he the said Parker became possessed as above mentioned, and to admit her under the protection & Care of him the said Parker, as the good Husband ought to do, or furnish her with such other assistance & property as in justice and agreeably to their marriage Vow he was in duty bound to render, hath refused & Still doth refuse; Your petitioner therefore prays that your honors may direct Subpoena or Subpoenas to issue command-ing &c. conformably to the Act of the General Assembly in that case made & provided; and that your Honors, the premises being considered, will grant your petitioner a divorce from the bed and board of the said Nathaniel and that your Honors may order and adjudge that the said Nathaniel pay to your petitioner such sum or sums of money, at such times and in such manner, as to your honors may seem proper, to her own use, for her seperate maintainance; and that your Honors may grant her such other relief in the premises, as may be legal &c.

> Mary Parker by her next friend
> Josiah Ramsey

State of Tennessee, Davidson County Sc.

Personally appeared before me Andrew Jackson one of the Judges of the Superior Courts of Law & Equity for the State aforesaid, Mary Parker & having been solemnly sworn saith that the contents of the above petition, and the facts contained therein are just and true; and that the Complaints made in said petition are not set forth through levity or col-lusion with said parker or any other person whatever, or for the mere purpose of being freed and seperated, but in sincerity and in truth, & for the causes mentioned in said petition. Sworn to & Subscribed this 29th day of April 1800.

Andrew Jackson   Mary Parker

Tr, TDaCo-MDSC Law Min. Bk., 1788–1803, pp. 674–675.

The Tennessee divorce statute required that the petitioner "exhibit an affidavit taken on oath or affirmation before one of the said judges, or some justice of the peace . . . that the facts contained in said petition are true to the best of his or her knowledge and belief." Ch. 19, 1799 Tenn. Pub. Acts (Sept. Sess.), reprinted in 1 Scott, *Laws of Tennessee* 645.

II. ANSWER OF
NATHANIEL PARKER

Mero District Superior Court, Nashville

[After April 29, 1800]

The Answer of Nathaniel Parker to the petition of Mary Parker his Wife. This Respondent Nathaniel Parker saying and reserving to himself all manner of benefit of exception to the many errors & imperfections in the said petition contained, for answer thereunto, or unto so much thereof as he is advised & believes is matereal for him to make answer unto, he answering says; That about the   ¹ day of   ¹ in the year 179 ¹ his said wife mary after having lived about one year with him as his wife left the house of this Respondent, when he was absent, without any good cause known to this Respondent for so doing; this respondent denies that he ever did beat, abuse or evilly treat his said Wife, as she has untruly charged, or threaten so to do, or render her life and Condition intolerable, or force her to leave him, or use her in any manner different from what a husband ought to use his Wife. This Respondent futher says, that the said petitioner informed this respondent before her departure from him; and after she had so left this Respondent, he says, she wasted and destroyed property & money of this Respondent to the amount of three hundred dollars, or thereabouts, contrary to the will and Consent of this respondent, & to his great injury; This respondent says that the said sum of three hundred dollars wasted as aforesaid, by the said petitioner is more than her share of all the property owned by this respondent would amount to, & that therefore this respondent does not think, nor can he believe the said petitioner is entitled or has any right to receive from this respondent any sum or sums of money whatsoever at any time or times, or in any manner whatever. This respondent admits, that the said petitioner and this respondent have lived separate and apart for about the space of   ¹ years and   ¹ months, occasioned by the obstinacy of the said petitioner and not by reason of any improper conduct of this respondent, as he was always willing & desirous, if she would return to his house & conduct herself as a Wife ought to do, to treat her well & tenderly as a husband ought to treat his Wife, & to provide for her every thing that was necessary & proper for her support, that his circumstances would enable him to do. This respondent therefore prays this Honorable Court to dismiss the said petition of the said Mary, & that this respondent may be hence discharged with his costs and charges wrongfully sustained.

Nathaniel Parker, by his Atto.
G. W. Campbell

Tr, TDaCo-MDSC Law Min. Bk., 1788–1803, pp. 675–676. Date is derived from Document I.

1. Thus in Tr.

III. MINUTE BOOK ENTRY

Mero District Superior Court, Nashville
Judges Jackson, White, and Campbell Presiding

Friday morning November 12th
1802

Court met agreeably to adjournment.
Present the Hon. David Campbell ⎫
    Andrew Jackson & ⎬ Esquires Judges.
    Hugh L White ⎭

. . . .

Pleas at Nashville before &c. November 12th 1802

Mary Parker by her next friend ⎫
    Josiah Ramsey ⎬ On a petition for
       agt. ⎭ a divorce.
Nathaniel Parker_____

Whereas heretofore, that is to say, on the twenty ninth day of April One thousand eight hundred, Mary Parker by her next friend Josiah Ramsey exhibited her petition to the Hon. Andrew Jackson one of the Judges of the Superior Courts of law & Equity for the State of Tennessee aforesaid, against Nathaniel Parker Defendant; which said petition followeth in these Words.[1] . . .

And the cause was continued from Term to term until this Term, to wit the first above mentioned. At which day come the parties, by their Attornies, and a Jury, to wit, Eli Hammon, Thomas Johnston, Isaac Phillips, John Brooks George Gillespie, Roger Qualls, William Anthony, John K. Wynne, Matthew Alexander, George Ridley, Charles M. Hall & William who being elected tried & Sworn the truth to speak upon the following issues of fact, to wit "Did Nathaniel Parker, the Defendant, treat Mary Parker the Complainant in a cruel manner as stated in the petition?"

"Did said Nathaniel Parker, by ill treatment, force the said Mary Parker to leave his house as stated in the petition." do say on their oath, "that, as to the first fact, Nathaniel Parker did not treat Mary Parker worse than she treated him." And as to the second fact they say, "that the said Nathaniel Parker did, by ill treatment, force the said Mary Parker to leave his house as stated in the petition."

MS, TDaCo-MDSC Law Min. Bk., 1788–1803, pp. 674–676.
The statute directed that if "either of the parties shall desire any matter of fact that is affirmed by the one and denied by the other, to be tried by a jury, the same shall be so tried in said court." Ch. 19, 1799 Tenn. Pub. Acts (Sept. Sess.), reprinted in 1 Scott, *Laws of Tennessee* 645. In *Parker* the jury rendered a special verdict in response to specific questions by the court.

1. The texts of Documents I and II follow at this point in the MS.

IV. THE DECREE OF THE COURT

Mero District Superior Court, Nashville
Judges Jackson, White, and Campbell Presiding

Mary Parker by Josiah
Ramsey her next friend
vs
Nathaniel Parker

[November 24, 1802]
Petition for a Divorce
from Bed and Board
Order and Decree

The following fact, at the request of the Petitioner, being found by a Jury, to wit, that the said Nathaniel Parker did, by ill treatment, force the said Mary Parker to leave his house as stated in the petition And that cause having come, on the 13th day of November[1] 1802, and this day to be heard on the Petition answer, fact found by the Jury and evidence admitted, which being heard and considered by the Court and Argument on both Sides being heard, it is thereupon ordered and Decreed, that the said Mary be separated and divorced from the Bed and Board of said Nathaniel Parker; and that the said Nathaniel Pay to the said Mary two hundred Dollars per annum to be paid Quarterly, to wit, the sum of fifty dollars at the end of the Present Term of this Court, and fifty dollars at the beginning of each succeeding Quarter; and that the said Mary by her next friend have Execution for any Payment that may remain due after the day hereby limitted for the Payment thereof; and it is further ordered and Decreed that said Nathaniel Parker pay the Costs of this Petition

Andrew Jackson
H. L. White

MS, PVT-Mrs. G. James Packard. Text in the hand of Nathaniel A. McNairy, Clerk, MDSC; autograph signatures. Date is taken from MDSC Law Min. Bk., 1788–1803, p. 705.

1. The jury returned its finding of fact on Nov. 12 (see Document III). The clerk corrected the error when he transcribed the MS into the court's minute book, 1788–1803, p. 705.

46. Witherspoon v. Jackson;
Jackson v. Witherspoon

1803
(Commercial Law)

EDITORIAL NOTE

These parallel cases represent the remaining two of the three actions that came before the Superior Court during Jackson's tenure in which Jackson himself was one of the litigants.[1] Although confusing, the pleadings in both cases reveal most of the factual elements underlying the litigation. Neither the pleadings nor the additional documentation that has been located for the cases, however, disclose the nature of the dispute out of which the litigation arose.

In November 1801 John Witherspoon filed a declaration in the Mero District Superior Court seeking a judgment against Jackson for (a) an unpaid $300 debt of Jackson's; (b) an additional $300, consisting of the consideration claimed for "a certain Grey horse and a note payable the fifteenth day of September 1796, for one hundred Dollars"; and (c) an additional $300, representing the consideration for still another gray horse and another note payable on September 15, 1796 (Document III). Jackson in turn filed a declaration seeking a judgment against Witherspoon for (a) an unpaid $200 debt of Witherspoon's; (b) an additional $200 that he had paid Witherspoon for "a certain gray gelding" that Jackson claimed had been "blind and otherwise diseased"; and (c) an additional $200 that he had paid Witherspoon for still another gray gelding that Jackson claimed had been "blind, & . . . afflicted with other diseases" (Document IV). At the court's May Term 1802, with Jackson presiding with Judges White and Campbell, the parties mutually agreed to submit the two suits to arbitration by David and Randal McGavock (Document V). The two arbitrators in turn selected Willie Blount as umpire in Jackson's suit against Witherspoon (see Document VI[B]). Awards

---

1. The third was *Jackson v. Kearby*, No. 36.

were returned to the court on May 16, 1803. Jackson and Witherspoon each were ordered to pay the other the sum of $150. Jackson was ordered to pay Witherspoon an additional $100, in return for which Witherspoon was ordered to execute a document releasing Jackson of all liability on the claims sued upon in *Witherspoon v. Jackson*. Each party was ordered to assume the costs of the other's suit (Document VI).

It is likely for several reasons that the subject matter underlying both suits was a single gray horse and a single promissory note for the sum of $100. Although it is, of course, possible that more than one such animal and more than one instrument payable on September 15, 1796, passed between Jackson and Witherspoon, the more likely explanation is that the horse and note referred to in the parties' declarations were those with which Witherspoon in December 1795 had purchased from Jackson a 525-acre tract of land identified as Patent 921 for the recited consideration of $200 (Document I). A receipt dated December 14, 1795, and introduced into evidence during the course of the litigation indicates that Witherspoon's payment for the tract consisted of (a) one gray gelding and (b) a $100 promissory note payable to Jackson on September 15, 1796 (Document II). That the horses described in both parties' declarations are all valued at $200[2] while the recited consideration for the conveyance of the land is $200 is not necessarily inconsistent with this interpretation. It is entirely possible that the parties contemplated that the $100 note and the value of the horse up to $100 were to serve as the consideration and that the value of the horse beyond $100 was to serve as security for Witherspoon's payment of the note.

In addition, the actual damages sought by each party fall short of the total amounts alleged in their declarations. Witherspoon's declaration on its face alleged damages amounting to $900, but Witherspoon actually sought only $500 from Jackson. Likewise, Jackson's declaration on its face alleged damages amounting to $600, but he actually sought only $500 from Witherspoon. When one considers that litigants normally sought to recover sums that exceeded the damages enumerated, it becomes even more apparent that the three separate claims set forth by each of the parties in reality were alternative pleadings upon the same facts.

Finally, of course, the arbitration awards refer only to one horse and suggest rather strongly that only one note was at issue. The arbitrators ordered each party to pay the other the sum of $150, which represented "the value of the Grey Horse . . . which was received by the Defendant from the plaintiff" (Document VI). By providing for payments that can-

---

2. Witherspoon alleged that the combined value of the horse and the $100 note was $300 (Document III). Jackson sued only upon the horse, which he valued at $200 (Document IV).

celed one another, the arbitrators, implicitly at least, appear to have agreed with Jackson's proof that the single horse transferred to him by Witherspoon had been unsound and thus without any value at all. Jackson, of course, was ordered to pay Witherspoon the additional sum of $100 with interest from December 14, 1795, which sum and date coincide with those for the single note executed by Witherspoon payable on September 15, 1796.

Jackson had purchased the 525-acre portion of Patent 921 at a sheriff's sale on December 8, 1795, six days before he sold it to Witherspoon. Patent 921 consisted in its entirety of 640 acres that had been granted to George Augustus Sugg by the state of North Carolina in November 1790.[3] Subsequent to Jackson's conveyance to Witherspoon in December 1795, two of Sugg's grantees, Jonathon Wisehart and William Harrison, on December 4, 1797, sold 500 acres of Patent 921 to Thomas Talbot.[4] On August 28, 1798, Talbot deeded into the remaining 140 acres of Patent 921 from another of Sugg's grantees, Micajah Barrow, and on the same date sold the entire 640 acres to Thomas Bedford.[5] None of the records that have been located indicates that, prior to the present litigation, Witherspoon might have litigated the title to Patent 921 with Bedford, that there ever was an adjudication that Talbot's or Bedford's title was superior to Witherspoon's, or that Witherspoon otherwise might have attempted to recover the consideration that he had paid Jackson for the tract.[6] Although the conveyance of Patent 921 to Witherspoon in 1795 thus unmistakably appears to have provided the underlying basis for the present litigation, the precise nature in which it did so remains undetermined.

Witherspoon, a nephew of the Reverend Charles Pettigrew's of Edenton, North Carolina, still was a resident of Wilkes County, North Carolina, when Jackson executed the conveyance to him in December 1795. He had participated in an unspecified business venture with Alexander Cunningham, however, in the Territory as early as 1791. In January 1799 Witherspoon had been commissioned by Governor Sevier as a justice of the Davidson County court, from which office he resigned in September 1803. As late as June 1800, Witherspoon had kept and operated a public mill in the county.[7]

3. DaCo Deed Bk. C, 497. Jackson paid only $5.25 for the tract.
4. See DaCo Deed Bk. E, 45.
5. DaCo Deed Bk. D, 489; DaCo Deed Bk. E, 94.
6. The significance of Witherspoon's reference to Aug. 10, 1800, remains undetermined (see Document III). Jackson on that date was in Warm Springs, Virginia. See AJ to Robert Hays, Aug. 10, 1800, *Jackson Papers*, I, 233.
7. Resignation of John Witherspoon, Sept. 12, 1803, Legislative Reports & Misc. 1803, T; Sarah M. Lemmon, ed., *The Pettigrew Papers (1685–1818)* (Raleigh, 1971), I, xii, 33; Sevier, *Commission Book*, 14; see Lewis v. Witherspoon, DaCo CPQS Min. Bk. D, 117 (1803); State v. Witherspoon, DaCo CPQS Min. Bk. C, 345 (1800); *Knoxville Gazette*, July 17, 1794.

I. DEED, JACKSON TO
JOHN WITHERSPOON

December 14, 1795

This indenture made this fourteenth day of December one thousand nine hundred and ninety five Between Andrew Jackson of the County of Davidson and Territory South of the river Ohio of the one part and John Wetherspoon of the County and Territory aforesaid of the other part, Witnesseth that in and for the consideration of two hundred dollars to me in hand paid the receipt whereof is hereby acknowledged hath and by these presents doth bargain and sell alien enfeoff and confirm unto the said John Wetherspoon his heirs and assigns forever a certain tract or parcel of land containing by estimation five hundred and twenty five acres be the same more or less, lying and being in the County of Sumner in the main East fork of stones river being part of a tract patented in the name of George A. Sugg by patent bearing date the 23rd of November, 1790, No. 921 and sold by the sheriff for the Public and County tax of the said George A. Sugg and conveyed by[1] the said Andrew by Nicholas Perkins Hardiman sheriff of Davidson which said tract [. . . .] Beginning at a poplar tree John Reeds' north West corner, Thence North two hundred and sixty two and half poles to a stake, Thence East three hundred and twenty poles to a stake, Thence South two hundred and sixty two and one half poles to a stake, Thence West three hundred and twenty poles to the beginning, Together with all woods waters mines minerals hereditaments of in and to the same belonging or in anywise appertaining to the same. To have and to hold the said bargained premises to the only proper benefit and behoof of him the said John Wetherspoon his heirs and assigns. And the said Andrew doth covenant and agree that he will warrant and defend the said bargained premises to the said John Wetherspoon his heirs and assigns from the claim of all persons legally claiming under him the said Andrew by virtue of a title from him but not from the legal claim or claims of any other person whatsoever. And it is further covenanted and agreed that should the above described land be taken by virtue of any other entry than that which the abovementioned patent issued upon then and in that case the aforesaid Andrew doth bind himself to restore to the said John Wetherspoon the consideration [. . .]ned recieved for said land with interest upon the value thereof from the date of the reciept of the said consideration which is mentioned in a reciept this day passed from the said Andrew to the said John Wetherspoon and it is the true intent and meaning of these presents that the said Andrew should not be liable in any

other way or manner or for any other matter or thing then is herein and
hereby expressed and agreed upon and herein expressly mentioned. In
witness whereof I have hereinto set my hand and seal the day and date
first afore written, in presence of Francis Hall and Geo. Nevill.

Andrew Jackson L.S.

Tr, TDaCo-DaCo Deed Bk. C, 480. Witherspoon's deed was proved in court on Jan. 5, 1796
(DaCo CPQS Min. Bk. B, 314) and was recorded on Feb. 8, 1796 (DaCo CPQS Min. Bk. C,
480).

  1. Thus in Tr; correctly: "to."

II. RECEIPT, JACKSON TO
JOHN WITHERSPOON

December 14th 1795

Then Recd. of John Witherspoon one Gray Horse formerly the prop-
erty of Benjamin Beshaw, and a note payable the fifteenth of September
1796 for one hundred Dollars it being in full Satisfaction for a Certain
Tract of Land Containing five hundred and Twenty five acres lying on the
East fork of Stones River this day Deeded by Me to the Said John
Witherspoon

Andrew Jackson

Test
Geo. Nevill

MS, PVT-William Waller, Sr. Endorsed: "Weatherspoon vs Jackson Rect Case Damage $500
[Jac]kson [vs Weathe]rspoon Rect."

III. DECLARATION OF
JOHN WITHERSPOON

Mero District Superior Court, Nashville

[November 1801]

State of Tennessee Mero District Ss.

John Weatherspon by his Attorney complains of Andrew Jackson in
custody &c. of a plea of Trespass on the Case; for that whereas the said

Andrew on the tenth day of August in the year 1800 at the County of Davidson was indebted to the said John in the sum of three hundred Dollars of lawful money; for so much money before that time had and received by the said Andrew to the use of the said John, and he the said Andrew, being so indebted, in consideration thereof, afterwards, that is to say, the same day and year aforesaid, at the County aforesaid, undertook and then and there faithfully promised the said John that he, the said Andrew, would well and truly pay and satisfy unto the said John, the said sum of three hundred Dollars, when he the said Andrew should afterwards be thereto requested.

And whereas the said Andrew, afterwards, that is to say, the same day and year last aforesaid, at the County aforesaid, was indebted to the said John in the sum of other three hundred Dollars of like lawful money, for a certain Grey horse and a note payable the fifteenth day of September 1796, for one hundred Dollars, before that time sold and delivered by the said John to the said Andrew, at his special instance and request; and he the said Andrew, being so indebted, in consideration thereof, afterwar[d]s, that is to say, the same day and year aforesaid; at the County aforesaid, undertook and then and there faithfully promised the said John, that he said Andrew would well and truely pay and satisfy to the said John, the said sum of three hundred Dollars when he should be afterwards thereto requeste[d].

And whereas the said Andrew had on the day and year last aforesaid received of him the said John, another gray horse and another note payable on the fifteenth day of September 1796, to the use of the said John, he the said Andrew, in consideration thereof did afterwards, to wit, the same day and year aforesaid, at the County aforesaid, undertook and faithfully promised the said John, that he the said Andrew would well and truly pay and satisfy to the said John so much money as the same were reasonably worth at the time of the delivery thereof when he the said Andrew should afterwards be thereto requested; and the said John avers that the last mentioned horse and note, so received by the said Andrew to the use of the said John, was reasonably worth, at the time of the delivery thereof, other three hundred Dollars of the lawful money, that is to say, at the County aforesaid, wherefo[re] the said Andrew afterwards, that is to say, the same day and year last aforesaid, there had notice from the said John, yet the said Andrew in no wise regarding his aforesaid several promises and undertakings made in manner aforesaid, but contriving and fraudulently intending craftily and subtilly to deceive and defraud the said John, hath not as yet paid or in any wise satisfyed the aforesaid several sums of money or any part thereof to the said John, altho' often thereto requested, by him the said John, but hath hitherto wholly refused and still refuses to pay or in wise satisfy the same to the said John, to the damage of the said John of five hundred Dollars, and thereof he brings his suit. &c.

Overton pro. que

Tr, TDaCo-MDSC Law Min. Bk., 1803–1805, pp. 43–44. Date is taken from *id.* at 43.

IV. JACKSON'S DECLARATION

Mero District Superior Court, Nashville

State of Tennessee Mero District, November Term 1801,

Andrew Jackson Esquire by his Attorney, complains of John Weatherspon, in custody of the Sheriff &c. of a plea of Trespass on the Case; for that whereas on the ¹ day of ¹ in the ¹ year, to wit at ¹ in the County of Davidson within the District aforesaid, in consideration, that the said Andrew, at the special instance and request of the said John, would buy of the said John a certain gray gelding of him the said John, at & for a certain large price or sum of money, to wit the sum of two hundred dollars to be paid by the said Andrew to him the said John for the same, he the said John then and there undertook & faithfully promised the said Andrew, that the said gelding was sound in all respects and the said Andrew in fact says, that he confiding in the said promise and undertaking of him the said John, so by him made as aforesaid, afterwar[d]s, to wit, on the day and year aforesaid, at ¹ in the County aforesaid at the special instance and request of him the said John did buy of him the said John the said gelding at and for the said price or sum of ¹ hundred Dollars, and then and there paid and satisfied him the said sum for the same, yet the said John, not regarding his said promise & undertaking so by him made as aforesaid; but contriving and fraudulently to injure the said Andrew, in this behalf, did not regard his said promise and undertaking, so by him made as aforesaid, but craftily & subtilly deceived the said Andrew in this, that the said gelding at the time of making the said promise and undertaking of the said John (& at the time the said gelding was sold by the said John to the said Andrew was not sound in all respects, but on the contrary thereof was unsound, that is to say, blind and otherwise diseased, to wit with ¹ at ¹ in the County aforesaid, whereby the said gelding then and there became & was of no use or value to the said Andrew, and afterwards, to wit on the ¹ day of ¹ at ¹ aforesaid, the said gelding's death was occasioned by his blindness & disease aforesaid, without having been of any use to the said Andrew

And for that whereas afterwards, to wit, on the same day and year aforesaid at   [1] in the County & District aforesaid, the said Andrew had bought of this Defendant John a certain other gray gelding of the said John's, and the said John then and there well knowing the said gelding to be unsound and labouring under & afflicted with blindness and otherwise diseased, to wit with   [1] then and there falsely & fraudulently bargained & sold the said gelding, as and for a gelding sound in all respects; to the said Andrew for a large sum of Money, to wit for two hundred dollars, which sum was then and there paid by the said Andrew to the said John for the said gelding which said gelding was then and there unsound, that is to say was blind, & was afflicted with other diseases, to wit with   [1] and so always afterwards thus remained to be untill the said gelding's death was occasioned thereby & was of no use or value to the said Andrew and thus the said John on the same day & year aforesaid, at   [1] in the County aforesaid, falsely and fraudulently deceived the said Andrew in selling him the aforesaid gelding in manner aforesaid; And for that whereas the said John afterwards, to wit, on the same day and year aforesaid, at   [1] in the District aforesaid, was indebted to the said Andrew in the sum of other two hundred Dollars for Money by the said John before that time had and received to the use of of the said Andrew and being so indebted, he the said John in consideration thereof, afterwards, to wit, on the same day and year aforesaid, at   [1] in the District aforesaid undertook & faithfully promised the said Andrew, to pay him the said last mentioned sum of Money, when he the said John should be thereto afterwards requested. Yet the said John (altho' often requested &c.) hath not paid the said Andrew the said sum of Money, nor any way satisfied him in the promises aforesaid, but he so to do hath hitherto wholly refused & still doth refuse, to the damage of the said Andrew five hundred Dollars—and therefore he Sues &c. and there are pledges &c.

Campbell pro Queto.

Tr, TDaCo-MDSC Law Min. Bk., 1803–1805, pp. 45–47.

1. Thus in Tr.

V. MINUTE BOOK ENTRY

Mero District Superior Court, Nashville
Judges Jackson, White, and Campbell Presiding

Tuesday Morning May 25th 1802.

Court met agreeably to adjournment.
Present the Hon. David Campbell ⎫
           Andrew Jackson & ⎬ Esqrs. Judges.
           Hugh L. White ⎭

John Witherspoon Plt. ⎫
      vs   ⎬ In Case.
Andrew Jackson—Deft ⎭

The parties mutually submit all matters in difference between them in this suit to the final determination of David McGavock & Randal McGavock, & their award, or the award of such person as they shall chuse for an Umpire thereupon is to be made the Judgment of the Court: And the same is ordered accordingly.—Vide

MS, TDaCo-MDSC Law Min. Bk., 1803–1805, p. 639. A similar entry for *Jackson v. Witherspoon* follows this entry in the MS.

VI. THE ARBITRATORS' AWARDS

Mero District Superior Court, Nashville
Judges White and Campbell Presiding

May 16, 1803

[*A. Witherspoon v. Jackson*]

The Arbitrators to whom the determination of the matters in difference between the parties aforesaid were submitted, by a rule of this Court, at May Term 1802 returned their award in these words—"whereas at a Superior Court of law held for the District of Mero, May Term 1802; a cause in the rule Court depending between John Weatherspon Plaintiff, & Andrew Jackson Defendant by consent of parties was refered to David McGavock & Randal McGavock to hear and determine all the matters in difference, & their award or the award of such person as they shall choose for an Umpire thereupon to be made the Judgment of the said Court. Now we the said David McGavock & Randal McGavock in pursuance of the said order or rule of reference having heard both the said parties their allegations & answers touching the matters in difference between them, and having thoroughly considered of the same, do award order and adjudge of & upon the premises in manner and form following, viz. First we do award that the said Andrew Jackson shall pay or cause to be paid unto the said John Weatherspon the sum of one Hundred Dollars on the first day of October next, with legal Interest thereon from the Fourteenth day of December 1795. We do also award and order that the said Andrew Jackson pay to the said John Weatherspoon the further sum of one hundred & fifty dollars on the said first day of October next, which last sum we esteem to be the value of the Grey Horse, of sound, which was received by the Defendant from the plaintiff. And we do also award and order that the said John Weatherspoon shall, upon payment of the said sums, execute unto the said Andrew Jackson a general release of the matters to us refered. And lastly we do award and order that the said Andrew Jackson pay the costs of the said suit. In witness whereof we have hereunto set our hands and seals the sixteenth day of May 1803.

D. McGavock (LS)
R. McGavock (LS)

[B. Jackson v. Witherspoon]

Whereas at a Superior Court of law held for the District of Mero, May Term 1802 a Cause in the said Court depending between Andrew Jackson Plt. and John Weatherspon Deft. by consent of parties was refered to David McGavock & Randal McGavock to hear and determine all the matters in difference, and their award or the award of such person as they shall choose for an Umpire thereupon, to be made the Judgment of the said Court. Now know ye that I Willie Blount Umpire indifferently chosen by the said David & Randal McGavock to act on & concerning the premises having deliberately heard and understood the griefs allegations & proofs of both the said parties, & willing (as much as in me lieth) to set the said parties at unity and good accord, do by these present arbitrate, award, order, decree and judge as followeth, that is to say, that the said John Weatherspon shall pay to the said Andrew Jackson the sum of one hundred & fifty dollars, on the first day of October next, and also that the said Weatherspon pay the costs of the said Suit. In witness whereof I have hereunto set my hand & Seal this 16th day of May 1803.

Willie Blount (Seal)

A. Tr, TDaCo-MDSC Law Min. Bk., 1803–1805, pp. 44–45. B. Tr, *id.* at 47–48.

47. Nusum v. Betts

1803
(Contracts)

EDITORIAL NOTE

In May 1802 Francis Nusum brought a covenant action in the Mero District Superior Court against William Betts to recover the compensation that he claimed for building a grist mill and dam for Betts. Nusum, through his counsel, Thomas Stuart, alleged that on August 15, 1800, he had agreed in writing to construct the mill and dam for Betts on the Little Harpeth River for $400 and that in the same writing Betts had agreed to furnish seven workmen, including two sawyers, and the necessary oxen to assist Nusum in transporting timber to the mill site. Nusum claimed that Betts had agreed to compensate him for time added to the completion of the work should he fail to provide the workmen and oxen. Nusum further alleged that Betts had failed to provide either the workmen or the oxen as promised before completion of the mill and dam in April 1801. In the declaration filed with the court in May 1802, Nusum sought $500 in damages (Document I). The defendant subsequently entered a pleading of performance of his obligation under the covenant (see Document II).

When the action went to trial on November 17, 1803, with Jackson and both his colleagues White and Campbell presiding, a jury returned a judgment for Nusum but only in the amount of $270 (Document II). Why the jury awarded $270 rather than $500 cannot be determined from the surviving documentation. It is possible that Nusum failed to prove either the $400 that the parties allegedly had agreed upon or the $100 that the plaintiff presumably sought as compensation for time lost. Another possibility is that the evidence demonstrated that Betts in fact already had performed at least part of his obligations under the covenant.[1]

1. Jackson had represented Betts, a Nashville ordinary keeper, in *Betts v. William T. Lewis,* which went to trial in the Davidson County court in October 1794. DaCo CPQS Min. Bk. B, 216, 403; DaCo CPQS Min. Bk. D, 2. Nusum has not been further identified.

I. DECLARATION OF
FRANCIS NUSUM

Mero District Superior Court, Nashville

May 1802

State of Tennessee Mero District to wit, May Term 1802 Francis Nusum complains of William Betts in custody &c. of a plea of Covenant broken, for that whereas the said Francis Nusum and the said William Betts made their certain writing obligatory at the District aforesaid, Sealed with the seals of the said Francis Nusum and William Betts on the fifteenth day of August in the year one thousand eight hundred, the date whereof is the same day and year, and which to the Court is now shewn, whereby the said Francis Nusum did agree to build a Grist Mill to run one pair of Stones with a place left for another pair on little Harpeth near the place the said Betts then lived and make all necessary bolting works to go by water likewise a good Dam and compleat all the works necessary to make a good Mill and deliver her to the said William Betts, as soon as it could be conveniently done after beginning the same the said Betts did agree by said writing to furnish seven hands including a pair of Sawyers, and the said Nusum by said writing agreed to furnish three hands in cluding a pair of Sawyers to work on said Mill, and in case either of their hands so funished should lose time, the parties agreed to make up in the work the time lost by either of their hands and as a compensation for the said work the said William Betts did agree to pay the said Francis Nusum the sum of four hundred dollars when ever the same should be compleated, and in Case there should be plank enough cut for the Mill before she should be finished, then said parties were not afterwards to be obliged to find Sawyers, but might put other hands in their room, & the said parties by said writing did further agree that said above mentioned hands were to do all the necessary halling, and said Betts was to find one pair of Oxen for that purpose. And said Plaintiff in fact saith that he began said Mill and dam on the ¹ day of ¹ in the year one thousand eight hundred, and furnished three hands including a pair of Sawyers to work on said Mill and that on the tenth day of April in the year one thousand eight hundred he compleated the building of a Mill for said Betts agreeable to said writing obligatory and all necessary bolting works to go by water on the twenty fifth day of December in the year 1801 and made a good dam agreeably to said writing obligatory, and delivered said Mill to the said William Betts, on the day and year last aforesaid. And said Plaintiff further in fact saith that said William Betts did not furnish seven hands including a pair of Sawyers to work on said Mill, but that the time so lost by said William in not furnishing hands amounted to   [1] days, and said plaintiff further in fact saith that said William Betts altho' often requested did not at any time make up for the time so lost. And said Plaintiff further in fact saith that the said William Betts altho' often requested hath not paid to the said Plaintiff said four hundred Dollars not any part thereof, nither before on nor since the time of the completion of said Mill & dam, contrary to the form and effect of said writing obligatory. Wherefore the said, Plaintiff saith that said Defendant altho' often requested hath not kept his said Covenant so made with said Plaintiff in form aforesaid but hath broken the same and to keep the same with the said Plaintiff hath hitherto wholly refused and still doth refuse to the damage of the said Plaintiff of five hundred Dollars, and therefore he brings Suit &c.

Thos. Stuart for Plt.

Tr, TDaCo-MDSC Law Min. Bk., 1788–1803, pp. 84–85.

1. Thus in Tr.

II. MINUTE BOOK ENTRY

Mero District Superior Court, Nashville
Judges Jackson, White, and Campbell Presiding

[November 17, 1803]

Pleas at the Court house in Nashville before &c. November Term 1803

Francis Nusum Plt.
    vs   }   In Covenant
William Betts Deft

William Betts was attached to answer Francis Nusum of a plea of Covenant broken. Damage five hundred Dollars. Whereupon the said Plaintiff by Thomas Stuart his attorney at May Term 1802 filed his Declaration upon the same in the words following[1] . . . .

And the Defendant William Betts by Jesse Wharton his attorney comes into Court and defends &c. and for plea saith, that the Plaintiff ought not to have and maintain his action thereof against him, because he says he hath not broken his covenant as the Plaintiff hath alledged but the same hath performed and of this he puts himself upon the Country And the said Plaintiff likewise.

And the Cause was continued from Term to Term untill this Term, to wit, the first above mentioned, at which day come the parties by their attornies and a Jury of Good and lawful men, to wit, Don Hill Matthew day, James Lauderdale, James Sawyers, John Lancaster, Nicholas Boyer Robert Ellise, John S Martin, John Payton, Willie Barrow, Josiah Fort & Eli Hammonds, who being elected tried, and Sworn the truth to speak upon the issue Joined upon their Oath do say that the said Defendant hath not performed the Covenant in the declaration mentioned but hath broken the same in manner and form as the Plaintiff against him in de-claring hath alledged and they do assess the Plaintiffs damages by reason of the nonperformance of that Covenant to two hundred and seventy dol-lars besides his costs. Therefore it is considered by the Court that Plaintiff recover against the said Defendant his damages aforesaid in form afore-said assessed, and his costs by him about—his Suit—in that—behalf ex-pended, and the said Defendant in mercy &c.

MS, TDaCo-MDSC Law Min. Bk., 1788–1803, pp. 84–86. Date is taken from *id.* at 84; judges' attendance is taken from *id.* at 59.

1. The text of Document I follows at this point in the MS.

Litigation: Equity Cases

48. Vannerson v. Montgomery
and McCormick

1800
(Procedure)

EDITORIAL NOTE

The equity proceedings in *Vannerson* illustrate the legal issues of a procedural nature that Jackson and his colleagues on the bench were called upon to resolve. At issue in *Vannerson* are questions relating to the manner in which cases came before the court on writs of certiorari from the county courts and to the authority of individual members of the court to enjoin enforcement of decisions by the full court.

William Vannerson arrived in Tennessee in March 1798 as an agent for David Ross at the ironworks that the latter had built in Sullivan County nearly a decade earlier.[1] Ross, a prominent merchant and shipowner in Petersburg, Virginia, who had served as commercial agent for Virginia for just more than a year during the Revolution, had secured the assistance of Patrick Henry as early as 1786 in convincing the North Carolina General Assembly to grant bounty lands in the westernmost part of the state to iron manufacturers. Ross had achieved that goal by 1788 and by 1801 had either deeded into or secured grants from the North Carolina, territorial, and Tennessee governments totaling more than 87,000 acres in the middle Tennessee counties of Sumner, Smith, and Wilson alone.[2]

---

1. See Document I. Williams estimates that Ross had his works in operation by the fall of 1789 or, at the latest, by February 1790. Samuel Cole Williams, "Early Iron Works in the Tennessee Country," 6 *THQ* 40 (1947).
2. *Knoxville Gazette*, May 6, 1801; William T. Hutchinson and William M. E. Rachal, eds., *The Papers of James Madison* (Chicago, 1963), III, 60 n.8; Williams, "Early Iron Works," 40. Ross and Henry also were principals in the formation in 1789 of the Virginia Yazoo Land Company. Williams, "Early Iron Works," 41.

Within the first decade of the start of production at his ironworks on the north fork of the Holston River, Ross's products were being shipped as far south as Natchez and New Orleans, and the small settlement of Rossville Ironworks had grown up around the site of Ross's furnace on the Sullivan County side of the river. Ross operated a store there[3] and leased out a portion of his land along Reedy Creek as a tavern. It was this "publick house and the farm thereunto belonging at the furnace on reedy Creek" that one of Ross's agents at Rossville, John McFarlane, leased in 1795 to William McCormick and Michael Montgomery (Document I).

Vannerson, who succeeded McFarlane as Ross's agent at the ironworks in March 1798, insisted that the 1795 lease was for the term of three years and that some commitment had been made to lease the tavern and the adjoining farm to one Matthew Nightingale upon the expiration of the lease at the end of 1798 (see Document IV).[4] Montgomery and McCormick claimed that the 1795 lease was for the term of thirty years. Vannerson, upon learning that Montgomery and McCormick intended to remain in possession of the premises beyond 1798, served eviction notices upon both of the tenants on October 1, 1798 (Document IV, Enclosures I and II).

When Montgomery and McCormick had not vacated the tavern by the next February, Vannerson secured a writ of forcible entry and detainer from the Sullivan County Court of Pleas and Quarter Sessions. The court, acting upon a jury inquiry conducted at the tavern before several of the justices, subsequently awarded Vannerson a writ of restitution and permitted one William Norris, an agent of Vannerson's, to enter into possession of the premises.

Before the writ of restitution was served upon the tenants, however, McCormick and Montgomery obtained from Judge Roane an injunction staying repossession of the tavern by Vannerson and a writ of certiorari directing the Sullivan County court to certify the forcible entry and detainer proceeding up to the Washington District Superior Court for a hearing at its March Term. When the court convened on March 14, Roane's writ was returned apparently unendorsed. Attached to the writ was a copy of the Sullivan County jury's verdict with the sheriff's endorsement that he had served the documents upon the tenants along with a certification by the Sullivan justices that the jury had found Montgomery and McCormick "Guilty of Forcibly detaining possession as complained of."[5] Counsel for Vannerson moved to quash the certiorari on the follow-

3. Williams, "Early Iron Works," 41; see *Knoxville Gazette,* Oct. 14, 1801.
4. Nightingale in fact already had begun cultivating portions of the farm in the late summer or early fall of 1798, but had been evicted by Montgomery and McCormick. See Document IV.
5. Bland Casebook, 5, Bland Papers, MdHi.

ing grounds. First, the state's constitution authorized the court to remove by certiorari only civil cases that were pending before inferior courts of record. The forcible entry proceeding, the plaintiff argued, had been in the nature of a criminal proceeding for breach of the peace that had been conducted not before a court of record, but at the site of the leased premises before several of the Sullivan justices. Second, the plaintiff asserted that, even had the court been authorized to remove the cause from the Sullivan court, there had not been a proper return made upon the writ of certiorari (Document II).

The court, speaking through Judge Roane, denied Vannerson's motion but, agreeing that there was nothing before the court because of the improper return, ordered at the defendants' motion the issuance of a second writ of certiorari returnable to the September Term and a stay of further proceedings in the county court (see Document III).[6] When the court's second writ was properly returned to its September Term 1799, the court reversed the county court's judgment and awarded Montgomery and McCormick possession of the premises based upon the tenants' production of a document purported to be the 1795 lease for a term of thirty years (Document I).

After the court had concluded its September Term and while the judges were in recess before reconvening the next March, Vannerson on September 14, 1799, applied for and received from Judge Campbell an injunction against enforcement of the court's September order on the ground that the language of the document produced by Montgomery and McCormick at the September hearing had been fraudulently altered from three years to read thirty years (Document IV).[7]

At the court's March Term 1800, Montgomery and McCormick, without filing answers to Vannerson's allegations of fraud, moved to dissolve Campbell's injunction on the ground that it had been improperly granted in the light of Jackson's decision for the court in *Mitchell v. Berry* (No. 19). The defendants argued that the effect of Judge Campbell's injunction had not been to stay the proceedings in a case before one of the county courts while the record of the case was brought up to the court on a writ of certiorari. Instead, they argued, the effect of Campbell's injunction had been to halt the enforcement of the court's own order in September reversing the Sullivan County court (Document V).

6. The court's order did not prevent an altercation on Mar. 18, the details of which are not revealed by the records, between Montgomery and Vannerson, Norris, and several others. See Indictment of William Vannerson, May 1799, Misc. Papers of Matthew Rhea, Records of Sullivan County, WPA Typescript, 19–20, T. Montgomery in turn obtained an indictment of Vannerson, Norris, and eight others for trespass vi et armis and assault and battery. The grand jury returned a true bill, and Vannerson was convicted at the Sullivan court's June Term 1799. *Id.*

7. Bland Casebook, 55, Bland Papers, MdHi.

Jackson agreed. Declaring that because "at Common Law whenever a Judgment is reversed the party is restored as of course," Jackson concluded that the court's reversal of the Sullivan court in September had constituted a final adjudication on the merits of the case, that the court's order restoring possession to Montgomery and McCormick did not require further proceedings that were subject to being enjoined, and that a single judge could not enjoin the enforcement of such a final adjudication by the full court (Document VI). Campbell disagreed, of course, asserting that before the injunction that he had issued during the court's recess could be dissolved, the defendants would need to file either an answer or a demurrer on the issue of fraud that Vannerson had raised. Although Judge Roane agreed with Campbell that in the English courts an injunction could not be dissolved without the filing of either an answer or a demurrer, he concluded that the English practice had been modified legislatively and that the court thus was free to review the grounds for injunctions issued by single judges during recess without the necessity of pleadings. Roane also agreed with Jackson that as a general rule an injunction could not be issued to stay the restoration of a party when a judgment by a lower court was reversed by the Superior Court. Judge Roane questioned, however, whether the court should not fashion an exception to the rule when the evidence of title proffered by the prevailing party was alleged to have been the product of fraud. Although thus clearly leaning toward the position that the court could intervene upon an allegation of fraud, Roane nevertheless abstained from rendering an opinion (Document VI).

With the court thus divided, the defendants withdrew their motion to dissolve Judge Campbell's injunction and filed answers denying Vannerson's allegations that the lease proffered in September had been the product of fraud.[8] The court, apparently concluding that Vannerson's assertion of fraud was without merit, subsequently dissolved Judge Campbell's injunction and restored possession of the disputed premises to Montgomery and McCormick.[9]

8. WDSC Eq. Rec. Bk., 1791–1803, pp. 78–88; WDSC Eq. Min. Bk., 1791–1804, p. 192; Bland Casebook, 61, Bland Papers, MdHi.
9. WDSC Eq. Min. Bk., 1791–1804, pp. 192–193.
Montgomery was the defendant in Nos. 30 and 32. McCormick has not been further identified.

I. LEASE AGREEMENT BETWEEN JOHN MCFARLANE, FOR DAVID ROSS, AND WILLIAM MCCORMICK AND MICHAEL MONTGOMERY

November 12, 1795

Articles of agreement made this twelfth day of November one thousand seven hundred and ninety five between John Mcfarlane for David Ross of the one part, and William McCormick and Michael Montgomery, the former of Sullivan County Western Territory south of the river Ohio, the latter of the County of Washington in the state of Virginia, witnesseth that the said William McCormick and Michael Montgomery hath this day rented the publick house and the farm thereunto belonging at the furnace on reedy Creek for the term of thirty years, from the first day of December One thousand seven hundred and ninety five, for which house and farm the said McCormick, and Montgomery, or Either of them are to pay to the said John Mcfarlane for the use of the said David Ross the sum of thirty pounds money of Virginia Each and every year during the term of the said agreement, but it is understood that the said Mcfarlane reserves to himself for the Benefit of his Employer, the fruit in the Orchard on the said farm which he wants for his own use, also the privalege of making roads through or Erecting buildings on all or any of the fields on said farm, for which privilage of making roads and building houses, the said Mcfarlane Engages to pay the said McCormick and Montgomery the damages the same will make or Ocasion as the same may, be asscertained by two honest men, one Chosen by each party as is Customary in such Cases, and it is further understood that the said McCormick and Montgomery are to repair the said publick house at their own proper Expence, also that they Engage to sow small grain on the fields of said farm Every other year during the residency of this agreement and to uphold the fences on the same, the said Mcfarlain Engages to pay the Expense of putting the same in good Order. in testimony whereof both parties hath hereunto set their hands and seales the day and year above written

for David Ross   John Mcfarlane (S)

William McCormick (S)

Michael Montgomery (S)

Tested
Ephm. Dunlop

Tr, TWashCo-WDSC Eq. Rec. Bk., 1791–1803, p. 85; marked "Exhibit" to Answer of Michael Montgomery, March 1800.

II. BLAND'S STATEMENT OF THE
CASE AND MINUTES OF THE
ARGUMENT OF COUNSEL

Washington District Superior Court, Jonesboro
Judges Jackson, Roane, and Campbell Presiding

[March 1799]
Vennerson agent of Ross vs: Montgomery
and McCormick.

This was a case of Forcible Entry and Detainer; on complaint made by Vennerson in behalf of Ross, to the Justices of the peace for the County of Sullivan that Montgomery and McCormick forcibly detained a certain Tenement from said Ross, they issued a warrant to the sheriff comanding him to summon a Jury in the usual form. Upon the inquest it appeared that Montgomery and McCormick had been put into possession of the premises by virtue of a Lease for years from an agent of Ross's, which Lease was then expired; the Jury without any Indictment being presented to them, found the said Montgomery & McCormick "Guilty of Forcibly detaining possession as complained of["] upon which restitution was awarded by the Justices; but before the Sheriff had made Restitution a Certiorari was obtained from one of the Judges of the Superior Courts in vacation returnabl[e] to the present Term; and now the Certiorari was found with an endorsement thus "Executed the Verdict as above stated,["] with a certificat[e] at the foot of it under the hand & seal of the Magistrates before whom it was taken that, that was the original verdict handed them by the Jury—also the warrant of the Justices comanding the sheriff to summon a Jury, which had been taken no manner of notice of.

It was objected by the counsel for Ross, first That this Court had no authority to grant a Certiorari inasmuch as the Constitution of this State (Art. 5. Sec 6) has only given them the power to remove a cause to this court from any inferior Court of *Record;* The proceedings in this case of Forcible Entry & Detainer were not before a Court of *Record.*

Secondly. The Constitution of Tennessee (Art 5. Sec 6) authorizes the Judges of the Superior Courts to remove *Civil* cases only by Certiorari, this is a Criminal case where the party is punished in a summary way by Indictment for breach of the peace.

Thirdly, Admitting the authority of this Court as to the former positions there is no return made on this Certiorari in consequence of which the proceedings are not superseded.

MS, MdHi-Bland Casebook, 4–7, Bland Papers (MS 134). Date is taken from *id.* at 1. Judges' attendance is taken from WDSC Eq. Min. Bk., 1791–1804, p. 148.

III. BLAND'S MINUTES OF
JUDGE ROANE'S
OPINION FOR THE COURT

Washington District Superior Court, Jonesboro
Judges Jackson, Roane, and Campbell Presiding

[March 1799]

Roane J: delivered the opinion of the Court. As to the first point, if the Statutes of England relative to Forcible Entry & Detainer are not tacitly abrogated by the Constitution of this state, the Justices before whom an Inquest of Forcible Entry is taken must as to that sit as a Court of *Record*.

As to the second position, as certiorari might in England issue from the Court of K. B. to any of the Inferior Courts to remove any cause whatsoever either Civil or Criminal by virtue of the general superintendant jurisdiction which that Court had over all the inferior Courts of the Kingdom; that superintendancy has been rec[o]gnized in the Superior Courts of this State antecedent to its having a Constitution and when the Constitution was made it affirmed a part of that superintendent jurisdiction but did not negative the rest, therefore we conceive the superintendancy which the Superrior Courts of Tennessee have over the Inf[e]rior is not at all abridged or curtailed, that being the case this Court had a right to remove *this cause.*

The last objection the Court are of opinion is well founded, there is certainly no return made on this Certiorari, there is nothing judicially before the Court, therefore they can take no notice of such papers as appear to have been foisted among those of this Court. The whole proceeding must remain in Statu quo

There was a motion made by the counsel for Ross to quash the Certiorari because it only called for the proceedings bettween Ross and Montgomery whereas they were between Ross and Montg[o]mery & *McCormick*[.] This motion was improper for the Court can't judge of the Certiorari till 'tis returned, therefore the motion should have been directed against the Order for the Certiorari, not the Certiorari itself[.] Wils: Rep: 111, 58[1]

On the motion of Geo: W: Campbell counsel for Montgemery & McCormick ordered by the Court that a Certiorari and Supersedeas issue pursuant to the prayer of the petition which is filed.

MS, MdHi-Bland Casebook, 7–10, Bland Papers (MS 134). Date is taken from *id.* at 1. Judges' attendance is taken from WDSC Eq. Min. Bk., 1791–1804, p. 148.

1. 1 Wils. 58, 111.

IV. PETITION OF WILLIAM
VANNERSON TO ENJOIN THE
COURT'S SEPTEMBER TERM
ORDER

Washington District Superior Court, Jonesboro

14 September 1799

State of Tennessee ⎫
Washington District ⎰   To the Honourable the Judges of the
Superior Court of Law and Equity, for the State of Tennessee Humbly
Complaining sheweth to your Honours, your Orator William Vannison,
agent for David Ross, being duly authorized, By the said David to do and
act in his stead, as fully and amply, as tho he was pers[onal]ly present, and
in pursuance of that authorety arrived in this State, in March One thousand seven hundred and ninety Eight and took posession and Charge of
all the said David Rosses lands, and Management of all his Other buisness whatever, and more perticularly that part of his Estate, known by the
name of the North fork, and part known by the name the Furnace, your
Orator further States, that before he left Virginia, he was Informed, by his
Employer David Ross, that that part of the Furnace Tract, Known by the
name of the Tavern House and some Out houses, necessary to the Carrying On of the said Tavern, was leased to a Certain William McCormick by
your Orators predicessor John S McFarlane but Expressd. much Satisfaction, that the time for which the lease was made would Expire some
time Shortly after your Orators arrival in this Country (towit) at the End
of the Year One thousand Seven hundred and Ninety Eight, That on your
Orators arival in this Country, he was also Informd. by John S. McFarlin,
that the premises before stated (towit) The Tavern hous, and some Out
houses necessary for the Carrying on of the said Tavern, ware leased
Jointly to William McCormick and also Informed your Orator, that the
time would Expire at the End of the Year One thousand seven hundred
and Ninety Eight, that your Orator than applyd. to Mr. McFarlain for a
Coppy of the lease, and was Informed by him, that by some accident he
had neglected to take a Copy, but at the same time Informed your Oretor,
that William McCormick had promised to deliver a Coppy when he
should be applyd to for it, that your Orator than became Satisfied sup-
posing that Mccormick was a man of Integ[rity] but he becoming more
acquainted with him and not Knowing how soon he might be deprived of
the Evidence of McFarlan (as he [was] about to leave the place) applied

to Mr. McCormick as well as your Orator recollects in Company with McFarlain, for a Copy of the aforsai[d] lease, and was told by him, that the lease was some where among his pap[ers] or was mislaid, and that he would hunt it up, and give a Copy some Other time, your Orator further states, that he had several Con[ver]sations with the said William McCormick about the time Concernin[g] his leaving the premises, at the Expiration of the time for which the[y] w[ere] leased, and Concerning Mathew Nightingail, who was by agreement with David Ross to Occupy the said premises when McCormick lef[t] them, and that he mentioned in the Course of some of those Conversa[tions] with McCormick, that he wished to make some repairs to the said premises for the more Comfortable reception of Nightaingale, and ab[solu]tely Obtain leave to do so. Your Orator further states, in pursuanc[e] of this disposition of things, Nightaingale had actually proceeded to fa[llow] up some land that belongd. to the aforsaid leased premises to prepa[re] it for small grain for the insuing year, and was informd. and [beli]eves that it was by the Express Consent of William McCormick, things ware in this situation, untill a Certain Michael Montgomery arived [in] the neighbourhood of the Furnace, where his Family lived, but from wh[ich] he had been absent Ever since your Orator arived in this Country, [and] untill Mathew Nightaingale was about to Seed the ground that [he] had fallowed as before stated, when One day on his way from t[he] north fork, to the Furnace, your Orator Met Nightaingale on his w[ay] to the north Fork after your Orator to Informed him that Montgomery [&] McCormick had discharged him from sowing the grain in the ground he had fallowed, altho the said Nightaingale had hire[d] a Boy bought grain and procured a plow for that purp[ose,] your Orator kept on in Company with Nightaingale, untill the[y] arrived at the Furnace, when Nightaingale went on to the store house & your Orator to the house where Montgomery & McCormick [were] he than applyd to McCormick to know if it was true that he had discharged Nightaingale from sowing the grain, and was answered in the afirmative, your Orator asked McCormick, in the Course of Conversation that was then had between them, if the lease under which he Claimed did not Expire at the ensuing Christmas or thereabout, he answered it did not for many years to Come, or words to that affect Your Orator than applyd to him to see the lease and was answered he should see it soon enough. McCormick, then to the best of your Orators recollection Called Muntgomery, down stairs, when your Orator applyd to them to shew their lease, and was answered he would see it time Enough, or words to that Import, and atho your Orator had it in his power to know, and had frequently heard, yet till that time he was not fully satisfyed that Montgomery actually was a Joint lessee of the premises, nor had your Orator untill than the least Idea, that the[y] would seriously pretend to hold the place

longer than the three Existing years, although there had been such a
thing whispered through the Neighbourhood before, but your Orator
Could not believe it, and he was the more Inclined not to believe it as
Mccormick had never mentioned such thing to your Orator Altho the[y]
had many Conversations on that head, and because before or about that
time the thing was whispering first through the Neighbourhood, McCormick had actually made some proposals to sell the then standing Crop,
on the place, and made some Other Arangements as your Orator has
been informed and believes to have been the place. Your Orator farther
states that about the time it was first whispered through the neighbourhood, that Montgomery and McCormick intended to hold the
premises before aluded to in this Bill for a longer time than three years to
begin from the time the lease was first made (towit) for a longer time than
three present years, and your Orator not Knowing of any means they had
of doing so but by force, was inclined to give them notice to quit possession marked (A) which notice your Orator prays may be Considered and
taken as part of this Bill your Orator than left them and was still in hopes
the[y] would leave the place, at the Expiration of their rightfull time, but
as the time ap[proa]ched, for their leaving the place, their deter-
minatio[n] for holding became more manifest, by their declaration
through out the neighbourhood. thus things stood untill the month of
February One thous[and] Seven hundred and ninety Nine, your Orator
having frequently given them to understand he wanted posession of the
premises before stated in th[is] Bill, and being as Often given to understand that they did not me[an] to give it up, your Orator procured a writ
of forcible Entery and det[ainer] to issue and in persuance thereof, a Jury
being summoned on the   [1] [day] of   [1] One thousand seven hundred
and ninety Nine, did appear [and] was sworn in due form of Law before
      [1] Esquires to Inquire [of] the force, than Complained of by your
Orator, for and in behalf of the said David Ross and after being so sworn,
and witnesses sworn on both si[des] your Orator demanded. to know by
his Counsel, under what title they Cla[imed] to hold the premises in question for a longer time than three years, which your Orator understood
and believes was before that time Expired your Orator doth farther state
that no title was then shewn what Ever by them or their Counsel, who
than appeared for them, altho the[y] were frequently requested to
produce it if any the[y] had. your Orator do[th] farther state, that it was
proven in that trial that Montgomery [&] McCormick had both said, as
well as your Orator recollects tha[t] they had leased for no longer time,
than three years, Or words to that import, and that it was farther proven
to be the underst[and]ing of their near neighbours, that the time for
which the[y] had lea[sed] the premises near Expired (towit) before the
then trial, your Ora[tor] doth further state that after the Evidence on

both sides ware go[ne] through, and the Counsel on both sides heard, the jury passed thereon, and the Virdict rendered by them, was that Michael Muntgomery and William McCormick held the premises herein recited by force or to that Import, whereupon there was a writ of rest[ituti]on awarded by the aforesaid Justices to your Orator, for and in beh[alf] of the aforsaid David Ross, and afterwards on the   ¹ day of   ¹ One thousand seven hundred and ninety Nine possession was given to W[illi]am Norris your Orators Agent in that behalf, your Orator doth farth[er] State that at March term of the Superior Court one thousand seven hundred and ninety Nine the said Michael Montgomery and William McCormick applyd for and Obtained, a Cerciorari from the [sa]id Superior Court, to bring up the proceedings had on the before mentioned Writ of forcible entry and detenure returnable to September term One thousand seven hundred and ninety nine and at September term acordingly the proceedings ware brought up and Entered up on the docket and at the Cauling of the Cause the said William McCormick and Michael Montgomery by their Counsel moved that the proceedings had before the Justices as before set forth in this Bill might be quashed and for Errors appearing in the face of the said proceeding, as your Orator has been Informed the[y] ware quashed, agreeable to the Motion, That then the said Michael Montgomery and William McCormick moved by their Counsil in Open Court that a writ of Rerestitution might be awarded by the said Court, which was objected to by your Orators Counsel unless they William McCormick and Michael Montgomery would produce some colour of title to the before mentioned premises, upon which the said Michael Muntgomery and William McCormick Confederating and Combining themselves together to defraud the said David Ross of the lawfull right and posession of the premises heretofore set forth, produced a lease purporting to be a lease given by John S. McFarlain, your Orators predecessor to the said Michel Muntgomery and William McCormick for thirty Years, and in Order to establish the said lease produced a Certain Ephreim Dunlap to Sware to the Execution thereof by the said John S. McFarlain and the said Dunlap being produced did sware to the Execution thereof by the said McFarlain, whereupon the Judges of the said Court did award that a writ of rerestitution to the said Michael Montgomery & William McCormick should issue, and your Orator doth Expressly Charge that the said paper purporting to be a lease for thirty years, Executed by the said John S McFarlin to the said Montgomery and McCormick Must have been altered by the said Muntgomery and McCormick or some other person from the term of three to the term of thirty years, or in some Other way procured a lease to be written for thirty years, when in truth and in fact there Ought to be a lease only for three, which term was Ended prior to the time of the trial herein set forth, to have been had befor the Justices aforesaid on the writ of forcible Entry and detainer Your Orator is much more Confirmed in his Opinion by the Conduct of the said McCormick and Montgomery who at all tim[es] and on all Ocasions Concealed said lease, from your Orator, and also frequently acknowledged, that their term, in the said premises would Expire in the [latter?] end of the year, One thousand seven hundred and n[inety] Eight, as your Orator has been informed, and verily believes. But now [so] it is may it please your honours, that the said Michael Montgomery and William McCormick, Combining and Confederating together, and w[ith] Other persons unknown to your Orator, whom when known your O[rator] prays, may be made defendents to this Bill, with apt words to Charge the[m] by procuring and producing the said faults and fradulent Instrument [of] writing, perporting to be a lease for thirty years, as before mentioned a[nd] designing to injure and Oppress the said David Ross in the premises, have Obtained a writ of rerest[it]ution to be awarded them for the said land and tennaments altho their title to the same has long since Expired, a[nd] no principle of write of Justice Could authorise them or Either of them to such Writ, all which actings and doings are inconsistant with Equ[ity] and good Conscience and tend most manifastly to the Injury and Opression of the said David Ross, your Orator therefore as the said David Ross, and had no adequete relief on the premises by the strict Rules of Common law proceedings and can be fully and afectually relieved in a Court of Equity Only, where such Cases and fradulently transactio[ns] will be discouraged, where frauds of Every kind are properly Cogniza[ble] and where ample relief Can be given to those who are Injured or serc[um]vented by the artful and neferious schemes and artifices of designing men, ha[s] Exhibited this his Bill of Complaint to this honourable Court, and prays that the said Michael and William and others their Confederates when discov[ered] may be made defendents thereto and be Compelled on their Corporal O[aths] true full and perfect answer to make to all and singular the premises [in] as full and ample manner as if the same were herein again repeated and more at large Interogated, and more Espacially that the said Mich[ael] and William may, answer and say, whether your Orator did not in Company with John S. McFarlin apply to the said William McCormick f[or] a Coppy of the lease under which he held the premises, and what ware his reasons for not giving it up to your Orator, and what Conversat[ions] passed between them on that visit. did not McCormick say he would give a Copy to your Orator at some Other time and if not what did he say. did any Conversation ever take place between your Orator and McCormick Concerning his leaving the premises at the End of the year One thousand seven hundred and ninety Eight did the[y] move off the premises at the end of the three years, for which their lease was made. did they not always or very Often report, through the Neighbourhood, that their time in the premises [expired] with the year, One thousand seven hundred and ninety Eight. if not at what time did they say the said lease would Expire, and if not what did the[y] say, Concerning it. did not your Orator Cause a writ of forcable Entry and detainure to issue & Cause a jury to Come and try the forcable detainure of the said McCormick & Montgomery. was there not a trial had on the premises and a verdi[c]t for the said David Ross. was it not demanded of the said McCormick and Montgomery on the trial by your Orator or his Counsel, for them to shew by what athority the[y] held the premises. and what answer did they make thereto, or what if any, title did the[y] shew. was it not proven on that trial, that Montgomery and McCormick had frequently said, their lease for the premises had Expired before the trial than had. if not what was then proven. was there more than One lease made by John S McFarlin for the before mentioned premises to the Knowledge of the said Montgomery and Macormick, or to the Knowledge of Ether of them. was the lease that was made by the said John S. Mcfurlin to the said Montgomery and Mecormick, made and delivered, for three years or for thirty, and who ware witnesses to the said lease if there ware more than one, what conversation had they, or whither of them with McFarlin when the said lease was made before, or at any time afterwards, Concerning the said lease. was the lease the[y] produced and had proven, by Ephreim Dunlap in the superior Court, Executed by John S. Mcfarlin as a lease for thirty Years. what persons ware present at the time the lease was Executed by John S. Mcfarlain and witnessed by Ephreim dunlap. Your Orator requests that your honours may grant him the states most gratious writ of Injunction directed &c &c to stay and injoin all further proceedings on said Judgement of the Court, and writ of rerestitution so by them awarded, and that your honours may Order and Decree, that the said injunction may be perpetual and all further proceedings on said writ for ever stayd. and injoined; and also that the said Michael Montgomery & William McCormick be Compelled by a decree of this honourable Court, to deliver up the said paper perporting to be a lease for the tenements for thirty years from John S Mcfarlin to the said Michael and William to be Cancelled, and that your honours may grant your Orator, for and in behalf of the said David Ross such other and further relief in the premises as may to you seem Conseistant with Equity and Justice and your Orator requests that the States writ of subpoena may be granted him directed &c &c to compell the said Michael and William to apear &c &c.

William Vennerson Agent for
Da[vid] Ross

William Vannerson agent for David Ross maketh Oath, that the sev[eral] Matters and things set forth in the foregoing Bill, to be of his Own knowledge are true, and those set forth which are not of his own knowledge he believes to be true Sworn to before me David Campbell one of the Judges of the superior Courts of Law and Equity for the State of Ten[ness]ee September 14th 1799.

David Campbell

Let Writs of Injunction and subpoena issue agreeable to the prayr of the above Bill.

D. Campbell

ENCLOSURE I[2]

William Vannerson to William McCormick

Rossville Ironworks
Octr. 1st 1798

Sir

When Mr. Mcfarlain was hear I applyd to him for a Coppy of the agreement made with you for rent of the houses and plantation at the Furnace. he informed me that there had been but one Copy of the agreement made and that was left with you; but that you ware to give a Copy at any time; I acordingly applyd to you for a Copy. I think in the presents of Mr. Mcfarlain and I have since made aplication to you but I have never yet seen the agreement. however it is understood that your time Expires with the present year, and that the propriator is in want of the place himself the insuing year. This has been Often mentioned between us in the Course of the past summer perticularly when you Obligingly permited me to do any repaires which would not Incammode your family. I am now going about those repaires and Expect possession of the premises in three months from this date. I am respectfully Sir Yr. Mo. Obt. Servt. &c.

William Vannerson for
David Ross

ENCLOSURE II[3]

William Vannerson to Michael Montgomery

Rossville Ironworks Octr. 1st 1798

Sir

I have understood that you are some way Concerned in renting the houses and plantation at present Ocupyd. by Capt. Wm. McCormick if so youl please to attend to a notice I have given Captain William McCormick a copy of which is below

I am Sir yr. Mo. Obt. Servt.

Wm. Vannerson for
David Ross[4]

Tr, TWashCo-WDSC Eq. Rec. Bk., 1791–1803, pp. 69–77. Those portions of the text that are supplied in brackets for the most part have been taken from Tr, T-WPA Records, WDSC Min. Bk. A, 43–48. Occasional, insignificant deletions and interlineations are not noted.

    1. Blank in Tr.
    2. Marked "A" in the margin of the Tr; inside address: "Captain William McCormick." The text of the enclosure is repeated in the Tr after Enclosure II and has been compared with the text reproduced here for accuracy and spelling variations and to supply missing and illegible words.
    3. Inside address: "Majr. Michael Montgomery."
    4. The text of Enclosure I follows at this point in the Tr.

V. BLAND'S MINUTES OF THE
ARGUMENT OF COUNSEL
ON THE MOTION TO DISSOLVE
THE INJUNCTION

Washington District Superior Court, Jonesboro
Judges Jackson, Roane, and Campbell Presiding

[ca. March 15, 1800]
Vannerson agent of D: Ross vrs Michael
Montgomery & Wm. McCormick.

The proceedings in the Inquest of Forcible Entry & Detainer having been brought up to last term in obedience to the Certiorari which was granted at March term 1799 (see ante 10) they were quashed for the manifold Errors apparent on the face of them—upon which the Defendants produced a Lease from Ross for the Lands in question and had a writ of Rerestitution awarded   During the recess of the Court and previous to their being restored to possession an Injunction was granted by his Honor Judge Campbell.

[John Rhea and Hugh Lawson White
for Defendants]

And now at this term the Counsel for the Defendants without answering Pleading or Demurring, Moved to dissolve the Injunction on the ground that it had been improvidently granted by one Judge out of Court—and argued that this was similar to the case of a Certiorari which had been decided in this Court (see ante 17)[1] where a Judge at his chambers had made a fiat for a Certiorari, the party was entitled to the opinion of the whole Court in session whether that fiat was properly made or not

[Jenkin Whiteside for Plaintiff]

Whiteside contra. I conceive there is a distinction between the cases— the one is a Petition to bring a Cause into Court the other is an original Bill of a Suit begun & now pending   here the Injunction is a thing accessory & collateral to that Suit and cannot be dissolved but by the regular mode of Plea Answer or Demurrer

MS, MdHi-Bland Casebook, 55–57, Bland Papers (MS 134). Bland's date is March 1800 (*id.* at 38); approximate date is derived from WDSC Eq. Rec. Bk., 1791–1803, p. 88.

1. *Mitchell v. Berry,* No. 19.

VI. BLAND'S MINUTES OF THE OPINIONS OF THE COURT

Washington District Superior Court, Jonesboro
Judges Jackson, Roane, and Campbell Presiding

[ca. March 15, 1800]

[The Opinion of Judge Jackson]

Jackson J: For my part I see no difference between the two cases. The intent of a Petition is to bring a Cause from an inferior to a Superior Court and have a Supersedeas to stop proceedings in the Court below, which is in effect an injunction. the object of Petition & Bill then is the same

This being the case, admit[ting] the facts as stated in the Bill to be true an injunction ought not to have been granted; because at Common Law whenever a Judgment is reversed the party is restored as of course, in this case the Judgment was reversed and a writ of Rerestitution awarded and I am of opinion it cannot be injoined.

[The Opinion of Judge Campbell]

Campbell J: It is my opinion that the Court have a control over the proceedings of a single Judge out of Court; but I conceive the case to be very different when we sit as Chancellors   It may be well to observe as a general rule that where the Practice of this country is unsettled it is proper to recur to that of England; now there is no instance mentioned in the Books where an Injunction has been dissolved on a motion similar to the Present—therefore this motion cannot be sustained.

[The Opinion of Judge Roane]

Roane J: I have on some little reflection found this case more difficult than I was at first awar of. It does seem to me that an Injunction could not be dissolved in England without Plea Answer or Demurrer (2 Eq: Ca: Ab: 172 contra),[1] but from our Act of Assembly I think there is a greater power given to the Courts in this Country the words of the Act (Iredell 434)[2] are "Any one Judge of the Court may in the Vacation, &c grant Injunctions, &c *but still subject to the controul and further order of the Court.*["] from hence I conclude that the Court have a right in this way to hear the Bill & see if there is sufficient foundation for an Injunction.

I agree with his Honor Judge Jackson upon the general principle that where a Judgment at Common Law is reversed an Injunction cannot be granted to stay the restoration of the party—but I take the present case of Forcible Entry & detainer to be some what different, for in this case the part[y] is not restored as of course but some shew of title must be made out in order to ground a writ of Rerestitution in the present case that was done by producing a Lease to the Court of Law which Lease it is stated in this Bill was fraudulently obtained indeed is a downright Forgery. now quære whether if that had have appeared to the Court of Law it would have granted a writ of Rerestitution, if not a Court of Equity might interfere. For my part I am in doubt on this subject; but were I to give an opinion as thus impressed I should say that Equity may interfere 3 Bacon 172[3] but I had rather take an advisari indeed must do so.

Upon which the motion was withdrawn, and the Defendants answered severally.

Injunction dissolved on Bill & Answer

MS, MdHi-Bland Casebook, 57–61, Bland Papers (MS 134). Bland's date is March 1800 (*id.* at 38); approximate date is derived from WDSC Eq. Rec. Bk., 1791–1803, p. 88.

1. 2 *General Abridgment of Cases in Equity* 172, 22 Eng. Rep. 147: "A Bill was brought to be *quieted in the Possession of a Right of Common,* and *to prevent Distresses;* and though the Plaintiff produced Affidavits of some fifty Years quiet Possession, and Evidence of their Right of Commonage in the Time of Q. *Eliz.* yet the Court refused to interpose till one or more Verdicts at Law; and dissolved Plaintiff's Injunction obtained for want of an Answer."

2. Iredell, *Laws of North Carolina* 434.

3. 3 Bacon, *Abridgment* 172: In a note to the definition of an injunction as a "prohibitory Writ, restraining a Person from committing or doing a Thing which appears to be against Equity and Conscience," the commentator notes that the definition includes "[a]n Injunction to stay Restitution upon an Indictment of forcible Entry."

49. Armstrong v. Tyrrell and Lytle

1802
(Enforcement of Judgments)

EDITORIAL NOTE

Jackson and the other Superior Court judges frequently were petitioned as a court of equity to enforce or to enjoin the enforcement of judgments that had been obtained at law. The present case and No. 51 represent attempts by petitioners to enjoin the enforcement of judgments.

Because records for the Mero District Superior Court of Equity are unavailable before 1803, the nature of Martin Armstrong's petition upon which Jackson and Judge Campbell issued their decree on May 26, 1802, is not known. The petition probably arose, however, out of the same facts that underlay an action brought almost simultaneously against Armstrong by William Lytle, Jr., one of the present party defendants.

According to Lytle's declaration in the latter case, Armstrong in August 1797 had executed a bill of exchange for the payment of $500 in silver to William Tyrrell. Tyrrell, according to Lytle, had presented the bill of exchange to Armstrong in February 1798, and Armstrong at that time had acknowledged having drawn the instrument.[1]

Tyrrell had died by July 1798, but before his death, he evidently had obtained a judgment against Armstrong for the $500 represented by the bill of exchange. Tyrrell satisfied a portion of his judgment by securing the public sale of a tract of land owned by Stockley Donelson, who, Tyrrell presumably believed, had been a partner of Armstrong's (see Document I).[2]

Claiming that Tyrrell had assigned Armstrong's bill of exchange to him, Lytle in May 1799 filed an action against Armstrong in the Mero District Superior Court of Law to enforce the instrument.[3] Contemporaneously with the filing of that suit, Lytle filed an answer to Armstrong's petition in the present case (see Document II). It thus seems quite likely that the basis for Tyrrell's earlier judgment against Armstrong was the bill

1. Lytle v. Armstrong, MDSC Law Min. Bk., 1788–1803, pp. 345–346 (1799–1800).
2. See Lytle v. Tyrrell's Estate, MDSC Law Min. Bk., 1788–1803, p. 273 (1798–1800). No record of the sale has been located.
3. Lytle v. Armstrong, note 1 above, 346.

of exchange that Armstrong had executed in 1797 and that Tyrrell subsequently had assigned to Lytle. Armstrong's equity petition evidently
was filed in an effort to enjoin further execution upon Tyrrell's judgment
by Lytle on the ground that the sale of Donelson's land in satisfaction of
the judgment had discharged him from further liability on the bill of
exchange.

Jackson and Judge Campbell conducted a hearing on Armstrong's petition in May 1802. The final decree that Jackson and Campbell issued on
May 26 (Document II) at best represented a partial victory for Armstrong. The court enjoined Lytle and Tyrrell's representatives from proceeding further against Armstrong with respect to a portion of Tyrrell's
judgment amounting to $102.50, which perhaps represented the price
that Donelson's land had brought at the sale. The court, however, apparently dismissed Armstrong's petition as to the residue of the judgment
and, indeed, provided that Lytle was to have the benefit thereof. The
court costs were divided among the parties.

Armstrong, a land-speculating partner of Governor Blount's, had secured a legislative commission as surveyor for the military reserve in
1783. Tyrrell had been commissioned as a surveyor by William Tyrrell
Lewis, surveyor general for the Western District of Tennessee, in 1796
and had been selected by Blount, Lewis, Donelson, and other land speculators to secure or to burn the land records by which they and others subsequently were implicated in the Glasgow Land Frauds. Before his death
in 1798, Tyrrell had been a partner of Lytle's in land speculation.[4] Lytle
has not been further identified.

4. KnoxCo Rec. Bk. 1, 1795–1799, p. 118; Thomas P. Abernethy, *From Frontier to
Plantation in Tennessee: A Study in Frontier Democracy* (Chapel Hill, N.C., 1932), 118,
172; see Lytle v. Tyrrell's Estate, note 2 above, 273.

I. DEPOSITION OF STOCKLEY
DONELSON

Mero District Superior Court, Nashville

October 25, 1800

Martin Armstrong Complainant In pursuance of a commission to
    vs   me directed from the Honorable
William Tyrrell   the Court of Equity in and for the
  and   Defendants District of Mero in the State of
William Lytle   Tennessee,[1] I John Manifee Es-
quire one of the Justices of the Peace in and for the County of Knox in the

said State have caused Stockley Donilson Witness on behalf of the Defendants to come before me at the dwelling House of John Stone in Knoxville on the twenty fifth day of October one thousand Eight hundred; and the said Stockley Donelson being solemnly sworn saith and deposeth as follows, (viz), That as well as he can now recollect William Tyrrell once told him the Deponent that the Sheriff had had Martin Armstrong the Complainant in custody on an Execution for five hundred Dollars; and that he Tyrrell knowing Armstrong and this Deponent had dealings together he had sold property and paid the Debt for the said Armstrong; and that this Deponent then replied to the said Tyrrell it was very well; and that he was glad it was the case; and this Deponent then understood it was his the Deponent's property the said Tyrrell had sold to pay the said Debt. The Deponent farther saith that at the time the said Debt was paid he did not believe nor does he now believe that he this Deponent was indebted to the Complainant Martin Armstrong in any *sum* whatever that there was and yet is a large account between the said Complainant and this Deponent unsettled and he cannot say certainly that he was not indebted to the said Complainant: but he does not believe that he was: This Deponent farther saith he would have been satisfied that the sum paid by the said Tyrrell for the said Complainant should have been settled for between the Complainant and this Deponent. [Ques]tion by Defendants Did you ever charge the Complainant with the said sum of five hundred Dollars as paid by Tyrrell for the Complainant? Answer I never did charge the Complainant therewith but had intended to have charged him with it or in settlement. Question by the Justice—Did you and Tyrrell ever come to a settlement? Answer—We did not: but Tyrrell must be indebted to me a large amount. And this Deponent farther saith not.

Sworn to and ⎫   Stockley Donelson
Subscribed before me ⎪
the said John Manifee ⎬
at the place and on ⎪
the day aforesaid. ⎭

John Menefee (Seal)

MS, TNJ-Stanley Horn Coll. Text in unidentified hand; autograph signatures.

1. At the request of a litigant, the Superior Court, sitting in equity, could issue a commission to obtain the deposition of a witness living outside the county or unable to attend court because of age or illness. Caruthers, *History of a Law Suit*, 34; Timothy Walker, *Introduction to American Law* (Philadelphia, 1837), 546–547. A 1782 North Carolina statute provided that "[c]ommissions to take testimony may issue, directed to any two justices of the peace, who shall have all the powers of commissioners of chancery." The measure also required that the opposing party be given notice before any testimony was taken under the commission. Ch. 11, 1782 Laws of N.C., reprinted in Iredell, *Laws of North Carolina* 432, 1 Scott, *Laws of Tennessee* 261. See also ch. 6, 1801 Tenn. Pub. Acts, reprinted in 1 Scott, *Laws of Tennessee* 685.

II. THE FINAL DECREE OF
THE COURT

Mero District Superior Court, Nashville
Judges Jackson, White, and Campbell Presiding

Mero District Sct   May Term 1802
　　Between   26th May 1802
　　　　　　Martin Armstrong: Complainant
　　　　　　　　　　and
　　William Tyrrell & William Lytle Defendants
　　This cause coming on this day to be heard on Bill and Answer which
being examined by the Court and the Argument of Counsil on both sides
heard and considered. It is ordered declared, and decreed that the said
William Tyrrell and William Lytle, their agents and attorneys and each of
them be perpetually enjoined from suing out Execution or proceeding
further on said Judgment recovered by said William Tyrrell against said
Complainant and mentioned in said Bill, as to one hundred and two Dollars and fifty Cents part of said Judgment; and that the Bill of the Complainant be dismissed as to the residue of said Judgment and the said
William Lytle have the benifit thereof; and it is further ordered, declared
and Decreed that the Defendant William Lyttle pay all Costs of said Suit,
which accrued at and previous to May Term one thousand seven hundred
and ninety nine of this Court, at which Term said William Lytle's answer
was filed, and that the Complainant pay all Costs subsequent to said Term
in this cause. Given under our hands in Open Court
　　　　　　　　　　David Campbell
　　　　　　　　　　Andrew Jackson

MS, TNJ-Stanley Horn Coll. Text in unidentified hand; autograph signatures. Judges' attendance is taken from MDSC Law Min. Bk., 1788–1803, p. 640, which records the attendance for the same date while the judges sat as a court of law. The reason for the absence
of Judge White's signature has not been determined.

50. Williams et al. v. Henderson & Company

1802
(Partition)

EDITORIAL NOTE

The present case was initiated in the Washington District Superior Court prior to February 1791 by the surviving principals in the Henderson & Company. The petitioners sought to partition a 200,000-acre tract of land in eastern Tennessee that had been granted to the company by the state of North Carolina. Still pending before the court when Jackson assumed his judicial duties in the autumn of 1798, the proceedings terminated only near the conclusion of his fourth year on the bench, when he and Judge Campbell in September 1802 issued a final decree effecting a division of the extensive Henderson grant.

Richard Henderson, a North Carolina lawyer and Superior Court judge, had organized the precursor of the Henderson & Company as early as 1764. With his Granville County law partner John Williams and Thomas Hart of Orange County, Henderson had planned to purchase and colonize a large portion of the extensive Indian lands that lay in western Virginia and North Carolina. In part because of his preoccupation with the Regulator movement in 1770–1771, Henderson and his associates were unable to pursue their colonizing plans beyond sponsoring two exploratory trips into the Kentucky region of western Virginia by Daniel Boone. Further encouraged by accounts of the areas that Boone brought back with him in 1771 and by the Cherokee Nation's having relinquished by treaty its claim to lands north of the Kentucky River, Henderson and his associates organized a new and larger company in August 1774 to purchase "a large Territory or Tract of Land . . . lying on the west side of the mountains on the waters of the Mississippi River, from the Indian Tribes now in possession thereof." In addition to Henderson, Williams, and Hart, the new Louisa Company consisted of Hart's brother Nathaniel, their brother-in-law John Luttrell of Chatham County, and William Johnston, a Hillsborough merchant.[1]

Henderson and Nathaniel Hart visited the region later in 1774 to initiate negotiations for a purchase of the Indian lands. Upon their return, Henderson and his associates on January 6, 1775, reorganized the Louisa Company as the Transylvania Company and added three associates: Williams's brother-in-law Leonard Henly Bullock; another brother of the Harts', David Hart; and James Hogg, a merchant and landowner from Hillsborough.[2] Under the terms of the company's articles of incorporation, the members were to be "copartners & Tenants in Common, by the Laws of England" with each, except for Bullock and David Hart, entitled to a one-eighth interest in

> a certain Territory or Tract of Land lying on the Ohio River & waters thereof, including the Rivers Cumber[l]and, Louisa &c. . . . That is to say each mans particular part to their and each of their respective use & uses, and to no other Intent or purpose whatever, And be it further known, that if any or either of the aforesaid partners, should Give, Grant, Sell, or Devise, or otherwise dispose of his particular part of the aforesaid Tract or Territory of Land to any other Person whatever, Such Donee, Grantee, or Divisee, shall by the rest of the Copartners be considered as Tenants in Common with them and have all the Rights, Privileges, & Immunities which the said Donor, Grantor, or Devisor could or might have had or enjoyed, from the benefit or advantage of the first purchase, made by him or them from Indians above . . . . and also if any or either of the said partners, their or either of their heirs [or] assigns shall die & depart this life without having first giving, Granted, Sold, devised or otherwise disposed of his or their particular part of the aforesaid Lands lying on the Ohio River & the waters thereof, purchased of the Cherokee Indians as aforesaid, that then & in that case the part of such person or persons so dying without having first disposed of the same as aforesaid, shall remain to devolve upon the right Heir or Heirs of such Decendant or Decendants, shall be considered as a Tenant or Tenants in Common, according to [the] Laws of England, with the other Copartners in the aforesaid Lands, & shall be entitled to have & receive all the rights, privileges, benefit advantages & emoluments which his, her, or their Predecessor or Predecessors could or might have had were he, she, or they, then living.

Bullock and Hart were entitled only to a one-sixteenth interest in the land.[3]

1. Kentucky Papers, 1CC, 2, Draper Coll., WHi; *DAB;* William S. Lester, *The Transylvania Colony* (Spencer, Ind., 1935), 4–9, 17–18; Archibald Henderson, "The Creative Forces in Western Expansion: Henderson and Boone," 20 *Am. Hist. Rev.* 86, 99–100 (1914).

2. Lester, *Transylvania*, 22–24; Shaw Livermore, *Early American Land Companies* (New York, 1939), 91–92. For Hogg (ca. 1729–1805), see Bernard Bailyn, *Voyagers to the West: A Passage in the Peopling of America on the Eve of the Revolution* (New York, 1986), 499–544.

3. Kentucky Papers, 1CC, 3–4, Draper Coll., WHi; Lester, *Transylvania*, 23.

Henderson, Williams, and Nathaniel and Thomas Hart returned to the region to resume negotiations with the Indians. The final discussions occurred during March 14–17, 1775, at Sycamore Shoals on the southern bank of the Watauga River, a tributary of the Holston River, near the present site of Elizabethton, Tennessee, where approximately 1,200 Indians had assembled to conclude negotiations with the North Carolina speculators. Under the terms of the conveyances executed by the parties on March 17, Henderson and his associates were granted approximately 20 million acres in the present states of Tennessee and Kentucky. The conveyances were represented by two deeds, the first of which transferred the larger Kentucky portion of the tract to Henderson and his associates and the second of which conveyed the smaller Tennessee portion.[4]

The Proclamation of 1763, however, had prohibited purchases of land from the Indians west of the Alleghenies. Moreover, the North Carolina General Assembly in May 1780 reclaimed most of the land in the company's purchase that lay within the state.[5] Henderson, therefore, subsequently sought to secure his title to the purchase from the Virginia and North Carolina legislatures. Virginia denied Henderson's request with respect to the Kentucky land, but compensated him for his loss with a portion of the original purchase.[6] In May 1783 the company petitioned the North Carolina assembly to recognize the validity of the Cherokee conveyances. The legislature concluded that the purchases had been illegal but that, because peaceful possession of the lands might be possible by virtue of the Henderson conveyances, compensation should be awarded the company.[7] Accordingly, the General Assembly granted to Henderson and his associates the 200,000 acres of land that eventually became the subject of the present litigation. The legislators provided that the tract was to lie within the following boundaries:

> Beginning at the old Indian town in Powell's valley, and running down Powell's river not less than four miles in width on one or both sides thereof to the junction of Powell's and Clinch river, then down Clinch river on one or both sides, not less than twelve miles in width, for the aforesaid complement of two hundred thousand acres.

Each of the company's principals was entitled to that portion of the tract that had been specified in the 1775 articles of incorporation. The grant

4. Lester, *Transylvania,* 31–34, 36–38; Samuel Cole Williams, "Henderson and Company's Purchase Within the Limits of Tennessee," 5 *Tenn. Hist. Mag.* 5, 9–11 (1919).

5. *N.C. State Records,* XXIV, 338; Williams, "Henderson and Company's Purchase," 17; see Lester, *Transylvania,* 29–31.

6. Thomas P. Abernethy, *From Frontier to Plantation in Tennessee: A Study in Frontier Democracy* (Chapel Hill, N.C., 1932), 24–27.

7. Williams, "Henderson and Company's Purchase," 23.

was conditioned upon the company's having entered and surveyed the tract by the last day of November 1783.[8]

The company failed to complete the survey within the prescribed time. Nonetheless, attributing the lack of compliance to "danger from the Indians, and the unsettled state of the country where the said lands lie," the North Carolina General Assembly in 1788 authorized the company to complete the survey "within twelve months after a peace shall be settled with the Indians."[9]

The company's survey was not completed until May 1791.[10] Prior to, and perhaps in contemplation of, the survey's completion, several of the company's surviving principals filed a petition initiating the present proceeding in the Washington District Superior Court for the partition of the North Carolina grant.[11] According to the court's initial minute book entry for the case in February 1791, the petitioner's bill was taken as confessed as against a number of the defendants, including Henderson's heirs. The court also ordered that notices be published in the *Cape Fear Gazette* and in the *Kentucky Gazette* for the benefit of the remaining defendants. The matter remained pending before the court, interrupted only by occasional orders by the judges that similar notices be published in additional newspapers, until September 1794, when the court directed that the petitioners' bill be taken as confessed as against the remaining defendants and "set for Trial at next Term." Thereafter, continuances were entered routinely at each term of court until well after Jackson's appointment to the bench.[12]

Jackson and Judges Roane and Campbell conducted a final hearing on

8. Ch. 38, 1783 Laws of N.C., reprinted in *N.C. State Records*, XXIV, 530–531. The statute granted the tract to Henderson and his associates as tenants in common and not as joint tenants. *Id.* §3.

9. Ch. 48, 1788 Laws of N.C.

10. A copy of the survey in an unidentified hand is located in Tennessee Papers, 5XX, 28ab–28gh, Draper Coll., WHi.

11. Williams et al. v. Henderson & Company, WDSC Eq. Min. Bk., 1791–1804, pp. 2–3 (1791). Throughout the court's records, the style of the case refers to "Henderson & Company" rather than to the Transylvania Company. Which of the petitioners enumerated by the court in its final decree in 1802 (Document II) actually had joined in filing the initial petition with the court more than a decade earlier is not entirely clear. The original petition has not been located. Both of the transcripts of the petition that have been found (see Document II, endnote) refer in their texts to John Williams, James Hogg, Thomas Hart, David Hart, and Leonard Henly Bullock as the petitioners. Bullock's, however, is not among the names enumerated in the transcripts as having appeared at the foot of the original document. The court's initial minute book entry for the case in 1791 adds to the confusion by listing Bullock and John Luttrell's widow, Susanna Umstead, among the party defendants. WDSC Eq. Min. Bk., 1791–1804, pp. 2–3. Bullock and Umstead, however, are referred to by the court in its final decree as two of the petitioners (see Document II).

12. WDSC Eq. Min. Bk., 1791–1804, pp. 2–3, 15, 26, 36–37, 49, 60, 66, 75, 79, 87, 96, 104, 111, 120, 126, 136, 148, 161.

the petition in March 1800 and mandated that a decree be prepared for their signatures in conformity with a partition deed that had been executed by the parties in August 1779 (see Document I).[13] Because of a series of continuances thereafter granted by the court,[14] the court's final decree was not forthcoming for more than two years later, on September 17, 1802. In the interim, Judge Roane had left the bench upon his election as the state's governor and had been succeeded by Hugh Lawson White. Since Judge White recused himself from consideration of the case, evidently because of his having represented the company in another matter before the court prior to his elevation to the bench,[15] the court's final decree bears only Jackson's signature and Judge Campbell's (Document II).

Tenants in common could always make a voluntary division of their land if all agreed. In *Williams,* however, several of the co-owners were minors or nonresidents who would not join in a voluntary partition. Hence, the plaintiffs were required to seek judicial relief. During the sixteenth century, a statutory right to compel partition became available to tenants in common. One or more tenants could sue the others under a writ of partition, and the court would divide the land into equal parts. Thereafter the parties would own their respective parcels in severalty.[16]

A series of post-Revolutionary North Carolina statutes authorized both the Superior Court and the county courts to partition real property. The tribunal was directed to appoint five commissioners, who in turn were charged with dividing the land. If necessary to achieve an equitable distribution, the commissioners could direct the recipient of the more valuable parcel to pay a compensating sum to the recipient of the less desirable tract. The commissioners' report was filed with the clerk of the appointing court.[17] No commissioners were named in *Williams,* presumably because the original tenants in common of the Henderson grant had executed a deed of partition in August 1779.[18]

13. The partition deed referred to in the court's final decree has not been located.

14. WDSC Eq. Min. Bk., 1791–1804, pp. 196, 211, 228, 254.

15. L. Paul Gresham, "The Public Career of Hugh Lawson White," 3 *THQ* 291, 293–294 (1944). The case was *Cocke v. Henderson & Company* (1796–1799), for which see Williams, "Henderson and Company's Purchase," 12–17; WDSC Eq. Min. Bk., 1791–1803, p. 162.

16. Robert Megarry and H. W. R. Wade, *The Law of Real Property,* 4th ed. (London, 1975), 427–428; 4 Tucker, *Blackstone's Commentaries* 188–190.

17. Ch. 24, 1789 Laws of N.C., reprinted in Iredell, *Laws of North Carolina* 678, 1 Scott, *Laws of Tennessee* 411; ch. 17, 1787 Laws of N.C., reprinted in Iredell, *Laws of North Carolina* 618, 1 Scott, *Laws of Tennessee* 385. See also ch. 11, 1799 Tenn. Pub. Acts, reprinted in 1 Scott, *Laws of Tennessee* 641.

18. The parties have not been further identified, except for Williams (1731–1799), for whom see Part IV.

I. MINUTE BOOK ENTRY

Washington District Superior Court, Jonesboro
Judges Jackson, Roane, and Campbell Presiding

March 13, 1800

At a Court of Equity begun and held in the State of Tennessee for the District of Washington in the Town of Jonesborough on the 13th day of March 1800. Present the Honorable

Archibald Roane ⎫
David Campbell & ⎬ Esquires Judges of
Andrew Jackson ⎭ said Court

Henderson & Company Compts. ⎫
            vs   ⎬ Original Bill
Henderson & Company Defts. ⎭

On the 14th of March 1800 this Cause Came to be heard on motion the Court order that a Decree be made in Conformity with a Deed of Partition made and Executed by John Williams James Hogg Richard Bullock Walter Alves Joseph Hart John Umstead Thomas Hart by his attorney Nathaniel Hart & Leonard Henderson Original Proprietors on the Eighth day of August one thousand Seven hundred and ninety Seven.[1]

MS, TWashCo-WDSC Eq. Min. Bk., 1791–1804, pp. 176–177.

    1. Correctly, on or about Aug. 20, 1779. See Document II.

II. THE COURT'S PARTITION

DECREE

Washington District Superior Court, Jonesboro
Judges Jackson, White, and Campbell Presiding

September 17, 1802

Be it remembered that heretofore John Williams Esquire of the County of Granville Leonard Henly Bullock of the same County James Hogg of orange County Thomas Hart, John Umstead and Susannah his wife & David Hart filed their Bill in the court of Equity for Washington District and therein stated That Richard Henderson late of Granville County Esquire deceased Nathaniel Hart late of   [1] County in Virginia Gentleman Deceased William Johnston late of Orange County Merchant deceased John Lutterel late of Chatham County Gentleman deceased in their life time that is to say in the year one thousand seven hundred and seventy five together with them the said John Williams James Hogg Thomas Hart, David Hart and Leonard Henly Bullock purchased of the nation of Cherokee Indians a very large and Valuable tract of land lying west of the Apalachian mountains of which the said Nation or tribe of Indians were then possessed, that is to say one eighth part of the lands so purchased to the said Richard Henderson, William Johnston John Lutteral John Williams James Hogg Nathaniel Hart and Thomas Hart each respectively and to their heirs and assigns for ever and one sixteenth part of said lands so purchased to the said Leonard Henly Bullock and to the said David Hart each respectively and to their heirs and assigns for ever to be held by them the said purchasers in severalty and not as Joint tenants (some proprietory rights only excepted) and that the said purchasers from the Indian Tribe or nation aforesaid obtained a Grant for the same lands conveying the right as aforesaid. And furth[er] that the General assembly of the state of North Carolina in May session in the year one thousand seven hundred and Eighty three taking into consideration the benefit which had accrued to the Said state by the peacible and secure settlement made by the citizens of the said state on part of said lands which lay within the limits of said state on amount of the purchase aforesaid and also considering the great trouble and expense of the persons so purchasing did by an act which they then passed Grant to the said Richard Henderson, Thomas Hart, John Williams William Johnston James Hogg, David Hart, Leonard Henly Bullock the Heirs and assigns or Devisees of the said Nathaniel Hart deceased and to the heirs and assigns or devisees of John Lutteral deceased and to Landon Carter heir of John Carter deceased and to the heirs and devisees of Robert Lucas deceased two hundred thousand acres (being part of the land purchased of the Indians as aforesaid) to be laid out in one survey and bounded as follows to wit Beginning at the old Indian Town in Powels Valley and Running down Powels River not less than four miles in width on one or both sides to the Junction of Powels and Clinch Rivers then down Clinch River on one or both sides not less than twelve miles in width for the aforesaid Complement of two hundred thousand acres, the said two hundred thousand acres to be divided amongst the Grantees last aforesaid in the following manner that is to say to the said Landon Carter and to the heirs and devisees of Robert Lucas ten thousand acres at the lower end thereof and of the remainder one eighth part to the said Richard Henderson one eighth to the said Thomas Hart one eighth to the said John Williams one eighth

to the said William Johnston one eighth to the said James Hogg one sixteenth part to the said Leonard Henly Bullock one sixteenth part to the
said David Hart one eighth part to the heirs assigns or devisees of the said
Nathaniel Hart deceased and one eighth part to the Heirs assigns or devisees of the said John Lutterel deceased to hold to them their heirs and
assigns or devisees respectively forever according to the aforesaid proportions in Severalty as tenants in Common and not as joint tenants. And
that the said Richard Henderson William Johnston Nathaniel Hart and
John Lutterel—in their life time to wit on or about the 20th day of august
in the year one thousand seven hundred and seventy nine together with
the Complainants John Williams James Hogg Thomas Hart Leonard
Henly Bullock and David Hart by a certain Deed of Covenant sealed with
their seals and subscribed with their names respectively intending to
make provision for a due and speedy partition of the lands purchased by
them of the Indians as aforesaid did contract bargain and agree among
themselves and did by the same writing bind themselves their heirs Executors administrators and assigns respectively either to other that in case
of the death of either of them the said parties in the said purchase before a
division of the Same lands should be made that then the surviving of them
should have full power and authority to make partition of the same lands
purchased of the Indians as aforesaid in the shares and proportions aforesaid and that the heirs or devisees of each deceased partner in Case such
heir or devisee should be an Infant should be bound to stand to and abide
by such partition or division as much as if such heir or devisee were of full
age and personally present and assenting to such division which Deed of
Covenant Complainants are ready to produce when required and further
that the [said] Richard Henderson departed this life in or about the year
1785 having first made his last will and testament in writing wherein hath
devised his part of land Granted by the General assembly aforesaid to be
sold for payment of his Debts and left Richard Henderson Archibald
Henderson and John Henderson his heirs. and further that Nathaniel
Hart aforesaid departed this life on about the month of July in the year
one thousand seven hundred and Eighty two having first made his last
will and Testament writing wherein he hath devised his Share of Said
lands so granted by the General Assembly as aforesaid to Nathaniel Hart
and also that the said John Lutteral departed this Life in or about the year
one thousand seven hundred and Eighty one having first made his last
will and Testament in Writing wherein he hath devised such part of the
said lands granted by the General Assembly as aforesaid as belonged
to him to be divided equally between his wife Susannah Lutterel now
Umstead and his brothers Hugh and William in fee. And likewise that the
said William Johnston departed this life on about the Month of May in
the year one thousand seven hundred and Eighty five having first made his

last will and Testament in writing wherein he hath devised his part of the lands so Granted by the General Assembly as aforesaid to his daughter Amelia Johnston now Amelia Alves in fee. and that John Umstead and Susannah Umstead intermarried with each other in the month   [1] year   [1] And that Amelia Johnston daughter and devisee of the said William Johnston intermarried with Walter Alves on or about the month of May in the year one thousand Seven hundred and Eighty seven and that the said Walter Alves is yet under the age of twenty one years that is to say of the age of Twenty years or thereabouts   And that the children and devisees of Nathaniel Hart or some of them are infants under the age of Twenty one years that is to say Nathaniel who is of the age of Eighteen years John who is of the age of fifteen years and Cumberland who is of the age of Eleven years and that the children and devisees of the said Richard Henderson or some of them are infants under the age of Twenty one years that is to say Archibald of the age of twenty years Leonard of the age of Sixteen years and John of the age of ten years and it is further stated that the said Complainants are desirous to have the said two hundred thousand acres divided to their respective rights agreable to the act of assembly aforesaid but by reason that the several Infants aforesaid are interested in the same lands and entitled to partition thereof and that the said Brothers of the said John Lutterel deceased and the said Landon Carter reside out of this State that is to say Landon Carter in Washington County in the state of Virginia and the said Hugh Lutterel and William Lutterel brothers of the said John Lutterel in   [1] County in the state of Georgia and are negligent or unwilling to make partition and that the heirs or devisees of Robert Lucas are also unknown to your orators. Whereby the complainants cannot but by the aid of this Honorable Court secure a division of the same Lands to be made—and further that the said John Lutterel in his life time co[n]veyed to several persons a part or parts of his share or eighth in the lands purchased of the Indians as aforesaid but to whom or what parts of his eighth the Complainants do not know and the Complainants believe that sales and Conveyances have been made in like manner by others of the said parties in the purchase from the Indians as aforesaid by reason whereof divers persons to Complainants unknown may have some legal or equitable interest in the lands Granted by the General Assembly as aforesaid. In Consideration whereof the said Complainants pray your Honors to appoint Guardians for the said Infants to answer for and take care of the rights of the said Infants respectively in the premises[2] and to Grant writs of Subpoena directed to the Guardians and also writs of Subpoena to be directed to the said Landon Carter and the said Hugh and William Lutterel brothers and devisees of the said John Lutterel and to the several persons when discovered who may have purchased from the said Partners or any of them and the Complainants pray that the division and partition of the said two hundred thousand acres— granted by the Assembly as aforesaid in such shares as therein mentioned agreeable to their respective rights may be made after such manner as to your Honors may seem best and that after such partition shall be made your Honors will be pleased to make such decree therein as may be necessary and proper. And afterwards the said Defendants having failed to plead answer or Demur to the said Bill it was taken pro confesso and appointed to be heard exparte. And afterwards to wit at March Term one thousand Eight hundred the said cause coming on to be heard it was ordered adjudged and honored that a division and partition of the said lands should be made in Conformity with a Deed of partition executed by John Williams James Hogg, Thomas Hart Richard Bullock, Walter Alves, Joseph Hart John Umstead Nathaniel Hart & Leonard Henderson original proprieters. And now to wit at September Term one thousand eight hundred and two the said Cause Coming on to be finally heard before the Honorable the Court of Equity it is ordered adjudged and decreed that a division and partition be made and that there be allotted to John Umstead and Susannah his wife Hugh Lutterel and William Lutterel Devisees of John Lutterel Deceased to be held in severelty the land in the letter marked Letter number 1 lott letter N. Number 2. as designated in a plott of the said lands lying in Powels Valley which plott is annexed to the said Partition Deed And that there be allotted to Thomas Hart to be held in severalty lott Number one and letter B lott Number 2 and letter M. as designated the said plott of said land in Powels Valley. And that there be allotted Richard Henderson Archibald Henderson and John Henderson Devisees Richard Henderson Deceased to be held in severalty lott Number one and J. lott Number 2 and letter C. as designated in the said plott of said [land] in Powels Valley. And that there be allotted to Walter Alves and Amelia his wife Devisee of William Johnston deceased to be held in severalty lotts number one and Letter L. Number 2 and letter D. as designated in said plott of said land in powels Valley—and that there be allotted to Nathaniel Hart deceased to be held on Severalty lott Number one and letter E. Number 2. and letter F. as designated in the said plot of said land in Powels Valley. And that there be allotted to Joseph Hart one of the [heirs] of David Hart Deceased and to the other heirs of David Hart deceased to be held in severalty the North Eastern Moiety of lott Number one and letter G. Number 2. and letter Q. as designated in the said plott of Said land in Powels Valley—and that there be allotted to Richard Bullock heir and Devisee of Leonard Henly Bullock Deceased to be held in Severalty the South Western moiety of said two last mentioned lott said two lotts mentioned hitherto be each divided by a line running paralel to the line of the north Eastern End of the Grant from the State of North Carolina to Richard Henderson & Company to wit North forty west. And that there be allotted to James Hogg to be held in severalty lotts Number one and letter H. Number 2. and letter P. as designated in Said plott of said land in Powels Valley. And that there be allotted to John Williams his heirs or devisees to be held in severalty lotts number one and letter O. number 2. and letter K. as originated on the said plott of Said land each of the lotts heretofore described and allotted as aforesaid containing Six thousand five hundred acres. Of that part of Company's lands lying on Clinch River that there be allotted to James Hogg to be held by him in severalty lotts Number one and letter A Number 2. and letter C. as designated in the plott of survey of said land annexed to said partition Deed. That there be allotted to John Williams his heirs or devisees to be held in severalty lotts Number one and letter C. Number 2. and letter B. as designated in said plott. That there be allotted to Nathaniel Hart heir of Nathaniel Hart Deceased to be held in severalty lotts number one and letter H. number 2, and letter D. as designated in said plott That there be allotted hereby is allotted to Richard Henderson Archibald Henderson and John Henderson heirs and devisees of Richard Henderson Deceased to be held in Severalty lotts number one and letter E. number 2 and letter H. as designated in said plott. That there be also hereby allotted to Joseph Hart and other heirs of David Hart the North Eastern Moiety of lotts number one and letter F. number 2. and letter G. to be held in severalty and to Richard Bullock heir of Leonard Henly Bullock to be held in severalty the south western moiety of the said two last mentioned lotts to be divided each in two equal parts by lines running parallal with the line of the north eastern and of the said grant to Henderson & company. That there be and so hereby is allotted to John and Susannah Umstead William Lutterel and Hugh Lutterel Devisees of John Lutterel Deceased to be held in Severalty lotts Number one and letter D. Number 2 and letter A. as designated in said plott. That there be and hereby is allotted to Walter Alves and Amelia his wife daughter and devisee of William Johnston Deceased to be held in Severalty lotts Number one and letter B. number 2. and letter E. as designated in said plott. That there be and hereby is allotted to Thomas Hart to be held in severalty lotts Number one and Letter G. number 2. and letter F. as designated in said plott Each of the lotts herein described lying on Clinch river containing five thousand three hundred and seventy five acres. And that there be allotted to the heirs and assigns or devisees of Landon Carter Deceased and to the heirs and assigns or Devisees of Robert Lucas Deceased to be held in Severalty Ten thousand acres off the lower end of said Survey or tract of two hundred thousand acres.

Given under our hands this seventeenth day of September in the year of our Lord one thousand eight hundred and two in open Court.

David Campbell
Andrew Jackson

Test
John Carter C.&.M.E }

Tr, TWashCo-WDSC Eq. Rec. Bk., 1791–1803, pp. 382–387. Judges' attendance taken from WDSC Eq. Min. Bk., 1791–1804, p. 287.

The court's decree contains a substantially verbatim recitation of the text of the petition, transcripts of which occur in WDSC Eq. Rec. Bk., 1791–1803, pp. 377–382, and in Kentucky Papers, 1CC, 227–233, Draper Coll., WHi, the latter of which is incomplete, in an unidentified hand, and endorsed: "Bill in Equity Henderson & Co. vs Henderson & Co. Copy."

1. Thus in Tr.

2. An infant could defend a lawsuit only by a guardian. If an infant was sued and had no guardian, the court in which the suit was pending would appoint a guardian ad litem whose sole function was to represent the minor. Courts exercised incidental power to name guardians ad litem. Caruthers, *History of a Law Suit,* 124; James Kent, *Commentaries on American Law* (New York, 1827–1828), II, 187.

51. Mitchell v. Claywell

1802
(Enforcement of Judgments)

EDITORIAL NOTE

Richard Mitchell in March 1800 filed a petition in the Hamilton District Superior Court of Equity to enjoin the enforcement of a judgment that Jesse Claywell had obtained against him on the law side of the court in 1798. Mitchell alleged that, at some time prior to 1794, Claywell had become indebted to him for $145. Mitchell claimed that Claywell subsequently had informed him that it would be impossible to repay the debt, but that he had agreed to turn over a horse to him as security for the repayment of the obligation. Mitchell asserted that he had agreed to take the horse and, upon Claywell's discharge of the debt, either to return the horse or to pay Claywell $200 and keep the animal. Claywell, according to Mitchell, recovered the horse in Mero District from Mitchell's brother, who had borrowed it for a trip to the district in 1794, in exchange for a promissory note renewing Claywell's existing obligation. Mitchell subsequently brought an action in his brother's name against Claywell to recover on the note. Claywell, denying that he had retrieved the horse, brought an action in July 1795 against Mitchell in the Hamilton District Superior Court of Law to recover the $200 that Mitchell had agreed to pay for the horse upon satisfaction of the original debt. The final disposition of Mitchell's action to recover his debt from Claywell is unknown, but Claywell was awarded a judgment at law in his suit against Mitchell.[1] By the time that Mitchell filed his petition in the present action, Claywell had secured an execution for the public sale of a portion of Mitchell's property to satisfy his judgment. Mitchell in the present case sought to enjoin the enforcement of the execution on Claywell's judgment (Document I).

Mitchell and his counsel, Hugh Lawson White, delivered the petition to Jackson on March 31, 1800. Jackson issued an injunction to stay fur-

---

1. Claywell v. Mitchell, HDSC Law Min. Bk. 3, p. 136; HDSC Law Rec. Bk., 1793–1798, pp. 290–291 (1798).

ther enforcement of Claywell's judgment until a hearing could be had on the petition and subpoenaed Claywell to enter an answer in the proceeding (Document I).

At September Term 1800, the court ordered that, because Claywell evidently was no longer a resident of the state, notice of the pending action be published for the defendant's benefit in the *Knoxville Gazette* (Document II). When Claywell had not filed an answer to the petition by April 1801, the court ordered that "the Bill of the Complainant be taken as confessed by the Defendant Jesse Claywell, and set for Trial next Term, Exparte."[2] At a final hearing on Mitchell's petition in October 1802, the court ordered that the complainant's bill be taken pro confesso and issued an injunction against further enforcement of Claywell's judgment (Document III).[3]

2. HDSC Eq. Min. Bk. 1, 1793–1808, p. 80. This procedure was prescribed by ch. 11, §3, 1782 Laws of N.C., reprinted in Iredell, *Laws of North Carolina* 32, 1 Scott, *Laws of Tennessee* 261. The purpose for delaying the hearing on the complainant's bill was to allow the defendant the first three days of the ensuing term in which to appear and offer a satisfactory reason for his absence at the previous term. *Id.* Upon demonstrating such a satisfactory reason, the defendant was entitled to have the court's pro confesso order rescinded and to be allowed to enter pleadings. *Id.*

3. For additional identification of Mitchell, see *Mitchell v. Berry,* No. 19. Claywell has not been further identified.

I. PETITION OF
RICHARD MITCHELL
Hamilton District Superior Court, Knoxville

March 31, 1800

To the Honorabl the Judges of the Superior Courts of law and Equity in and for the state of Tennessee now Sitting in Equity for the District of Hamilton in the state aforesaid.

Humbly complaining Shew Unto your Honors, your Orator Richard Mitchell of the county of Hawkins in said state That a Number of years Since your Orator being in the State of North Carolina met with a Certain Jessee Claywell late of the County of Knox in the state first aforesaid when and where the said Jesse became indebted to your Orator in about the sum of one hundred and forty five Dollars which he did then nor at any time Since pay. That some time afterwards the said Jesse Came to Knoxville in the state of Tennessee and within the District aforesaid where your Orator being in conversation with the said Jesse was informed by him that it was out of his power to pay the said Sum of money which he was indebted to your Orator but that he had a Sorrel mare a running Nag which he would put into the possession of your Orator as a Security for the said Debt and that you Could and should Keep the said mare until the said Jesse should discharge the said debt at which time your Orator must return the said mare to the said Jesse or pay him in place of the mare two hundred Dollars—that is fifty five Dollars more than the Debt which the Said Jesse owed your Orator—your Orator being willing to secure the payment of said Debt agreed to take the mare aforesaid on the terms proposed and did accordingly take her and agreed with the said Jesse to give him his Obligation with Joseph Greer Security that he would Comply with the said agreement and your Orator having prepared such an Obligation ready for Signature the said Jesse being present said he would have Obligation nor Security that he was willing to take your Orator's word and tore up the Obligation upon this your Orator took the said mare and went to his residence in Hawkins County and after having kept the mare some time and finding the mare was an expence to him and discerning no prospect of soon receiving his pay Came down to Knoxville with a view of seeing the said Jesse receiving his pay and returning the mare But upon arrival was informed the said Jesse was out on Bull Run some distance from Knoxville your Orator then disappointed returned home some time after this the said Jesse Come to the house of your Orator and wanted the mare but being still unable to discharge the Debt due to your Orator and also unable in any other way to secure the payment thereof at a future day your Orator refused then to give up the mare. Sometime after this as well as your Orator recollects in the year one thousand seven hundred and ninety four the said mare having been then in your Orator's possession about Six months the Brother of your Orator Thomas Mitchell being about to set out for Mero District your Orator lent to him the said mare to ride to the said District at the same time informed the said Thomas of the manner in which your Orator had become possessed of said mare— your Orator further sheweth That the Said Thomas Set out with the said mare and as he informed your Orator rode her to mero District and some time after his arrival in mero District as your Orator has been also informed he there met with the said Jesse who at that time also wanted the said mare telling the said Thomas if he could get the said mare it was in his power to make something by racing on her but the said Jesse at the same time informed the said Thomas he was not in fund sufficient to discharge the Debt due to your Orator as aforesaid and thereby redeem the said mare but that he would give his Note or Obligation for the said Sum of money due to your Orator and at the same time get some person that would be his security for the payment of the said Sum of money and the said Thomas as he informed your Orator believing it would be as much to your Orators advantage to have the said obligation with security for the said debt as to hold the mare in security therefore did agree that on receiving the said Obligation given by the said Jesse and another person as his security for the payment of the said Sum of money he would accomodate the said Jesse and give up the said mare and immediately the said Jesse with some other person (whose name your Orator does not now recollect as his security made and executed to the said Thomas an Instrument of writing binding them selves to pay to him the sum of one hundred and fifty Dollars or redeliver the said mare; and your Orator further sheweth that the reason why the sum Expressed in the said Instrument of writing was one hundred and fifty Dollars; was because neither the said Jesse nor the said Thomas Could accurately recollect the sum due to your Orator and therefore the said Jesse would have that Sum inserted saying if it was more than the sum due your Orator he knew would have the mistake in the sum corrected as soon as the said Jesse could see him. your Orator further sheweth that as he is informed and surly believes the said Thomas on receiving the said Obligation did deliver the said mare to the said Jesse. And your Orator doth charge that the said Jesse never afterwards did deliver the said mare to your Orator but kept and appropriated her to his own Use. And Some time after wards your Orator discovering no prospect of receiving his pay from the said Jesse commenced Suit in the name of Thomas Mitchell on the Obligation aforesaid against the said Jesse and his security aforesaid But now so it is may it please your Honors that the said Jesse Combining and Confederating with divers others persons who are at present unknown to your Orator) but whose names when discovered your Orator prays may be herein inserted and they made parties hereto with apt words to charge them to injure and Oppress your Orator pretending that the said mare had been Sold by the said Jesse to your Orator and that your Orator was to pay, for her two hundred Dollars or return her to the said Jesse and also pretending that the said Jesse had never received the said mare from your Orator or any other person on your Orators behalf did cause a suit to be instituted in the Superior Court of Law for the District of Hamilton aforesaid and under the pretent aforesaid at a time when your Orator had no Oppertunity of procuring his testimony recovered a Judgment against your Orator for the sum of two hundred Dollars and Costs of suit; and farther intending to injure and oppress your Orator did cause an Execution to be issued on the said Judgment against the goods and chattles lands and tenements of your Orator which Execution has been levied on the property of your Orator to satisfy the said Judgment and Cost amounting to the sum of two hundred and fifty four Dollars and Sixty Six cents or there about and the property of your Orator is now liable to be sold to satisfy the said Judgment and Costs: All which actings and doings are contrary to Equity and good

Conscience and tend to the manifest injury of your Orator: In tender consideration whereof and forasmuch as your Orator is without remedy by the strict rules of the common law and can only be relieved in your Honorable Court of Equity where matters of this nature are not only cognizable but achievable against; To the End therefore that the said Jesse Claywell and his Confederates when discovered may full true direct and perfect Answer make to all and Singular the matters and things here in before Set forth and contained and that in as full positive a manner as if the same were herein again repeated interogated and more particularly, Did the said Jesse at the place herein befor stated or at any other and what other place become indebted to your Orator in the sum of one hundred and forty five Dollars, or any other and what other sums? Did the said Jesse to secure the payment of the same put in possesson of your Orator a certain Sorrel mare on the conditions before set forth or any other and what other Conditions; did your Orator offer Bond and Security to comply withe the said conditions as before set forth? Did the said Jesse refuse said Bond? what did he say on such refusal? Did your Orator take the said mare home with him as before set forth? Did your Orator return to Knoxville as before stated and for the purpose aforesaid? Did the said Jesse afterwards Come to your Orator for the said mare as set forth in the bill? Did your Orator refuse to give her up and what reason did he assign for such refusal? Did your Orator lend the said mare to Thomas Mitchell to ride to mero District as in this Bill set forth? in what year was it? Did the said Thomas ride the said mare to mero District? Did the said Thomas see the said Jesse in mero District Did the said Jesse want the said mare as in this bill set forth? Did the said Thomas deliver up the said mare on account of your Orator to the said Jesse? On what time did he deliver her up? Did the said Jesse and any other person and if any other whats it his mare enter on Instrument of writing to Thomas Mitchell as before set forth? What did the said Thomas receive for delivering up the said mare? Did the said Jesse afterwards redeliver the said mare to your Orator? what become of the said mare? was a suit instituted on the Instrument of writing given to Thomas Mitchel as herein before set forth? Did the said Jesse institute or Cause to be instituted and prosecuted to Judgment a suit against your Orator under the pretences herein before set forth or any other and what other pretences? Did he recover a Judgment against your Orator? On what claim was the suit brought and Judgment recovered against your Orator? In what Court was the said Suit instituted and the Judgment recovered? What is the amount of the said Judgment and Costs? Did an Execution issue on said judgment? was the Execution levied as in the bill set forth? Your Orator prays the premises considered that your Honors may grant not only a writ of Injunction to Stay all further pro-

ceedings on the said Judgment and Execution against him until the min-
uts of this his bill be heard in your Honorable Court: but also a Writ of
subpoena requiring and Commanding the said Jesse on a certain day and
under a certain pain to be and appear before your Honors in your Honorable Court of Equity for the District of Hamilton and then and there on
his Corporal Oath to answer all and singular the matters and things
herein before Contained your Orator further prays that on the hearing of
this his Bill your Honors may decree that the Judgment obtained by the
said Jesse and the costs of the said suit may be perpetually injoined and
also that your Honors may decree to him all and every such other and
further relief as the nature of his Case may require and to your Honors
shall seem consistant with Equity and good Conscience and he as in duty
bound shall ever pray &c

White
Council for Complainant

State of Tennessee Sst.
This day Richard Mitchel the Complainant Appeared before me Andrew
Jackson Esquire One of the Judges of the Superior Courts of Law and
Equity in and for the state aforesaid and made Oath in due form that the
facts stated in the within Bill as of his own knowledge are true and those
that are not Stated as of his own knowledge he believes to be true.

Richard Mitchell

Sworn and Subscribed this 31st ⎫
day of March 1800 before me   ⎭
   Andrew Jackson

March 31st 1800

To the Clerk and Master in Equity for the District of Hamilton in the state
of Tennessee
   Let Writs of Injunction and Subpoena Issue agreeable to the prayer of
the Bill.

Andrew Jackson

Tr, TKL-HDSC Eq. Rec. Bk. B, 1797–1804, pp. 235–238.

II. PUBLISHED NOTICE TO
JESSE CLAYWELL

[January 7, 1801]

STATE OF TENNESSEE,
   Hamilton District
In Equity, September term, 1800,
Richard Mitchell, comp't.
   Against,   Bill to enjoin
Jesse Claywell, defendant.

FORASMU[C]H as it hath been made appear to the honorable the judges of the court of Equity, for the district aforesaid, that Jesse Claywell, the defendant, in the above named suit, is not an inhabitant of this state, therefore cannot be met with to be sued with process issuing out of this court. It was therefore ordered, that the said Jesse Claywell file his answer to the complainant's bill of complaint, against next March term of this court, or the bill will be taken *pro confeso* against him, and that this be published in the Knoxville Gazette, once.

                 JOSEPH GREER, C M. E.

Printed copy, *Knoxville Gazette,* Jan. 7, 1801.

III. THE FINAL DECREE
OF THE COURT

Hamilton District Superior Court, Knoxville
Judges Jackson, White, and Campbell Presiding

[October 8, 1802]

Richard Mitchell Complainant
     against   Injunction Bill
Jesse Claywell   Respondant

Exparte—This cause came on to be heard at this Term and the following Decree was made up and signed by   [1]

Richard Mitchell
     vs   In Equity Hamilton District
Jesse Claywell

Be it remembered that heretofore, to wit, at march Term one thousand eight Hundred Richard Mitchell filed his Bill of complaint against Jesse

Claywell in the Court of Equity for Hamilton District in the State of Tennessee and therein complained in substance as follows[2]. . . . And afterwards at September Term of said Court one thousand eight Hundred it appearing to the satisfaction of said Court, that the said Defendant was an Inhabitant of the state of Tennessee the said Court ordered the said defendant should file his answer to said Bill again March Term of said Court one thousand eight hundred and one otherwise the said Bill should be taken pro Confesso, and the copy of said order should be published once in the Knoxville Gazette And afterwards to wit at March Term 1801 of said Court appearing to said Court that said Defendant had not filed answer to said Bill; and that due publication of said order had been made, on motion of said Complainant by his Council was ordered by said Court that said Bill should be taken pro confesso. And now to wit at September Term 1802 said cause coming on to be heard exparte before the Honorable David Campbell and Andrew Jackson Esquires two of the Judges &c. and the Matters and things therein being fully understood and considered It is ordered adjudged and decreed that the said Judgment and costs recovered by the said Defendant against the said Complainant be and hereby are perpetually injoined; and the said Judges do hereby order adjudge and decree that the said Jesse Claywell his agents Attories and all others be and hereby are perpetually injoined from proceeding to inforce the payment of said Judgment and Costs or either of them. and it is further ordered and decreed by said court that Jesse the Defendant do pay the Costs of this suit.

Given under our hands in open Court at Knoxville in the state of Tennessee this eighth day of October one thousand eight Hundred and two.

Test
Joseph Greer   Clerk

David Campbell
Andrew Jackson

Tr, TKL-HDSC Eq. Min. Bk. 1, 1793–1808, pp. 129–132; HDSC Eq. Rec. Bk. B, 1797–1804, pp. 238–240. Date and judges' attendance are taken from HDSC Eq. Min. Bk. 1, 1793–1808, p. 126. The absence of White's signature from the decree is due, no doubt, to his representation of Mitchell when the latter's petition was presented to Jackson on Mar. 31, 1800 (see Document I).

1. Thus in Tr.
2. The court's decree contains a substantially verbatim recitation of the text of Document I at this point in the Tr.

PART III

A Chronology of Jackson's Legal Career

THIS CHRONOLOGY COVERS the period of Jackson's practice in the county and superior courts and his tenure upon the bench. Each term of the county and superior courts at which Jackson is known to have been active is listed. For the practice period, the number of Jackson's pretrial appearances is provided, and those of his cases that went to trial or were otherwise disposed of are listed, along with a parenthetical indication of the nature and final disposition of each case. For the judicial period, the number of trials or nontrial final dispositions of cases is provided for each term, and only those cases that are printed in this volume are listed. Because the sources are fragmentary, the information provided is necessarily incomplete and varies in its accuracy from term to term.

For Jackson's practice period, the style of each action that Jackson tried is listed under the term at which it was argued or tried, with his client's name printed in italics and the result indicated. The cases printed in this volume are listed in capital letters under the courts to which each document printed in those cases has been attributed, again with Jackson's clients' names italicized.

The following abbreviations represent Jackson's co-counsel:

HL	Hopkins Lacy
JL	Josiah Love
JCM	James Cole Mountflorence
JO	John Overton
HT	Howell Tatum

Primary sources for the Chronology include the minute and record books and dockets for the various courts and, for events of general importance in Jackson's legal career, *Jackson Papers,* I.

1784 ca. December
Begins reading law in the office of Spruce Macay, Salisbury, N.C.

1787 ca. March
Begins reading law in the office of John Stokes, Montgomery
   Co., N.C.

September
Licensed to practice in the North Carolina county courts (Sept.
   26).

November
ROWAN COUNTY COURT OF PLEAS AND QUARTER SESSIONS
   Admitted to practice (Nov. 6).
SURRY COUNTY COURT OF PLEAS AND QUARTER SESSIONS
   Admitted to practice (Nov. 13).
GUILFORD COUNTY COURT OF PLEAS AND QUARTER SESSIONS
   Admitted to practice (Nov. 20).
ROCKINGHAM COUNTY COURT OF PLEAS AND QUARTER
SESSIONS
   Admitted to practice (Nov. 26).

December
RANDOLPH COUNTY COURT OF PLEAS AND QUARTER SESSIONS
   Admitted to practice (Dec. 11).

1788 February
ROCKINGHAM COUNTY COURT OF PLEAS AND QUARTER
SESSIONS
   O'Neal v. *Terrant* (case; confession of judgment).

March
RANDOLPH COUNTY COURT OF PLEAS AND QUARTER SESSIONS
   Appointed county solicitor; files 5 indictments (3 true bills
      returned).
   State v. Davenport (unknown; AJ moves for issuance of scire
      facias; further disposition unknown).
   State v. Pearce (profane swearing; guilty verdict).
   Tatum v. Tate (on AJ's motion, court orders "that Adam Tate,
      Esquire, Coroner of Rockingham County, be fined 50 Lb.
      Nisi for failing to return a writ of Fiere Facias against John
      May").

1788 (continued)

May
WASHINGTON COUNTY COURT OF PLEAS AND QUARTER
SESSIONS
Admitted to practice (May 12).

August
Issues challenge to Waightstill Avery (Aug. 12).
GREENE COUNTY COURT OF PLEAS AND QUARTER SESSIONS
Admitted to practice (Aug. 5).
WASHINGTON COUNTY COURT OF PLEAS AND QUARTER
SESSIONS
Carney v. Mitchell (case; further disposition unknown).[1]

November
Licensed to practice in Superior Court (Nov. 3).
MERO DISTRICT SUPERIOR COURT
Admitted to practice; appointed state's attorney (Nov. 3);
files 4 indictments.
Routh v. Rains (case/appeal; jury for Routh).
STATE v. DOLLISON, No. 1 (robbery; not-guilty verdict).

1789 January
DAVIDSON COUNTY COURT OF PLEAS AND QUARTER SESSIONS
Admitted to practice (Jan. 5); makes pretrial appearances in
at least 8 cases.
Bosley v. Cripp's Heirs (attachment; final default judgment).
Bosley v. *Lewis* (case; jury for Lewis; appeal granted).
Donaldson v. Boyles (case; jury assessment of damages on
prior default judgment).
Foster v. *Thomas* (case; jury for Foster; appeal granted; fur-
ther disposition unknown).
Robertson's Executors v. Brock (case; jury for Robertson's
Executors; appeal granted but forfeited for failure of Brock
to post appeal bond).
Tait v. Fulton (case; final default judgment).
Tait v. Riston (attachment; final default judgment).
SUMNER COUNTY COURT OF PLEAS AND QUARTER SESSIONS
Admitted to practice (Jan. 12).

1. The only evidence of AJ's having served as counsel of record for Carney is the endorsement of the writ issued in the case on Aug. 19, 1788: "Jacks & All. Atto." Writ, Aug.
19, 1788, Paul Fink, PVT.

1789 January (continued)
> *Bowman* v. Sutton (appeal; jury for Bowman).
> McKain v. *Douglass* (appeal; jury for Douglass).
> Peyton v. *Martin* (slander; nonsuit).

April
DAVIDSON COUNTY COURT OF PLEAS AND QUARTER SESSIONS
> Makes pretrial appearances in at least 9 cases.
> *Cartwright* v. Brock (attachment; final default judgment).
> *Creton* v. Cribbens (case; jury assessment of damages on
> prior default judgment).
> Freeland v. *Robertson* (caveat; jury for Robertson).
> *Glaves* v. Chambers (attachment; final default judgment).
> *Hood* v. Montgomery (case; jury assessment of damages on
> prior default judgment).
> *McFarlin* v. Brock (case; jury for McFarlin; appeal granted;
> further disposition unknown).
> *Robertson* v. Clark (attachment; final default judgment).
> *Rowan* v. Lenier (case; jury for Rowan).
> *Strong* v. Hays (case; jury assessment of damages on prior
> default judgment).
SUMNER COUNTY COURT OF PLEAS AND QUARTER SESSIONS
> Makes pretrial appearance in at least 1 case.
> Hayes v. *Hamilton* (case; dismissed).
> Payton v. *Martin* (AJ and JO) (slander; jury for Payton; ap-
> peal granted Payton).

May
MERO DISTRICT SUPERIOR COURT
> Appointed state's attorney (May 4); files 1 indictment for
> which no true bill returned.
> *State* v. Casselman (trespass; guilty verdict).
> *State* v. Casselman (trespass, assault and battery; guilty plea).
> STATE v. HENDRIX ET AL., No. 2 (horse stealing; not-
> guilty verdict as to Hendrix).
> *State* v. Loggans (perjury; not-guilty verdict).
> *State* v. Rains (trespass, assault and battery; guilty verdict).

July
DAVIDSON COUNTY COURT OF PLEAS AND QUARTER SESSIONS
> Makes pretrial appearances in at least 19 cases.
> *Archer* v. Skinner (appeal; jury for Archer).

1789 **July** (continued)

> BARTON AND SHAW v. *ROBERTSON*, No. 3 (case; jury for plaintiffs; appeal granted; further disposition unknown).
>
> *Bentley* v. Dodge (attachment; discontinued).
>
> Bosley v. *Forde* (case; jury assessment of damages on prior default judgment).
>
> *Bosley* (AJ and JL) v. Lenear (case; jury for Bosley).
>
> *Condry* (AJ and JL) v. Chambers (attachment; jury assessment of damages on prior default judgment).
>
> Crutcher v. *Bosley* (case; jury for Crutcher).
>
> Demonbreun v. *Smith* (case; jury for Demonbreun).
>
> *Edgar* v. Grant (case; confession of judgment).
>
> *Edgar* (AJ and JL) v. Hay (case; confession of judgment).
>
> *Erwine* (AJ and JL) v. Lenear (case; confession of judgment).
>
> Fago v. *Moore* (scire facias; jury for Fago).
>
> *Hays* v. Sugg (case; confession of judgment).
>
> *Martin* v. Brock (case; jury for Martin).
>
> *Martin* v. Martin (appeal; jury for defendant).
>
> *Martin* v. Martin and Loggins (case; confession of judgment by Loggins; further disposition unknown).
>
> *Maxel* v. Bell (debt; jury assessment of damages on prior default judgment).
>
> MELDRUM v. CLARK, No. 4 (case; jury for Meldrum; AJ appeals to Mero District Superior Court).
>
> *Owens* v. Fulton (attachment; jury assessment of damages on prior default judgment).
>
> Rice v. Hay and *Bosley* (debt; jury for Rice).
>
> *Stump* (AJ and JL) v. Murdock (case; jury assessment of damages on prior default judgment).
>
> *Tait* (AJ and JL) v. Hay (case; confession of judgment).
>
> *Wilson* v. Baker (attachment; final default judgment).

SUMNER COUNTY COURT OF PLEAS AND QUARTER SESSIONS

> Makes pretrial appearances in at least 2 cases.
>
> McKain v. *Roberts* (trover; jury for Roberts).
>
> *Murry* v. White (attachment; final default judgment).

October

DAVIDSON COUNTY COURT OF PLEAS AND QUARTER SESSIONS

> Makes pretrial appearances in at least 7 cases.
>
> *Bosley* v. Crutcher (debt; jury for Bosley).
>
> *Bosley* v. Crutcher (debt; jury for Bosley).

1789   **October** (continued)

Crow v. *Lancaster* (appeal; jury for Crow).

Crutcher v. *Bosley* (case; judgment for Crutcher; appeal granted).

Crutcher v. *Bosley* (covenant; jury for Bosley).

Edgar v. Forde (debt; jury for Edgar).

Green (AJ and JL) v. Dodge (attachment; abatement).

HAMPTON v. *BOYD AND FOSTER* (AJ and HT), No. 5 (trespass vi et armis; AJ makes initial appearance for defendants; continued).

Hoggatt v. *Nelson* (case; confession of judgment).

Loggins v. *Coonrod* (attachment; court awards Loggins judgment *respondeat ouster;* appeal granted; further disposition unknown).

Sumner County Court of Pleas and Quarter Sessions

Makes pretrial appearances in at least 4 cases.

State v. Cotton (assault and battery; AJ as "Atto. for the State" prepares indictment; further disposition unknown).[2]

November

Mero District Superior Court

Court does not convene for November Term.

December

Elected attorney general, Mero District, by N.C. General Assembly (Dec. 21).

1790   **January**

Davidson County Court of Pleas and Quarter Sessions

Makes pretrial appearances in at least 6 cases.

Sumner County Court of Pleas and Quarter Sessions

Makes pretrial appearances in at least 2 cases.

McGary v. Cartwright (case; non prosequitur).

Shelby v. *Bushnell* (debt; jury for Shelby).

April

Davidson County Court of Pleas and Quarter Sessions

Makes pretrial appearances in at least 10 cases.

HAMPTON v. *BOYD AND FOSTER* (AJ and HT), No. 5 (jury for Hampton; appeal granted).

2. There is no record of AJ's having been appointed state's attorney for Sumner County. No further records have been found concerning this case.

1790 **April** (continued)

>Harrington v. *Brown* (debt/appeal; jury for Brown)
>*Maxwell* v. Robertson (case; jury assessment of damages on prior default judgment).
>MURFREE v. *LEEPER* (AJ and JO), No. 7 (caveat; jury for Murfree).
>SUMNER COUNTY COURT OF PLEAS AND QUARTER SESSIONS
>*Blackmore* v. Desha (case; jury for Desha).
>*Steel* v. Lynn (case; jury for Steel).

May

>MERO DISTRICT SUPERIOR COURT
>Makes pretrial appearance in at least 1 case.
>Payton v. *Martin* (AJ and JO) (slander; nonsuit).
>*State* v. Gambell (petit larceny?; not-guilty verdict).
>*State* v. Hay (perjury; not-guilty verdict).
>*State* v. Lane (assault and battery; guilty verdict).
>*State* v. O'Neal (forgery; not-guilty verdict).
>*State* v. Thomas (mismarking; guilty verdict; new trial granted).
>*State* v. White (murder; jury returns manslaughter verdict).

July

>DAVIDSON COUNTY COURT OF PLEAS AND QUARTER SESSIONS
>Makes pretrial appearances in at least 9 cases.
>SUMNER COUNTY COURT OF PLEAS AND QUARTER SESSIONS
>Makes pretrial appearance in at least 1 case.

October

>DAVIDSON COUNTY COURT OF PLEAS AND QUARTER SESSIONS
>Makes pretrial appearances in at least 7 cases.
>Crutcher v. *Moore* (case; jury for Crutcher).
>Demonbreun v. *Coonrod* (debt; jury for Demonbreun).
>*Edgar* v. Brock (debt; jury for Edgar).
>Hickman v. *Crutcher* (case; jury for Hickman).
>*Moore* v. Clark (appeal; jury for Moore).
>*Payne* v. McFaddin (case; jury for Payne; appeal granted; further disposition unknown).
>Rice, Sappington & Company v. *Lenear* (case; jury for Rice, Sappington & Company).
>*Tait* v. Marney (case; jury for Tait).
>*Tait* v. Nelson (covenant; jury for Tait).

1790 October (continued)
SUMNER COUNTY COURT OF PLEAS AND QUARTER SESSIONS
Makes pretrial appearances in at least 6 cases.
Butler v. Cotton (appeal; jury for Cotton).
Hampton v. *Shaw* (debt; dismissed).
Hays (AJ and JL) v. Smith (covenant; jury for Hays).

November
MERO DISTRICT SUPERIOR COURT
Court convenes Nov. 1, adjourns Nov. 2; no recorded appearances by AJ.

December
Licensed to practice in the territorial courts (Dec. 15).

1791 January
DAVIDSON COUNTY COURT OF PLEAS AND QUARTER SESSIONS
Presents license (Jan. 10); makes pretrial appearances in at least 8 cases.
SUMNER COUNTY COURT OF PLEAS AND QUARTER SESSIONS
Makes pretrial appearances in at least 8 cases.
Scott v. *Hardin* (AJ and HL) (case; jury for Hardin).

February
Appointed attorney general, Mero District (Feb. 15).
WASHINGTON DISTRICT SUPERIOR COURT
Secures issuance of writ in *Shelby* v. Greer (Feb. 18) (debt; further disposition unknown).[3]

April
Arbitrates with Robert Weakley claims of Isaac Thomas, William Brown, and James Hamilton (Apr. 18).
DAVIDSON COUNTY COURT OF PLEAS AND QUARTER SESSIONS
Makes pretrial appearances in at least 9 cases.
Boyd v. Forde (debt; jury for Boyd).
Green v. Johnston's Executors (interpleader; jury for Green).
Johnston's Executors v. *Green* (AJ and JO) (attachment; jury assessment of damages on prior default judgment).
Sugg (AJ and JCM) v. Barrow (appeal; jury for Sugg; court grants Barrow's motion in arrest of judgment).

---

3. The only evidence of AJ's representation of Shelby is the endorsement on the verso of the writ: "A Jackson." Writ, Feb. 18, 1791, Paul Fink, PVT.

1791 **April** (continued)

SUMNER COUNTY COURT OF PLEAS AND QUARTER SESSIONS
Makes pretrial appearances in at least 8 cases.
Cartwright (AJ, JO, and JCM) v. Thompson (covenant; jury for Cartwright).
Cotton v. *Turney* (case; dismissed).
Edwards v. Fotwine (appeal; judgment for Fotwine).
Hendricks v. *Sutton* (case; nonsuit).

May

MERO DISTRICT SUPERIOR COURT
Assumes office as attorney general (May 2); makes pretrial appearances in at least 2 cases.
Bosley v. *Lewis* (case; petition for certiorari denied).
MURFREE v. *LEEPER* (AJ and JO), No. 7 (continued to November Term).
Territory v. Aherrin (murder; guilty verdict).
Territory v. Blevins (trespass, assault and battery; guilty verdict).
Territory v. Bushnell (scire facias; court judgment for the Territory).
Territory v. Collins (trespass, assault and battery; guilty verdict).
Territory v. Crabtree (horse stealing; not-guilty verdict).
Territory v. Hampton (trespass, assault and battery; guilty verdict).
Territory v. Hardin (perjury, not-guilty verdict).
Territory v. Hardin (perjury; nolle prosequi).
Territory v. Rains (assault and battery; Rains fined by court and imprisoned).
Territory v. Sugg (trespass, assault and battery; not-guilty verdict).

July

DAVIDSON COUNTY COURT OF PLEAS AND QUARTER SESSIONS
Makes pretrial appearances in at least 7 cases.
Berry v. *Gower* (covenant; jury for Berry).
Demonbreun v. *Clark* (case; jury for Demonbreun).
Erwine v. *Bosley* (debt; jury for Erwine).
Fago v. *Shaw* (case; confession of judgment).
Finn v. *Frazer* (scire facias; jury for Frazer).
GILMORE v. *WILLIAMS*, No. 6 (allegation that Williams is a slave; jury for Williams).

1791 **July** (continued)

> Hadley v. *Shaw* (case; jury for Hadley).
> *Jennings* v. Skerrett (attachment; conditional default judgment).
> *Rogers* v. Forde (case; jury for Rogers).

SUMNER COUNTY COURT OF PLEAS AND QUARTER SESSIONS

> Makes pretrial appearances in at least 6 cases.
> Cartwright v. *Shaw* (AJ and JL) (case; confession of judgment).
> Cotton v. *Mansker* (case; jury for Cotton).
> *Kuykendall* v. Morgan (case; nonsuit).

August

WASHINGTON DISTRICT SUPERIOR COURT

> Chamberlain v. *Hamilton* (ejectment; final disposition unknown).[4]
> Scales v. *Rice* (covenant; final disposition unknown).[5]

October

DAVIDSON COUNTY COURT OF PLEAS AND QUARTER SESSIONS

> Makes pretrial appearances in at least 9 cases.
> Demonbreun v. *Tait* (trover; jury for Demonbreun).
> *Edgar* v. Forde (scire facias; court judgment for Edgar).
> *Jennings* v. Skerrett (attachment; jury assessment of damages on prior default judgment).
> *Payne* v. Hampton (scire facias; defendant's sureties exonerated upon surrender of principal).
> *Starks* v. Johnston (interpleader?; jury for Starks; appeal granted).
> Territory v. *Shearman* (AJ and JO) (petit larceny; not-guilty verdict).

SUMNER COUNTY COURT OF PLEAS AND QUARTER SESSIONS

> Makes pretrial appearances in at least 3 cases.
> Gipson v. *Sheppard* (appeal; dismissed).

---

4. The only evidence of AJ's representation of Hamilton is the MS pleading, in AJ's hand and bearing his signature, that was filed with the court at August Term 1791. Pleading, August 1791, Stanley Horn Coll., TNJ.

5. The only evidence of AJ's representation of Rice is the MS pleading in AJ's hand and bearing his signature that was filed with the court at August Term 1791. Pleading, August 1791, Rocky Mount Historical Ass'n.

1791   **October** (continued)

Mountflorence v. *Kuykendall* (case; nonsuit).

Payton v. *Mansker* (trover; discontinued).

Robinson v. Gipson (appeal; dismissed).

Spencer v. *Kuykendall* (case; dismissed).

November

MERO DISTRICT SUPERIOR COURT

Makes pretrial appearance in at least 1 case.

Bosley v. Crutcher (debt; jury for Bosley).

Boyd v. Shaw (unknown; confession of judgment).

Frazier v. Wicoff (case; jury for Frazier).

Minor v. *Martin* (AJ and JO) (trover; witnesses fail to appear; further disposition unknown).

MURFREE v. *LEEPER* (AJ and JO), No. 7 (Murfree's motion to quash writ of certiorari denied).

Robertson's Executors v. Lenier (certiorari; judgment for Robertson's Executors).

Territory v. McKain (horse stealing; guilty verdict; new trial granted).

Territory v. Wallace (rape; not-guilty verdict).

1792   **January**

DAVIDSON COUNTY COURT OF PLEAS AND QUARTER SESSIONS

Makes pretrial appearances in at least 11 cases.

John Edgar & Company v. McPherson (attachment; jury assessment of damages on prior default judgment).

Frazer v. Wicoff (case; jury for Frazer; new trial granted).

Gowen v. *Bosley* (debt; jury for Gowen).

Hay (AJ and JL) v. Rains (scire facias; jury for Rains; appeal granted).

Kuykendall v. Johnston (case; jury assessment of damages on prior default judgment).

McNeely v. *Smith* (scire facias; jury for McNeely; AJ files motion in arrest of judgment).

Rice & Company v. *Hay* (debt; jury for Rice & Company).

Sanders v. Coonrod (scire facias; jury for Sanders).

SUMNER COUNTY COURT OF PLEAS AND QUARTER SESSIONS

Makes pretrial appearances in at least 2 cases.

Carter v. Billew (case; jury for Carter).

Payton v. *Love* (case; jury for Payton).

1792   (continued)

April

DAVIDSON COUNTY COURT OF PLEAS AND QUARTER SESSIONS
Makes pretrial appearances in at least 6 cases.
Barnes v. Gunn (debt/appeal; jury for Barnes).
Bosley v. Gunn (covenant; jury for Bosley).
Cotton v. *Loggins* (appeal; jury for Cotton).
Demonbreun v. *Lockett* (scire facias; confession of judgment).
Edgar v. *Bosley* (case; jury for Edgar; appeal granted; further disposition unknown).
Fago v. *Clark* (appeal; jury for Clark).
Frazer v. Wicoff (case; jury for Frazer).
Gibson v. *Cunningham* (case; jury for Gibson; appeal granted; further disposition unknown).
Kitt v. *Hay* (scire facias; jury for Kitt).
Murry v. Crutcher (covenant; jury for Murry).
Quarles & Company v. Sevier (case; jury for Quarles & Company).
Robertson v. *Hay* (case; jury for Robertson).
Tait v. Hay (scire facias to revive former judgment; court judgment for Tait).
SUMNER COUNTY COURT OF PLEAS AND QUARTER SESSIONS
Makes pretrial appearances in at least 2 cases.
Douglass v. Bowman (attachment; jury assessment of damages on prior default judgment).
Shelby v. *Espy* (scire facias; jury for Shelby).

May

MERO DISTRICT SUPERIOR COURT
Makes pretrial appearances in at least 14 cases.
Bosley v. Sugg (case; jury for Bosley).
Nash v. *Armstrong* (AJ and JO) (trespass, assault and battery; jury for Armstrong).
TAIT v. DEADERICK, No. 8 (debt; files answer for Deaderick; jury for Deaderick).
Territory v. Billow (felony; guilty verdict).
Territory v. Bosley (perjury; not-guilty verdict).
Territory v. Pillow (trespass, assault and battery; guilty verdict).

1792   (continued)

July
DAVIDSON COUNTY COURT OF PLEAS AND QUARTER SESSIONS
Makes pretrial appearances in at least 18 cases.
SUMNER COUNTY COURT OF PLEAS AND QUARTER SESSIONS
Makes pretrial appearances in at least 6 cases.
Douglass v. Kuykendall's Administrator (case; dismissed).

September
Appointed judge advocate, Davidson County militia (Sept. 10).

October
DAVIDSON COUNTY COURT OF PLEAS AND QUARTER SESSIONS
Makes pretrial appearances in at least 16 cases.
SUMNER COUNTY COURT OF PLEAS AND QUARTER SESSIONS
Makes pretrial appearances in at least 4 cases.
Hall v. Kuykendall's Administrator (case; dismissed).
Haynes v. *Turney* (case; dismissed).

November
MERO DISTRICT SUPERIOR COURT
Makes pretrial appearances in at least 19 cases.

1793   ### January
DAVIDSON COUNTY COURT OF PLEAS AND QUARTER SESSIONS
Makes pretrial appearances in at least 39 cases.
Quarles & Company v. Baker (debt; final default judgment).
Sugg v. Hague (debt; final default judgment).
Sugg v. Hague (debt; final default judgment).
Sugg v. Hague (debt; final default judgment).
Tait & Company v. Lane (debt; final default judgment).
SUMNER COUNTY COURT OF PLEAS AND QUARTER SESSIONS
Makes pretrial appearances in at least 4 cases.

April
DAVIDSON COUNTY COURT OF PLEAS AND QUARTER SESSIONS
Makes pretrial appearances in at least 19 cases.
Bell v. Hague (appeal; jury for Bell).
Blackamore v. Sugg (case; jury for Blackamore).
Boyd v. *Crutcher* (case; jury for Boyd).
Boyd v. Richards (case; jury for Boyd; appeal granted; further disposition unknown).

1793 **April** (continued)

Boyd v. Rowan (case; jury for Boyd).

Deaderick v. Boyd (case; confession of judgment).

Gower v. Talbot (covenant; jury for Gower).

Lockett v. *Barnes* (covenant; jury for Lockett).

Loggins v. *Grant* (AJ and JO) (case; jury for Loggins).

Lynn v. Gunn (case; jury assessment of damages on prior default judgment).

Nelson v. *Love* (case; jury for Nelson).

Price v. Cox (covenant; jury for Price).

Quarles & Company v. Donelson (debt; jury for Quarles & Company).

Shaffer v. *Montgomery* (case; jury for Shaffer).

Shaw v. Martin (unknown; jury for Shaw).

Stump v. *Lockett* (case; jury for Stump).

Stump v. *Moore* (covenant; jury for Moore; appeal granted).

Sugg v. Crutcher (case; jury assessment of damages on prior default judgment).

Sugg v. Hay (case; confession of judgment).

Sugg v. Lane (case; jury assessment of damages on prior default judgment).

Sugg v. Moore (case; jury assessment of damages on prior default judgment).

Tait & Company v. Armstrong (debt; jury for Tait & Company).

Tait & Company v. Hay (debt; confession of judgment).

Tait & Company v. Hay (debt; confession of judgment).

Tait & Company v. Maclin (debt; jury for Tait & Company).

Tait & Company v. Robertson (debt; jury for Tait & Company).

Talbot v. Mountflorence (debt; jury assessment of damages on prior default judgment; appeal granted).

Thomas v. White (attachment; final default judgment).

Thornberry v. Bosley (covenant; jury for Thornberry).

SUMNER COUNTY COURT OF PLEAS AND QUARTER SESSIONS

Makes pretrial appearances in at least 5 cases.

Carter v. Hardin (scire facias; jury for Hardin; new trial granted).

Gilbreath v. McKain (debt; jury for Gilbreath).

Hendricks v. *Sutton* (case; arbitration award for Hendricks).

Quarles & Company v. McKain (debt; final default judgment).

Spencer v. Hendricks (attachment; final default judgment).

1793   (continued)

May
MERO DISTRICT SUPERIOR COURT
Makes pretrial appearances in at least 15 cases; files 2 indictments for which no true bills returned.

Bell v. Rowan (case; jury assessment of damages on prior default judgment).

HAY v. HICKMAN, No. 9 (case; files declaration for Hay; referred to panel of arbitrators).

Smith v. Fletcher's Administrators (covenant; jury for Smith).

Territory v. Cotton (perjury; not-guilty verdict).

Territory v. Cotton (perjury; not-guilty verdict).

Territory v. Deaderick (scire facias; rescinded).

Territory v. Deloach (scire facias; rescinded).

Territory v. Eagon (perjury; not-guilty verdict).

Territory v. Franklin (scire facias; rescinded).

Territory v. Frazier (scire facias; rescinded).

Territory v. Frazier (scire facias; further disposition unknown).

Territory v. Kuykendall (scire facias; rescinded).

Territory v. McKain (grand larceny; guilty verdict).

Territory v. McKain (horse stealing; guilty verdict).

Territory v. McKain (scire facias; rescinded).

Territory v. Moser (petit larceny; guilty verdict).

Territory v. Payton (scire facias; rescinded).

Territory v. Perry (scire facias; rescinded).

Territory v. Skelly (scire facias; rescinded).

Territory v. Smith (scire facias; jury for Territory).

Territory v. Sugg (counterfeiting; not-guilty verdict).

Tison v. Gilbert (case; jury for Tison).

July
DAVIDSON COUNTY COURT OF PLEAS AND QUARTER SESSIONS
Makes pretrial appearances in at least 24 cases.

Boyd v. Edmondson (case; jury for Edmondson; appeal granted; further disposition unknown).

Bradford v. Clark (debt; confession of judgment).

Bradford v. Clark (debt; confession of judgment).

Demonbreun v. *Rice* (scire facias; jury for Demonbreun).

Hickman v. *Reed* (debt; confession of judgment).

James v. *Bosley* (covenant; jury for James).

McGavock v. *Hickman* (debt; jury for McGavock).

1793   **July** (continued)

> *Sharp* v. McNairy (unknown; AJ tenders himself as surety
> for Sharp, but McNairy already has pleaded an abatement;
> further disposition unknown).
>
> *Sugg* v. Sugg (case; jury for plaintiff Sugg; appeal granted).
>
> *Thornberry* v. Stump (case; jury for Thornberry).

SUMNER COUNTY COURT OF PLEAS AND QUARTER SESSIONS

> Makes pretrial appearances in at least 7 cases.
>
> *Gillaspy* v. McColgin (debt; jury for Gillaspy).
>
> *Hendricks* v. Hays (case; dismissed).
>
> *Kennedy* v. White (case; dismissed).
>
> Lewis v. *Worldly* (case; jury for Worldly; appeal granted).
>
> *Mitchell* v. Kuykendall (case; dismissed).

October

DAVIDSON COUNTY COURT OF PLEAS AND QUARTER SESSIONS

> Makes pretrial appearances in at least 32 cases.
>
> *Barrow* v. Lancaster (covenant; confession of judgment).
>
> *Cartwright* v. Cofield (debt; jury for Cartwright).
>
> Irvin v. *Donelson* (case; jury for Donelson).
>
> McGavock v. *Hamilton* (case; jury for McGavock).
>
> McNAIRY v. EDGAR & TAIT, No. 15 (ejectment; makes
> initial appearance for Tait; continued).
>
> *Quarles & Company* v. Bucchanan (scire facias; jury assess-
> ment of damages on prior default judgment).
>
> *Ross* v. Cannon (attachment; jury assessment of damages on
> prior default judgment; new trial granted Ross).
>
> *Tait & Company* v. Shaw (debt; jury for Tait & Company).
>
> Territory v. *Clark* (petit larceny; not-guilty verdict).
>
> Territory v. *Hutchison* (assault and battery; not-guilty
> verdict).
>
> Wilson v. *Boyd* (case; jury for Wilson).

SUMNER COUNTY COURT OF PLEAS AND QUARTER SESSIONS

> Makes pretrial appearances in at least 12 cases.
>
> Allison v. *Turney* (case; dismissed).
>
> *Carter* v. Hardin (scire facias; jury for Carter).
>
> Desha v. *Parker* (appeal; nonsuit).
>
> *Douglass* v. Payton (case; jury for Douglass).

November

MERO DISTRICT SUPERIOR COURT

> Makes pretrial appearances in at least 19 cases.
>
> *Crutcher* v. Walker (case; jury for Crutcher).

1793 **November** (continued)

  HAY v. HICKMAN, No. 9 (arbitration award for Hickman).

  Talbot v. Mountflorence (debt/appeal; jury for Talbot).

  Territory v. Abell (assault and battery; confession of guilt).

  Territory v. Allen (scire facias; court judgment for Territory).

  Territory v. Clark (scire facias; court judgment for Territory).

  Territory v. Dean (scire facias; court judgment for Territory).

  Territory v. Massingale (scire facias; court judgment for Territory).

  Territory v. Moore (buggery; not-guilty verdict).

  Territory v. Smith (scire facias; court judgment for Territory).

  Territory v. O'Conner (petit larceny; guilty verdict).

1794 **January**

  DAVIDSON COUNTY COURT OF PLEAS AND QUARTER SESSIONS

  Makes pretrial appearances in at least 23 cases.

  Able v. *Frazier* (case; jury for Able).

  Cartwright v. Coonrod (covenant; jury for Cartwright).

  Crutcher v. *Rice* (covenant; confession of judgment).

  Cunningham v. *Armstrong* (unknown; jury for Cunningham).

  Davis v. Allison (attachment; jury assessment of damages on prior default judgment).

  Frazer v. Porter (covenant; jury assessment of damages on prior default judgment).

  Good v. Moore (case; jury assessment of damages on prior default judgment).

  Hamilton v. *Talbot* (covenant; jury for Hamilton).

  Lewis v. *Fergison* (case; jury for Lewis).

  Maclin v. Barton (covenant; jury assessment of damages on prior default judgment).

  McDowel v. Lockett (covenant; jury for McDowel).

  Moore v. Sugg (case; jury for Moore; appeal granted).

  Overall v. King (attachment; jury assessment of damages on prior default judgment).

  Rodgers v. Mosier (covenant; jury assessment of damages on prior default judgment).

  Ross v. Cannon (attachment; jury assessment of damages on prior default judgment).

  Stump v. Robertson (case; jury for Stump; appeal granted).

  Walker v. Mays (case; jury for Walker).

  Wilson v. *Gibson* (case; jury for Wilson).

1794   January (continued)
SUMNER COUNTY COURT OF PLEAS AND QUARTER SESSIONS
    Makes pretrial appearances in at least 8 cases.
    Blackmore v. *Robinson* (case; nonsuit).
    Crutcher v. *McKain* (covenant; mistrial; new trial granted).
    Dean v. *Scoby* (case; abatement).
    Desha v. *Parker* (case; jury for Desha).
    Desha v. *Parker* (debt; confession of judgment).
    Hamilton v. Payton (attachment; jury assessment of damages
        on prior default judgment).
    Kenny v. Hardin (covenant; discontinued).
    McFarland v. *Kuykendall* (covenant; nonsuit).
    Thompson v. *McKain* (covenant; jury for Thompson).

April
DAVIDSON COUNTY COURT OF PLEAS AND QUARTER SESSIONS
    Makes pretrial appearances in at least 24 cases.
    Christmas v. Hudson (case; jury for Hudson; new trial
        granted).
    Cocke v. Payton (caveat; jury for Payton).
    Lewis v. *Mays* (covenant; jury for Lewis).
    McNAIRY v. *EDGAR & TAIT*, No. 15 (juries' verdicts; ap-
        peals granted).
    Pierce v. *McQuilliam* (case; jury for Pierce).
    Sharp v. Mountflorence (attachment; jury assessment of dam-
        ages on prior default judgment).
    Shelby v. *Lucas* (debt; jury for Shelby).
    Todd v. *Boyd* (debt; jury for Todd).
    Tucker v. Hand (case; jury for Tucker).
    Williams (AJ and JO) v. Thompson (scire facias; judgment
        for Williams).
SUMNER COUNTY COURT OF PLEAS AND QUARTER SESSIONS
    Makes pretrial appearances in at least 5 cases.
    Bradford v. White (covenant; dismissed).
    Crutcher v. *McKain* (covenant; jury for McKain; new trial
        granted).
    Cummins v. Wyer (slander; jury for Wyer).
    Douglass v. Wotwood (unknown; compromised).
    Glaves v. Dougherty (attachment; jury assessment of dam-
        ages on prior default judgment).
    Hainey v. Spencer (covenant; mistrial).
    Lusk v. Holley (covenant; court grants AJ's post-trial motion

1794   **April** (continued)

that execution be issued against sheriff of Tennessee County for detaining Lusk's judgment).

McFarland v. *Condry* (scire facias; court releases Condry from fine).

McKain v. *Hendricks* (AJ and JO) (case; dismissed).

Maclin v. McKain (covenant; jury for Maclin).

May
MERO DISTRICT SUPERIOR COURT

Makes pretrial appearances in at least 14 cases.

Campbell v. Gimson (covenant; jury for Campbell).

Hart v. *Prince* (case; jury for Prince).

Montgomery v. Armstrong (covenant; jury assessment of damages on prior default judgment).

Morgan v. Sugg (qui tam; confession of judgment).

MURFREE v. *LEEPER* (AJ and JO), No. 7 (jury for Leeper).

Territory v. Bradly (petit larceny; guilty verdict).

Territory v. Cotton (scire facias; court judgment for Territory).

Territory v. Cotton (scire facias; court judgment for Territory).

Territory v. Dobbins (scire facias; court judgment for Territory).

Territory v. Eagon (scire facias; court judgment for Territory).

Territory v. Eastis (felony; final disposition unknown).

Territory v. Hays (horse stealing; not-guilty verdict).

Territory v. Hogan (riot; not-guilty verdict).

Territory v. McFarlin (scire facias; rescinded).

Territory v. Rains (trespass, assault and battery; guilty verdict).

Territory v. Roberts (trespass, assault and battery; confession of guilt).

Territory v. Smith (scire facias; court judgment for Territory).

Territory v. Smothers (scire facias; rescinded).

July
DAVIDSON COUNTY COURT OF PLEAS AND QUARTER SESSIONS

Makes pretrial appearances in at least 19 cases.

Boyd v. Demonbreun (scire facias; confession of judgment).

Boyd v. *Espy* (case; jury for Boyd; appeal granted but withdrawn after settlement).

1794   July (continued)

> *Bucchanan* v. Moore (case; jury for Moore; appeal granted; further disposition unknown).
> *Cassellman* v. Robertson (case; jury for Cassellman).
> *Christmas* v. Hudson (case; jury for Hudson).
> *Gower* v. Nelson (attachment; jury assessment of damages on prior default judgment).
> *Hawkins* v. O'Neal (attachment; jury for O'Neal).
> *Hinds* v. Gibson (covenant; jury assessment of damages on prior default judgment).
> Maclin v. *Anderson* (case; jury for Anderson).
> McEwen v. *Robertson* (scire facias; jury finds Robertson's pleadings to be true as a matter of fact; court judgment for McEwen).
> *McGinnis* v. Blackamore (case; jury for McGinnis; appeal granted).
> *Mays* v. Rounsevall (covenant; jury assessment of damages on prior default judgment).
> Parker v. *Skinner* (covenant; jury for Parker).
> *Sevier* v. Cox (attachment; jury for Sevier).
> *Skelly* v. Betts (appeal; jury for Skelly).
> *Sugg* v. Sugg (alias scire facias; final default judgment).
> *Tait* v. Burke (alias scire facias; final default judgment).
> *Walker* v. Hay (scire facias; final default judgment).
> *Weakley* v. Witt (attachment; final default judgment).

SUMNER COUNTY COURT OF PLEAS AND QUARTER SESSIONS
> Makes pretrial appearances in at least 2 cases.
> Catron v. *Wiggins* (case; jury for Catron).
> Crutcher v. *McKain* (covenant; jury for Crutcher).
> MacFarland v. *Kuykendall* (covenant; jury for MacFarland).
> Sugg v. *Thompson* (case; nonsuit).
> *Wells* v. Anderson (deceit; dismissed).

October

DAVIDSON COUNTY COURT OF PLEAS AND QUARTER SESSIONS
> Makes pretrial appearances in at least 9 cases.
> *Betts* v. Lewis (case; jury for Betts).
> *Crockett* v. Hickman (covenant; jury for Crockett).
> *Deaderick* v. Erwine (case; jury for Deaderick).
> *Deaderick* v. Erwine (debt; jury for Deaderick).
> *Ewing* v. Lewis (debt; jury for Ewing).
> *Ewing* v. Lewis (debt; jury for Ewing).
> *Ewing* v. Rodgers (case; confession of judgment).

1794 October (continued)
  Gamble v. Baker (covenant; jury assessment of damages on prior default judgment).
  Johnston v. Hopkins (case; jury for Johnston).
  Lewis v. *Bosley* (covenant; jury for Lewis; appeal granted Lewis).
  Lewis v. *Bosley* (covenant; jury for Bosley; appeal granted; further disposition unknown).
  Lyons v. Carmichael (attachment; jury assessment of damages on prior default judgment).
  Searcy v. Armstrong (attachment; jury assessment of damages on prior default judgment).
SUMNER COUNTY COURT OF PLEAS AND QUARTER SESSIONS
  Makes pretrial appearances in at least 5 cases.
  Roberts v. Cotton (trespass vi et armis; dismissed).

November
MERO DISTRICT SUPERIOR COURT
  Makes pretrial appearances in at least 11 cases.
  Clark v. *Kell* (appeal; jury for Clark).
  Demonbreun's Administrator v. Hay (covenant; jury for Demonbreun's Administrator; court grants AJ's motion for new trial).
  HANNAH v. CUMMINS, No. 11 (slander; jury for Hannah).
  Hawthorn v. Rains (case; jury for Hawthorn).
  Johnston v. Nelson (equity; probably tried at Nov. Term but final disposition unknown).
  KING v. COX, No. 10 (case; final default judgment).
  Martin (AJ and JO) v. Minor (fieri facias; court awards execution for costs only).
  Moore v. Sugg (case/appeal; jury for Moore).
  Nelson v. *Hart* (appeal; final disposition unknown).
  Shanon v. McCamey (unknown; jury for Shanon).
  Territory v. Campbell (assault and battery; not-guilty verdict?)
  Territory v. Elliot (riot; probably tried at Nov. Term but final disposition unknown).
  Territory v. Elliot (riot; probably tried at Nov. Term but final disposition unknown).
  Territory v. Grayson (petit larceny; not-guilty verdict).
  Territory v. Grayson (petit larceny; guilty verdict).
  Territory v. Hogan (riot; confession of guilt?)

1794   November (continued)

    Territory v. Lancaster (trespass, assault and battery; guilty
      verdict).

    Territory v. Lewis (assault and battery; guilty verdict).

    Territory v. Loggins (horse stealing; nolle prosequi).

    Territory v. Nullerfield (assault and battery; AJ files indict-
      ment; no true bill).

    Territory v. Payton (scire facias; court judgment for
      Territory).

    Territory v. Rider (petit larceny; guilty verdict; new trial
      granted).

    Territory v. Robertson (trespass, assault and battery; guilty
      verdict).

1795   January

    DAVIDSON COUNTY COURT OF PLEAS AND QUARTER SESSIONS

    Makes pretrial appearances in at least 12 cases.

    Barnes v. *Lewis* (case; jury for Barnes; appeal granted).

    Johnston v. Hopkins (scire facias; final default judgment).

    McGavock v. *Bosley* (trespass quare clausum fregit; jury for
      McGavock).

    McPherson v. *Nash* (case; jury for Nash).

    Matlock v. *Searcy* (case; jury for Matlock).

    Ross v. *Shannon* (covenant; jury for Shannon).

    Shannon v. Ross (covenant; jury for Shannon; new trial
      granted).

    SUMNER COUNTY COURT OF PLEAS AND QUARTER SESSIONS

    Makes pretrial appearances in at least 2 cases.

    Bledsoe's Executors v. *Thompson* (trover/conversion; dis-
      missed).

    Carr v. Fisher (deceit; dismissed).

    CUMMINS v. PEAIRS, No. 12 (case; files declaration for
      Cummins; continued).

    Hainey v. Spencer (covenant; abatement).

    Hardin v. Chambers (debt; confession of judgment).

    Parker v. Penny (assault and battery; dismissed by
      agreement).

    Penny v. *Parker* (case; dismissed by agreement).

    Steel's Administrator v. McKinsey (debt; confession of
      judgment).

1795 (continued)

April

DAVIDSON COUNTY COURT OF PLEAS AND QUARTER SESSIONS
Makes pretrial appearances in at least 11 cases.
Deal v. *Mitchel* (covenant; jury for Deal).
Erwine v. Nash (attachment; jury assessment of garnishee
  Nash's land; new trial granted Nash).
Lancashire v. *Rains* (case; jury for Rains).
Parks v. Stump (detinue; jury for Stump; appeal granted).
Shannon v. Pearl (attachment; jury assessment of damages on
  prior default judgment).
Sugg v. Hay (scire facias; jury for Sugg; appeal granted).
SUMNER COUNTY COURT OF PLEAS AND QUARTER SESSIONS
Makes pretrial appearances in at least 5 cases.

May–June

Travels to Philadelphia to sell land and purchase inventory for
  store to be opened with Samuel Donelson; returns to Knoxville by June 9 and to Davidson County by June 18.
MERO DISTRICT SUPERIOR COURT
Court convenes and appoints Samuel Donelson attorney for
  the territory pro hac vice in AJ's absence (May 11).

July

DAVIDSON COUNTY COURT OF PLEAS AND QUARTER SESSIONS
Makes pretrial appearances in at least 5 cases.
Bell v. Malett (case; jury for Malett; appeal granted).
Cross v. Davie (covenant; jury assessment of damages on
  prior default judgment).
John Edgar & Company v. *Rice* (alias scire facias; jury for
  John Edgar & Company).
Erwine v. Nash (attachment; new jury assessment of Nash's
  land; confession of judgment).
Anthony Foster & Company v. Clark (case; jury for An-
  thony Foster & Company).
McPherson v. *Bosley, Rice,* and Loggins (scire facias; court
  enters judgment for McPherson against Loggins upon spe-
  cial verdict exonerating Bosley and Rice).
Maxell v. *Wilcox* (attachment; court enters judgment for
  Maxell on special verdict).
Melvin v. Lewis (covenant; jury for Melvin; appeal granted).

1795 **July** (continued)

> *Sugg* v. Sugg's Heirs (alias scire facias; final default judgment).

SUMNER COUNTY COURT OF PLEAS AND QUARTER SESSIONS

> Makes pretrial appearances in at least 5 cases.
>
> *Hainey* v. Spencer's Administrator (covenant; jury for Hainey).
>
> Sugg v. *Standly* (debt; non prosequitur).

October

DAVIDSON COUNTY COURT OF PLEAS AND QUARTER SESSIONS

> Makes pretrial appearances in at least 5 cases.
>
> Erwine v. *Black* (covenant; jury for Erwine).
>
> *Hand* v. Maclin (case; jury for Hand; appeal granted but withdrawn).
>
> *Montgomery* v. Forde (debt; confession of judgment).
>
> *Shannon* v. Ross (covenant; jury for Shannon).
>
> *Sugg* v. Maclin (appeal; court grants AJ's motion to quash appeal and enters judgment).

SUMNER COUNTY COURT OF PLEAS AND QUARTER SESSIONS

> Makes pretrial appearances in at least 4 cases.
>
> BARTON v. HANNAH, No. 13 (debt; jury returns special verdict, Oct. 6; court takes under advisement).
>
> *CUMMINS* v. PEAIRS, No. 12 (jury for Peairs; appeal granted).
>
> Douglass v. *Gatlin* (case; jury for Gatlin).
>
> *Mercer* v. Perry (slander; dismissed).

November

MERO DISTRICT SUPERIOR COURT

> Makes pretrial appearances in at least 19 cases.
>
> *Armstrong* v. Sloan (covenant; jury for Armstrong).
>
> BARTON v. HANNAH, No. 13 (court issues advisory opinion, Nov. 17).
>
> Bosley v. *Allison* (AJ and JO) (appeal; jury for Allison).
>
> *Demonbreun's Administrator* v. Hay (covenant; jury for Demonbreun's Administrator).
>
> McNAIRY v. *EDGAR & TAIT*, No. 15 (AJ appointed arbitrator).
>
> *PROTZMAN* v. ROBERTSON, No. 14 (covenant; court enters judgment for Protzman upon special verdict).
>
> *Sugg* v. Hay (scire facias/appeal; jury for Sugg).

1795   **November** (continued)
   Territory v. Brown (scire facias; court judgment for
      Territory).
   Territory v. Campbell (fieri facias; final disposition
      unknown).
   Territory v. Harrison (assault and battery; guilty plea).
   Territory v. Harrison (scire facias; court judgment for Terri-
      tory remitted).
   Territory v. Robertson (unknown; Robertson fined by court).

   December
   Elected to represent Davidson County as delegate to Knoxville
   convention to frame first Tennessee constitution (Dec. 19).

1796   **January–February**
   Attends Tennessee Constitutional Convention, Knoxville (Jan.
      11–Feb. 6).
   Arbitrates McNAIRY v. *EDGAR & TAIT*, No. 15, with JO and
   HT (Feb. 23).

   March
   Purchases Hunter's Hill.

   April
   DAVIDSON COUNTY COURT OF PLEAS AND QUARTER SESSIONS
      Makes pretrial appearances in at least 2 cases.
      Gibbs v. Hickman (covenant; jury for Gibbs).
      Robertson v. *Allison* (attachment; motion in abatement
         granted; AJ's motion for appeal granted).
      Smith v. McGee (case; confession of judgment).
   SUMNER COUNTY COURT OF PLEAS AND QUARTER SESSIONS
      Makes pretrial appearance in at least 1 case.
      Government v. *Gillaspie* (misdemeanor in keeping ferry;
         guilty verdict; AJ's motion in arrest of judgment granted).
      Kuykendall v. Wright (attachment; jury assessment of dam-
         ages on prior default judgment).
      Lynn v. Fryal (scire facias; dismissed).
      Lynn v. Jimason (scire facias; dismissed).
      Patton v. White (attachment; jury assessment of damages on
         prior default judgment).

1796 (continued)

May–June
Travels to Philadelphia to sell land and to purchase inventory.
MERO DISTRICT SUPERIOR COURT
Court convenes and appoints Samuel Donelson attorney general pro hac vice in AJ's absence (May 10).

July
Licensed to practice in Tennessee courts (July 5).
DAVIDSON COUNTY COURT OF PLEAS AND QUARTER SESSIONS
Makes pretrial appearances in at least 2 cases.
SUMNER COUNTY COURT OF PLEAS AND QUARTER SESSIONS
Makes pretrial appearance in at least 1 case.
Douglass v. Bowman (scire facias; final default judgment).

October
Elected to U.S. House of Representatives (Oct. 22).
DAVIDSON COUNTY COURT OF PLEAS AND QUARTER SESSIONS
Makes pretrial appearance in at least 1 case.
Bosley v. White (case; jury for Bosley).
White v. *Bosley* (case; jury for Bosley).
SUMNER COUNTY COURT OF PLEAS AND QUARTER SESSIONS
Makes pretrial appearance in at least 1 case.
Wotwood v. Graves (covenant; dismissed).

November
MERO DISTRICT SUPERIOR COURT
Court convenes and appoints Samuel Donelson attorney general pro hac vice (Nov. 15).

December
Travels to Philadelphia for convening of Congress.

1797 January–March
Attends Congress (through Mar. 3).

May
MERO DISTRICT SUPERIOR COURT
Samuel Donelson appointed attorney general pro hac vice (May 10).
Quarles & Company v. Sharp (case; jury for Sharp; AJ's motion for new trial denied).

1797 (continued)

September
Elected to U.S. Senate by Tennessee General Assembly.

November
Attends Congress (beginning Nov. 22).
MERO DISTRICT SUPERIOR COURT
John C. Hamilton assumes office as attorney general (Nov. 13).
READING v. DOUGLASS, No. 16 (case; AJ files declaration
for Reading).

1798 **January–April**
Attends Congress (through Apr. 16).

May
MERO DISTRICT SUPERIOR COURT
Lenier v. *Hadley* (detention of slaves; jury for Hadley).

August
With George M. Deaderick, arbitrates McConnell v. Snoddy
(Aug. 18).

September
Appointed by Gov. Sevier to Superior Court of Law and Equity,
ad interim (Sept. 20).
HAMILTON DISTRICT SUPERIOR COURT (at least 34 trials or
nontrial final dispositions).
Takes oaths of office (Sept. 24); attends entire term.

November
MERO DISTRICT SUPERIOR COURT (at least 23 trials or nontrial
final dispositions).
Attends entire term.
READING v. DOUGLASS, No. 16 (jury for Douglass).

December
Elected judge, Superior Court of Law and Equity, by Tennessee
General Assembly over Bennett Searcy by vote of 18–13
(Dec. 20); commissioned by Gov. Sevier (Dec. 22).

1799   **March**
WASHINGTON DISTRICT SUPERIOR COURT (at least 7 trials or
nontrial final dispositions).
Attends entire term.
GRUNDY'S EXECUTORS v. HARMON, No. 31 (debt/ap-
peal; AJ, for the court, sustains lower court's denial of de-
fendant's plea in abatement; defendants ordered to
answer).
VANNERSON v. MONTGOMERY AND McCORMICK,
No. 48 (forcible entry and detainer/certiorari; motion to
quash writ of certiorari granted; new writ issued).
HAMILTON DISTRICT SUPERIOR COURT (at least 26 trials or
nontrial final dispositions on dates AJ attends).
Attends Mar. 24–28; absent Mar. 29–Apr. 6.
LOVE v. DUNCAN, No. 21 (certiorari; jury for Love; motion for new trial continued to September Term).
MAGOFFIN & SON v. ACKLIN, No. 41 (debt; jury for Ma-
goffin & Son).

May
MERO DISTRICT SUPERIOR COURT (at least 24 trials or nontrial
final dispositions).
Attends entire term.

September
WASHINGTON DISTRICT SUPERIOR COURT (at least 9 trials or
nontrial final dispositions).
Attends entire term.
CRAFT v. FLORA, No. 20 (assumpsit/certiorari; motion to
quash certiorari denied; continued; further disposition
unknown).
CRAIG v. MONTGOMERY, No. 30 (debt; AJ, for the court,
refuses to admit deposition proffered by Craig).
EMBREE v. McFERRAN, No. 17 (assumpsit/certiorari; jury
for Embree).
MITCHELL v. BERRY, No. 19 (debt/certiorari; supersedeas
set aside).
VANNERSON v. MONTGOMERY AND McCORMICK,
No. 48 (court reverses lower court and awards possession
to defendants, which award subsequently is enjoined by
Judge Campbell during vacation).

1799   **September** (continued)
   STATE v. THOMPSON ET AL., No. 18 (assault and bat-
      tery/certiorari; proceedings quashed).
   HAMILTON DISTRICT SUPERIOR COURT (at least 36 trials or
      nontrial final dispositions).
   Attends entire term.
   FINLEY v. McCLUNG, No. 22 (ejectment; jury for
      McClung; motion for new trial denied).
   LOVE v. DUNCAN, No. 21 (motion for new trial denied;
      judgment entered for Love).

   November
   MERO DISTRICT SUPERIOR COURT (at least 22 trials or nontrial
      final dispositions).
   Attends entire term.

1800   **March**
   WASHINGTON DISTRICT SUPERIOR COURT (at least 12 trials and
      nontrial final dispositions).
   Attends entire term.
   CRINDER v. WILLSON, No. 23 (trespass quare clausum
      fregit; Crinder's motion to introduce third-party testimony
      denied; further disposition unknown).
   McKINLEY AND HOLMES v. ROGERS & HAGAN, No.
      24 (assumpsit; defendant's motion to strike granted; fur-
      ther disposition unknown).
   VANNERSON v. MONTGOMERY AND McCORMICK,
      No. 48 (Judge Campbell's injunction dissolved).
   WILLIAMS ET AL. v. HENDERSON & COMPANY, No.
      50 (partition; final hearing; decree ordered prepared).
   HAMILTON DISTRICT SUPERIOR COURT (at least 51 trials or
      nontrial final dispositions).
   Attends entire term.
   SMITH v. FITZGERALD, No. 25 (trover; jury for
      Fitzgerald).
   STATE v. McKEE, No. 26 (horse stealing; guilty verdict; mo-
      tion in arrest of judgment denied).

   May
   MERO DISTRICT SUPERIOR COURT (at least 60 trials or nontrial
      final dispositions).
   Attends entire term.

1800   **May** (continued)

STOTHART v. STUART, No. 27 (case; jury for Stothart; Stuart's motion for new trial denied).

VAUGHN v. BARNES, No. 42 (debt; jury for Vaughn; new trial granted).

STATE v. LAVENDER, No. 29 (assault and battery; jury discharged; case dismissed).

STATE v. PIERCE, No. 28 (horse stealing; guilty verdict; motion in arrest of judgment denied).

August–September

Visits mineral springs, Bath Co., Va., with Rachel (ca. Aug. 10–early Sept.); returns to Jonesboro by Sept. 5.

September

WASHINGTON DISTRICT SUPERIOR COURT (at least 11 trials or nontrial final dispositions).

Attends entire term.

CRAIG v. MONTGOMERY, No. 30 (debt; Craig's motion for presumption re: statute of limitations denied; further disposition unknown).

GRUNDY'S EXECUTORS v. HARMON, No. 31 (defendants' demurrer denied; judgment for Grundy's Executors).

STATE v. MONTGOMERY, No. 32 (perjury; not-guilty verdict).

HAMILTON DISTRICT SUPERIOR COURT (at least 35 trials or nontrial final dispositions).

Attends entire term.

November

MERO DISTRICT SUPERIOR COURT (at least 47 trials or nontrial final dispositions).

Attends entire term.

COTTON v. LEWIS, No. 33 (case/appeal; Cotton's demurrer to Lewis's plea in abatement overruled; writ quashed).

1801   **March**

WASHINGTON DISTRICT SUPERIOR COURT (at least 8 trials or nontrial final dispositions).

Attends entire term.

HALL v. AMIS ET AL., No. 34 (debt/certiorari; jury for Amis; motion for new trial denied).

1801 **March** (continued)
> MOORE v. GAINS, No. 35 (case/appeal; writ of error quashed).
> HAMILTON DISTRICT SUPERIOR COURT (at least 30 trials or nontrial final dispositions).
> Attends entire term.

> **May**
> MERO DISTRICT SUPERIOR COURT (at least 35 trials or nontrial final dispositions).
> Attends entire term.
> VAUGHN v. BARNES, No. 42 (special verdict returned).

> **September**
> Administers oath of office to Gov. Archibald Roane, Tennessee House of Representatives chamber, Knoxville (Sept. 23).
> WASHINGTON DISTRICT SUPERIOR COURT (at least 5 trials or nontrial final dispositions).
> Attends entire term.
> MOORE v. GAINS, No. 35 (second writ of error quashed).
> HAMILTON DISTRICT SUPERIOR COURT (at least 21 trials or nontrial final dispositions).
> Attends entire term.
> JACKSON v. KEARBY, No. 36 (ejectment; jury for AJ).

> **November**
> MERO DISTRICT SUPERIOR COURT (at least 44 trials or nontrial final dispositions).
> Absent Nov. 12–14; attends Nov. 15–25.
> GREER v. EMERSON, No. 37 (trespass; jury for Greer; motion for new trial denied).
> STATE v. BEELER, No. 40 (horse stealing; guilty verdict).
> STATE v. CHILDRESS, No. 38 (murder; jury returns guilty verdict of manslaughter; court allows plea of benefit of clergy).
> STATE v. WHITFORD, No. 39 (assault/appeal; state's motion for trial de novo denied; court reverses guilty verdict).
> WITHERSPOON v. JACKSON; JACKSON v. WITHERSPOON, No. 46 (trespass on the case; declarations filed).

1802 **February**
> Enters into business partnership with Thomas Watson and John Hutchings (Feb. 16).

1802 (continued)

March

WASHINGTON DISTRICT SUPERIOR COURT (at least 11 trials or nontrial final dispositions).
Attends entire term.

HAMILTON DISTRICT SUPERIOR COURT (at least 41 trials or nontrial final dispositions).
Attends entire term.
MAGOFFIN & SON v. ACKLIN, PERRIN, AND COMBS, No. 41 (motion for execution withdrawn).

April

Commissioned major general, Tennessee militia (Apr. 1).

May

MERO DISTRICT SUPERIOR COURT (at least 49 trials or nontrial final dispositions).
Attends entire term.
ARMSTRONG v. TYRRELL AND LYTLE, No. 49 (petition to enjoin enforcement of judgment; court enters decree).
EDGAR & TAIT v. NEVILLE, No. 43 (debt; plaintiff nonsuited; nonsuit set aside).
VAUGHN v. BARNES, No. 42 (court enters judgment for Barnes on special verdict).
STATE v. WATSON, No. 44 (incitement to murder; presentment returned; continued).
WITHERSPOON v. JACKSON; JACKSON v. WITHERSPOON, No. 46 (submitted to arbitration).

September

WASHINGTON DISTRICT SUPERIOR COURT (at least 10 trials or nontrial final dispositions).
Attends entire term.
WILLIAMS ET AL. v. HENDERSON & COMPANY, No. 50 (court enters final partition decree).

HAMILTON DISTRICT SUPERIOR COURT (at least 32 trials or nontrial final dispositions).
Attends entire term.
MITCHELL v. CLAYWELL, No. 51 (petition to enjoin enforcement of judgment; court enters final decree).

1802 (continued)

November
MERO DISTRICT SUPERIOR COURT (at least 62 trials or nontrial final dispositions).
Attends entire term.
EDGAR & TAIT v. NEVILLE, No. 43 (jury for Edgar & Tait).
PARKER v. PARKER, No. 45 (petition for divorce from bed and board; court enters final decree).
STATE v. WATSON, No. 44 (not-guilty verdict).

1803 **March**
WASHINGTON DISTRICT SUPERIOR COURT (at least 21 trials or nontrial final dispositions).
Attends entire term.
HAMILTON DISTRICT SUPERIOR COURT (at least 37 trials or nontrial final dispositions on dates AJ attends).
Attends Mar. 28–Apr. 5; absent Apr. 6–12.

April–July
Travels to Philadelphia; arrives in Washington Co., Va., by Apr. 11; arrives in Philadelphia by May 5; arrives at "Redstone old Fort 30 miles above Pittsburgh" en route to Tennessee by May 26; at Hunter's Hill by July 4.

May
MERO DISTRICT SUPERIOR COURT.
Absent entire term.

July–November
Quarrels with John Sevier.

August–October
Considers resigning from the bench.
Dissolves business partnership with Thomas Watson (Aug. 6).

September
WASHINGTON DISTRICT SUPERIOR COURT (at least 9 trials or nontrial final dispositions on dates AJ attends).
Attends Sept. 5, 14, 15; absent Sept. 6–13, 16.
HAMILTON DISTRICT SUPERIOR COURT (at least 34 trials or nontrial final dispositions).
Attends entire term.

1803 (continued)

November
MERO DISTRICT SUPERIOR COURT (at least 44 trials or nontrial final dispositions).
Attends entire term.
NUSUM v. BETTS, No. 47 (covenant; jury for Nusum).

1804 **March**
WASHINGTON DISTRICT SUPERIOR COURT (at least 10 trials or nontrial final dispositions on dates AJ attends).
Attends Mar. 7–13; absent Mar. 5–6.
HAMILTON DISTRICT SUPERIOR COURT (at least 26 trials or nontrial final dispositions on dates AJ attends).
Attends Mar. 26–31, Apr. 2–9; absent Apr. 10.

April–June
Enters business partnership with John Coffee (Apr. 6); Jackson & Company licensed to operate retail store in Davidson County (Apr. 19).
Travels to Philadelphia to purchase inventory for Jackson & Company; arrives in Abingdon by Apr. 13; arrives in Washington by Apr. 28; arrives in Philadelphia by May 3; arrives in Pittsburgh en route to Tennessee by June 2; returns to Hunter's Hill on June 19.

May
MERO DISTRICT SUPERIOR COURT
Absent entire term.

July
Tennessee General Assembly accepts AJ's resignation from the bench (July 24).

PART IV

A Biographical Register

Jackson's Legal Colleagues in Western North Carolina, the Territory South of the River Ohio, and Tennessee, 1787–1804

COMPILATION OF A COMPREHENSIVE biographical register of the scores of superior and inferior court judges who held office under the North Carolina, territorial, and Tennessee governments between 1787 and 1804 and of the many attorneys who were admitted to the bar during Jackson's legal career has proved to be impossible. The editors thus have included here sketches of (a) all judges of the western North Carolina, territorial, and Tennessee Superior Court of Law and Equity between 1787 and 1804 and all judges of the federal district and circuit courts in Tennessee between 1797 and 1804; (b) a number of the justices of the courts of pleas and quarter sessions for Davidson, Sumner, and Tennessee counties who occupied the bench during AJ's practice before those courts and a smaller number of the justices of other county courts who held office during AJ's tenure on the bench; and (c) most of the lawyers for whom biographical data are available who were admitted to practice before the Superior Court between 1787 and 1804 and a number of attorneys who were admitted to practice before the state's various county courts.

Each entry consists of three sections, except when such a format is not possible because of insufficient data. The first contains information, when available, about the subject's educational background and admission to the bar. The second contains additional biographical information, primarily relating to the subject's legal career. The third section supplies citations of sources. Cross-references in the entries are indicated by the use of capitals and small capitals.

These sketches are provided primarily for the purpose of indentification. No attempt has been made to be comprehensive either biographically or bibliographically. Standard sources are provided and relied upon when available; other references are provided when no standard sources are available or when the cited materials contain data that are not found in standard sources.

DAVID ALLISON (d. 1798). Admitted to practice, Washington County Court of Pleas and Quarter Sessions, May 12, 1788, the date of AJ's admission. Licensed to practice, territorial courts of law and equity, December 1790.

Appointed clerk pro tempore, Davidson County Superior Court of Law, May 1789. Commissioned clerk, Mero District Superior Court of Law, December 1790; resigned before May 1792. Appointed by Governor William Blount as deputy paymaster of federal troops and county militia units, ca. 1790. Moved to Philadelphia as a business agent for William, John Gray, and Thomas Blount, 1792. Speculated with William Blount in land extending from South Carolina to present state of Arkansas, much of it located in Tennessee. Became a partner in the Philadelphia mercantile firm of John B. Evans & Company, which did a substantial business in the Cumberland basin, 1795. Purchased from AJ all the land that he and JOHN OVERTON marketed in Philadelphia, 1795 and 1796, in exchange for notes on which he defaulted when he became bankrupt in 1797. Sent to a Philadelphia debtors' prison, July 1797, where he remained until his death.

MDSC Law Min. Bk., 1788–1803, pp. 7, 63; WashCo CPQS Min. Bk. 1, p. 322; Blount, *Journal,* 43, 46; *Jackson Papers,* I, 58 n.2.

JOSEPH ANDERSON (1757–1837). Studied law in New Jersey. Licensed to practice, Delaware, ca. 1785. Licensed to practice, Pennsylvania, April 1787. Licensed to practice, Tennessee county courts and Superior Court, April 1796.

Son-in-law of ALEXANDER OUTLAW. Although Anderson did not practice in Delaware, where he taught school for two years, or in Pennsylvania, he applied as a resident of Delaware to President Washington for appointment as a judge, Territory South of the River Ohio, June 1790. Primarily because of a controversy surrounding Anderson's unsettled account of some $20,000 with the United States as paymaster of the Third New Jersey Regiment during the Revolution, Washington denied Anderson's application and appointed William Peery. Upon Peery's resignation from the position in December 1790 without ever having taken his seat, Anderson renewed his application for the office. Although having eluded the procedures prescribed by Congress for the settlement of claims relating to military service and having instead secured by February 1791 an administrative decision by the War Department to consider the matter of his account with the United States as closed, Anderson encountered a further obstacle in his effort to secure the appointment when a rumor reached Washington about a transaction that had occurred between the candidate and a distinguished war veteran from Wilmington, Peter Jaquett. Anderson did not produce the original instrument that had been the basis of the transaction, a bond of indebtedness executed by Anderson payable to Jaquett. Neither did the candidate reveal that under a subsequent agreement between the two parties, Anderson had obligated himself to liquidate his debt by making payments to Jaquett from his anticipated judicial salary.

Apparently satisfied by a certificate of Jaquett's hastily produced by Anderson that placed the transaction in a favorable light, however, Washington submitted his nomination of Anderson to the Senate on Feb. 25, 1791. The Senate confirmed the nomination the next day. Disturbed when Jaquett subsequently asserted that he had not revealed the full truth about the Wilmington transaction in the certificate that Anderson had secured and submitted to the President, Washington turned for counsel to Secretary of State Jefferson. After a hasty review of the evidence and apparently after having given some thought to withdrawing the nomination and to urging the Senate to revoke its confirmation, Jefferson finally put aside his doubts about Anderson's fitness for judicial office and advised the President that the weight of the evidence was favorable to the candidate. Washington concurred, and Anderson's commission was delivered to him on Mar. 4, 1791. He assumed office on July 15, 1791.

Served as delegate to the convention that framed the first Tennessee constitution, 1796. Resigned from the bench to accept appointment to U.S. Senate, 1797, to fill the unexpired term of William Blount and served until 1815. Comptroller of the U.S. Treasury, 1815–1836. Died in Washington, D.C.

Joseph Anderson to George Washington, June 25, 1790, Series 7, Washington Papers, DLC (Reel 119); *BDAC;* Julian P. Boyd, ed., *The Papers of Thomas Jefferson* (Princeton, N.J., 1974), XIX, 382, 387–388, 390–392, 400–401; *DAB;* Green, *Lives of the Judges,* 2.

WILLIAM PRESTON ANDERSON (1775–1831). Licensed to practice in the Tennessee courts, December 1797. Admitted to practice, Davidson County Court of Pleas and Quarter Sessions, January 1798. Admitted to practice, Mero District Superior Court, May 1798.

Appointed by President Adams, U.S. attorney, Eastern District of Tennessee, April 1798. Resigned before July 1802. Acquired lease interest in "house of entertainment" at Clover Bottom with AJ and John Hutchings, March 1805. Entered into partnership with AJ's mercantile partner John Coffee for speculation in unoccupied land in middle Tennessee, 1807. Served on AJ's military staff before War of 1812. By 1823 had moved to Craggy Hope, near Winchester, Tennessee. No records are available to determine whether Anderson practiced in the Franklin County courts before his death at Winchester in 1831.

Agreement, AJ and John Hutchings with William Preston Anderson, Mar. 15, 1805, Dyas Coll., Coffee Papers, THi; DaCo CPQS Min. Bk. C, 34; MDSC Law Min. Bk., 1788–1803, p. 211; Bassett, *Correspondence*, III, 422 n. 2; Gordon T. Chappell, "The Life and Activities of General John Coffee," 1 *THQ* 129 (1942); *JES*, I, 267, 268; *Nashville Republican & State Gazette*, May 24, 1831; Sevier, *Commission Book*, 5; see *Knoxville Gazette*, Aug. 4, 1802; Anderson to James Winchester, Aug. 18, 1823, Winchester Papers, THi.

SAMUEL ASHE (1725–1813). Presiding judge, North Carolina Superior Court of Law and Equity that examined and issued license to AJ to practice in the state's county courts, September 1787. A former assistant attorney for the Crown in the Wilmington District, Ashe by 1774 had become perhaps the most substantial lawyer in the state to identify himself unreservedly with the more aggressive elements of the Revolution. Represented New Hanover, North Carolina Provincial Congress, 1775–1776. Represented Wilmington District, North Carolina Provincial Council, 1775–1776. President, North Carolina Council of Safety, 1776. Member of the committee appointed to frame a constitution for the state, 1776. Elected judge, North Carolina Superior Court of Law and Equity, December 1777, and served on the bench until his election as governor of the state, November 1795.

Cheney, *North Carolina Government*, 151, 155–58, 360, 366 n.1; *DAB*.

WAIGHTSTILL AVERY (1743–1821). B.A., College of New Jersey, 1766. Studied law in Somerset County, Maryland, with Littleton Dennis. Licensed to practice in North Carolina, 1769. Licensed to practice in the territorial courts of law and equity, November 1790.

Master, Nassau Hall Grammar School, College of New Jersey, 1766–1767; Crown attorney, Mecklenburg Co., North Carolina, 1775–1776. Member, North Carolina Provincial Congress, 1775–1777. Signer of the Mecklenburg Resolutions, 1775. Served as North Carolina attorney general, 1777–1779. Practiced in Washington, Greene, and other county courts in present Tennessee, ca. 1778—1796. Appointed state's attorney, Court of Oyer and Terminer, Washington and Sullivan counties, August 1782. Recommended to President Washington by John Sevier as William Peery's successor as judge, Territory South of the River Ohio, January 1791.

Before applying to read law with SPRUCE MACAY, AJ is reported to have sought unsuccessfully to read with Avery. According to tradition, the dispute between AJ and Avery in Jonesboro in August 1788 that prompted AJ's note to Avery of August 12 (*Jackson Papers*, I, 12) arose from Avery's having insulted AJ during the course of litigation in which the two men represented opposing parties. Although the Washington District Superior Court did meet in Jonesboro in August 1788, the incident between AJ and Avery could not have concerned in any direct way litigation pending before this court. Although the court's minute books have not survived, the court by statute (ch. 24, § 1, 1784 Laws of N.C., reprinted in *N.C. State Records*, XXIV, 689) was required to convene its August Term on the fifteenth day of the month, at least three days after the incident had occurred. Moreover, in August 1788, AJ as yet had been licensed to practice only in the state's county courts (see License, Sept. 26, 1787, p. 3; *Jackson Papers*, I, 10) and thus could not have been serving as counsel of record in any case before the district Superior Court when the dispute with Avery took place. If AJ's note was prompted by a disagreement with Avery over an action in which the two lawyers represented opposing parties rather than by some other matter that happened to erupt "in the presence of a court and a larg audianc," the case was probably one that was tried or that was pending trial at the session of the Washington County court that had convened on August 11, the day before AJ's note to Avery. Because the court's minute book entries for August Term 1788, as for most other of its terms, fail to identify counsel of record in any of the cases tried before that tribunal, however, the possibility cannot be verified.

John Sevier to George Washington, Jan. 17, 1791, Ser. 7, Washington Papers, DLC (Reel 119); Greene County Court Records, THi; WashCo CPQS Min. Bk. 1, pp. 168, 335–341; Avery Sketch, North Carolina Papers, KK, Draper Coll., WHi; Avery Sketch, Samuel C. Williams Papers, THi; John Allison, *Dropped Stitches in Tennessee History* (n.p., 1897), 110–11; John S. Bassett, *The Life of Andrew Jackson* (New York, 1911), I, 12; Blount, *Journal*, 35; Cheney, *North Carolina Government*, 182, 195 n.47; *General Catalogue of Princeton University 1746–1906* (Princeton, 1908), 80, 91; "The Records of Washington County," pt. 1, 5 *AHM* 349 (1900).

REDMOND DILLON BARRY (b. 1766). Probably the same Redmond Barry who was graduated B.A., 1787, and received an LL.B., 1792, Trinity College, University of Dublin. He is reported also to have been awarded M.A. and M.D. degrees by Trinity College, but there are no records of his having been awarded the latter degrees by that institution. Reported to have read law with John Breckinridge in Kentucky before moving to Tennessee. Admitted to practice, Mero District Superior Court, November 1800; Sumner County Court of Pleas and Quarter Sessions, April 1801.

Member of the Irish bar, 1792. Reported to have practiced medicine in Liverpool before moving to the United States.

SumCo CPQS Min. Bk. 3, p. 298; MDSC Law Min. Bk., 1788–1803, p. 373; George D. Burtchaell, ed., *Alumni Dublinenses: A Register of the Students, Graduates, Professors, and Provosts of Trinity College, in the University of Dublin* (London, 1924), 45; Jay G. Cisco, *Historic Sumner County, Tennessee* (Nashville, 1909), 220.

SAMUEL BARTON (1749–ca. 1814). Assumed office as justice, Davidson County Court of Pleas and Quarter Sessions, October 1783, and remained on the bench throughout AJ's practice before that court. Had been a member, Cumberland Association Committee, January–August 1783, and had been appointed entry-taker, Davidson County, October 1783. Appointed treasurer and trustee of Nashville by North Carolina General Assembly, 1784. Appointed major, Davidson County militia, 1784; nominated for brigadier general, Mero District cavalry, November 1788. Moved to Wilson County, Tennessee, in 1798.

Ch. 47, § 2, 1784 Laws of N.C. (Apr. Sess.), reprinted in *N.C. State Records*, XXIV, 616, 617; DaCo CPQS Min. Bk. A, 2, 6; Wilson County Wills & Inventories, 1803–1814, p. 389; Blount, *Journal*, 41; Brown, "Tennessee County Courts," 411 (Table 16); Dixon Merritt, *The History of Wilson County* (Lebanon, Tenn., 1961), 295; Quarles and White, *Three Pioneer Documents*, 23, 39.

THEODORICK BLAND (1776–1846). Admitted to practice, Washington County Court of Pleas and Quarter Sessions, May 1799. Read law in Tennessee, ca. 1799–1801.

Born in Virginia. Was practicing in Mercer and Garrard counties in Kentucky by October 1798. After concluding that "the opening for my profession in this State is not to compare to what it is in Tennessee," moved from Danville, Kentucky, to Bluff City, Tennessee, to practice in the courts at Jonesboro, ca. October 1798. Practiced with his cousin TOWNSHEND STUART DADE in Washington District and Hamilton District Superior Court, March 1799–March 1801. Practiced in the district court and the county courts at Abingdon, Virginia, May 1800–March 1801, upon the recommendation of JENKIN WHITESIDE. Moved to Baltimore, Maryland, ca. 1801. Elected to the Maryland House of Delegates,

1807, and subsequently to the Maryland Senate. Appointed associate judge, Sixth Judicial District, Maryland, 1812. Appointed by President Monroe as a commissioner to South America, November 1817. Judge, U.S. District Court, District of Maryland, 1819–1824. Chancellor, Maryland High Court of Chancery, 1824–1846. Compiled and published *Bland's Chancery Reports* (1846). His unpublished casebook, which is preserved in MdHi, is a principal source for the present work.

Affidavit of Theodorick Bland, Sept. 10, 1819, Letters of Application and Recommendation During the Administration of James Monroe, 1817–1825, RG 59, DNA; Theodorick Bland to Sophia Bland, Oct. 11, 1798, and May 6, 1800, Bland Papers, MdHi; WashCo CPQS Min. Bk., 1798–1799, p. 36; W. Calvin Chesnut, "The Work of the Federal Court of Maryland," 37 *Md. Hist. Mag.* 361, 366 (1942); Henry D. Harlan, "The Names of the Great Lawyers on the Fringe of the Baltimore Supreme Bench Court Room," 37 *Md. Hist. Mag.* 264–65 (1942); Judicial Conference of the United States, *Judges of the United States*, 2d ed. (Washington, D.C., 1983), 41; see Bland to Sophia Bland, July 15, 1800, Bland Papers, MdHi.

WILLIE BLOUNT (1768–1835). Professed to have attended College of New Jersey and King's College, but there are no records of his attendance at either institution. Licensed to practice, territorial county courts, April 1794. Admitted to practice, Knox County Court of Pleas and Quarter Sessions, May 1794. Licensed to practice, Superior Court, Territory South of the River Ohio, October 1795.

Half-brother of territorial Governor William Blount, whom he served as a personal secretary before beginning practice of law. Judge, Superior Court of Law and Equity, 1796. Was serving as a justice, Knox County Court of Pleas and Quarter Sessions, in February 1802. Moved from Knoxville to Montgomery County, ca. 1802. Published *A Catechetical Exposition of the Constitution of the State of Tennessee* (1803). Represented Montgomery and Stewart counties, Tennessee House of Representatives, 1807–1809. Governor of Tennessee, 1809–1815. Unsuccessful candidate for governor, 1827. Represented Montgomery County, Tennessee Constitutional Convention, 1834.

Tennessee Papers, 1XX42, Draper Coll., WHi; KnoxCo CPQS Min. Bk. O, 1792–1795, p. 163; *BD–Tenn. Assembly*, I, 56–57; Blount, *Journal*, 96, 115; Caldwell, *Bench and Bar*, 31; *DAB*; John Dobson, *The Lost Roulstone Imprints* (Knoxville, 1975), 57; Sevier, *Commission Book*, 2; White, *Messages*, I, opp. 162.

LUKE BOWYER (b. 1745). Probably read law under Gabriel Jones in Augusta County, Virginia. Admitted to practice, Botetourt County, Virginia,

1770. Admitted to practice, Washington County Court of Pleas and Quarter Sessions, February 1780. Admitted to practice, Knox County Court of Pleas and Quarter Sessions, July 1792. Admitted to practice, Claiborne County Court of Pleas and Quarter Sessions, March 1802.

Listed among Botetourt County subscribers to Blackstone's *Commentaries on the Laws of England,* 1771–1772. Attorney for the Crown, Botetourt County, before 1776. State's attorney, Watauga Association, Washington County, 1776. Represented Washington County, North Carolina House of Commons, 1778. County solicitor, Claiborne County Court of Pleas and Quarter Sessions, December 1801–September 1802. Was serving as justice, Claiborne County Court of Pleas and Quarter Sessions, in February 1812 and as late as February 1823.

Claiborne County CPQS Min. Bk. 1, 1801–1803, pp. 4, 11, 71; Claiborne County CPQS Docket, 1812–1814, p. 7; Claiborne County CPQS Min. Bk., 1821–1824, p. 204; KnoxCo CPQS Min. Bk. O, 1792–1795, p. 4; *BD–Tenn. Assembly,* I, 63–64; "The Records of Washington County," pt. 2, 6 *AHM* 57 (1901); "Subscribers in Virginia to Blackstone's Commentaries on the Laws of England, Philadelphia, 1771–1772," 1 *WMQ* (ser. 1) 183 (1921); Samuel Cole Williams, "Tennessee's First Lawyer," *Proceedings of the Forty-Fifth Annual Session of the Bar Association of Tennessee* (Nashville, 1926), 116, 117, 118.

DRURY WOOD BREAZEALE. Licensed to practice in Tennessee county courts, April 1796. Licensed to practice, Superior Court, April 1797. Admitted to practice, Knox County Court of Pleas and Quarter Sessions, April 1796; Grainger County Court of Pleas and Quarter Sessions, December 1796.

Resigned as county solicitor, Grainger County, March 1797. Maintained an active practice in Knox County. Served as one of three attorneys representing the state in impeachment proceedings against Judge DAVID CAMPBELL, December 1798. Commissioned by Governor WILLIAM C. C. CLAIBORNE as attorney general, Jefferson County, Mississippi Territory, April 1802.

Grainger County CPQS Min. Bk., 1796–1802, pp. 16, 20; KnoxCo CPQS Rec. Bk., 1795–1799, p. 85; Rowland, *Courts of Mississippi,* I, 47; Sevier, *Commission Book,* 1, 4; White, *Messages,* I, 85.

DAVID CAMPBELL (1750–1812). Licensed to practice in Virginia, August 1780.

Son-in-law of ALEXANDER OUTLAW. Clerk, Washington County Court, Virginia, January 1777–August 1780. Elected assistant judge for Washington District, North Carolina Superior Court, November 1784, but declined the office. Elected judge, Superior Court, State of Franklin, March

1785. Represented Greene County, North Carolina House of Commons, 1787. Judge, Washington District, North Carolina Superior Court, 1787–1790. Appointed by President Washington as judge, Territory South of the River Ohio, June 1790. Commissioned by Governor Sevier as judge, Superior Court of Law and Equity, October 1797, and remained on the bench throughout AJ's tenure as one of his colleagues on the court.`

Writing to President Washington about various candidates' qualifications to receive appointment as judge of the new federal district court in Tennessee, AJ observed: "I think Mr. Campbell a good upright Citizen, but his abilities as a lawyer never can be Considered as Competant to that appointment, and the duties appertaining thereto." Jackson's opinion of Campbell did not change once he joined him on the bench. Lamenting the departure from the bench of his respected colleague ARCHIBALD ROANE to assume his new duties as governor, AJ wrote to his brother-in-law ROBERT HAYS in August 1801: "[I]t is well known I cannot Expect much beneficial aid from the Talents of Judge Campbell, altho an agreable companion" (AJ to Hays, Aug. 24, 1801, *Jackson Papers*, I, 252).

Campbell survived two legislative impeachment efforts. The first, in December 1798, arose from his having ordered the release on constitutional grounds of a federal official named as defendant in a civil action in a county court and from his absence at the Mero District Superior Court's May Term 1798. The second, in October 1803, was prompted by allegations that he had accepted a bribe from a party to litigation pending before the Hamilton District Superior Court. Resigned from the bench, 1807. Appointed by President Madison as a judge in the Mississippi Territory, March 1811, a position that he assumed in November of that year and held until his death the following year.

AJ to Washington, Feb. 8, 1797, *Jackson Papers*, I, 121; *BD-Tenn. Assembly*, I, 113; Blount, *Journal*, 29; Carter, *Territorial Papers*, VI, 191 n.10, 238; *N.C. State Records*, XIX, 487; Sevier, *Commission Book*, 4; White, *Messages*, I, 73–98, 154–159; Williams, *Lost State of Franklin*, 57–58, 298–299.

GEORGE WASHINGTON CAMPBELL (1769–1848). B.A., College of New Jersey, 1794. Licensed to practice in Tennessee courts, March 1798. Admitted to practice, Knox County Court of Pleas and Quarter Sessions, April 1798.

Born in Scotland. Moved with his parents to Mecklenburg County, North Carolina, 1772. Reported to have taught school in Trenton, New Jersey, upon graduation from college. Practiced in North Carolina before moving to Knoxville to practice, ca. March 1798. Represented Judge DAVID CAMPBELL in Campbell's impeachment proceedings, October 1803. Served in U.S. House of Representatives, 1803–1809. Judge, Tennessee Supreme Court of Errors and Appeals, 1809–1811. Represented Tennessee, U.S. Senate, 1811–1814, 1815–1818. Appointed secretary of the treasury by President Madison, February 1814, but resigned because of ill health the next October. U.S. minister to Russia, 1818–1820. Served as a member of the French Spoliation Claims Commission, 1831. Lifelong personal and political ally of AJ's.

KnoxCo CPQS Rec. Bk., 1795–1799, p. 318; *Knoxville Register,* Sept. 25, 1798; *BDAC; DAB; General Catalogue of Princeton University 1746–1906* (Princeton, 1908), 108; *Jackson Papers,* I, 290 n.1; Weymouth T. Jordan, "George Washington Campbell of Tennessee: Western Statesman," *Florida State University Studies,* No. 17 (Tampa, 1955); Sevier, *Commission Book,* 6; White, *Messages,* I, 85–86.

LANDON CARTER (1760–1800). Reported to have attended Liberty Hall (Davidson College), Mecklenburg County, North Carolina.

Son of John Carter, chairman of the Watauga Association. Succeeded his father as entry-taker, Washington County, 1780. Received legislative appointment as auditor, Washington District, 1782. Represented Washington County, North Carolina House of Commons, 1783, 1784; Senate, 1789. Speaker of the Senate, member of the Council of State, and secretary of state, State of Franklin, 1785. Assumed office as justice, Washington County Court of Pleas and Quarter Sessions, May 1788, the same term that AJ was admitted to practice before that court. Represented Washington County as delegate to the convention that met at Fayetteville, North Carolina, in 1789 to ratify the U.S. Constitution. Commissioned lieutenant colonel commandant, Washington County militia, and justice, Washington County Court of Pleas and Quarter Sessions, October 1790. Clerk and master in equity, Washington District Superior Court, September 1793, March 1794. Commissioned treasurer, Washington and Hamilton districts, September 1794, April 1796, April 1798. Represented Washington County as delegate to the convention that framed the first Tennessee constitution, 1796, where both he and AJ were aligned with the faction led by Governor William Blount. Commissioned justice, Carter County Court of Pleas and Quarter Sessions, April 1796. Commissioned brigadier general, Washington District, November 1796.

WashCo CPQS Min. Bk. 1, p. 323; *Knoxville Gazette,* Feb. 13 and July 17, 1794; *BD-Tenn. Assembly,* I, 130; Barnhart, "The Tennessee Constitution of 1796," p. 543 n.41; Blount, *Journal,* 29, 30, 101; *DAB;* Sevier, *Commission Book,* 1, 3, 6, 10; Williams, *Lost State of Franklin,* 299–301; Samuel Cole Williams, comp., "Western Representation in North Carolina Assemblies, 1776–1790," ETHS *Publ.* No. 14, p. 110 (1942).

WILLIAM CHARLES COLE CLAIBORNE (1775–1817). Reported to have attended Richmond Academy. Attended College of William and Mary, ca. 1790. Studied law in Richmond, ca. 1792. Licensed to practice law in the territorial courts, May 1794. Admitted to practice, Knox County Court of Pleas and Quarter Sessions, August 1794. Licensed to practice in Tennessee, April 1796.

After leaving the College of William and Mary, Claiborne secured a position in the office of John Beckley, clerk of the U.S. House of Representatives, in New York and Philadelphia. Apparently upon the advice of John Sevier, who at the time was a representative from North Carolina, he returned to Virginia to study law. While in Richmond, he was a member of the city's Independent Literary Society, 1793. After reportedly establishing his practice first in Sullivan County, he maintained an active practice in Knox County.

Claiborne represented Sullivan County as a delegate to the convention that framed the first Tennessee constitution, 1796, where both he and AJ were aligned with the faction led by Governor William Blount. He was commissioned by Governor Sevier as "Judge Protemporary of the Superior Courts of Law and Equity," September 1796; resigned, 1797. Described as having "the best practice of any man at the Bar" and as being "as much respected as any practitioner" in Tennessee, Claiborne was recommended to President Washington in December 1796 for appointment as judge of the new federal district court in the state. Describing Claiborne as "an amiable young man," AJ nonetheless advised Washington that the candidate lacked "sufficient Experience to fill such an important office" (AJ to Washington, Feb. 8, 1797, *Jackson Papers*, I, 122). Claiborne succeeded AJ as the state's delegate to the U.S. House of Representatives, 1797, and served until 1801. Appointed by President Jefferson as governor of the Mississippi Territory, May 1801. Governor, Territory of Orleans, 1804–1812; Louisiana, 1812–1816. Represented Louisiana in the U.S. Senate from March 1817 until his death.

David Ross to William Claiborne, Dec. 6, 1796, and William Fleming to Washington, Dec. 10, 1796, Ser. 7, Washington Papers, DLC (Reel 119); William C. C. Claiborne to [Henry Lee], May 28, 1793, in *Calendar of Virginia State Papers . . . Preserved in the Capitol at Richmond* (Richmond, 1886), VI, 384–385; KnoxCo CPQS Min. Bk. O, 164; Barnhart, "The Tennessee Constitution of 1796," p. 543 n.41; *BDAC*; Blount, *Journal*, 96; *DAB*; *A Provisional List of Alumni . . . of the College of William and Mary in Virginia, from 1693 to 1888* (Richmond, 1941), 12; Dunbar Rowland, ed., *Official Letter Books of W. C. C. Claiborne, 1801–1816* (Jackson, 1917), I, 2, 3, 5; Sevier, *Commission Book*, 2.

LARDNER CLARK (d. 1801). Attended College of New Jersey, ca. 1773–1774.

Merchant in Philadelphia in 1780. Had moved to Kaskaskia by 1783 to establish mercantile firm in partnership with William Wycoff, Jr. Had opened a store in Nashville by October 1783. Became owner or partial owner with Wycoff of more than 24,000 acres in Davidson County and in western and middle districts, 1784–1790. Received legislative appointments as trustee of Davidson Academy and as trustee of Clarksville, Tennessee, 1785. Entered into partnership with JAMES COLE MOUNT-FLORENCE and William Tyrrell Lewis for mining salt in Davidson County, 1788. Assumed office of justice, Davidson County Court of Pleas and Quarter Sessions, January 1791. Increasing demands of creditors in Detroit (see, for example, No. 4) and Philadelphia and the failure of his Kaskaskian partnership with Wycoff in 1790 forced Clark to dispose of most of his property holdings before moving to Kaskaskia in 1795.

Commissioned by Governor Arthur St. Clair as clerk, Court of General Quarter Sessions of the Peace; clerk, Orphans Court; prothonotary, Court of Common Pleas; and recorder of deeds, Randolph County, Territory North of the River Ohio, October 1795. Had resigned all offices except that of recorder before leaving Randolph County, ca. 1800, for St. Genevieve.

DaCo CPQS Min. Bk. A, 400; *Archives of the State of New Jersey,* ser. 1 (Paterson, N.J., 1902), XXIX, 496; Carter, *Territorial Papers,* III, 442, 489, 523; Brown, "Tennessee County Courts," 386, 388; William A. Provine, "Lardner Clark, Nashville's First Merchant and Foremost Citizen," 3 *Tenn. Hist. Mag.* 33, 36, 116, 119, 125 (1917). In 1793, Clark and AJ were the only subscribers to the *Knoxville Gazette* in Davidson County. *Knoxville Gazette,* Dec. 29, 1792. The inventory of Clark's estate, filed in Davidson County Court of Pleas and Quarter Sessions in July 1802, lists a commentary on Blackstone, a manual for justices of the peace, and a copy of Sir Thomas Jones's *The Reports of Several Special Cases Adjudged in the Courts of King's Bench and Common Pleas at Westminster, in the Reign of King Charles II* (1729). DaCo Wills & Inventories, II, 264.

TOWNSHEND STUART DADE (b. 1774). Licensed to practice in the Tennessee courts, October 1798. Admitted to practice, Grainger County Court of Pleas and Quarter Sessions, November 1798.

Practiced with his cousin THEODORICK BLAND in Washington District and Hamilton District Superior Court, March 1799–March 1801, and, after Bland's return to Virginia, as late as April 1802 (see Dade to AJ, Apr. 12, 1802, *Jackson Papers,* I, 293). Represented AJ in *Jackson v.*

Kearby, No. 36. Returned to King County, Virginia, where he resided as late as 1829.

Grainger County CPQS Min. Bk., 1796–1802, p. 74; Stella P. Hardy, *Colonial Families of the Southern States of America,* 2d rev. ed. (Baltimore, 1958), 493; Bishop Meade, *Old Churches, Ministers and Families of Virginia* (Philadelphia, 1857), II, 190; Sevier, *Commission Book,* 7; see Theodorick Bland to Sophia Bland, Oct. 4, 1799, Bland Papers, MdHi; Dade to AJ, Feb. 25, 1829, AJ Papers, DLC (Reel 36).

JOHN DICKINSON (1781–1815). Dartmouth, 1797. Read law with JOHN McNAIRY and with JOHN OVERTON, 1801. Admitted to practice, Mero District Superior Court, May 1800; Davidson County and Sumner County Courts of Pleas and Quarter Sessions, July 1800.

Born in Charlestown, New Hampshire. Reported to have been persuaded to move to Tennessee by MOSES FISK and to have taught school in Knoxville after his arrival in the state. Clerked in the office of JOHN OVERTON, inspector of the revenue in Tennessee, 1801. Clerk, U.S. District Court, District of West Tennessee, 1802–1806. Elected an alderman for the newly incorporated town of Nashville, 1806.

John McNairy to John Overton, Jan. 16, 1801, Murdock Coll., Overton Papers, THi; Overton to Dickinson, Jan. 23, 1801, Claybrooke and Overton Papers, THi; DaCo CPQS Min. Bk. C, 292; MDSC Law Min. Bk., 1788–1803, p. 320; SumCo CPQS Min. Bk. 3, p. 262; Caldwell, *Bench and Bar,* 32; Clayton, *Davidson County,* 198; *Dartmouth College and Associated Schools General Catalogue, 1769–1940* (Hanover, N.H., 1940), 87; Samuel Cole Williams, "Moses Fisk," ETHS *Publ.* No. 20, p. 30 (1948); see *Tennessee Gazette,* Apr. 6, 1803, and *Impartial Review,* Jan. 3, 1807.

JAMES DOHERTIE. Admitted to practice, Davidson County and Sumner County Courts of Pleas and Quarter Sessions, July 1793. Admitted to practice, Mero District Superior Court, May 1795. Licensed to practice in Tennessee courts, July 1796.

DaCo CPQS Min. Bk. B, 99; MDSC Law Min. Bk., 1788–1803, p. 130; SumCo CPQS Min. Bk. 2, p. 60; Sevier, *Commission Book,* 2.

JOHN DONELSON, JR. (1755–1830). Brother-in-law of AJ, ROBERT HAYS, and THOMAS HUTCHINGS; brother of SAMUEL DONELSON and WILLIAM DONELSON. Assumed office as justice, Davidson County Court of Pleas and Quarter Sessions, April 1788; commissioned, December 1790; served only through January 1791.

Blount, *Journal,* 41; Brown, "Tennessee County Courts," 385, 411 (Table 16); Donelson Family Genealogical Charts, *Jackson Papers,* I, 417.

SAMUEL DONELSON (ca. 1759–1803). Licensed to practice in territorial county courts, November 1794; Superior Court, December 1795. Admitted to practice, Davidson County and Sumner County Courts of Pleas and Quarter Sessions, January 1795. Licensed to practice in Tennessee courts, July 1796.

Brother-in-law of AJ, ROBERT HAYS, and THOMAS HUTCHINGS; brother of JOHN DONELSON, JR., and WILLIAM DONELSON; son-in-law of DANIEL SMITH. County solicitor, Davidson County Court of Pleas and Quarter Sessions, 1795–1797. Appointed county solicitor, Robertson County Court of Pleas and Quarter Sessions, July 1796. Resigned as county solicitor, Sumner County Court of Pleas and Quarter Sessions, April 1798. Appointed attorney for the territory pro hac vice, Mero District Superior Court, May 1795 (in AJ's absence), May 1796 (in AJ's absence), November 1796, May 1797.

DaCo CPQS Min. Bk. B, 231, 345, 391; SumCo CPQS Min. Bk. 2, p. 80, Min. Bk. 3, p. 148; MDSC Law Min. Bk., 1788–1803, pp. 130, 164, 179, 195; Blount, *Journal*, 103, 115; Donelson Family Genealogical Charts, *Jackson Papers*, I, 417; Sevier, *Commission Book*, 2; "Sketches of Sevier and Robertson Counties," 5 *AHM* 314 (1900). The inventory of his estate lists ten identified law books and an additional "One Lot Law Books." Donelson Inventory, Nov. 1, 1804, SumCo Records (unprocessed), T.

WILLIAM DONELSON (1756–1820). Brother-in-law of AJ, ROBERT HAYS, and THOMAS HUTCHINGS; brother of JOHN DONELSON, JR., and SAMUEL DONELSON. Commissioned justice, Davidson County Court of Pleas and Quarter Sessions, August 1796. Commissioned lieutenant colonel, Davidson County militia, October 1794.

Blount, *Journal*, 102; Donelson Family Genealogical Charts, *Jackson Papers*, I, 417; Sevier, *Commission Book*, 12.

EDWARD DOUGLASS, JR. (1745–1825). Reported to have read law, but where and with whom not identified.

Commissioned justice, Sumner County Court of Pleas and Quarter Sessions, December 1790, April 1796. Represented Sumner County as a delegate to the convention that framed first Tennessee constitution, 1796, where both he and AJ were aligned with the faction led by Governor William Blount. Commissioned lieutenant colonel commandant, Sumner County militia, October 1796. Represented Sumner County, Tennessee Senate, 1797–1799; Sumner and Wilson counties, 1805–1809; Sumner County, 1819–1821. Died in Wilson County.

Barnhart, "The Tennessee Constitution of 1796," p. 543 n.41; *BD-*

Tenn. Assembly, I, 211; Blount, *Journal,* 44; Sevier, *Commission Book,* 39, 40.

GEORGE DUFFIELD (1767–1823). A.B., 1787, A.M. 1790, University of Pennsylvania. Probably the same George Duffield who was admitted to the bar, Lancaster County, Pennsylvania, 1792. Licensed to practice in the Tennessee courts, December 1798. Admitted to practice, Hamilton District Superior Court, October 1801.

Son-in-law of LANDON CARTER. Reported to have practiced in Philadelphia before moving to Greeneville, Tennessee, in 1798. Practiced regularly in the Washington District and Hamilton District Superior Court while AJ was on the bench (see, for example, No. 24). Having received recommendations from JOSEPH ANDERSON, JOHN RHEA, and numerous county court justices, Duffield was appointed by President Jefferson as one of the judges of the Superior Court, Territory of Orleans, March 1805. Resigned because of ill health, July 1805. Reported to have been offered appointment to Tennessee Supreme Court of Errors and Appeals to succeed HUGH LAWSON WHITE, February 1815. Died in Elizabethton, Tennessee.

Duffield File, Letters of Application and Recommendation During the Administration of Thomas Jefferson, 1801–1809, RG 59, DNA; HDSC Law Min. Bk. 3, p. 249; Carter, *Territorial Papers,* IX, 415, 417; Edward Potts Cheney and Ellis Paxson Oberholtzer, *University of Pennsylvania* (Boston, 1901), II, 15; Clayton, *Davidson County,* 93; *General Alumni Catalogue of the University of Pennsylvania* (Philadelphia, 1917), 22; Frank Merritt, *Early History of Carter County 1760–1861* (Knoxville, 1950), 193–94; J. I. Mombert, *An Authentic History of Lancaster County in the State of Pennsylvania* (Lancaster, 1869), 431; Sevier, *Commission Book,* 7. As a trustee for Greeneville College, Duffield helped to raise funds for the institution's library and secured for it a portion of the Philadelphia library of the Reverend William Hollingshead. Richard H. Doughty, *Greeneville One Hundred Year Portrait [1775–1875]* (Greeneville, 1975), 156. Duffield Academy, established in Elizabethton in 1806, was named in his honor. Merritt, *Early History of Carter County,* 125, 194.

EPHRAIM DUNLOP. Admitted to the bar, Botetourt County, Virginia, 1770; Fincastle County, Virginia, 1773. Licensed to practice in the North Carolina county courts, 1778. Admitted to practice, Washington County Court of Pleas and Quarter Sessions, November 1778. Licensed to practice in the territorial county courts, November 1790. Admitted to practice, Knox County Court of Pleas and Quarter Sessions, October 1792.

Deputy attorney for the Commonwealth, Washington County, Virginia, 1777. State's attorney, Washington County Court of Pleas and Quarter Sessions, 1778–1782. Appointed state's attorney, Sullivan County Court of Pleas and Quarter Sessions, November 1779.

KnoxCo CPQS Min. Bk. O, 7; WashCo CPQS Min. Bk. 1, p. 183; Blount, *Journal,* 35; Ramsey, *Annals,* 189; "The Records of Washington County," pt. 1, 5 *AHM* 358, (1900); Lewis P. Summers, *History of Southwest Virginia 1746–1786, Washington County, 1777–1870* (Richmond, 1903), 260, 353, 834, 835.

ROBERT EDMONDSON (d. 1816). Justice, Davidson County Court of Pleas and Quarter Sessions, 1789–1803, a tenure encompassing AJ's practice before that court. Commissioned justice, Montgomery County Court of Pleas and Quarter Sessions, January 1799. Represented Davidson County, Tennessee House of Representatives, 1801–1803.

DaCo CPQS Min. Bk. A, 295; Edmondson Resignation, Legislative Reports and Miscellaneous 1803, Box 1, T; *BD-Tenn. Assembly,* I, 228; Sevier, *Commission Book,* 34. The inventory of his estate, filed Apr. 26, 1816, lists a copy of Haywood's *The Duty and Office of Justices of Peace, . . . According to the Laws of the State of North-Carolina* (1800).

THOMAS EMMERSON (1773–1837). Reported to have attended Hampden-Sydney College. Admitted to practice, Hamilton District Superior Court, September 1803; Knox County Court of Pleas and Quarter Sessions, October 1803.

Moved to Tennessee from Virginia, ca. 1800. Resigned as justice, Knox County Court of Pleas and Quarter Sessions, October 1803. Appointed by Governor Sevier as judge, Superior Court, to succeed HUGH LAWSON WHITE, 1807; served through 1809. Returned to private practice in Knoxville with PLEASANT M. MILLER. Clerk, Supreme Court of Errors and Appeals, 1810–1816. Collaborated with JOHN OVERTON in the publication of the first two volumes of *Tennessee Reports* (1813–1817). Elected mayor of Knoxville, 1816. Judge, First Circuit Court, Tennessee, 1816–1819. Judge, Supreme Court of Errors and Appeals, 1819–1822. Upon retirement from the bench, moved to Jonesboro, where he edited the *Washington Republican and Farmers' Journal,* beginning in 1833, and an agricultural journal, the *Tennessee Farmer,* 1834–1837.

Thomas Emmerson to John Sevier, Oct. 11, 1803, Governors' Papers, 1803–1809, T; HDSC Law Min. Bk. 3, p. 327; KnoxCo CPQS Min. Bk. 4, p. 174; Henry F. Beaumont, "Biography of Thomas Emmerson," 9 *AHM* 141–142 (1904); Caldwell, *Bench and Bar,* 17; Weston A. Goodspeed, *A History of Tennessee from the Earliest Time to the Present*

(Nashville, 1886), 817; Green, *Lives of the Judges*, 62; Samuel Cole Williams, *Phases of the History of the Supreme Court of Tennessee* (Johnson City, 1944), 16–17.

ANDREW EWING (1740–1813). Member and clerk, Cumberland Association Committee, January–August 1783. Commissioned clerk, Davidson County Court of Pleas and Quarter Sessions, December 1790; served throughout AJ's practice before the Davidson court. At his death, the office of clerk went to his son, Nathan Ewing, who held the position until 1830.

Blount, *Journal*, 43; Clayton, *Davidson County*, 92; Quarles and White, *Three Pioneer Documents*, 23, 39. His collection of some seventy-four volumes, including an occasional law book such as Vattel's *The Law of Nations* (1787), is itemized in the inventory filed with the Davidson court Nov. 12, 1813. DaCo Wills & Inventories, V, 262–263.

ROBERT EWING (1760–1832). Son-in-law of EPHRAIM MCLEAN. Assumed office as justice, Davidson County Court of Pleas and Quarter Sessions, January 1789, the term at which AJ was admitted to practice before that court; commissioned, December 1790; remained on the bench through July 1792, when he moved to Logan County, Kentucky.

After having moved to Davidson County from Virginia in 1784, Ewing represented the county in the North Carolina House of Commons, 1787, 1789; delegate to the convention that met at Fayetteville, North Carolina, to ratify the U.S. Constitution, 1789. Member, Kentucky House of Representatives, 1797; Kentucky Senate, 1806–1818; Speaker of the Kentucky Senate, 1818. Served as brigadier general during the War of 1812. Died in Logan County, Kentucky.

BD-Tenn. Assembly, I, 239; Blount, *Journal*, 41; Brown, "Tennessee County Courts," 411 (Table 16).

MOSES FISK (ca. 1759–1843). A.M., Dartmouth, 1786; A.M. (honorary), Yale, 1793. Studied divinity. Licensed to practice in the Tennessee county courts, October 1797; Superior Court, January 1798.

Tutor, Dartmouth College, 1788–1795. Published tracts on slavery and liberty while at Dartmouth. Moved to Tennessee as an agent for Governor William Blount, 1796. Commissioned justice, Smith County Court of Pleas and Quarter Sessions, October 1799. Appointed one of three commissioners to settle Tennessee-Virginia boundary, 1802. Recommended to President Jefferson by Tennessee congressional delegation for appointment as commissioner of bankruptcy, District of West Tennessee, 1803. Commissioned by Tennessee General Assembly to compile all North Carolina and territorial statutes in effect in Tennessee, 1803; never completed. With SAMPSON WILLIAMS established Fisk Female Academy, Hilham, Tennessee, 1803; elected trustee, Davidson Academy, 1804. A corresponding member of the Massachusetts Historical Society and the American Antiquarian Society, Fisk published a text on English grammar and articles on early Tennessee settlements and North American archaeology for the eastern societies' journals.

Joseph Anderson et al. to Thomas Jefferson, Jan. 6, 1803, Letters of Application and Recommendation During the Administration of Thomas Jefferson, 1801–1809, RG 59, DNA; George T. Chapman, *Sketches of the Alumni of Dartmouth College* (Cambridge, 1867), 41; *Dartmouth College and Associated Schools General Catalogue, 1769–1940* (Hanover, N.H., 1940), 76; Sevier, *Commission Book*, 4, 50; Samuel Cole Williams, "Moses Fisk," ETHS *Publ.* No. 20, pp. 17, 23–24, 28–29, 31–32 (1948).

THOMAS GRAY (1745–1829). Licensed to practice in the territorial courts, January 1796; Tennessee courts, April 1796.

Appointed by President Washington, U.S. attorney, District of Tennessee, February 1797; served until ca. April 1798; appointed by President Adams, U.S. attorney, District of East Tennessee, February 1801.

Blount, *Journal,* 116; *JES,* I, 226–227, 267–268, 384–385; *National Banner,* Oct. 3, 1829; Sevier, *Commission Book,* 2.

JOSEPH GREER (1754–1831). Son of Andrew Greer, one of the first justices of the Washington County Court of Pleas and Quarter Sessions. Commissioned justice, Knox County Court of Pleas and Quarter Sessions, January 1793, August 1796. Served as clerk and master in equity, Hamilton District Superior Court, throughout AJ's tenure on the bench.

Blount, *Journal,* 71; Sevier, *Commission Book,* 28; Maggie H. Stone, "Joseph Greer, 'King's Mountain Messenger': A Tradition of the Greer Family," 2 *Tenn. Hist. Mag.* 40–42 (1916); see HDSC Eq. Rec. Bk. B, 1–435 *passim.*

JOHN C. HAMILTON (d. 1833). Credited by his uncle, Chowan County attorney William Cumming, with having "received the Rudiments of his Law Education at Edinburgh and at Westminster" and with having "studied the common Law at Lincolns Inn." Possibly the same Hamilton who matriculated at Edinburgh University, 1775, 1776; there are no records of his ever having been admitted to Lincoln's Inn. Licensed to practice in the Tennessee county courts, April 1797; Superior Court, January 1799. Admitted to practice, Carter County Court of Pleas and Quarter Sessions, July 1797; Davidson County and Sumner County Courts of Pleas and

Quarter Sessions, January 1798; Mero District Superior Court, November 1800.

A native of Pennsylvania, Hamilton was recommended for appointment as U.S. attorney, District of North Carolina, 1789. Commissioned state's attorney, Mero District, September 1797. Judge, Ninth Circuit Court, Tennessee, 1823–1833. Writing in 1830 to secure James Knox Polk's influence with AJ and HUGH LAWSON WHITE for an appointment to the federal bench in Missouri, Hamilton observed: "When those gentlemen knew me as a lawyer I knew nothing of law, I fear. They both entertain an unfavorable opinion of my legal acquirements."

William Cumming to Samuel Johnston, Oct. 17, 1789, Feb. 10, 1790, Ser. 7, Washington Papers, DLC (Reel 121); Hamilton to James Knox Polk, Dec. 20, 1830, *Correspondence of James Knox Polk* (Nashville, 1969), I, 365; Carter County CPQS Min. Bk., 1797, Carter County Records, THi; DaCo CPQS Min. Bk. C, 30; MDSC Law Min. Bk., 1788–1803, p. 399; SumCo CPQS Min. Bk. 3, 145; Matriculation Register, Edinburgh University; *National Banner & Nashville Daily Advertiser,* Mar. 11, 1833; Sevier, *Commission Book,* 4, 7; Samuel Cole Williams, *Beginnings of West Tennessee in the Land of the Chickasaws 1541–1841* (Johnson City, 1930), 219.

JOSEPH HAMILTON (1763–1834). Reported to have attended Liberty Hall Academy and to have been admitted to the bar in Virginia, ca. 1784. Admitted to practice, Washington County Court of Pleas and Quarter Sessions, May 1788. Licensed to practice in the territorial courts, November 1790. Admitted to practice, Knox County Court of Pleas and Quarter Sessions, July 1792.

Son-in-law of ALEXANDER OUTLAW. Maintained an active practice in Knox County. Clerk, Greene County Court of Pleas and Quarter Sessions, 1785; Jefferson County Court of Pleas and Quarter Sessions, 1792–1821. Commissioned county solicitor, Hawkins County, February 1791. Elected trustee of Blount College, 1795; Greeneville College, 1795; Washington College, 1795; Maury Academy, Jefferson County, 1807. Represented Greene and Jefferson counties, Tennessee Senate, 1823–1825. Died in present Hamblen County, Tennessee.

KnoxCo CPQS Min. Bk. O, 4; WashCo CPQS Min. Bk. 1, p. 322; *BD-Tenn. Assembly,* I, 326; Blount, *Journal,* 35, 46, 63.

DAVID HAY (d. ca. 1801). Assumed office as justice, Davidson County Court of Pleas and Quarter Sessions, July 1788; commissioned December 1790; served through October 1793. Elected sheriff, Davidson County, July 1786, July 1787. Appointed director and trustee of Nashville, July

1790. Commissioned first major, Davidson County militia, June 1791, October 1796.

DaCo CPQS Min. Bk. A, 124, 176; DaCo Wills & Inventories, I, 171; Blount, *Journal*, 41, 52; Brown, "Tennessee County Courts," 411 (Table 16); Sevier, *Commission Book*, 12.

ROBERT HAYS (1758–1819). Brother-in-law of AJ, JOHN DONELSON, JR., SAMUEL DONELSON, WILLIAM DONELSON, and THOMAS HUTCHINGS. Represented Davidson County, North Carolina House of Commons, 1787. Assumed office as justice, Davidson County Court of Pleas and Quarter Sessions, April 1788; commissioned, December 1790, April 1796. Elected colonel, Mero District cavalry, July 1790; commissioned lieutenant colonel commandant, January 1797. Appointed by President Washington as U.S. marshal, District of Tennessee, February 1797; reappointed by President Adams, December 1800; had been removed from office by December 1803.

DaCo CPQS Min. Bk. A, 377; Donelson Family Genealogical Charts, *Jackson Papers*, I, 417; *BD-Tenn. Assembly*, I, 349–350; Brown, "Tennessee County Courts," 411 (Table 16); *JES*, I, 226–227, 362–363, 460; Sevier, *Commission Book*, 3, 12.

THOMAS HUTCHINGS (1750–1804). Brother-in-law of AJ, JOHN DONELSON, JR., SAMUEL DONELSON, WILLIAM DONELSON, and ROBERT HAYS. Commissioned justice, Davidson County Court of Pleas and Quarter Sessions, August 1796. Had represented Sullivan County, North Carolina House of Commons, 1786, and had served as clerk, Hawkins County Court of Pleas and Quarter Sessions, 1787.

BD-Tenn. Assembly, I, 395–396; Sevier, *Commission Book*, 12.

HARRY INNES (1752–1816). Reported to have attended the College of William and Mary and to have read law under George Wythe. Admitted to practice in the Virginia courts, 1773.

Assumed office in Nashville as one of three judges, U.S. Circuit Court for the Sixth Circuit, April 1801; served and held court in Nashville with JOHN MCNAIRY and WILLIAM MCCLUNG until 1802. Judge, U.S. District Court, District of Kentucky, April 1789–1801, 1802–1816. Had practiced law in Bedford County, Virginia, before appointment in 1782 as assistant judge, Supreme Court of Judicature, District of Kentucky. Moved to Kentucky, 1783. Elected attorney general, Kentucky District, October 1784. Was a member of the Political Club of Danville along with JOHN OVERTON and other Kentucky lawyers. Subsequently implicated in the Spanish Conspiracy, 1794.

U.S. Circuit Court, Western District of Tennessee, Minute Book, 1800–

1846, pp. 1, 14, RG 21, DNA; *DAB;* Harry Phillips, *History of the Sixth Circuit* (n.p., [1976]), 148; Mary K. Bonsteel Tachau, *Federal Courts in the Early Republic: Kentucky, 1789–1816* (Princeton, 1978), 31–32, 47–50.

JOHN FINLEY JACK (1766–1828). Dickinson College, 1794, in the same class as RANDAL MCGAVOCK and JESSE WHARTON. Admitted to practice, Knox County Court of Pleas and Quarter Sessions, January 1799; Grainger County Court of Pleas and Quarter Sessions, November 1799; Hamilton District Superior Court, March 1799.

Clerk, Grainger County Court of Pleas and Quarter Sessions, 1808–1810; Circuit Court, 1810–1824. Represented Claiborne, Grainger, and Campbell counties, Tennessee Senate, 1803–1807, 1813–1815.

Grainger County CPQS Min. Bk., 1796–1802, p. 113; HDSC Law Min. Bk. 3, p. 175; KnoxCo CPQS Rec. Bk. 1, p. 407; *BD-Tenn. Assembly,* I, 400; Weston A. Goodspeed, *A History of Tennessee* (Nashville, 1886), 856; George L. Reed, ed., *Alumni Record of Dickinson College* (Carlisle, Pa., 1905), 43.

JOHN KIRKPATRICK (d. 1806). Assumed office as justice, Davidson County Court of Pleas and Quarter Sessions, April 1788; commissioned, December 1790, August 1796; served on the bench throughout AJ's practice before the Davidson court.

Blount, *Journal,* 41; Brown, "Tennessee County Courts," 411 (Table 16); *Impartial Review & Cumberland Repository,* Apr. 19, 1806; Sevier, *Commission Book,* 12. The inventory of his estate lists some fifty volumes, including for the most part histories and various works on divinity. DaCo Wills & Inventories, III, 137.

HOPKINS LACY (1763–1831). Admitted to practice in the following territorial county courts of pleas and quarter sessions: Washington County, May 1790; Davidson County, July 1790; Sumner County, July 1790; Knox County, July 1792; Jefferson County, 1793. Licensed to practice in the territorial county courts, December 1790; Tennessee county courts, February 1797. Admitted to practice, Mero District Superior Court, May 1791.

Appointed county solicitor, Sumner County Court of Pleas and Quarter Sessions, October 1790; Davidson County, March 1791. Commissioned attorney general, Washington District, March 1794; reappointed July 1796. Appointed clerk, Territorial Assembly, 1794. Represented Sevier County, Tennessee House of Representatives, 1809–1811. Moved to Morgan County, Alabama, where he resided until his death.

DaCo CPQS Min. Bk. A, 363; KnoxCo CPQS Min. Bk. O, 4; MDSC

Law Min. Bk., 1788–1803, p. 30; SumCo CPQS Min. Bk. 1, pp. 26, 29; WashCo CPQS Min. Bk. 1, 436; *BD-Tenn. Assembly,* I, 435, 836; Blount, *Journal,* 43, 48–49, 90; Sevier, *Commission Book,* 2, 3.

SETH LEWIS (1764–1848). Studied law under JOSIAH LOVE, 1790–1793. Admitted to practice, Davidson County Court of Pleas and Quarter Sessions, July 1795. Licensed to practice in the Tennessee courts, April 1796; Mero District Superior Court, May 1796; Williamson County Court of Pleas and Quarter Sessions, May 1800.

Commissioned justice, Davidson County Court of Pleas and Quarter Sessions, June 1794. Represented Davidson County, Tennessee House of Representatives, 1796–1797. Appointed by President Adams as chief justice, Mississippi Territory, May 1800; resigned April 1803. Commissioned attorney general for Adams, Jefferson, Wilkinson, and Claiborne counties, Mississippi Territory, April 1807; resigned, 1808. Appointed judge, Parish of St. Martin, Attakapas County, Orleans Territory, 1810; resigned, 1812. Appointed judge, Fifth Judicial District, Louisiana, 1813; remained on the bench until 1840.

Autobiographical Memoir of Seth Lewis, 1848, p. 20, McRaven Coll., T; DaCo CPQS Min. Bk. B, 264; MDSC Law Min. Bk., 1788–1803, p. 163; Williamson County CPQS Min. Bk. 1800–1812, p. 5; *BD-Tenn. Assembly,* I, 447–448; Carter, *Territorial Papers,* V, 215; *JES,* I, 354–355; Rowland, *Courts of Mississippi,* I, 18, 59; Dunbar Rowland, ed., *Official Letter Books of W.C.C. Claiborne, 1801–1816* (Jackson, 1917), VI, 172.

JOHN LOVE. Admitted to practice, Hamilton District Superior Court, September 1799.

Was counsel of record for the accused in *State v. McKee,* No. 26.

HDSC Law Min. Bk. 3, 1793–1809, p. 186.

JOSIAH LOVE (d. 1793). Admitted to practice, Davidson County Court of Pleas and Quarter Sessions, October 1788; Superior Court of Davidson and Sumner Counties, November 1788; Mero District Superior Court, May 1791. Licensed to practice in the territorial courts, December 1790.

Maintained a larger practice before his death late in 1793 than any other lawyer in Davidson County. Frequently acted as co-counsel with AJ and HOWELL TATUM. Jackson apparently assumed much of Love's practice beginning in 1794. Love had been an unsuccessful candidate for judge of the Superior Court of Davidson County, December 1787, and had been appointed state's attorney, Davidson County Court of Pleas and Quarter Sessions, October 1788. SETH LEWIS read law under him, 1790–1793.

Lewis Memoir, 20; DaCo CPQS Min. Bk. A, 242; MDSC Law Min. Bk., 1788–1803, pp. 2, 30; Blount, *Journal,* 43; Brown, "Tennessee County Courts," 394; *Knoxville Gazette,* Jan. 2, 1794; *N.C. State Records,* XX, 202. That Lewis was accurate in recalling that Love had had an "excellent library" is suggested by the appearance in July 1794 of advertisements in the *Gazette* in which the executor of Love's estate notified the public of the pending sale of "a large number of LAW BOOKS" that had belonged to Love. See, *e.g., Knoxville Gazette,* July 31, 1794.

JOHN LOWREY. Licensed to practice in the territorial county courts, April 1793; Superior Court, October 1794; Tennessee courts, October 1796. Admitted to practice, Knox County Court of Pleas and Quarter Sessions, May 1793.

Commissioned county solicitor, Sevier County, October 1794; state's attorney, Hamilton District, July 1796; was serving in that capacity as late as March 1801. Represented Blount County, Tennessee House of Representatives, 1809–1811; Blount and Sevier counties, Tennessee Senate, 1817–1821; Blount, McMinn, and Monroe counties, Tennessee Senate, 1827–1829.

Indictment of David Nelson, March 1801, HDSC Records, TKL; KnoxCo CPQS Min. Bk. O, 38; *BD-Tenn. Assembly,* I, 460; Blount, *Journal,* 78, 102; Sevier, *Commission Book,* 2.

SPRUCE MACAY (d. 1808). B.A., College of New Jersey, 1775.

Jackson studied law under him for a year beginning in late 1784 or early 1785. Was practicing in Washington County Court of Pleas and Quarter Sessions as early as August 1781. Elected to Council of State, North Carolina, June 1781, May 1782, May 1783. Received legislative appointment as judge, Court of Oyer and Terminer, Washington and Sullivan counties, May 1782. Represented town of Salisbury, North Carolina House of Commons, 1784–1785. Elected judge, North Carolina Superior Court of Law and Equity, December 1790; remained on the bench until his death.

Cheney, *North Carolina Government,* 215, 360, 367 n.9; *General Catalogue of Princeton University 1746–1906* (Princeton, 1908), 98; *N.C. State Records,* XVI, 95, 175, XVII, 812, 896, XIX, 59, 123, 202, 331; "The Records of Washington County," pt. 2, 6 *AHM* 86 (1901).

CHARLES McCLUNG (1761–1835). Licensed to practice, Tennessee county courts, May 1796.

Frequently handled AJ's legal affairs in Knox County (see, for example, AJ to McClung, [April 1801], *Jackson Papers,* I, 243; see also *id.,* App. III, for several deeds beginning with AJ, by McClung, to Robert

Holt, Apr. 13, 1801). Commissioned clerk, Knox County Court of Pleas and Quarter Sessions, June 1792; held the office until 1834. Had moved to present site of Knoxville from Pennsylvania in 1788. Served as Knox County trustee, 1794–1806. Represented Knox County as a delegate to the convention that framed the first Tennessee constitution, 1796, where both he and AJ were aligned with the faction led by Governor William Blount. Was a partner in the mercantile firms of McClung & Son, Knoxville, and McClung & Campbell, Campbell's Station, ca. 1816. Died in Harrodsburgh Springs, Kentucky.

Barnhart, "The Tennessee Constitution of 1796," p. 543 n.41; Blount, *Journal*, 61; Rothrock, *French Broad-Holston Country*, 446–447; Sevier, *Commission Book*, 2.

WILLIAM MCCLUNG (1758–1811). Reported to have been graduated from Washington College, 1785.

Appointed by President Adams one of three judges, U.S. Circuit Court for the Sixth Circuit, February 1801; assumed office in Nashville, October 1801; served with HARRY INNES and JOHN MCNAIRY until 1802. Had declined appointment by President Washington as U.S. attorney, District of Kentucky, May 1794. Had represented Nelson County, Kentucky House of Representatives, 1793; Senate, 1796–1800. Appointed judge, Mason County Circuit Court, 1804. Brother-in-law of Chief Justice John Marshall.

U.S. Circuit Court, W.D. Tenn., Min. Bk., 1800–1846, p. 14, RG 21, DNA; Harold Chase et al., comps., *Biographical Dictionary of the Federal Judiciary* (Detroit, 1976), 183; *JES*, I, 160, 383, 385; H. Levin, ed., *The Lawyers and Lawmakers of Kentucky* (Chicago, 1897), 668; Mary K. Bonsteel Tachau, *Federal Courts in the Early Republic: Kentucky 1789–1816* (Princeton, 1978), 56–57, 72.

RANDAL MCGAVOCK (d. 1843). Dickinson College, 1794, in same class as JOHN FINLEY JACK and JESSE WHARTON. Admitted to practice "by consent of the Court & Barr," Davidson County Court of Pleas and Quarter Sessions, January 1796, and upon production of license, April 1797; Sumner County Court of Pleas and Quarter Sessions, January 1796. Licensed to practice in Tennessee county courts, July 1796; Superior Court, January 1798. Admitted to practice, Mero District Superior Court, May 1798.

Was serving as clerk, U.S. District Court, District of Tennessee, 1801; clerk, U.S. Circuit Court for the Sixth Circuit, District of West Tennessee, 1802; clerk, Mero District Superior Court, 1803–1804. Served as circuit court clerk, Davidson County, 1810–1834; mayor of Nashville, 1824. Moved to Williamson County, where he resided until his death.

DaCo CPQS Min. Bk. B, 301, 392; MDSC Law Min. Bk., 1788–1803, p. 211; SumCo CPQS Min. Bk. 2, p. 97; Clayton, *Davidson County*, 92, 198, 426; *Nashville Whig*, Sept. 30, 1843; George L. Reed, *Alumni Record of Dickinson College* (Carlisle, Pa., 1905), 44; Sevier, *Commission Book*, 2, 5; see Certificate of AJ's Attendance, MDSC, November 1803, Treasury Records, T; *ASP*, Class X, I, 321; *Tennessee Gazette*, July 20, 1804.

LACHLAN McINTOSH (1725–1806). Licensed to practice, Superior Court of Tennessee, June 1798.

Moved from Scotland to Georgia, 1736. Represented Parish of St. Andrew, Provincial Congress, 1775; Georgia, Continental Congress, 1784. Served as counsel for Zachariah Cox's Tennessee Yazoo Land Company, ca. 1797–1798, and was associated with William Blount in land speculation. Was one of three attorneys representing the state in impeachment proceedings against Judge DAVID CAMPBELL, December 1798. Died in Savannah, Georgia.

DAB; Jackson Papers, I, 213 n.1.

EPHRAIM McLEAN (1730–1823). Assumed office as justice, Davidson County Court of Pleas and Quarter Sessions, January 1785; commissioned, December 1790, August 1796. Before moving to Davidson County, had served as member, Rowan County Committee of Safety, North Carolina, 1775; had been elected justice, Rowan County Court of Pleas and Quarter Sessions, December 1776; had represented Burke County, North Carolina House of Commons, 1777–1778, Senate, 1779–1780. Represented Davidson County, North Carolina House of Commons, 1784. Appointed tax collector, Davidson County, June 1784. Moved to Greenville, Kentucky, 1820, and resided there until his death.

McLean Sketch, Provine Papers, T; Blount, *Journal*, 41; Brown, "Tennessee County Courts," 411 (Table 16); Sevier, *Commission Book*, 12.

ANDREW McNAIRY. Licensed to practice in the Tennessee county courts, November 1796.

Brother of JOHN McNAIRY. Commissioned clerk, Mero District Superior Court, March 1792; reappointed May 1796; had resigned by November 1802.

MDSC Law Min. Bk., 1788–1803, pp. 176, 674; Blount, *Journal*, 56; Stephen S. Lawrence, "The Life and Times of John McNairy," (M.A. thesis, Middle Tennessee State Univ., 1971), 28; Sevier, *Commission Book*, 3.

JOHN MCNAIRY (1762–1837). Read law under SPRUCE MACAY. Admitted to practice, Rowan County Court of Pleas and Quarter Sessions, May 1784; Washington County Court of Pleas and Quarter Sessions, May 1788.

Married the widowed sister-in-law of JAMES and ELIJAH ROBERTSON; brother of ANDREW MCNAIRY. Elected by North Carolina General Assembly as judge, Superior Court of Davidson County, December 1787, over JOSIAH LOVE and HOWELL TATUM. Appointed by President Washington as one of three judges, Territory South of the River Ohio, June 1790. Elected one of three judges, Superior Court of Tennessee, April 1796, but declined the office. Appointed by Washington as U.S. district judge, District of Tennessee, February 1797.

By Act of Feb. 13, 1801, the U.S. District Court for the District of Tennessee was abolished, and the authority and jurisdiction formerly exercised by that court were vested in the U.S. Circuit Court for the Sixth Circuit that met biannually for the District of East Tennessee in Knoxville and for the District of West Tennessee in Nashville (Act of Feb. 13, 1801, § 24, 6th Cong., 2d Sess., *Acts of Congress*, 1544). McNairy by operation of law became one of three judges of the U.S. Circuit Court for the Sixth Circuit (see House and Senate Debate, 7th Cong., 1st Sess., *Acts of Congress*, 64–65, 114); assumed office as one of three judges, U.S. Circuit Court for the Sixth Circuit, October 1801; served with HARRY INNES and WILLIAM MCCLUNG until 1802.

By Act of Apr. 29, 1802, the U.S. Circuit Court for the Sixth Circuit was abandoned and was replaced in Tennessee by a U.S. District Court for the District of East Tennessee and a U.S. District Court for the District of West Tennessee (Act of Apr. 29, 1802, §§ 16, 21, 7th Cong., 1st Sess., *Acts of Congress*, 1338–1339). By operation of law, McNairy again became U.S. district judge for both the District of East Tennessee and the District of West Tennessee (*id.* § 17) and held court biannually at Knoxville and Nashville. Remained on the bench until retirement, May 1833.

Had represented Davidson County as a delegate to the convention that framed the first Tennessee constitution, 1796, where both he and AJ were aligned with the faction led by Governor William Blount.

U.S. Circuit Court, W.D. Tenn., Min. Bk., 1800–1846, p. 1, RG 21, DNA; WashCo CPQS Min. Bk. 1, p. 323; *JES*, I, 50, 226–227; Stephen S. Lawrence, "The Life and Times of John McNairy" (M.A. thesis, Middle Tennessee State Univ., 1971), 5–6, 9, 22, 53, 96; Harry Phillips, *History of the Sixth Circuit* (n.p., [1976]), 166–167; Sevier, *Commission Book*, 4.

ISAAC MCNUTT. Licensed to practice in the territorial county courts, October 1795; Superior Court of Tennessee, July 1796. Admitted to practice, Sumner County and Davidson County Courts of Pleas and Quarter Sessions, January 1796.

Appointed county solicitor, Davidson County, April 1797. Eventually moved to Orleans Territory, where he received an appointment as justice of the peace, Parish of Rapide, March 1809.

DaCo CPQS Min. Bk. B, 301, 391; SumCo CPQS Min. Bk. 2, p. 97; Blount, *Journal*, 114; Dunbar Rowland, ed., *Official Letter Books of W.C.C. Claiborne, 1801–1816* (Jackson, 1917), IV, 386; Sevier, *Commission Book*, 2.

PLEASANT MOORMAN MILLER (1773–1849). Reported to have studied law under Judge Archibald Stewart, Staunton, Virginia. Licensed to practice in the Tennessee county courts, June 1797; Superior Court, March 1798. Admitted to practice, Carter County Court of Pleas and Quarter Sessions, July 1797; Knox County Court of Pleas and Quarter Sessions, 1800.

Son-in-law of Governor William Blount. Served in U.S. House of Representatives, 1809–1811. Moved to Madison County, Tennessee, ca. 1824, where he practiced until his election as chancellor, West Tennessee Chancery Division, 1836. Remained on the bench until 1837. Moved to Gibson County, Tennessee, ca. 1847, where he resided until his death.

Carter County CPQS Min. Bk., 1797, Carter County Records, THi; BDAC; BD-Tenn. Assembly, I, 519–520; Weston A. Goodspeed, *A History of Tennessee* (Nashville, 1886), 819; Sevier, *Commission Book*, 4, 6.

THOMAS MOLLOY (d. 1801). Assumed office as justice, Davidson County Court of Pleas and Quarter Sessions, October 1783, and remained on the bench throughout AJ's practice before that court. Had been a member of the Cumberland Association Committee, January–August 1783. Received legislative appointment as trustee of Nashville, 1784. Commissioned register, Davidson County, December 1790. Died during visit to Raleigh, North Carolina, leaving his estate in trust to an emancipated slave.

DaCo Wills & Inventories, II, 245–247; Blount, *Journal*, 43; Brown, "Tennessee County Courts," 387–388, 411 (Table 16); Quarles and White, *Three Pioneer Documents*, 23, 39; *Tennessee Gazette*, Feb. 17, 1802. Among the eleven volumes itemized in the inventory of his estate is Blackstone's *Commentaries on the Laws of England*. DaCo Wills & Inventories, II, 320.

JAMES COLE MOUNTFLORENCE (d. 1820). Studied philosophy and mathematics, University of Paris. Probably studied law under William Richard-

son Davie, under whose patronage at the close of the American Revolution he secured a license to practice in North Carolina. Represented
clients in some ten cases before being formally admitted to practice,
Davidson County Court of Pleas and Quarter Sessions, April 1790; admitted, Sumner County Court of Pleas and Quarter Sessions, April 1790.
Licensed to practice in the territorial Superior Court, December 1790;
admitted to practice, Mero District Superior Court, May 1791.

Born in Paris; moved to North Carolina ca. 1778, where in December
of that year he was teaching "the Greek, Latin and French languages,
with arithmetic, the principles of Mathematics, Geography and Book-
keeping" at New Bern. After having obtained his license, moved to Nashville and began practicing, ca. October 1788. Entered into partnership
with LARDNER CLARK and William Tyrrell Lewis for mining salt in Davidson County, 1788. Represented Davidson County as a delegate to the
convention that met at Fayetteville, North Carolina, to ratify the U.S.
Constitution. Returned to France as trade and land speculating agent
of the Blounts in late 1791. Remained in France except for trips to the
United States, 1793–1795; an aide to the American consul to the French
Republic, 1796–1797. Appointed by President Adams as U.S. commercial agent at Paris, February 1801.

Lafayette to Alexander Martin, Jan. 29, 1826, Misc. File, THi; Thomas
Jefferson to William Blount, Aug. 17, 1791, and Jefferson to William Short,
Nov. 16, 1791, Charles T. Cullen, ed., *The Papers of Thomas Jefferson*
(Princeton, 1986), XXII, 45, 46n, 301–302; Mountflorence to Richard
Caswell, Dec. 23, 1778, N.C. *State Records*, XIII, 335–336; Mountflorence to Jefferson, Nov. 12, 1791, *Jefferson Papers*, XXII, 293; Mountflorence File, Letters of Application and Recommendation During the Administration of John Adams, 1797–1801, RG 59, DNA; DaCo CPQS
Min. Bk. A, 244–340 *passim*, 349; MDSC Law Min. Bk., 1788–1803,
p. 30; SumCo CPQS Min. Bk. 1, p. 24; *ASP*, Class I, II, 8–9, 11; Blount,
Journal, 43; Cheney, *North Carolina Government*, 768; *JES*, I, 384–
385; Alice B. Keith, ed., "Letters from Major James Cole Mountflorence
to Members of the Blount Family . . . January 22, 1792–July 21, 1796,"
14 N.C. *Hist. Rev.* 253–254, 283 (1937); William A. Provine, "Lardner
Clark, Nashville's First Merchant and Foremost Citizen," 3 *Tenn. Hist.
Mag.* 116 (1917). Evidently owned several law books while practicing in
Tennessee, including Charles Viner's twenty-three-volume *A General
Abridgement of Law and Equity* (1741–1753). See DaCo CPQS Min.
Bk. B, 84.

JAMES MULHERIN (d. 1826). Assumed office as justice, Davidson County
Court of Pleas and Quarter Sessions, October 1784, and remained on the

bench throughout AJ's practice before that court. Was a surveyor and part-time teacher.

Harriette Simpson Arnow, *Flowering of the Cumberland* (New York, 1963), 172–173; Brown, "Tennessee County Courts," 411 (Table 16); *Nashville Banner*, May 4, 1826.

ALEXANDER OUTLAW (1738–1825). Admitted to practice, Knox County Court of Pleas and Quarter Sessions, July 1792. Licensed to practice in the Tennessee courts, April 1796.

Father-in-law of JOSEPH ANDERSON, DAVID CAMPBELL, and JOSEPH HAMILTON. Commissioned justice of the peace, Washington County, Virginia, November 1782. Moved to Greene County, 1783. Represented Greene County, North Carolina House of Commons, 1784, 1788, 1789; a delegate to the convention that met in Fayetteville, North Carolina, to ratify the U.S. Constitution, 1789. Commissioned justice, Greene County Court of Pleas and Quarter Sessions, November 1790; justice, Jefferson County Court of Pleas and Quarter Sessions, June 1791, April 1796. Represented Jefferson County as a delegate to the convention that framed the first Tennessee constitution, 1796, where he opposed the Blount faction with which AJ was aligned. Represented Jefferson County, Tennessee House of Representatives, 1796–1797; represented Jefferson and Cocke counties, Tennessee Senate, 1799–1803; was Speaker of the Senate, 1799. Died in Dallas County, Alabama.

KnoxCo CPQS Min. Bk. O, 4; Barnhart, "The Tennessee Constitution of 1796," p. 543 n.41; *BD-Tenn. Assembly*, I, 562–63; Blount, *Journal*, 34, 63; Sevier, *Commission Book*, 1, 26; Williams, *Lost State of Franklin*, 324–325.

JOHN OVERTON (1766–1833). Studied law in Kentucky ca. 1787–1788, but with whom has not been determined. Admitted to practice, Davidson County and Sumner County Courts of Pleas and Quarter Sessions, April 1790; Superior Court of Davidson County, May 1790; Mero District Superior Court, May 1791. Licensed to practice in the territorial Superior Court, December 1790; Superior Court of Tennessee, April 1797.

Brother-in-law of HUGH LAWSON WHITE and JOHN WILLIAMS. Moved from Louisa County, Virginia, to Danville in present-day Kentucky, ca. 1787, and began practice with his brother James. Was a member of the Political Club of Danville along with HARRY INNES and several other Kentucky lawyers; also a member of the Kentucky Society for Promoting Useful Knowledge, 1787. Moved to Nashville, March 1789, and began practice in the Davidson County Court of Pleas and Quarter Sessions in April. During the next year, he represented clients in at least six cases in the Davidson court before being formally admitted to practice, April 1790. Frequently served as co-counsel with his close friend AJ, with whom he boarded at the Donelson farm. Became a partner of AJ's in land speculation beginning in May 1794 (see Agreement, May 12, 1794, *Jackson Papers*, I, 46–48). Represented Sumner County as a delegate to the convention that met at Fayetteville, North Carolina, to ratify the U.S. Constitution, 1789. Appointed by President Washington as supervisor of the revenue, District of Tennessee, Territory South of the River Ohio, February 1795; appointed inspector of the revenue, District of Tennessee, June 1795. Elected to succeed AJ as judge, Superior Court of Tennessee, August 1804; served until abolition of the court effective Jan. 1, 1810. Elected judge, Supreme Court of Errors and Appeals, November 1811; resigned, 1816. Collaborated with THOMAS EMMERSON in publishing the first two volumes of *Tennessee Reports* (1813–1817). After retiring from the bench, Overton devoted much of his attention to his widespread business interests and to the promotion of AJ's political career.

Overton to Robert C. Foster, May 8, 1827, Dickinson Papers, THi; DaCo CPQS Min. Bk. A, 282–310 *passim*, 349; MDSC Law Min. Bk., 1788–1803, pp. 18, 30; SumCo CPQS Min. Bk. 1, p. 23; Blount, *Journal*, 43; *DAB; JES*, I, 173–74, 180–81; *Kentucky Gazette*, Dec. 15, 1787; Sevier, *Commission Book*, 4; Thomas Speed, *The Political Club Danville, Kentucky 1786–1790*, Filson Club Publ. No. 9 (Louisville, 1894), 38, 87; *Tennessee Gazette*, Aug. 15, 1804; Samuel Cole Williams, "Western Representation in North Carolina Assemblies, 1776–1790," ETHS *Publ*. No. 14, p. 110 (1942). An inventory of Overton's law library taken in 1808 itemizes more than 160 volumes. Inventory of Books, 1808, Box 12, Claybrooke and Overton Papers, THi. Overton evidently served as an agent for eastern publishers seeking professional subscribers to such secondary legal works as Comyns's *Digest of the Laws of England*. See numerous subscription agreements, Claybrooke and Overton Papers, THi.

ISHAM ALLEN PARKER. Licensed to practice in the territorial county courts, October 1795; Superior Court of Tennessee, November 1796. Admitted to practice, Davidson County Court of Pleas and Quarter Sessions, January 1796; Mero District Superior Court, November 1796.

Commissioned justice, Davidson County Court of Pleas and Quarter Sessions, 1804. Kept an inn in Nashville, ca. 1802–1804.

DaCo CPQS Min. Bk. B, 301; MDSC Law Min. Bk., 1788–1803, p. 176; Blount, *Journal*, 114; Clayton, *Davidson County*, 89, 197; Margaret B. DesChamps, "Early Days in the Cumberland Country," 6 *THQ* 221 (1947); Sevier, *Commission Book*, 3.

NICHOLAS PERKINS (1779–1848). Admitted to practice, Davidson County Court of Pleas and Quarter Sessions, July 1800; Mero District Superior Court, November 1800; Sumner County Court of Pleas and Quarter Sessions, October 1800.

Moved from Pennsylvania to Knoxville and, in 1797, to Mero District. Appointed by President Jefferson as register of Land Office, Washington County, Mississippi Territory, December 1805. Served as attorney general, Washington District East of Pearl River, Mississippi Territory, 1809. Returned to Tennessee, 1810. Represented Williamson County, Tennessee Senate, 1815–1817; House of Representatives, 1841–1843.

DaCo CPQS Min. Bk. C, 293; MDSC Law Min. Bk., 1788–1803, pp. 272–273; SumCo CPQS Min. Bk. 3, p. 276; *BD-Tenn. Assembly,* I, 579; *JES,* I, 11, 13; *Knoxville Gazette,* Mar. 27, 1797; Rowland, *Courts of Mississippi,* I, 10, 64.

FRANCIS ALEXANDER RAMSEY (1764–1820). Served as clerk, Hamilton District Superior Court of Law, throughout AJ's tenure on the bench. Moved from Pennsylvania to Washington County, ca. 1783. Commissioned clerk, Washington District Superior Court of Law, November 1790; clerk, Hamilton District Superior Court of Law, 1793. Had served as secretary to the Jonesboro convention called to draft a constitution for the State of Franklin, 1785. Assumed office as justice, Knox County Court of Pleas and Quarter Sessions, January 1802. Clerk, Knox County Circuit Court, 1810–1820.

KnoxCo CPQS Min. Bk. 3, p. 279; Blount, *Journal,* 38; Elizabeth S. Bowman, "Swan Pond: Francis Alexander Ramsey's Stone House, A Tennessee State Shrine," ETHS *Publ.* No. 27, pp. 13–14, 16, 18 (1955).

JOHN RHEA (1753–1832). B.A., College of New Jersey, 1780. Licensed to practice in the territorial courts, November 1790; Tennessee courts, April 1796. Admitted to practice, Knox County Court of Pleas and Quarter Sessions, July 1792; Carter County Court of Pleas and Quarter Sessions, July 1797.

Born in Ireland; emigrated 1769. During the territorial period, probably maintained a larger practice in the Knox County Court of Pleas and Quarter Sessions than any other lawyer practicing before that court. Commissioned county solicitor, Sullivan County, November 1790; Greene County, 1796; Carter County, July 1797. Appointed county solicitor, Knox County, July 1792; resigned, October 1799. Had served as clerk, Sullivan County Court of Pleas and Quarter Sessions, 1785–1790. Represented Sullivan County, North Carolina House of Commons, 1789; Tennessee House of Representatives, 1796–1799; as a delegate to the convention that met at Fayetteville, North Carolina, to ratify the U.S. Constitution, 1789; as a delegate to the convention that framed the first Tennessee constitution, 1796, where both he and AJ were aligned with the faction led by Governor William Blount. Jackson suggested to President Washington in 1797 that Rhea be considered as a candidate for appointment as judge of the new federal district court, indicating that the bar viewed him and JOHN OVERTON as "possessing the greatest Legal abilities—of any gentlemen" in the state (AJ to Washington, Feb. 8, 1797, *Jackson Papers*, I, 122). Served in the U.S. House of Representatives, 1803–1815, 1817–1823.

Carter County CPQS Min. Bk., 1797, Carter County Records, THi; KnoxCo CPQS Min. Bk. O, 4, 5; KnoxCo CPQS Min. Bk. 2, p. 54; Barnhart, "The Tennessee Constitution of 1796," p. 543 n.41; *BDAC; BD-Tenn. Assembly*, I, 617; Blount, *Journal*, 35, 39; *DAB; General Catalogue of Princeton University 1746–1906* (Princeton, 1908), 101; Sevier, *Commission Book*, 1.

ARCHIBALD ROANE (1759–1819). A.B., Liberty Hall Academy, 1789. Admitted to practice, Washington County Court of Pleas and Quarter Sessions, May 1788; Knox County Court of Pleas and Quarter Sessions, July 1792. Licensed to practice in the territorial Superior Court, November 1790.

Was practicing in Greene County in May 1790. Commissioned county solicitor, Greene County, November 1790. Was serving as clerk and master in equity, Washington District Superior Court, February 1793. Maintained an active practice in the Knox County court after 1792. Attorney general, Hamilton District, 1794–1796. Represented Jefferson County as a delegate to the convention that framed the first Tennessee constitution, 1796, where both he and AJ were aligned with the faction led by Governor William Blount. Elected one of three judges, Superior Court of Tennessee, August 1796; served until inaugurated governor of Tennessee, September 1801; appointed judge, Second Circuit Court, November 1811; served until elected judge, Supreme Court of Errors and Appeals, October 1815. Governor of Tennessee, 1801–1803. Represented Knox County, Tennessee Senate, September–November 1811.

Greene County Records, THi; KnoxCo CPQS Min. Bk. O, 4; WashCo CPQS Min. Bk. 1, 322; Barnhart, "The Tennessee Constitution of 1796," p. 543 n.41; *BD-Tenn. Assembly*, I, 621–622; Blount, *Journal*, 34–35; *DAB; Knoxville Gazette*, May 4, 1793; *Washington and Lee University Alumni Directory 1749–1964* (Lexington, 1964), 251; Samuel Cole Williams, *Phases in the History of the Supreme Court of Tennessee* (Johnson City, 1944), 23.

ELIJAH ROBERTSON (1744–1797). Brother of JAMES ROBERTSON. Assumed office as justice, Davidson County Court of Pleas and Quarter Sessions, October 1784, and remained on the bench throughout AJ's practice before that court. Represented Davidson County, North Carolina Senate, 1783; House of Commons, 1785, 1788. Commissioned lieutenant colonel commandant, Davidson County militia, June 1791. Between September 1787 and June 1791, he was granted or deeded more than 32,000 acres of land in Davidson County and in the middle and western districts of the Military Reserve; also owned more than 19,000 acres in Sumner County in 1789.

   BD-Tenn. Assembly, I, 628; Brown, "Tennessee County Courts," 385–386, 411 (Table 16).

JAMES ROBERTSON (1742–1814). Brother of ELIJAH ROBERTSON. Assumed office as justice, Davidson County Court of Pleas and Quarter Sessions, October 1783, and remained on the bench throughout AJ's practice before that court. Had been a justice of the Washington County Court of Pleas and Quarter Sessions, February 1778, and a member of the Cumberland Association Committee, January–August 1783. Received legislative appointment as trustee, Davidson Academy, 1785. Represented Davidson County, North Carolina House of Commons, 1786; Senate, 1787–1788, 1798–1799. Appointed by President Washington as brigadier general, Mero District, February 1791; resigned, 1794. Represented Davidson County as a delegate to the convention that framed the first Tennessee constitution, 1796, where both he and AJ were aligned with the faction led by Governor William Blount.

   Barnhart, "The Tennessee Constituion of 1796," p. 543 n.41; *BD-Tenn. Assembly,* I, 629–631; Brown, "Tennessee County Courts," 411 (Table 16); *DAB; JES,* I, 75–76; Quarles and White, *Three Pioneer Documents,* 23, 29; "The Records of Washington County," pt. 1, 5 *AHM* 344 (1900).

EDWARD SCOTT (d. 1844). Licensed to practice in the Tennessee county courts, October 1798. Admitted to practice, Knox County Court of Pleas and Quarter Sessions, 1799.

   Commissioned county solicitor, Knox County, January 1800. Declined appointment by President Jefferson as commissioner of bankruptcy, District of East Tennessee, August 1803. Was one of three attorneys who represented Judge DAVID CAMPBELL during impeachment proceedings, October 1803. Appointed by Jefferson as U.S. Attorney, District of East Tennessee, January 1805; tenure ended by February 1807. Register of the Land Office, District of East Tennessee, 1808–1815. Judge, Second Circuit Court, Tennessee, ca. 1815–1844. Compiled and published two-volume *Laws of the State of Tennessee* (1821).

Edward Scott to Thomas Jefferson, Aug. 22, 1803, Letters of Application and Recommendation During the Administration of Thomas Jefferson, 1801–1809, RG 59, DNA; *JES*, I, 481–482; Rothrock, *French Broad-Holston Country*, 481; Sevier, *Commission Book*, 6, 31; White, *Messages*, I, 158; see *JES*, II, 53.

BENNETT SEARCY (d. 1819). Admitted to practice, Davidson County Court of Pleas and Quarter Sessions, January 1789; Sumner County Court of Pleas and Quarter Sessions, October 1796; Mero District Superior Court, November 1796. Licensed to practice in the territorial Superior Court, December 1794; Superior Court of Tennessee, July 1796.

Commissioned county solicitor, Sumner and Tennessee counties, December 1790. Commissioned clerk and master in equity, Mero District Superior Court, June 1791; was serving in that capacity as late as 1806. Was defeated by AJ for election by the Tennessee General Assembly as judge of the Superior Court, December 1798. Judge, Fifth Circuit Court, Tennessee, 1814–1817. Died in Montgomery County.

DaCo CPQS Min. Bk. A, 259; MDSC Law Min. Bk., 1788–1803, p. 176; SumCo CPQS Min. Bk. 2, p. 113; Ursula S. Beach, *Along the Warioto* (Nashville, 1964), 78, 138; Blount, *Journal*, 43, 51, 103; Sevier, *Commission Book*, 2; Samuel Cole Williams, *Phases of the History of the Supreme Court of Tennessee* (Johnson City, 1944), 7; see *Impartial Review & Cumberland Repository*, July 5, 1806.

ROBERT SEARCY (1768–1820). Licensed to practice in the Tennessee county courts, January 1797; Superior Court, February 1798. Admitted to practice, Davidson County Court of Pleas and Quarter Sessions, April 1797; Sumner County Court of Pleas and Quarter Sessions, October 1797; Mero District Superior Court, May 1798.

Commissioned justice, Davidson County Court of Pleas and Quarter Sessions, January 1799; treasurer, Mero District, September 1797, September 1799. Served as clerk, U.S. District Court, District of Middle Tennessee; clerk to Commissioners of North Carolina Land Claims; and U.S. paymaster. Owned with his brother a mercantile firm in Nashville, ca. 1802–1806.

DaCo CPQS Min. Bk. B, 392; MDSC Law Min. Bk., 1788–1803, p. 211; SumCo CPQS Min. Bk. 3, p. 138; Clayton, *Davidson County*, 203; Enoch L. Mitchell, "Robert Whyte, Agrarian, Lawyer, Jurist," 10 *THQ* 9–12 (1951); *Nashville Gazette*, Sept. 2, 1820; Sevier, *Commission Book*, 3–5, 7, 14.

DAVID SHELBY (ca. 1763–1822). Commissioned clerk, Sumner County Court of Pleas and Quarter Sessions, December 1790; justice, Sumner County Court of Pleas and Quarter Sessions, April 1796. Had represented Sumner County as a delegate to the convention that framed the first Tennessee constitution, 1796, where both he and AJ were aligned with the faction led by Governor William Blount.

Barnhart, "The Tennessee Constitution of 1796," p. 543 n.41; Blount, *Journal,* 43; Jay G. Cisco, *Historic Sumner County* (Nashville, 1909), 104; Sevier, *Commission Book,* 39.

DANIEL SMITH (1748–1818). Traditionally credited with having attended the College of William and Mary, but there are no records of his attendance at that institution; his education more likely was confined to the practical surveying experience gained under the tutelage of Thomas Walker, an Albemarle County, Virginia, physician.

Father of GEORGE SMITH; father-in-law of SAMUEL DONELSON. Had served as a justice of the peace in Washington County, Virginia, 1776; sheriff, 1781–1782. Assumed office as justice, Davidson County Court of Pleas and Quarter Sessions, October 1783; served through October 1786; appointed justice, Sumner County Court of Pleas and Quarter Sessions, November 1786, and reappointed, August 1796. Received legislative appointment as trustee of Nashville, 1784. Represented Sumner County as a delegate to the convention that met at Fayetteville, North Carolina, to ratify the U.S. Constitution, 1789. Appointed by President Washington as secretary, Territory South of the River Ohio, June 1790. Represented Sumner County as a delegate to the convention that framed the first Tennessee constitution, 1796, where both he and AJ were aligned with the faction led by Governor William Blount. Completed AJ's unexpired term in the U.S. Senate, 1798–1799, and served again, 1805–1809.

Barnhart, "The Tennessee Constitution of 1796," p. 543 n.41; *BDAC; BD-Tenn. Assembly,* I, 680; Brown, "Tennessee County Courts," 411 (Table 16); *DAB;* Walter T. Durham, *Daniel Smith: Frontier Statesman* (Nashville, 1976), 4–10, 51, 80–81, 91, 97, 113, 122; Sevier, *Commission Book,* 39.

GEORGE SMITH (1776–1849). Reported to have attended College of William and Mary, although there are no records of his attendance at that institution. Licensed to practice in the Tennessee county courts, May 1797; Superior Court, October 1798. Admitted to practice, Davidson County and Sumner County Courts of Pleas and Quarter Sessions, July 1797.

Son of DANIEL SMITH. Appointed county solicitor, Sumner County, April 1798. Represented Sumner, Smith, Wilson, and Jackson counties, Tennessee House of Representatives, 1801–1805.

DaCo CPQS Min. Bk. B, 407; SumCo CPQS Min. Bk. B, 131, 148; *BD-Tenn. Assembly,* I, 680; Sevier, *Commission Book,* 4, 7.

JOHN STOKES (1756–1790). Jackson read law with him beginning ca. Mar. 1787. Represented Montgomery County, North Carolina House of Commons, 1786–1787; Rowan County, House of Commons, 1789; Rowan County as a delegate to the convention that met in Fayetteville to ratify the U.S. Constitution, 1789. Elected to the Continental Congress from Montgomery County, December 1787, but apparently never took his seat. Elected judge, Morgan District Superior Court, December 1788; resigned by November 1789; elected assistant judge, Morgan District Superior Court, December 1789. Appointed by President Washington as judge, U.S. District Court, District of North Carolina, August 1790; served until his death in October 1790.

Samuel A. Ashe and Stephen B. Weeks, eds., *Biographical History of North Carolina* (Greensboro, 1908), VII, 448; Cheney, *North Carolina Government,* 217, 223, 659, 740 n.46, 750, 769; N.C. *State Records,* XXI, 184, 197–98, 412, 717.

THOMAS STUART (1762–1838). Admitted to practice by consent of the court and bar, Davidson County Court of Pleas and Quarter Sessions, April 1796, and upon production of license, July 1797; Sumner County Court of Pleas and Quarter Sessions, July 1796. Licensed to practice in the Tennessee county courts, April 1797; Superior Court, December 1798.

Jackson recommended him to President Jefferson for appointment as U.S. attorney, District of West Tennessee, in June 1802 as "a man of respectability, and of considerable Standing at the Barr" (AJ to Jefferson, June 16, 1802, *Jackson Papers,* I, 300); appointed, July 1802; reappointed, January 1803. Elected judge, Fourth Circuit Court, Tennessee, November 1809; remained on the bench until February 1836.

DaCo CPQS Min. Bk. B, 317; SumCo CPQS Min. Bk. 2, p. 106; *JES,* I, 433, 437; *Knoxville Gazette,* Aug. 4, 1802; Park Marshall, "Judge Thomas Stuart," 8 *Tenn. Hist. Mag.* 92, 97–98 (1924); Sevier, *Commission Book,* 4–5.

HOWELL TATUM (1753–1822). Admitted to practice, Davidson County and Sumner County Courts of Pleas and Quarter Sessions, July 1789; Mero District Superior Court, May 1791. Licensed to practice in the Tennessee courts, July 1796.

Frequently served as co-counsel with AJ and JOSIAH LOVE. Had been an unsuccessful candidate for judge of the Superior Court of Davidson County, December 1787. Commissioned state's attorney, Mero District,

July 1796. Jackson suggested to President Washington in February 1797 that he and several other lawyers be considered for appointment as judge of the new federal district court in Tennessee (AJ to Washington, Feb. 8, 1797, *Jackson Papers*, I, 122). Commissioned judge, Superior Court of Law and Equity, May 1797; resigned, September 1798. It was to his seat on the Superior Court that AJ received a temporary appointment from Governor Sevier on Sept. 20, 1798. After retiring from the bench, he became a partner in a Nashville mercantile firm and apparently returned to practice for an undetermined period of time in June 1808. Served as AJ's topographical engineer during the New Orleans campaign, 1814–1815. Returned to Rutherford County, Tennessee, and was appointed keeper of the federal military store in Nashville.

DaCo CPQS Min. Bk. A, 292; MDSC Law Min. Bk., 1788–1803, p. 30; SumCo CPQS Min. Bk. 1, p. 18; Curtis C. Davis, "Howell Tatum," unpubl. sketch on file with the AJP Project, 1, 3–4; *Impartial Review & Cumberland Repository*, June 23, 1808; Sevier, *Commission Book*, 2; Samuel Cole Williams, *Phases of the History of the Supreme Court of Tennessee* (Johnson City, 1944), 14. Tatum's journal as AJ's topographical engineer at New Orleans appears in published form in *Smith College Studies in History*, No. 7 (1921–1922).

ROBERT WEAKLEY (1764–1845). Assumed office as justice, Davidson County Court of Pleas and Quarter Sessions, April 1789, and remained on the bench throughout AJ's practice before that court. A surveyor and planter, he had represented Davidson County as a delegate to the convention that met at Hillsborough, North Carolina, to ratify the U.S. Constitution, July–August 1788. Represented Davidson County, Tennessee House of Representatives, 1796–1799; represented in varying sequence Davidson, Dickson, and Williamson counties, Tennessee Senate, 1799–1805, 1807–1809, 1819–1821, 1823–1825; served in the U.S. House of Representatives, 1809–1811. Represented Davidson County as a delegate to the Tennessee Constitutional Convention, 1834.

BDAC; BD-Tenn. Assembly, I, 768–769; Brown, "Tennessee County Courts," 411 (Table 16); Cheney, *North Carolina Government*, 766.

JESSE WHARTON (1776–1833). Dickinson College, 1794, in the same class as JOHN FINLEY JACK and RANDAL MCGAVOCK. Admitted to the bar, Albemarle County, Virginia. Licensed to practice in the Tennessee county courts, April 1798; Superior Court, November 1798. Admitted to practice, Davidson County and Sumner County Courts of Pleas and Quarter Sessions, July 1798; Mero District Superior Court, May 1799.

Elected county solicitor, Davidson County, January 1801. Represented

Davidson County, Tennessee House of Representatives, 1801–1803; represented Tennessee, U.S. Senate, 1807–1809, 1814–1815. Commissioned justice, Davidson County Court of Pleas and Quarter Sessions, 1817.

DaCo CPQS Min. Bk. C, 77, 360; MDSC Law Min. Bk., 1788–1803, p. 252; SumCo CPQS Min. Bk. 3, p. 160; *BDAC; BD-Tenn. Assembly,* I, 773–774; Clayton, *Davidson County,* 89; George L. Reed, ed., *Alumni Record of Dickinson College* (Carlisle, Pa., 1905), 44; Sevier, *Commission Book,* 6–7.

HUGH LAWSON WHITE (1773–1840). Studied law under ARCHIBALD ROANE and intermittently under James Hopkins, Lancaster, Pennsylvania, ca. 1794–1795. Licensed to practice in the Tennessee county courts, October 1796; Superior Court, October 1797. Admitted to practice, Knox County Court of Pleas and Quarter Sessions, October 1796.

Brother-in-law of JOHN OVERTON and JOHN WILLIAMS (1778–1837). Maintained an active practice in the Knox County court. Had served as secretary to Governor William Blount, 1793, and had been appointed deputy clerk, Knox County Court of Pleas and Quarter Sessions, May 1793. Was one of three attorneys who represented the state in impeachment proceedings against Judge DAVID CAMPBELL, December 1798. Elected judge, Superior Court of Law and Equity to succeed ARCHIBALD ROANE, September 1801; resigned, 1807. Represented Knox County, Tennessee Senate, 1807–1809, 1817–1819. Appointed by President Jefferson as U.S. Attorney, District of East Tennessee, March 1808; tenure ended before June 1809. Elected judge, Supreme Court of Errors and Appeals, 1809; submitted resignation in December 1814 effective April 1815.

Retired to law practice in Knoxville and to duties as president of the Tennessee State Bank. Declined offers to return to the bench as a judge of the Supreme Court of Errors and Appeals, 1822, 1824. Elected to succeed AJ in U.S. Senate, 1825; resigned, 1840. After breaking with AJ politically, was a presidential candidate in 1836 and received the electoral votes of Tennessee and Georgia.

KnoxCo CPQS Min. Bk. O, 54; KnoxCo CPQS Rec. Bk. 1, p. 152; *BDAC; BD-Tenn. Assembly,* I, 776–777; *DAB;* L. Paul Gresham, "Hugh Lawson White, Frontiersman, Lawyer, and Judge," ETHS *Publ.* No. 19, p. 24 (1947); Gresham, "The Public Career of Hugh Lawson White," 10 *THQ* 293, 295, 300, 317 (1951); *JES,* II, 74, 123–24; Sevier, *Commission Book,* 3–4; White, *Messages,* I, 85.

JAMES WHITE (1749–1809). Reported to have attended a Jesuit college, St. Omer, France, and the University of Pennsylvania College of Medicine, although there are no records of his having been graduated from the latter institution. Licensed to practice in the territorial courts, December 1790.

Admitted to practice, Davidson County Court of Pleas and Quarter Sessions, January 1791.

Appointed state's attorney, Davidson County Court of Pleas and Quarter Sessions, January 1791. Had represented Davidson County, North Carolina House of Commons, 1785; Territorial Assembly, 1794–1795. Had represented North Carolina as a delegate to the Continental Congress, 1786–1788; Territory South of the River Ohio as a delegate to the U.S. Congress, 1794–1796. Moved to Territory of Orleans, 1799. Appointed parish judge, Parish of Attakapas, Territory of Orleans, 1807; remained on the bench until his death. Grandfather of Edward Douglass White, Chief Justice, United States Supreme Court, 1910–1921.

DaCo CPQS Min. Bk. A, 401; *BDAC; BD-Tenn. Assembly,* I, 780–81; Blount, *Journal,* 43; Carter, *Territorial Papers,* IX, 749, 835.

JENKIN WHITESIDE (1772–1822). A.B., 1792, A.M., 1795, University of Pennsylvania. Reported to have studied law under John Marshall, Richmond, Virginia. Licensed to practice in the Tennessee courts, April 1798. Admitted to practice, Knox County Court of Pleas and Quarter Sessions, April 1798; Washington County Court of Pleas and Quarter Sessions, May 1798.

Moved from Virginia to Knoxville, 1798, and practiced there and apparently in the district and county courts at Abingdon, Virginia, until he assumed the office of attorney general, November 1801. Represented the state in impeachment proceedings against Judge DAVID CAMPBELL, October 1803. Served as the state's attorney general until 1807. Elected to U.S. Senate, 1809; resigned to return to practice in Nashville, 1811.

KnoxCo CPQS Rec. Bk. 1, p. 318; WashCo CPQS Min. Bk., 1798–1799, p. 5; *BDAC; BD-Tenn. Assembly,* I, 787; *General Alumni Catalogue of the University of Pennsylvania* (Philadelphia, 1917), 24; *Knoxville Register,* Oct. 16, 1798; Kenneth McKellar, *Tennessee Senators as Seen by One of Their Successors* (Kingsport, 1942), 122–23; *Nashville Constitutional Advocate,* Oct. 22, 1822; Sevier, *Commission Book,* 6; Whiteside Sketch, McRaven Coll., THi; see Theodorick Bland to Sophia Bland, May 6, 1800, Bland Papers, MdHi.

ROBERT WHYTE (1767–1844). Variously reported to have attended Edinburgh University or the University of Glasgow. Probably studied law in Virginia. Licensed to practice in the Tennessee courts, September 1802. Admitted to practice, Mero District Superior Court, November 1803; Davidson County Court of Pleas and Quarter Sessions, January 1804.

Son-in-law of James Glasgow, North Carolina secretary of state. Erroneously credited with having been a member of the faculty of the College of William and Mary as a professor of languages, instead of Charles

Bellini, Professor of Modern Languages at the College, ca. 1779–1803. Claimed by one biographer to have been the same "Robert White" who represented Lenoir County, North Carolina Senate, 1797, and Glasgow County, Senate, 1798, and the same "Robert Whyte" who represented Greene County, Senate, 1800. Was one of three attorneys who represented Judge DAVID CAMPBELL during impeachment proceedings, October 1803. Appointed by Governor Joseph McMinn as judge, Supreme Court of Errors and Appeals, 1816; remained on the bench until 1834.

DaCo CPQS Min. Bk. D, 167; MDSC Law Min. Bk., 1788–1803, p. 59; Scope and Content Note, Whyte Papers, THi; Enoch L. Mitchell, "Robert Whyte, Agrarian, Lawyer, Jurist," 10 *THQ* 3–5 (1951); White, *Messages,* I, 158; see Cheney, *North Carolina Government,* 236–237, 241.

JOHN WILLIAMS (1731–1799). Admitted to the bar in Williamsboro, North Carolina.

Elected judge, North Carolina Superior Court of Law and Equity, February 1779; remained on the bench until his death; was a member of the court when AJ was examined and licensed to practice, September 26, 1787. Had served as deputy attorney general, 1768. Had represented Granville County, North Carolina Provincial Congress, 1775; House of Commons, 1778; Speaker, House of Commons, 1778. Had represented North Carolina as a delegate to the Continental Congress, 1778, 1779.

BDAC; Cheney, *North Carolina Government,* 155, 203, 360.

JOHN WILLIAMS (1778–1837). Admitted to practice, Knox County Court of Pleas and Quarter Sessions, January 1803; Hamilton District Superior Court, April 1803.

Brother-in-law of JOHN OVERTON and HUGH LAWSON WHITE. Was one of three attorneys who represented Judge DAVID CAMPBELL during impeachment proceedings, October 1803. Attorney general of Tennessee, 1807–1808. Represented Tennessee in the U.S. Senate, 1815–1823; defeated for reelection by AJ. Appointed by President John Quincy Adams as chargé d'affaires to the Central American Federation, 1825; served until December 1826. Represented Knox and Anderson counties, Tennessee Senate, 1827–1829.

HDSC Law Min. Bk. 3, p. 311; KnoxCo CPQS Rec. Bk. 4, p. 101; *BDAC; BD-Tenn. Assembly,* I, 794; White, *Messages,* I, 158.

SAMPSON WILLIAMS (1762–1841). Commissioned justice, Davidson County Court of Pleas and Quarter Sessions, June 1794; justice, Sumner County Court of Pleas and Quarter Sessions, January 1799. Clerk,

Smith County Court of Pleas and Quarter Sessions, 1799–1804. A native of South Carolina, he had arrived in Davidson County ca. 1780 and had served as sheriff, Davidson County, 1789–1794. Represented Sumner County, Tennessee Senate, 1799–1801; Jackson, Smith, Sumner, and Wilson counties, Senate, 1805–1807; Jackson, Franklin, Overton, Smith, Warren, and White counties, Senate, 1811–1813. With MOSES FISK established Fisk Female Academy, Hilham, Tennessee, 1803.

DaCo CPQS Min. Bk. A, 293, 364, 402, Min. Bk. B, 149; *BD-Tenn. Assembly,* I, 797; Blount, *Journal,* 96; Weston A. Goodspeed, *A History of Tennessee* (Nashville, 1886), 828; Sevier, *Commission Book,* 40.

JAMES WINCHESTER (1752–1826). Commissioned justice, Sumner County Court of Pleas and Quarter Sessions, December 1790, and remained on the bench throughout AJ's practice before that court. Commissioned lieutenant colonel commandant, Sumner County, December 1790. Had represented Sumner County as a delegate to the convention that met at Hillsborough, North Carolina, to ratify the U.S. Constitution, 1788. Appointed by President Washington as one of five members of Legislative Council, Territory South of the River Ohio, 1794. Represented Sumner County, Territorial Senate, 1794, 1795; Tennessee Senate, 1796; Speaker of the Senate, 1796. Became a joint tenant with AJ and JOHN OVERTON for the purpose of laying off a portion of the Rice grant as the town of Memphis, January 1819.

Agreement, AJ with Overton and Winchester, Jan. 7, 1819, Shelby County Deed Bk. 1, pp. 133–135; *BD-Tenn. Assembly,* I, 810–811; Blount, *Journal,* 44; Cheney, *North Carolina Government,* 767; *DAB;* Sevier, *Commission Book,* 39.

Appendix

The Russell Bean Anecdote

The Russell Bean anecdote illustrates the difficulties that were encountered by the editors in their attempt to document the often colorful incidents for which Jackson's legal career has traditionally been best known.

The earliest account of the Bean incident that has been located occurs in an extract from an article about Jackson in the London *Atlas* that was printed in the *United States Telegraph* on March, 19, 1830:

> The character of the President is not sufficiently appreciated in this country. He is, by the majority of the English, believed to be an intemperate soldier: the reverse is the case: he is cool, cautious, and prudential. He once held a judicial situation in the United States, a fact not generally known in this country. While he administered the laws in that capacity, he distinguished himself for acuteness and moderation. A friend of ours, who was resident in America at that period, related an anecdote of the President, which exhibits his personal courage and presence of mind in a favorable light, although we should not desire to see an English judge perform a similar feat. A notorious burglar was one day cited in Court, but did not appear, and Jackson ordered an officer to apprehend him. In a short time the officer returned, and informed him that they could not take the fellow, who soon overpowered him. 'Then get another man to assist you,' replied Jackson. Accordingly two officers went, but with no better success, when Jackson desired them to add a third. The three went, but they were also defeated; the burglar proving too powerful an opponent for their unified strength. 'What,' said Jackson, 'have the three men failed?—then I must go myself.' And he descended from the judgment seat, went out of Court, and in a few minutes returned with his prisoner, whom he took without any assistance.

In 1843 Amos Kendall published an account of a similar incident in one of the installments to his *Life of Andrew Jackson:*

> [Jackson's] first court was held at Jonesborough, where an incident occurred illustrative alike of the rudeness of the times and the firmness of the new judge.
> (8.) A man named Russell Bean was indicted for cutting off the ears of his infant child in a drunken frolic. He was in the courtyard; but such was his strength and ferocity, that the sheriff, not daring to approach him, made a return to the court that 'Russell Bean will not be taken.' Judge Jackson, with his peculiar emphasis, said that such a return was an absurdity, and could not be received. 'He must be taken,' said the judge, 'and, if necessary, you must sum-

mon the *posse comitatus*.' The mortified sheriff retired, and waiting until the court adjourned for dinner, summoned the judges themselves, as part of the *posse*. Conceiving that the object of the sheriff was to avoid a dangerous service under cover of the judges' refusal to obey the summons, Judge Jackson instantly replied, 'Yes, sir, I will attend you, and see that you do *your* duty.' Learning that Bean was armed, he requested a loaded pistol, which was put into his hand. He then said to the sheriff, 'Advance and arrest him; I will protect you from harm.' Bean, armed with a dirk and brace of pistols, assumed an attitude of defiance and desperation. But when the judge drew near, he began to retreat. 'Stop and submit to the law,' cried the judge. The culprit stopped, threw down his pistols, and replied, 'I will surrender to you, sir, but to no one else.'[1]

Kendall's account apparently was based upon one of several interviews of Jackson that had been conducted by Kendall's nephew, James McLaughlin, in early 1843. On January 3, 1843, McLaughlin wrote to Kendall from the Hermitage that he was enclosing "an account of an encounter which the Genl. when a judge had with a felon." The enclosure has not been located, but McLaughlin in the same letter observes:

> The account is substantially but not literally correct. The correct statement is as follows. 'The man had in a fit of jealousy with his wife cut off the ears of his child and afterwards went armed to the teeth to avoid apprehension. The sheriff had summoned ten men to take him but they were afraid. The judge then told him to summon the whole posse. He did so but returned the same answer to the judge and at the same time apologized for his want of success. The Judge told him to excuse himself if he could to his fellow citizens and country. The court, consisting of Judge Campbell, Rowen and Jackson, then adjoined to dine. On their way to the hotel the Sheriff summoned the judges. The first two put themselves upon their dignity and declined serving but Jackson with readiness assented and having armed himself advanced to the felon and told him that if he did not surrender he would shoot him down. He said he would do so but he was afraid of the people. The Judge told him he should be perfectly safe from the people and he immediately surrendered and Jackson handed him over to the custody of the sheriff.[']'[2]

Jackson reviewed each installment of Kendall's *Life* before it was published. Kendall sent the first installment to AJ for his review in October 1843. In August 1844, Kendall forwarded the fifth installment, along with copies of Nos. 3 and 4, to AJ. Kendall's account of the Bean incident occurred in No. 3. When AJ acknowledged receipt of installment No. 5, he wrote to Kendall that Nos. 3 and 4 had not accompanied No. 5, as Kendall had indicated, but had "come on Some time before." In his letter to Kendall of September 10, AJ makes corrections to No. 5. If AJ made any corrections to No. 3, they have not been located. Jackson's memory by 1843, of course, had become less than entirely accurate. He wrote

---

1. Amos Kendall, *Life of Jackson*, No. 3 (New York, 1843), pp. 102–103.
2. James A. McLaughlin to [Amos Kendall], Jan. 3, 1843, AJ Papers, DLC (Reel 55).

to Kendall, for instance, that he had resigned from the bench in 1799 or 1800.[3]

Still another account, which does not name Bean as the recalcitrant accused and which specifies murder as the offense in question, occurs in an unpublished journal kept by the young lawyer William Frierson Cooper shortly after Jackson's death in June 1845.[4]

Fifteen years later, Parton printed two embellished versions of the incident in his biography of Jackson. Although both versions identify Bean, one separates the date of the incident from the prosecution of Bean for the mutilation offense. Acknowledging that the "popular story" had been "going the rounds of the papers for about forty years," Parton nevertheless asserted that it contained some element of truth:

> This story I have in several different versions, cut from newspapers of various dates, which show that, like the steam engine, it is a growth, rather than an invention, each period contributing some little addition to the delightful whole.[5]

Variations on the Parton account have been repeated by subsequent Jackson biographers and Tennessee writers.[6]

Jackson's apparent silence upon reviewing Kendall's account of the Bean story may be interpreted as a confirmation by Jackson that, to his failing recollection, the anecdote had some basis in fact. Implicit in all of the varying accounts of the Bean incident, however, is that the proceeding in which Bean had been summoned to appear was one that was pending before Jackson and his colleagues in the Superior Court. The editors have been unable to locate any records for a criminal or civil action in the Superior Court between 1798 and 1804 in which Bean was named as a defendant. Indeed, the only court record possibly relating to the Bean anecdote that has been found by the editors is a warrant issued in February 1802 by a justice of the Washington County Court of Pleas and Quarter Sessions for Bean's arrest "for having feloniously and on purpose maimed and disfigured an infant child by having cut off both its ears."[7] The editors have not discovered any documentation linking Jackson with the prosecution of Bean in the Washington County court in 1802.

3. Kendall to AJ, Oct. 21, 1843, Bassett, *Correspondence*, VI, 235–236; Kendall to AJ, Aug. 28, 1844, *id.* at 316; AJ to Kendall, Nov. 13, 1843, *id.* at 241–242; AJ to Kendall, Sept. 10, 1844, *id.* at 318.

4. Entry, June 10, 1845, Journal and Letterbook of William Frierson Cooper, THi.

5. James Parton, *Life of Andrew Jackson* (New York, 1860), I, 166–167, 228–229.

6. *E.g*, John Allison, *Dropped Stitches in Tennessee History* (n.p., 1897), 119–121; Augustus C. Buell, *History of Andrew Jackson* (New York, 1904), I, 132–133; Robert V. Remini, *Andrew Jackson and the Course of American Empire, 1767–1821* (New York, 1977), 115.

7. Warrant, Feb. 12, 1802, Paul M. Fink, PVT.

Glossary

Legal Terms Employed in the Tennessee Courts

Accord and satisfaction: A new contract and performance that takes the place of and settles a predecessor contract; usually a compromise settlement of a contractual dispute or problem.

Alias fieri facias: A second writ of fieri facias issued when the prior writ was ineffective. See *Fieri facias.*

Assumpsit: A common-law form of action to obtain damages for the nonperformance of a contract that is not written or under seal.

Capias ad respondendum: A writ ordering the sheriff to arrest a named person and hold him until he is to appear in court and answer a civil suit.

Capias ad satisfaciendum: A writ ordering the sheriff to seize a named party and detain him until the damages or debt he owes has been paid or otherwise discharged.

Curia advisare vult: A phrase indicating that the court will postpone decision to permit further consideration and study of the point at issue.

Dedimus potestatem: A judicial commission authorizing a specific individual to take the depositions of certain witnesses, administer oaths, or perform other legal duties.

Elegit: A writ of execution permitting a judgment creditor to have the defendant's personal property sold to pay the debt; if this was not enough, the creditor also could get control of part of the defendant's lands and take his rents and profits to discharge the obligation.

Fieri facias: A writ ordering the sheriff to seize the debtor's property, sell it, and use the proceeds to satisfy a judgment against the debtor.

Forcible entry and detainer: A common-law offense of wrongfully taking possession of land and tenements; also a proceeding to return the land to its rightful owner.

Imparlance: Time given to either of the parties to an action to answer the pleading of the other; also a discussion between the parties to a pending action that might effect an amicable settlement of the controversy.

In fieri: In process.

Indictment: A formal accusation by a grand jury that a named person has committed a criminal offense; in the normal course of events, the indictment leads to a trial of the accused. See *True bill.*

Injunction: An order from a court commanding that a party do, or refrain from doing, some act.

Jeofail, statute of: A statute permitting a pleader to acknowledge an error in the form of his proceedings and to correct it by amendment.

Non assumpsit: Defendant's response to an action of assumpsit; a denial of the alleged promise upon which the suit is based. See *Assumpsit.*

Non est factum: A plea that denies the validity of a legal instrument, such as a bond, upon which suit is being brought.

Non est inventus: The sheriff's report on his failure to find an individual whom he was ordered to arrest; literally, "He has not been found."

Orator: The plaintiff in a suit in chancery.

Onus proband: Burden of proof.

Per curiam: By the court as a whole.

Precept: An order, writ, warrant, or process; specifically, an authoritative order to an officer that he perform some act.

Presentment: An accusation made by a grand jury independent of the prosecutor; the presentment may become the basis of an indictment.

Pro confesso: A default judgment taken against a defendant in an equity suit.

Procedendo: An order from a higher court to a lower court to proceed to judgment on a matter before it.

Puis darrein continuance: A plea alleging a defense that has arisen after an action has been initiated and after the first phase of pleading has been completed.

Respondeat ouster: A judgment against the defendant's dilatory plea; after this judgment, the pleading continues.

Scire facias: A writ requesting some judicial action based upon a written record; commonly used by creditors against defaulting garnishees to discover and identify the garnishee's property.

Scire facias ad audiendum errores: A common-law writ available to a plaintiff in error who had assigned errors to compel the executors or administrators of the deceased defendant in error to participate in the hearing on the alleged errors.

Solvit ad diem: The defendant's plea in a debt action on a bond that he paid the money on the date due.

Supersedeas: A writ from an appellate court ordering a trial court to suspend execution of a judgment that is being appealed.

Traverse: A denial.

Trespass quare clausum fregit: The common-law action for damages for unlawful entry or trespass on land.

Trespass vi et armis: The common-law action for damages sustained by the plaintiff because of force used by the defendant against the plaintiff's person or property.

True bill: The endorsement made by a grand jury upon a bill of indictment when they find sufficient evidence to warrant a trial of the person charged with a criminal offense. See *Indictment.*

Venire facias: A writ summoning a person to service as a grand juror.

Writ of error: A writ from an appellate court ordering a lower court to send it the record of a case tried in the lower court so that the appellate court might examine the record and correct any errors that might have been made.

Writ of error coram vobis: A writ of error from an appellate court to a trial court ordering the latter to correct an error of fact made in deciding a case before it.

Writ of restitution: A writ issued after the reversal of a judgment that orders the sheriff to return to the defendant the property taken from him in executing the judgment.

Index